Visual Basic Object and Component Handbook

PRENTICE HALL PTR MICROSOFT® TECHNOLOGIES SERIES

NETWORKING

- Microsoft Technology: Networking, Concepts, Tools
  Woodard, Gattuccio, Brain
- NT Network Programming Toolkit
  Murphy
- Building COM Applications with Internet Explorer
  Loveman
- Understanding DCOM
  Rubin, Brain
- Web Database Development for Windows Platforms
  Gutierrez

PROGRAMMING

- Introduction to Windows 98 Programming
  Murray, Pappas
- Developing Professional Applications for Windows 98 and NT Using MFC, Third Edition
  Brain, Lovette
- Win 32 System Services: The Heart of Windows 98 and Windows NT, Third Edition
  Brain
- Multithreaded Programming with Win32
  Pham, Garg
- Visual Basic 6: Design, Specification, and Objects
  Hollis
- ADO Programming in Visual Basic 6
  Holzner
- Visual Basic 6: Error Coding and Layering
  Gill
- Visual C++ Templates
  Murray, Pappas
- Introduction to MFC Programming with Visual C++
  Jones
- MFC Programming in C++ with the Standard Template Libraries
  Murray, Pappas
- COM-CORBA Interoperability
  Geraghty, Joyce, Moriarty, Noone
- Distributed COM Application Development Using Visual Basic 6.0
  Maloney
- Distributed COM Application Development Using Visual C++ 6.0
  Maloney
- Understanding and Programming COM+: A Practical Guide to Windows 2000 DNA
  Oberg
- ASP/MTS/ADSI Web Security
  Harrison
- Microsoft Site Server 3.0 Commerce Edition
  Libertone, Scoppa
- Building Microsoft SQL Server 7 Web Sites
  Byrne
- Visual Basic Object and Component Handbook
  Vogel, Peter

ADMINISTRATION

- Windows 2000 Registry
  Sanna
- Configuring Windows 2000 Server
  Simmons
- Tuning and Sizing NT Server
  Aubley
- Windows NT Cluster Server Guidebook
  Libertone
- Windows NT 4.0 Server Security Guide
  Goncalves
- Windows NT Security
  McInerney
- Supporting Windows NT and 2000 Workstation and Server
  Mohr
- Zero Administration Kit for Windows
  McInerney
- Designing Enterprise Solutions with Microsoft Technologies
  Kemp, Kemp, Goncalves

PRENTICE HALL PTR MICROSOFT® TECHNOLOGIES SERIES

Peter Vogel

Visual Basic Object and Component Handbook

Prentice Hall PTR, Upper Saddle River, NJ 07458
www.phptr.com

Library of Congress Cataloging-in-Publication Data

Vogel, Peter
Visual Basic Object and Component handbook / Peter Vogel
p. cm. -- (Prentice Hall series on Microsoft technologies)
Includes bibliographical references and index.
ISBN 0-13-023073-1
1. COM (Computer architecture) 2. Microsoft Windows (Computer file)
3. Electronic data processing--Distributed processing. I. Title. II. Series.
QA76.9.A73 O24 1999
005.2'768--dc21 99-056388

Editorial/Production Supervision: *Joanne Anzalone*
Acquisitions Editor: *Tim C. Moore*
Marketing Manager: *Bryan Gambrel*
Manufacturing Buyer: *Maura Goldstaub*
Cover Design: *Anthony Gemmellaro*
Cover Design Direction: *Jerry Votta*
Series Design: *Gail Cocker-Bogusz*
Technical Reviewers: *Don Merusi and Richard Campbell*

Prentice-Hall, Inc.
Upper Saddle River, NJ 07458

Printed in the United States of America

10 9 8 7 6 5 4 3 2

ISBN 0-13-023073-1

Prentice-Hall International (UK) Limited, *London*
Prentice-Hall of Australia Pty. Limited, *Sydney*
Prentice-Hall Canada Inc., *Toronto*
Prentice-Hall Hispanoamericana, S.A., *Mexico*
Prentice-Hall of India Private Limited, *New Delhi*
Prentice-Hall of Japan, Inc., *Tokyo*
Pearson Education Asia Pte. Ltd.
Editora Prentice-Hall do Brasil, Ltda., *Rio de Janeiro*

DEDICATION

Since this book was a labor of love,
it is dedicated to my wife Jan, the love of my life.

CONTENTS

PART TWO Building *63*

THREE Coding Objects *65*

FOUR Objects *103*

SIX Interfaces *175*

FOREWORD

by Ken Getz

I've known Peter Vogel for a number of years now. Peter likes to talk. I've seen him speak at conferences, and I've had dinner with him. He likes to talk a whole lot. Serious talking here. But the funny thing is, he knows what he's talking about. Unlike many who talk in mass quantities (publicly or privately), Peter's really on top of things, and I always learn something from him. Yes, I may learn that the average temperature inside a frog's mouth is the same as the ambient temperature in the surrounding environment (ignoring wind chill), but it's always something.

When Peter came to me and asked me to write a foreword for his book, I realized that this was my chance to make sure his readers understood just how much he's respected in the development community, and how much people enjoy hearing him speak in 3-D. He's always among the top rated speakers at conferences he speaks at, and he's been editing the Smart Access newsletter for a few years now, adding his own brand of wit and commentary each month. I'm sorry, dear reader, that you'll have to content yourself with Peter in 2-D (and no pictures, to boot), but after having read early chapters of the book, it's clear that Peter's knowledge and dry, somewhat sarcastic tone comes across. No doubt about it—only Peter Vogel could have written this book.

And why should you want to read this book? I've seen lots of books on components, and the technology behind them. What's different about this book is that it's focused on practical techniques. Peter has devoted a great deal of time to coming up with useful and interesting samples, documenting them well, and (my favorite part) demonstrating why he's made the choices he's made, based on timings and comparisons. I appreciate that attention to detail, and I hope you will, too. If you're intent on digging into the details on the grungy underpinnings of COM, this probably isn't the book for you. There are many good books on that topic (and Peter makes solid recommendations to those other books when necessary).

Just perusing a few chapters, I learned new details of creating ActiveX controls and about working with COM Add-ins for VB. Even if you're an experienced component developer, I'm betting that you'll find something new to dig into in this book. I'm looking forward to reading the whole thing, and feel sure that this book will enhance your library as well. My theory on technical books is that if some example code in the book saves me even one hour of personal effort, the book has paid for itself. I think you'll find this book provides you with many, many hours of unspent effort on your part, making it a worthy contribution to your programming efforts.

Along the way, you may even find out how many windows there are in the Empire State Building, or the boiling point of bleach. You never know, with Peter. But it's always an interesting ride.

PREFACE

In the Microsoft and Windows world, objects and components form the foundation on which everything else rests. The mortar for this foundation is Microsoft's Component Object Model (COM) specification and implementation. The COM specification describes how objects can be assembled into components and how components can work together to form applications. The implementation of COM in the Windows operating system provides the support to take advantage of this powerful technology. To participate in the world of COM, you need to create components that will work with any other COM-compliant development tool and application.

I wrote this book to provide the working Visual Basic programmer with something that I wanted: A one-volume reference to writing COM-based objects and components using Visual Basic. My goal was to provide, in one place, in plain language, everything that the Visual Basic programmer would need to know to create components.

COM and Visual Basic

COM is constantly evolving. Currently COM is being expanded into the COM+ specification in Windows 2000. In both the COM and COM+ models, developers create objects and then combine them to form components. Once built, your components can be integrated with applications built with other development tools ranging from C++ to Delphi to Object COBOL. COM-based applications that can use your components include both Microsoft Word and Internet Information Server. Building on COM, Microsoft has also defined a series of environments—including Microsoft Transaction Server and ActiveX Data Objects—that require objects with specific characteristics. It's a very big world out there.

Fortunately, Microsoft has provided a terrific tool for creating objects: Visual Basic. Much of the drudgery involved in creating COM objects and components is taken care of automatically by Visual Basic so that you can concentrate on solving problems. There's still a lot that you have to know, as this book demonstrates, but Visual Basic lets you concentrate on the important issues.

I've taken a very practical approach in this book. Throughout the book, I'm going to tell you two things:

1. If you want to do this using Visual Basic, here's the code that you should write.
2. If you write this code, here's what Visual Basic will do.

Or, more simply: If you want this, code this; if you code this, you'll get this. Where Visual Basic gives you different implementation choices, I've described the costs and benefits from a design and maintenance point of view for each choice. I've also provided benchmarking information on the impact on your code's performance. I can't tell you what the right answer is for each one of these choices, because too much depends on what you are trying to accomplish with your program. However, if you're wondering what threading model to use or whether to declare your parameters as ByVal or ByRef, this book will give you the background to make an informed decision.

I've given design considerations precedence over performance. I don't want to suggest that performance isn't important—the application with the sub-two-second response time and a few bugs will be implemented before the application with plus-six-second response time and no bugs. But for your application to succeed, you must first get the design right and then make the adaptations necessary to get the performance you need. I firmly believe that it's often better to abandon a project than compromise the design in order to meet the performance goals. For most applications, the life cycle cost of a bad design will swallow whatever benefits the application was supposed to deliver.

Good design and good performance are not incompatible. If the design is right, then you will probably find that modifying it where necessary to improve the performance is relatively straightforward. Throughout this book I will be pointing out where you have opportunities to ensure that your component will run quickly, along with the costs and benefits of building your component that way.

The Knowledge Gap

Back in the early '80's, I started out programming on mainframe computers and creating linear programs—programs that started executing on the first line of code and kept going until they got to the end of the code. I inserted Do loops, If…Then statements, and subroutines or functions to break up the monotony, but mostly my programs began at the beginning and ran until the end.

Programming doesn't work that way anymore. My first exposure to this new world was when I started creating programs using Visual Basic 3.0. My first exposure to "programmer's culture shock" was when Visual Basic introduced me to event-driven programming. In event-driven programming I had to give up control over the execution of my program; the events that were triggered by the user determined the order in which my code executed.

When I started developing programs in Visual Basic, I also began to work with the objects that made up the Visual Basic environment. I had experimented with object-oriented programming earlier in my career by learning Smalltalk, the language that pioneered object-oriented development. I discovered that, while I had learned the syntax of the language and could write Smalltalk code, I still couldn't create Smalltalk applications. I just didn't know where to begin. Visual Basic turned out to be the tool that moved me from the world of linear programming to the world of working with objects.

For the last three years, in addition to developing Visual Basic applications, I've been teaching Visual Basic to developers for Learning Tree International. Many developers in my classes suffered the same problem that I had in getting started with object oriented development. These programmers found themselves in the position of knowing all the necessary syntax, but unsure about how to put it all together. Experienced developers in my classes found that they knew only part of what Visual Basic could do for them.

It was to address this gap between knowledge and performance that I wrote this handbook. In addition to teaching and developing, I wanted to provide developers not only with the knowledge on how to use Visual Basic's ability to create objects, but also the "when and why" of using objects.

The Handbook

I edit the Smart Access newsletter (the leading source for technical information on Microsoft Access). While working for Learning Tree, I also wrote a course on developing Web-based applications. If you read the various magazines about programming with Visual Basic, then you've probably read an article that I've written. As a result, I've had a lot of experience in explaining technical concepts to programmers. More important, I've had a lot of feedback from students, teachers, authors, peers, and others on what works and doesn't work. I've learned that the key to presenting information successfully is to provide a solid structure to organize the material.

This handbook's structure is simple. The first three parts of the handbook discuss designing objects, creating objects and components, and integrating components into specific environments. The fourth part is a "heads-up" look at what changes you can expect in Windows 2000.

Part 1 of this book covers the issues involved in designing objects. In this part, I discuss what you should consider when designing the interface for your objects. Among other topics, I'll look at deciding when you should use a method or a property, and how to derive your object design from your data design. I also show you how to use Visual Modeler, the object design tool that comes with Visual Basic.

Part 2 provides you with a complete guide to creating objects and components, including the code you need to write to implement methods, properties, and events. You'll see how to develop objects that act as collections and how to create objects that create other objects. In this part I also show you how to combine your objects to create components and cover both the why and how of implementing interfaces. Thanks to Visual Basic, your components can be as complicated as Microsoft's Data Access Objects or as simple and powerful as ActiveX Data Objects.

The examples in Part 2 are deliberately simple: Just enough code to demonstrate the technique. However, objects are really interesting only when they are put together and interact with each other. To demonstrate this, most of the chapters in Part 2 end with a case study that shows the various techniques in action. Even in these final sections, I've kept the standard "business" code to a minimum so that you can concentrate on the code that makes the objects work. The error handling that a real business application would require is missing, for instance.

With a foundation on how to build objects and components in place, Part 3 looks at how to create objects that will work in the specialized environments that Microsoft has defined. You'll see how to create an object that can pass data into to ActiveX Data Objects and what you must do to create a component that will work with Microsoft Transaction Server. In Part 4, I look at what Windows 2000 developers can expect to find under COM+ and Component Services.

Benchmarks

Throughout Part 2 of this book I've given examples of the impact on execution time of the programming decisions that you will make. If you are trying to decide whether to use a ParamArray or a set of optional parameters, these benchmarks should provide you with the information to make a performance-based decision. However, performance isn't everything, as you know if you've ever tried to maintain someone else's "highly optimized" code. And, in many cases, a foolish emphasis on writing the fastest code leads to introducing bugs. To paraphrase the immortal words of the authors of *The Fundamentals of Programming Style*, to some programmers, efficiency often seems to mean getting to the wrong answer as fast as possible.

Overreliance on benchmarks can be a mistake. As you look at the benchmark results remember that I repeated most operations 1000 times. So, when I say that an operation took 2 milliseconds on my computer, that really means that one execution took 2/1000 milliseconds. You should recognize that even a difference of an order of magnitude may translate into less than a millisecond. Do you really need to worry about a millisecond? And, if you do, shouldn't you be writing this code in C and not Visual Basic? If you are concerned about the assumptions that I've made, you can find the code in Appendix B, the Benchmarking Code appendix. You can also download the code (and the COM Add-in that generated it) from my Website at `www.phvis.com`.

Keep in Touch

I've had a lot of fun writing this book and exploring Microsoft's world of objects. I wrote the book because I wanted to provide a single reference to all the information that you might need when building components with Visual Basic. I hope you get as much satisfaction out of using this book as I did writing it. If you have any questions, issues, concerns, or recommendations don't hesitate to drop me a line at `peter.vogel@phvis.com`. You're also welcome anytime at the PH&V Information Services website at `www.phvis.com`. In addition to finding the Visual Basic COM Add-in that generated the benchmarks in Part 2, you'll find white papers on a variety of topics in application development.

And, for those of you who've read Ken's Foreword: the Empire State Building has 6,500 windows (though I suspect that the number has been rounded), and the boiling point of bleach (typically, water with a 5% solution of NaOCI) is close to the boiling point of water at 212F/100C.

ACKNOWLEDGMENTS

There were a lot more people involved in creating this book than the author. Tim Moore approached me about writing a book for Prentice Hall after reading a short article of mine in a magazine. Tim nursed me through the proposal stage and answered my numerous questions as this project progressed. Also, he was unbelievably patient with me as the book expanded and I missed one deadline after another. This book means a lot to me, and it's here because of Tim. Thanks, Tim!

Tim also lined up two reviewers to provide feedback as this book wended its way to completion: Don Merusi and Richard Campbell provided me with great feedback, didn't hesitate to point out where I had lost my way (or just said something really, really dumb), and encouraged me when the amount of work involved seemed endless. There's only so much that they could do, however, and the errors that remain despite their best efforts are mine alone.

When the book neared completion, I was left in the excellent hands of Joanne Anzalone. Jo not only patiently answered all of my questions about what was going to happen to my baby next, but fielded my many changes, fixes, and backtracks as we neared production. The book looks good because of Jo and I was lucky to get to work with her.

Over the years an enormous number of people have helped me understand how to use Visual Basic in an object-oriented world. I can't list them all here but special mention must go to Guy Eddon. Like myself, Guy is a teacher for Learning Tree International. He is also the author of Learning Tree's Visual Basic and COM course. Teaching Guy's course over the last three years has given me the opportunity to constantly explore and refine my understanding of COM. It's also a great course.

Paul Litwin, Ken Getz (who graciously consented to write the foreword for this book), Michael Kaplan, Stephen Forte, and Richard Campbell have also been part of the group that has educated me and helped me out of the pits that I have dug myself into. Rob MacDonald took the time to give me his insights into the world of ADO data providers as did Mike Gunderloy, who also shared with me chapters on his upcoming book on ADO. I must also, at least, give a mention to all the people who answered questions from me in the newsgroups, all the people I've taught who've taught and challenged me, and all the authors of the courses and books that helped me understand this fabulous technology—thank you.

Going back to the beginning of my work with computers, I have to thank Herman Kempe. Herman not only laid the groundwork that let me become a programmer and developer, he insured that I always kept my eye on the business that my programs would support.

Finally, a special thanks to Jim and Jean Irvine. In addition to being my in-laws, Jim's artistry and Jean's penmanship turned by scribbled graphics into something that was actually usable. I feel that graphics can often help explain things better than words can and, thanks to Jean and Jim, we had some to include in this book.

PART ONE

Designing

While the technical aspects of building objects are easy to grasp (especially with Visual Basic), the major problem in using objects is in deciding where they fit in your design. This part of the book introduces the fundamental concepts behind using objects and introduces a process for determining what objects make up an application, based on the application's data design. This section also introduces Visual Basic's tool for developing your object design—Visual Modeler and discusses the value of design tools like Visual Modeler before showing you how to use it.

In This Part

ONE

Designing Components

When Visual Basic 4.0 came along and gave me the ability to create objects, I found myself reading a lot of articles about how I could now introduce a "middle layer" between the user interface and the database. These articles were usually accompanied by a certain amount of hand waving about the "business rules" that would be implemented in that middle layer. I found these articles less than helpful.

Rather than talk in these abstract terms, I want to take a very practical look at how you might actually design objects when developing an application. Since I began life developing database applications for business, I describe how objects fit into that environment.

This chapter will show you where and when you will want to use objects. You'll see how objects fit into the application development process, outline the reasons why you might want to use objects, and dispel some myths about Object Oriented Programming (OOP). I define what an object is in terms that make sense to a developer. You'll also be introduced to Microsoft's model for creating applications by combining objects. Finally, I discuss the issues and conventions that you should consider as you start to design your objects.

Defining Objects

An object is just a program. Unlike other applications, though, an object is built with the expectation that it will be used from some other program. In order to make its functionality available to other programs, the object exposes its subroutines and functions as a set of methods and properties. In order to communicate with the programs that use it, an object fires events. For objects to work effectively with other programs, there must be a standard that describes how objects are built and a means for objects to communicate with the programs that use them.

When you are building objects and components in Visual Basic, you are taking advantage of Microsoft's COM specification. COM stands for Component Object Model and describes how collections of objects (components) can communicate with applications and objects in other components. The "COM Vision" is that everything from applications to operating systems can be built as a collection of cooperating components that can be snapped in, replaced, and upgraded independently of each other. There are a number of services built on top of COM, as shown in Figure 1–1. The specifications that are important to component developers are the ones that describe ActiveX components, ActiveX Controls, and Automation.

ActiveX Controls describe objects that must be hosted by some other object (the text box that you pull onto your Visual Basic form is an ActiveX Control). ActiveX components are objects that can be hosted directly by the operating system (DAO is a good example of an ActiveX component). Automation describes the communication protocol that is used by applications to create and manage ActiveX components.

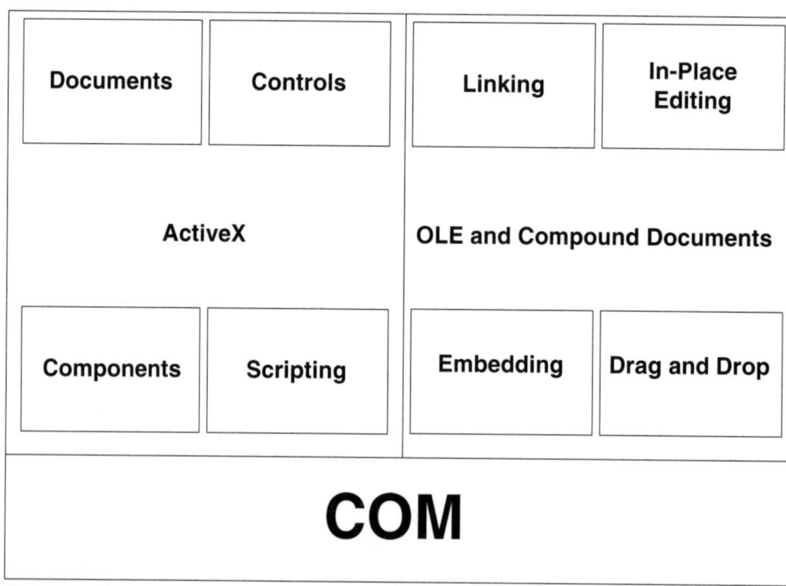

Figure 1–1 *COM is the basis for a number of technologies that Microsoft uses in developing their applications.*

Microsoft developed the COM specification for very mercenary reasons. They wanted to create large, complex applications that could be easily enhanced. Microsoft was in a unique position to develop and exploit such a specification. In their application business (best represented by Microsoft Office), Microsoft needed a specification like COM that would let them build large applications as a series of small components. In their operating system business (Windows 95, 98, NT, and 2000) Microsoft had the ability to provide that environment. The Microsoft tools group could build the development environments that would deliver applications built on the specification. And, coming full circle, the consumer applications would both exploit COM and reveal its deficiencies, driving new development. By releasing their tools into the developer community, Microsoft would simultaneously generate a revenue stream from those tools and cement the popularity of COM by building a third party market around it.

Designing Objects

There are a number of different ways that you can approach working with objects. In this chapter, I discuss two different perspectives. The first perspective is that of the database application developer, a programmer who builds applications for a business. The second perspective is that of a Visual Basic developer, someone who has built a number of Visual Basic applications and is looking for ways to increase their productivity.

Objects for the Database Developer

For me, getting the database design correct is paramount. If the database design accurately represents the way that the users need the data, then building applications to use the data will be simple. If, on the other hand, the database doesn't accurately reflect the way that the company does business, then the application developers will be forced to generate a considerable amount of extra code to handle the deficiencies in the design of the database.

In the sample application that I use in this book, I assume that the database design for the application has been developed. I'm stepping into the project at the point where I must begin the process of designing the objects that the application requires. While this is a viable way to design an application, it's certainly not the only one. In other methodologies, the database design is done during the object-oriented analysis of the business problem or after it.

For my example, I use a database that a typical wholesaling company might develop. This database contains information about products that the company buys from its vendors and sells to its customers. The company needs a database containing tables that hold information about customers, their orders, and the company's products (see Appendix A for an overview of the company, a description of the database, and a discussion of the database's design).

Since the data is held in a relational database, there are a number of tables that divide what users might regard as a single item into several tables.

While the users of the company's database would probably regard a sales order as a single "thing", in the relational database a sales order is divided into at least two tables: the sales order header (I'll call it the OrderHeader table) and the sales order detail (the OrderDetails table). If you've worked with relational databases long enough, this division seems almost natural to you, no matter how odd it may seem to your users.

This difference in attitude between developers and users often doesn't become clear until the database is made available to the users so that they can do their own reporting. All of a sudden, the company's end users start complaining about how awkward it is to get information because they have to combine the OrderHeader, OrderDetail, and Customer tables to get any useful information on customer orders. Many companies create data warehouses just so these tables can be recombined into a single Orders table.

It's important that you, as a developer, realize that your users are correct and that the imposition of the relational model does distort the data. More important, the multiple tables required by your relational model add complexity to your programs. Dividing up the data into multiple tables requires you to use complex queries to retrieve information about one "thing"—the sales order. While the relational model still forms the strongest and most flexible means of storing data, it can add some unnecessary complexity to your applications. Fortunately, just as your users find it simpler to work with denormalized data, your programs can be made simpler by using objects to retrieve all the data on a single object.

Objects also solve a significant flaw in the relational model. The relational data model has no special cases. The relational model does not let you store sales order data one way and have product information stored in a different way. Yet, as a developer, you know things about the OrderHeader data that should let you to work with it more effectively than is allowed by the standardized format of the relational database. Once you start thinking about the meaning of your data and let that control how you want to work with it, you are well on the way to working with objects.

I'm not advocating creating denormalized operational databases. The relational model still provides the most rigorous basis for defining and organizing data. It's worth remembering, though, that your data is not actually stored in tables. If you lift up the hood on your database engine, you will find that your data is stored in some proprietary format that facilitates rapid retrieval—which is not in tables. The database engine only makes it appear that your data is stored in tables. The result of making it appear that your data is stored in tables is that the data is easier to work with (i.e., you can use SQL!). Since the format of the data is already being disguised in order to make it easy to work with, creating objects simply lets you insert an additional layer of programming that makes developing your application even easier.

Objects and the Visual Basic Programmer

The methodology that I just described certainly isn't the only way to develop an object-oriented design. Other methodologies start by determining what objects make up the application, and then determining what data is required for those objects. Once the data needs for the application are determined through an object-oriented analysis, a database structure is developed to hold that data. Whatever method you use, you need to have a preliminary version of your objects and data models before you start writing code.

Using objects does not mean writing less code, at least not in the short run. There's no magic here—all the code that you would write in a non-object oriented program will still be written. If you've been dividing your programs up into subroutines and functions, you will find that Visual Basic lets you repackage that functionality into methods and properties in objects. However, all the complexity of converting from the "relational world" view of the database tables to the "real view" of the sales order can be segregated into your objects. Your applications become significantly simpler as you export complexity to the object.

By moving your code into objects, you separate it from the code that manages your user interface. This allows you to work on different parts of your project in parallel. One developer can work with users to build a user interface that matches the business workflow. Other developers can build the objects that the user interface requires in order to provide users with the services they need. The application's user interface acts as a client to the application's objects. To succeed with this strategy it's important that your object model (your objects and their methods, properties, and events) be specified early so that user interface developers can write code to use it.

The lowest level of that specification is COM itself. COM provides you with a great deal of freedom in selecting your development tools. You can build your objects and user interfaces using any tool you want because COM is a language-neutral specification. The Microsoft COM model ensures that any object that you create using Visual Basic, or any other COM-compliant tool, can be used by any other program executing on your computer, regardless of the language that either program was written in. Through Distributed COM (DCOM), you are free to access objects on other computers on your network or even over the Internet.

In effect, when you create objects in Visual Basic, you are adding to the inventory of objects available for use on your network. In the same way that normalizing your data creates data structures that can be used by many applications, creating objects creates "bundles of functionality" that can be used by many programs. Once you segregate the code to access your data into objects, you greatly increase the chances that you can re-use that code again in some other application. Initially, writing object-oriented code will not reduce the code that you must create but there is a potential, through re-use, that you will have less to write in subsequent applications.

The idea that using objects will lead inevitably to code re-use is a myth. Simply starting to use objects will not cause programming teams to begin to re-use code. Experience with our clients at PH&V Information Services has shown us that implementing code re-use has very little to do with the programming language used. The key factors are the way that the IT department is organized and how employees are rewarded.

Even without code re-use, working with objects is a tremendous boon for the developer. The objects that I use in my program can represent many things: a printer, a textbox on a form, a customer, the serial port on my computer, or a transaction. Regardless of whether the object represents some data in a database, a physical object like a printer, or an ephemeral activity like a transaction, I need know only three things about the object:

1. What properties I can read and write
2. What methods I can invoke
3. What events I can respond to

As a developer, I would like to package up my programs into objects to give other developers (and myself) access to my applications. I want to be able to fully describe my application (no matter how complex it is) in terms of its methods, properties, and events. Visual Basic and COM let me do this. This is also the way that Microsoft develops its applications. Excel, for instance, is a component that consists of over 130 different objects.

When you build objects and assemble them into components, you are really working in a client/server model. Your objects will provide a set of services to the programs that use them. Programs (the clients in this model) will request services from your component by setting and reading your object's properties and invoking your object's methods. Your objects (the servers) will communicate with those programs by firing events. Thanks to DCOM, you can even end up moving your objects to some server and have them accessed over the network in a true, networked client/server model.

For the rest of this book, I refer to the programs that use the components that you develop as your components' clients. And, as a good designer, it's your responsibility to provide your clients with good service.

An Object Model Case Study

One danger in developing objects based on your database design is that you may simply create an object for each table in your database. This would defeat the purpose of using objects in your application. One of the reasons that you use objects is to hide from the application the details of the data model. Objects transform the relational model into a "real world" model of objects. One of the benefits of this approach is that you can modify your data model and only have to change the functionality of a few objects. Without objects you would have to modify every application that used the changed tables.

In Figure 1–2, I show some of the tables that would make up the database of my wholesaling company.

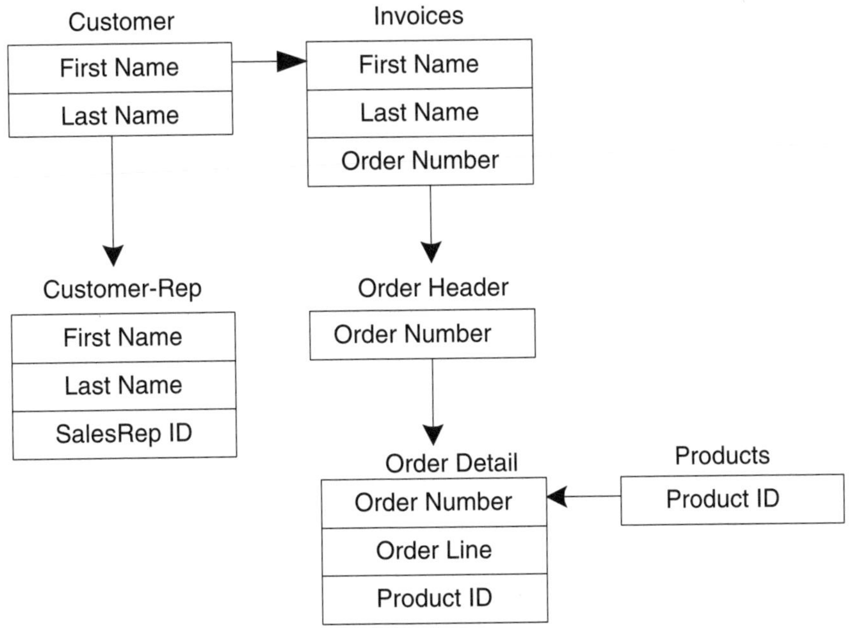

Figure 1–2 *The data model for the WholesaleManagement component defines the tables used by the company's applications.*

Object Overview

It may seem pretty obvious that whatever application is developed for this company is going to have Product, SalesRep, Customer, OrderHeader, and Invoice objects. These five objects would be used by the applications that retrieve and update information in the Product, SalesRep, Customer, Invoice and OrderHeader tables. But, while it may seem obvious that these objects are necessary, that doesn't mean that it's true.

There's no one model that will meet the needs of a retail company. When you design your objects, you'll have to take into account the way that your particular company works and how your clients will want to interact with your components. To do that effectively, you have to develop a set of scenarios that describes how your objects are used and make sure these correspond to your actual business practices. The way that your objects are used in these scenarios will define the objects you need and the methods, properties, and events they must have.

As I noted before, there are several design methodologies that will allow you to analyze business problems and develop object-based solutions. Scenario based design methodologies are usually referred to as "use-case." In general, however, even with these methodologies the data design remains a separate task from the object design. Since we don't yet have enterprise-level object databases, the objects that your applications use will not correspond to the tables that hold your data.

I describe here one possible design for the objects that make up the Wholesale system, based on the way that I assume that my fictional wholesaler works. For instance, my design does not include an Invoice object. Since there is a one to one relationship between the records in the Invoice table and the OrderHeader table, I need only one Order object to access both tables. If I believed that, at some point in the future, there was going to be a one-to-many relationship between these two tables, then I would design in a separate Invoice object.

The SalesRep table supports the information behind the SalesRep object. In addition, every Customer has a SalesReps collection which contains one SalesRep object for each representative that the customer does business with. The same is true for the SalesRep object: It has a Customers collection that contains one Customer object for each customer that the SalesRep serves. Both the Customers collection and the SalesReps collection are based on the same table, CustomerSalesRep. The CustomerSalesRep table has one record for every customer–salesrep combination. The information in this table determines what SalesRep objects to put in each Customer's SalesReps collection, and what Customer objects to put in each SalesRep's Customers collection.

Collections form an important part of many object models. A collection is a group of related items that the object's client may need to process without knowing how many or what objects are in the collection. A collection allows the client to simply ask for the next object in the collection without knowing anything about that next object.

At this stage in the process, I'm not too concerned with how I will create these objects or what code I will use to implement this model. All I want to do is get the objects designed correctly, confident that Visual Basic has all the tools to allow me to create my objects.

In the database model, the OrderDetail table links the OrderHeader table to the Product table in the same way that the CustomerRep table links the SalesRep and Customer tables (see Figure 1–3). Just as the SalesRep has many Customers, the OrderHeader has many Products.

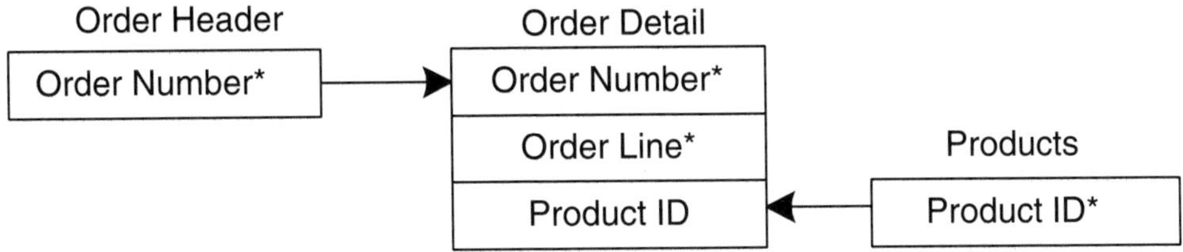

Figure 1–3 *The OrderDetail records links Orders to Products in a relationship that allows Products to be on many orders.*

The OrderDetail record contains information that can't be found in either the OrderHeader or the Product table. This information includes the quantity of the product purchased on this order, for instance. As a result, I need an OrderDetail object to provide access to this information. In my design, then, the OrderHeader object will have an OrderDetails collection which will have one object for each OrderDetail in the order. Similarly, the Customer object will have a CustomerAddresses collection with a Customer-Address object for each address that a customer has.

Object Relationships

In Figure 1–4, I show the WholesaleManagement object model that I've developed. In this model the Order object is placed under the Customer object in a parent/child relation. The same kind of relationship exists for OrderDetail/ Order objects, and Customer/CustomerAddress objects. On the other hand, the Customer, Product, and SalesRep objects have no "parent" object, indicating that they can be created independently of any other object.

In the Microsoft COM world, the parent/child relationship between objects frequently indicates that the child object can be created from the parent object using some method of the parent object. An example is the Recordset object in Microsoft's Data Access objects (DAO). In DAO, the Recordset object is a child of the Database object and is created using the Database object's OpenRecordset method. A parent/child relationship is usually defined because the child draws some information from the parent object in the process of being created. For instance, in creating an Order object, the Order must know what customer it is being created for in order to get the appropriate delivery address. To make sure this happens, an Order object can be created only through the CreateOrder method of the Customer object.

The parent/child relationship also suggests that the child object can't exist without the parent object. As an example, in the WholesaleManage-

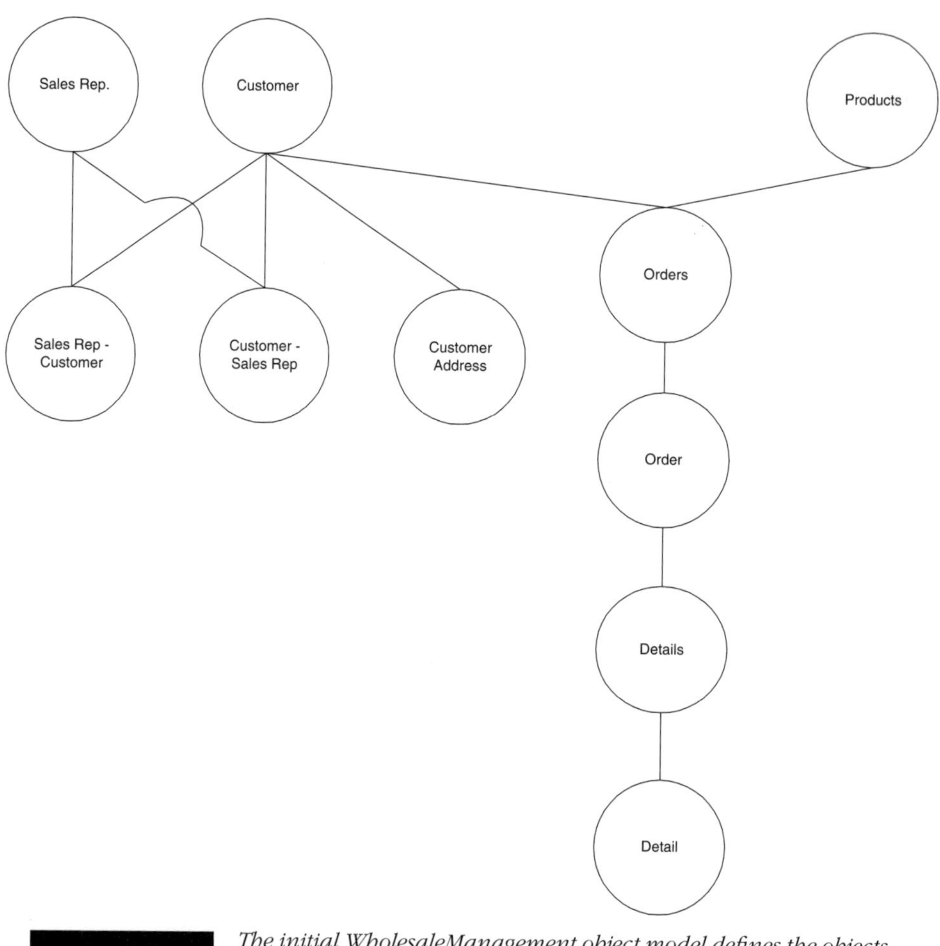

Figure 1–4 *The initial WholesaleManagement object model defines the objects that will be used by the company's applications.*

ment model a CustomerAddress object should always have a corresponding Customer object.

The parent/child relationship always implies an access path: that you can retrieve a related child object from the parent object. Collections figure strongly in this kind of relationship. In the WholesaleManagement model, for instance, a Customer object retrieved from a SalesRep's Customers collection will be a Customer served by that SalesRep. This does not mean that the only way to retrieve a Customer object is through a SalesRep object. In the model that I've developed, for instance, it's possible to retrieve a Customer object just by knowing the Id that uniquely identifies the Customer. It will not be possible, in this model, to retrieve an OrderDetail without using an Order object.

If you've come to the COM environment from another object development environment, you may be expecting more from the parent/child relationship than COM offers. The parent/child relationship, in the Microsoft COM model, does not imply any shared functionality. The Order object does not inherit any of the capabilities of the Customer just object because it is a child of the Customer object.

These objects, with their relationships, form the WholesaleManagement model. I'll call this model the WholesaleManagement object model because it forms the basis of all of the applications used to manage the wholesale operation in this company. All of these objects compiled into a DLL or EXE file would form a single component, which I'll call the WholesaleManagement component.

Object Detail

In creating the WholesaleManagement object model from the data model, two of the tables in the data model (the Invoices and CustomerRep tables) have disappeared. The design of the individual objects also blurs the division between the tables.

The Order object, for instance, has a CustomerName property. The customer name is stored on the Customer record but will frequently be required when working with the OrderHeader object. It would place a burden on the application if, after retrieving an Order object, it was necessary to retrieve a complete Customer object just to get the customer name. Similarly, the OrderDetail object contains a ProductDescription property that contains the description for the product purchased on that line of the order. In the data model for the application, the product description is kept in the Product table but it will be used so frequently with the OrderDetail object that it makes sense to provide it from the OrderDetail object.

The OrderDetail and OrderHeader object will also have properties that violate the relational model. In the relational model, it's considered an error in design to store calculated fields. So, as an example, the OrderDetail record does not have a LineCost field which contains the result of multiplying the quantity ordered by the product price. Nor does the OrderHeader table have a TotalCost field containing the sum of all of the OrderDetail records for the Order. Calculated fields are generally left out of data models because the individual fields might be changed without the calculated fields being recalculated.

In the WholesaleManagement object model, however, the OrderDetail does have a LineCost property and the OrderHeader has a TotalCost property. In both cases, reading these properties will cause code within the object to execute and calculate the necessary values using the current data stored in the database.

Using objects can also ensure that the same process is followed by every application that performs some activity. In this particular company, calculating the TotalPrice of an order can be a complicated process. When calculating an order's price, there are volume discounts that reduce the cost of the order if the total price is over some level, among other interesting wrinkles. By embedding the code to calculate the order's cost in the Order object, the model guarantees that this calculation is always done correctly (or, at least, always done the same way) by the applications that use this object. This is typically what's meant by using objects to implement business rules.

Just as properties blur the divisions between tables, the events that the WholesaleManagement objects fire will also combine information from different parts of the data model. For instance, each customer has a credit limit which determines the largest unpaid balance the customer can have outstanding. Adding OrderDetails to an Order will increase the cost of the order and may drive the cost of the order over the customer's credit limit. In the Warehouse model, as OrderDetails are added to an Order, the total customer unpaid balance will be calculated and compared to the customer's credit limit. The Order object will fire a CreditLimitViolation event to notify the application should the customer's credit limit be exceeded. This event is based on an analysis of data drawn from the Customer, OrderHeader, and OrderDetail tables.

Handling Interfaces

While COM doesn't support inheritance, it does support polymorphism. Polymorphism is the term used to describe how the same method can be used to perform different functions. Polymorphism is something that you already take advantage of in working with any programming language. In Visual Basic, for instance, you can use the Print command to print both string and numeric variables, though the underlying machine code behind these activities is very different. In the spirit of polymorphism, when the Visual Basic designers created the Form object they gave it a Print method for writing data to the form.

Every object that you create has an interface. An object's interface is made up of the methods, properties, and events that an object exposes. Within Visual Basic you can create an interface that can be implemented many different ways. This form of polymorphism allows a single object's interface to be shared among several different, but related, objects.

In the Warehouse object model, for instance, the Order object represents three different kinds of orders. While the Order object has a single Post method, which starts the process of sending the product on the order to the customer, the Post method does very different things for each of the three different order types.

• For a rush order, the Post method checks that sufficient quantity is in stock, reserves the ordered quantity, generates a "high priority" notice at the shipping dock, and adds a "rush" premium to the customer's bill.

• For a standard order, the Post method sends a notice to the warehouse to pull the quantity ordered and send it to the shipping dock.

• With a back order, the Post method actually sends an order to one of the company's vendors to purchase enough stock to cover the customer's order.

In the WholesaleManagement object model, a single Order interface contains all the methods and properties common to all the different kinds of orders. This interface includes the Post method which performs the appropriate activity for the kind of order being processed. However, the WholesaleManagement model also includes the BackOrder, RushOrder, and StandardOrder interfaces, which have properties and methods that are peculiar to the different kinds of orders. The BackOrder interface, for instance, has a CancelVendorOrder method that cancels the order placed to our company's vendor. The RushOrder interface has a PremiumPrice property so that the client can set the extra charge for placing a rush order.

Designing the Object Interface

When designing an object interface, you are determining what methods, properties, and events your object will expose. One of the key decisions that you have to make is how you are going to expose your object's functionality. Your object will do many things. You have to decide whether your object's clients will get to that functionality through methods or properties (or both).

This is an area that I always found very intimidating—I was terrified that I was going to do something stupid. As I suggest throughout this section, the key to success in designing objects is knowing your customers and the way that they will use your components. No one should know your customers better than you (otherwise, they'll become someone else's customers), so no one can do a better job of designing objects for them than you.

Properties and Methods

Some definitions of properties and methods have made the distinction between them seem very clear cut. Traditionally, properties are described as the data stored in the object. Another standard description of properties is that they represent the status of the object. This is contrasted with the standard definition of a method, which is some activity that the object can perform. The distinction between methods and properties is by no means as sharp as these definitions suggest. In fact, the distinction between methods and properties is purely arbitrary. Deciding whether your object needs a method or a property is a design decision that is completely in your control as an object designer.

As you will discover when creating your own objects, properties and methods are both implemented by writing code. Methods are implemented by writing subroutines and functions. Properties are implemented by writing Property Lets and Property Gets—which look very much like subroutines and functions.

One example of the overlap between properties and methods can be seen in the Visual Basic Form object. The Form object has Top and Left properties, which can be read to determine where the Form is displayed on the screen. The Top property gives the distance, in twips, from the upper edge of the screen to the top of the Form. The Left property gives the distance in twips from the left edge of the screen to the left edge of the Form. What's interesting about these properties is that changing them causes the Form to relocate on the screen—surely an action. In fact, the Form also has a Move method that, when passed the position to move the Form to, relocates the Form. As a result of using this method, the Top and Left properties are updated. When the designers of the Form object wanted to expose the functionality that relocated a Form on the screen, they implemented it both as a property and as a method.

This kind of overlap between the effect of changing a property and the result of invoking a method can lead to a lot of fruitless discussion about which technique is better, changing the property or invoking the method. In a well-designed object, either choice should cause exactly the same code to execute. Properties and methods just provide a means for exposing the functionality that you build into your object. You are free to decide, when exposing some of your object's functionality, whether to use a property or a method (or both) as part of your object's interface.

The key factor in determining whether you should add a property or method to your object's interface has very little to do with any technical considerations. The most important consideration is how the functionality is regarded by the object's clients—which means understanding how your users think about their business.

In a set of objects for a bank, you might design an Account object which represents one customer's bank account. It might make sense to you to give that object a Balance property, which could be used to extract the current balance for the account. As my bank manager explained to me, though, that wouldn't be a good match to the way that bank employees think about a bank account's balance.

In the banking world, determining the balance of an account (especially a daily interest account) is a very complicated process. Calculating a balance involves determining what transactions are pending, what transactions are fully processed, and the amount of earned interest to apply. To someone familiar with the world of banking, it makes sense for the Account object to have a CalculateBalance method rather than a Balance property. The CalculateBalance method would determine the account balance, and pass the result back to the calling program.

It's not hard to imagine an interface that might confuse you because it doesn't meet the expectations that you have. A developer could, for instance, create a Car object that would plot a route to a location and calculate the gas that would be consumed. In order to use the object, a badly designed interface might require you to use a Go property that you would set to the name of the city that you wanted to go to. A better interface might would a PlotRoute method that accepted a city name, or a Destination property that should be set to the end of the trip.

Interface Guidelines

There aren't many generally accepted conventions in the area of object interface design. So, among the components that you work with, you can probably find some support for any specific object interface that you want to implement.

Given that there's probably already too much variety in component interfaces, you should try to avoid introducing new conventions unless they reflect some new functionality in your component. For instance, if you have a method that produces text on paper or the screen, call it "Print" not "Output," because Print is a common method on many objects. Go back to your scenarios and look at the dozen or so most likely ways that your object is going to be used. Look at similar objects that are used in similar situations and mimic their interfaces—it just makes life easier for your developer.

As with User Interface design, the first rule is to be consistent. You need to be consistent not just within your component, but within the environment in which your objects will be used. Rather than starting from scratch, try to pick an interface design standard that is common among developers who will be using your objects. And, regardless of what standard you pick, stick to it.

PROPERTIES AND METHODS • Where you do find yourself having to create new interface elements, there are some very general guidelines that you can follow when designing your interface. To begin with, you want to ensure that common tasks are performed easily: The most frequently performed tasks should require setting a single property or calling a single method. Going back to your original scenarios will help you determine what the most common tasks are.

Any common task that requires several values to be passed to it should probably be a method. If you expose this functionality through multiple properties, then you require the developer to set each of those properties to accomplish the task. Methods accept multiple values as parameters more easily than properties. If you use a method to implement the functionality, the client can call the single method, passing the necessary parameters.

In general, anything that reflects an object's current state should be a property. Typical examples in database applications are properties like Connected, DataLoaded, and Updated. For objects with a visible user interface, standard properties include items like Visible, BorderStyle, and Enabled.

If the functionality strongly lends itself to being a set of properties, you can eliminate the need to a number of properties by establishing a set of default values for those properties. If you do this, it may well be that the most common tasks will require only one of the properties to be set. The default values can either be predefined or based on values set in another property. In the WholesaleManagement model, shipping an order is one of the most common activities. However, this activity doesn't require the Order object's ShipToAddress property to be set before the Ship method is invoked. The Order object's ShipToAddress property defaults to the Customer's ShipTo address in the CustomerAddress table (and to the customer's billing address if no ShipTo address exists).

If a group of properties must be set in a specific order, then it implies that some action is being taken on each property. Since an action is implied, the functionality should probably be exposed as a method. The same is true of reading properties. If the order that the properties are read in has an effect on the object, then you should probably define the functionality as a method.

In general, if retrieving a property's value has a side effect (i.e., data is written to the database, or a change is made to the object's internal data), then you should probably treat the functionality as a method. The Remote Data Objects component has a routine called MoreResults that returns True if there is another Resultset to process. Even though this routine returns a value, this functionality is defined as a method because it also causes the next Resultset to be made available for processing.

One of the key differences between a method and a property is that the method can accept multiple values while properties generally accept only one (though there is an exception to that rule, as you'll see in Part 2). This difference creates a relationship between methods and properties. You can set up a method that accepts a series of parameters and then duplicate those parameters as properties of the object. The developer then has a choice in how to invoke the functionality.

As an example, Microsoft's latest model for accessing data, ActiveX Data Objects (ADO), includes a Connection object. The Connection object has both an Open method that accepts a ConnectionString parameter and a property called ConnectionString. A developer working with ADO can either set the ConnectionString property and call the Open method without parameters, or call the Open method and pass a ConnectionString as a parameter.

While duplicating method parameters as properties increases flexibility, it's not clear to me that there's any real benefit to this design. It's almost always more efficient to pass a group of parameters to an object as part of calling the method. The alternative is to make two trips to the object: one to set the property and one to call the method.

Making method parameters available as properties increases the amount of code required to build the object, lengthening the development process, and increasing the opportunity for bugs. Overlapping properties and parameters also make the object harder to understand for the client developer. I find myself constantly asking questions like, "If I set the ConnectionString property to one value and pass a different value as a parameter, which one is used?" (Generally, the standard is for the parameter passed to the method both to take precedence over the property value and to reset the property to the parameter's value.)

In earlier versions of COM, methods that required many parameters were difficult to work with. If you wanted to pass only the fifth parameter to a method, you had to supply five commas to the method to indicate all of the parameters that you had skipped. Now, named parameters allow the developer to specify which parameters are being supplied without all the commas. In addition, the IntelliSense feedback built into the most recent versions of Microsoft's tools provides developers use with instant feedback on a method's parameters.

Events

You can think of events in a number of different ways:

- Events are used by objects to coordinate activities with their clients. This is what a Command Button object does when it fires a Click event. It allows the Form that the button is part of to react to the button being clicked.
- Events provide the object developer with a way to run a subroutine in the client. A Command button fires a Click event to run the corresponding Click subroutine in the button's host Form.
- Events also provide the object developer with a way to pass data from the object to the client. The KeyDown event of a Form, for instance, passes parameters that tell the developer what keys on the keyboard were being pressed, what mouse button was clicked, and where the mouse pointer was at the time of the event.

While you can use events to meet any of these needs, you may not need to use events at all—many components do not fire events. Components that do fire events impose some performance costs on their clients

As you build your object, you'll want to consider when in your code you'll want to notify your clients or pass information to them. This means considering what conditions may occur as the code in your methods executes. If you want to notify your object's client of that condition, an event may be an appropriate way to send the notification. Before you jump to that solution, you should at least consider some of the other alternatives. These include:

- Providing a property in your object that your clients can check (a Status property, for instance). This method requires that your clients constantly check the property to determine your object's state. It also increases the chances for error should the client program fail to check your object's status at some critical moment. However, this technique does free your client to check the property when it is convenient to the client and ignore it the rest of the time.
- Implementing your method as a function that can return a value. With this technique you return a value to the client with the results of executing the method. This technique works well when you are returning a single value. However, if you are returning a number of data items or data and an error code, your code can get more complicated (I discuss various solutions to this situation in the chapter on Coding Objects).
- Requiring your object's clients to give your component a reference to an object in the client. The client can pass an object to your component either by setting one of your object's properties or passing the object as a parameter when calling a method. Your object can then invoke methods or set properties of the client's object when appropriate to pass information back to the client (this technique is known as a callback). The callback technique duplicates the functionality of an event, but are usually more efficient.
- Having your method accept parameters and modifying the value of one of the parameters in your component to indicate the results of your processing. Modifying parameters passed to a routine is a bad programming practice, as I discuss in Part 2.

Using events to communicate from your object to its clients avoids these problems. You can pass as much or as little information as you want when firing an event. In general, components that fire events make life easier for client developers. If a developer wants to respond to an event fired by your object, the developer just has to drop some code into an event routine. Visual Basic is fundamentally an event-driven development tool, so components that fire events fit more cleanly into the Visual Basic model than components that do not.

Also, many code-completion development environments (like Visual Basic) provide support for events. If you select an object and an event from the dropdown list boxes at the top of the Visual Basic code window, the editor will automatically write out the event's Public Sub line for you. This support is one of the main reasons for using events instead of callback functions.

Events also allow you to communicate when your object's clients don't call a method of the object. This situation occurs when an object has code that executes in parallel (and independently of) the program that created it. Returning a value from a method or altering a method's parameters requires the client to call a method of your object. These two techniques won't work when your object is running in parallel with its client and doesn't require the client to call a method.

Using events does have one major complication. When a client responds to an event fired by your object, the code that executes in the client can contain a reference back to your object. While responding to one of your events, a client could call another method of your object. As a result, if you fire events then you're going to have to address re-entrancy issues. The main issue with re-entrancy is determining whether a call to a method or a property of your object during an event will cause problems. For instance, a call to a method of your object might cause you to fire the event again, triggering the client code that causes the event to re-fire, trapping the client and your object in an endless loop.

If you fire an event when some condition occurs, you'll need to decide if you want to fire the event no matter how the condition occurs. It's not unusual for an object to provide several different ways to accomplish the same thing. One example is a Text Box, which can have its text changed both by the user through the user interface and through code in the application.

In the Text Box example, the designers chose to have the Change event fire both when the text is changed in the user interface and when it is changed through code. During the Form Load of many of my programs, I frequently load Text Boxes with default values, triggering the Text Box's Change event. I also sometimes put code in the Change event to edit input from the user. To prevent this code from running during the Form Load event, I have to add some extra code that checks whether the Change event is being fired because the Text Box is being changed from the user interface or from the Form Load event. It's a pain.

If you want to save some time for developers like me who are using your object, there are a couple of solutions to this problem. You can limit your events to specific situations (the Change event fires only when the code is changed from the user interface) or provide two events (ChangeFromUI and ChangeFromCode). All of these decisions should be made at the design phase for your objects.

Naming Names

Once you've defined your object's methods, properties, and events you'll have to assign names to them. This is not a trivial task. The names that you assign are the part of your object's documentation that developers will see most. When assigning names to your methods and properties there are some general rules that you should follow.

The first two rules are simple:

- Property names should be nouns.
- Methods names should be verbs.

These basic naming rules help to enforce the design decisions you made as you exposed your object's functionality as methods and properties.

I always recommend that you use a standard naming convention for all of the variables that you use in your program. The convention that I use, which you'll see in the code in this book, is a simplified version of the Reddick Visual Basic for Applications (RVBA) naming convention. RVBA is a variation on the Hungarian naming convention. RVBA applies a prefix that consists of a three character, lowercase string to each variable name. The prefix indicates the variable's data or object type. When setting up your object's interface, however, I don't recommend that you use the Hungarian convention. The standard in the COM world is that object names are all plain English words: Print, Visible, etc.

The industry standard is to use plain English words. This works to the developer's advantage in the Visual Basic world as the IntelliSense list boxes allow the programmer to pick out a method or property by typing the first few characters of a property or method's name. Imagine what would happen if the RVBA naming convention was applied to methods that return strings. All of these methods would have to begin with the letters "str" (see Figure 1–5). Many of an object's method names, which originally began with unique characters, would now share their first three characters. Where the methods could originally have been selected from the IntelliSense list boxes with one or two keystrokes, now a minimum of four is required. The IntelliSense list boxes would require more space to display the longer names, and so on. The operational problems created don't seem to justify the benefits provided by the naming convention.

The names of parameters passed to methods and returned by events also do not have prefixes applied to them. Ideally, the name you give to all of these items will allow the developer to determine what the method/property/event/parameter does without having to look it up in the Help system.

There are some rules that do apply to these names. One is that the names should contain no blanks ("ConnectionString", not "Connection String" or "[Connection String]"). In the Visual Basic world, another standard is to capitalize the initial letter of the words that make up the name. In the Java and JavaScript world, though, the standard is to leave the initial letter of the name in lowercase ("connectionString", not "ConnectionString"). Since COM allows your components to be used from all of these languages, you should determine which languages will be the primary environment for your component. A component that is primarily used for client-side scripting from within a Web browser will normally be interacting with JavaScript, for instance, and should follow that language's naming convention.

Event name conventions also vary from environment to environment. In the environment dominated by Java and JavaScript events that occur after something has happened are normally prefixed with the word "on" ("onClick", not "Click" or "OnClick"). In the Dynamic HTML model, Microsoft

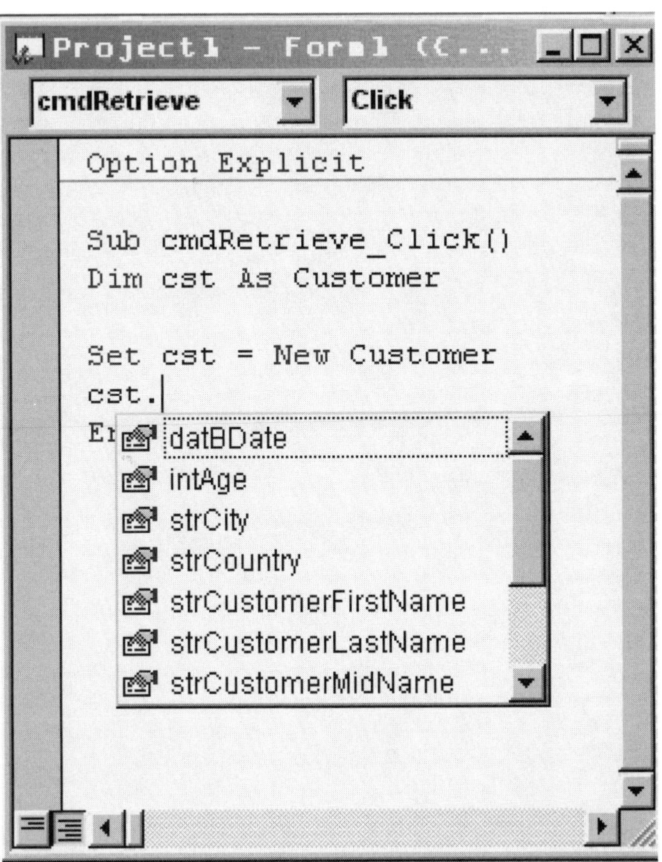

Figure 1–5 *Applying a naming convention to method and property names reduces the help that IntelliSense can provide to the developer.*

has followed this convention. Again, if this is the environment that your component will be used in predominately, this is the naming convention that you should follow for your Events.

Public and Private Interfaces

Having spent some time looking at the interfaces for our objects, it's time to back up one level and look at the components that are made up of these objects. Every component has an interface that it exposes to its clients. That interface is made up of the combined interfaces of the objects that make up the component.

In addition to the public interface exposed to your clients, your component may also have a private interface. Just as the developer of an application may create a series of objects to improve the design of the application, a component developer may break up the functionality of the component into a series of objects. Using objects makes it easier to develop components in the same way that using objects makes it easier to develop applications. As a result, your component may include objects that are used by the other objects in the component but aren't intended to be used by the component's clients. Those objects that are internal to the component form a private interface that is hidden from your clients.

Even the objects that are part of the component's public interface may not expose all of their methods and properties to their clients. Some of an object's methods may be designed to be used only by other objects in the component. These "hidden" methods and properties form another aspect of your object's private interface.

In the WholesaleManagement object model, there's an object that isn't displayed to the component's clients. This is the InventoryUpdate object, which handles all changes to the quantity on hand. Since the company wants to keep very close track of inventory levels, changing an inventory quantity involves a certain amount of logging and transaction management. All of that code is segregated into the InventoryUpdate object. The component's clients never access this object directly. Instead, the clients remove items from inventory only indirectly by creating an Order for that item.

An example of a method that is "hidden" from the clients that use the component can be seen in the Product object. This object has a method called SetQuantity that can change the value of the quantity in stock for any product. This method is not available to the WholesaleManagement component's clients and is used only by the InventoryUpdate object. Both the InventoryUpdate object and the Product object's SetQuantity method are available to the other objects in the WholesaleManagement component as part of the component's private interface.

Other parts of an object's private interface are obsolete methods and properties. As your component is enhanced, you may decide to phase out some method or property. In this situation you may not want to remove the obsolete method or property because clients that depend on those items will immediately stop working. On the other hand, you don't want new applications that use your component to invoke the now-phased-out method. COM allows you to hide the obsolete parts of your interface so that they can still be called from your clients but will not be visible to developers.

Root Objects

The model that I've described so far is missing one significant feature. The object model provides no way to process all the Customers, SalesRep, or Product objects in the system. This kind of processing is typically associated with collections.

For Figure 1–6 I've developed a revised version of the model that does allow those objects to be processed. This model includes a Company object, which provides access to SalesReps, Customers, and Products collections. These collections, in turn, contain all the SalesRep, Customer, and Product objects. The Company object does not need to be created by the application programmer. Instead the Company object is available as soon as any program starts to use the WholesaleManagement component. In this respect, the Company object is like the DBEngine object in DAO or the Application object in Excel, Word, and Visual Basic.

Unlike the previous objects, the Company object is independent of any table in the company database. The WholesaleManagement system doesn't store any data about the company as a whole, so there's no need for a Company table. While I've stressed a development process that moves from the data design to the object design, that doesn't mean that you can't create objects that don't correspond to items in your data model.

Though it doesn't have a table behind it, the Company object has some methods that are very important to the overall design of this system. In the WholesaleManagement object model, I want to ensure that new customer records are created in a highly controlled manner. To ensure this, Customer objects can only be created by using the CreateCustomer method of the Company object.

The Company object also provides an entry point to the object model. Most applications that use the WholesaleManagement component will begin by using one of the methods or collections of the Company object. As you'll see in the chapter on Components, because of the way that COM handles objects, most models will require you to define a "root object" that provides an entry point for your component.

Summary

In this chapter I looked at what an object is: a program designed to be used by other programs. I took a standard business application and showed how objects could be used to move complexity out of your program and into a component. As you begin to integrate objects into your development activities, you must develop the scenarios that describe how those objects are going to be used. In

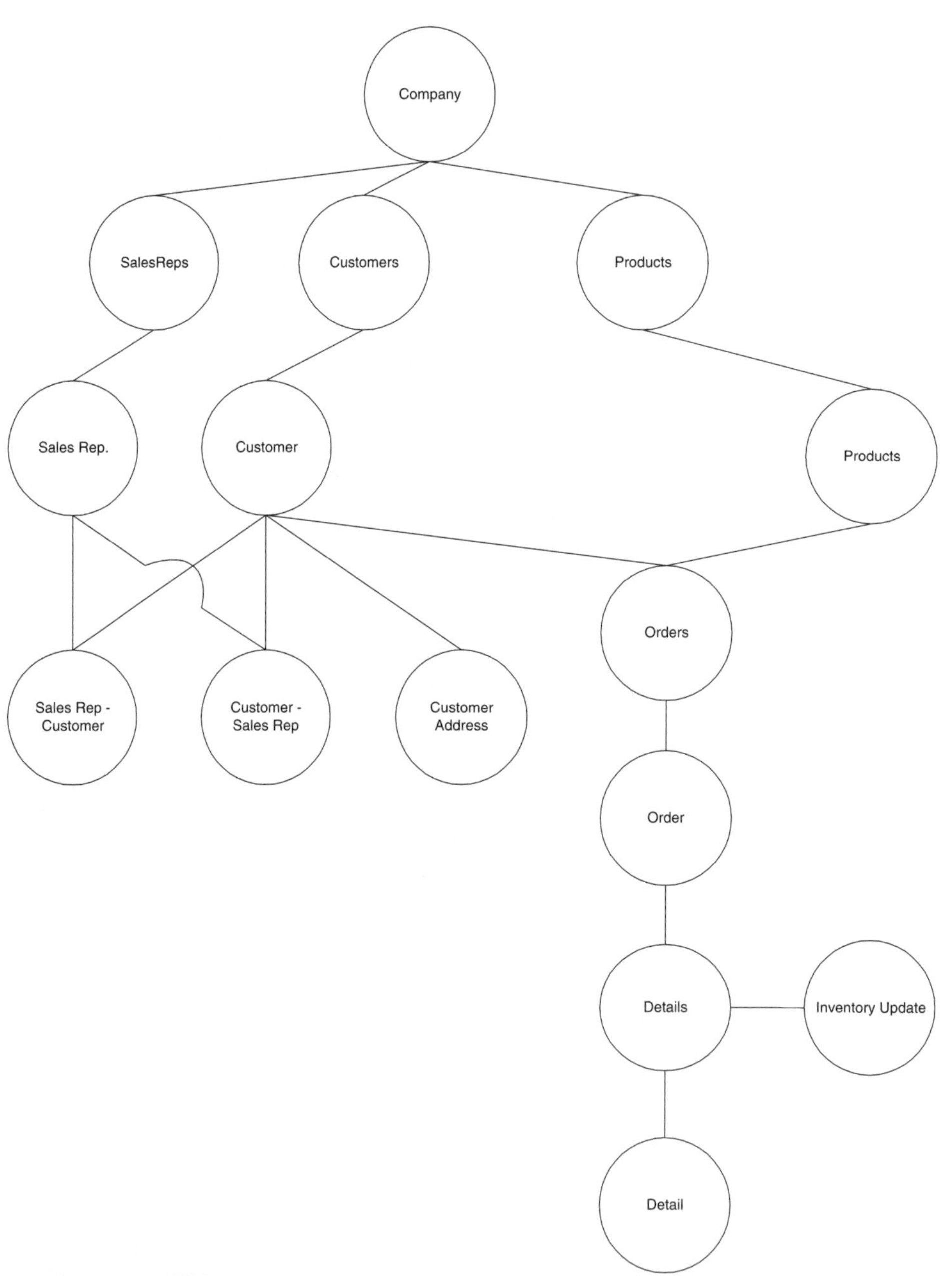

Figure 1–6 *The final version of the WholesaleManagement object model includes both private and public objects.*

this chapter you've learned about the issues that you should consider when designing your object to meet the needs of those scenarios.

Visual Basic comes with Visual Modeler, a tool to help you document the objects that make up your component. In the next chapter, I show you how to use Visual Modeler, starting from the initial design stages right through to having Visual Modeler generate the initial code for your objects for you.

In Part 2 of this book, I show you how to implement all of the features of WholesaleManagement object model. This will include how to create all of the different kinds of objects that I've outlined in this chapter. Part 2 also discusses how you can debug your code as you develop your objects. I look at the different compile options that you can take when you create and EXE and DLL from your component's code, and what effect they have on your components.

Getting used to working with objects means getting used to designing objects. The best way to do that is to build some object models. One exercise that I recommend is designing the tables that would have to underlie an object model that you are familiar with. In the DAO object model, for instance, there would have to be a table to store the information necessary for the Database object. This table would include fields for the database name and whether or not there is an active transaction. DAO would also require a table to list all of the WorkSpace objects, with fields that included the workspace name and the access type (ODBC or ODBCDirect). Another useful exercise is to take an existing application and consider the objects that you would need if you converted it into a component.

If you are interested in more information on the topics in this chapter, there are some excellent references available. The best book on the COM technologies for non-C programmers is *Understanding ActiveX and OLE* by David Chappell from Microsoft Press. The only article on object design that I've found is "The Basics of Programming Model Design" by Dave Stearns of Microsoft Corporation. Fortunately, it's very good. It was published in the June 1998 issue of the MSDN newsletter and can be found on the Microsoft Website at http://msdn.microsoft.com/library/techart/msdn_basicpmd.htm.

TWO

Visual Modeler

Visual Modeler is a graphical tool that allows you to describe the objects that make up an application. It draws its vocabulary of graphical elements from the Unified Modeling Language (UML). Visual Modeler is a subset of the tools that come with Rational Software Corporation's object modeling tool, Rational Rose.

In this chapter I'll introduce you to the basics of UML and how it is implemented in Visual Modeler. You'll see how to use Visual Modeler to build models of your components and how to turn those models into code. I'll also show you how to reverse engineer an existing Visual Basic project. More important, there are some issues that you need to think about before you even start to use a tool like Visual Modeler. To begin with, it's important to understand what a modeling tool will and won't do for you. That means understanding what Visual Modeler is and where it fits in your development activities.

Modeling Tools and Health Clubs

Before discussing how to use Visual Modeler, you should decide how a modeling tool will fit into your development methodology. Tools like Visual Modeler are like health club memberships—more people buy them than actually use them. Most people seem to feel that

1. Using a tool like Visual Modeler is a good thing (in some moral sense of the word "good").
2. If only they had a modeling tool, they would use it.

Most people buy health club memberships for the same reasons. They believe that they would be better off if they exercised regularly and that they would exercise regularly if they only had a facility they could go to. The reverse is usually true: People who already exercise regularly benefit from health club memberships. However, all the people who do exercise on a regular basis had to start sometime and perhaps buying a membership is your starting point.

If you are interested in graphically laying out your object-based designs, then Visual Modeler may be the right choice for you. However, if you aren't already doing this kind of design work, you probably won't start just because you have a tool that will help you do it.

I'm not saying that planning your component isn't a good thing to do. For components with a lot of objects, planning is essential if you want to avoid constantly rebuilding your component as you learn about how you want to use it. However, there are many ways to design components, ranging from using a large pad of paper to building prototypes to sitting and thinking quietly. My personal feeling is that using a tool to help you design your components does not necessarily make you a better developer than some one who does not. Even if you are using diagrams as part of your design process it isn't necessarily true that adopting a standard set of symbols (like UML) will cause you to do a better job.

While UML is said to be "process neutral" (meaning it can be used with a variety of methodologies), I'll be discussing it in terms of the use-case methodology. Use-case isn't the only game in town. Another methodology is Kent Beck and Ward Cunningham's CRC (for Classes-Responsibility-Collaboration) which can also be used to design object-oriented solutions.

Should you be investigating design strategies and tools to help you do a better job? The answer is a definite "Yes!" One of the benefits of having a tool like Visual Modeler ship with Visual Basic is that you can experiment with the tool to see if it works for you. Just don't think that buying a health club membership will get you in shape or that, if Visual Modeler and UML don't work for you, modeling isn't useful. Adopting Visual Modeler also means adopting a specific and disciplined way of building components.

Visual Modeler Benefits and Limitations

If you do want to use Visual Modeler, you should realize what it will, and will not, do for you.

What Visual Modeler Does

Visual Modeler will provide you with a means of documenting your object oriented design. Given that description of Visual Modeler, there are three main benefits that you will get from using it:

- First, the documentation that Visual Modeler produces will provide you with a tool for communicating with other developers familiar with UML.
- Second, Visual Modeler will provide you with an unambiguous way of recording the design decisions that you make. When reviewing your Visual Modeler-based design material, you will spend less time going "Now, what did I mean by that?"
- Finally, when you have finished working with Visual Modeler, you can have it generate the skeleton of the Visual Basic Class modules that correspond to your graphical design. You will still need to write the code to implement your methods, properties, and events, but much of the grunt work will be taken care of for you.

As an example, in the WholesaleManagement application, the forms that make up the User services are being outsourced to a company specializing in User Interface (UI) design. Only the business objects are going to be built by the company's developers. This division of labor is one of the reasons that a Visual Modeler diagram is being generated. The model will serve two purposes:

1. It will be used to communicate the design of the business objects to the UI development team.
2. The model will be used to generate the skeletons for the component development team to fill in, in parallel with the UI team.

You can also have Visual Modeler examine an existing Visual Basic project and take its best shot at generating a diagram that corresponds to your project. That diagram can give you a clearer picture of the modules that make up an existing application. The alternative is to try to decipher what the application does by plowing through the code in the application's Class modules. As an example of what Visual Modeler produces when reverse engineering an existing project, Figure 2–1 shows the diagram generated for the AEClient application that comes with the Application Performance Explorer in Visual Studio 6.

What Visual Modeler Doesn't Do

As my description suggests, what you can't expect from Visual Modeler is that it will help you design your component, except in an indirect fashion. To use Visual Modeler, you will have to develop the discipline of creating a Class diagram and working with the methodology that Visual Modeler is based on.

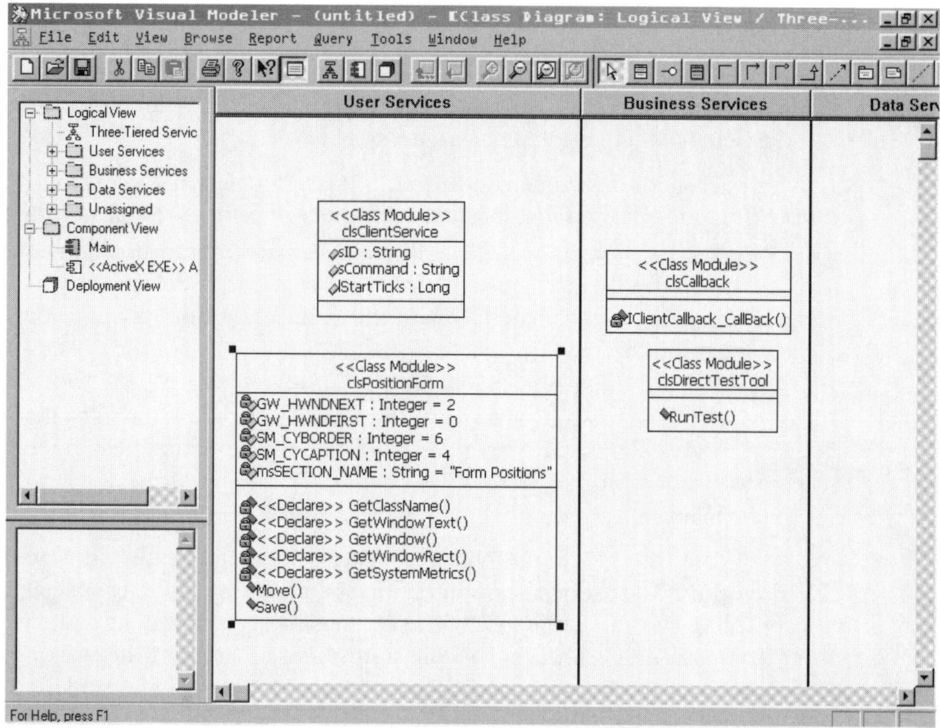

Figure 2–1 *A Visual Modeler Model.*

This may force you to think through your design in a more thorough fashion than you might otherwise do.

However, you should not expect Visual Modeler to make suggestions about which objects you need in your component, about whether or not your component should be compiled as an EXE or a DLL, or about any of the other design decisions that you will wrestle with.

The lack of help that UML gives you in designing your database is not unusual. In the database modeling world, the standard technique for documenting database designs is entity-relation (ER) diagrams. With ER diagrams, you make the decisions about what tables you need, what fields that they should have, and so on. ER diagrams provide you with a standard way of recording all of that information in a graphical format. On the other hand, ER diagrams do not help you design your data model. This is different from, for instance, the FORML modeling technique. FORML only asks you to record the basic facts about your data. When you have provided that information, a FORML-based tool will actually generate your database design, based on the information that you provided. Like ER diagramming tools, Visual Modeler provides you with a way of recording designs. Unlike FORML, Visual Modeler does not help you to design your component.

A Word From the Wise

I don't want to suggest that the discipline of a methodology or the process of documenting your design decisions is unimportant. To quote one of the authors of UML, Grady Brooch:

> "[the] primary product of a development team is not beautiful documents ... Rather, it is good software that satisfies the evolving goals of its users and the business. Everything else is secondary. Unfortunately, many software organizations confuse 'secondary' with 'irrelevant.'... Modeling is a central part of all of the activities that lead up to the deployment of good software. We build models to communicate the desired structure and behavior of our system. We build models to visualize and control its architecture. We build models to better understand the system we are building, often exposing opportunities for simplification and reuse. We build models to manage risk."

UML Benefits and Limitations

In a team environment, the importance of a common, unambiguous method for communicating information is essential to ensuring that every team member knows what the other team members intend to do. A formal language like UML removes ambiguity from the discussion by using symbols that, unlike words in natural languages like English, mean exactly one thing.

UML was developed by integrating the best features of a number of existing modeling languages. The language is supported by a number of organizations (including Microsoft) and is an official standard of the Object Management Group. It is a graphical language for creating diagrams like the ones that Visual Modeler produces.

An ideal formal language would be so easy to read that ordinary users could be quickly taught to check the formal descriptions produced by the developers. Better yet, users could produce those descriptions themselves. Since UML is too technical for most people to become comfortable with until they've had some months of training and experience, UML will probably never become an effective tool for communicating with end users. That doesn't mean it isn't an effective tool among developers and developer teams.

UML, through the use of rules that control how the symbols that make it up can be used, does provide some error checking for the diagrams that you create with it. If you enter inconsistent data into a UML modeling tool, the tool can inform you that you've broken one of the rules in UML's grammar. Notice that the tool can't tell you if the diagram that you've entered matches what your users need you to build. The best that any UML tool can do is tell you that what you've entered doesn't make sense in terms of the UML grammar.

Methodology

While UML is a language for creating diagrams, it also assumes that you are using a methodology that will require you to create those diagrams at the appropriate point in your development process.

The methodology that UML is based on involves developing a set of "use cases." A use case describes an interaction between one or more actors and an application. For the WholesaleManagement component, actors might include data entry clerks, sales representatives, company management, and customers. An interaction with the application would include adding a new customer, updating an order, and requesting a report (among other activities).

From a set of use cases, you can determine what objects your system will require and design your classes accordingly. The process of recognizing actors and objects in the use cases still depends on the ability of the designers rather than applying rules from the underlying methodology.

A sample use case for the WholesaleManagement system might look like this:

Use Case for WholesaleManagement System

Overview

This use case describes how a sales representative updates a customer's order.

Primary Actor

Sales representative

Secondary Actor

Customer

Starting Point

The customer's order has been entered into the system and the customer is requesting a change to the order.

Ending Point

The order is updated or the updates are rejected.

Measurable Results

The order is updated to reflect the change requested by the secondary actor.

Flow of Events

The case begins when the actor requests the display of a specific customer order to make a change requested by the customer. The actor will then make the change to the order requested by the secondary actor.

The order may not have any dates changed to a date prior to the current date. The customer number on the order may not be changed. These two changes will cause the change to the order to be rejected.

Alternative Flow of Events

If the order does not exist, the actor will be advised that the order does not exist and given the opportunity to search for it.

When the order is displayed, if it is not an order for the requested customer, the actor will be able to list orders for the customer.

From this use case (and others generated in the analysis phase of a project) you would probably identify sales representatives as one set of actors in this system. Objects indicated by this case might include orders and a searchable collection of orders.

UML is also designed to work best when used on certain kinds of problems. The UML methodology tends to assume that you are creating a business application. While it wouldn't be wrong to use UML to design a utility like Microsoft Word or a real-time process control system, those kinds of applications aren't what the designers of UML were considering as they developed the tool. UML is also intended to help develop the characteristics of, and the relationships among, the objects in the application. A UML based tool like Visual Modeler does not, for instance, provide much support for the details of user interface design.

To help you determine what objects will be required in your system and what attributes they must have, UML allows you to create a series of graphical models, each of which is a simplified version of the information in your use cases. A Sequence Diagram, like the one shown in Figure 2–2 for instance, shows when activities occur in relationship to each other but not necessarily where (e.g., on the client, on the server, at the warehouse, at home).

Generating these diagrams forces you to think about the information that each diagram requires. Without creating a Sequence Diagram, you might not consider the order of operations for some of your cases. However, just by placing all of your cases on a Sequence Diagram, you are obliged to consider

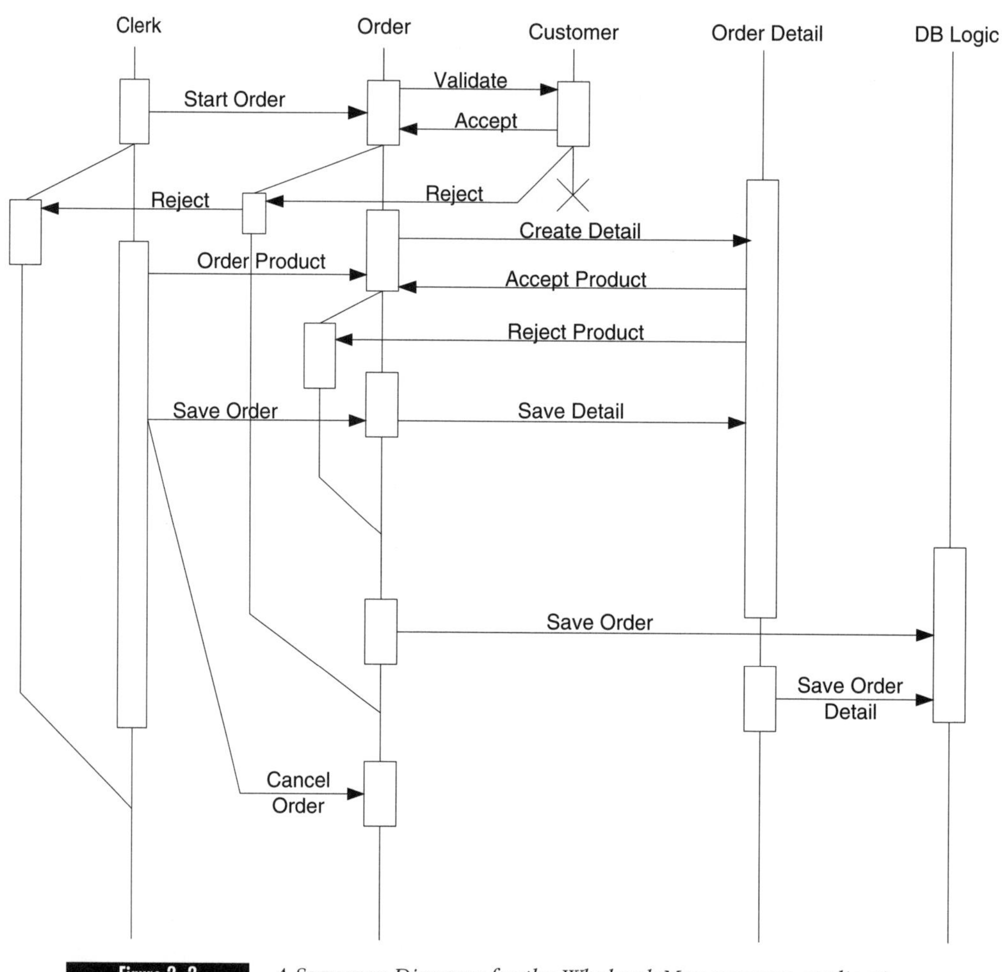

Figure 2–2 *A Sequence Diagram for the WholesaleManagement application.*

how they relate to each other. In many cases, the process of creating the diagram might be more valuable to you than the final product.

Implementation

UML, while it specifies how the design process is carried out, does not specify how the design is to be implemented. For instance, UML does not require you to use any particular language when you go to write code for your classes.

Most use cases include some set of restrictions on what can be done in the use case. A use case for creating a sales order, for instance, might indicate that an order cannot be created unless the customer has a specific credit rating. These restrictions correspond to what are frequently called "business rules." Use cases also include measurable results: what effect the performing this case will have. The use case for creating the sales order might state that the measurable results include creating a sales order, generating a shipping order, and reducing the quantity of a product in inventory.

Using UML in your design does not require you to implement the business rules in your application program, in the objects used by the program, or in triggers and stored procedures in a database. UML is language neutral. The code to perform the activities in the use case can also be implemented in any one of a number of locations without violating any part of the UML methodology.

Never-the-less, the more of the concepts that UML depends upon that exist in your development tool, the easier it will be to go from the UML description to the code. For example, Class Diagrams (one of the UML diagrams that Visual Modeler allows you to create) document the classes that your application needs. This documentation includes listing the methods and properties for each class, plus the relationships among the classes. A language and development environment that allows you to create classes, methods, and properties will make it much easier to implement your UML documented design.

UML and Visual Basic

If you choose to implement your business rules with a development tool that allows you to create middle-tier objects, the conversion from the UML diagram to the executing code will be much easier. Visual Modeler, for instance, can generate Visual Basic Class modules directly from Visual Modeler Class Diagrams because there is a one-to-one correspondence between many UML concepts and Visual Basic code structures. From your Class Diagram, Visual Modeler can write out the declarations for all of the methods, properties, and events that you've specified in the diagram.

Some essential elements of a Visual Basic implementation don't have a counterpart in UML. In other words, UML provides no way for you to specify some required attributes of your Visual Basic project. As a result, some information specific to implementing a UML design in Visual Basic is supplied through the use of UML stereotypes. Where many different implementations are possible, a UML stereotype describes a specific way of implementing part of the diagram. For instance, specifying that a particular diagram is to use the << ActiveX DLL >> stereotype will cause Visual Modeler to create a Visual Basic project with its compile options set to create an ActiveX DLL.

In addition, some concepts have only partial matches in the Visual Basic environment. UML includes the concept of packages, which are bundled groups of functionality. The closest that Visual Basic comes to this concept is a single project or a Microsoft Transaction Server package, neither of which are an exact match to a UML package.

And, of course, some features supported by UML aren't present in Visual Basic. Not all of the relationships that can exist between classes in a UML model are supported by Visual Basic, for instance. Dependency, where one class depends upon the methods and properties of another class, is not directly supported by Visual Basic. Since Visual Modeler lets you create these dependency relationships, you will find that when you generate code from Visual Modeler that not all of the information in your diagram is translated into code.

Working With Visual Modeler

You can start Visual Modeler from two locations: from the Add-Ins menu of Visual Basic or from the Windows Start menu (you'll find Visual Modeler under Visual Studio | Visual Studio Enterprise Tools). If you don't start Visual Modeler from Visual Basic, you may run into problems if you intend to generate code during your Visual Modeler session. When you generate code from Visual Modeler without starting it from Visual Basic, Visual Modeler always starts a new copy of Visual Basic. If Visual Basic takes too long to start, Visual Modeler simply gives up and does not create any code.

The alternative is to start Visual Modeler from Visual Basic. To do this, you must first add Visual Modeler to your Add-Ins menu by setting both the Visual Modeler Add-In and the Visual Modeler Menus Add-In to Loaded under the Tools | Add-In Manager menu choice. Once you've loaded these two add-ins, you can start Visual Modeler by selecting either Reverse Engineering Wizard or Browse Class Diagram from the Add-Ins | Visual Modeler menu.

If you pick Browse Class Diagram, the Class Diagram that you open must match the already existing modules in your program. The match is case sensitive: A class module in your Visual Basic project called Class1 won't match a module in Visual Modeler called CLASS1. Normally, you will use this option to open a Class Diagram that has been created in conjunction with your project.

Selecting Reverse Engineering Wizard will generate a Class Diagram that matches your project (including any objects selected in your project's References list). Reverse engineering will also add the model to your Visual Basic project in a folder called Related Documents.

Reverse Engineering With Visual Modeler

What this all suggests is that you shouldn't try to create a Class Diagram for an existing project and then try to integrate it into your project—trying to resolve the differences between the Visual Modeler and Visual Basic versions of your project will drive you mad. The easiest way to begin a Visual Modeler model, at least if you intend to generate Visual Basic code, is by selecting Reverse Engineering from within a Visual Basic project. You should take this option even if you've just started a new project and it has nothing in it.

If you are reverse engineering a project that contains objects, the first page of the Wizard allows you to select which objects you want to reverse engineer (see Figure 2–3). For most programs, selecting ActiveX controls on this form will substantially lengthen the time needed to produce the diagram as Visual Modeler will also generate icons for every ActiveX control in the project. The second page of the Wizard requires that you assign each module in the program to one of the three layers that make up a Visual Modeler project: User services, Business services, and Data services (again, see Figure 2–3). You make the assignment by selecting a service in the lower left window and then dragging a module from the top window. The assignments that you make here can be changed later, so don't panic if you're not sure which level to put a particular module in.

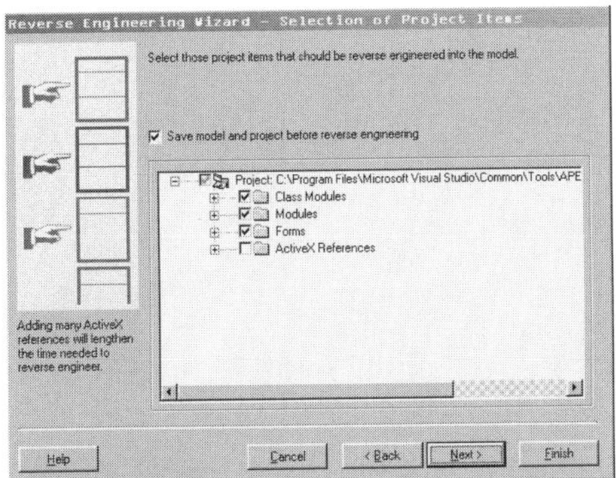

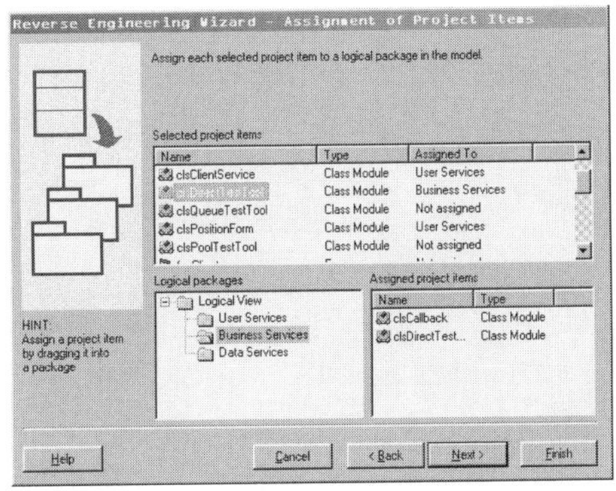

Figure 2–3 *The first two screens of the Visual Modeler Reverse Engineering Wizard.*

Before generating a diagram, Visual Modeler provides an estimate of how long the process can be expected to take. For the AEClient application in the Application Performance Explorer project, Visual Modeler's estimate was 51 minutes. To make the test more realistic, I ran the Wizard on a 32 meg, P100 laptop and loaded Microsoft Word to work on other projects while Visual Modeler ran in the background. The analysis ended up taking two hours but did not interfere with my work in Word.

The Visual Modeler Display

When Visual Modeler starts up, it displays three windows (see Figure 2–4):

- The pane on the right is used to display the various diagrams that you work with. Initially, this displays the three-part Class Diagram window that is the main diagram in the Logical View. Also minimized in this pane is the Log window. This displays information about the results of converting your diagram to code or running a check on your model.

• The top left pane is the Explorer or Browser window (the documentation uses both terms, I will use Explorer window). This window lets you review or select the elements that make up your Visual Modeler design.

• The pane in the lower left corner is the Documentation window, which displays the text documentation associated with the currently selected diagram or item on the diagram.

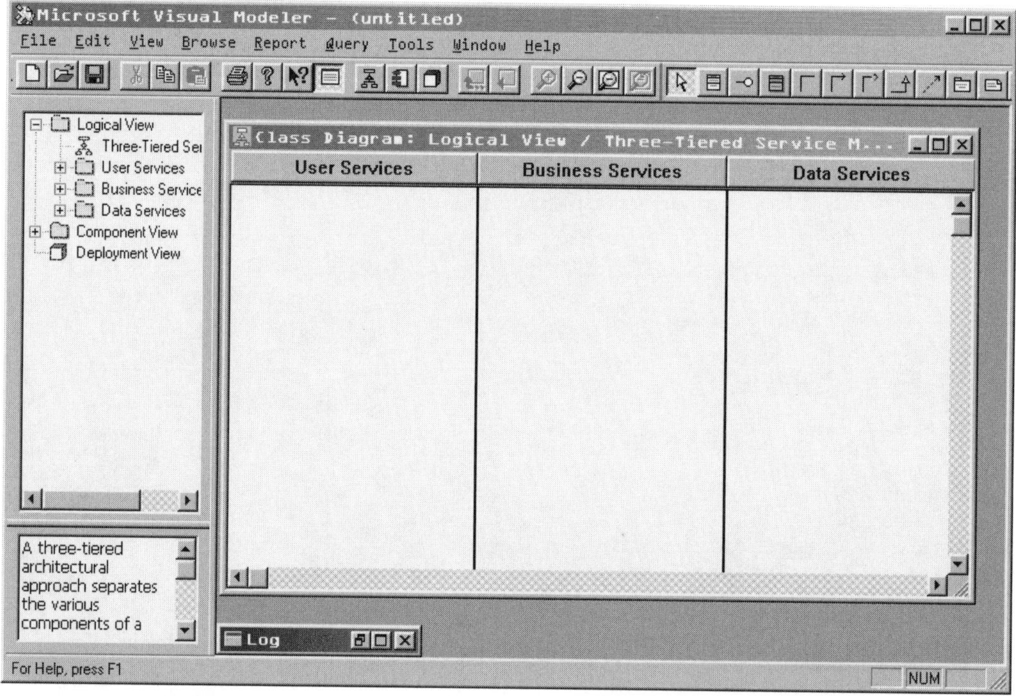

Figure 2–4 *Visual Modeler's initial display, showing the Logical View of the project.*

The Visual Modeler Help file includes an excellent tutorial to get you started with Visual Modeler (though I feel the tutorial starts you off creating the wrong diagram). In this chapter, I'll provide you with more background on Visual Modeler than the tutorial does (among other things, I'll cover the diagrams that the tutorial ignores). Throughout, my emphasis will be on what a component developer needs to know to use Visual Modeler effectively.

MANIPULATING ITEMS AND DIAGRAMS

A Visual Modeler project consists of diagrams and the items that appear on the diagrams. The Class Diagram, for instance, is used to display Class items, which describe the classes that make up your project. Both items and the diagrams that they appear on are displayed in the Explorer window that sits in the upper left corner of the Visual Modeler window. Diagrams can also include notes, text boxes, and lines that indicate relationships between items (see Figure 2–5). Visual Modeler organizes diagrams into three views:

Logical View, for Class Diagrams

Component View, for Component Diagrams

Deployment View, for the single Deployment Diagram

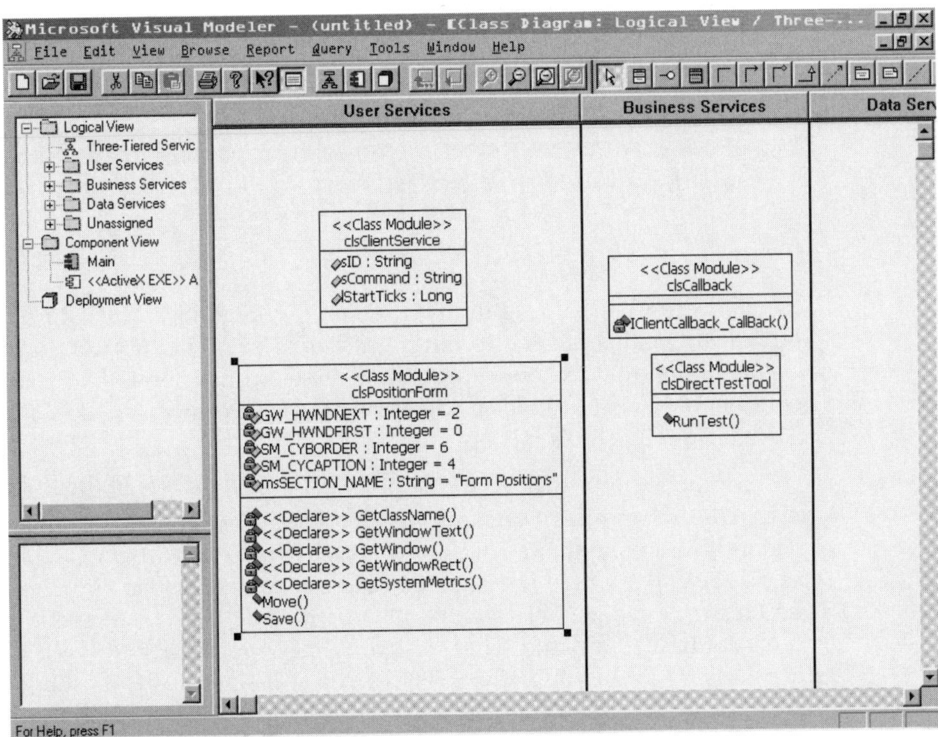

Figure 2–5 *A sample Visual Modeler Class Diagram.*

Double-clicking on a diagram in the Explorer window opens the diagram in a window in the pane on the right. Double-clicking on an item in the Explorer window, instead of double-clicking a diagram, opens the item's Specifications form, again in the pane on the right. The Specifications form for an item can also be opened by right-mouse clicking on an item and selecting Open Specification. An item's specification consists of a set of tabs that organize the information about the item. For a Class module, the Specification information includes the name of the class and information on how code for that class is to be generated.

Items can be added directly to a diagram or dragged from the Explorer Window onto the diagram. You can add an item to multiple diagrams. If you do, changes made in one occurrence of the item will appear in all of them.

One side effect of Visual Modeler's ability to have one item on several diagrams is that creating a brand new item by copying an existing one requires some special handling. If you just copy and paste a Class, for instance, the Class that you paste will be treated as another instance of the original rather than as a new item. If you want to create a new Class by copying an existing one, you'll need to follow these steps:

Select the item that you want to copy

Copy the item

Change the name of the original item

Paste the item

When you paste the item, it will still have its original name. Since you have changed the name of the original item, you have ensured that the pasted copy will have a different name than the original and will be treated as a separate item.

Items can be removed from a diagram by right-mouse clicking on them and selecting either Delete (to remove the item from the diagram) or Delete from Model (to remove the item from the project completely). If your diagram gets cluttered, Visual Modeler will clean up the layout if you select Layout Diagram from the Tools menu.

The initial view that Visual Modeler displays is the tool's Logical View, which consists of Class Diagrams that you use to define the classes and the relationships among them. I wasted a lot of time trying to figure out how to use Visual Modeler until I realized that the Logical View is the wrong place to start creating a model. This is especially true if, like I did, you intend to generate Visual Basic code from your design. While you can define classes in the Class Diagram, many of the options that you will want to set in order to generate Visual Basic code can't be set on this diagram. To set those options, I discovered that I must assign my Classes to Components, which are defined in Component View. The best place to start working with Visual Modeler is Component View.

Component View

Visual Modeler's Component View allows you to diagram the components (EXE's and DLL's) that make up your model. A Component is made up of one or more of the classes that you define in the Class Diagram. Each Visual Modeler Component will create a Visual Basic project when you generate code for it. Visual Modeler Component items allow you to specify options that will be used when you generate your Visual Basic code.

ADDING COMPONENTS AND COMPONENT DIAGRAMS

Clicking on the plus sign beside Component View in the Explorer window reveals that it already contains a sample Component Diagram called Main. This Main diagram can be renamed but not deleted. You can add new Component Diagrams by right-clicking on the Component View folder and selecting New | Component Diagram.

The WholesaleManagement model consists of two components. One component contains only the Customer object while all of the other objects (Company, Product, OrderHeader, etc.) are in the second component. The Customer object is kept in a separate component because it will be re-used. In addition to the WholesaleManagement application, many of the company's other systems will also need to use the Customer object. By putting it in a separate component, the Customer object can be used in a variety of applications without having to include the whole WholesaleManagement component in every application.

Once a Component Diagram is displayed, you can add new Components to it. To add a new Component, click on the Component button in the toolbar and then click on the diagram where you want it to appear. The Component will be added to the diagram and to the Explorer window in the same folder as the diagram that you added it to. Figure 2–6 shows the Component view of the WholesaleManagement system with the Customer and Wholesale-Objects components displayed.

Another way to create Components is to right-mouse click on the Component View folder in the Explorer window and select New | Component from the popup menu. This process creates a Component in the Explorer window but does not add it to any Component Diagram (you can add it to a diagram later by dragging it out of the Explorer window and dropping it on a Component Diagram).

DEPENDENCIES

When you've put more than one Component on a menu, you can indicate relationships between them. You can show that one Component is dependent on another by drawing a Dependency line between them. With Components, Dependency relationships indicate that an object in one Component calls an object in the other Component. You draw a dependency line by clicking on the Dependency button on the toolbar, clicking on the calling Component in the relationship and dragging to the second Component. A dependency relationship between Components has no effect on the generation of your Visual Basic code. The relationship shown in Figure 2–6 indicates that the WholesaleObjects component is dependent on the Customer Component.

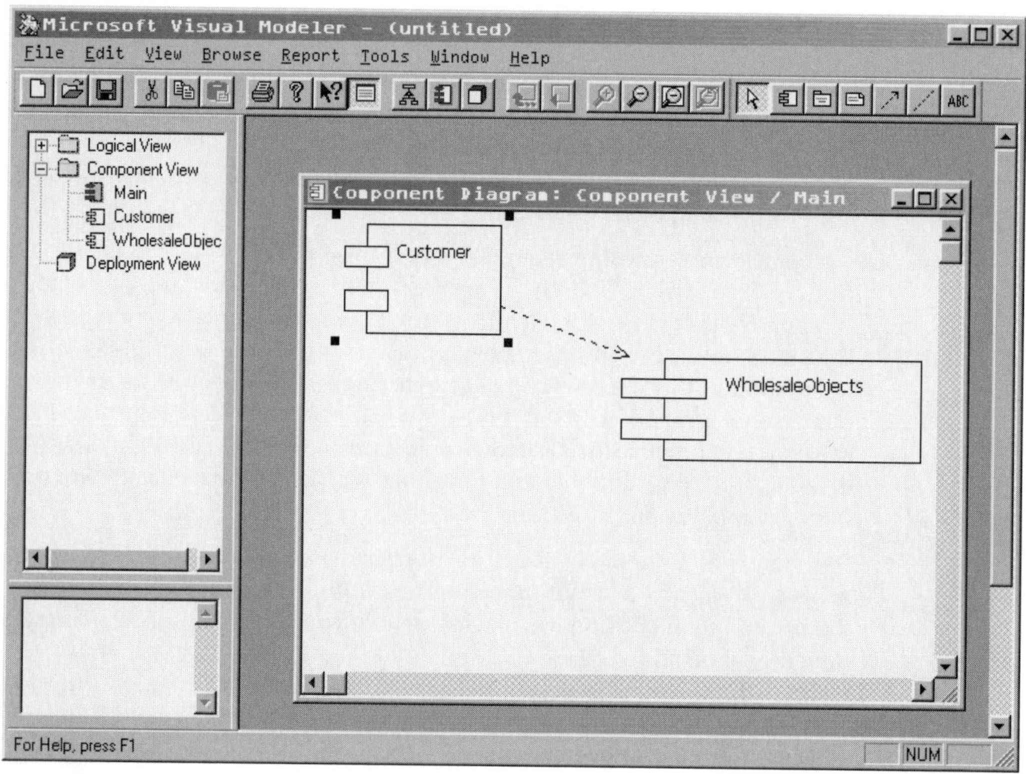

Figure 2–6 *The WholesaleManagement system is made up of two components. One holds the Customer object while the rest of the objects are held in the WholesaleObject component.*

COMPONENT SPECIFICATIONS

A Component's Specifications form allows you to set information about the component. Later, during code generation, Visual Modeler will use this information to control the way that code is generated for the component. A Component's Specifications form is broken up into two tabs: General and Realizes (see Figure 2–7).

The General tab allows you to specify a Component name, Documentation, Stereotype, and Language. Information entered into the Documentation window in the Specifications form will be included on Visual Modeler reports, added as comments to generated code, and displayed in Visual Modeler's Documentation window when the component is selected.

The default Language for a Component is 'Analysis' and is effectively "no language." To specify a particular language, use the Language drop down listbox.

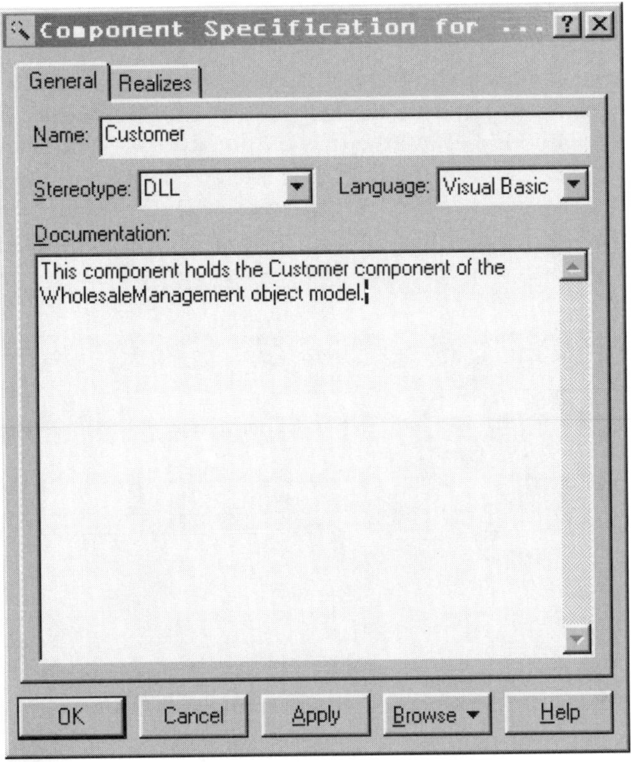

Figure 2–7 *The Specifications form for a Component.*

The Language listbox will show all of the supported languages that have been installed for Visual Modeler. In a complete installation of Visual Studio, that will include Visual Basic, Visual C++, and Visual J++.

Not surprisingly, if you are creating a model that will generate Visual Basic code you should set the Language listbox to Visual Basic. Selecting Visual Basic will add a Visual Basic tab to the Specifications form. This tab lists Visual Basic specific options for the Component (you will have to close and reopen the Component's Specifications form to view the tab). Selecting Visual Basic also makes the various stereotypes that control code generation available for you to choose.

Once you've selected the Language, you can now select the appropriate stereotype for the Component. While the Stereotype listbox gives you a number of choices, the only relevant options for generating components in Visual Basic are DLL and EXE, which create an ActiveX DLL or EXE, respectively.

The Realizes tab (see Figure 2–8) in the Component Specifications form lists Class items in the model that can be associated with the Component. The Classes associated with the Component will be included in the Visual Basic project generated from the Component. The Realizes tab on the Specifications form can list either just the Classes already associated with the Component or all the Classes in the model (checking the 'Show all classes module' at the top of the tab switches between the two lists). To assign a Class to the Component, right-mouse click on a Class in the list and select Assign. A red checkmark appears beside each Class associated with the Component.

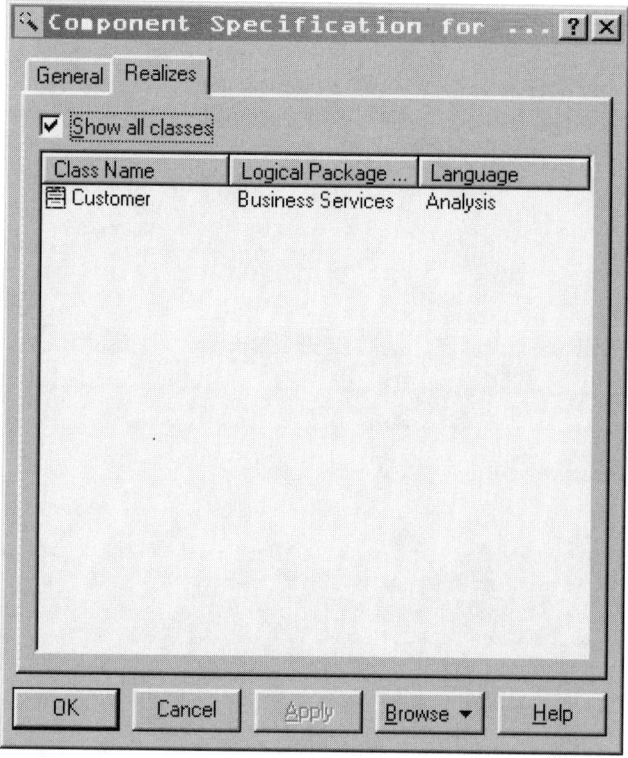

Figure 2–8 *The Realizes tab lists the Classes that make up a Component.*

Class Diagram

With Components defined, you can return to the Logical View and begin designing your Classes. The Logical View is organized around the three-tiered Class Diagram and the three areas that it defines: User, Business, and Data Services. The three-tier Class Diagram integrates information from single-tier

Package Overview Diagrams in each of the three service areas. You can add additional single- and three-tier Class Diagrams to the model. The various Class Diagrams appear under the Logical Services entry in Visual Modeler's Explorer window.

Once you open a Class Diagram, you can add Class items to it by clicking on the Class object on the tool bar and then clicking on the diagram. As you create Class items, they appear both in the diagram and in the Explorer window. Like Components, Class items can also be added to the Logical View without placing them on a specific diagram. In the Explorer window each Class appears under the User, Business, or Data service folder, depending on where they were added in the three-tier diagram.

For the WholesaleManagement application, all of the objects that will be created by the company's developers will be Business Services objects. The objects to access data will be provided by Microsoft's ActiveX Data Objects and the company outsourced the UI development. Had the model needed to show these additional items, you could have added Class Utility items to the diagram. These are very similar to Class items but are used for Visual Basic objects that aren't going to be implemented as Class modules (e.g., Forms and Modules).

Each Class item appears with three bands (called compartments) across it. The top compartment displays the Class name and stereotype, the middle compartment lists all the properties that you define for the Class, and the bottom compartment lists the Class's methods. Figure 2–9 shows a Class module with several properties and methods, along with its Specifications form. By right-mouse clicking on the Class and selecting Options from the popup menu, you can select which compartments you want to have displayed or suppressed.

CLASS SPECIFICATIONS

The Class Specifications form consists of the General, Methods, Properties, Relations, Components, and Visual Basic tabs. The Components tab allows you to assign the Class to an existing Component item. The Component that the Class is assigned to controls the Stereotypes that you can use with the Class (which is why you should create your Components first). This is the tab that would be used to assign the Customer object to the Customer component and the remaining objects in the model to the WholesaleObjects component.

The General tab on the Specifications form lets you set the Class module name, Stereotype, and documentation. The Stereotype specifies the kind of Class module that will be generated by Visual Modeler. The various stereotypes that you can use to control your code generation are listed in Table 2.1.

The Method tab allows you to create methods for your Class. Double-clicking on the window in the Methods tab brings up the Method Specifications form. The Methods Specifications form allows you to specify the type of

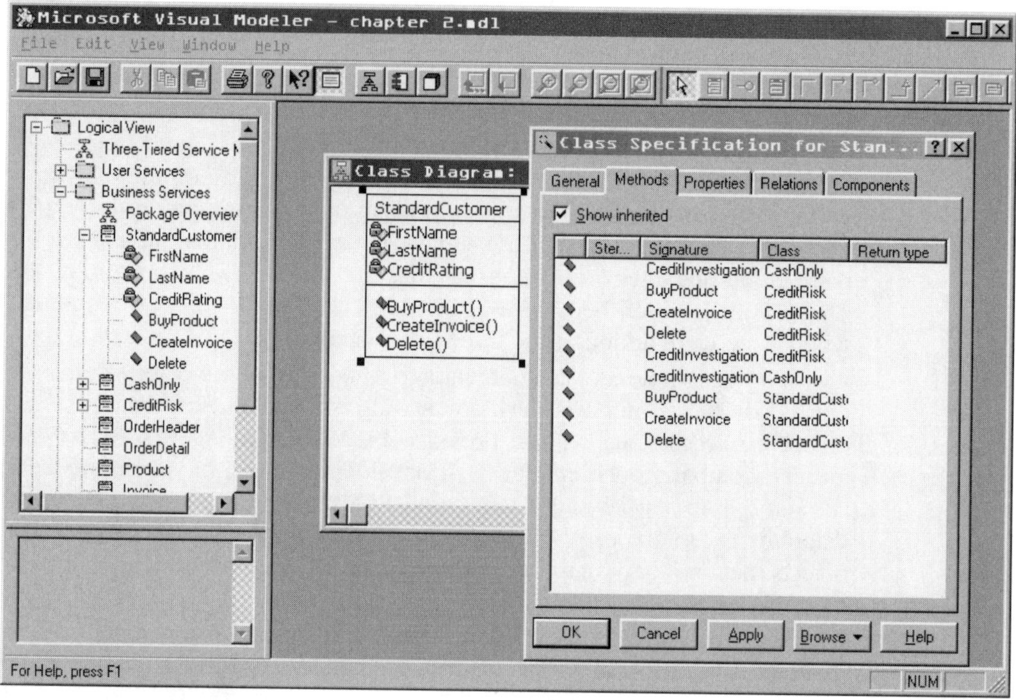

Figure 2–9 *A Visual Modeler Class description and its Specifications form.*

Table 2.1 Stereotype Options for Class Modules

Stereotype Name	Description
Class	(Default) Generate a Visual Basic Class module.
Control	No code will be generated. Use this for classes that are required by the model but are not required in code or that you don't want generated by Visual Modeler.
Interface	Generates a class module. There's a shortcut for creating this kind of module: Just click on the Interface button on the toolbar.
Module	Generates a standard Basic module.
All others	Classes with these stereotypes are created during the reverse engineering process but are not generated by Visual Modeler.

method, the data type of the value returned by the method, and the parameters required. Methods also have Stereotypes which control whether the method is to be generated as a property, method, or event. The Property tab allows you to establish a name, data type, and initial value for your properties.

One benefit of working with Visual Modeler is that it emphasizes the fundamental similarity of methods, properties, and events. Methods and properties are both thinly disguised functions and subroutines: In Visual Modeler it just depends on what stereotype you define them with. As I'll discuss later, events are just a way for objects to call subroutines in the clients that are using them.

The Company object in the WholesaleManagement system has a method that creates a Customer object. The Specifications form for this method allows you to define this method. To begin with, you can use the form to assign the name CreateCustomer to the method. You can also specify the method's return type as Customer. When a method returns an object as the CreateCustomer method does, you must define the object to be returned before you can set the return type of the method. In this case, that means that the Customer object must be added to the Class Diagram before the CreateCustomer method can be fully specified.

The CreateCustomer method accepts only one parameter, which can also be specified on this form. The required parameter is called CustomerName and it is a string data item. Since this function is a standard method, no stereotype is required. The method will be called by the object's clients so the method must be flagged as Public.

CLASS ASSOCIATIONS

Once you have multiple Class modules on a diagram, you can establish relationships among them. There are really just two kinds of relationships: Association (bidirectional, unidirectional, or aggregate) and Generalization. All associations are generated by clicking on the Associations button on the toolbar, clicking on one of the Class modules, and then dragging to the other Class module involved in the relationship to draw a line between them. The lines that join items can be bent to make the diagram easier to read: Just click on the line and drag it to add a corner.

Association Types • In UML, an association means that one object's state depends on another object. In the WholesaleManagement system, the OrderDetail object depends on the OrderHeader object. To know the state of an OrderDetail, you would have to know about the OrderHeader object: Is the order a backorder, a rush order, and so on. But the Order object also depends on the OrderDetail object—an order cannot be shipped unless there's enough product in stock to satisfy each OrderDetail. This relationship is a bi-directional association and is drawn as a single line.

On the other hand, a Product object's state does not depend on the OrderDetail objects that exist for it. A Product object may exist without any OrderDetail objects, for instance. An OrderDetail does depend on a Product object—if a Product is deleted, then all the OrderDetails for that object are also deleted. This is a unidirectional relationship and is drawn as a line with an arrow at the end of the line with the controlling (or supplier) object. (In this case, the arrow points to the Product object.)

An aggregate association indicates that one object is subordinate to another object. In the previous two examples, the OrderHeader/OrderDetail relationship is best described as an aggregate association. This association is drawn as a line with a diamond at the end with the object that controls the other object (in this case, the OrderHeader object). Figure 2–10 shows some of the associations in the WholesaleManagement component.

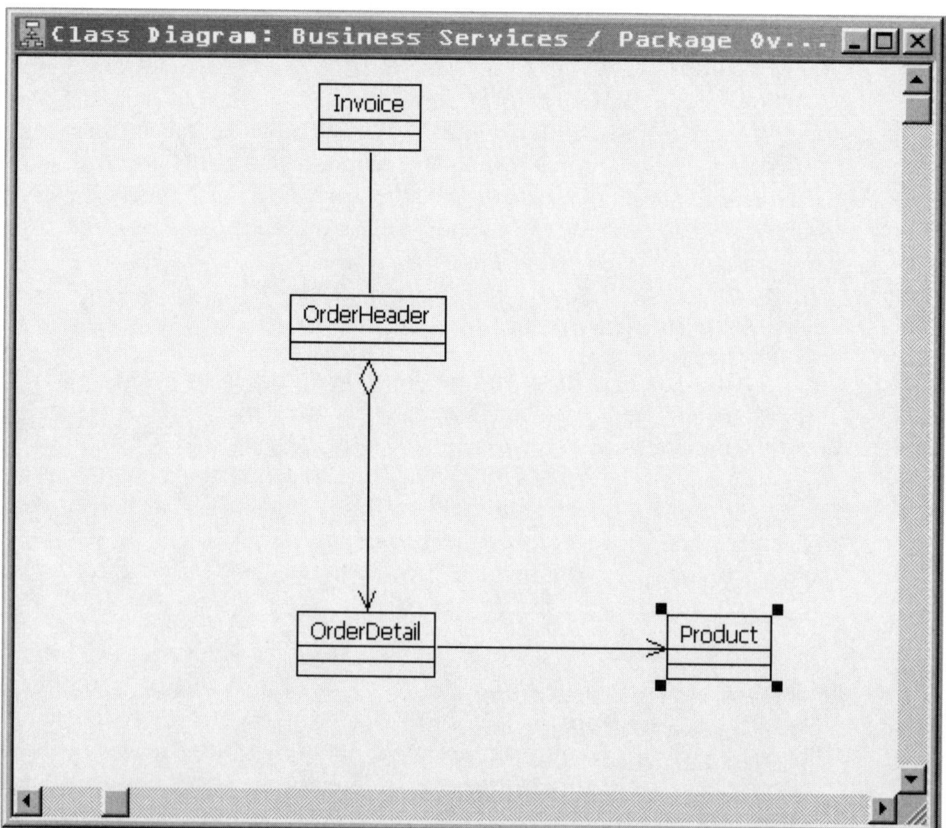

Figure 2–10 *The three kinds of association supported by Visual Modeler.*

When code is generated for objects in an association, variables are added to the Class modules that are created. For uni-directional associations, the controlling object in the class will have a variable added to it that can refer to the other object in the association. In a bi-directional association, both Classes get an object variable that can refer to the other object. Aggregates have no effect on code generation.

GENERALIZATION • A Generalization association represents inheritance. Inheritance occurs when one class (the subclass) implements the methods and properties of another class (the superclass), along with the superclass's functionality. When code is generated for this relationship, Visual Modeler will

- place an Implements statement in the subclass's module. This statement will force the subclass to have all the methods, properties, and events of the superclass. If the superclass has a method called Post, then the subclass will be given a method called Post.
- add code to all of the subclass's methods and properties to call the corresponding routines in the superclass. If the superclass has a method called Post, then the subclass's Post method will call the Post method on the superclass object.

Only the public interface (the methods and properties exposed by the Class for use) of the superclass will be implemented in the subclass.

Subclasses don't inherit from anything but the Class that they are immediately connected to. As an example of what this means, the WholesaleManagement application has several different kinds of customers: Standard, CreditRisk, Premium, and CashOnly, among others (see Figure 2–11). The CreditRisk customer has a Generalization association with the StandardCustomer Class. As a result, the CreditRisk customer will have all of the public methods and properties of the Standard customer. These methods include the CreateInvoice method.

The CreditRisk customer class also has some additional methods of its own. The CreditRisk customer object has a CreditInvestigation method, for instance, that the StandardCustomer object does not have. If the CashOnly customer was made a subclass of the CreditRisk customer, it would not inherit the methods and properties of the Standard Customer. Instead, the CashOnly customer would inherit only those methods and properties native to its immediate superclass: the CreditRisk customer. As a result, the CashOnly customer would inherit the CreditInvestigation method but not the CreateInvoice method.

RELATIONSHIP SPECIFICATIONS • You can add all of these relationships to your diagram by clicking on the various Association buttons in the toolbar, clicking on the controlling object, and then dragging to the other object in the relationship. Once a relationship has been created, you can set the association's multiplicity. Multiplicity refers to how many of each object can exist in the association. You set multiplicity by right-mouse clicking on an end of an association line and selecting either "1" or "0..*". A 1 indicates that there is

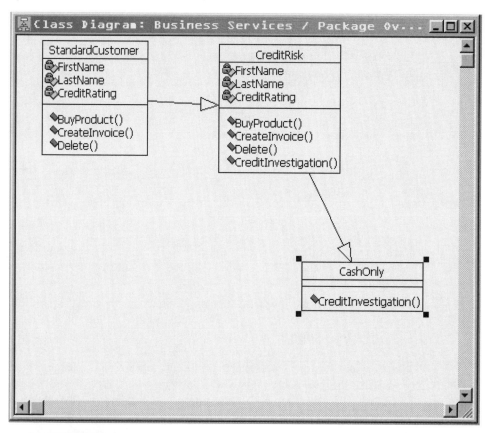

Figure 2–11 *In this relationship, the Standard object is a superclass to the CreditRisk object and CreditRisk is a superclass to CashOnly.*

always and only one occurrence of the object in the association. A "0..*" indicates that there may be none or many objects in the relationship. In the WholesaleManagement component there is a relationship between Order-Headers and Customers. At the Customer end, the multiplicity is "1" because there is always and only one Customer object in the relationship. At the OrderHeader end, the multiplicity is "0...*) because there may be no orders or many orders for a Customer.

You cannot describe the "at least one and possibly more" relationship in Visual Modeler. You cannot, for instance, indicate that every customer has at least one address, but may also have more. You could, however, indicate that a customer has exactly one billing address and may have zero or more other addresses (e.g., billing, contact).

Roles • In any association, the relationship between the two objects may not work the same way in both directions. For example, in the WholesaleManagement system, the SalesRep and Customer relationship is identical in both directions: a Customer may exist without Salesreps and vice-versa. You could say that a Customer "has" a Salesrep and a Salesrep "has" a customer.

On the other hand, the relationship between an OrderHeader and an OrderDetail line is different depending on which object you are working with. To begin with, an OrderHeader can exist without an OrderDetail, but an OrderDetail cannot exist without an OrderHeader. In this situation, the association between an OrderHeader and an OrderDetail is said to have two roles. The OrderHeader "has" an OrderDetail while an OrderDetail "belongs" to an OrderHeader (or "is part of" an OrderHeader).

Visual Modeler lets you describe the different roles in an association by using the Specifications form for the association. Double-clicking on the association line brings up the Specification form for the association. There is one General tab and an additional tab for each role in the relationship. On the General tab you can assign a name to the association and to each role (you can also enter the documentation for the association). On the tab for each role, you can enter documentation for the role, change the role's name, and indicate if the role is Public or Private. Setting the role to Public or Private controls how the variable that will refer to the other object in the relationship is declared when the code for the class module is generated.

Code Generation

To generate code, click on the Component or Class for which you want to generate code and select Generate Code from the pop-up menu to start the Code Generation Wizard (the Wizard will let you add additional Classes from the Logical View, if needed). The Wizard will let you override some of the settings that you've made in the specification forms and set some additional options for the project as a whole. Among other features, the Wizard will add standard error handling routines to your program.

After Visual Modeler generates your skeleton code you can return to Visual Basic and begin adding code to those routines in order to implement your object's methods and properties. If you add new methods and properties to your project you will also want to add them to the Visual Modeler model (unless you intend to abandon your model). The simplest way to add those new methods and properties is to select the Reverse Engineering Wizard from the Visual Basic Add-Ins | Visual Modeler menu.

The relationship between an ongoing Visual Basic project and its Class Diagram is a brittle one and easily broken. Once you generate code, you will no longer be able to change the implementation type of any Classes—you will have to delete the old Class and create a new one. If you want to move methods from one Class to another after you have added code to them, you must do it in Visual Basic. If you move the methods in Visual Modeler the method definition will appear in its new location but the code that you've written for it will be left behind. And, as I noted above, reverse engineering can be time consuming. Resist the temptation to generate code any earlier than you have to.

CODE GENERATION OPTIONS

Setting the options that control how Visual Basic is generated is critical to getting the code that you want. Many of these options will be obscure to you until you have some more familiarity with how Visual Basic code is used to create objects. You may want to skip this section and return to it after reading Part 2.

To set the default options to be used when generating code for each type of item (e.g., Classes, Components, Methods) go to Visual Modeler's Tools | Options menu choice and select the Visual Basic tab. The options that you set here can be overridden on an item by item basis from the Visual Basic tab in an item's Specifications form. For instance, from a Component's specification tab you can set Project file name for that Component instead of taking the default. The options that will have the most impact on how your object's code is generated are listed in Table 2.2.

Table 2.2 Component Specification Options

Object Type	Option	Static
Method	IsStatic	Set to True, it causes the method to be declared Static.
	EntryCode	Specifies text to be added to the beginning of the routine.
	ExitCode	Specifies text to be added to the end of the routine.
	OperationName	The name to be assigned to the method.
Class	GenerateInitialization	If True, adds an Initialize event routine to the Class module
	GenerateTermination	If true, adds a terminate event routine to the Class module.

Table 2.2 Component Specification Options (Continued)

Object Type	Option	Static
	Collection	The name of the object to use when creating a collection object. This defaults to using Visual Basic's Collection object, but if you create your own collection object (as described in the chapter on interfaces) you will want to use its name here.
Generalization	ImplementsDelegation	When a class implements another class, causes the class methods to consist of calls to the methods and properties of the original class.
Property/Role	GenerateDataMember DataMemberName	If GenerateDataMember is True, creates a private variable in the class module to hold the value for a Property. DataMemberName specifies the name to be used for the variable.
	GenerateGetOperator GenerateSetOperator GenerateLetOperator	If set to True, Visual Modeler adds the Property routines that save and return the value passed to the property to a private variable in the Class module.
	WithEvents, New, Subscript, IsConst	The variable generated is declared with the WithEvents, Const, and New keywords if these options are True. If Subscript is set to "(), a dynamic array is created. If Subscript is set to some value, the variable is declared as an array of the size specified by value.

The values for the options can be changed in the specification form by double clicking on them. The options can be set to various literal values or to some tokens whose values will change depending on the situation. The tokens that you can use include

$class: the name of the Class

$operation: the name of the method

$package: the name of the package

$relationship: the name of the dependency relationship between two items

$supplier: the name of the supplier in an association relationship

$type: the type of method (Sub, Function, Property)

Option Sets • Clicking on the Edit Set button in the specification form will bring up the Options screen from which you can change any of the options without double-clicking them (see Figure 2–12).

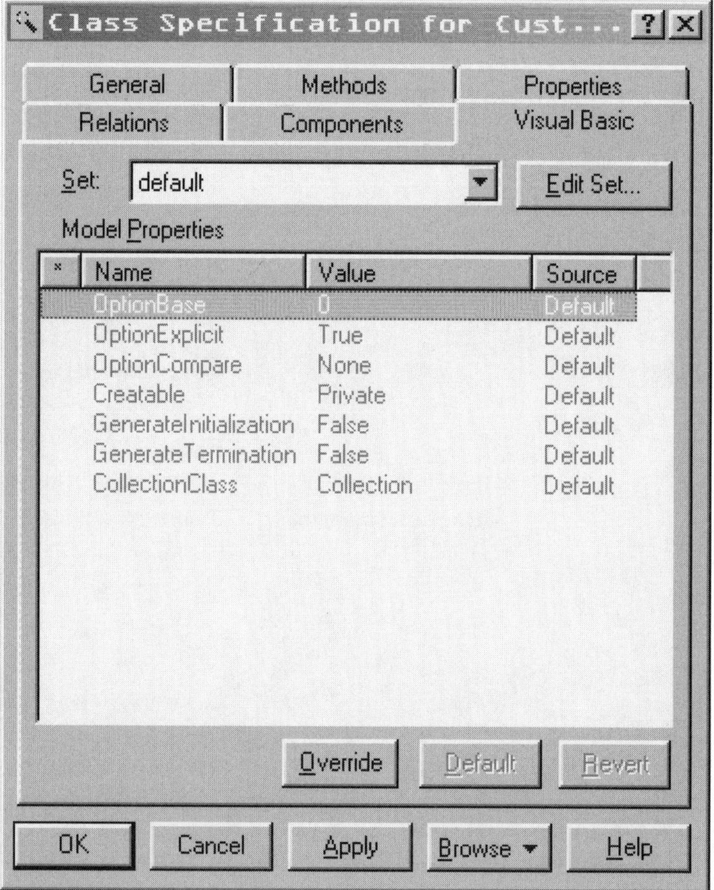

Figure 2–12 *The Set Options dialog allows you to create a new, named Option by clicking on the Clone button.*

If you have a set of options that you will use many times, you can add them to the list of pre-defined option sets displayed in the Visual Basic tab's Set listbox. Once you have set the values of the options in the Options dialog, click on the Clone button to assign a name to your current settings so that you can re-use them.

In any Specifications form, on the Visual Basic tab, the column on the right lists which group of settings a value comes from or indicates if you have overridden the setting for this option.

Non Code-Generation Related Features

Several parts of Visual Modeler have no impact on code generation and are provided purely for documentation purposes.

Text Boxes and Notes

Visual Modeler allows you to add two kinds of documentation to a diagram. You can, for instance, add Text Boxes to a diagram. Text Boxes are static text displayed on the diagram. To add a Text Box, just click on the Text Box button on the tool bar, then click and drag on a diagram to size your box. You must enter text into the Text Box as soon as you have created it because blank Text Boxes are removed from the diagram. You can move a Text Box or change its text at any time just by clicking on it.

Notes, on the other hand, are associated with a specific item on the diagram. You create a Note in the same way that you create a diagram item: click on the Note button on the toolbar and then click on the diagram. To enter text into a Note or to move it to another location, just click on the Note. To associate a Note with an item, click on the Anchor Note to Item button on the toolbar, click on the Note and drag to the item with which you want to associate the note.

The Deployment Diagram

The Deployment Diagram lets you show the hardware and networks that your application will be implemented on. A Deployment Diagram consists of Nodes which represent processing points. Nodes are joined together with Connections, which represent the ability of the Nodes to communicate. Figure 2–13 shows the diagram for the WholesaleManagement component. As the diagram shows, the application will be implemented on a network consisting of an application server, a database server, and multiple pc's.

The only Specifications that you can associate with a Connection are a Name, Documentation, and Characteristics (Characteristics are entered on a free form text field on the Connection's Details tab). The Node's Specifications form lets you include a list of Processes for the device on the Node's Details tab. Processes added to this window appear in the Explorer window under the Node they belong to. For each Process you can provide a name, documentation, and a priority (all on the General tab). Nodes can also be added by right-mouse clicking on a Node in the Explorer window and selecting New | Note.

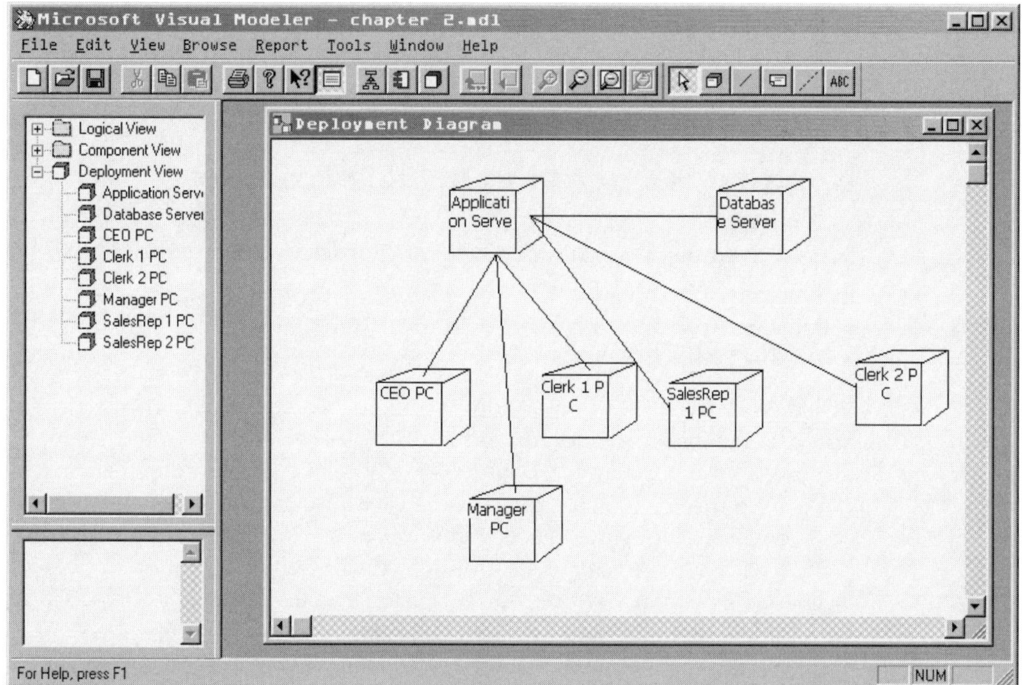

Figure 2–13 *The WholesaleManagement Deployment Diagram.*

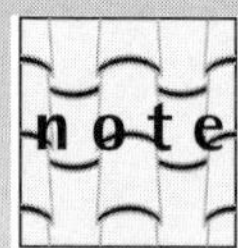

There is only one deployment diagram for each Visual Modeler project.

Packages

All of the objects that appear in the Explorer Window, except for Nodes and the folders native to Visual Modeler (e.g., Logical View), can be organized into Packages. Packages can be added to Component and Class diagrams to represent a group of Classes or Components.

Packages are most important when used with the Class diagram. On a Class diagram a Package represents a set of Classes that are highly cohesive with each other (many dependency relationships) but not with other Classes: a package of services. Added to a Component Diagram, a Package indicates a subsystem. There is no Visual Basic construct that corresponds to a Package during code generation.

To add a Package to Visual Modeler, right-mouse click on any of the folders in the Explorer window and select New | Package. A new Package will appear as a folder underneath the folder that you clicked, ready to be renamed.

Once you've created a package, you can view its Specifications by double-clicking on the folder in the Explorer window. A Package's specification consists of the documentation text associated with it (entered on the General tab) and a list of the Components, Component Diagrams, or Class Diagrams that make up the Package (listed on the Detail tab). Items are added to a Package three ways:

1. Drag items in Visual Modeler's Explorer window to the Package folder (this is the only way to add existing items to a Package).
2. Right-mouse click on the Package, select New, and from the menu select the item to add.
3. In the Package's specification window select its Detail tab. Right-mouse click in the window on the tab and select New (in Logical View) or Insert (in Component View) to create a new item.

Packages can be added to diagrams either by dragging them to the diagram in the Explorer window itself, or dragging them onto the diagram when it is open in the right side pane. Dependency lines can be drawn from Classes, Components, or other Packages to a Package. A Class Package can also be flagged as Global, indicating that it represents a component that can be called from anywhere. The Global Adornment is set on the Details tab of the Package's specification.

Reports

From Visual Modeler's File menu you can choose to print two different reports. Selecting Print Diagrams allows you to print any combination of the Logical View's Class diagrams, Component View's Component Diagrams, or the Deployment Diagram. You cannot choose which of the diagrams in each category that you want to print, but you can choose to print just the current diagram.

You can choose to print just the Top Level diagram in the Logical and Component Views. In Logical View, this is the three-tier Class diagram. In Component view, it is the diagram called Main.

Integration

You can seamlessly upgrade from Visual Modeler to Rational Rose, maintaining all of your existing diagrams. Visual Modeler also integrates with Visual Component manager, and the Microsoft Repository. I'll discuss both Visual Component Manager and the Repository in the chapter on Deploying, along with some of the other tools that ship with the Enterprise edition of Visual Basic.

You can save just your Logical View into Microsoft Repository through the Tools | Export to Repository menu choice and retrieve it through Tools | Import from the Repository. Saving the model to the Repository saves it in UML format.

Alternatively, you can save all of the information in Visual Modeler to Visual Component Manager through the Tools | Publish to VCM menu choice. In order to use Visual Component Manager to save Visual Modeler models, the Visual Component Manager must have the VCM tool information.

Summary

In this chapter I've introduced you to a tool for documenting your object designs. Visual Modeler can provide you with a standard way of recording information about your design by using UML notation. You've been introduced to UML and seen how Visual Modeler can be used to record the design decisions that you make about your components. I've discussed what you can expect from Visual Modeler so that you are clear on the benefits that you can get from using it. You've also had a look at all of Visual Modeler's views, from the Component level right through to the Deployment diagram.

The only real way to become proficient with Visual Modeler is to create some models. If you've tried working through an object model for some existing application or some set of objects (e.g., DAO), you might want to try documenting that model in Visual Modeler.

In the next part of this book, I'll discuss the code that you can put in the Class modules that you've designed. I'll show you how to create methods, properties, and events. You'll also learn about the various options that you can set (both at the Project and Class level) that control when and how your objects are created. Through the use of the Implements keyword, you'll see how Generalization relationships are created in Visual Basic.

If you're interested in more on designing objects, *Applying UML and Patterns: An Introduction to Object-Oriented Analysis and Design* by Craig Larman shows how UML can be used with a variety of different methodologies while showing you how to use UML. *VB6 UML* by Jake Sturm from Wrox Press discusses the relationship between UML and Visual Basic. There are some excellent whitepapers on both the Rational Rose and Microsoft sites, though neither site makes them easy to find. "Optimizing Software Teamwork" by John R. Rymer from Upstream Consulting is on the Rational Rose site at http://www.rational.com/sitewide/support/whitepapers/dynamic.jtmpl?doc_key=100860. Additional papers can be found on the Rational Rose site at http://www.rational.com/products/rup/prodinfo/whitepapers/index.jtmpl. The quote by Grady Brooch is taken from "The Visual Modeling of Software Architecture for the Enterprise" which can be found at http://msdn.microsoft.com/library/backgrnd/html/msdn_visualmod.htm and is an excellent overview of the importance of modeling and Rational Rose's unified process.

PART TWO

Building

This part begins by reviewing the features of the VBA language that are relevant to the object developer, including how VBA works with objects. The issues around combining objects into components are covered next, leading up to when and how to use interfaces. The code to create callbacks and collections is included. The final chapter in this section shows how to package your component and deploy it, along with information on how to get the best performance out of your component. Programming efficiencies and trade offs are demonstrated through benchmarks for those situations when raw speed is your most important design goal.

In This Part

THREE

Coding Objects

Before working with objects, I'm going to explore some fundamentals of the Visual Basic for Applications (VBA) language that relate to object development.VBA is the programming language that comes with the Visual Basic development package (it's also the language that comes with Word, Excel, and other Microsoft products). Since this is the language that you will use to create your objects, you need to understand the object- and component-related parts of it fully.

The topics in this chapter include the fundamentals of using objects—an important topic to know if you're going to build objects for others to use. I also go into some depth on parameters, user-defined data types, and enumerated variables. All of these topics have important implications when working with objects. While I've assumed that you have a command of VBA or you wouldn't be reading this book, there are nuances and "gotchas" about these topics that you need to know if you're going to build sophisticated objects.

Parameters

VBA routines are used to define methods and properties and, like ordinary subroutines and functions, method and property routines can accept parameters. I have discovered that as I build more powerful and flexible methods they have acquired more and more parameters. Passing parameters to methods (and, as you will see, to properties) allows the developer using your object to exercise more control over how your object's code executes and what it does. I use parameters to pass data to be used for updates, as switches to control the execution of code, and as holding areas for data to be passed back to the calling program.

One of the other things I've discovered is that, as I've added more parameters, not all of the parameters are required all the time. While a method may accept eight or nine parameters, typically a programmer will need to pass only two or three on any particular call. Not surprisingly then, I've come to make more and more use of optional parameters so that programmers can skip the parameters they don't need. In this section I show you how to use parameters effectively.

Beginning with version 4, Visual Basic has allowed you to define subroutines and functions that have Optional parameters. This feature allows you to define multiple parameters for your routine but require only some of the parameters to be passed when the routine is called. It wasn't until Visual Basic 5 that full support for Optional parameters was provided in Visual Basic.

Benchmark: Calling Subroutines With Multiple Parameters

Calling a subroutine and passing multiple parameters doesn't take much time. Calling a subroutine with a single literal integer parameter took 2 milliseconds. Calling a subroutine with 30 literal integer parameters took only 9 milliseconds. And, remember, this is the time to make 1,000 calls.

The data type used for parameters has an impact on calling time. Passing a single string literal took 3 milliseconds (compared to 1 for an integer) and 171 milliseconds for 30 parameters (a 57-fold increase).

Passing variables rather than literals speeds up calling routines. A single integer parameter took only 1 millisecond when passed as a variable and 60 parameters took only 5 milliseconds. Passing a string variable takes about as long as passing a numeric variable. This speed increase is due to Visual Basic passing only a reference to the variable's memory location.

Using variants as parameters doesn't make much difference in the time to call a routine when passing literals. When larger numbers of parameters were passed, the time to pass integer literals to variant parameters was greater than the time to pass string literals to variant parameters. Passing integers in a call to a subroutine expecting variants took about as long as calling a subroutine with explicitly declared parameters when the calling data was a literal. However, when passing a variable, passing an explicitly declared string to a routine with parameters declared as variables increased the calling time, typically by a factor of 5.

The conclusions that you can draw are that passing literal strings takes longer than passing literal numerics, and that passing additional string parameters increases the calling time disproportionately. As a programmer, wherever possible you should pass variables rather than literals and match the data type of your variable to the data type of the parameter. As an object developer, you want to declare your parameters as a specific data type wherever possible, use as few string parameters as possible, and keep the number of parameters low.

Optional Parameters

In order to indicate that one of a routine's parameters is optional when declaring the routine, you must precede the parameter name with the keyword Optional. Once you indicate that a parameter is optional, all subsequent parameters to that routine must also be marked as Optional. This declaration is not correct because a non-optional parameter follows an Optional parameter:

```
Public Sub BadRoutine (Optional FirstParam As String, _
                       SecondParam As String)
```

This routine's declaration is fine because the Optional parameter is not followed by any required parameters:

```
Public Sub GoodRoutine (FirstParam As String, _
  Optional SecondParam As String, _
  Optional ThirdParam As String)
```

The GoodRoutine can be called either with or without the second and third parameters:

```
GoodRoutine "Hi"
GoodRoutine "Hi", "Hello"
GoodRoutine "Hi", "Hello", "Greetings"
```

Benchmark: Calling Subroutines With Optional Parameters

Calling a subroutine with Optional parameters has no appreciable effect on the calling time as long as the parameters are passed. Passing variables to Optional parameters takes about as long as passing variables to non-optional parameters. The same is true when passing literals. I tested this code only with string data and with the parameters declared to match the data passed to them.

However, if parameters are not passed, then the calling time for the routine increases significantly. A single parameter routine took twice as long to call if no Optional parameters were passed, and a routine with 30 parameters took five times as long to call if no parameters were passed.

You have no control over whether someone using one of your routines will pass all, or even most, of your parameters. You create Optional parameters just to allow your users to avoid passing values. However, from a performance point of view, a routine with the right parameters for the user's needs is preferable to a routine with a large number of parameters where typically only a few parameters will be used.

ParamArrays

The last parameter in a routine's parameter list can be designated as a ParamArray. When a routine is passed more values than it has parameters, the extra values will be placed in the ParamArray, if one is present. The ParamArray variable must be declared as a variant.

I've always envied the ability of functions like C's printf which can accept an indeterminate number of parameters. ParamArrays let you do the same thing with routines in Visual Basic. If you wanted to create a method that would concatenate as many values as were passed to it, you would use a ParamArray. As an example, this subroutine will accept as many parameters as the programmer wants to pass to the routine:

```
Public Sub ParamArrayEx (FirstParam As String, _
    ParamArray SecondParam() As Variant)
```

In the ParamArrayEx routine, the first parameter passed to the routine will be placed in the FirstParam variable. Any other values passed to the routine will be placed in SecondParam. SecondParam will be an array with one entry for every parameter after the first, non-optional parameter. In this example, the values "So Long" and "Goodbye" will be placed in the ParamAarry called SecondParam:

```
ParamArrayRoutine "Hello", "So Long", "Goodbye"
```

If you use a ParamArray, you'll probably want to know how many entries the array holds. You can determine the number of entries in the ParamArray by passing the array to the UBound function, like this:

```
intArrayEntries = UBound(SecondParam) + 1
```

Since UBound returns the number of the last position in the array and the first entry in a ParamArray is always 0, you must add 1 to the value returned by UBound to get the total number of entries in the array. UBound will return –1 if no entries have been placed in the ParamArray.

Normally, I use a For Each…Next loop to process ParamArrays. As an example, this routine uses a For Each construct to concatenate all the entries in the ParamArray into the variable varString:

```
Dim varEntry As Variant
For Each varEntry In SecondParam
    varString = varString & varEntry
Next
```

You cannot mix Optional parameters and ParamArrays—if you use a ParamArray none of the preceding parameters can be Optional. You cannot use the ReDim keyword with ParamArrays.

Benchmark: Calling Subroutines With ParamArrays

Unlike using Optional parameters, ParamArrays impose a significant overhead on calling a procedure. Calling a routine with a single parameter took 3 milliseconds. Passing a single parameter to a routine with a single ParamArray took 17 milliseconds, a 6-fold increase. Increasing the number of literal parameters passed to a ParamArray increased the calling time but not proportionately. Calling 30 parameters took 167 milliseconds, only 10-fold increase.

Passing variables helps, especially as the number of parameters increases. Passing a single variable to a ParamArray took 12 milliseconds (compared to 17 for the literal), and passing 30 variables took only 28 milliseconds (compared to 167 for literals). This is still 5 times longer than the time to pass variables to explicitly declared parameters.

In general, ParamArrays should be avoided unless absolutely needed.

Named Parameters

Visual Basic allows users to omit Optional parameters by using a comma to indicate that a parameter has been skipped. This routine, for instance, has all of its parameters declared as Optional:

```
Public Sub OptionalRoutine (Optional FirstParam As String, _
    Optional SecondParam As Variant)
```

As a result, any of the following ways of calling the routine are legal:

```
OptionalRoutine
OptionalRoutine "Hi"
OptionalRoutine , "Hello"
OptionalRoutine "Hi", "Hello"
```

In addition, you can specify which parameters are being passed by referring to them by name using the := operator (required parameters can also be passed by name):

```
OptionalRoutine FirstParam := "Hi"
OptionalRoutine SecondParam := "Hello"
OptionalRoutine SecondParam := "Hello", FirstParam := "Hi"
```

Named parameters, in conjunction with IntelliSense, have made it important that you provide meaningful names for your parameters. IntelliSense will provide a tool tip to your object's users to help them fill in the parameters (see Figure 3–1). This tool tip will be more useful if your parameter names give your users some indication of what data should be provided as the parameter.

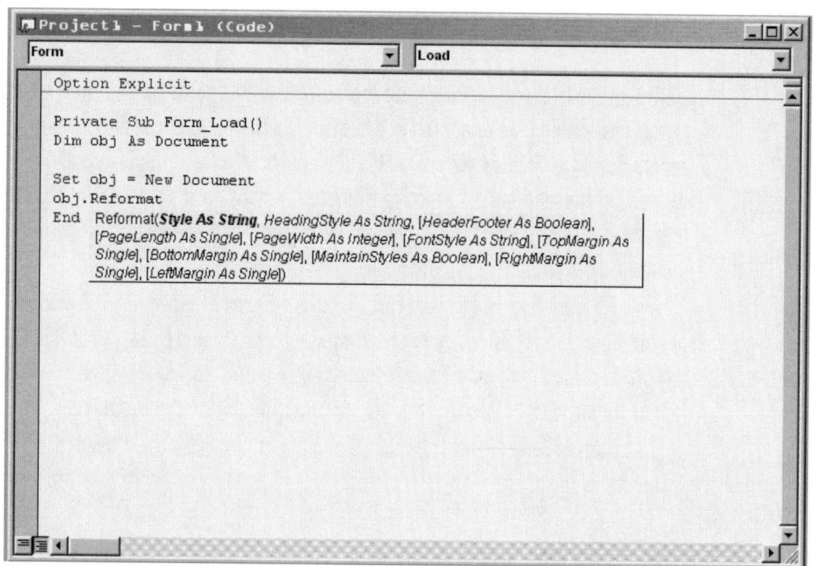

Figure 3–1 *The IntelliSense ToolTip support for parameters. Note that the Optional parameter names are enclosed in brackets.*

Here's an example from some code that I found in a program that I was maintaining. In this code, the developer called the Reformat method but needed to provide only two of the many Optional parameters that the method supports. When I found the code, the developer hadn't taken advantage of named parameters, which generated some pretty obscure code:

```
obj.Reformat, , , , , , , ,True, , 6
```

While the code worked fine, as a favor to the next programmer, I rewrote it to use named parameters. Since the object's developer had used meaningful names for the routines parameter, the result is code that's considerably easier to read:

```
obj.Reformat MaintainStyles:=True, LeftMargin:=6
```

Again, like method names, the current practice is not to use a naming convention for parameter names that provides any technical information about the parameter.

Benchmark: Using Named Parameters

No appreciable performance is incurred when using named parameters. Again, I tested only by passing string literals or string variables with the data types on the parameters declared to match the data passed to them.

Default Values

If you are going to allow your users to omit parameters, you will probably need to provide a default value for any missing parameters in order to prevent your code from abending. From Visual Basic 5 on, you have two ways of supplying default values for Optional parameters: declarative or programmatic.

The declarative method allows you to specify, as part of declaring the parameter, the value to be provided when the user omits it:

```
Public Sub OptionalMethod _
    (Optional FirstParam As String = "X", _
     Optional SecondParam As Integer = 2)
```

The declarative technique allows you to supply a constant value as the default value for the parameter. You can use literal values (as I did in the example), Constants, or a combination of both. You cannot use a function name, public variable, or a reference to a control on a form as the default value. In the following example, I use a Constant to set the default value for an Optional parameter:

```
Const DefaultLimit As Integer = 200
Public Sub ConstMethod _
    (Optional FirstParam As Integer = DefaultLimit)
```

The programmatic method allows you more flexibility than the declarative method. In the programmatic method you pass the parameter to the IsMissing function. This function returns True if the parameter passed to it was not provided when the routine was called. If the function returns True, you can then perform any action that you want in order to provide a value for the missing parameter. In this example, the routine calls a function to determine a value for the missing parameter:

```
Public Sub ConstMethod _
    (Optional CreditLimit As Variant)
If IsMissing(CreditLimit) Then
    CreditLimit = CalculateDefaultCreditLimit()
End If
```

Wherever possible, the declarative method is preferable to the programmatic method. The declarative method places all the information about the parameter in a single place: the parameter's declaration. The programmatic method, on the other hand, provides no direct connection between the parameter and its default value. The next programmer who works on the code, in order to find out if a default value is provided for the parameter, must search through the routine for any use of the IsMissing function.

The main attraction of the programmatic method is its flexibility. With the programmatic method you can do anything that you want to set the default value for the parameter. There is a price for that flexibility, however.

To begin with, you must declare your parameter as Variant in order to use the IsMissing function with it. When variables are declared as Variant, you lose much of the error checking that Visual Basic will do for you automatically. With a Variant parameter, for instance, if you pass a string value to a parameter that expects numerics, no error is raised. Sooner or later, though, that string value will cause your program to abend. If the parameter had been declared with a numeric data type, Visual Basic would have raised an error message when you attempted to compile your program (a much better time to find your errors).

One of the results of these differences between the two methods is that the declarative method runs faster than the programmatic method, even if you are just using the IsMissing function to provide a literal value.

Benchmark: Using Default Values With Parameters

Adding default values to Optional parameters slows down your program if the parameters aren't supplied. While calling a procedure with a single Optional string parameter took 1 millisecond and a procedure with 30 parameters took only 3 seconds, supplying default values and omitting the passed variables significantly added to the run time. Calling a routine with a single Optional string parameter took 3 seconds. Using 30 Optional parameters took 100 milliseconds (a roughly proportional increase).

Using IsMissing to handle missing parameters and supply a default value greatly increases the time to call a routine. A routine with a single parameter to be checked took 8 milliseconds to process, while a routine with 30 parameters took 309 milliseconds (not a proportional increase).

If you are going to use Optional parameters, you would be better off to provide default values in the parameter's declaration instead of using IsMissing.

There is no way to use the declarative method with a ParamArray. You can use the IsMissing function to determine if there are entries in the array before using a ParamArray, as follows:

```
Public Sub ArrayMethod _
    (ParamArray Recipients() As Variant)
If Not IsMissing(Recipients) Then
    ...processing of Recipients...
End If
```

You can also use the UBound function to check for entries in a ParamArray (if UBound returns –1, then the ParamArray is empty). One of the reasons that I recommended using a For Each...Next loop to process an array is that the For loop will be skipped automatically if the array is empty. Which method you use will depend on personal preference, clarity of the code, and the standards in your shop.

ByVal and ByRef

There are two ways that parameters can be passed to a routine. When you declare the parameters for a method, you can indicate which mechanism you want. Your two choices are ByRef (the default mechanism) and ByVal.

ByRef indicates that the only thing to be passed to the routine is the address of the data. As a result, with ByRef, the program calling the subroutine and the subroutine both update the same location in memory. In effect the program and the subroutine are updating the same data (see Figure 3–2). With a ByRef parameter, code in the routine that updates the parameter is also updating the variable used by the calling program, as in this example:

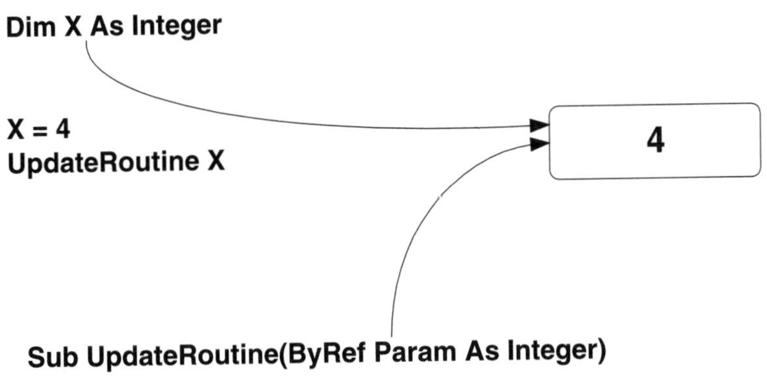
Dim X As Integer
X = 4
UpdateRoutine X
4
Sub UpdateRoutine(ByRef Param As Integer)
End Sub

Figure 3–2 *The ByRef passing mechanism: both the calling program and the called routine are updating the same memory location.*

```
X = 4
UpdateRoutine X
'X will now be equal to 5, the value set in UpdateRoutine
MsgBox X

Sub UpdateRoutine(ByRef Param As Integer)
    Param = 5
End Sub
```

I feel that it's a bad practice for a routine to update the parameters passed to it because it makes the code harder to read and maintain. Routines that update parameters drive me crazy and have cost me untold hours when debugging other people's code. If I know that a method will not update any parameters passed to it then I can, when reading code, ignore the effect of the method on the data passed to it. If a routine might update the parameters passed to it, then I have to figure out what the routine does to the parameters before I can go on to understand how the program is working.

If I have a method that is return a value to the calling program, I will write the method as a function. Using a function clearly indicates to subsequent readers of the program that the method returns a value and what variable is updated with that value. Rewriting the previous example gives this clearer, easier to maintain code:

```
X = 4
Y = UpdateRoutine(X)
'Y will be equal to 5, the value set in UpdateRoutine
Msgbox Y

Function UpdateRoutine(Param As Integer)
    UpdateRoutine = 5
End Sub
```

When parameters are passed ByVal, instead of ByRef, a separate copy of the data is made for the routine. The routine is then passed the address of this copy of the data. If the routine makes any changes to its parameters, those changes are made to the routine's private copy and have no effect on the calling program's data (Figure 3–3).

Optional parameters can be specified as either ByRef or ByVal as follows:

```
Sub OptionalByVal (Optional ByVal X As Integer, _
    Optional ByRef Y As Integer)
```

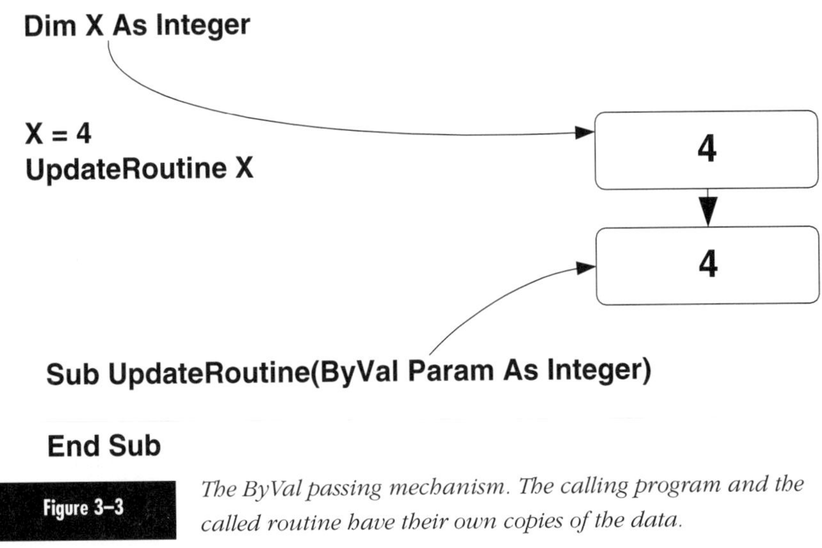
Dim X As Integer
X = 4
UpdateRoutine X
4
4
Sub UpdateRoutine(ByVal Param As Integer)
End Sub

Figure 3–3 *The ByVal passing mechanism. The calling program and the called routine have their own copies of the data.*

note

Don't worry about the syntax of the Optional and ByRef/ByVal options. If you get the order of the Optional and ByRef/ByVal keywords out of order, Visual Basic will quietly correct it for you.

While using ByVal enforces better coding practice by ensuring that updates to parameters are not passed back to the calling program, there is a cost in performance. In general, ByVal parameters will take longer to process than ByRef parameters.

Benchmark: Using ByVal Parameters

All the previous tests have been using the default setting for this option—ByRef. I reran the tests, setting all parameters to ByVal for both integer and variable data/literals and numerics.

When passing literal values to a procedure, declaring parameters as ByVal doesn't have much effect on the time to make a call.

However, passing variables to a procedure and declaring parameters as ByVal does significantly increase the time to make a call for most data types. For instance, the time to call a procedure, passing variants and using ByRef variant parameters, varied from 1 millisecond for a single parameter to 3 milliseconds for 30 parameters. Using ByVal parameters, the time went from 2 milliseconds for the single parameter to 36 milliseconds for 30 parameters. Integer parameters were, on the other hand, unaffected by being passed ByRef or ByVal.

The biggest impact was on string parameters. With ByRef, the timings varied from 1 millisecond for a single parameter to 29 milliseconds for 30 parameters. If the parameters were declared as ByVal, those times went to 3 milliseconds for the single parameter to 29 milliseconds for 30 parameters. Not as bad as using variants, but still a hefty increase over using ByRef parameters. If, in addition to passing string parameters, the calling routine had its parameters declared as variant, the calling time varied from 3 milliseconds for a single parameter to 56 milliseconds for 30 parameters.

While declaring parameters ByVal has benefits from a design point of view, unless you are using integer parameters, you can expect to take a performance hit.

Having said that, there are some cases where you will have no choice as to which passing mechanism to use. Some clients will accept only ByVal parameters. As you will see, parameters that are User Defined Types must be passed ByRef. Literal values are always passed ByVal. ParamArrays cannot be specified as being either ByRef or ByVal. In a ParamArray, the individual elements of the array are passed ByRef, so changes made to entries in the array are visible to the calling program.

User Defined Types

A User Defined Type (UDT) allows the programmer to create a complex data type by combining the Visual Basic data types like String, Double, and Integer. The following code defines a Customer data type made up of string, numeric, and date values:

```
Type Customer
    Name As String
    CreditLimit As Currency
    BirthDate As Date
End Type
```

With this new data type declared in a Class or Basic module, you can then declare variables of that data type, just as you would with intrinsic Visual Basic data types. The individual parts of the data type, referred to as elements, are accessed using a syntax similar to the syntax used for object's properties.

You cannot declare a UDT in a private Class module. That means that you can't declare a UDT in a Standard EXE's Class module since Class modules in these kinds of projects are private. You also cannot declare a UDT in a Class module whose Instancing property is set to Private (more on Instancing in the chapter on Components).

This code declares the variable udtSales as being of type Customer and then sets two of its elements to my name and birthdate:

```
Dim udtSales As Customer
udtSales.Name = "Peter Vogel"
udtSales.BirthDate = "31/05/53"
```

On occasion, you will want to use UDTs with your methods and properties. If you have a set of values that must be passed as a group to your method or property, it may be simpler to pass a UDT rather than create multiple parameters.

I frequently use UDTs when an object's method or property must return multiple values. In the WholesaleManagement component, for instance, the Customer object reads a customer record and needs to return a number of different pieces of data (e.g., the customer's name, address, credit rating, etc.). Another example of where UDTs are useful are methods that can generate an error and need to return both the data requested and information about the error. There are several ways to handle a method that returns multiple values:

- Have the code in the method set other properties of the object
- Fire an event
- Return an object
- Modify the parameters passed to the method
- Return a "special value" under some circumstances
- Return a UDT

The first two methods (setting multiple properties of the record or firing an event) fit best with an object-oriented design methodology. I'll discuss using events in the next chapter. Using properties to return multiple data values causes developers to write code like the following example. This sample code calls the GetCustomerData method of the cst object to load various properties of the cst object. These properties are then used to update the corresponding fields on the form:

```
cst.GetCustomerData "Jane Doe"
Form1.txtName = cst.CustomerName
Form1.txtBDate = cst.CustomerBirthDate
Form1.txtCreditLimit = cst.CustomerCreditLimit
```

While using properties works well from a design point of view, repeated trips to the object can slow your application's performance as I discuss in the chapter on Deploying. The performance hit is especially large if the object is compiled as an ActiveX EXE or is running over the network using DCOM.

Returning an object is an excellent practice from an object-oriented design point of view. The returned object can have multiple properties, one for each value that the routine must provide. This code shows this technique in action by having the GetCustomerMethod return a customer object:

```
Dim cstObj As CustomerObject

Set cstObj = obj.GetCustomerData
Form1.txtName = cstObj.CustomerName
Form1.txtBDate = cstObj.CustomerBirthDate
Form1.txtCreditLimit = cstObj.CustomerCreditLimit
```

In this scenario, the objOrder object is running on a remote server, so repeatedly accessing its properties could be time consuming. However, the cstObj is set up as an object running on the same computer as the client. As a result, reading the cstObj object's properties won't slow down your code as much. However, even under this scenario, a pure object-oriented solution might impose more overhead than you want to incur.

As I've discussed, I think that modifying the parameters passed to the routine is a poor practice and should be avoided wherever possible.

Returning a "special value" (e.g., the way that the UBound function returns –1 for an empty array) works in only a limited number of situations—typically where the routine needs to return either data or an error code, but never both. If the routine can return a wide variety of data, it can become difficult to select a "special value" that won't be mistaken for real data. Where both data and an error code need to be returned or it's hard to find a "special value," a common practice is to expose a Status property to hold the error code.

Returning a UDT can be an effective compromise between an object-oriented design and performance. While not as good a practice as returning an object (since it's less object-oriented), using a UDT does provide better performance then returning an object. In Visual Basic 6, returning a UDT from a method is straightforward, but the technique requires a workaround in earlier versions of Visual Basic.

With Visual Basic 6, methods can both accept and return UDTs, as this function does:

```
Public Function UDTRoutine (CustomerData As Customer) _
    As Customer
```

A developer could call the function like this, both passing a UDT and accepting the function's return value into a UDT variable:

```
Dim udtData As Customer
udtData.Name = "Peter Vogel"
udtData.BDate = "31/05/53"
udtData.CreditLimit = 200
udtData = obj.UDTRoutine(udtData)
```

Benchmark: Passing and Returning User Defined Types

If you have a large number of parameters to pass, there's a significant performance gain to be made by passing a UDT. Since UDTs must always be passed ByRef, effectively only one address has to be passed for all the procedure's parameters. For UDTs varying from a single string element to 30 string elements, the time to pass a parameter was effectively the same, 1 to 2 milliseconds.

However, returning a UDT takes significantly longer then returning an equivalent amount of data in a single variable. I tested with UDTs containing 1 to 30 string elements, each containing a single character, and with a string variable containing 1 to 30 characters. Processing time varied from 17 (for a UDT with a single string element) to 583 milliseconds (for a UDT with 30 string elements) to return the UDT. Returning a string variable took about 10 milliseconds, regardless of size.

UDT Workarounds

In Visual Basic 5.0, you cannot pass or return UDTs to methods. In addition, some containers that your object operates in may not allow you to use UDTs. To get around these problems, you can move data from string variables into and out of a UDT by using the LSet keyword. The LSet keyword allows you to move data from one UDT to another. The technique works by moving the data out of a complex UDT into another UDT that consists of a single string element. This string element can then be used anywhere a normal string variable would be used. The process is then done in reverse to move the data out of the simple UDT and back into the original, more complex UDT (see Figure 3–4).

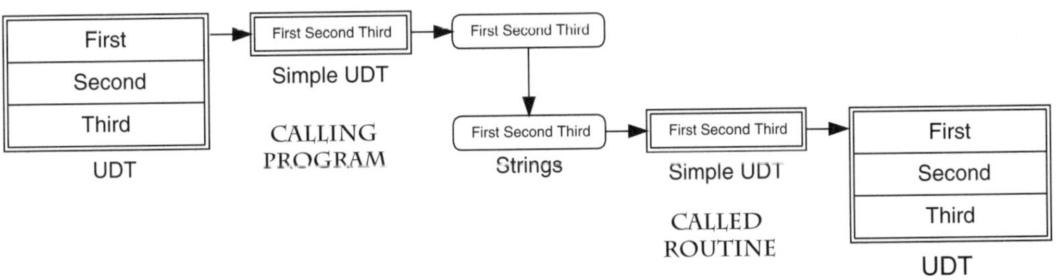

Figure 3–4 *Using a User Defined Type where UDTs are not supported.*

If you are going to use this technique, you must make sure that the two UDTs involved are the same length. You must also declare any string elements in your UDT as fixed length strings so that the length of the various elements in the UDT won't change. In this Type declaration, the Name element has been fixed at 20 characters:

```
Type Customer
    Name As String * 20
    BirthDate As Date
    CreditLimit As Currency
End Type
```

The UDT that this data will be passed to must also be a fixed length string and be large enough to hold Customer type variable. While you could calculate how big the variable needs to be, it's probably simpler just to declare a variable of the UDT type and use Visual Basic's Len function to find out how long the type is:

```
Dim cst As Customer
'display length for variable of type Customer
MsgBox Len(cst)
```

Now that you know how big a Customer variable is, you can declare a simpler UDT that will be big enough to hold a Customer variable's data:

```
Type CustHold
    HoldData As String * 36
End Type
```

As an example, the following code uses the CustHold and Customer data types I previously defined. This code sets the values of the Customer variable elements and then uses the LSet command to move the data into a CustHold type variable:

```
Dim cstData As Customer
Dim cstStore As CustHold

cstData.Name = "Peter Vogel"
cstData.Bdate = "31/05/53"
cstData.CreditLimit = 200

LSet cstStore = cstData
```

Moving the data to cstStore effectively places the data in the string element cstStore.HoldData. This String element can be used anywhere a string variable can be used. UDTRoutine can now be rewritten to accept and return a string instead of the UDT I used originally:

```
Public Function UDTRoutine (CustomerData As String) _
                                            As String
```

The UDTRoutine can now be passed the string variable cstStore.HoldData:

```
UDTRoutine(cstStore.HoldData)
```

Within UDTRoutine, the string variable passed to the routine is moved into a simple UDT. Once there, an LSet can be used to move it from that simple UDT into a Customer type variable:

```
Public Function UDTRoutine (CustomerData As String) _
                                        As String
Dim cstRStore As CustHold
Dim cstRData As Customer

cstRStore.HoldData = CustomerData
LSet cstRData = cstRStore
If cstRData.CreditLimit > 1000 Then ...
```

With the data in a Customer type variable, the UDTRoutine can access the various element type (e.g., CreditLimit). When processing is complete, the UDTRoutine returns the data to a simple UDT variable (again using LSet). Once back in the simple UDT, the string element of the UDT can be returned from the function:

```
LSet cstRStore = cstRData
UDTRoutine = cstRStore.HoldData
End Function
```

The program that called UDTRoutine now accepts the return value into the simple UDT and uses an LSet to move the data back into a Customer type variable:

```
cstStore.HoldData = UDTRoutine(cstStore.HoldData)
LSet cstData = cstStore
Form1.txtCreditLimit = cstData.CreditLimit
```

UDT Support

You will, of course, have to provide developers using your object with information about the structure of your UDTs. Fortunately, you can count on Visual Basic's IntelliSense to provide most of that information. Information about UDTs declared in your Class modules is automatically included in the information provided to IntelliSense. Developers who add your component to their project's References list will find that your UDT name appears in the list of data types that they can use when they type in a Dim statement. When developers use variables declared as your data type, IntelliSense will prompt them with the list of elements for your UDT (see Figure 3–5).

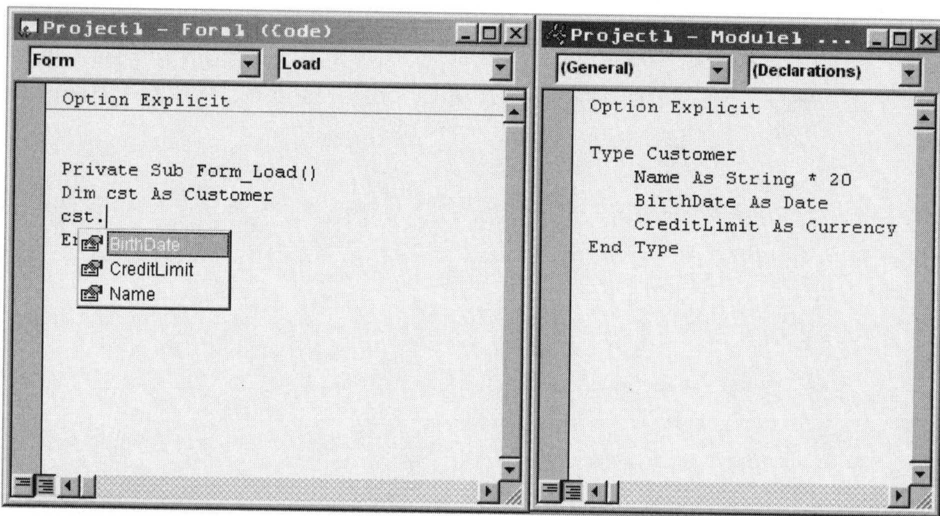

Figure 3–5 *IntelliSense support for UDT elements.*

UDT parameters cannot be Optional and must be passed ByRef. This means that some containers, which require methods whose parameters must be passed ByVal, will not accept an object with UDT parameters.

Enums

Enumerated data types are like UDTs in that they allow you to design a custom data type. While a UDT lets you define the kind of data that the variable can hold (some combination of strings, doubles, etc.), enumerated variables allow you to specify the values that your variables hold. Among other features, enumerated data types let you create predefined constants.

An enumerated variable is defined with an Enum declaration. An Enum defines the name of your new data type and lists the values that variables of this type are to have. This Enum declaration defines a data type called CustomerStatus and indicates that variables of this type are to have one of three values (-1, 0, and 1):

```
Enum CustomerStatus
    Invalid = -1
    NoStatus = 0
    Valid = 1
End Enum
```

Enums can be placed in the Declarations section of any Visual Basic module. Once you've defined the data type you can declare variables as that type:

```
Dim cstStatus As CustomerStatus
```

Variables declared as an Enum are actually Long variables and can hold any numeric integer value from roughly negative two billion to positive two billion. What's key about Enums is that the values established in the Enum's definition can be used by name. Given the definitions above, the variable cstStatus will have IntelliSense support for the values Invalid, NoStatus, and Valid like this:

```
    cstStatus = Invalid
    If cstStatus = NoStatus Then
```

Used in a Class module, an Enum effectively defines a set of predefined constants that can be used with variables, properties, and parameters. Using Enums makes life easier for developers who use your object. Instead of having to look up the appropriate values for a property or parameter, IntelliSense will provide them with a list of meaningful names for any variable or property declared as that data type (see Figure 3–6). Enums also reduce the cost of maintenance for programs using your objects by making the programs easier to read and understand.

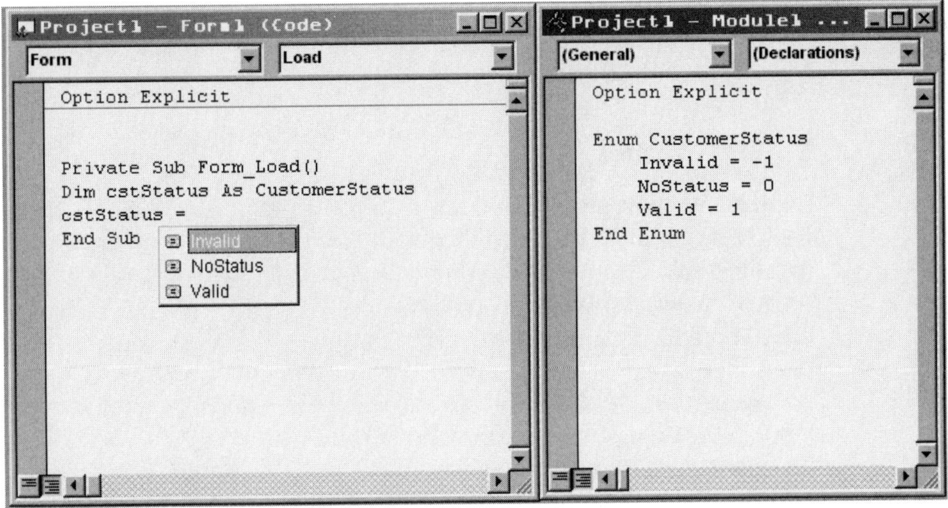

Figure 3–6 *IntelliSense support for an Enum.*

When defining an Enum, you don't have to specify the values to be assigned to the Enum's entries. If you don't specify a value, each Enum entry is given a value one greater than the previous value. In this example, the

Enum has been declared with a combination of explicit values and automatically generated ones:

```
Enum EmployeeStatus
    NewHire
    Probation
    Standard
    Retired = 200
    Terminated
    Disabled
End Enum
```

The EmployeeStatus Enum defines six predefined values: NewHire, Probation, Standard Retired, Disabled and Terminated. The NewHire value will be equal to 0 (as the first value in the Enum) and Probation will have a value of 1 (one more than the previous value of New). Retired will have the value of 200 that it has been explicitly set to, and Terminated will have a value of 201 (one more than the previous value of Retired). Explicit values can be set using literals (as I did with the Retired value), constants, or expressions made up of constants and literals:

```
Const UpperLimit As Integer = 200
Enum MemberStatus
    NewMember
    Probation = UpperLimit/2
    Standard = UpperLimit
    Expired = 255
End Enum
```

Naming Names

The naming convention for Enums is to put a prefix on the names of the values to prevent them from colliding with Enums defined in other components. Rewriting the CustomerStatus Enum for use in the WholesaleManagement project, I would probably define it as:

```
Enum CustomerStatus
    wmInvalid = -1
    wmNoStatus = 0
    wmValid = 1
End Enum
```

If two items in your project's References define Enums with the same name, the Enum from the component higher in the Reference lists will be used. If you do have two components that declare Enums with the same name, you can specify which Enum that you want by explicitly using the component name with the Enum name, like this:

```
Dim cstStatus As WholeSaleManagement.CustomerStatus
```

Enums can be used in a variety of places and are not restricted to defining Properties. Once a developer adds your object to their project, they can use your Enum's values as predefined constants. A project using the WholesaleManagement component, for instance, would be able to use the values defined in the CustomerStatus Enum like this:

```
If frmCustomer.txtStatus = wmInvalid Or _
   frmCustomer.txtStatus = wmNoStatus Then
    Msgbox "Customer not valid for this operation."
End If
```

While you can use an Enum value with any variable, if a variable isn't defined with the Enum's datatype (e.g., EmployeeStatus) then IntelliSense won't provide a dropdown list of the Enum's values.

Benchmark: Using CONST, Enum, Literals, and Variables

I first tested assigning values by setting a single integer variable to values from a CONST, Enum, literal, and another variable. I then tested again using a string value of "X" in a CONST, literal, and another string variable. The results of assigning the numeric, whether literal, variable, CONST, or Enum were the same: 2 milliseconds. The results of assigning the string value were the same in all situations, also: 4 milliseconds.

Powers of 2

If you define an Enum as powers of two (0, 2, 4, 8, 16, 32, 64, ...), you can work with them using the logical operators Or and And. The Or operation effectively adds together two numbers and the And operation tells you what values were Or'ed together.

The EmployeeStatus Enum, for instance, might include several statuses that aren't exclusive. An employee might be both Standard and on Probation, first instance, or Disabled and Retired. If the Employee object has only a single Status property, the Or operation can be used to pack several statuses in one property. The first step is to define all of the enumerated values as powers of two, like this:

```
Enum EmployeeStatus
     NewHire = 0
     Probation = 2
     Standard = 4
     Retired = 8
```

```
    Terminated = 16
    Disabled = 32
End Enum
```

With this Enum in the Customer Class, a client can use this code to set a Customer's Status property to both Disabled and Retired:

```
cst.Status = Retired Or Disabled
```

In order to test which values were used to set the Status property, you use the And operator in conjunction with the Status that you want to test for. In order to test for the Retired status, I would use:

```
cst.Status And Retired
```

This statement will return a positive value if the Status property contains the Retired value and zero if it does not. Since any non-zero value is treated as True by VBA, you can test for the presence of the Retired value in the Status property with this statement:

```
If cst.Status And Retired Then
```

The Basics of Objects

Visual Basic makes it easy for a programmer to work with objects as part of building an application. The simplest objects to work with are the ActiveX Controls that you add to your form. To use a control you just refer to it by the value in the control's Name property. If you have a control named txtMyName, you can set its Text property with this code:

```
txtMyName.Text = "Peter Vogel"
```

You can work with ActiveX Controls so simply because ActiveX Control objects are created as soon as you draw them on your form. Other objects require that you write a little more code before they can be used.

Adding Objects

To use an object other than an ActiveX Control, you begin by associating that object with your project. You do this by going to the Project | References menu choice. From the References list you then select the component that the object is part of. When you are looking at your project's References list (see Figure 3–7), you are seeing a list of all of the components that are installed on your computer and available for use. The items at the top of the list are the objects that the application requires in order to work (for Visual Basic that includes the objects that make up the VBA language itself).

Ever since Visual Basic 3, elements of the VBA language have been moving out of the language itself and into a set of libraries and objects that ship with VBA. You don't notice because, when the VBA interpreter hits a word (.e.g .,"CreateRecordset") that it doesn't know, VBA will scan the components in the References list to find an object with a method or property that matches this word. If you've ever used "Date()" or "Now()", you've been calling methods of the "_DateTime" library rather than functions built into the VBA language. You can change the order of the items in the References list to control which objects are found first when Visual Basic goes searching.

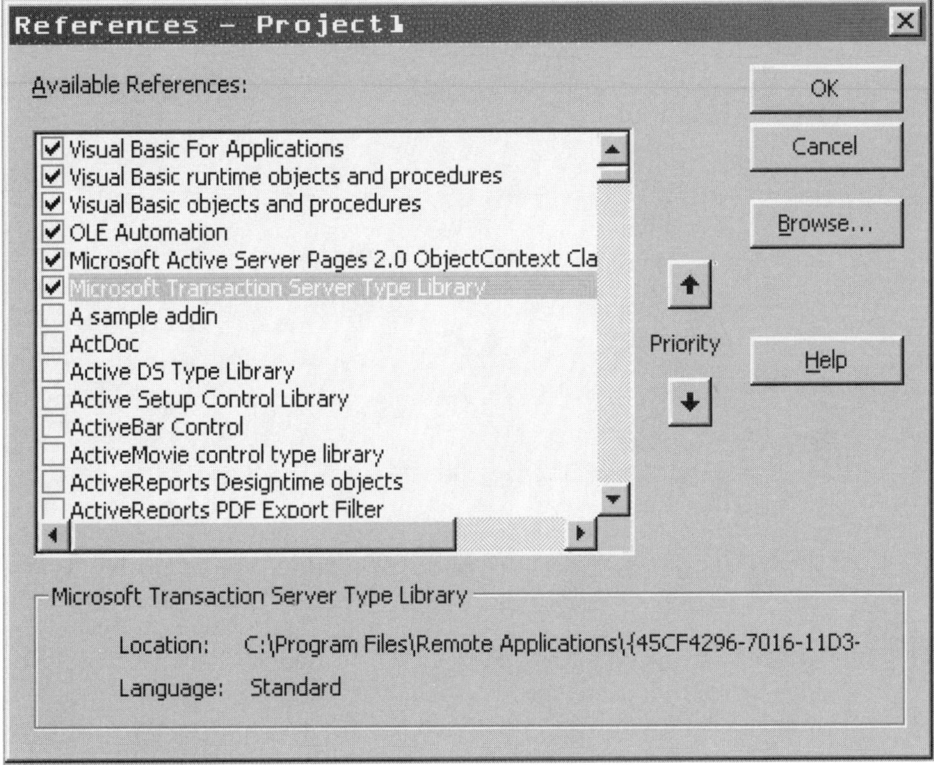

Figure 3–7 *A Visual Basic project's References list.*

Once you select a component from the References list, Visual Basic loads the information about the objects that make up the component from the component's type library. The type library may be a separate file (with the extension .TLB) distributed with the component, or may be embedded in the DLL or EXE files that make up the component.

Working With Objects

Some of the objects on the References list are almost as obliging as ActiveX Controls in making themselves available for use. For instance, if you check off Microsoft Data Access Objects on your project's References list, the DBEngine object is automatically available for use. Like an ActiveX control, you can manipulate it by referring to it by name. This code creates a Workspace object by using the DBEngine's CreateWorkspace method. Since the DBEngine object is available as soon as your application starts running, these could be the first two lines of code in your program:

```
Dim wks As Workspace
Set wks = DBEngine.CreateWorkspace()
```

NEW AND CREATEOBJECT

Most objects, though, will require you to create them explicitly before you use them. To use the Connection object in the ActiveX Data Objects component, it's not enough just to check ADO off on your References list. You must create a Connection object using the New keyword:

```
Dim con As Connection
Set con = New Connection
```

You can also use the CreateObject function to create an object:

```
Dim con As Connection
Set con = CreateObject("ADODB.Connection")
```

Both of these methods used the object's progid to identify the object to be loaded. Typically, but not always, the progid consists of the name of the component followed by the name of the object within the component that you want to use. Both code samples started the Connection object from the ADODB component. In the example that used the New keyword, I omitted the name of the component ("ADODB") and just used the name of the object ("Connection"). You'll get the progid for the components and objects on your server from the documentation for the relevant product.

There's a certain amount of danger involved in omitting the component name when using the New keyword. If you have both the DAO and ADO components checked off on your References list and then create a Recordset object without specifying the component, you may get a DAO Recordset or an ADO Recordset. Which one you get will be determined by which component appears first in your References list.

GETOBJECT

There is one exception to the requirement that your application must create the object before using it. If the object is already loaded into memory and can be shared with your application, then you can use the GetObject function. The GetObject function allows your project to connect to an already loaded version of an object. This code uses the GetObject function to get a reference to the Application object in a running copy of Microsoft Excel:

```
Dim xcl As Excel.Application
Set xcl = GetObject("Excel.Application")
```

These commands are discussed in more depth in the chapter on Components.

Instantiation

I'll bite the bullet here and introduce some terminology. While terminology is important (if only so that you can read more about developing components), it doesn't do you much good in creating components—the focus of this book. This section exists primarily for anyone who reads this book and says "Well, he didn't even mention 'instantiation'."

When you load a Class module into memory to create an object, you are said to be creating an "instance" of the object. Since you can have multiple copies of a Class module loaded simultaneously, you can have many instances of an object in use at a time. The process of creating an object from a Class module is known as "instantiating" that Class.

Note that you instantiate Classes, not objects. An object (an executing program in memory) is what you get when you instantiate a Class (a description of an object in code). Get this wrong and the OOP bullies will make fun of you.

Object References

All of these code samples used the Set command to get a reference to an object and store it in an object variable. The object variables wks, con, and xcl which I used in the preceding examples are your way of communicating with object once it is loaded into memory and executing.

You don't always have to use the Set command to get a reference to an object. This code, for instance, defines the Collection object that comes with VBA and adds the cst object to the Collection:

```
Dim col As Collection
Dim cst As Customer

Set col = New Collection
Set cst = New Customer
col.Add cst
```

In the above code, all that is actually added to the col Collection object is a reference to the cst object. After the code finishes executing, there will be two object variables pointing at the Customer object: the cst object variable and the first entry in the col Collection. Both of these lines of code, for instance, would do the same thing and run the Customer object's Delete method:

```
cst.Delete
col(1).Delete
```

Since all that is added to a Collection is a reference to the object, there is no reason that you can't add the same object to a Collection object multiple times. This code adds two references to the same Customer object to the col Collection:

```
Set cst = New Customer
col.Add cst
col.Add cst
```

ACTIVEX CONTROLS

With ActiveX controls, the process of working with objects is simpler than the code that I've been showing you. You don't have to use New, CreateObject, or Set with an ActiveX control. These steps are unnecessary with ActiveX Controls because Visual Basic:

- Automatically loads all of the controls on any Form as the Form is loaded.
- Creates an object variable for each control.
- Uses the value in the control's Name property to name the object variable.

Since most developers have their first exposure to working with objects through ActiveX Controls, I often feel that it's too bad that Visual Basic takes care of so much of the object-related housekeeping. In my classes, when I expose programmers to using the New and Set keywords, it often seems like a foreign and awkward process to them. I try to reassure those programmers that this process is what they've been using all along, it's just that Visual Basic has been taking care of it for them.

VARIABLES

Object variables are enough like ordinary variables to make you feel comfortable about using them. Object variables are also sufficiently different from ordinary variables, though, that failing to understand the differences can get you into trouble.

When you work with data in your Visual Basic program you create a variable to hold your data. If you want to store data in a variable, you will create a variable of type String, Double, Long, or one of the other supported Visual Basic data types. All of the following statements mark out a section of memory large enough to hold the specified kind of data and assign a name to that location:

```
Dim dbl As Double
Dim strFirstName As String
Dim curSalaries(9) As Currency
```

The first line of code, for instance, allocates enough memory to hold a Double numeric value and assigns the name dbl to that location. After this point in the program, you can use the dbl variable as a holding place for numeric data. You could say that this Dim statement, when executed, creates a Double variable called dbl. In Visual Basic, the Dim statement not only defines the variable but sets it to some initial value: 0 for numerics, a zero length string ("") for string variables.

You might be tempted to say that the following line of code creates a variable of, presumably, type CommandButton:

```
Dim cmd As CommandButton
```

However, it would be wrong to say that you create a CommandButton with this line of code. You would not expect a CommandButton to appear on your form when the code executes, for instance. If you tried to alter any of the properties of this CommandButton, you would get an error. This code, for instance, is guaranteed to cause an error when executed because the object variable cmd doesn't refer to any loaded CommandButton:

```
Dim cmd As CommandButton
cmd.Caption = "Click Here"
```

OBJECT VARIABLES

There is an important distinction to be made between ordinary variables and object variables. The Dim statement that declared the variable cmd created not an object and not a variable, but an object variable. An object variable provides the programmer with the ability to communicate with an object. An object variable provides a way to manipulate the object's properties, call its methods, and respond to its events.

Every object (even an ActiveX Control) is a program that Windows loads into memory and starts running. When you draw a Command button on your form, you are loading a copy of the CommandButton program into memory. Your code needs some way to communicate with that other program and the object variable provides that mechanism. You use the object variable to call the methods and functions in the object. The syntax in your code is to follow the object variable name with a period and then the name of a method or property or property from the object. This code, for instance, creates an ADO connection object, then sets a property and calls the object's Open method, all through the object variable:

```
Dim conn As ADODB.Connection
Set conn = New ADODB.Connection
conn.CursorLocation = adUseClient
conn.Open "File Name=c:\MyData.UDL"
```

CALLBYNAME

You can also access an object's methods or properties using the CallByName function. This function accepts an object variable, the name of a method or property, a constant that indicates the kind of access, and a variant array of the data to be passed to the method or property being called. There are four kinds of access that you can use with CallByName: Call a method, read a property, set a property, write a property. The equivalent call to the Connection object that I used in my previous example, rewritten to use CallByName, would look like this:

```
Dim conn As ADODB.Connection
Set conn = New ADODB.Connection
conn.CursorLocation = adUseClient
CallByName conn, "Open", _
    vbMethod, "File Name=c:\MyData.UDL"
```

▲ Case Study: Experimenting With Objects

One way to see the effect of working with object variables is to create a sample object and manipulate it from your program. To get ready for this experiment start Visual Basic and create a Standard EXE project. With the project create, from the Project menu select Add Class Module. From the following dialog, select Class Module and click on the Open button to add an empty Class module to your project and open it for editing.

CODING THE OBJECT

Like a Form, a Class module fires events. While a Form fires many different events (Load, UnLoad, Resize, etc.), a Class module fires only two: Initialize and Terminate. The Initialize event is roughly equivalent to a Form's Load event in that it fires as the Class module's code is loaded into memory. The Terminate event is like a Form's Unload event in that it fires as the object is unloaded from memory. For this experiment, put a MsgBox that identifies the event being fired into the Initialize and Terminate events. The code in your Class module should look like this:

```
Private Sub Class_Initialize()
    MsgBox "Creating a Class1 object"
End Sub
Private Sub Class_Terminate()
    MsgBox "Destroying a Class1 object"
End Sub
```

You are now well on your way to creating an object. At this point, you have the simplest object possible in the world (no methods, no properties, no events, just messages displayed as the object is created and destroyed), but it will still be an object.

Adding a property to a Class module isn't very difficult, either, as any public variable will appear as a property to a program that uses this Class. The experiment requires that this simple object have a property called Data, which you can define by adding this line to the [Declarations] area of your Class module:

```
Public Data As String
```

Now you're ready to create a program to use the object that's defined by your Class module.

CODING THE PROGRAM

To start creating a program to use the object that you just defined, double-click on the Form in your project to open it in design view. Add a single CommandButton to the Form and then double-click on the button to view the button's Click event. In the Click event add this code to work with your object. (I've numbered the lines for reference in the following discussion; you shouldn't type the numbers in.)

```
    Private Sub Command1_Click()
 1. Dim clsOne As Class1
 2. Dim clsTwo As Class1

 3. Set clsOne = New Class1
 4. clsOne.Data = "First created"

 5. Set clsTwo = clsOne
 6. Msgbox "Data for clsOne: " & clsOne.Data
 7. Msgbox "Data for clsTwo: " & clsTwo.Data

 8. Set clsOne = Nothing
 9. Msgbox "Data for clsTwo: " & clsTwo.Data

10. Set clsOne = New Class1
11. Msgbox "Data for clsOne: " & clsOne.Data

12. Set clsOne.Data = "Second created"
13. Msgbox "Data for clsOne: " & clsOne.Data
14. Msgbox "Data for clsTwo: " & clsTwo.Data

15. Set clsOne = Nothing
16. Set clsTwo = Nothing

    End Sub
```

As you enter this code you'll notice that Visual Basic provides the same IntelliSense support for your Class as it does for every other Class that you may use.

RUNNING THE EXPERIMENT

The next step is to run the program and click on the button to see what results you get. If you do, you should get the following series of message boxes (I've labeled this list for reference in the following discussion):

```
A.  Creating a Class1 object
B.  Data for clsOne: First created
C.  Data for clsTwo: First created

D.  Data for clsTwo: First created

E.  Creating a Class1 Object
F.  Data for clsOne:

G.  Data for clsOne: Second created
H.  Data for clsTwo: First created

I.  Destroying a Class1 object
J.  Destroying a Class1 object
```

WORKING WITH OBJECTS

So what's happening here? In the program, lines 1 and 2 create object variables that can refer to Class1 objects. This creates the situation shown in Figure 3–8: the program has two object variables called clsOne and clsTwo, but no objects. Line 3 actually creates a Class1 object using the New keyword. An object is a loaded copy of a Class module. As the object is created from the Class1 module, the first MsgBox dialog (line A) is displayed when the object's Initialize event fires and "Creating a Class1 object" is displayed.

Figure 3–9 shows the situation after line 3 executes. The program and a Class1 object are both loaded into memory and executing. The clsOne object variable has a reference to the Class1 object which allows the program to communicate with, and control, the object. In line 4, the program uses the clsOne object variable to set the object's Data property to "First Created" as shown in Figure 3–10.

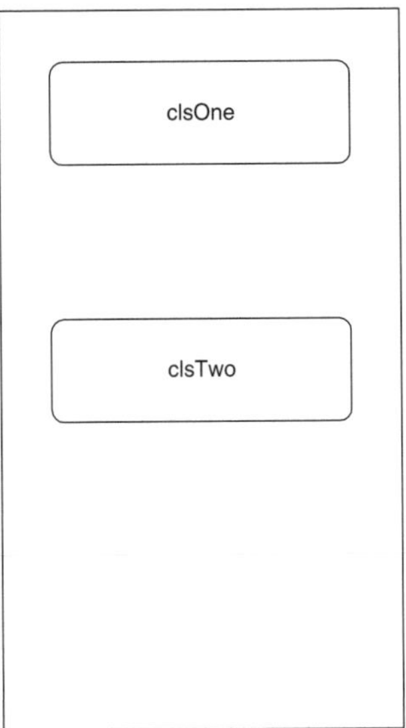

Figure 3–8 *A program with two object variables.*

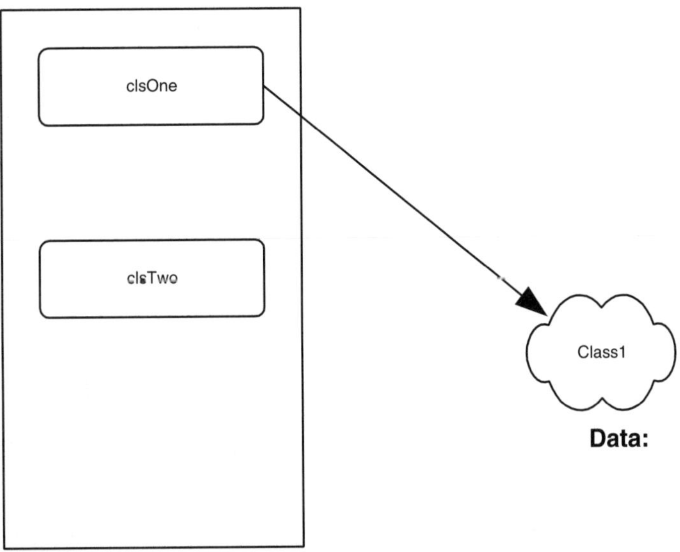

Figure 3–9 *A program with a Class1 object loaded.*

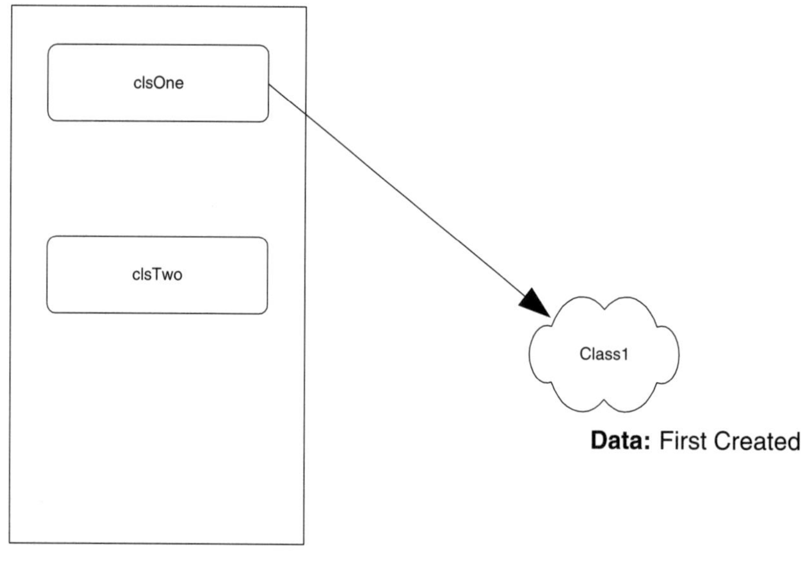

Figure 3–10 *Setting the Class1 object's Data property.*

Line 5 sets the object variable clsTwo equal to clsOne. No new object variable is created. If a new object had been created, a "Creating a Class1 Object" message would appear. Instead, at this point, both the clsOne and clsTwo object variables are referring to the same Class1 object (see Figure 3–11). As a result, when lines 6 and 7 display the Data property for the two object variables, the value is the same: "First created" (display lines B and C). It's important to realize that the reason the Data property for the two object variables is the same is not because they are copies of each other. The Data property for the two object variables is the same because the two object variables are referring to the same object.

In Line 8, clsOne is set to Nothing which breaks the object variable's reference to the Class1 object. This creates the situation shown in Figure 3–12, with the object variable clsTwo referring to the object and clsOne referring to nothing. To demonstrate this, line 9 uses the clsTwo object variable to display the Data property of the object, which is still "First created" (display line D).

Line 10 creates a new Class1 object, triggering the "Creating a Class1 object" message on line F. Figure 3–13 shows the result, with two Class1 objects loaded and referred to by the two object variables. To prove this, line 11 displays the value of the Data property for the new object, which is blank (display line E). Line 12 then sets the Data property of the new Class1 object to "Second created" as shown in Figure 3–14. Lines 13 and 14 display the two different property values in the two different objects (display lines G and H).

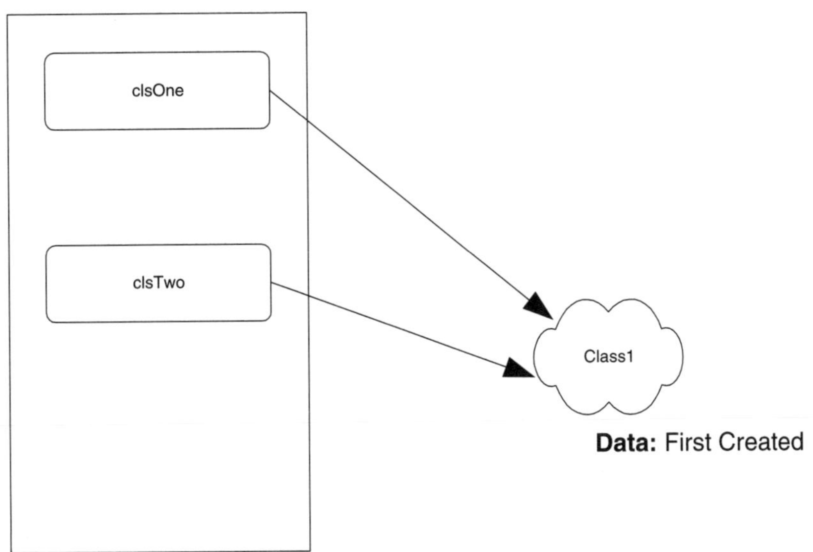

Figure 3–11 *Two variables referring to the same object.*

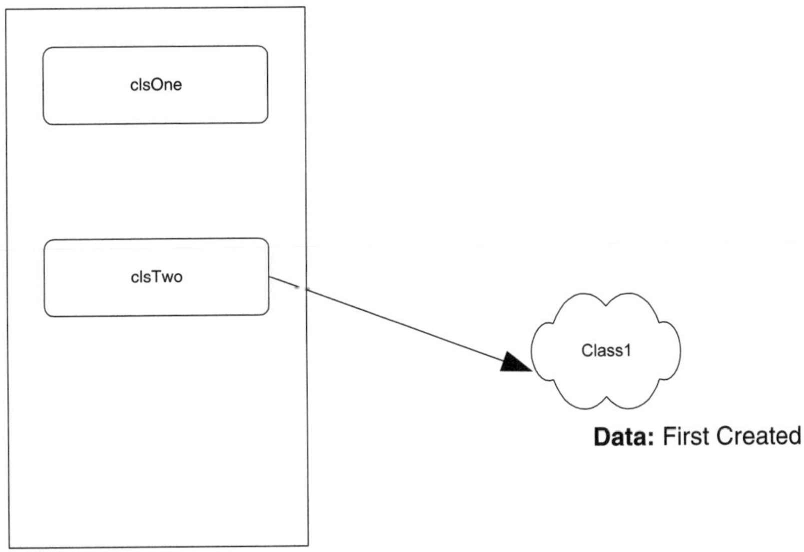

Figure 3–12 *Disconnecting clsOne from the Class1 object.*

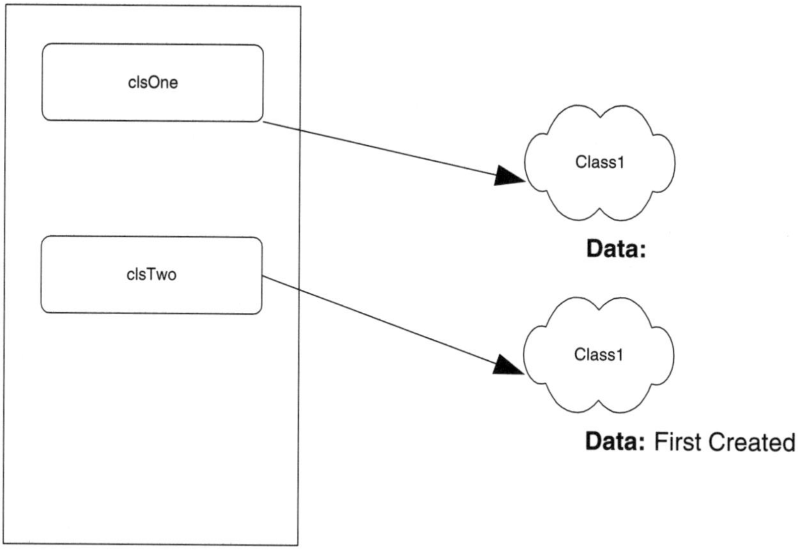

Figure 3–13 *A program with two object variables.*

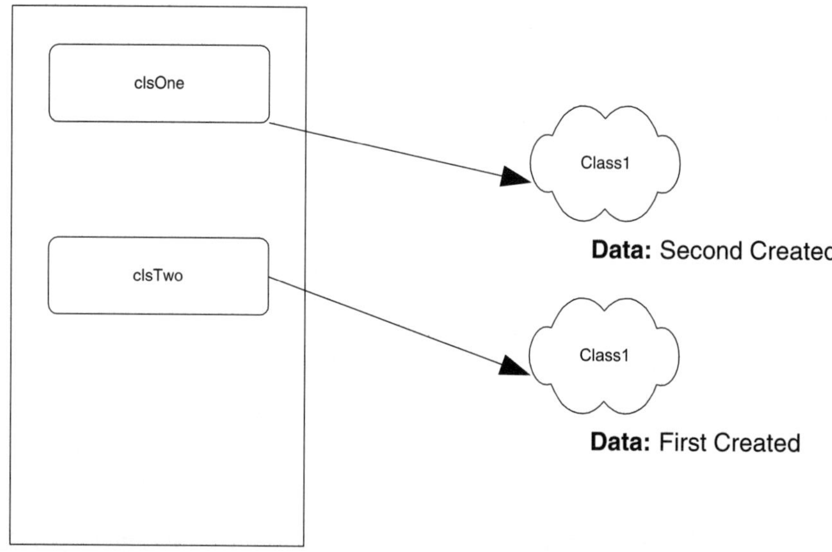

Figure 3–14 *Setting the Data property of the second Class1 object.*

In line 15, the clsOne object variable is set to Nothing. This breaks the connection between the second Class1 object and the only object variable that was using it. When an object has no object variables referring to it, Visual Basic and Windows remove the object from memory. This triggers the object's Terminate event, giving the message "Destroying a Class1 object" on display line I (Figure 3–15). Line 16 sets the object variable clsTwo to Nothing, breaking the variable's connection to the first Class1 object that was created back on line 3 of the program. As the object is unloaded from memory, it fires its Terminate event, giving the message seen on display line J (Figure 3–16).

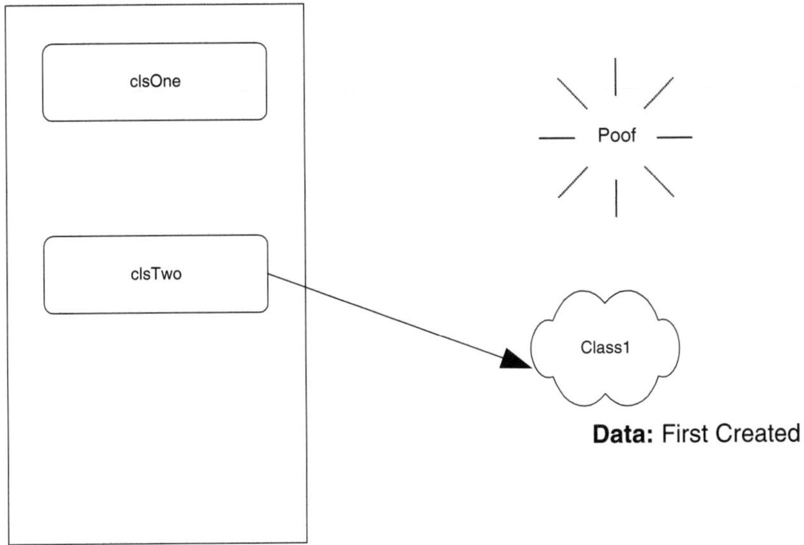

Figure 3–15 *Destroying the second Class1 object.*

EXPERIMENTAL LESSONS

There are a number of lessons that you can take away from this Case Study:

1. An object variable is *not* an object.
2. An object is a separate program loaded into memory and running in conjunction with your program.
3. An object variable provides you with a conduit through which you can manipulate an object.
4. Over the life of a program, an object variable can refer to several different objects.
5. At any time, an object variable points to one object or Nothing.

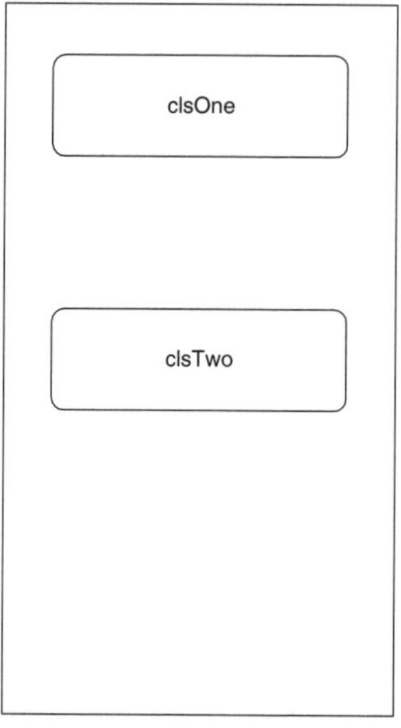

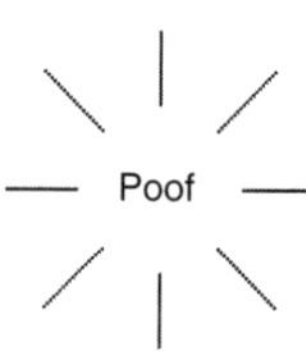

Figure 3–16 *Destroying the first Class1 object.*

6. At any time, an object may have one or more object variables referring to it.
7. An object may, over its life, be referred to by several different object variables.
8. An object will be removed from memory when no object variable refers to it.

Saying that an object variable refers to an object is a simplification of what's actually going on. In the chapter on Interfaces I'll return to this topic to refine what's happening when you use an object variable with an object.

ByVal and ByRef Object Parameters

Now that you've solidified your knowledge of object variables, I can finish the discussion of the ByVal and ByRef passing mechanisms. When you pass an object variable as a parameter, the effect of ByVal and ByRef is a little more complicated than it is with the intrinsic data types like String, Date, Integer, and so on.

The first thing to remember is that, regardless of whether you use ByVal or ByRef, you are always passing the object variable, not the object itself. As a result, the routine that receives the parameter will always be working with the same object as the calling program. This is because passing an object variable as ByVal does not make a copy of the object, just of the object variable. Regardless of which mechanism is used, the called routine receives a reference to the same object as the called routine. With ByRef, the called routine just gets its own private copy of the object variable. So, if the called routine changes a property of the object, that change will be visible to the calling program, no matter how you passed the object variable to the routine.

The difference between passing an object variable either ByVal or ByRef only matters if the called routine's code points the object variable at some other object. Walking through the steps as an object variable is passed to a routine ByVal, you have

1. Visual Basic creates a copy of the object variable.
2. The new object variable is pointed at the existing object.
3. The new object variable is passed to the called routine.

If the routine changes its copy of the object variable to point at some other object, that change will have no effect on the object variable used by the calling program.

On the other hand, if the object variable is passed ByRef and the called routine points the object variable at a different object, the calling program will then find that its variable now points to the new object (Figure 3–17).

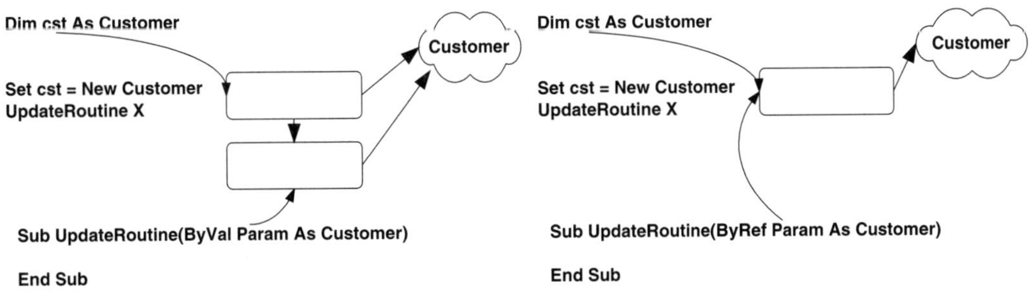

Figure 3–17 *Using ByVal and ByRef to pass an object variable.*

Benchmark: Passing Object Parameters

Passing object variables ByRef is considerably faster than calling ByVal. A routine accepting an object variable ByRef runs in 1 millisecond, while a routine accepting the object variable ByVal took 3 milliseconds. There is no difference in the time to pass a parameter for an ActiveX EXE or an ActiveX DLL.

Summary

In this chapter I reviewed the fundamentals of how Visual Basic programmers use objects. While building, rather than using objects, is the focus of this book, it's important to understand how your users are going to interact with the objects that you create. Understanding the relationship between object variables and the objects that they connect to is also fundamental to understanding interfaces, one of the topics in the Chapter on interfaces and a key part of the COM specification.

You've also got a thorough understanding of parameters and, especially, Optional parameters. Powerful methods and (as you'll see in the next chapter) complex properties require multiple parameters. Being able to make effective use of UDTs and ParamArrays gives you tremendous flexibility in creating objects. I also showed you how you can use enumerated variables to establish predefined constants and additional support for developers using your objects.

While there are a number of books that discuss the Visual Basic product with its editors and tools, very few books concentrate on the features of the VBA language itself. A good book is ***Visual Basic Language Developer's Handbook*** by Ken Getz and Mike Gilbert from Sybex Press. And, of course, the reference manuals and Help files that ship with Visual Basic provide the official descriptions of these keywords and how they work.

FOUR

Objects

In the Microsoft and Windows world, objects form the foundation on which everything else rests. In the COM model, developers create objects and then combine them to form components. Components then form the building blocks for creating applications. The new paradigm for creating programs is based on designing applications as a series of interacting objects.

In order to build more sophisticated applications, I began to participate in the world of COM by creating objects in my applications. The most important thing that I learned about this whole discussion is that objects, object models, classes, components, and all the rest of the topics covered in this book didn't change what I did as a developer. I had been writing subroutines and functions as part of creating Visual Basic applications, and I found that I kept on writing subroutines and functions as I moved into the world of object-oriented development. Objects provided a powerful way of packaging up my code to make it more useful. When I looked at how much I been able to do with the object models provided by DAO, ADO, and Visual Basic itself, it made me want to build my own object models.

In this chapter I show you how to create an object in Visual Basic. You'll see how to define methods, properties, and events. You'll also learn how to design objects that clients can save and restore from one execution of the application to another. You'll build on the VBA knowledge that you already have to create flexible methods that accept multiple parameters. You'll find out how to create properties that accept multiple parameters and mimic some of the behavior of a full-fledged collection object. At the end of this chapter, I bring many of the concepts that make up the chapter together by showing you how to create an object with asynchronous methods: methods that continue to execute after control returns to the client that called them.

Working With Class Modules

The code that you put in a Class module describes how the object created from it will behave. To put it another way, a Class module is a description of an object. A Class module is no different from any other program that you have written: The code you put in the source file describes how the program loaded into memory will behave.

The major difference between a Class module and a standard program is that a Class module provides a more explicit interface than a typical program. If a program exposes its functionality to other programs at all, it does it as an undifferentiated mass of subroutines and functions. A Class module organizes its functionality and allows programmers to use it by performing one of three activities:

- Reading or setting properties
- Invoking methods
- Responding to events

These three items (properties, methods, and events) describe everything that you need to know about an object in order to use it.

When you create an object you define it to your users in terms of the properties, methods, and events that you expose. As a result, the documentation about an object organizes itself around these three topics. However, when providing documentation about your object, it's also important to provide the developer with an overview that indicates how you expect those methods, properties, and events to be used together.

Classes

The Class module itself has three properties when used as part of a Standard EXE: Name, DataBindingBehaviour, and DataSourceBehaviour (see Figure 4–1). The most important is the Name property (I discuss the two DataBinding properties in the chapter on data objects). The Class module's Name property establishes the name that developers will use when creating an object from your Class.

For the case study in the previous chapter, I had you leave the Name property of the Class module at its default value of Class1. Both of the objects created from that module would be said to be of the same Class, the Class1 class. This is exactly what happens when, for instance, you create a Recordset object using ADO: You are creating an object created from the Recordset Class module.

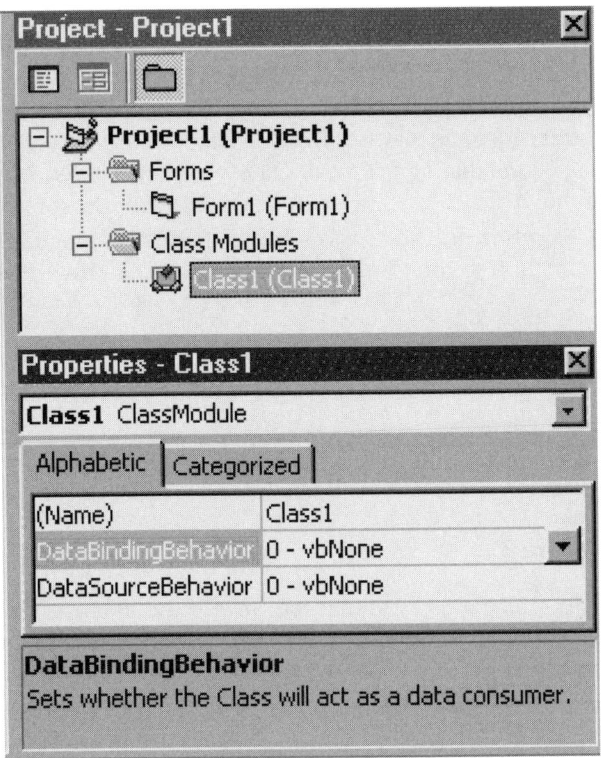

Figure 4-1 *A Class module's property list.*

Objects created from the same Class will have the same set of properties, events, and methods. Defining a new Class consists of defining the methods, properties, and events that objects created from that Class will have in common. Individual objects created from the same Class will differ in terms of the data that the object presents to the user. For instance, two objects of the same Class will have different values for their properties. While you may have two CommandButton objects on your form, they will have different values in their Name properties (Command1 and Command2).

In a true object-oriented world, one of the characteristics of an object is that it has "identity." You can access any object provided that you know its identity, because no two objects will be identical. In the COM world, things are a little different: You keep track of objects through the object variables that point to them. However, you should also consider making sure that you define at least one property (like Name) that you can use to uniquely identify all of the objects currently in use.

Defining Methods

I've always found methods the easiest part of an object to create. Even before I came to Visual Basic I had been writing my programs as a collection of subroutines and functions that I called as I needed. In Visual Basic, those subroutines and functions that I put in my Class modules suddenly appeared to programs using the object as methods (provided I declare the routines as Public).

To return to the Class1 object of the previous example, adding a SayHello method to the Class requires me to write only this Public subroutine:

```
Public Sub SayHello()
    MsgBox "Hello"
End Sub
```

To use this method, a developer using my object would write this code:

```
Dim cls As Class1
Set cls = New Class1
cls.SayHello
```

To create a method that returns a value, I just use a function instead of a subroutine. This function returns True if the current date is a weekday (Monday to Friday):

```
Public Function ValidWorkDay() As Boolean
    Dim intWeekDay As Integer
    intWeekDay = WeekDay(Date)
    If intWeekDay < 6 And _
       intWeekDay > 1 Then
        ValidWorkDay = True
    Else
        ValidWorkDay = False
    End If
End Function
```

Using this method would require code like this:

```
Dim cls As Class1
Dim bolResult As Boolean
Set cls = New Class1
bolResult = cls.ValidWorkDay()
```

Since a function returns a value, a function should be declared with a data type (ValidWorkDay is declared as Boolean in the previous sample code, for example). If you don't supply a data type when creating your function, the method will return a variant value.

Benchmark: Returning Values

In order to get any difference at all between functions returning the different data types, I had to execute each call 5000 times (rather than my normal 1000 iterations) So, while there are differences between the various data types, they are very, very small. The results for each data type (in milliseconds) from the fastest to the slowest were:

Boolean/Double/Integer: 6
Long/Byte/Currency/Single: 7
Date: 8
String: 11
Variant: 13

The relative position of the numerics to each other shifted with each run, so the difference between Boolean, Double, Integer, Long, Date, Single, Byte and Currency should be ignored. The results then boil down to numeric data types being faster than String data and String data being faster than Variant.

Like most programmers these days, I follow a convention when creating names for the variables in my programs. In the preceding code sample, I gave the variable intWeekDay the three letter prefix 'int' to indicate that it holds integer values. However, despite the fact that the ValidWorkDay function has a data type, I did not give its name a prefix to indicate that it returns a Boolean value. Even where a function is being used to create a method, general practice is to not use a naming convention but just to give the function a name that describes what the method does (see Figure 4–2 for an example).

You will, in the code in this book, often see me prefix private module level variables with "m_". Module level variables (variables declared in the General Declarations section at the top of the module) are available to all the routines in the Class module. If they are declared using either the Dim or Private keywords, then the variables are not visible to routines outside of the Class module. Borrowing a term from more object-oriented languages like SmallTalk, these variables are referred to as "member" variables and prefixed with "m_".

Defining Properties

Properties allow you to expose the functionality of your object as a set of data values that can be read or set. A property can be defined one of two different ways: through Public variables or through a set of Property procedures.

PUBLIC VARIABLES

The simplest way to add a property to a Class module is to define a Public variable in the Declarations section of the Class module. This method usually turns out to be inadequate for the needs of your object. It almost always turns out that you need some code in your Class module to execute when the

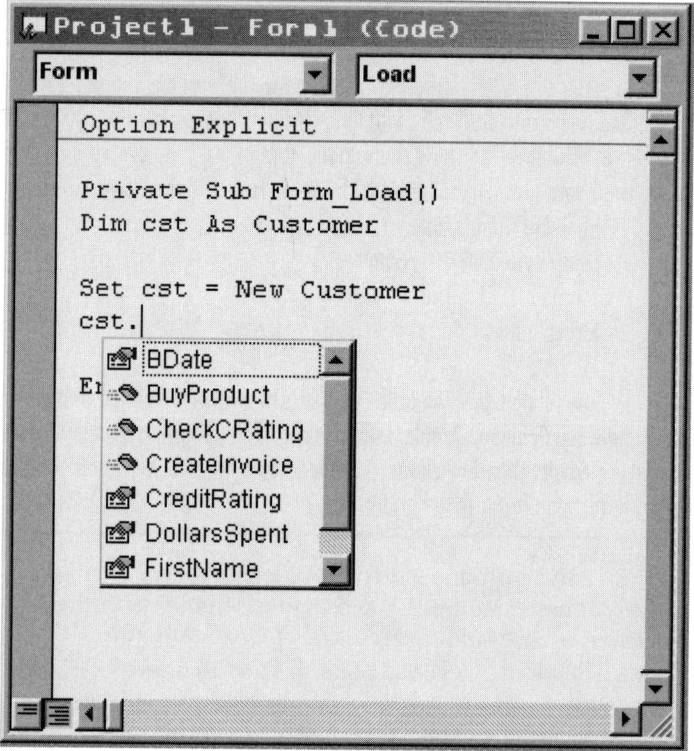

Figure 4–2 *The IntelliSense drop list of methods and properties for an object. Note that the names of the methods and properties do not reflect any naming conventions.*

property is read or changed. At the very least, when your users set the value of a property in your object, you will probably want to run some code to validate the value that they pass to your object.

When Visual Basic first gained the ability to define Class modules with properties, the underlying mechanism used when a Public variable defined a property was different from the mechanism used for Property Procedures. One side effect of these differences was that properties created through Public variables were faster to set and read than properties created through Property Procedures. With Visual Basic 6, however, this difference has disappeared. If you create a property by using Public variables, Visual Basic 6 creates the appropriate Property Procedures for you behind the scenes.

PROPERTY PROCEDURES

If you want to have some routine execute when your property is read or written, you must define the property through a set of Property Let, Property Get, and Property Set routines. These routines execute automatically as your properties are used. They are:

PROPERTY GET • A Property Get routine is run each time your property's value is read (when the calling program "gets" the property value).

PROPERTY LET • A Property Let routine is run every time your property has its value changed. This routine's name comes from the now obsolete Basic keyword Let, which used to be required in an assignment statement.

PROPERTY SET • A Property Set should be used in place of a Property Let whenever the property's data type is an object.

Benchmark: Properties

You have three ways of implementing properties or "property-like" behavior: Public variables, Property Procedures, and methods that accept and return values. The performance cost of the techniques are similar, with a spread of less than 70 milliseconds over 1000 iterations among all three. However, on all of my test runs, the Public variables had the fastest response, followed by methods, with Property Procedures taking the most time.

Initially, Property Procedures looked odd to me. I soon realized that they looked very much like my old familiar subroutines and functions, as I discuss in this section .

PROPERTY LET

The WholesaleManagement component contains a Customer object, which allows developers to access information about a single customer. When a Customer object is created, the developer needs a way to associate the object with a particular customer's data. This is done through the Customer object's CustNum property. In the WholesaleManagement component, the CustNum property is implemented by a Property Let routine, which contains the code to retrieve data from the appropriate customer record:

```
Dim rst As Recordset

Public Property Let CustNum (CustomerNumber As String)
Set rst = New Recordset
rst.Open("DSN=WholesaleDatabase", _
     "Select * From Customer Where CustNo = '" _
        & CustomerNumber & "'")
End Property
```

As you can see, a Property Let looks very much like a subroutine; passed a value it performs some operation.

The name of the Property Let statement provides the name for the property. To use the CustNum property to retrieve the data for Customer 46513, the developer would write code like this (after adding the WholesaleManagement component to the project's References list):

```
Dim cust As Customer
Set cust = New Customer
cust.CustNum = "46513"
```

PROPERTY GET

With only a Property Let routine written, the CustNum property will be a read only property. In order to allow users to read the CustNum property, you will have to write a Property Get routine. You must set the name of the routine—which is the same as the name of the property—to whatever value you want the Property routine to return.

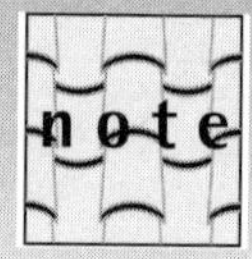

To me, a Property Get looks very much like a function. Like a function, a Property Get returns a value to the calling routine. In a function you set the value to be returned by setting the name of the function to that value. A Property Get works the same way; you set the name of the Property Get routine to the value to be returned.

Here's the code for the CustNum Property Get, which allows developers to retrieve the CustNo field for the customer represented by the object:

```
Public Property Get CustNum() As String
CustNum = rst("CustNo")
End Property
```

PROPERTY SET

You need to write a Property Set routine (instead of a Property Let) only if your property accepts an object value and you want the developers using your project to use a Set statement to set the property's value. You don't have to use a Property Set, even if your property accepts an object value. These two implementations of a property with an object data type, work equally well:

```
Public Property Let LetObject(inObject As Form)
End Property

Public Property Set SetObject(InObject As Form)
End Property
```

The only difference between the two implementations of the properties is in the code that the developer uses to change the value of the property:

- If you implement the property using a Property Let, then the developer will not be able to use a Set statement when changing the value of the property.
- If you implement the property with a Property Set, then the developer will have to use a Set statement when changing the value of the property.

A developer using the LetObject and SetObject properties defined above, would use this code (where frmMain is the name of a form):

```
obj.LetObject = frmMain
Set obj.SetObject = frmMain
```

Using a Property Set procedure is the better practice when defining properties that accept objects because it matches the way that Visual Basic works.

When you have a property that accepts objects, you must remember that any assignments within your property procedure will have to use the Set statement. This includes setting the name of the property in the Property Get procedure to the value to be returned.

The following example shows some typical code for a property with an object data type. The Property Let accepts an object variable and stores the reference in a private variable called m_HoldForm. In the Property Let, the assignment of InObject to m_HoldForm requires a Set statement, as would any assignment of any object variable.

```
Dim m_HoldForm As Form
Public Property Let LetObject(InObject As Form)
    Set m_HoldForm = inObject
End Property
```

The Property Get returns the value of whatever is stored in m_HoldForm. Since the LetObject routine is defined with an object data type (Form), a Set statement is required when the name of the property is assigned the value of m_HoldForm in the Property Get:

```
Public Property Get LetObject() As Form
    Set LetObject = m_HoldForm
End Property
```

Note that these Set assignment statements used in the LetObject routines are internal to the object. Since the property was implemented with a Property Let instead of a Property Set, the developer using this property would not use the Set keyword when setting this property. Instead, the developer could change the value of the LetObject property with code like this (again, frmMain is the name of a form in the client project):

```
obj.LetObject = frmMain
```

COMBINING LET AND SET

You can use all three Property Procedures for a single property. When a Property Let and a Property Set are declared for the same property, the developer can use either of these lines of code to change the property value:

```
obj.LetSetProperty = varValue
Set obj.LetSetProperty = varValue
```

When the developer uses the "Set" syntax, the Property Set routine in the Class module will be run. When the non-Set syntax is used, the Property Let routine will be run. By having both a Set and a Let you can duplicate, as an example, the behavior of the ActiveConnection property in the ADO Recordset object. The ActiveConnection property can accept either a Command object (using the Set syntax) or String data by using the non-Set syntax. A typical combination of a Set and a Let might look like this:

```
Dim m_cst As Customer

Public Property Let Customer (CustId As Variant)
Set m_cst = New Customer
m_cst.Id = CustId
End Property

Public Property Set Customer(Customer as Variant)
Set m_cst = Customer
End Property

Public Property Get Customer() as Variant
Set Customer = m_cst
End Property
```

The Property Let statement expects to be handed a CustId value as a string. It uses that information to create a Customer object and sets the private member variable m_cst to refer to that object. The Property Set, on the other hand, expects to be passed a Customer object and so just sets the m_cst variable to refer to the object. Since the result of using either the Let or the Set is the creation of a Customer object, the Property Get returns the m_cst variable that refers to the Customer object.

If you do use both a Set and a Let, you will have to declare your property as type Variant so that you can accept different data types in the different routines (e.g., Object in the Set routine, String in the Let routine).

Benchmark: Property Lets for Objects

Since you can use Property Lets with object data types, you may want to know if there's a performance difference between using a Property Let or a Property Set. The answer is, not much. While using a Property Let to accept an object variable was slower, it was only by some 20 milliseconds over 1000 iterations.

Benchmark: Returning Properties and UDTs

When multiple values have to be returned from a function, you can pass the data back in a UDT or in a property. Ignoring the cost of creating the object, I first tested setting 1 to 30 properties in an object (using Public string variables), returning the object, and reading the properties. I then set 1 to 30 string elements of a UDT, returned the UDT, and read the elements. The object was faster than the UDT for a DLL. The more data that I had to return, the larger the difference. With 30 properties/elements to set, the object took only 191 milliseconds while the UDT took 453. That difference was maintained even when a small number of properties was involved: With 2 properties, the object took only 13 milliseconds while the UDT took 23 milliseconds. However, if the object was defined in an out-of-process EXE, using the object could take 3 times longer than the UDT. If you are compiling your object as an EXE you should return UDT's in preference to setting multiple properties.

PROPERTY EXIT

Within a Property procedure, you can use a Property Exit statement to prevent the code following the statement from being executed. There will be times when you don't want a property to be read or written, and so want to exit the Property Procedure before taking any action (see Figure 4–3 for block diagrams demonstrating the use of Property Exit).

In the Customer object, for instance, most of the properties of the object (e.g., Name) should not be read or written until the developer has used the object's CustNum property to associate the object with a record. In the Customer object, the CustNum property retrieves the customer data into a Recordset object that is declared at the module level. In the following version of the Name Property procedures, the code first checks to see if the Recordset is Nothing, which indicates that no data has been retrieved. If no data has been retrieved, the Name property returns an error code indicating that the property isn't ready for use:

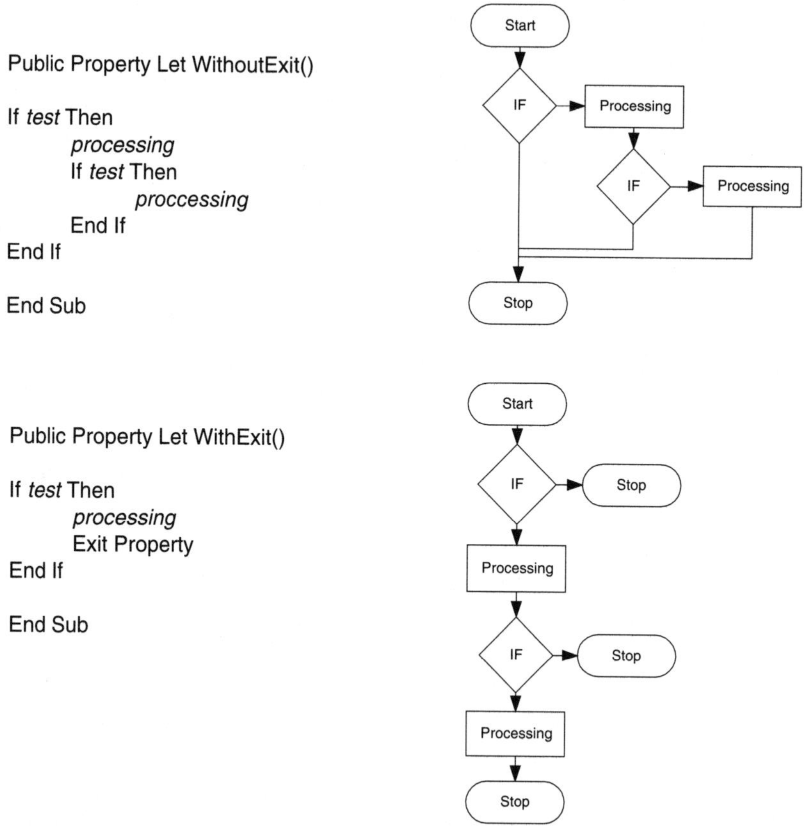

```
Public Property Let WithoutExit()

If test Then
        processing
        If test Then
                proccessing
        End If
End If

End Sub
```

Start
IF
Processing
IF
Processing
Stop

```
Public Property Let WithExit()

If test Then
        processing
        Exit Property
End If

End Sub
```

Start
IF
Stop
Processing
IF
Stop
Processing
Stop

Figure 4–3 *Using Property Exit vs. If blocks.*

```
Public Property Let Name (CustomerName As String)
    If rst Is Nothing Then
      Err.Raise 445
      Exit Property
    End If
    rst("CustName") = CustomerName
    rst.Update
End Property

Public Property Get Name () As String
    If rst Is Nothing Then
      Err.Raise 445
      Exit Property
    End If
    Name = rst("CustName")
End Property
```

I lived through the ideological wars over structured vs. unstructured coding. People just aren't talking about it anymore. I was always on the side of structured code and, fortunately for me, that's the side that won. Using an Exit Property statement may look like a deviation from the standards of structured code. Structured code, after all, suggests that every routine should have one entry point and one exit point. For Property Procedures, the entry point is the Property Let, Get, or Set statement, and the exit point is the End Property statement. I disagree.

I feel that using Exit Property statements usually results in simpler code. Rewriting the Property Let above to eliminate the Exit Property results in this:

```
Public Property Let Name (CustomerName As String)
    If rst Is Nothing Then
      Err.Raise 445
    Else
      rst("CustName") = CustomerName
      rst.Update
    End If
End Property
```

As you can see, the main body of the routine (the update of the Recordset) is nested inside the Else statement. In this routine, because the body is so short, the code is still easy to read. However, where the body of the routine is quite long, or contains several If blocks, I feel that not using the Exit Property statement adds an unnecessary level of complexity to the program.

I use structured code to make my code easier to read, both for myself and the programmers who come after me and have to maintain my code. In the original version of the Property Let, using Exit Property made my intent when I wrote the code clear: If rst isn't set, skip the rest of the routine. Using the If block instead of the Exit Property suggests that part of the routine may still be valid if the Recordset isn't Nothing.

MULTIPLE PARAMETER PROPERTIES

A property may accept more than one parameter. When a property accepts multiple parameters, all but the last one appear to the developer using the property as indexes to the property. Defining properties with multiple parameters lets you create properties that mimic the syntax of a collection or a list.

This code shows a Property Get declared with multiple parameters:

```
Public Property Get IndexProperty (IndexValue As Integer) _
    As String
End Property
```

A developer reading this property would use this syntax:

```
strValue = obj.IndexProperty(2)
```

The "2" that the developer provided as an index to the property IndexProperty would be passed into the Property Get routine as the IndexValue parameter.

The corresponding Property Let for this property would be declared like this:

```
Public Property Let IndexProperty (IndexValue As Integer, _
    InValue as String) As String
End Property
```

The developer setting this property would use this syntax

```
obj.IndexProperty(1) = "New value"
```

The "1" that the developer provides as an index to the property is passed to the IndexProperty's Property Let routine in the IndexValue parameter. The value that the developer wants to set the property to would be passed in as the InValue parameter. Putting this together, you can create a property that provides access to a list.

In the following code, I declare a module level array called m_strArray that can be shared among all the routines in the Class module. In the Class's Initialize event, I use the ReDim command to add the first position in the array:

```
Dim m_strArray() As String

Private Sub Class_Initialize()
    ReDim m_strArray(0)
End Sub
```

The following Property Let procedure accepts an index and a value. The Let procedure checks to make sure that there is a position in the array that corresponds to the index. If the array isn't big enough, the code then uses the ReDim statement to add new positions to the array. Finally, the procedure assigns the value passed in to the position in the array specified by the routine's first parameter:

```
Public Property Let ListProperty (Index As Integer, _
                                 InValue As String)
If Index > UBound(m_strArray) Then
    ReDim Preserve m_strArray(Index)
End If
m_strArray(Index) = InValue
End Property
```

This is the corresponding Property Get that returns the value in the array for the position specified by the index passed to the routine (or raises an error if the index is outside of the bounds of the array):

```
Public Property Get ListProperty (Index As Integer) as String
```

```
    If Index < LBound(m_strArray) Or _
       Index > UBound(m_strArray) Then
        Err.Raise 452
    End If
    ListProperty = m_strArray(Index)
End Property
```

Your Property Let, Get, and Set routines can accept as many parameters as allowed by any other Visual Basic subroutine or function.

You cannot create a property by declaring an array as a Public variable in a Class module's Declarations section. If you want a property that acts as a list, you will have to implement the property using Property procedures.

When you create a Property Procedure with multiple parameters, the number of parameters must be consistent among the Get and Set or Let procedures. This means that the Set and Let procedures must have one more parameter than the corresponding Get. The data types of the parameters must match among the Get, Set, and Let procedures for a property. If the first parameter of a property's Get is an integer, then the first parameter of the corresponding Set or Let must also be an integer, and so on for any other parameters in the Property Procedures.

OPTIONAL PARAMETERS • Optional parameters can be used with Property Procedures, though the rules are slightly different than for the subroutines and functions that you use to define your methods. In a Property Let or Set, the final parameter holds the value that the property is being set to, and so is treated as a special case: it cannot be Optional or a ParamArray. The parameters prior to the final parameter follow the same rules for using the Optional and ParamArray keywords as for a function or subroutine:

- The Optional and ParamArray parameters must be the last parameters in the group.
- If you use a ParamArray parameter you cannot use Optional parameters.

The following routines are a valid Property Get and Let combination. The property Let has two index parameters (FirstIndex and Index) and a parameter to accept the property's value (InValue). The second parameter (Index) is declared Optional even though it is followed by the required InValue parameter. This is because the final parameter for the Property Procedure is treated as a special case:

```
Public Property Let OptionalProperty _
    (FirstIndex As Integer, _
     Optional Index As Integer, InValue As String)
```

```
End Property

Public Property Get OptionalProperty _
    (FirstIndex As Integer, _
     Optional Index As Integer)
End Property
```

Since the Property Let has its second parameter marked as Optional, a developer could set the property with either of these statements (let us hope the Let procedure has some code to handle the situation when the Optional parameter is not supplied):

```
obj.OptionalProperty(1, 1) = "New Value"
obj.OptionalProperty(1) = "New Value"
```

You can specify default values with the Optional arguments as you would with a subroutine or function (Figure 4–4 shows the structure of optional parameters in a Property Procedure).

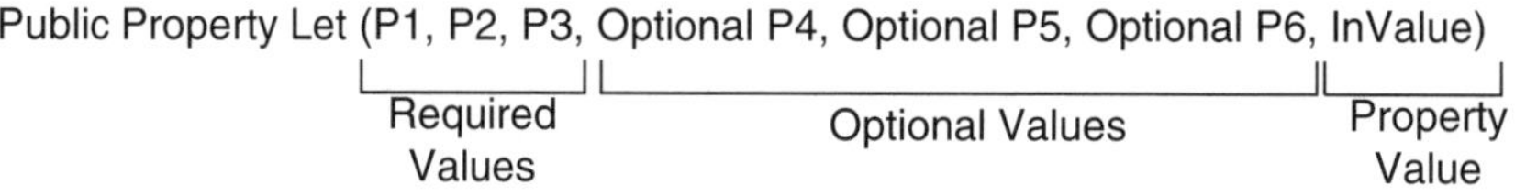
Public Property Let (P1, P2, P3, Optional P4, Optional P5, Optional P6, InValue)
Required Values
Optional Values
Property Value

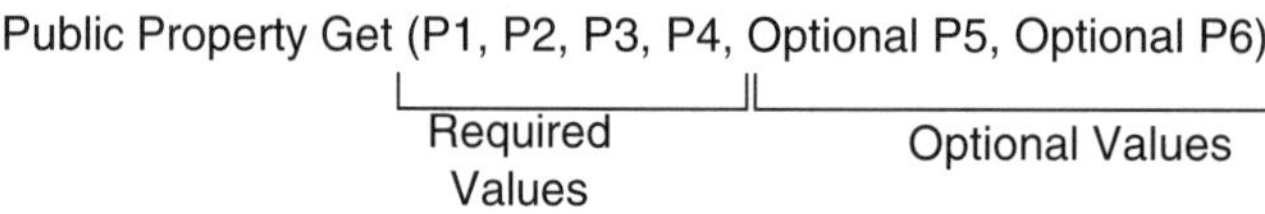
Public Property Get (P1, P2, P3, P4, Optional P5, Optional P6)
Required Values
Optional Values

Figure 4–4 *Optional parameters in Property Procedures.*

You don't have to match the "optionality" of parameters. If the first parameter in a Get is optional, the first parameter in the corresponding Property Let or Property Set does not have to be.

NAMED PARAMETERS • Developers can use named parameters with Properties, though the syntax is a little awkward. This code sets the value of the Index parameter using a named parameter and passes the property the value "New Value":

```
obj.OptionalProperty(Index:=1) = "New Value"
```

BYVAL AND BYREF • The final parameter of a Property Let is always passed ByVal, so the Property procedure gets its own copy of the data. As a result, changes made to the final parameter will not be seen by the calling program. The other parameters can be passed either ByVal or ByRef.

PROPERTY DATA TYPE

When a property is defined by declaring a public variable, the data type for the variable determines the data type of the property. Adding this line of code to a Class module's Declarations section will create a property called State with a data type of Boolean:

```
Dim State As Boolean
```

Where properties are defined through the use of Property Lets, Gets, and Sets, the data type of the property is set by

- The data type of the last parameter passed to the Property Let and Property Set
- The data type returned by the Property Get

If these data types do not agree exactly your code will not compile. Standard Visual Basic data type conversions are not performed to reconcile property data types. You can not, for instance, declare the parameter passed to a Let as an Integer variable and have the corresponding Get declared as Double. Even declaring a Let procedure as Form and the Get procedure as the more general Object is forbidden.

Where a property has multiple parameters, the last parameter in the list sets the property type for a property Let or Set. This property Let creates a Boolean property because the last parameter is of type Boolean:

```
Public Property Let MultProperty (Index1 As Integer, _
    Index2 As Variant, InValue As Boolean)
```

The data type for the last parameter in a Set procedure must be an object variable. Property routines may also be used to create properties that are of a User Defined Data Type. These statements create a property of type Customer, for instance:

```
Type Customer
    Name As String
    BirthDate As Date
    CreditLimit As Currency
End Type

Public Property Get UDTProperty() As Customer
End Property

Public Property Let UDTProperty (CustData As Customer)
End Property
```

You cannot implement a UDT property by declaring a Public variable in a Class module's Declarations section. If you want a property that's a UDT, then you will have to use Property procedures. You also cannot define a Property as being a UDT unless the UDT is declared in a Class module of a public component. This means that you can't have a UDT type property in a Standard EXE unless you

- Move the Type declaration to a Class module in a ActiveX EXE or ActiveX DLL
- Compile the new project
- Add the resulting component to your project's References list

If two items in your project's References list define UDTs with the same name, the UDT from the component higher in the References list will be used. If you don't want to take a chance on which UDT's component is higher in the References list, you can specify which UDT that you want by explicitly using the component name with the UDT name, like this:

```
Dim cstStatus As PHVISWholeSaleManagement.Customer
```

While I'm always pretty specific about talking when methods and properties, they can also be generically referred to as members. A Class module with three methods and two properties would be said to have five members.

Debugging Error Handling

Under the Tools | Options menu choice on the General tab, you'll find three settings for handling errors. These options apply only when your object is running in the Visual Basic IDE (i.e., while you are debugging your object).

If you select Break on All Errors, Visual Basic will stop on any line that raises an error, regardless of what error handling you have in place. So, with this code

```
On Error Resume Next
X = Y/0
```

Visual Basic will stop and highlight the second line (where the code divides by 0). This is despite the On Error code that would normally cause Visual Basic to ignore the error and continue to the next line. Basically, Break on All Errors disables your error handling code while you are debugging. This is the option that you should use when you are trying to determine what problems exist in your code.

If you select Break on Unhandled Errors, Visual Basic treats your code as it will after you compile it—if an error occurs, Visual Basic will run the relevant error handling routine. Only if there is no active error handler (i.e., none of the code leading to the error contained an On Error statement) will Visual Basic stop, display an error, and highlight the line in error. This is the setting to use when testing your error handling code. However, if there is an unhandled error in one of your Class modules, Visual Basic will stop on the line in the client that called the routine in the object that caused the error.

The middle option, Break in Class Module, acts like Break on Unhandled Errors but, when the line in error is in your Class module, Visual Basic will stop on the line in your Class module that caused the error. In addition, any error handling code in the client is ignored while your Class module code is executing. So, if the client has an On Error Resume statement in effect when an error occurs in your Class module, the On Error statement will be ignored with this setting. Any On Error statements in your Class module will, however, be honored. This is the setting that you will use when you are testing the error handling within your Class module independently of the error handling code in your client.

You can change the way that Visual Basic handles errors by right-mouse clicking in the Code window and selecting Toggle from the popup menu.

Persisting Objects

Strictly speaking, this section belongs in the chapter on components because persisting objects requires that your objects be compiled in an ActiveX EXE or an ActiveX DLL. With Visual Basic 6, Class modules in ActiveX EXE or DLL projects acquired a new property called Persistable. Since this chapter has introduced Properties and persistence has much to do with saving property values, I'm going to discuss it here.

Persistence Events

Setting the Presistable property to 1 (Persistable) adds three new events to your Class module: InitProperties, ReadProperties, and WriteProperties. Setting the Persistable property to 1 also gives the Class module the ability to be converted into a string of bytes. Among other features, this allows programs using your object to save it to permanent storage (typically, a file on the hard disk).

The three new events that are added to the Class module give you the ability to manage your object's internal data as your object is saved and restored. The InitProperties event is fired when a client first creates your object. The WriteProperties event is fired just before the client converts your object to an array of bytes. The ReadProperties event is fired when your object is recreated by the client (something that's possible only when the object is saved through the persistence mechanisms). In Figure 4–5 you can see the events as they appear in the Class module.

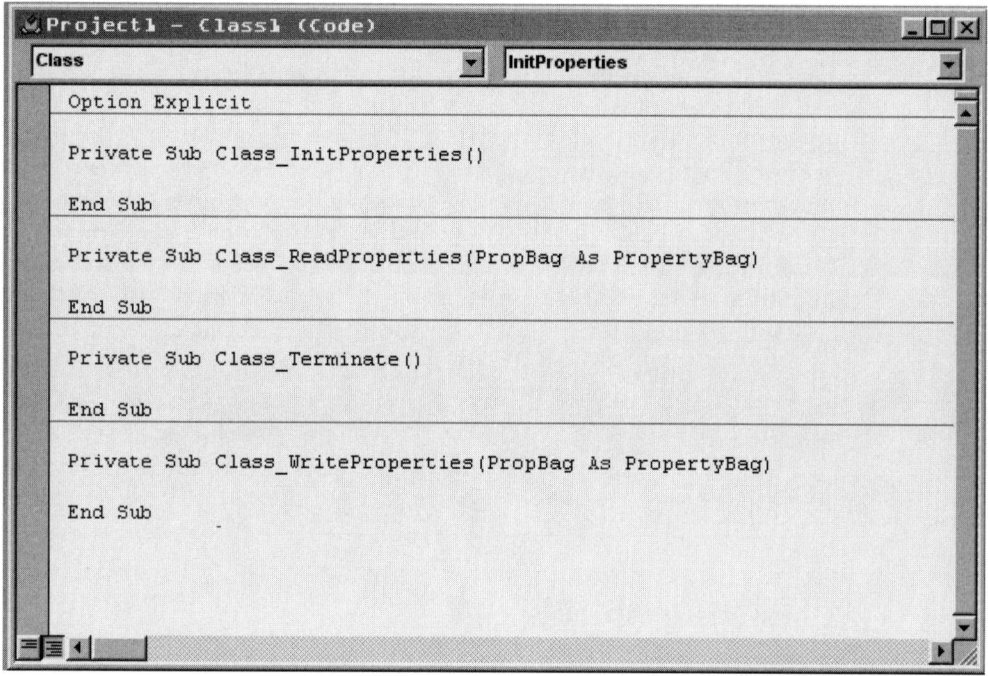

Figure 4–5 *A persistable class with the supporting events.*

InitProperties is the event that you should use to set the default initial values for any internal variables. While you could use the Initialize event for this, the Initialize event will fire whenever the object is loaded into memory. By using the InitProperties and ReadProperties event, you can distinguish between when an object is being created for the first time (the InitProperties event fires) and when it is being recreated (the ReadProperties fires). The WriteProperties event gives you an opportunity to save data that represents the object's current state just before it is removed from memory.

For some ActiveX objects (particularly ActiveX Controls), these events fire either just after the Initialize event (InitProperties and ReadProperties) or just before the Terminate event (WriteProperties). At this point, the client using the object may not have access to the object through the object variable. Raising errors from within your object in these events, therefore, may cause an application using your object to crash.

Saving an Object

A client that wants to save your object must first create a PropertyBag object. Using the methods and properties of the PropertyBag object allows a client to convert a presistable object into a savable format (an array of bytes). In the following example, I've assumed that I have created an object called PersistObject that has its Persist property set to Persistable. This client code creates the object and then immediately adds it to a PropertyBag:

```
Dim pso As PersistObject
Dim prb As PropertyBag

Set pso = New PersistObject
Set prb = New PropertyBag

prb.WriteProperty "PObject", pso
```

As the code shows, to add something to a PropertyBag the client uses the PropertyBag's WriteProperty method. The WriteProperty method must be passed a name and the item to be saved. In this case, the client has used the name PObject and passed a reference to the PersistObject that it created.

When the WriteProperty method executes and stores the object, your object's WriteProperties event will fire. Your WriteProperties event is passed a reference to the PropertyBag that it is being saved in. You can, at that point, add items to the PropertyBag using the WriteProperty method. In the following example, the object's code saves the current date to the PropertyBag under the name "CDate":

```
Private Sub Class_WriteProperties(PropBag As PropertyBag)
   PropBag.WriteProperty "CDate", Now()
End Sub
```

This mechanism allows your client to save your object in a PropertyBag. As part of being saved, your object can save any information that it needs. Typically, you will store whatever information you need to resume processing where you left off when your object is restored.

Saving the PropertyBag

Unfortunately, like any other object, the PropertyBag is destroyed when the client stops running. In order to save the object more permanently, the client must save the contents of the bag somewhere safe. To do that, the client can use the PropertyBag's Contents property which returns an array of bytes that represents the contents of the bag. The following code stores the Contents property of the PropertyBag in a file called "c:\ThisObject.BIN":

```
Dim intFileNum As Integer
intFileNum = FreeFile()
```

```
Open "C:\ThisObject.BIN" For Binary As intFileNum
Get intFileNum, , prb.Contents
Close intFileNum
```

Restoring the object from the file is very similar to the process involved in saving it. Since the client in my previous example saved the PropertyBag's contents to a file, the client must read the contents back from the file and into a PropertyBag's Contents property. The only real difference between saving and restoring is that the contents of the file can't be read directly into the Contents property of a PropertyBag. In the following code, the client reads the file into a variant, then moves the variant into the PropertyBag's Contents property:

```
Dim prb As PropertyBag
Dim varFileContents As Variant
Dim intFileNum As Integer

intFileNum = FreeFile()
Set prb = New PropertyBag

Open "C:\ThisObject.BIN" For Binary As intFileNum
Get intFileNum, , varFileContents
Close intFileNum

prb.Contents = varFileContents
```

Restoring the Object

With the PropertyBag now filled again, the client can use the PropertyBag's ReadProperty method to recreate the object. The ReadProperty method is passed the name of one of the entries in the bag and returns the value saved under that name. This code returns the object stored under the name PObject:

```
Dim pso As Class1
Set pso = prb.ReadProperty("PObject")
```

When the PropertyBag's ReadProperty method executes to retrieve an object, your object's ReadProperties event fires. As in the WriteProperties event, your object is passed a reference to the PropertyBag and can read from the bag any values that it stored there. In the following code, PersistObject uses the ReadProperty event to retrieve the value stored under the name CDate:

```
Private Sub Class_ReadProperties(PropBag As PropertyBag)
Dim dteCurrentDate As Variant

dteCurrentDate = PropBag.ReadProperty("CDate")

End Sub
```

Figure 4–6 shows the full processing cycle for object persistence.

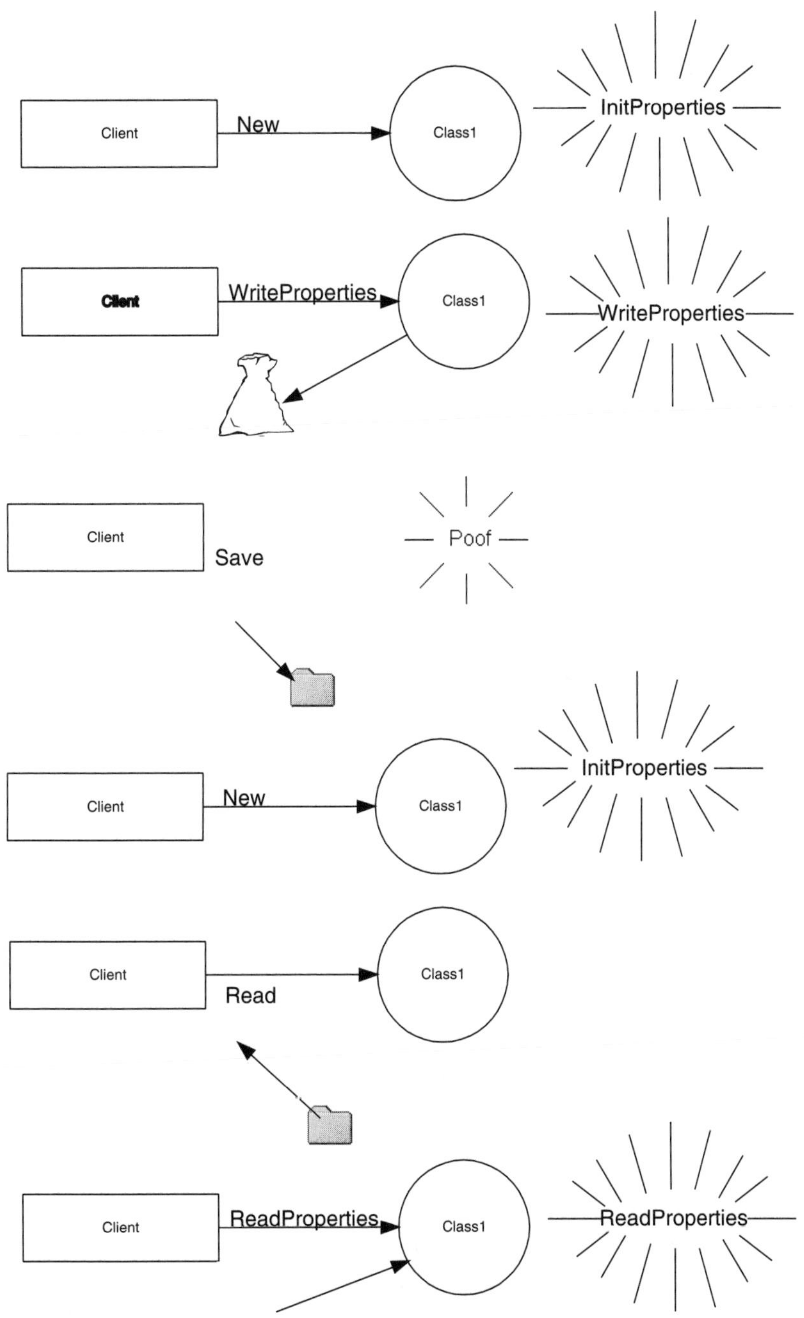

Figure 4–6 *The object persistence life cycle. The client calling ReadProperties and WriteProperties Methods triggers events in your object.*

You cannot use the ReadProperty method in the WriteProperties event. The client that issues the WriteProperty method can not read values stored in the PropertyBag by the object that the client is storing.

Other Uses

A client can store the contents of a PropertyBag's Contents property anywhere that is convenient for the application. The Contents property of a PropertyBag can be assigned directly to the Body property of a Microsoft Message Queue message, for instance, allowing the object to be recreated by whatever application picks up the message. A client doesn't have to store the contents anywhere: The PropertyBag provides a simple way for a client to create a copy of a persistable object. This code writes an object to a PropertyBag only so that it can be read out into a new instance of the object:

```
Dim pso As PersistObject
Dim pso2 As PersistObject
Dim prb As PropertyBag

Set pso = New PersistObject
Set prb = New PropertyBag

prb.WriteProperty "PObject", pso
Set pso2 = prb.ReadProperty("PObject")
```

Me

Within an object, the Me keyword can be used to refer to the object that the code is part of. If you had a object called MyObject and wanted to add a property to MyObject that returned a reference to itself, you could use this code:

```
Public Property Set SelfReference() As MyObject
    Set SelfReference = Me
End Property
```

You can also use the Me keyword to run methods of the object that your code is part of. If you wanted to execute a method called MyMethod from code within the same class object, you could just use this code:

```
Me.MyMethod
```

The Me keyword can be especially useful in working with the PropertyBag as it lets you retrieve (or set) a property value by calling the property routine itself. This technique ensures that, should you change the way that the property works, the PropertyBag based routines continue to work correctly. For instance, you might have set up a property so that it stores a value in a private member variable defined in the Class module. You might be tempted just to write the value of that variable out to the PropertyBag. Later, however, you change the property procedures so that they read and write one element in a UDT. In order for your object to continue to work, you must now remember to change the WriteProperties and ReadProperties routine to work with the UDT. On the other hand, if you use the Me keyword to run the property routines, they will take care of retrieving and updating the correct value, regardless of how it's stored.

This code, for instance, loads a value called CurrentName by reading the CurrentName property of the object that the WriteProperties routine appears in:

```
Private Sub Class_WriteProperties(PropBag As PropertyBag)
   PropBag.WriteProperty "CurrentName", Me.CurrentName
End Sub
```

This code, on the other hand, retrieves the CurrentName property from the PropertyBag and sets the CurrentName property of the object:

```
Private Sub Class_ReadProperties(PropBag As PropertyBag)
    Me.CurrentName = PropBag.ReadProperty("CurrentName")
End Sub
```

Me refers to the object that you define in the container—the properties, methods, and events that *you* create. The Me keyword does not refer to the methods, properties, and events of your object's container. For instance, to refer to the Class module's Initialize event, you use Class_Initialize, not Me_Initialize. In the third part of this book we'll be creating objects in UserDocuments and UserControl containers, which have properties and methods that you can manipulate from your code. To refer to the methods and properties of the UserDocument or UserControl you use "UserDocument" or "UserControl", not "Me."

Managing State

As an object developer, you are not responsible for persisting your object. Your responsibility is to create ReadProperty and WriteProperty events that will store and retrieve enough information for your object to resume processing. You can, as part of your WriteProperties event, save objects that your object is dependent on and that you have references to. Then, in your ReadProperty event, you can recreate those objects as part of restoring your object. Even in this case, though, you merely save your data to the PropertyBag passed to your WriteProperties event. It is the responsibility of the client to save the Contents of the PropertyBag somewhere.

These activities are usually referred to as managing your object's state. In order to resume processing from the point where your object was saved, you must store enough internal data to know where you left off. This information represents the state of your object at the time that it was saved. Restoring these values is referred to as restoring your object's state.

Typically, saving and restoring state is dependent on saving and restoring the current values of the properties exposed by your object in the client's PropertyBag. However, you're not restricted to those properties or to storing everything in a PropertyBag. There may be additional values, not related to your properties, that you will need to store to maintain state. Alternatively, you may find that only a subset of your object's properties needs to be tracked. You could use the ReadProperties and WriteProperties events to update the Registry with data rather than use the PropertyBag.

I'll be returning to the PropertyBag and looking at its methods in more detail in the chapter on ActiveX controls.

Events

Understanding how to use events can often be difficult for object developers. At least it was for me. I came to realize that events exist to make communication between an object and its client into a two way street. A program communicates with an object by calling the object's methods or setting the object's properties. In return, objects communicate with the programs using them by using Events. In the same way that clients can call routines in an object, Events provide objects with a way of running procedures in the client. When a CommandButton object wants to tell the form that it is sitting on that the user has clicked on the button, it fires a Click event and so runs the form's CommandButton_Click procedure.

In designing objects, I frequently find occasions when I want to communicate with the program that is using my object. This communication generally has one of two forms:

- Notifying the client of some occurrence
- Passing information to the client

One of the important things to realize about events is that they are a relatively expensive way to communicate with the program using the object. In this chapter I describe how to use Events, and in later chapters I outline some of the alternatives.

Some terminology first: an object that fires events is said to be an event source. Most of the ActiveX Controls that you place on your form are event sources, firing Click, LostFocus, and Exit events to notify their host form that something has occurred in the control's life. I don't write code for most of the events fired by most of the Controls on my forms (on CommandButtons, for instance, I've probably only ever used their Click event). When I do write an event routine, my program is classified as an event sink—a place that accepts events.

DECLARING EVENTS

There are two parts to using an event: declaring it and firing it. You must declare your events before you can fire them by using the Event keyword in the Declarations section of a Class module. The simplest declaration just establishes a name for the event. This example defines an event called Click:

```
Event Click
```

FIRING EVENTS

To fire an event, you use the RaiseEvent keyword followed by the name of the event that you want to fire. To fire the Click event declared above, you would add this code to a Class module:

```
RaiseEvent Click
```

This RaiseEvent statement fires an event named Click from the object—but that doesn't mean that the event will be received. The client has to participate in receiving any event that you fire. The clients using your object may choose not to accept any events fired by your object. Alternatively, clients may choose to accept your object's events but only to respond to some of the events that you fire.

When the RaiseEvent statement is executed, control passes to the client's event procedure (if it exists). If your object is compiled as part of a standard EXE or in an ActiveX DLL, processing in your object will not proceed until the client's event procedure completes. To put it another way, event processing is synchronous for ActiveX DLL's. If your object is compiled as an ActiveX EXE, your object does not have to wait for the client's event procedure to finish processing, as shown in Figure 4–7.

If an object is compiled into an ActiveX EXE, the object can be shared among many clients. When several clients have object variables pointing at the same object, firing an event can run event procedures in all of those programs. When multiple clients are receiving events from a single object, Microsoft's documentation is ambiguous on what order the clients will receive the event. Some documentation indicates that the order is not guaranteed. Other documentation states that the clients will receive the events in the order that they got their references to the object.

WITHEVENTS

In order to accept events from an object, the client must declare the object variable that points to your object using the WithEvents keyword. This puts

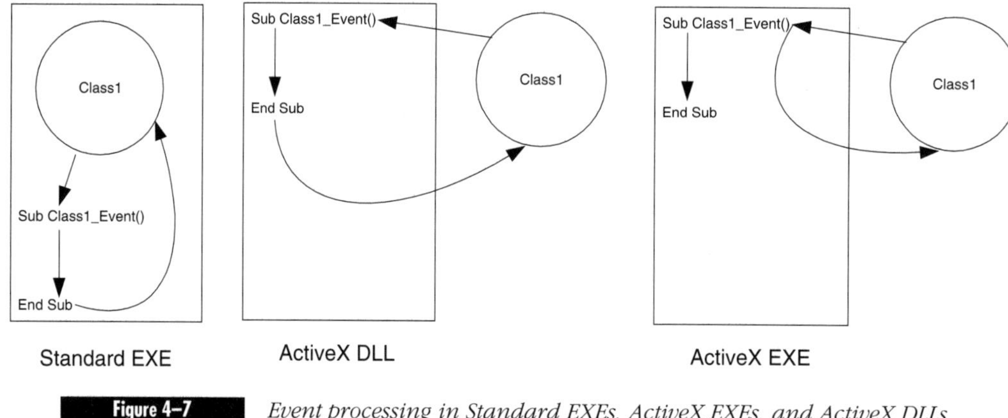

Figure 4–7 *Event processing in Standard EXEs, ActiveX EXEs, and ActiveX DLLs*

some limitations on how the object variable can be declared: The variable can't be declared with the New keyword, it must be declared in the Declarations section of a Class module, and it can't be declared as an array. There is a naming convention that prefixes the names of object variables declared using WithEvents with a "w":

```
Dim WithEvents wcstOrder As Customer
```

EVENTS WITH PARAMETERS

You can also declare an event so that it can pass data to the client when it fires. Events with parameters allow your object not only to notify the client that something has occurred, but also to pass information from your object to the client. In addition, the client can use the Event's parameters to return data to your object.

You declare an Event that returns data by specifying the number of parameters and their data type in the Event declaration. The following declaration defines an Event called OutOfStock that is used by the Product object in the WholesaleManagement component. This event is fired when the code in the object determines that there isn't enough product on hand to satisfy the order. The event passes two pieces of information to the client: the quantity available and the status of the product:

```
Event OutOfStock(QtyOnHand As Integer, Status As String)
```

As with methods and functions, general practice is not to use a naming convention with event parameters.

In Visual Basic 6, event parameters can be Enums or UDTs. In Visual Basic 5, or with clients that don't support UDTs, parameters are limited to the intrinsic data types (string, integer, etc.). In these situations, if you want to use a UDT, you (and the clients using your object) will have to use the same workarounds that I suggested when using UDTs with methods. Event parameters cannot be Optional or ParamArrays in either Visual Basic 5 or 6.

The RaiseEvent can use any combination of literals, constants, or variables to pass data to the client. The RaiseEvent corresponding to the OutOfStock declaration might look like this:

```
strStatus = "BackOrder"
RaiseEvent OutOfStock(rst("StockQty"), strStatus)
```

You cannot use named parameters in a RaiseEvent statement.

Benchmark: Events With Multiple Parameters

Adding additional parameters to an event increases the time to process the event, but not proportionately. Raising an event 1000 times took 10 milliseconds with one parameter passed. With 30 parameters, the time increased to 183 milliseconds, an 18-fold increase in time against a 30-fold increase in the number of parameters.

BYVAL AND BYREF • You can declare Event parameters as being either ByVal or ByRef. Declaring an Event parameter as ByRef allows clients to pass data back to your object. When a client modifies the value of a ByRef parameter, the value is passed back to your object. You can use this to let a client tell your object what action to take when an Event occurs.

In the OutOfStock event, for instance, the WholesaleManagement system allows the client's Event procedure to change the Status property to indicate whether the order should be cancelled or a backorder created. The client does this by setting the Status property passed in the Event to either "Cancel" or "BackOrder". The Status property will be declared as ByRef by default in the OutOfStock event but, in the following code, I've rewritten the event declaration to make the passing mechanism for Status explicit. I also made the QtyOnHand parameter ByVal to prevent changes to the client being passed back to my object:

```
Event OutOfStock(ByVal QtyOnHand As Integer, _
    ByRef Status As String)
```

When using ByRef parameters, the code in the object must pass a variable rather than a literal value in order for data to be returned from the client. The following code uses the strStatus variable as the second parameter to the OutOfStock event to hold the value returned by the client. The code to fire the event and respond to the Status setting looks like this:

```
Dim strStatus As String

strStatus = "BackOrder"
RaiseEvent OutOfStock(rst("StockQty"), strStatus)

Select Case strStatus
    Case   "BackOrder"
           BackOrderProcessing
    Case   "Cancel"
           CancelOrderProcessing
Select End
```

A client that uses the Product object might contain this code:

```
Dim WithEvents prd As Product
Public Sub prd_OutOfStock(StockQty As Integer, _
                         Status As String)
If frmCustomer.txtPriority = "Urgent" Then
    Status = "BackOrder"
Else
    Status = "Cancel"
End Sub
```

If you have an object that is being used by multiple clients then, when you fire your event, each of the clients will execute their code for that event, one after the other. If the event has been declared with a ByRef parameter, then, if one of the clients changes the value of the ByRef parameter, all subsequent clients that respond to the Event will see that new value.

There is a relatively obscure bug that occurs with ByRef parameters with Events when

- You create an ActiveX Control object
- The developer using your Control loads it dynamically using Visual Basic 6.0's new Load command
- Your code passes data through Event parameters
- The data type of the data that you are passing does not match the data type of the variable in the Event declaration

In these circumstances, the data will always be passed ByVal, even if you indicate that you want it passed ByRef. The solution is to make sure that you match the data type used in the declaration of your event when passing parameters.

Benchmark: Events With ByVal Parameters

Changing Event parameters to ByVal substantially lowers the cost of raising the event. While raising an event with a single parameter took 10 milliseconds with ByRef parameters, it took only 5 seconds with ByVal parameters. Furthermore, adding additional parameters had little or no effect. As the number of parameters increased to 30, the time to raise the event varied randomly between 5 and 8 milliseconds.

SOME RESTRICTIONS

Adding events to your object can limit the number of places that it can be used. Objects that fire events and are executing on a remote computer using DCOM must be configured with very specific security (see the articles Q179835 and Q171456 in the Microsoft Knowledgebase for a discussion of these settings). As I discuss in the chapter on Interfaces, there are also limitations imposed on the developer when using multiple interfaces with an object that fires events. If a developer chooses to use your object without declaring it using the WithEvents keyword, they can avoid most of these problems.

In addition, when you have many clients accepting Events from a single object, Visual Basic's event processing degrades very quickly (i.e., if many clients have object variables declared WithEvents and referring to the same object). This is because, after firing an event, an object must wait until all the clients sinking the event have executed their code before control will return to the object (see Figure 4–8). Alternatives to using events include setting a property to indicate the results of an operation, or returning data when a client calls a method. These techniques are discussed in the section of this chapter on Methods.

A more flexible alternative is to use callbacks. Since an object can only be shared among multiple clients if it is compiled as an ActiveX EXE, I defer discussion of this technique until the chapter on Components. No matter what alternative you take, if you don't use Events, your object (while it may perform better) will be harder for developers to work with.

The ObjPtr Function

Visual Basic 6 introduced (or, at any rate, documented) the ObjPtr function. Passed an object variable, this function allows you to retrieve the location in memory for the object that the variable refers to. As an example, the following code sets the variable lngMemoryLocation to the location in memory for the object referred to by the obj variable:

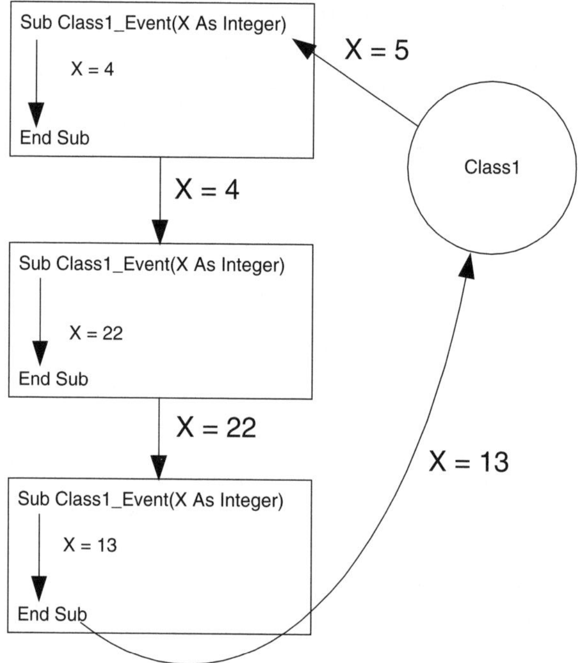

Figure 4–8 *Event processing with multiple clients and ByRef parameters.*

```
Dim lngMemoryLocation As Long
Dim obj As Class1

Set obj = New Class1
lngMemoryLocation = ObjPtr(obj)
```

I think that it's probably just as well to stay away from this function except when working with some product that requires you to provide the address in memory for an object (I don't know of any that do). One of the wonderful things about working with a high-level development language is that it conceals from the developer what the underlying computer is doing. Every time that I have written programs that accessed specific locations in memory, or otherwise involved myself with the hardware that my programs run on, I've been sorry. I've paid for whatever benefits I've received with additional maintenance costs, more frequent failures at both design time and run time, longer testing cycles, and more expensive upgrades (ask anyone who used API calls in Windows 3.1 and had to rewrite them all for Windows 95).

Since ObjPtr has been added to Visual Basic, there have been a number of hacks suggested that make use of it. In the current implementation of COM, the position four bytes in from the address returned by ObjPtr holds the object's reference count. The reference count is the object's internal count of the number of object variables that are currently referring to the object. This number is incremented and decremented each time that you use a Set command to access or (with Nothing) stop accessing an object.

Using the ObjPtr function to get the address of an object does not change the object's reference counter. You can, however, use the value returned by ObjPtr to create a reference to the object. Once you've retrieved the address with ObjPtr, you can copy the address into an object variable to create a reference to the object without incrementing the object's reference count. A typical example of this technique in action looks like this:

```
Private Declare Sub RtlMoveMemory Lib "Kernel32" _
    (pDest As Any, pSource As Any, ByVal ByteLen As Long)
Dim lngMemLocation As Long
Dim obj As SomeObject
Dim objHold As SomeObject
Dim objHack As SomeObject

Set obj = New SomeObject
lngMemLocation = ObjPtr(obj)
rtlMoveMemory objHold, lngMemLocation,4
Set objHack = objHold
```

Using this technique, you can play all sorts of tricks with your objects, almost all of which lead to a General Protection Fault. While you can use ObjPtr to get a reference to an object without incrementing the object's reference count, sooner or later you must destroy that object variable. You will do this either by setting the object variable to Nothing or letting the variable be destroyed when the routine that it's declared in ends. At that point, Visual Basic will use the information in the variable to find the object that the variable referred to and reduce that object's reference count. Since the object has more variables referring to it than are indicated by the object's reference count, the reference count will be reduced to zero while some object variables are still in use. Guaranteed GPF.

ObjPtr: Just say no.

▲ Case Study: Asynchronous Methods

In this section I want to look at a special type of method that you can create in your object. Among other things, this example gives me a chance to demonstrate some of the techniques that I've discussed in this chapter.

When you call a method in an object, processing stops in the calling program until the method finishes executing. This is called a synchronous call. On occasion, though, you will want your object to return control to the client and continue processing. This kind of method is said to implement an asynchronous call.

Using the Timer Object

There's no direct way to create an asynchronous method in a Visual Basic component. What you can do, however, is write a method that starts code running in your object after control is returned to the client. One way to do that is to add a form to your Visual Basic project and place a Timer control on the form. You could also use the SetTimer API call, but I prefer to stay away from API calls (and, by using the Timer control, I can demonstrate using the WithEvents keyword).

Very little needs to be done in the method called by the client. The method's code will only set the properties of the Timer control so that the Timer will fire an event in the near future. The method then ends, returning control to the client. When the Timer fires its event, any code that you have written for the Timer control's event will start running independently of the client.

One problem with this mechanism is that a Timer event normally fires an event in the Form that the Timer control has been placed on. It would be more convenient to have the code that's executed by the Timer event reside in your Class module. The simplest way to do this is to declare an object variable in your Class module that refers to the Timer, and capture events fired by the Timer through that object variable in your Class module.

The code to declare the Timer object variable and set it to fire a Timer event in the Class module looks like this:

```
Dim WithEvents tim As Timer
```

The Dim statement for the object variable tim uses the WithEvents keyword in order to capture the events fired by a Timer object.

The Asynchronous Method

The next step is to create the method that will be called by the client. The following code shows a typical example of this kind of method called, in this case, StartAsynchronous. When the client calls the StartAsynchronous method, the code in the method sets the variable to point to the Timer on the Form, and then sets the Timer's Interval property to 55 milliseconds (the smallest interval recognized by the Timer). This will cause the Timer1 object to fire a Timer event after 55 milliseconds have passed. The routine then ends, returning control to the client:

```
Public Sub StartAsynchronous()
    Set tim = Form1.Timer1
    tim.Interval = 55
End Sub
```

The next routine added to the Class module captures the Timer event fired by the Timer1 control. The event routine's name consists of the object variable name and the name of the event itself:

```
Private Sub tim_Timer()
    tim.Interval = 0
    …code to process…
End Sub
```

The first thing that routine does is set the Timer's Interval property to 0 to prevent the event from firing again. Within the Timer event you can place any code that you need. If you want the code to execute continuously, you can either:

- leave the Interval property at some value greater than 0 so that the event keeps firing and executing the code.
- add a loop to the Timer event code so that the routine never stops running.

Notifying the Client

Within the class, you may want to use the RaiseEvent keyword to fire events to pass information back to the client. This version of the Timer event code uses a loop and passes the number of times that the loop has executed back to the client:

```
Event StillRunning (LoopCount As Integer)

Private Sub tim_Timer()
Dim ctr As Integer
    tim.Interval = 0
    Do While True
      ctr = ctr + 1
      RaiseEvent StillRunning(ctr)
    Loop
End Sub
```

Shutting the Object Down

If you do set up the code to execute continuously, then you will have a problem in getting the component to shut down. Even if the client sets its object variable to Nothing, the component will not be removed from memory as long as it is executing code. One way to handle this is to add another method or property to the object that will allow the client to signal to the object when processing is to stop.

USING A PROPERTY

You might, for instance, want to give the object an Enabled property that will allow you to control the object's processing loop. If the Timer event code contains a loop, you can simply end the loop when the property is set. Here's what that code looks like:

```
Dim m_enabled As Boolean

Public Property Let Enabled(Enable As Boolean)
    m_enabled = Enable
End Property

Private Sub tim_Timer()
    Set tim = Form1.Timer1
    tim.Interval = 0
    Do While m_enabled = True
      …code to process…
    Loop
End Sub
```

If you set this component up as an ActiveX EXE then all that's necessary to start the component is to call its StartAsynchronous method. If you set up the component as an ActiveX DLL, for reasons that I discuss in Chapter 6 in the section on Threading, you'll need to add a DoEvents statement in the client after calling the StartAsynchronous method. The code in the client to enable the object, then start the processing, and finally stop the object looks like this:

```
Dim asn As AsyncObject

Set asn = New ASyncObject
asn.Enabled = True
asn.StartAsynchronous
DoEvents
asn.Enabled = False
```

The problem with this technique is that control may never return to the calling object if the processing loop doesn't release control long enough for the client to move to the next line of code. (This is especially true during debugging.)

USING AN EVENT

As an alternative to using a method, you could have your object fire an event back to the client, passing a parameter that the client can use to stop processing. In Figure 4–9 you can see a diagram that represents the relationship between the client and an asynchronous object. The code in the object looks like this:

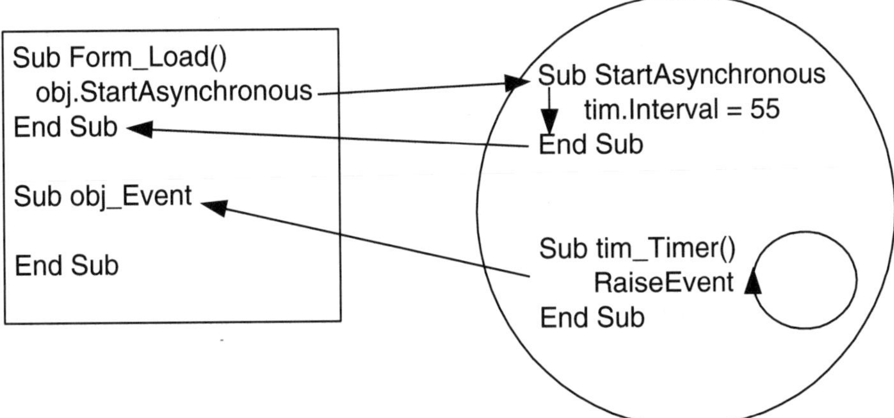

Figure 4–9 *A client with an asynchronous object. After StartAsynchronous finishes, control returns to the client. Control is also handed back when the RaiseEvent executes.*

```
Event ContinueProcessing(ByRef Cancel As Boolean)

Private Sub tim_Timer()
Dim Cancel As Boolean
    Set tim = Form1.Timer1
    tim.Interval = 0
    Do While Cancel = False
      ...code to process...
      RaiseEvent ContinueProcessing(Cancel)
    Loop
End Sub
```

This version of the object's code declares an Event called ContinueProcessing that passes a Boolean variable called Cancel to the client. In the processing loop in the Timer event, the code raises the event each time through the loop. If the Cancel parameter is set to False, then the loop will terminate. The code in the client to start processing and handle the event looks like this:

```
Dim WithEvents asn As AsyncObject

Private Sub Form_Load()
    Set asn = New ASyncObject
    cls.StartAsynchronous
End Sub

Private Sub asn_ContinueProcessing(Cancel As Boolean)
    Cancel = True
End Sub
```

This version of the client's code declares the object variable using the WithEvents keyword in order to catch events fired by the object. The client's ContinueProcessing event accepts the Cancel parameter which, in this example, is immediately set to False in order to stop processing.

Summary

This chapter revolved around how you can define your object. You saw how to give your object methods, properties, and events. You also saw that you can use User Defined Types, enumerated types, and Optional parameters when creating your routines (though you can't use Optional parameters with Events). I showed you the effect of using ByVal instead of ByRef when passing parameters and how to use parameters when creating properties.

At this point, you probably want to cement your knowledge by creating some objects of your own. One of the exercises that you might want to try is to recreate some of the objects in the DAO model. While you don't have to put much code behind those routines, you could try your hand at implementing the CreateRecordset method that has optional parameters and returns an object, or the Fields collection which gives you access to a group of fields. At the end of Chapter 1, I suggested that you take an existing application and develop an object model for it. You could now go back and write the code that would define the objects that make up that model.

This chapter has provided you with the foundation to use objects effectively in your programs. In the next chapter I look at how you can combine objects to create components that can be shared among many clients.

A book that looks at developing with Visual Basic from a design (rather than a coding) point of view is *Visual Basic 6: Design, Specification and Objects* by Billy S. Hollis from Prentice Hall Computer Books. Another useful book is *Professional Visual Basic 6.0 Business Objects* by Rockford Lhotka from Wrox Press. While it does discuss the mechanics of defining properties, methods, and events, the book's primary focus is on how to convert business requirements into Visual Basic objects.

F I V E

Components

From DAO to ADO and from Excel to Visio, components have come to dominate the Windows software landscape. In Chapter 3, I showed you how to define objects by giving them methods, properties, and events. Now that you know how to create objects, you can combine them to create components. The issues involved here can get confusing, so this chapter will let you know what your choices are and what the results of your decisions will be.

Visual Basic 5 and 6 allow you to combine the objects that you develop into components that can be as simple or as complicated as you need. This chapter looks at the properties of the Class module itself and shows you how to use the Instancing property to integrate your objects into a component. The relationships that exist among objects become important as you build your component, so I also look at the various strategies that you can use in defining your component. This chapter also introduces you to the differences between an ActiveX EXE and an ActiveX DLL (and you'll see how to debug them both). You'll also find out how some of the features of the language (CreateObject, GetObject) and the development environment (the References list) relate to working with Components.

Using Components

As developer, Visual Basic makes it very easy for me to use components in building my applications—or to build other components. From the Visual Basic Project menu, if you select References, you will get a list of all the components available for use from your computer. I can use those components (like ActiveX Data Objects) to build my own components. I have to admit that I also still get a kick out of seeing the components that I've built in Visual Basic on this list.

What appears on the References is all the components available for use—not just the components that can be useful from Visual Basic. Many of the components listed aren't useful except to the applications that they were developed for.

The References List

The References list is built by examining the registry entries on your computer. Most, but not all, of the entries on the References list are components installed on your computer (see Figure 5–1). Some of the references may be to components installed on some other computer on your network. When you access those components, your request will be routed through DCOM and the objects will be created and executed on the other computer.

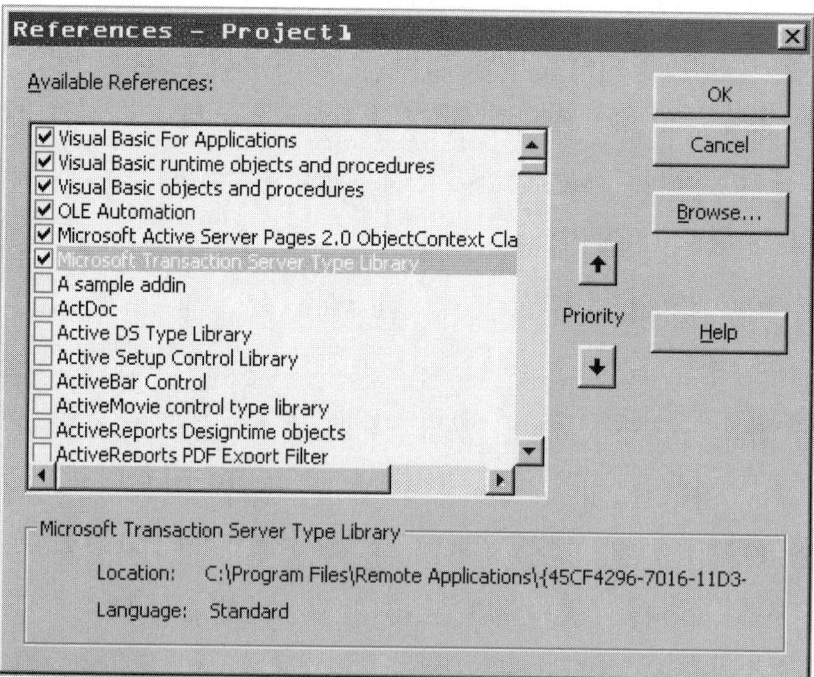

Figure 5–1 *The References Dialog lists all components installed on the computer. The checked-off components are the ones that Visual Basic will provide IntelliSense support for.*

If you select an entry from the References list, Visual Basic looks for the component's type library, which describes the objects that make up the component. Using the type library information, the Visual Basic compiler can speed access to the object's methods and properties at run time by bypassing some of the COM interfaces. You can also use the New keyword to create objects from any component selected on your References list. The term for these benefits is "early bound" because you have bound your code to the object as early in the process as you can, during coding.

IntelliSense support in the Visual Basic IDE is provided through the type library. Since the IntelliSense lists are drawn from the type library rather than from an examination of the object, the IntelliSense list may not accurately reflect the object. The Form in Visual Basic, for instance, has a Print method that doesn't appear in any of the IntelliSense lists, but the method can still be used. The type library information is also used to check your use of an object's methods and properties to warn you of errors at compile time, preventing your code from failing at run time. Some components (the early versions of Outlook, for instance) ship without type libraries, making them considerably harder to work with.

CreateObject in Detail

You can also work with objects without using the References list by creating instances of the objects with the CreateObject function. The CreateObject keyword accepts the ProgId for an object in a component, looks up the ProgId in the registry to get the necessary information on the object and its component, and creates the object. Since using the CreateObject defers getting information on the object until the code actually executes, you get no type library support while writing your code. This means no IntelliSense support and that Visual Basic cannot check your use of the object's methods and properties until your code actually executes, leaving you open to more run time errors. In addition, at run time, your application will have to determine if a method exists and what parameters it accepts, causing your methods to take longer to execute. You also can't react to events fired by an object created with the CreateObject function. The term for this situation is "late bound" because you bind your code to the object at the last possible moment, when you call the method or set the property.

CreateObject does provide more flexibility than using the New keyword. Since the CreateObject function accepts the ProgId as string you can write code that dynamically creates objects. This code, for instance, asks the user for a ProgId and then creates the corresponding object:

```
Dim obj As Object
Dim strProgId As String
    strProdId = InputBox("Enter a ProgId")
Set obj = CreateObject(strProdId)
```

In Visual Basic 6, You can also use CreateObject to access an object defined on another computer in the network. The second parameter to the

CreateObject function is the name of the server that the object is to be created on. Supplying the second parameter to the CreateObject function effectively routes your request through DCOM. The new version of this code accepts both a ProgId and a server name before calling the CreateObject function:

```
Dim obj As Object
Dim strProgId As String
Dim strServerName As String
    strProdId = InputBox("Enter a ProgId")
    strServerName = InputBox("Enter a Server name")
    Set obj = CreateObject(strProdId, strServerName)
```

You can combine use of the References list and CreateObject to create an instance of an object. This code, for instance, assumes that Excel has been selected in the project's References list before using the CreateObject function to create an instance of Excel's Application object:

```
Dim WithEvents exl As Excel.Application
Set exl = CreateObject("Excel.Application")
```

With this code, the only penalty that you will pay in using CreateObject is some overhead in initially creating the object. You will catch events fired by Excel and have IntelliSense support while writing your code. There is no performance hit in accessing the object's methods and properties. Of course, once you've added the component to your References list, it would be an unusual situation where you wouldn't use the New keyword.

GetObject

CreateObject has a close equivalent in the GetObject function. The GetObject function accepts either the name of a file or a ProgId.

When passed the name of a file, GetObject will use the file's extension to determine which application is associated with the file. GetObject will then instantiate the object and pass it the name of the file to open. This code will open Microsoft Access which will, in turn, open the MyDatabase.MDB file:

```
Dim obj As Object
Set obj = CreateObject("MyDatabase.MDB")
```

GetObject can accept a progId as its second parameter. When passed a progId without a filename, GetObject returns a reference to an already existing instance of the object, if one exists.

If multiple copies of the object are executing, GetObject does not guarantee which one the reference it returns will point to.

If you pass GetObject a ProgId and a zero length string ("") as a filename, GetObject functions like CreateObject. This code, for instance, creates an instance of the Excel.Application object:

```
Dim WithEvents exl As Excel.Application
Set exl = GetObject("","Excel.Application")
```

In this book, wherever I refer to the CreateObject function, you can assume that the material also applies to the GetObject function.

Component Definitions

Strictly speaking, a component is a compiled program with specific sets of functions that are required by COM. As a Visual Basic developer, I use a more practical definition: A component is a collection of objects compiled into an EXE or DLL file for use by other applications.

Components and Applications

Unlike an application, a component can simply be a collection of objects with no central application driving the objects. The ActiveX Data Objects component is an excellent example of a component that has no internal application. The objects that make up ADO are used by other programs to access data sources. While you can't "run" ADO, you can use its objects.

Applications can also be compiled as components instead of standard EXEs (see Figure 5–2). When an application is compiled as a component, then the objects that make up the application can be used by other programs. Compiling a project with Class modules as a Standard EXE locks those objects inside the application where they can't be used by other applications. The best example of applications compiled as a components is probably Microsoft Office. Each of the members of Office is a component whose objects can be used by other applications.

I often think of myself as an "Office Developer" because I frequently use the Office components as part of my development tool kit. I've built numerous Access applications, for instance, that used Excel to format data or graph output. I've done this by using the components that make up Excel from within my Access VBA code.

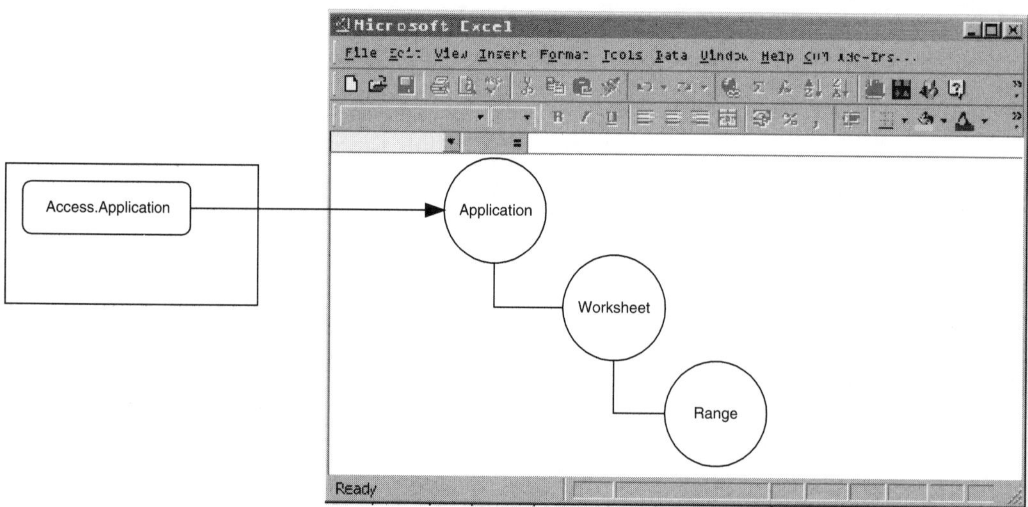

Figure 5–2 *Applications can use components and be compiled as components themselves. When compiled as a component, the applications objects can be used by other programs.*

Objects and Components

The objects that make up a component typically have some relationship with each other. To begin with, all of the objects in the component will be available at the same time. In addition, the objects may depend on each other to accomplish some task. In DAO, for instance, the Database, Workspace, Recordset, QueryDef, and TableDef objects are all part of the same component. Once your application starts using DAO, it can access any of these objects. The objects are related in different ways: a QueryDef object can be accessed only through a Database object, a Recordset can be created only from a Database or QueryDef object.

In the ADO component, the relationships among the objects that make up the component are considerably looser (see Figure 5–3). It is possible, in ADO, to create a Recordset object independently of any other object in the ADO component. It is also possible to create a Recordset from a Connection object or to use a Connection object with a Recordset to connect to a data source. The relationship between the objects in the ADO component are very fluid and range from parent/child, to completely independent, to peer-to-peer. While DAO and ADO are both components, the relationships between the objects that make them up are very different.

When I began using ADO, coming from several years of developing with DAO, I found ADO's flexibility difficult to work with. I was used to components with fixed relationships between their objects. ADO, which allows its objects to work together in a variety of ways, was a real break with the traditions of component design that I was used to. As an object developer, ADO provided me with a model for developing my own components (which had always had very rigid relationships) that I hadn't considered before.

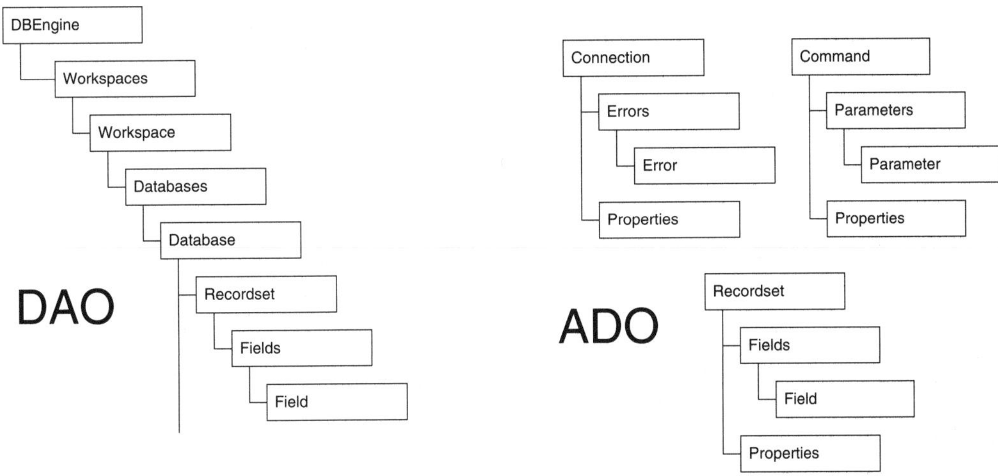

Figure 5-3 *While the ADO object model has relatively few relationships between its objects, the DAO model is highly structured.*

Not long ago, these relationships among the objects in a component would have been referred to as an object model. The phrase "programming model" has been proposed as a more descriptive term. A programming model describes the set of interfaces exposed for a client to work with. Like a user interface for an application, a programming model conceals the complexity of the component behind a set of properties, methods, and events that make the component easy to work with. Terminology is far from settled in this area. I'll stick to the terms object (something created from a single Class module) and component (a group of objects meant to be used together, typically compiled into one file).

Defining a Component

The first step in creating a component in Visual Basic is to open Visual Basic and select either ActiveX DLL or ActiveX EXE as the project type (The differences between the two types are discussed in Chapter 6). This will open a Visual Basic project with a single Class module. Unlike a standard EXE with its

Forms and Modules, an ActiveX component frequently contains only Class modules.

COM Interfaces

When you select any of the ActiveX project choices from the Visual Basic startup screen, you are actually providing directions to the Visual Basic compiler. Your selection tells the compiler to add a set of standard COM interfaces to your program as part of compiling it. These interfaces allow other COM-compliant programs to talk to your component. The fundamental interface is called IUnknown and is used by other COM components to gain access to your methods and properties (all COM interface names are prefixed with the letter I).

In the COM world, an interface is a set of functions. The IUnknown interface, for instance, defines three functions:

ADDREF • called by any application using an object to add one to the object's references counter.

RELEASE • called by any application as it gives up the object to subtract one from the object's references counter.

QUERYINTERFACE • allows a client to gain access to the other interfaces supported by your component.

If you define an object variable as being of type Object, Visual Basic will access the methods and properties of the object that it references through the QueryInterface function of the IUnknown interface. If you define an object variable as being of a specific type (e.g., Excel.Application), your program can use the IDispatch interface of the object, if it exists. Figure 5–4 shows the standard notation for showing the interfaces on a COM object. Going through the IDispatch interface is faster than going through the IUnknown interface.

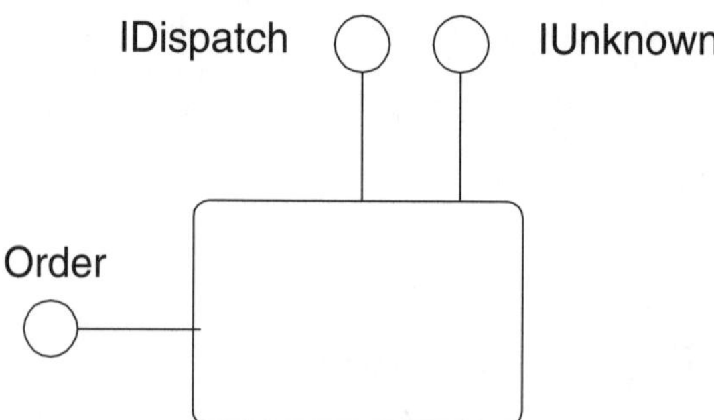

Figure 5–4 *This is a COM diagram showing an Order object with three interfaces. COM defines the IDispatch and IUnknown interface while the programmer has defined the Order interface.*

When I first started exploring COM, I looked at the C++ references and was overwhelmed by the amount of code that I would have to write to create the methods and functions of these required interfaces. Fortunately, as a Visual Basic programmer, the IUnknown and IDispatch interfaces (and the other interfaces that COM requires) are all added to my component automatically. Nor, as a Visual Basic programmer, do I have to worry about using the AddRef and Release methods. Those functions will be run automatically as clients make use of my object or as I make use of other objects.

In addition to the COM interfaces, your object always has at least one other interface. The functions that you create to define your object's methods and properties form an interface for your object.

Visual Basic also adds the code to your object to remove your object from memory. When your object's references counter gets to zero, that code will be run to destroy your object. In this book I won't be discussing the COM underpinnings for Visual Basic much, but the references that I've included at the end of each chapter list books on this topic if you want to know more.

The Visual Basic compiler will also create a type library for your component and generate progIds for all of the objects in your component. The progIds for your objects will be in the format componentname.objectname. For my sample component, the progId for the Company object will be PHVIS_WholesaleManagement.Company.

Initial Project Options

The most obvious result of choosing to create an ActiveX DLL or EXE on Visual Basic's startup screen is that some of the options in your Project are set for you. You can review and change those options through the Properties menu choice on the Project menu. The options that are relevant to a component developer can be found on the General and Component tabs and are shown in Table 5.1.

Table 5.1 Project Property Settings for ActiveX DLL and ActiveX EXE Domponents

Tab	Property	ActiveX EXE Setting	ActiveX DLL Setting
General	Type	ActiveX EXE	ActiveX DLL
	Startup Object	(None) Sub Main	(None) Sub Main
	Threading Model	Thread per Object	Apartment Threaded, Single Threaded

Table 5.1 Project Property Settings for ActiveX DLL and ActiveX EXE Domponents (Continued)

Tab	Property	ActiveX EXE Setting	ActiveX DLL Setting
Component	Start Mode	StandaloneActiveX Component	N/A
	Remote Server	Checked, Unchecked	Checked Unchecked
	Version Compatibility	All options	All options
Compile	DLL Base Address	N/A	A memory address

By changing the Type, Start Mode, and Threading Model values you can convert an ActiveX DLL to an ActiveX EXE, or even back to a standard EXE. Over the next two chapters, I discuss the effect of these settings on your component's performance.

Assigning Names

There are some Project properties that I set as soon as I start to create a component. On the Make tab, I set the Project Name text box to a name for my component. The text that I enter here will be displayed in the References dialog, which is where developers will select my component. This name will also appear in the Object Browser as the name of one of the libraries used by developers who use my component. Setting the Project Name early also prevents me from having lots of entries in my References list, all labeled "Project1."

I entered "PHVIS_WholesaleManagement" as my Project Name for the WholesaleManagement component. I included my company's name (PH&V Information Services) in the component's name to prevent this name from duplicating the name of some other component on the user's computer.

I also set the Project Description property when I start a project. The Project Description is the text that will be displayed at the bottom of the Object Browser dialog in its description pane. For the WholesaleManagement component, I set the Project Description property to "PH&V Wholesale Management Objects".

Adding Objects

The next step in creating your component is to add Class modules for each object that makes up your component. For the WholesaleManagement component, that means adding Class modules for Order, Product, and other objects that make up the object model. This process is identical to adding objects to a standard project. As you set the Name property of each object, you'll notice that the Class modules in an ActiveX component have several more properties than Class modules in a standard EXE. Most of this chapter will consist of looking at the effects of setting the Instancing property.

Testing

In parallel with developing the component, I also develop a separate Standard EXE application to test my component. If I've decided to compile my project as an EXE, then this "test bed" project must be created in a separate instance of Visual Basic. If I've decided to compile my project as an ActiveX DLL, then I can simply add another project to the running version of Visual Basic.

Just as you can convert your ActiveX EXE to an ActiveX DLL, you can switch from one testing strategy to another. Initially, I may have created my component as an ActiveX DLL. If I did, I normally would have added the test bed project to the same instance of Visual Basic as the component. Later, though, I might convert my component to an ActiveX EXE, which means that that my test bed must now be moved to a separate project.

When you save your Visual Basic environment, you save a VBP (Visual Basic Project) file for each project that you had open. If you have more than one project open, you also save a VBG (Visual Basic Group) file, which lists all the open projects. To open the individual projects that made up the group, just make sure that you select the VBP file for the project on the Existing tab of Visual Basic's Open Project dialog. So, to convert from an ActiveX DLL testing strategy to an ActiveX EXE strategy, I first shut down Visual Basic, saving all my changes. I then start two copies of Visual Basic, opening the individual VBP files for the ActiveX EXE and the test bed project.

Adding a Test Bed Project to an ActiveX DLL Project

This method will work only for ActiveX DLL projects.

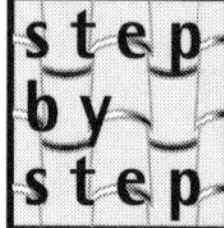

1. From the File menu, select Add Project.
2. Select Standard EXE and press the Enter key.
3. When the new project is added, right-mouse click on the Project name in the Project Explorer window and select Set as Start Up. Setting the new project as the Start Up project causes it to be executed when you press F5 or click on the Run button.
4. From the Project menu, select References to display the list of available objects.
5. In the References list, find the name of the ActiveX DLL project that you want to test (it should be the first unchecked item on the list).
6. Click on the ActiveX DLL in the list to select it.
7. Click on the OK button to close the References list.

Creating a Test Bed Project for an ActiveX Component

This method will work for ActiveX DLL and ActiveX EXE projects.

1. From the Project menu, select Properties.
2. On the Component tab, in the Start Mode box, make sure that the ActiveX Component option is selected.
3. Click on the OK button to close the Project Properties dialog.
4. Click on the Run button to start the ActiveX component project running. Starting the ActiveX component running makes it available for use by other programs.
5. Start another copy of Visual Basic running.
6. Select Standard EXE and press the Enter key.
7. Make sure that the name of the new project does not match the name of the ActiveX component.
8. From the Project menu, select References to display the list of available objects.
9. In the References list, find the name of the ActiveX DLL project. (The list is sorted alphabetically, so a project called "Xylophone" will be well down in the list.)
10. Click on the ActiveX component in the list to select it.
11. Click on the OK button to close the the References list.

For the WholesaleManagement project, I started another instance of Visual Basic and created a Standard EXE project called WholesaleTestBed. The TestBed project consists of a few forms that will create an instance of the WholesaleManagement component and exercise the objects that make it up. The forms don't have much more on them than some Command Buttons to start my test code running and some text boxes for entering and displaying test data.

If, in an ActiveX DLL, you use API calls that depend on your component executing in the same process as the client, this debugging process will probably fail. To test these kinds of components, you'll have to add a standard module to your component and put a routine in it to test your component. You can then call this routine from Visual Basic's Immediate window by typing in the routine's name and pressing the Enter key.

DEBUGGING OPTIONS

When your test bed program is not part of your Visual Basic project, the first time that you start the component executing you will be presented with the Debugging tab of the Project Properties dialog. This tab lets you set some options that will start your test bed project running automatically. With ActiveX DLL and EXEs you have three choices:

START PROGRAM. • You must supply the complete path name to the program's EXE. Presumably, this is the compiled version of the test bed program that will exercise your component. If you are confident about the code in your test bed program, you can compile it and save yourself starting another copy of Visual Basic. I don't use this very often because I frequently find that when I get unexpected results from my testing it's often my test bed program that is at fault.

START BROWSER WITH URL. • This will open a Web browser and have it request the Web page at a URL that you specify. I use this option when my test bed program is an ASP page or a page that uses an ActiveX control that I'm developing.

WAIT FOR COMPONENTS TO BE CREATED. • This is the default option and the one assumed in the step by-step examples. This option just makes your component available for use and waits for your test bed program to request one of the objects in the component. This debugging option works even if your component is going to be created by a client running on another computer and accessing your component through DCOM.

Simple and Complex Components

The simplest component consists of a single object, one that can be created using the New command. In the WholesaleManagement component, the Product object is that kind of object. B

```
Dim WithEvents prd As Product

Sub Form_Load
    Set prd = New Product
End Sub
```

To work this way, the Product Classs' Instancing property must be set to either SingleUse or MultiUse.

Instancing for Simple Objects

The Class module's Instancing property controls the visibility of the object to the component's clients and how the object will be loaded into memory. The MultiUse setting, for instance, means that:

- The object can be created at any time by any client
- Only one copy of the component is loaded, and all the instances of the object are created from it

There are four settings that can be used for ActiveX DLLs: Private, PublicNotCreatable, MultiUse, and GlobalMultiUse. ActiveX EXE projects can also set the Instancing property to SingleUse and GlobalSingleUse. Like MultiUse, SingleUse objects can be created by any client with the New command. However, when a Class module's Instancing property is set to SingleUse and multiple instances of the object are created, each instance of the object is run in a separate process with its own copy of the component loaded (see Figure 5–5).

While you don't have a choice between Single and MultiUse with ActiveX DLL projects, you will have to choose between those options for objects in your ActiveX EXE projects. Normally MultiUse is the best choice, but there are some benefits to using SingleUse. In this section, I discuss the trade-offs between Single and MultiUse objects in ActiveX EXE components.

SINGLEUSE VERSUS MULTIUSE EFFICIENCY ISSUES

The discussion around SingleUse and MultiUse can get confusing, so I'll start with a simple case: a component with a single object.

I've sometimes heard developers say that using MultiUse is always the most efficient choice. The basis for this claim is that the code for a SingleUse object is loaded each time it is requested by a client. Loading an object means loading the whole component that the object is part of. If the component is

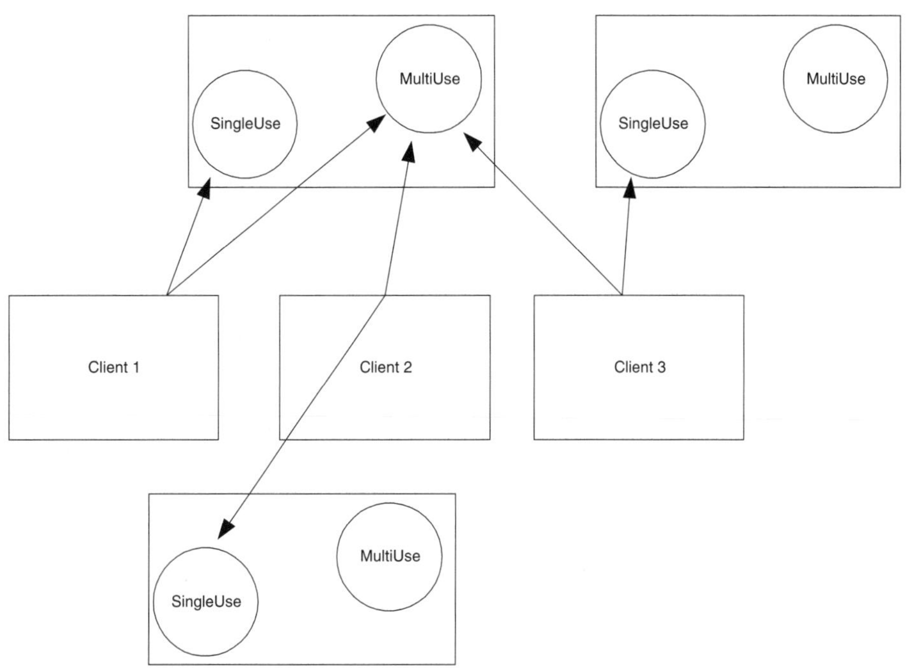

Figure 5–5 *For a MultiUse object, one copy of the component is shared among many objects. For a SingleUse object, each instance of the object comes from a separate component.*

large, this could have a significant impact on the client's performance as it waits for the component to load. A SingleUse object also creates a separate process to run in. Starting a new process is another resource-intensive activity that will slow down the object's creation.

MultiUse objects have their code loaded when the first instance of the object is created. Since the code is shared, it will stay in memory as long as one instance of an object in the component is left alive. Only the first time that a MultiUse object is created does a client have to wait for the code to load.

It's worth pointing out that you get the benefits associated with MultiUse objects only as long as the object remains in memory. As soon as no client is using any of a component's object it will be removed from memory and will have to be reloaded when next requested.

The first thing to note is that if there will be only one copy of your object loaded at a time, the distinction between SingleUse and MultiUse isn't important from an efficiency point of view. This is the typical situation for components that execute on the same computer as the client. On a single computer, in all probability only one application will be using any particular component and, so, only one copy of the component will be loaded. In a DCOM environment, though, where the component is executing on a server and may be accessed by any computer on the network, a component may be loaded many times.

However, even in a DCOM environment, if a component is used infrequently there may not be many efficiency gains in declaring an object as MultiUse. After all, the chances of finding an infrequently used component in memory are small. There are also other solutions to keeping objects loaded. One of the reasons that Microsoft developed Microsoft Transaction Server (MTS) was to provide a tool for keeping objects alive when they weren't being used.

There are two other points worth making here about efficiency and the MultiUse setting. The first is that, regardless of the Instancing setting, each instance of the object will run its Initialize procedure as the object is created. If this process is a significant part of the object's load time, the difference in load time between SingleUse and MultiUse will be minimized.

The second point is that, regardless of the Instancing setting, each object will get their own copy of memory for the data that the object uses. While a MultiUse object's code is shared, each instance of an object's data is kept separate. You won't save much memory if the object has little code but works with large amounts of in-memory data (data kept in large arrays, for instance).

Benchmark: SingleUse versus MultiUse

To test the effect of SingleUse and MultiUse, I created two objects in an ActiveX EXE. Both objects, in their Initialize event, dimensioned an array of 1000 rows by 1000 columns, declared as double. Each instance of the class effectively allocated itself several megabytes of memory as part of its initialization.

My testbed program then created multiple copies of both objects. The test was simple: How many objects could be created before my testbed computer (with 64 megabytes of RAM) would crash. I could create a virtually unlimited number of copies of the MultiUse object. I could create less than 20 of the SingleUse.

If you run the test yourself (or use my sample code), you can use the System Monitor (on Windows 98) or Performance Monitor (on Windows NT) to watch the impact of creating the objects. To get the most informative view add the Unused Physical Memory chart to the monitor and (for System Monitor) set the response time to 1 second from its default of 5 seconds before running the sample code. After starting the sample application, you can switch to System Monitor or Performance Monitor and watch the impact.

In my tests creating the MultiUse objects resulted in small drops in free physical memory which the system soon recovered. With the SingleUse object, free physical memory dropped steadily towards zero as more objects were created.

Not surprisingly, creating a SingleUse object takes longer than creating a MultiUse object. Typically, a SingleUse object took 25% longer to create than its MultiUse equivalent. So, when creating EXE components that may be loaded multiple times on the same computer, MultiUse objects will scale better than SingleUse.

With those warnings, MultiUse objects do, in general, conserve computer resources. MultiUse objects can have queuing problems, though. Where many instances of an object share the same code, an application may end up waiting to execute portions of the code while some other client uses the object. SingleUse objects do not have queuing problems since each client has their own copy of the code.

Another benefit of SingleUse objects is that they are more fault tolerant than MultiUse objects. Each instance of SingleUse object is run in a separate process, which isolates it from interacting with other components or clients. Because of this isolation, should a SingleUse object fail, it shouldn't cause any other application to fail also.

As I suggested in the discussion of MultiUse objects, SingleUse objects will, in general, use more resources than a MultiUse object. If there are a lot of simultaneous instances of a SingleUse object created, then there will be many copies of the code loaded. This will put a strain on your server's resources. This strain can probably be relieved by adding more memory to your server, moving to a multiprocessor platform, or implementing some other hardware fix.

There's a Catch-22 here. If you have a MultiUse object that isn't as responsive as you want due to queuing problems, it's because there are many instances of the object loaded. If you switch it to SingleUse, you may end up overloading your computer because all of those instances consume resources. The moral is, "If you switch an object from MultiUse to SingleUse to improve responsiveness, watch your computer's performance to ensure that it doesn't run out of resources."

So, what's the best choice? Ignoring the data sharing issues, which I discuss next, MultiUse is probably the best choice for a component that isn't used much. With MultiUse, every once in a while a client will find the component already loaded and so save the time to load it again. MultiUse is also a good choice for a heavily used component where responsiveness isn't critical because of the increased likelihood of finding the component already loaded. SingleUse is the best choice for a heavily used component where responsiveness is vital and the server resources to support multiple copies of the object are available. If you're choosing between Single and MultiUse based on fault tolerance, perhaps you should do more testing of your component instead.

As you'll see, though, if the objects in a component need to share information, the decision to use SingleUse or MultiUse will depend on the relationships between the objects rather than the frequency of use.

Sharing

The MultiUse setting becomes more important because of the way that non-Class modules are shared in a component. While each object in a component has its own data, the non-object portions of a component are shared. In a component, any standard Modules and Forms are shared among all the objects created from the component.

For an ActiveX DLL, this means that Forms and standard Modules are shared among all the objects created from the component. If the developer declares variables in a standard Module in the program, then those variables will be accessible from any object created from the component. If any code in an object changes a value in a variable declared in a Module, that change will be visible to all the other objects created from that component. This allows the various instances of the object to communicate with each other through variables declared in standard Modules.

The situation for ActiveX EXE components is slightly different, as ActiveX EXE objects can have their Instancing properties set to SingleUse or MultiUse. If an object is marked SingleUse, a new copy of the component will be loaded each time an object is created. Since each object may have a component to itself, there is no other object to share information with.

If an ActiveX EXE's objects are marked MultiUse, then only one copy of the component will be loaded. Like an ActiveX DLL, all the instances of the objects created from a single ActiveX EXE component will share the Modules and Forms in the component. An ActiveX EXE component, is shared among all the clients running on the computer. This allows objects created by different clients to communicate with each other through variables declared in Modules. Table 5.2 summarizes the various options.

Table 5.2 How Data Is Shared Among Objects in Components

Object Setting	Component Type	
	ActiveX EXE	**ActiveX DLL**
MultiUse	Forms and Modules shared among all clients	Forms and Modules shared among objects for the same client
SingleUse	No shared data	N/A

A typical use of shared data is a semaphore. A semaphore is a software switch that is used to signal that some resource is in use. A program checks the semaphore before starting to use the resource and, if the semaphore is set, waits for the semaphore to be cleared. Once the application finds the semaphore cleared, the application sets it to indicate that the resource is in use, uses the resource, and then clears the semaphore to indicate that the resource is available for use.

In the Wholesale component, the Customer object has a method called CreditCheck. This method contains code to dial up a credit management firm and electronically request a credit rating for the customer represented by the object. However, the company has only one modem connected to their server and so only one client can make the phone call at a time. For this reason, the Customer Class module is set to MultiUse and a global variable called bolModemInUse declared in a Basic Module in the component. The code for dialing the credit management firm looks like this:

```
Public Sub CreditCheck()
Do While bolModemInUse
    ...code to wait for modem to become available
Loop

bolModemInUse = True
...code to use the modem...
bolModemInUse = False
End Sub
```

The variable bolModemInUse is declared in a standard Module like this:

```
Global bolModemInUse As Boolean
```

Assuming that the component was compiled as an ActiveX EXE, the component will be shared among all the clients using objects in the component. In the CreditCheck event, the code checks to see if the variable bolModemInUse is set to False. Since the variable was declared in a Basic Module, it is shared among all the WholesaleManagement components executing on that computer. If any of the other Customer objects currently running have set the bolModemInUse variable, the CreditCheck routine will go into a loop until that other Customer object sets the variable to False. Once the variable is set to False, the loop will end and the next Customer object can use the modem (see Figure 5–6).

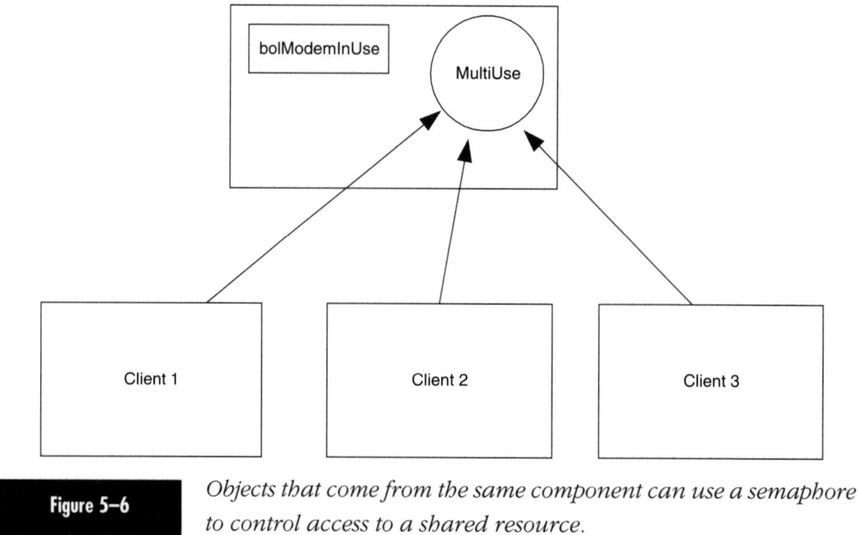

Figure 5–6 *Objects that come from the same component can use a semaphore to control access to a shared resource.*

Had the component been compiled as an ActiveX DLL, only the Customer objects created by a single client would share the bolModemInUse variable.

To sum up for single object components: MultiUse conserves resources and can give faster response when creating new objects. MultiUse objects can share data between objects (ActiveX DLL) and clients (ActiveX EXE). MultiUse objects may have responsiveness problems when many objects are loaded. SingleUse objects will take longer to load successive instances of the same object compared to MultiUse, but will be more fault-tolerant and will avoid queuing problems. SingleUse objects do not share data and shouldn't be used if your objects must communicate with each other (unless you provide some other way to share data).

Complex Components

Components get more complex as more objects are added to them and you define relationships between the objects in the component. As you've seen, choosing between SingleUse and MultiUse has an impact on how many copies of a component will be loaded and how objects in the same component can share information with each other.

In this section I discuss what happens when a component contains many objects. For me, defining the architecture of my components—the relationships between the objects—is the critical part of creating a component. To keep the discussion focused, I begin by assuming that the objects in the component have no relationship with each other (i.e., the objects are not in a parent/child relationship or members of a collection).

MULTIPLE SINGLEUSE COMPONENTS

So what happens when a component containing both SingleUse and MultiUse classes is loaded? COM specifies some of what happens, but not everything.

Let me begin with a simple case: a component that contains two SingleUse objects called SingleA and SingleB. A client creates an instance of object SingleA, causing the component to be loaded into memory. The client then creates an instance of the object SingleB. COM does not load a new copy of the component into memory even though SingleB is marked as SingleUse and the component is already loaded. Only if the client attempts to create a second instance of a SingleA or SingleB object will another copy of the component be loaded.

It's helpful to think of the SingleUse object as a single potential instance of the object. When a client creates an instance of a SingleUse object, it uses up that one potential instance in the component. COM will load another copy of the component if the client asks for a second instance of the object. If a second instance of a SingleUse object is requested, since the one potential instance has already been used, COM will load a second copy of the component (see Figure 5–7).

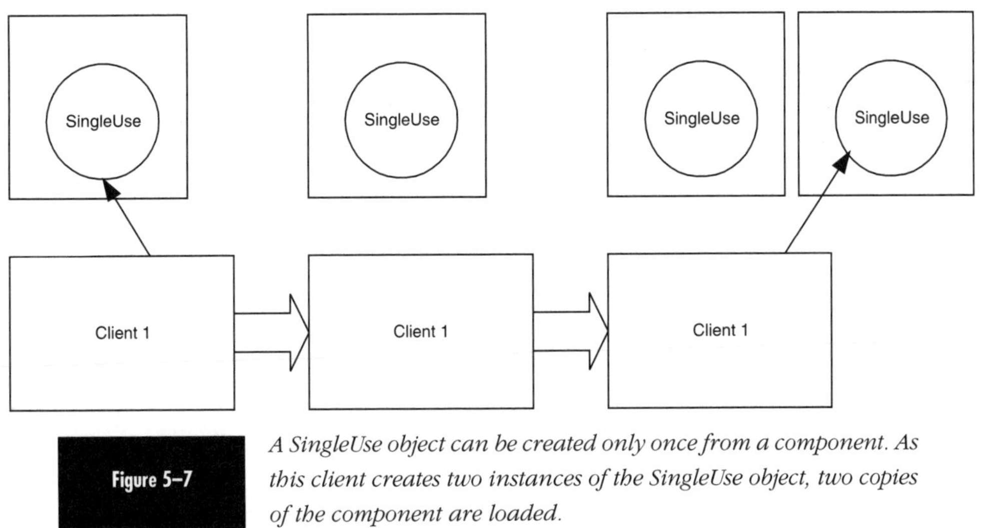

Figure 5–7 *A SingleUse object can be created only once from a component. As this client creates two instances of the SingleUse object, two copies of the component are loaded.*

Even if an instance of a SingleUse object is destroyed because no client is referring to it, that instance of the object is considered to be used. Should a client create another copy of the SingleUse object, a new copy of the component will be loaded into memory.

MULTIUSE AND SINGLEUSE COMPONENTS

For a more complicated situation, take a component with one SingleUse object (called Single) and one MultiUse object (called Multi). The client creates an instance of Single, causing the component to load into memory. The client now creates several instances of the Multi object. Since the Multi object has been marked as MultiUse, a second copy of the component will not be loaded.

Now the client creates a second instance of the Single object. Since the one potential instance has already been used, a second copy of the component will be loaded. If the component depends on the objects communicating with each other through a shared standard module, this component will now fail.

At this point the client has two copies of the component loaded because the client created two instances of the SingleUse component. Now, the client creates another Multi object. Here's where COM does not specify all of the activities that take place. COM does not guarantee from which copy of the component the new Multi object will come. One Multi object may be updating a variable in the first component loaded while another Multi object may be updating a variable in the second component loaded.

When multiple objects exist in a component and they share information with each other, the choice between Single and MultiUse becomes a matter of controlling when a new component is loaded to memory.

CONTROLLING COMPONENT CREATION

There are a couple of ways to control how many copies of a component are loaded. The first is to set the Instancing property of all of the Class modules in your component to MultiUse. If the component is an ActiveX EXE, this guarantees that only one copy of the component will be loaded for all clients and they will be able to communicate with each other. If the component is an ActiveX DLL, this strategy guarantees that only one copy will be loaded for each client, no matter how many objects are created.

Another tactic is to have only one SingleUse object in a component. Provided that

- no client creates more than one instance of the SingleUse object
- the SingleUse object is created first

each client will get their own personal copy of the component. This tactic works well when a component has a principal object that all the other objects in the component depend upon. Using this design allows the objects in the component to communicate with each other but not with other instances of the same component.

You have to guarantee that clients will access the SingleUse object in your component first. The first client that accesses an object from the component will cause the component to be loaded. If another client creates a MultiUse object from the component, it will get an object from the already loaded component and not from its own copy of the component. The first client to create an instance of the component's SingleUse object will use up the one potential instance of the SingleUse object in the loaded component. When the second client finally creates an instance of the SingleUse object, it will cause a second copy of the component to be loaded. The second client will now be drawing its objects from two components and may run into difficulties if the objects are expected to share data.

A good example of the "one SingleUse" design would be any of the Office components. Excel, for example, has a SingleUse object called Application which must be created before any other object in the component can be used. All the other objects in Excel depend on the Application object and are created from it. Creating two Excel Application objects will cause Excel to be loaded twice. In each instance of the Excel component, the objects can communicate with each other but not with the objects in the other loaded instance of Excel.

Using Objects in the Same Component

The New keyword uses a special mechanism to create objects in a very efficient manner that is different from the mechanism used by the CreateObject function. This means that an object will be created differently depending on whether the New keyword or the CreateObject function is used. This difference is important when an object creates another object in the same component.

The difference is also important when your object is running within Microsoft Transaction Server, as I discuss in the chapter on Transaction Server.

If you use New from an object in your component to create an instance of another object within the same component, another copy of the component will not be loaded. In other words, when using the New keyword, all other objects within the component are treated as MultiUse.

On the other hand, if you use the CreateObject function from an object in your component to create a SingleUse object, a new copy of the component will be loaded, even if the object is part of the same component. The CreateObject function creates instances as if the request came from a client outside the component.

Regardless of how they are created, SingleUse objects have an impact on debugging because you can't load more than one copy of a SingleUse component in the Visual Basic development environment. When debugging, once you've created your SingleUse object, you will not be able to create another one in the same debugging session.

Global Objects

A Class' Instancing property can also be set to Global. Global objects are available to the client that references the component without having to use the New statement. It appears to the developer that an instance of the object is available as soon as their application starts running. In fact, Global objects are not created until one of their methods or properties is used.

Using a Global Object

Global objects are objects that are automatically created. If you've used DAO, you will recognize the DBEngine object as a Global object. Once you've selected DAO from your project's References list, you can immediately start writing code that uses the DBEngine's methods and properties without having to create an instance of the object.

In the WholesaleManagement component, the Company object has its Instancing property set to Global. Once a developer adds a Reference to the PHVIS_WholesaleManagement component to their Project they can use the CreateCustomer method of the Company object to create a Customer object:

```
Dim cst As PHVIS_WholesaleManagement.Customer
Set cst = CreateCustomer
```

Your component's clients won't explicitly create an instance of your Global object (in fact, any attempt to do so will generate a syntax error). This isn't true of the other objects in the same component as your Global object. If, in the WholesaleManagement's Product object, I wanted to use the methods and properties of the Customer object, I would have to create an instance of it:

```
Dim cst As Customer
Dim cmp As Company
Set cst = cmp.CreateCustomer
```

Benchmark: Global Calls versus MultiUse Calls

When using Global objects I wanted to know if the overhead on calling a Global object differed significantly from calling a method on any other kind of object. My testing showed no appreciable difference in calling methods on a Global object versus calling methods from a MultiUse object.

One interesting use of Global objects is to create complex predefined constants. You can add Property Get procedures to your Global object to return complex values. The code in the procedure can do whatever processing that you need to create the value. The developer using your component can just use your property as if it were a predefined constant.

Global Instancing

Global objects come in two varieties for ActiveX EXE projects: GlobalMultiUse and GlobalSingleUse. For an ActiveX DLL, you can select only GlobalMultiUse.

If a Global object's Instancing property is set to GlobalSingleUse, then each client will create its own copy of the Global object. As a result, each client that uses the Global object will load a separate instance of the component that the object is part of. If the Instancing property of your object is set to GlobalMultiUse, then only one copy of the component will be loaded and it will be shared among all of the clients using the component.

Component Design Strategies

At this point, deciding on a SingleUse/MultiUse strategy for your component probably sounds horribly complicated. In practice, I've found that there are really just three strategies: Share All, One Copy Each, and Multiple Copies/No Sharing (see Figure 5–8). The first thing to remember is that if the objects in your component don't communicate with each other then it doesn't matter how many copies of the component are loaded: You can make the decision based on the efficiency issues that I discussed earlier.

Even where the objects are related, picking a SingleUse/MultiUse strategy doesn't have to be difficult if you stick to the three basic structures for you components.

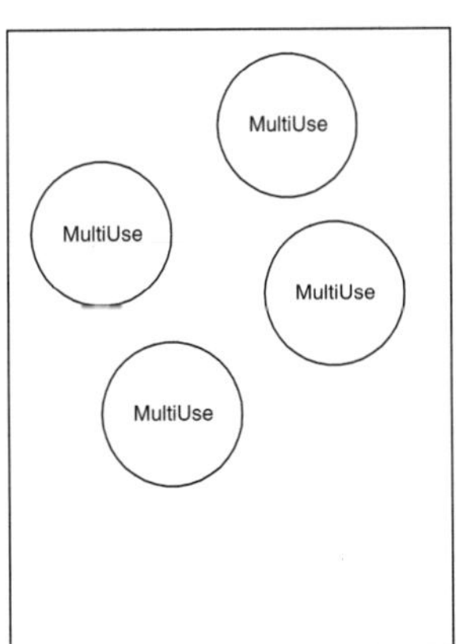

Share All

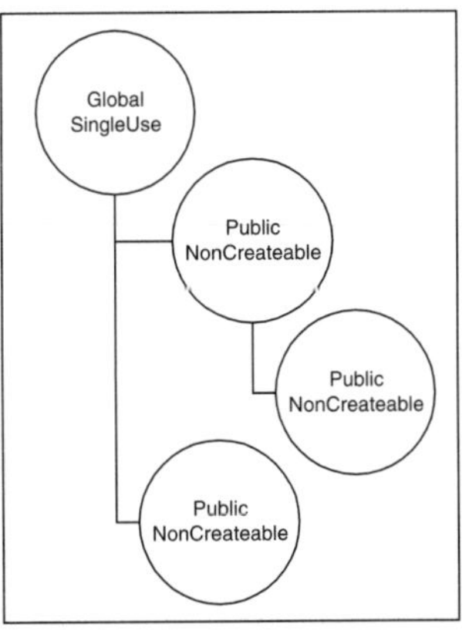

One Copy Each

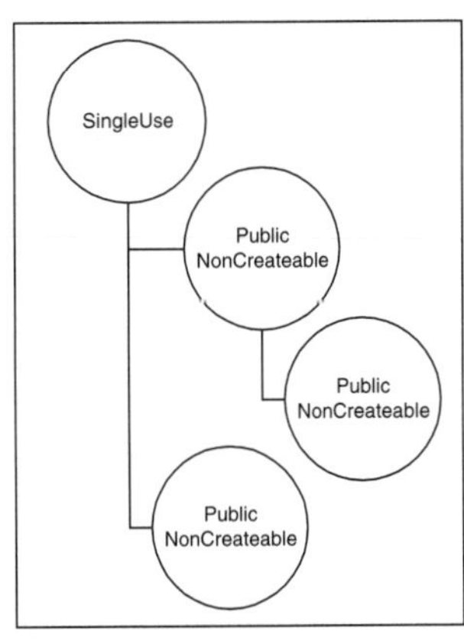

Multiple Copies/No Sharing

Figure 5–8 *The three strategies that you can use when designing your component.*

ActiveX EXE

Since ActiveX EXEs are shared among all the clients using the component, I begin by looking at them.

SHARE ALL

If you want your ActiveX EXE component shared among all clients, you should set all your objects, including your Global objects, to MultiUse. Setting any object to SingleUse will cause the second client that uses the SingleUse object to load a new copy of the component. Once the second copy of the component is loaded, clients won't be able to determine which copy they are creating objects from, and so won't know if the objects are communicating with each other.

In a Share All strategy, the objects that make up the component are usually independent of each other. If the objects do share resources, there can be problems with concurrency when two objects attempt to update or use a shared resource at the same time. Semaphores can assure that you don't have two components attempting to use some resource at the same time. Concurrency is discussed in more depth in the chapter on Microsoft Transaction Server.

ONE COPY EACH

If you want each client to have its own copy of the component (and only one copy) make sure that

- The client will access a SingleUse object first
- The client will not create a second instance of any SingleUse object in the component

It doesn't matter how many of your objects (including Global objects) are marked SingleUse as long as none of them will ever have more than one instance created and a SingleUse object is accessed first. The danger with letting a MultiUse object be created first is that two clients might end up sharing a component before one of the clients creates a SingleUse object that causes a second copy of the component to be loaded.

The strategy that I usually follow when designing components is to make the Global object the only SingleUse object. I then design my model so that this GlobalSingleUse object must be created first because the client must use the object's methods or properties to access any other object in the model. Because a client can't create a second instance of a Global object, my clients cannot create a second instance of the component's only SingleUse object.

In DAO, for instance, most activities require you to use either the OpenDatabase or CreateDatabase methods of the Workspace object before doing anything else. Since Workspace objects can be retrieved only through the

Workspaces collection of the DBEngine object, this guarantees that the DBEngine object is created before any other activity is performed. The DBEngine object is declared SingleUse, ensuring that each client gets its own copy of the DAO component.

As I have noted, there is one exception to the rule that creating a SingleUse causes a new copy of the component to be created. When SingleUse objects are created from other objects within the same component using the CreateObject function a new copy of the component will be loaded. You can cause the "one copy each" strategy to fail by having an object in your component create an instance of the Global object using the CreateObject function.

MULTIPLE COPIES/NO SHARING

You can also design your component to allow your clients to load multiple, independent copies of the component. The strategy is the same as the previous strategy with a SingleUse object that must be accessed first. In this strategy, though, the initial object is not a Global object. Since the initial object is not Global, the client can create multiple instances of the SingleUse object and so load multiple copies of the component.

At this point, it becomes important to control from which copy of the component new objects are created. In the next section, I show you how to set the Instancing property so that clients have to use methods of objects in the component to create new objects. Since an object, if it uses the New command, always creates objects from its component, this allows you to control where new objects come from.

Returning to the example of the components that make up Microsoft Office, this is the strategy that they follow. It is possible, for instance, to create multiple instances of the Excel.Application object. Each time you create an instance of the Excel.Application object, it causes a separate copy of Excel to load. Once the Excel component is loaded, you must use the methods and properties of the Application object to create the other objects in the Excel object model. As a result, the data in each instance of Excel is kept separate from data in the other instances of Excel that are currently loaded.

ActiveX DLL

If you are following a strategy where each client gets its own copy of the component, it may be simpler just to compile your component as an ActiveX DLL. The objects in an ActiveX DLL are not shared among clients. Objects in an ActiveX DLL are always MultiUse, so a client cannot load a second copy of the component by creating an object.

Returning to DAO, the strategy that it follows is to use a Global object and to prevent all other objects from being created by the client. The DAO component is compiled as a DLL, ensuring that each client gets its own copy of the component. The DBEngine object is declared as Global and the other objects in the component can only be created using the DBEngine's methods or properties.

Often, the only reason a component is compiled as an ActiveX EXE is because it may be run as a standalone application in addition to being used as a component. I show you how to do that in the next chapter.

Objects That Create Objects

As you can see, preventing clients from creating objects can be very important to the architecture of your component. To prevent a client from creating the objects that it uses, you can set the object's Instancing property to PublicNotCreatable. A PublicNotCreatable object can be used by the component's clients and can be created by other objects in the same component. The object cannot, however, be created by a client.

In the WholesaleManagement component, for instance, I set the Order class Instancing property to PublicNotCreatable. Any attempt by a client program to create this object using either New or CreateObject will cause an error. To create an Order object, the client must use the CreateOrder method of the Customer object. A simplified version of the code for this method looks like this:

```
Public Function CreateOrder()
Dim ord As Order
    Set ord = New Order
    Set CreateOrder = ord
End Function
```

The code from the WholesaleManagement's Order object first creates an instance of an Order object, using the New keyword. The routine then sets the function's name to the new object, causing the function to return the object to the client that called the method.

A client would create an order by first retrieving a Customer object and then using that object's CreateOrder method:

```
Dim ordMyOrder As PHVIS_WholesaleManagement.Order
Dim cust As PHVIS_WholesaleManagement.Customer

Set cust = Customers("Peter Vogel")
Set ordMyOrder = cust.CreateOrder
```

Using a method to create an object provides you with control over how the object is created. If I wanted to ensure that the Order object was created only once, I could use this code:

```
Public Function CreateOrder()
Dim ord As Order
Static bolCreated As Boolean
    If bolCreated Then
      Msgbox "Order already created"
    Else
      Set ord = New Order
      Set CreateOrder = ord
      bolCreated = True
    End If
End Function
```

This version of CreateCustomer sets a variable called bolCreated to True the first time that an order object is created. Before creating the object, the code checks bolCreated to see if the Order object has already been created and, if it has, the Customer object will not create another Order object.

Controlling the creation of SingleUse objects isn't the only reason to use a method to create an object. You may also want to use a PublicNotCreatable object to set some initial properties of the object, add it to a collection, or perform some other processing before turning the object over to the requesting client.

In the WholesaleManagment component, for instance, an order is created from a CustomerObject because the order will belong to that customer. The CreateOrder routine creates this binding by setting the Order object's CustomerId property to the Id for the Customer object that is executing the method. Assuming that the customer object keeps the customer number in a variable called strCustomer, here's what that code looks like:

```
Public Function CreateOrder()
Dim ord As Order
  Set ord = New Order
  ord.CustomerId = strCustomer
  Set CreateOrder = ord
End Function
```

This technique of creating a method for an object that is used to create another object helps define the structure of an object model. In the Figure 5–9, I show the DAO QueryDef and Recordset objects. The parent/child relationship of the QueryDef and the Recordset object indicates that a method of the QueryDef object must be used to create a Recordset (the QueryDef's OpenRecordset method, to be exact). As I discussed before, the parent/child relationship in a COM object model can indicate a variety of relationships. The creation relationship, where an object is used to create a PublicNotCreatable object, is one of the most common.

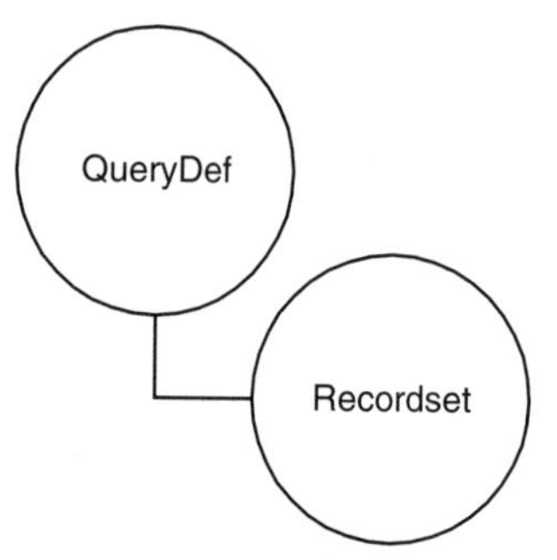


```
Dim qdf As QueryDef
Dim rec As Recordset

Set qdf = dbs.QuerDefs("MyQuery")
Set rec = qdf.OpenRecordset()
```

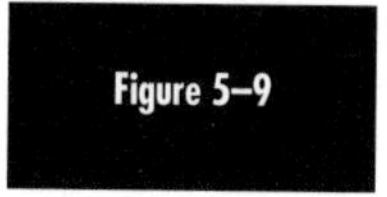

The relationship between the QueryDef and Recordset objects in DAO exists because the QueryDef object's OpenRecordset method is used to create a Recordset object.

Initializing

There are additional benefits to using a strategy that specifies a SingleUse object as the entry point for the component. You can place any activities that are common to all objects in the component in the entry object's Initialize event.

In the WholesaleManagement component, for instance, most of the objects read and write information to the company database. It's important, then, that the database be opened before any of the objects in the component attempt to access it. The entry point object for the WholesaleManagement component is the Company object, so I put this code in the Company object's Initialize event:

```
Private Sub Class_Initialize()
    Set dbs = con.Open "DSN=Wholesale;"
End Sub
```

In this example, the dbs variable is declared in a standard Module so that it can be shared among all of the objects.

▲ Case Study: The WholesaleManagement Components

The number of decisions that you have to make may seem overwhelming at this point, so I'm going to look at the WholesaleManagement model and how it could be implemented. In this example, I concentrate on the definition of the Class modules and ignore the issues around defining the methods, properties, and events.

The first question is how many components the various objects should be distributed over. As indicated in the chapter on Visual Modeler, I've chosen to implement the WholesaleManagement model in two components. One component contains only the Customer object, which can be used by a number of other applications that don't need the rest of the objects in the model. All the rest of the objects are in another component. The two components are called WholesaleCustomer and WholesaleManagement.

The next decision is whether the objects should be DLLs or EXEs. I've chosen to implement both objects as ActiveX DLLs, primarily for performance reasons. There is also a real possibility that the WholesaleManagement component may be moved to a server and run under Microsoft Transaction Server (MTS). MTS requires that all of the components it manages be DLLs.

The Customer object has its Instancing property set to MultiUse so that it can be created just by using the New command. Because the Customer object is the only object in its component, it couldn't be set to PublicNotCreateable as there is no other object to create it. Since an application may need to have several Customer objects in use at a time, the object couldn't be made Global.

On the other hand, in the WholesaleManagement component, the Company object has had its Instancing property set to Global so that its methods and properties are available whenever required by the client. All of the other objects in the component have their instancing property set to PublicNotCreateable. As a result, I have a great deal of control over when, and how, these objects are created. The design strategy that I've implemented is that any client will have only one instance of the WholesaleManagement object loaded, though they may have multiple instances of most of the objects (e.g., Customer, Order, Product, but not Company because it is Global).

Since the only way to work with any object in the WholesaleManagement component is to use a method or property of the Company object, I can be assured that the Company object will be created before any other object. In order to get an Order, for instance, the client must use the Orders property of the Company object.

The Company object exposes Orders, Customers, Products, and SalesReps properties. Supplying an index to any of these properties returns the appropriate object. Only SalesReps is implemented as a complete collection with a SalesReps object. Since the Company object will be created before any other object, these collections are loaded in the Company's Initialize event.

The Company object also has CreateCustomer, CreateOrder, CreateProduct, and CreateSalesRep methods. These methods are implemented as functions that accept the parameters necessary to define their object, and return a Customer, Order, Product, or SalesRep object.

Summary

In this chapter I described the issues that arise when you combine your objects into components. I gave you a definition of a component and used your new knowledge to review the Visual Basic References list, CreateObject, and GetObject. You also got a quick look at the underlying COM technology that allows components to work together.

Much of this chapter looked at the various component design strategies that result from setting the Class module's Instancing property. If your objects don't share any data, the only decision that you have to make is whether to use MultiUse (one copy of the component loaded and queuing problems) or SingleUse (many copies of the component loaded and no queuing problems). If your objects do communicate, or you want to control how an object is created, you may want to set your objects to PublicNotCreateable. Global Instancing lets you define an object that your clients don't have to create.

I also introduced you to the distinction between ActiveX EXEs and DLLs (there are more differences between them, which I return to in a later chapter). ActiveX EXEs are shared among all the clients on the same computer, while DLLs are private to the client that loaded them. Among other differences, I showed you how to debug each type of component.

The more you use these concepts, the more familiar you will become with them. It's especially important that you become comfortable with the various strategies for creating components.

There are a couple of ways that you can experiment with the information in this chapter. One way is to determine what strategy is being used by various object models that you work with. What strategy does ADO use, for instance? Or Access?

Another way of working with building components is to redesign a component that you are building into each of the three strategies. Could you build your application as an ActiveX EXE with its objects shared by multiple clients? What problems would this create? If the problems outweigh the benefits, would it be better to create your component as an ActiveX DLL? What object should be your SingleUse object? Can it be your Global object? How will you control creation of other objects in the component?

One of the standard works on building components is Dan Appleman's book *Developing COM/ActiveX Components with Visual Basic 6: A Guide to the Perplexed* from Sams. The book goes into more detail on COM interfaces and the history of ActiveX than I feel is necessary, but provides a thorough technical background on the issues involved.

In the next chapter I show you how to work with the more private parts of your component. This includes setting up your ActiveX EXE so that it can run as a standalone application or as a component. You'll also see how to add collections to your component and create objects that return other objects. The next chapter also discusses creating a private interface through the use of hidden objects and methods. Finally, I introduce the Implements keyword that, among other things, allows you to create multiple objects that support a single interface.

S I X

Interfaces

In this chapter I discuss how your component can tailor the way that it exposes its methods, properties, and events to its clients in order to meet your design goals. One of the topics in this chapter—Visual Basic's Implements keyword—is fundamental to the way that COM works. However, I also look at how you can hide parts of your component from your clients to create a private interface accessible only from within the component itself. You'll see how to set properties on your object's routines to control the way that they interface with other clients, including the Object Browser. You'll also learn how to add a collection to your component.

In this chapter I have two case studies. The first case study shows you how interfaces allow you to enhance your component without having the clients that use it fail. The second case study looks at a replacement for using Events that allows your objects to communicate with the clients that are using it in a more efficient manner.

Object Interfaces

When I create objects and components I decide what methods, properties, and events they should expose. Effectively, I'm designing an interface to my object—not a user interface, but an interface for the client programs that will use my component. In the COM world, the term interface means a collection of methods and properties. COM assigns names to the interfaces that you create that allow clients to use your objects. A component could be said to be a collection of interfaces rather than a collection of objects.

In this section, I show you how to add multiple interfaces to your objects. You'll see how you can group methods and properties into named groups. More important, I also discuss why you would want to have a Class module with more than one interface.

COM Interfaces

As I mentioned in the chapter on Objects, Visual Basic provides your object with a set of methods that are required by the COM specification. That set of methods—AddRef, Release, and QueryInterface—are grouped together as the IUnknown interface. From the very beginning, then, your object has had several interfaces: The one that you defined and the ones that Visual Basic provided to meet the COM specification. Figure 6–1 shows the standard graphic notation for a single object with multiple interfaces.

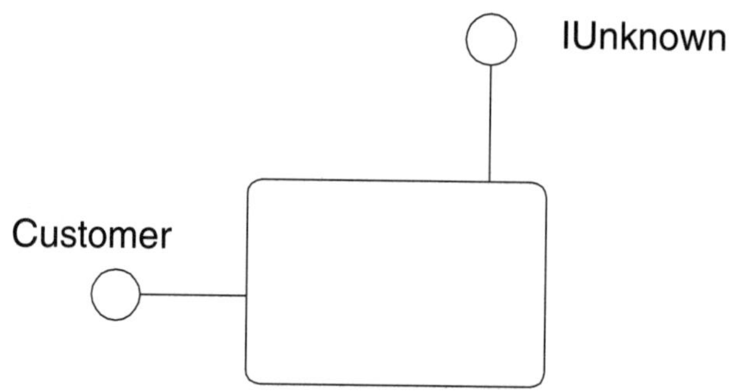

Figure 6–1 *A COM object (the Customer object) with the IUnknown and Customer interfaces.*

The number of interfaces that Visual Basic adds to your application can be large. When you create an ActiveX control, for instance, Visual Basic adds more than a dozen interfaces to your object. In fact, what distinguishes one type of object (like an ActiveX Control) from another type of object (like an ActiveX Document) are the COM specific interfaces that the object exposes. All COM objects must have the IUnkown interface, for instance, but only objects that support Automation must have the IDispatch interface.

Clients that are designed to use a specific kind of object look for and expect to find specific interfaces. By example, a Visual Basic form requires those dozen or so interfaces that Visual Basic adds to any ActiveX Control that you build.

Objects that are designed to work in a specific environment expect that the host environment will expose certain interfaces. Some ActiveX controls, like the Frame control, can't be used in Microsoft Access because the Access Form does not support some of the interfaces that the control requires (for the Frame control, that's the methods and properties that make up the ISimpleFrame interface). Your Visual Basic component will be able to work only in the environments that support the interfaces that it depends on.

Visual Basic and Interfaces

Up until now, the code that I've shown has always declared any object variables with the same name as the Class that they were referring to. An object variable created to point to a Customer object was declared as type Customer:

```
Dim cst As Customer
Set cst = New Customer
```

It's tempting to think that the object variable refers to the object itself, but that's not the case. Instead, the object variable points to just one interface on the object. A Visual Basic object variable gives you access to the methods and properties for only one of the interfaces that your object may have. So, while all objects have multiple interfaces, you've only seen the methods and properties of one of the interfaces.

When you create a Class module and add routines to it, you could say that you are creating the Class's "native" interface, the interface defined by the procedures in the class module. This native interface takes the same name as the Class module.

Any additional interfaces that you add to a Class are copies of some other class module's native interface.

INTERFACES AND OBJECT VARIABLES

In my previous code examples, then, when I declared an object variable as type Customer, I was saying that I wanted to use the Customer interface of the Customer class. If I wanted to access the methods and properties of the IUnknown interface for the Customer object, I would have to declare a variable with type IUnknown (see Figure 6–2). The resulting code would look like this:

```
Dim cst As IUnknown
Set cst = New Customer
```

In the preceding code, the New keyword will cause an instance of the Customer Class module to be loaded into memory to create a Customer object. The cst variable, because it is declared as type IUnknown, will allow

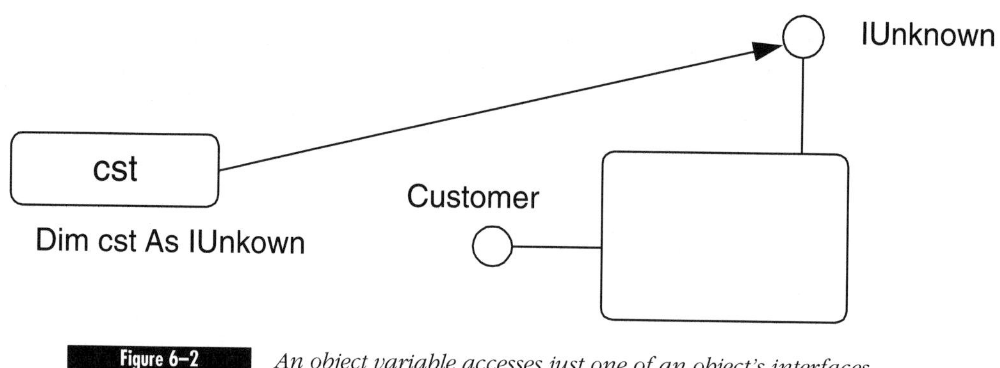

Figure 6–2 *An object variable accesses just one of an object's interfaces.*

me to access the methods that make up the Customer object's IUnknown interface: the Addref, Release, and QueryInterface methods.

Declaring references to the IUnknown interface doesn't let you call any of the methods that make up the IUnknown interface.

Back in the chapter on VBA, in the tutorial on using objects and object variables, I had two object variables referring to the same object. The code for that looked like this:

```
Dim cst1 As Customer
Dim cst2 As Customer

Set cst1 = New Customer
Set cst2 = cst1
```

After this code has executed, both the cst1 and cst2 object variables would refer to the same Customer object.

USING MULTIPLE OBJECT VARIABLES

Where multiple object variables point to the same object, the variables don't all have to be of the same type. In the previous example, I could have one of the object variables refer to the Customer object's IUnknown interface by declaring the variable as type IUnknown:

```
Dim cst1 As Customer
Dim cst2 As IUnknown

Set cst1 = New Customer
Set cst2 = cst1
```

When this code finishes executing, both variables will still point to the same Customer object. The cst1 object variable will provide access to all the methods and properties that make up the Customer interface. The Customer interface will consist of all of the methods and properties defined in the Customer Class module itself. The cst2 object will provide access to those methods that make up the IUnknown interface

With Visual Basic, when you declare a variable as type Object, the variable will refer to the object's native interface. This code will create a Customer object and provide access to the methods and properties of the Customer interface through the cst variable:

```
Dim cst As Object
Set cst = New Customer
```

Visual Basic uses the data type of the object variable to provide IntelliSense support. When you declare a variable as type Object, Visual Basic can't determine what interface you are using. With a variable declared as Object, you'll have to remember what method and properties make up the object's native interface because IntelliSense won't be able to prompt you with its dropdown lists.

SUMMING UP

Interfaces are sufficiently important that I take a moment here to summarize the previous discussion. An interface is a named collection of methods, properties, and events that an object implements. The New command determines which Class module is loaded into memory and so controls what code is called when a method or property in an interface is called. The data type of the variable that refers to an object will control which interface you will have access to. An object can have many interfaces, including its native interface (the methods and properties defined within the Class module). Different object variables that refer to the same object can access different interfaces of the object if they are declared differently.

Figure 6–3 shows an object with two interfaces and three object variables referring to the object. One object variable refers to the IUnknown interface, one refers to the object's native interface with a typed variable, and the last refers to the object's native interface through a variable declared as type Object.

Using COM Interfaces

When I'm teaching Visual Basic, the immediate reaction of most of the programmers in my class when introduced to interfaces is "Why would I want to do this?" I've always found that to be a difficult question to answer without first going into some detail on how to add an interface to an object. So, first I show

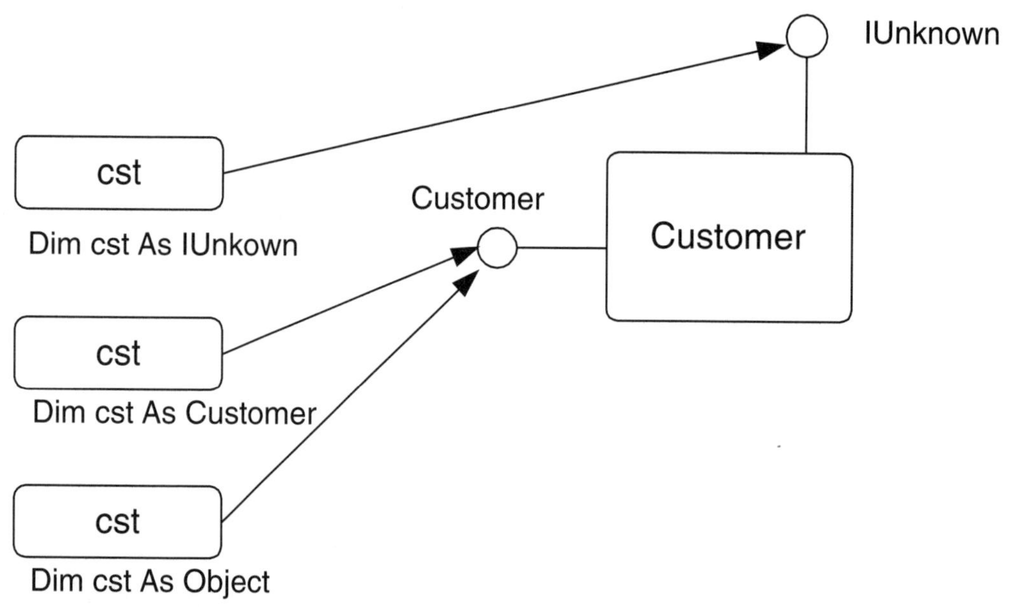

Figure 6–3 *Two COM objects and a client with multiple references to one object.*

you how to add an interface to your application and then give you all the reasons why you would want to. In the meantime, you'll have to trust me: Interfaces are important to you. Among other benefits, interfaces solve a major problem when it comes time to release any enhancements to your component.

Adding Interfaces

You've been defining native interfaces every time you created an object. Adding a Class module to a Visual Basic project and filling it with Public subroutines and functions defines an interface. To add a second interface to your Class you put the Implements keyword followed by a Class module name in the General Declarations section at the top of your Class module. Your Class module will pick up the interface of the Class module used by the Implements statement. For instance, this line adds the Customer interface to the Class that it is placed in:

```
Implements Customer
```

The Class module whose name appears in the Implements statement must be a Class module in the same project as the Class it is it added to, or an object defined in one of the components checked off in the project's References list.

Once you have added the Implements statement to your Class module, it is still your responsibility to write the procedures that make up the interface. In fact, Visual Basic will not let you compile your project until you have added to your Class module all the methods and properties that make up the interface.

For instance, in the WholesaleManagement component, the Customer Class module has an interface that includes an Id property and a CreditInvoice method. Any Class module that implements the Customer interface must also have an Id property and a CreditInvoice method in its version of the Customer interface. You are not required to add the Events that make up the Implemented Class module.

Visual Basic makes it easy to add these members of an interface after you add the Implements statement. Once you add an Implements statement, the Object listbox in the upper left corner of the Class module code window will include the name of the Class referenced by the statement. When you select that Class in the Object listbox, the Procedures/Events listbox in the upper right corner of the window will list all of the methods and properties for that Class.

In Figure 6–4, I show the CashOnly Class module, which contains the statement Implements Customer. In the figure, the Customer object has been selected in the object listbox. The Procedures/Events listbox shows all of the methods and properties for that interface. Selecting the CreditInvoice method from the Procedures/Events listbox would add this code to the CashOnly Customer Class module:

```
Private Function Customer_CreditInvoice() As String
End Sub
```

A procedure that implements a method or property in an interface has a name made up of the name of the Class that the method came from, followed by an underscore, followed (finally) by the name of the method. This naming convention isn't all that unusual in Visual Basic. The Visual Basic convention for Event procedures works the same way: object name, underscore, event name.

Procedures that implement methods or properties for an interface are also marked as Private. As a result, the CreditCheck routine will not appear as a method of the CashOnly Class. This makes sense: the method is not part of the CashOnly native interface and shouldn't be a Public member of the CashOnly module. The CreditCheck method is a member of the Customer interface and appears as a public member of that interface.

ACCESSING INTERFACE ROUTINES

The only way to run the code that you put in the private Customer_CreditCheck routine is through an object variable that refers to the Customer interface. Now that the CashOnly Class module is implementing the

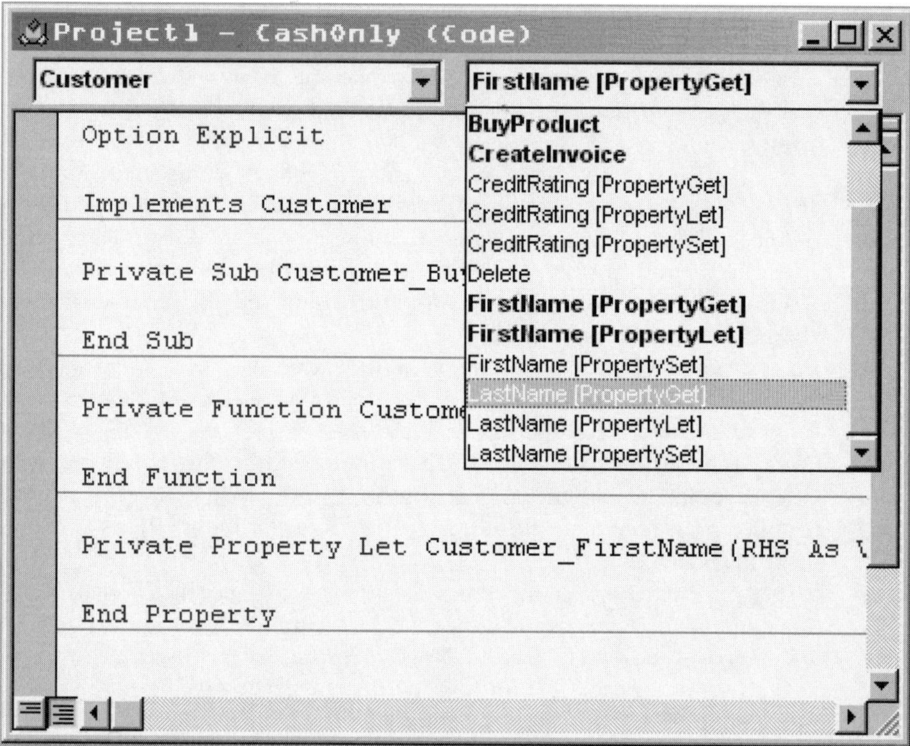

Figure 6–4 *A Class module that implements a second interface.*

Customer interface, clients would use this code to run the CreditCheck method found in the CashOnly object:

```
Dim cst As Customer
Set cst = New CashOnly
```

As the code shows, the Class module loaded into memory by the New command is the CashOnly module. Since it's the CashOnly module that's loaded into memory, that's the code that will be executed. However, since the cst variable was declared as Customer, the methods and properties that will be available through the cst variable will be the ones that make up the Customer interface (e.g., Id, CreditInvoice). This code will run the code in the private Customer_CreditInvoice method in the CashOnly module:

```
Dim cst As Customer
Dim strResult As String

Set cst = New CashOnly
strResult = cst.CreditInvoice
```

What if the CashOnly Class module contained some additional methods or properties that weren't part of the Customer Class? Since those methods and properties would make up the CashOnly Class native interface, then the client would need an object variable declared as type CashOnly to access that functionality.

In the following code, the cst object variable refers to the methods and properties that make up the Customer interface. The cho variable will provide access to whatever methods and properties make up the CashOnly object's native interface:

```
Dim cst As Customer
Dim cho As CashOnly
Set cst = New CashOnly
Set cho = CashOnly
```

The declarations for the methods and properties for a procedure that implements a method or property from an interface must be identical to the way that the routine was declared in the original Class. The only exception is that, even if a Public variable was used to create a property in the original Class module, Property Procedures must be used in the Class with the Implements statement.

REDUCING CODE

The word "implements" has the meaning of "making something happen." As the term Implements implies, you must add code to the Class module before these routines will actually do anything. The CashOnly Class adopts the Customer interface but must still make the interface functional by implementing the methods and properties through code. The CashOnly Class does not inherit the functionality of the Customer interface, it only commits you to implementing those methods and properties. While the method and property declarations are added by Visual Basic, it is your responsibility to put the code in those routines to make something happen when they are called. When an interface is added to a Class module, no code or functionality is imported from the Class module that defined the interface. I realize that I am belaboring this point, but many object developers have trouble with the Implements statement simply because they expect it to do more than just commit you to creating the appropriate methods and properties.

Implementing an interface does not mean that you have to copy all the code from the Customer Class module to the CashOnly Class module. Instead, the CashOnly module can create a Customer object of its own and use the Customer object's methods and properties.

The process of creating an object so that you can call it from another object that implements its interface is so common it even has a name: delegation.

Here's how the CashOnly Class could implement a CreditCheck method by delegating the work to a Customer object's method (Figure 6–5 shows the relationship between the client, the object and the delegated object):

```
Dim cst As Customer
Private Sub Class_Initialize()
    Set cst = New Customer
End Sub

Private Function Customer_CreditCheck() As String
Dim strPeturnValue As String
    strReturnValue = cst.CreditCheck
    Customer_CreditCheck = strReturnValue
End Sub

Private Sub Class_Terininate()
    Set cst = Nothing
End Sub
```

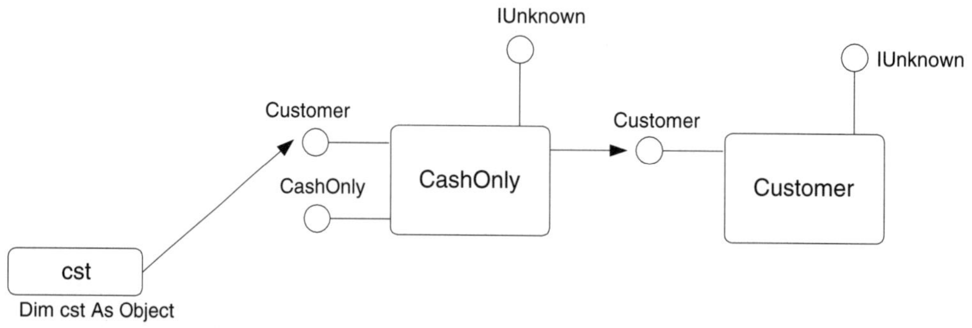

Figure 6–5 *A client accessing an object that has delegated its functionality to another object.*

In this sample code, the CashOnly Class module creates a Customer object in its Initialize event (i.e., as the CashOnly object is loaded into memory). The variable is declared at the module level so that it is available to all the routines that make up the Class. Declaring the variable at the module level also ensures that the variable will not be destroyed until the CashOnly object is unloaded from memory.

The code in the Customer_CreditCheck routine the code calls the CreditCheck method of the Customer object used by the CashOnly module. The value returned by the call to the Customer object is used as the value returned by the Customer_CreditCheck method. In effect, the CashOnly Class uses a Customer object to implement the Customer's CreditCheck method.

Of course, the design for the CashOnly Class may require that its CreditCheck method not work the same way as the Customer's CreditCheck method. In that situation, the CashOnly code won't be able to delegate the CreditCheck processing to a Customer object. In that case, the code for the CreditCheck method might look like this:

```
Private Function Customer_Creditcheck() As String
Customer_CreditCheck = "No Credit"
End Sub
```

Benchmark: Calling Implemented Methods

I tested to see if there was any difference between calling a method, calling a method implemented in another Class, and calling a native method in a Class that implemented another interface. I tested with both a DLL and an EXE. There was no appreciable difference among the three cases.

IMPLEMENTS AND EVENTS

Interfaces in Visual Basic ignore Events. The Implements keyword makes no attempt to ensure that events defined in the interface Class module are also defined in the implementing Class module.

You also can't receive events through any interface except the Class module's native interface. In order for a client to receive events from a Class module that fires Events, the client must use a WithEvents variable that refers to the Class module's native interface. In fact, a variable that points to an implemented interface can't even be declared with the WithEvents keyword.

A client that wanted to use the Customer interface of the CashOnly object and receive events fired by the Class will need two object variables. The client will have to declare an object variable of type Customer to access the methods and properties in the Customer interface. In order to capture events fired by the CashOnly object, the client would also have to declare a variable of type CashOnly (the native interface) using the WithEvents keyword. Event routines could then be created using the variable that referred to the CashOnly interface. The code looks like this:

```
Dim WithEvents cho As CashOnly
Private Sub Form_Load()
```

```
Dim cst As ICustomer
    Set cst = New CashOnly
    Set cho = cst
End Sub

Private Sub cho_CustomerOverDrawn()
'Event routine to capture events fired by
'the CashOnly object
End Sub
```

CLASS MODULE TYPES

With the introduction of interfaces, you have three ways of looking at Class modules:

- Class modules that contain code to implement only their native interface
- Class modules that contain code to implement multiple interfaces
- Class modules that contain no code other than method and property declarations

The last group of Class modules exists only to define an interface to be implemented by other Classes. These modules are sometimes referred to as interface modules/classes or virtual classes. As I suggest in this chapter, you should create two Class modules for each object that you want to have in your component. One Class module should contain only the declarations for the object's methods and properties. The second Class module will implement the interface defined by the first Class module.

There are a number of naming conventions that are used with interfaces. I follow a couple of them, but ignore some others. For instance, where a Class module exists solely to define an interface and contains no code of its own, the naming convention is to begin the Class module name with the letter I. If the Customer module contained no code other than the declarations of its methods and properties, then its name, under this convention, should be ICustomer. I follow this convention in my code. Some naming conventions prefix the name of the modules that implement an interface class with the letter c. The Class Modules that implement the ICustomer interface would be called "cCustomer" and "cCashOnly" under this convention. This is a convention that I don't follow since I prefer my Class modules to have names that don't describe, in any way, how they work.

Why Interfaces?

As I said earlier on, your immediate reaction on being exposed to interfaces is probably "Why bother?" If interfaces also automatically included the functionality behind the interface, eliminating the need for delegation, the usefulness of interfaces might be more obvious. Even without inheriting functionality, interfaces are important and perform several essential functions.

MANAGING DEVELOPMENT

The use of objects provides project managers with a way to split the development of a project among many developers while ensuring that the design of the application is maintained. The process works as follows:

1. In the initial stages of a project, the objects that make up an application can be defined.
2. Interface Class modules are then created for each of the objects and distributed to all of the project's developers.
3. Developers then create Class modules that implement the interfaces defined at the start of the project.

Since Visual Basic will not compile a Class module unless it correctly defines the interfaces it implements, this technique ensures that all Class modules conform to the specifications established at the start of the project. Among other benefits, this methodology allows one group of developers to work closely with the users to build the user interface that calls the objects that make up the application. Another group of developers can work separately on building the objects that the user interface depends on. Interface Class modules and the Implements keyword help ensure that the two groups stay in sync.

EXTENSIBILITY

Many systems allow developers to add new objects to the system. Microsoft Transaction Server, for instance, is designed to allow you to place objects and components under its control. In Part 3 of this book I show how to create components to work with MTS, ActiveX Data Objects, and the Visual Basic development environment. In order to integrate your component into these environments, you must implement the interfaces that the environment requires. In the same way, you can use interfaces to allow developers to integrate their objects with your component.

Interfaces allow developers to specify what methods and properties the objects added to their application must have. The developers for Microsoft Transaction Server, for instance, require that all components that want to make full use of MTS implement a specific set of methods. To make sure that this is done correctly, MTS provides a set of interface classes that MTS compatible modules must implement.

EARLY BINDING

What if you have a routine that accepts, as a parameter, more than one kind of object? In the WholesaleManagement component, the CreateOrder method of the Product object must be passed a Customer object. The CreateOrder method should be able to accept any kind of Customer object, from Premium to NoCash.

There are a couple of ways to handle this situation. You could declare the parameter as Object:

```
Function CreateOrder (OrderCustomer As Object) As Order
```

This technique will let the CreateOrder routine accept any kind of object. There are a number of problems with this solution, however. First, the method will accept any kind of object, not just Customer objects. If you inadvertently call the CreateOrder method and pass it a SalesRep object, the error won't be caught by Visual Basic. Also, when writing the code for the object, you won't get any IntelliSense support because to work its magic IntelliSense needs to know which interface you are using. And, as I pointed out in the chapter on objects, when an object variable is declared as type Object, your application runs slower.

Another solution is to write different versions of the routine for each type of Customer object:

```
Public Function CreateOrderPR (OrderCustomer As Premium) _
                            As Order
Public Function CreateOrderCO (OrderCustomer As CashOnly) _
                            As Order
```

While this solution gives you faster code because the parameter's declaration matches the kind of object passed to, there are other problems. To begin with, you will have a lot more code to write as you create different versions of the routine for each kind of Customer object. With different versions of the same routine, there is a real possibility that one version of CreateOrder may not match the other versions. In addition, if you define a new type of Customer, you will have to come back and add a new version of the CreateOrder routine.

There is a third, and better, solution as shown in Figure 6–6. All of these different versions of the Customer object could be designed to implement the Customer interface. With this design you can declare the CreateOrder's parameter to point to the Customer interface of the object passed to it, regardless of the object's type.

```
Public Function CreateOrder (OrderCustomer As Customer) _
                          As Order
```

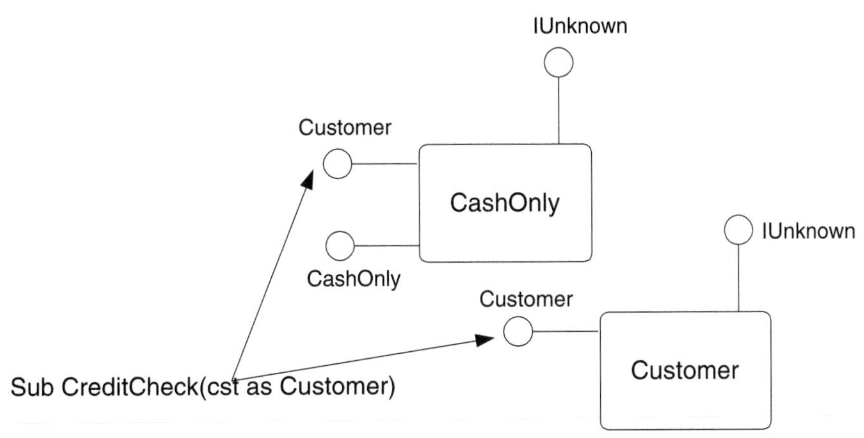

Figure 6–6 *Many objects, all implementing the same interface, can be passed to the same parameter.*

With this declaration of the CreateOrder method, you write only one routine and get the benefits of early binding. The only restriction is that you can only use the OrderCustomer variable to access the methods and properties of the Customer interface.

ACCESSING NATIVE FUNCTIONALITY WITH TYPEOF • If the CreateOrder routine must call some method that is part of the object's native interface, you'll need some way to determine what kind of object was passed to the routine. Without the ability to determine what kind of object has been passed, you can't determine what native methods are available to call. The TypeOf keyword allows you to test for the kind of object referred to by a variable. To work with the object's native interface, you will have to use a variable declared as the appropriate type. Here's a version of the CreateOrder method that includes special processing for the Premium and CashOnly object types:

```
Public Function CreateOrder (OrderCustomer As Customer) _
                             As Order
Dim cho As CashOnly
Dim prm As Premium

If TypeOf OrderCustomer Is Premium Then
    Set prm = OrderCustomer
    'Premium customer specific processing
ElseIf TypeOf OrderCustomer Is CashOnly Then
    Set cho = OrderCustomer
    'CashOnly customer specific processing
End If
End Sub
```

The TypeOf keyword can only be used in If statements and in conjunction with Object types.

OTHER INTERFACE BENEFITS

In addition to the benefits of interfaces that I've already discussed, here are some other reasons that you might find yourself wanting to use interfaces:

ORGANIZING COMPLEX OBJECTS. • If you have an object with many methods and properties, there may be no one client that will need to access them all. Instead, you may find that there are specific groups of methods and properties that are useful to particular clients. Grouping these "bundles of functionality" into interfaces can make your object easier for developers to use. In the WholesaleManagement component, a Customer object has two interfaces: one includes the methods and properties for recording sales and the other provides the methods for updating customer information.

MTS SECURITY • Microsoft Transaction Server allows you to restrict a client to using specific interfaces on an object. Since Customer object's functionality was split into two interfaces, it was possible, using MTS security, to limit access to the Customer interface methods to head office personnel without adding any code to the component.

IMPLEMENTING A COMMON INTERFACE. • In the WholesaleManagement component, there are different kinds of customer: Standard, CreditRisk, Premium, CashOnly. All of these kinds of Customershare some common functions, which other objects in the component depend upon. By implementing the Customer interface in these different Class modules, you ensure that these objects will work with any other object or application that can interact with a Customer object. The code in the CreditCheck method of the CashOnly Class module is nothing like the code in the Premium Class module, but both objects do have a CreditCheck method as part of their Customer interface. Developers find that your objects are easier to use because they are so similar.

Versioning

I've saved the most important topic for last. When you create an object and distribute it to other developers, they may well start writing clients that set your object's properties and call its methods. If you release a new version of that object that causes those clients to stop working, you can make life difficult for the people who depended on your object. At least it did for the developers who were dependent on the first component that I developed. I discovered the hard way that there were a number of changes that I could make to my components that would cause a client that used it to fail. Those changes included (but are not limited to)

- Removing a method or property
- Changing the data type of a parameter to a method or property
- Adding a new required parameter to a method or property
- Removing a parameter (of any kind) from a method or property

Any changes that you make of the type described here that cause a client to fail are said to "break the object's interface."

Changes that you can make that won't break your object's interface and cause a client to stop working include

- Adding a new method or property
- Enhancing code within a routine
- Adding a new interface
- Adding an optional parameter to a method or property
- Adding a new Class module

Some changes to your component's objects are unavoidable. You might discover a problem in a method that can only be solved by having the client program pass a new parameter to the method. In this situation you must change the component, break the object's interface, and re-issue the component, notifying developers that programs which use the component will have to be rewritten. Not making the change will leave the clients that use your object exposed to failure: they simply cannot continue using the old version of your code.

Many changes are discretionary, though. If you are adding functionality or enhancing some existing feature, you will want to issue a new version of your component that won't cause existing clients to fail.

Interfaces allow you to re-issue your object so that clients can continue to use the old functionality and ignore the new functionality. All that you need to do, when enhancing your component, is create a new interface that supports your new functionality. When you release your component, developers accessing the old interface will still be able to use your component. When a developer wants to access your enhancements, they can change the data type of their object variables and recompile their applications.

It's for this reason, managing the development of your object, that I recommend that you always create an interface Class module for every Class module that you create. In the next section, I show you how you can use interfaces to insulate your component's users from your changes.

▲ Case Study: Managing Versions

In Figure 6–7, I show a project with a single Customer Class module. It implements a method called CreditCheck. This version of the CreditCheck method requires no parameters.

The code in the client to use the Customer Class looks like this:

```
Dim cst As Customer
Set cst = New Customer cst.Id = txtCustonterld
txtCRate = cst.CreditCheck
```

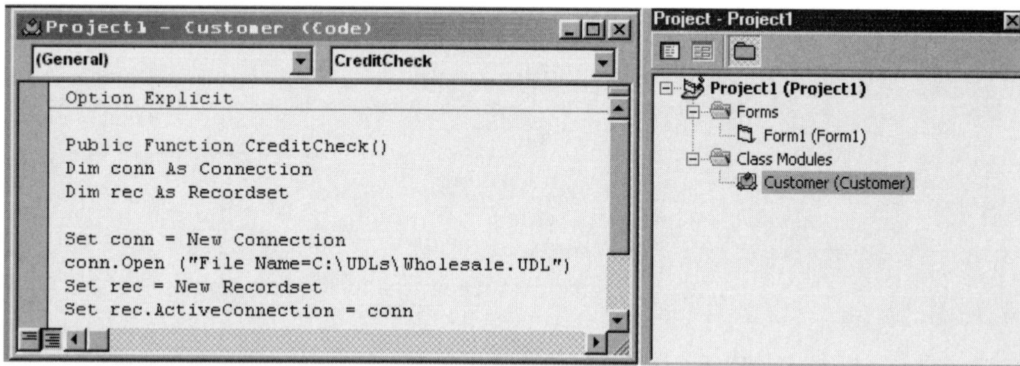

Figure 6–7 *A class implemented without interfaces.*

However, after releasing the Customer object you realize that there is a fundamental problem with the CreditCheck method. The credit checking process, as it is currently designed, not only returns the customer's credit rating but also does all the processing to determine what the customer credit rating is. This recalculation of the customer's credit rating is time consuming and, for most purchases, unnecessary. In fact, the performance of the applications that use the WholesaleManagement component is unacceptable because of how long the CreditCheck method takes to execute.

You decide to alter The CreditCheck method to accept a required parameter that indicates whether to just return the CreditRating or recalculate the rating. Using an Enumerated value, clients can use either of these two lines of code to call the CreditCheck method:

```
'calc credit rating
txtCRate = cst.CreditCheck(wblCalcCredit)

'report credit rating
txtCRate = cst.CrsditCheck(whlRptCredit)
```

Unfortunately, when users install this new version of the component on their computers, any client that calls the CreditCheck method without this required parameter abends. How could you have avoided this?

There are a couple of solutions. First, of course, you could have made the parameter optional and made one of the processing options the default value. For instance, if you don't pass a parameter, the code could assume that the whlCalcCredit was passed. The problem with this solution is that if a programmer inadvertently omits the second parameter for this method, they get the slowest possible processing. Ideally, errors of omission should either be impossible or have minimal consequences.

A better solution is possible, provided that you design the Class module with an interface module in the first place. In Figure 6–8, I show the design that I've recommended. In this version of the application, there is a Class module called ICustomer that does nothing but define the interface for all Customer-type objects. The Class module Customer contains the statement Implements ICustomer and holds code to implement the ICustomer interface.

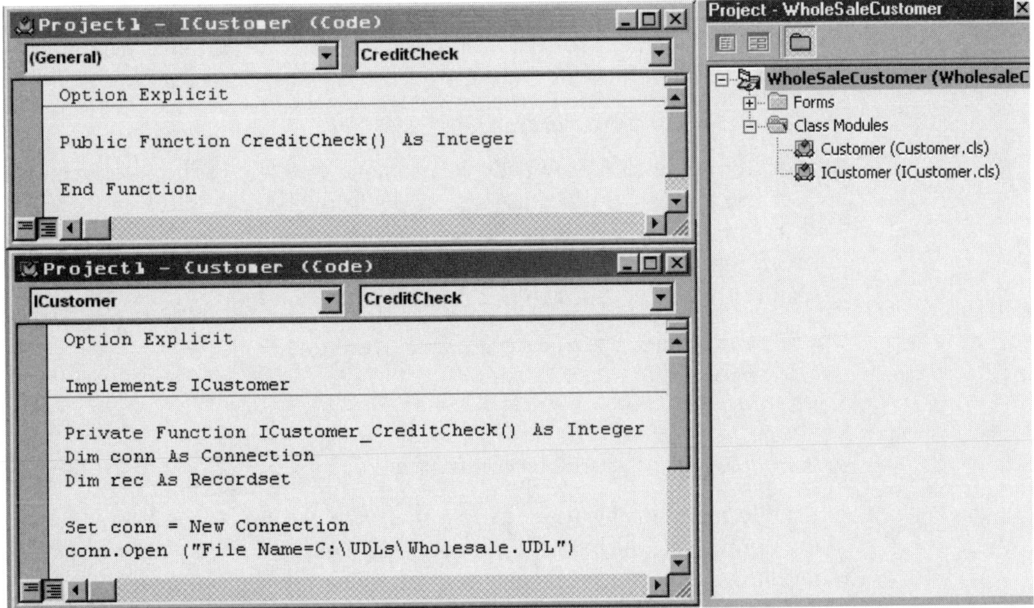

Figure 6–8 *A class implemented through an interface.*

In the version of this project that didn't use interfaces, the code in the client to use the original version of the Customer object's CreditCheck method would have looked like this:

```
Dim cst As Customer
Set cst = New Customer
cst.Id = txtCustomerld
Me.txtCRate = cst.CreditCheck
```

The code required by my recommended version would look like this:

```
Dim cst As ICustomer
Set cst = New Customer
cst.Id = txtCustomerld
txtCRate = cst.CreditCheck
```

The only thing that has changed in this version of the code is that the cst variable is declared as type ICustomer instead of Customer.

When you realize that you need to upgrade the CreditCheck method and release the new version of the Customer object you perform the following steps:

1. Add an ICustomer2 Class module which defines all of the same methods, properties, and events of the ICustomer module but replaces the old declaration of the CreditCheck method with the new version.
2. Add this statement to the Customer Class module to have it implement the ICustomer2 interface along with the existing ICustomer interface:

   ```
   Implements ICustomer2
   ```

3. Add the code to support the ICustomer2 versions of the interface. This does not mean duplicating the code from the old interface, since an ICustomer2 routine can call the appropriate ICustomer method already existing in the Class. A typical ICustomer2 routine might just contain a call to the existing ICustomer version of the routine:

   ```
   Private Sub ICustomer2_SendInvoice
   ICustomer_SendInvoice
   End Sub
   ```

4. Compile and release your component.

While many of the routines that make up the ICustomer2 interface just call the equivalent ICustomer routine, not all will do so. The code for the new CreditCheck method, for instance, is different from the version in the ICustomer interface. Thanks to interfaces, the code for the old version of CreditCheck remains available through the ICustomer interface. The new CreditCheck method is available through the ICustomer2 interface. Clients that use your program will continue to run because they will still have access to the ICustomer interface.

At some convenient time, developers can edit their clients to use the ICustomer2 interface with the enhanced version of the CreditCheck method.

The revised version of the code that switches over to use the new version of the CreditCheck method looks like this:

```
Dim cst As ICustomer2
Set cst New Customer
cst.Id = txtCustomerld
txtCRate = cst.CreditCheck(whlGetCredit)
```

In the chapter on deployment I'll discuss some of the support that Visual Basic provides to help you maintain compatibility.

Hiding Interfaces

I've found that what's left out of an interface is often as important as what's put in. Many of the components that I've developed contain elements that I don't want to expose to the clients that use it. In the same way that I use objects to build my Visual Basic applications, I use objects to build my Visual Basic components. While many of the objects in my components are designed to be used by the component's clients, some of the objects are not. These hidden objects are ones that I developed to support the processing in the visible objects in my component and I don't want my components' clients to use them.

Visual Basic offers you two alternatives for hiding parts of your component.

Hiding Methods and Properties with Friend

To begin with, it's not unusual for me to have methods or properties for some of my objects that shouldn't be available to clients using the component. In the WholesaleManagement component, the function that adjusts the quantity in stock for a product is an example of a routine that should be hidden from the component's clients.

The quantity in stock for any product can be changed for a variety of reasons, including:

- When goods are received, this method must be called to increase the quantity recorded in stock
- When goods are sold, it must be called to lower the quantity in stock
- Returned goods also cause an adjustment in the inventory amount
- When an inventory count is done, once a year, the quantity in stock frequently needs to he adjusted

Keeping an accurate track of the quantity in inventory is an important part of running a wholesale company. In the same way that a bank must keep careful track of how much money is in the vault, a wholesaling company must know how much product it has on hand.

Changing the quantity in inventory isn't a simple update, either. What should an application do, for instance, if inventory is to be removed from stock but the balance on hand is zero? What sort of logging should be done as the inventory balances are adjusted? How should record locking be handled when multiple clients attempt to update the same product's record?

Since the inventory balance can be changed for so many reasons, many objects in the WholesaleManagement component could end up having routines to change the balance on hand. Rather than have a separate routine to adjust the inventory for every different process, the WholesaleManagement component has a single SetInventory method as part of the Product object. In Figure 6–9 you can see the relationships among the objects.

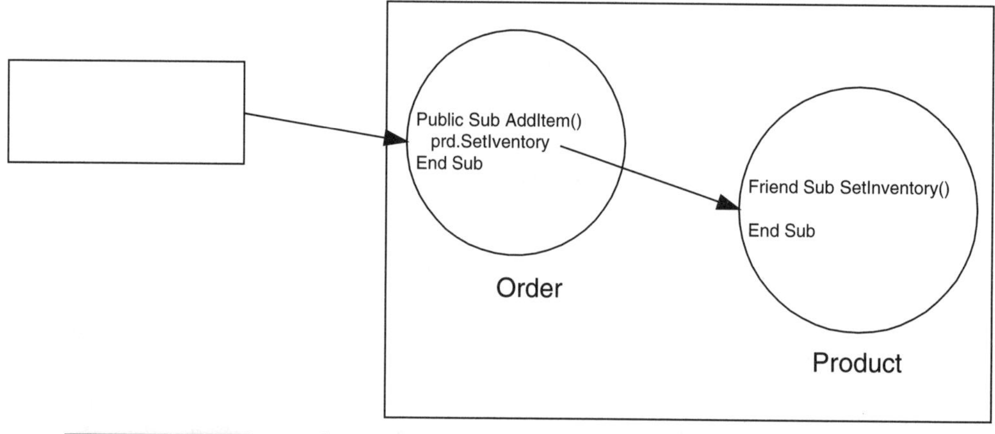

Figure 6–9 *An object with methods not visible outside of the component, but used by other objects in the component.*

Other objects in the WholesaleManagement component, after performing whatever processing they require, can call the SetInventory method to adjust the quantity in stock for a product. However, client programs that are using the component should not be able to call this method. Instead, client programs should be able to have only the inventory on hand adjusted indirectly. As part of making a sale, or instance, a client would use the AddItem method of the Order object. Adding an item to an order should result in a reduction in inventory.

In the component, then, the SetInventory method must be available to other members of the component as a method of the Product object, yet hidden from any clients using the component. If the SetInventory routine was declared as Public, it would be available as a method. However, the method would also be available to any client using the component.

Declaring the routine as Private would hide the routine from the component's clients. However, the routine can now be called only by other routines in the Product Class module, which makes it unavailable to the other objects in the component.

Declaring the routine as Public and placing it in a standard module would hide it from the component's clients, while making it available to other objects in the component. Putting the routine in a module, however, means that the code is shared among all the objects created from the component. This can make the object code difficult to write as the routine will have to keep separate the data for each object using it. Also, the code won't have access to the variables declared in the object that called it. If the routine is called frequently, one object may end up waiting to use the routine while some other object is running the procedure.

The best solution is to leave the code in the Product Class module, but to declare the method as Friend, rather than Public or Private. The declaration for the routine looks like this:

```
Friend Sub SetInventory(NewAmount As Integer)
End Sub
```

Declared like this, the SetInventory method will appear as a method of the Product object, but only to objects in the same component.

Procedures declared as Friend are ignored by the Implements statement. The Implements statement requires only you that you provide the public interface for a Class module.

Properties can also be declared with Friend, provided the property is defined through Property Procedures (you can't declare a variable with Friend). The declarations for Property Procedures made using Friend look like this:

```
Friend Property Let Inventory(Inventory As Integer)
End Property

Friend Property Get Inventory() As Integer
End Property

Friend Property Set Inventory(Inventory As IInventory)
End Property
```

By declaring a Property Get as Public and a Property Let as Friend, you can create a method that is publicly read-only but can be written by other objects in the same component.

You can get the effect of the Friend declaration for variables, User Defined Types, and enumerations by declaring them in a standard Basic module. Declaring these data items in the Basic module conceals them from clients using your component. Declaring a variable as Public in a module makes it available to all the objects in the component. UDT's and enumerated data types are Public by default.

Hiding Objects

As I said at the start of this section, as with building applications, I have found that building components by using objects is a cost effective design strategy. Of course, a component has to consist of a set of objects so that it can be used by other applications. But a component might also contain objects that aren't intended to be used by the component's clients. Instead, these objects are included in the design to make the program easier to maintain, and aren't intended for use by the component's clients.

In the WholesaleManagement component, it turns out that more than just one function was required to maintain the inventory level. Rather than continue to add Friend methods to the Product object, these routines were moved to a separate Class module called InventoryUpdate. Like the SetInventory method, this object's methods and properties must be hidden from the component's clients while still being available to the objects within the component. To hide an object from a component's client, all that is necessary is to set the object's Instancing property to Private.

User Interfaces

A component, at one extreme, may not have any user interface at all. At the other extreme, a component may have a complete user interface. DAO is an example of a component that has no user interface, while Excel and Word are examples of components with complete user interfaces. RDO (which will display a dialog requesting your password) occupies the middle area between these two extremes, popping up a simple user interface occassionally.

Standalone Components

If your application has a complete user interface, you will want to compile it as an EXE so that end users can run your component from the Windows Start menu or Windows Explorer. When you compile your program as an EXE, your code will need to distinguish between two situations:

- When your component is being loaded into to memory to be run as a standalone program
- When it is being loaded by a client to get access to the objects that make up the component

In order to check how your component is being loaded, you have to add a routine that will be run regardless of which scenario your object is being loaded in. To specify a routine to be run when the component is loaded into memory, go to the General tab of the Project | Properties menu choice. On this tab, set the Startup Object list box to Sub Main. This setting causes a subroutine called Main to be run every time your component is loaded, regardless of the cause.

With the start object set, you must now create the Main routine for your component. This routine must be in a Basic module so, if one isn't already part of your project, you must add one. Once you've added a Basic module to your component you add the Main subroutine to it (the routine can be declared either Public or Private):

```
Private Sub Main()
End Sub
```

In this routine, you can check the StartMode property of the App object to determine what caused your application to be loaded into memory. When the StartMode property is set to the enumerated constant vbSModeAutomation, your component is being loaded because a client has created one of the objects that make up your component. When StartMode equals vbSModeStandalone, the component is being run by the user from Windows as an application in its own right. Typically, when your component is being started in the standalone mode, you will want to display the initial form in your application. A typical Main subroutine looks like this:

```
Private Sub Main()
     If App.StartMode = vbSModeStandalone Then
       …display initial form
     End If
End Sub
```

Suppressing the UI

Thanks to DCOM, your component does not have to execute on the same computer as its client. Instead, the component may execute on a server on the network and be accessed remotely by the client. In this scenario, any user interface components in the component will display on the server's screen. These displays will be unavailable to your client but will cause your component to hang until someone responds to its messages. You can suppress MsgBox and InputBox UI components by selecting an option in Visual Basic.

I've found this option useful in at least two scenarios. I sometimes place InputBoxes or MsgBoxes in my component as part of the component's development process (this is especially true for components that I develop for Internet applications where debugging facilities can be primitive). I also have included InputBoxes or MsgBoxes as part of my component's user interface when the component was going to execute on the same computer as the client. However, when I move that component to a server and have it accessed over the network using DCOM, I need to suppress those same InputBoxes and MsgBoxes.

Rather than go through my application looking for all the places where these dialogs are used, I can suppress them with Visual Basic's Unattended Execution option. You can find this checkbox on the General tab of the Project | Properties menu choice. Setting this choice will cause all the output generated by InputBoxes and MsgBoxes to be routed to a log file. If you have any Forms in your project this option is disabled, and, once it has been set, you won't be able to add any Forms to your project.

Under Windows NT, all messages will be written to the Windows Application log unless you use the App object's StartLogging method. Under Windows 95/98, the entries are made to C:\Windows\VBEvents.Log, unless, again, you have used the StartLogging method. Entries for a MsgBox and an InputBox in the log file look like this:

```
InformationApplicationc:\fred.log:ThreadID:-804793,Logged:
    InputBox: Project1, InputBox prompt, returned
InformationApplicationc:\fred.log:ThreadID:-804793,Logged:
    MsgBox:  , MsgBox prompt
```

Logging

The App object also provides you with a simple way to log the activities performed by your application without using InputBoxes or MsgBoxes. The LogEvents method allows you to write text to the log file. The LogEvent method accepts two parameters: the text to be written to the log file and an integer event type.

Logging will not occur while you are running your application in the Visual Basic IDE. Logging isn't activated until you compile your program and run it outside of Visual Basic.

The following code writes the text "Checkpoint 1" to the log file with no event type:

```
App.LogEvent "Checkpoint 1"
```

Event types are really only relevant under Windows NT and should be avoided unless you intend to follow the guidelines given in the Win32 SDK. The three options are vbLogEventTypeError, vbLogEventTypeWarning, and vbLogEventTypeInformation.

Under Windows 95/98, LogEvents are written to the file "C:\Windows\VBEvents.Log" unless you override the file name by using the App object's StartLogging method. Under Windows NT, LogEvents are written to the

Windows NT Application log (see Figure 6–10) unless you override the log with a file name and set the StartLogging method's second parameter to vbLogToFile. To use the Windows NT Application log, just leave the file name parameter blank. As noted, with Unattended Execution set, MsgBox and InputBox log entries are also written to the log file set in the StartLogging method.

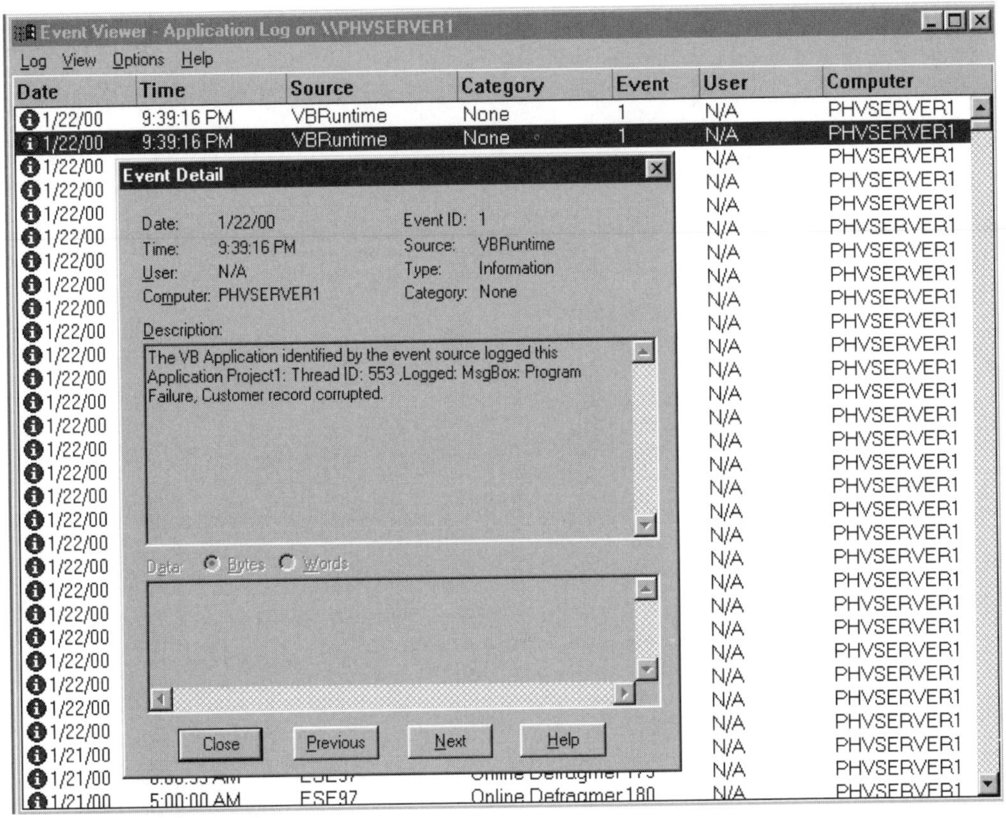

Figure 6–10 *The Windows NT Application Log showing logged Visual Basic events.*

The StartLogging method accepts two parameters, the file to write to and a flag indicating how the logging is to be done. Table 6.1 provides a list of all of the logging options. The meaning of any particular option varies, depending on whether your component is running under Windows 95/98 or Windows NT.

The documentation is confusing on the logging options, suggesting that vbLogToFile does something different than vbLogAuto if no log file is specified. However, since there doesn't seem to be any way to use StartLogging without specifying a file name, this distinction is moot.

You should avoid the vbLogToNT option unless your component will never be used under Windows 95/98.

Table 6.1 Logging Options

Constant	Windows 95/98	Windows NT	Combine With Other Options?
VbLogAuto	Logs messages to the file specified in the StartLogging method.	Logs messages to the Windows NT Application Event Log, with VBRunTime used as the application source and App.Title appearing in the description.	No
VbLogOff	Turns all logging off, including events resulting from InputBoxes and MsgBoxes	Same as Windows 95/98	No
VbLogToFile	Same as vbLogAuto	Logs messages to the file specified in the StartLogging method.	No
VbLogToNT	Causes object to abend	Same as vbLogAuto unless the event log is unavailable, when it is the same as vbLogOff.	No
VbLogOverwrite	Causes the log file to be recreated each time the application starts.	No effect unless combined with vbLogToFile.	Yes
VbLogThreadID	Causes thread ID to be added to the message, in the form [T:0nnn]. Default if the application is multithreaded	Same	Yes

This code will start logging to the file C:\MyApp.Log. For the second parameter, this command combines the auto log option with the overwrite option using an Or:

```
App.StartLogging "C:\MyApp.Log", _
    vbLogAuto Or vbLogOverWrite
```

Procedure Attributes

Once you have created your methods, properties, and events, you can set some additional properties for them using the Procedure Attributes dialog on Visual Basic's Tools menu. While most of the attributes that you can assign are relevant only to ActiveX Controls, you can use the Procedure Attributes dialog to tailor the methods, properties, and events for an object. First, a quick detour to discuss Dispatch Ids.

Dispatch Ids

When your object is compiled, all of its methods and properties are assigned a dispatch id (or dispid). When you compile a program, the calls to an object's methods are replaced with calls to specific dispids (provided that your object variable isn't declared as type Object). Some dispids are defined by specification. Whatever method or property has the dispid of 0, for instance, will act as the default property or method for the object. This means that code that refers to your object without specifying a method or property will run the code for the member that has the dispid 0. Typical examples are the Text property of a TextBox control or the Item method of a collection.

Among other features, the Procedure Attributes dialog lets you assign dispids to your methods and properties.

Basic Attributes

To use the Procedure Attributes dialog, you must have the Class module that you want to work with open. The initial format for the dialog lets you select one of the methods, properties, or events from the Class module in the Name ComboBox at the top of the form (see Figure 6–11). Only Public methods or properties will be listed. Once you select an item from the list, you can enter text in the Description TextBox or a number in the Help Context Id TextBox.

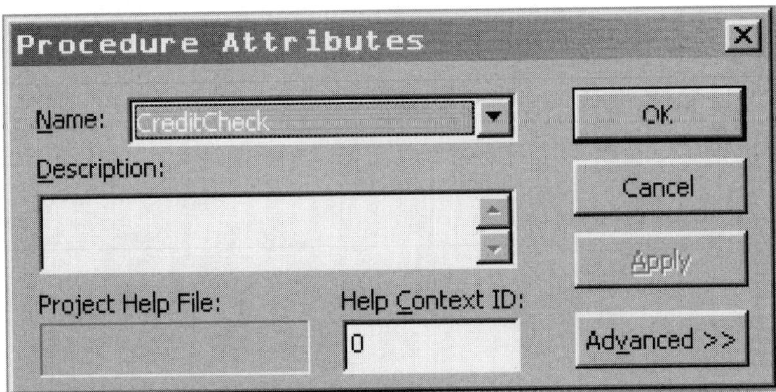

Figure 6–11 *The Basic Procedure Attributes dialog*

The text that you enter in the Description TextBox will be included in the object's type library. The Object Browser will display this text when you select the method. The number in the Help Context Id must refer to a topic in the Help file for the project (you set the Help file for the project in the General tab of the Project | Properties menu choice).

Pressing the Advanced button displays some the rest of the attributes that you can set for your object.

Advanced Attributes

The options available from the Advanced section of the Procedure Attributes dialog will vary depending on whether you are setting attributes for a method, property, or event (see Figure 6–12). For methods and events you can only set the Procedure Id and Display Attributes. Only properties make use of all of the features of the dialog.

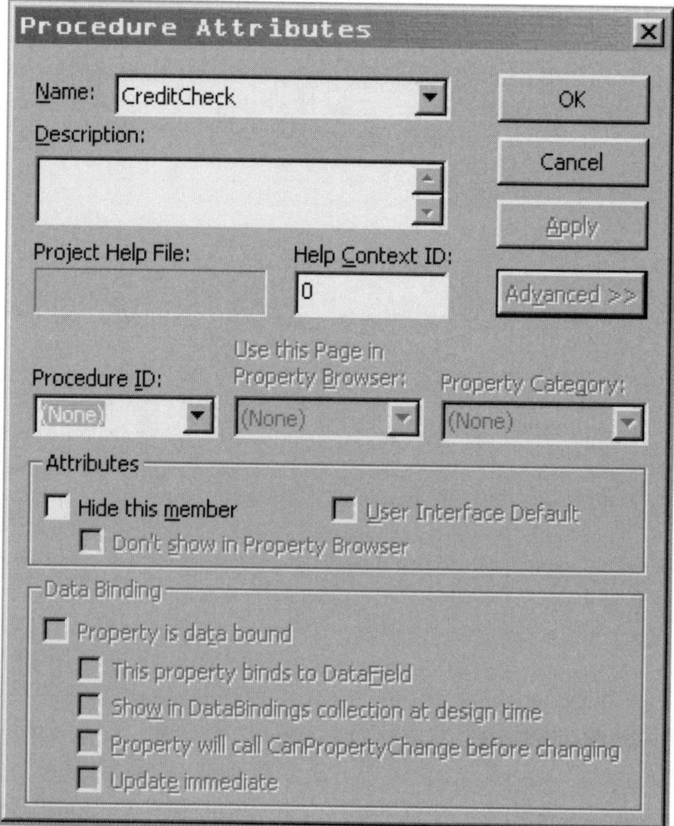

Figure 6–12 *The Advanced Procedure Attributes dialog*

The Procedure Id ComboBox lets you assign dispids to the method, property, or event that you are working with. Rather than list the numbers of the defined dispids, this ComboBox lists by name the events, properties, and methods that have these dispids. You can also enter a dispid (if you know it) instead of selecting a name from the list. As I show you in the section on creating collections, the dialog does not list the names of methods or properties that are normally hidden.

Selecting a dispid for your method, property, or event does not add any functionality to your application. Once you select a dispid, it is your responsibility to add the appropriate code to the routine to cause it to carry out the expected function. Setting a dispid, however, can change the way that clients use your object. Marking one of your routines as the default method or property causes that code to be accessed when a client uses your object without specifying a method or property.

Only one method or property can be marked as the default member.

Once you make a method or property the default property, it automatically becomes Public. Changing the routine's declaration to Friend or Private will not hide it from the clients that use the object, though it will disappear from the Procedure Attributes dialog box. If you want to hide the property or method you must set the dispid back to (None) and then change the declaration. If you have already changed the declaration to Friend or Private, you'll have to change the declaration back to Public (in order to display the property or method in the dialog) before changing the dispid to (None).

Selecting the Hide this member CheckBox on the dialog will prevent the method or property from appearing on the IntelliSense dropdown for the object. Events marked as hidden will not appear in the Event/Procedure ComboBox in the code module editor. Also, the methods, properties, and events marked as hidden will not be listed for the object in the Object Browser. IntelliSense will not list these items, either. Clients can still set hidden properties, call hidden methods, and respond to hidden events.

In general, the hidden attribute is used when you want to phase out an existing feature of your object. By hiding the method, property, or event you discourage its use in new development but continue to make it available for programs that already use the feature.

Changing the attributes for a method, property, or event will break the interface that they are part of. If you implement another class interface, you inherit the attributes for the methods and properties for that interface. Since the inherited methods and properties are declared as Private, you cannot change their attributes in the Procedure Attributes dialog.

I discuss the rest of the options on this dialog in the chapter on ActiveX Controls.

Creating a Collection Interface

Collections are an important part of many components' interfaces. I use collections frequently in my component because they provide a way for a client to process all of the available instances of an object without knowing what objects exist or how many of them there are. In DAO, for instance, I can process all the tables in a database with this code:

```
Dim tbl As TableDef
For Each tbl In dbs.TableDefs
     'process table
Next
```

By adding collections to my components, I provide the same capability to my clients.

In the WholesaleManagement object model, there are two collections available from the Company object: Orders and Products. These collections allow the client to browse all of the orders and products in the system, and to retrieve an order or customer by providing the appropriate Id to the collection. The following code would be used by a client to browse the Orders collection, looking for an order whose Overdue property is set to True. Once found, the code uses the Order's CustomerId property to retrieve the associated Customer object from the Customers collection:

```
Dim ord As Order
Dint cst As Customer

For Each ord In Order
     If ord.Overdue Then
       Set cst = Customers(ord.CustomerId)
     End If
Next
```

Defining A Simple Collection

If all that the component provides is the ability to extract an object from a collection, you can simulate some of the functions of a collection by adding a single property to the object that owns the collection. In the WholesaleManagement component, the Orders property of the Company object allows clients to select Orders in the system much like a true collection. To create a property that mimics a collection, you define the Property Procedure routines so that they accept an index along with whatever value the property is to be set to.

The following code shows a typical collection in use. The code requests the second item in the collection by passing an index ("2") to the property. The object that is returned then has its DeliveryDate property updated:

```
Company.Orders(2).DeliveryDate = txtDate
```

Since the Company object in the WholesaleManagement component is a Global object, it doesn't have to be referenced in the code, so I'll omit it for the rest of the examples in this chapter to simplify the examples.

To create a property that accepts an index and a value, you define the property with two parameters for the Property Let or Set, and one parameter for the Property Get. Here are the declarations for the Company object's Orders property:

```
Public Property Let Orders(index As Variant, _
    Order As IOrder)
End Property

Public Property Set Orders(index As Variant, _
    Order As IOrder)
End Property

Public Property Get Orders(index As Variant) As IOrder
End Property
```

In these routines, the index parameter is declared as a Variant so that it can accept both numeric and string values. This matches the features of a standard collection, which allows you to request items from the collection, using either numerics or strings. When the client passes a number as the index to a collection, the routine must return the object in that position in the collection (passing in the number 2 returns the second member in the collection). If the client passes in a string, the member of the collection with that name is returned (in the Orders collection, passing in an Order Id retrieves the corresponding order).

LOADING THE COLLECTION

Before the client can request a member of the collection, the collection must be loaded with objects. There are two strategies that you can follow when adding a collection. The first method is to create all the objects that the collection is to hold when the component starts. The second strategy creates the objects only as they are needed.

I'll begin by looking at the code used when the collection's objects are created when the component is started. Typically, this is done in the Initialize event of the object that owns the collection. This code, for instance, creates an Order object for every record in the SalesOrder table and adds it to a Private collection object in the Company module (I could also have declared m_Orders using Visual Basic 6's new Dictionary object instead of a Collection):

```
Dim m_Orders As Collection

Private Sub Class Initialize()
Dim rec An Recordset
Dim ord As Order

Set m_Orders = New Collection
Set rec = New Recordset
rec.Open("DSN=Wholesale;", "Select OrderId From Orders;")

Do Until rec.EOF
    Set ord = New Order
    ord.Id = rec("OrderId")
    m_Orders.Add ord, rec("OrderId")
    rec.MoveNext
Loop

rec.Close
Set rec = Nothing
End Sub
```

The routine begins by creating the m_Order collection object which will be used inside the Company object to hold all the Order objects. The m_Order collection is declared as a module level variable so that the collection is available to the other routines in the module.

After the collection is created, the routine reads all of the records from the Orders table and creates an Order object for each one. Setting the Order object's Id property to the OrderId field from the recordset causes the code in the Order object to retrieve the data for that order. With the Order object created and initialized, a reference to it is added to the m_Order collection. The OrderId for the Order is used as the name for the item in the collection.

RETURNING A COLLECTION

With the collection created and loaded, the Orders property of the Company object could just return the m_Order collection to the client:

```
Public Property Get Orders() As Collection
    Set Orders = m_Orders
End Sub
```

In fact, the m_Order collection could just be declared as a Public variable in the Company Class module. Clients using the component would then have direct access to the collection and be able to perform all the standard activities on the Orders collection object returned by this routine. This would include using the Collection object's Add, Remove, and Count functionality.

The following is the code the client might use to retrieve the collection from the Company object and display the number of objects that it contains:

```
Dim ors As Collection
Set ors = Company.Orders
MsgBox ors.Count
```

The problem with this technique is that it allows the client to add objects other than Order objects to the collection. You also give up the ability to track when objects are added and removed from the collection and to take action when they are.

MANAGING THE COLLECTION

Establishing a set of Properties to manage the collection allows you to control how objects are retrieved and updated in the collection. The following Properties in the Company object allow the user to retrieve and update members of the m_Order collection, and would provide a framework for adding code to control the process.

The Get procedure returns the item in the collection specified by the index. This routine may be the only procedure that you need if all that is required is read-only access to the objects in the collection:

```
Public Property Get Orders(Index As Variant) As IOrder
    Set Order = m_Orders(Index)
End Property
```

The following Set procedure allows the client to add new items or replace items in the collection by number. When the index passed to the Set is one greater then the number of items in the collection, an item is added to the end of the collection. If the index is greater than the number of items in the collection, an error 381 ("Invalid property array index") is raised. If the index matches an existing item in the collection, the new object replaces the old object. Replacing an object is a three-step process: The object is added before the order currently in that position in the collection, the Delete method for the item to be replaced is called to perform any database activity, and then the item is removed from the collection:

```
Public Property Set Orders(Index As Integer, _
                        OrderItem As IOrder)
    If m_Orders.Count = Index - 1 Then
        m_Orders.Add OrderItem, Order.Id
    ElseIf m_Orders.Count < Index Then
      Err.Raise 381
    Else
        m_Orders.Add OrderItem, Order.Id, index
        m_Orders(Index + 1).Delete
        m_Orders.Remove Index + 1
    End If
End Property
```

If you do allow updates to the collection, you will also need to provide the client with a read-only Property that returns the number of items in the collection so that clients can find out where the end of the collection is:

```
Public Property Get OrderCount() As Integer
    OrderCount = m_Orders.Count
End Property
```

If you allow the client to add to the collection, you will probably also want to provide a method that, passed an index to the collection, removes an item from it:

```
Public Sub OrderRemove(Index As Integer)
    m_Orders.Remove Index
End Sub
```

To simplify adding objects to the end of the collection, you could make the index parameter to the Property Set method optional and, when it is omitted, always add the object to the end of the collection. In this case you will also need to either make the OrderItem parameter optional (since an optional parameter can't be followed by a required parameter) or reverse the order of the parameters so that the index parameter is the second parameter. Alternatively, you could provide an Add method to add items to the end of the collection and allow deletes but not replacements of existing members.

As you can see, things get more complicated if you want to give the client the ability to add and remove objects from the collection. At this point, the appropriate strategy is to add a complete collection object to your component.

A Complete Collection

To create a complete implementation of a collection you'll have to add another object to your component. The WholesaleManagement component includes an Orders object that has Add, Remove, and Item methods, plus a Count property just like the Collection object. The Company object still owns the collection and must create it as part of its Initialize event and destroy it in the Terminate event. Figure 6–13 shows the relationships among the various objects.

The Company object's Initialize event contains the code to load the collection that used to be in the Company object:

```
Dim m_Order As Orders
Private Sub Initialize()
    Set m_Order = New Orders
End Sub

Private Sub Terminate()
    Set m_Order = Nothing
End Property
```

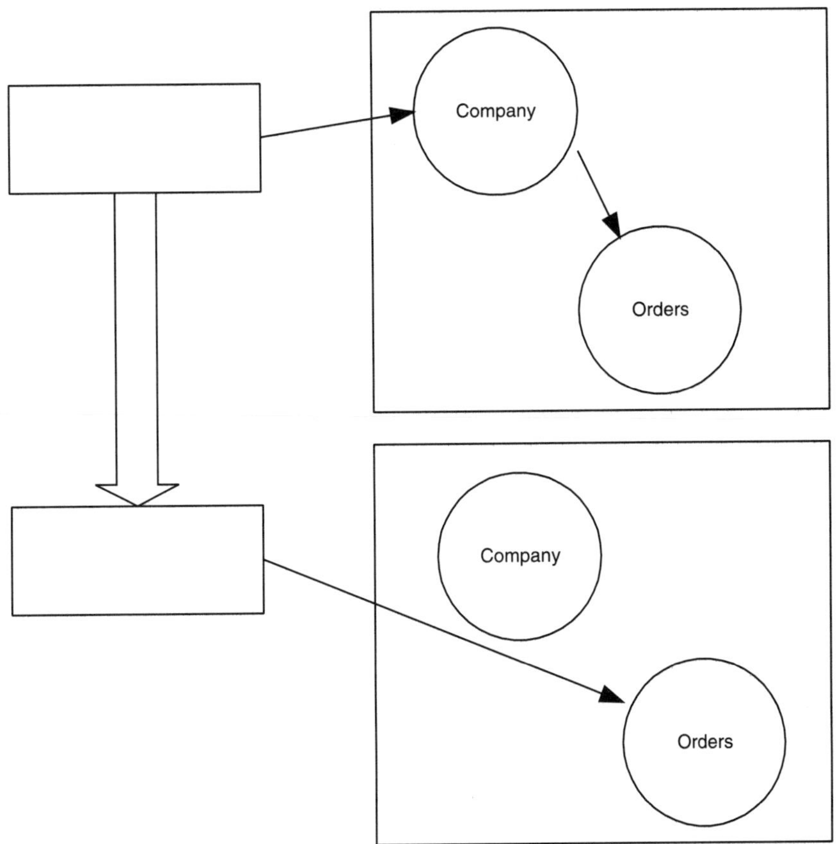

Figure 6–13 *A client accesses the Company object to retrieve the Orders object. The client can then access the Orders object directly.*

The Company object's Orders property now returns its internal Orders object to the client:

```
Public Property Get Orders() As Orders
    Set Orders = m_Order
End Property
```

Once in the client's hands, the Orders object, in order to mimic a collection, will need an Item, Add, Remove, and Count routines. For the first version of the Orders object I show the code that uses a collection object internal to the Orders object to hold the Order objects that it manages. To begin with, the Orders object's Initialize and Terminate events will create and destroy this internal collection:

```
Dim m_coll As Collection
Private Sub Class_Initialize()
Set m_coll = New Collection
End Sub

Private Sub Class_Terminate()
Set m_coll = Nothing
End Sub
```

The Initialize event of the Orders object would also contain the code to read all the records from the database, create an object for each record and add them to the m_coll collection (as shown earlier in this chapter). With the collection created, the Orders object must now have the methods to mimic the collection object's Item, Get, Add, and Remove members. Since this version of the Orders object uses a collection internally, all that's necessary in this version is to call the equivalent method of the internal collection:

```
Public Function Item(ByVal Index As Variant)
    Set Item = m_coll(Index)
End Function
Public Property Get Count() As Integer
    Count = m_coll.Count
End Property
Public Sub Add (OrderIn As Order)
    m_coll.Add OrderIn
End Sub
Public Sub Remove(ByVal Index As Variant)
    m_coll.Remove Index
End Sub
```

The Index parameter in these routines uses ByVal to mimic the declaration of the index parameter of the collection object. The Item method should be set as the default method for the object.

ENUMERATING A COLLECTION

Most collections can be used in a For Each...Next structure which allows you to retrieve each member of a collection. The process of working through all the members of a collection is referred to as enumerating the collection (not to be confused with enumerated data types or iterating through an array). The For statement in the For Each...Next structure takes an object variable and the name of a collection:

```
For Each variablename In collectioname
```

The For statement sets the object variable to refer to each item in the collection in turn. The body of the For Each...Next structure normally contains code that works with the methods and properties available through the object variable. This code, for instance, does a recalculating credit check on every object in the Customers collection:

```
Dim cst As Customer
For Each cst In Customers
    cst.CreditCheck whlRecalcCredit
Next
```

In order for your collection object to participate in a For Each statement, the object must have a method that returns the next object in the collection. The method must be defined as a function that returns a reference. In order to identify the function as the one to call in the For Each statement, you must give the method a dispid of –4 in the Procedure Attributes dialogue.

The standard is to call this method NewEnum though it's the dispid that actually identifies the procedure to the For Each...Next structure. In addition, this method is normally set as hidden.

An enumeration routine for the Orders collection that uses a Collection internally is simple to write—you just delegate the method to the internal collection's NewEnum method. The Visual Basic collection's enumeration method's name begins with an underscore, a standard for hidden methods. Because of that leading underscore, when calling the method you must enclose the name in brackets to prevent syntax errors. The resulting routine looks like this:

```
Public Function NewEnum() As IUnknown
Dim unk As IUnknown
    Set unk = m_coll.[_NewEnum]
    Set NewEnum = unk
End Function
```

A Large Collection: Simple Version

The strategy of loading all the objects in the internal collection makes sense only if the number of objects in the collection is small: typically less than a dozen. If the number of objects in the collection is large, the resources that must be devoted to the collection and the time it takes to load the collection will make the object awkward to use. When the number of objects in the collection is large, it's better to create each object as it is requested. To handle those situations, I developed the routines that I show you in this section.

In the next version of implementing a collection, I assume that the number of orders is so large that creating all of the objects in the Initialize event would be too time consuming. Instead of an internal collection to hold all the Order objects, an internal Recordset is used. The Recordset is declared at the module level, so that it is available to every procedure in the module. The Recordset is retrieved in the Initialize event (and destroyed in the object'sTerminate event).

```
Dim rec As Recordset

Private Sub Class_Initialize()
Set rec = New Recordset
rec.CursorType = adOpenStatic
rec.LockType = adLockOptimistic
rec.Open "Select Orderld From Orders;", "DSN=Wholesale;"
End Sub

Private Sub Class_Terminate()
rec.Close
Set rec = Nothing
End Sub
```

Remember that if all that the component needs is the ability to retrieve an object from the collection, then all you need to write is a Get Property Procedure that returns a member of the collection.

In the WholesaleManagement component, the Company object could have an Orders property that would return the next Order object. In this scenario, the Orders Get Property Procedure uses the index passed to it to find a record in the internal Recordset. The following code demonstrates that technique.

The routine uses Visual Basic's VarType function to determine the datatype of the index passed to the routine. The VarType function accepts a Variant type variable holding data in one of the basic data types (string, boolean, etc.) and returns a value indicating the data type. If the index is a string value, the Recordset's Find method is used to locate the matching record in the Recordset. If the index is numeric, the routine uses the Recordset's AbsolutePosition property to move to the requested position in the Recordset.

```
Public Property Get Orders(Index As Variant) As Order
Dim ord As Order
If VarType(Index) = vbString Then
    rec.Find "OrderId = '" & Index & "'"
    If rec.NoMatch Then
      Err.Raise 381
    End If
Else
    If Index > rec.RecordCount Then
      Err.Raise 381
```

```
        End If
    rec.AbsolutePosition = Index
    End If

    Set ord = New Order
    ord.Id = rec("OrderId")

    Set Orders = ord
    End Property
```

Once the appropriate record is found, an Order object is created, initialized with the data in the record by setting its Id property to the records OrderId field, and the object returned to the client.

Using a Recordset to implement the collection means that the collection will reflect the status of the data in the database. As a result, the objects available through the Orders collection will be affected by updates performed against the database by other users. What the effect will be will be depends on the kind of Recordset used.

If a Static Recordset is used (as in the preceding example), changes to the data in the database will not be reflected in the Recordset. Clients will find that accessing the collection by index number will be reliable: If the client repeatedly asks for the second record in the collection, the same record will be returned each time. However, updates to a record in the Recordset may fail if the record has been updated in the database by another user (though this will depend on what record locking scheme is being used).

If a Dynamic record set is used, then the data will reflect the current state of the data in the database. However, accessing records with a numeric index may not be reliable because records deleted or added by other users will cause the records in the Recordset to be reordered.

A Large Collection: Complete Version

If more than the ability to retrieve an Order is required, then the component will have to include a collection object of your own design. This is the strategy used in the Wholesale Management component (see Figure 6–14).

The code required in the Orders object when a Recordset is used to implement the collection is different from the code required when an internal collection is used. The Count property is relatively easy to implement, since it just returns the Recordset's RecordCount property:

```
Public Property Get Count() As Integer
    Count = rec.RecordCount
End Property
```

The code for the Item method must find the record specified by the index, create an object for it, and then return the object to the client:

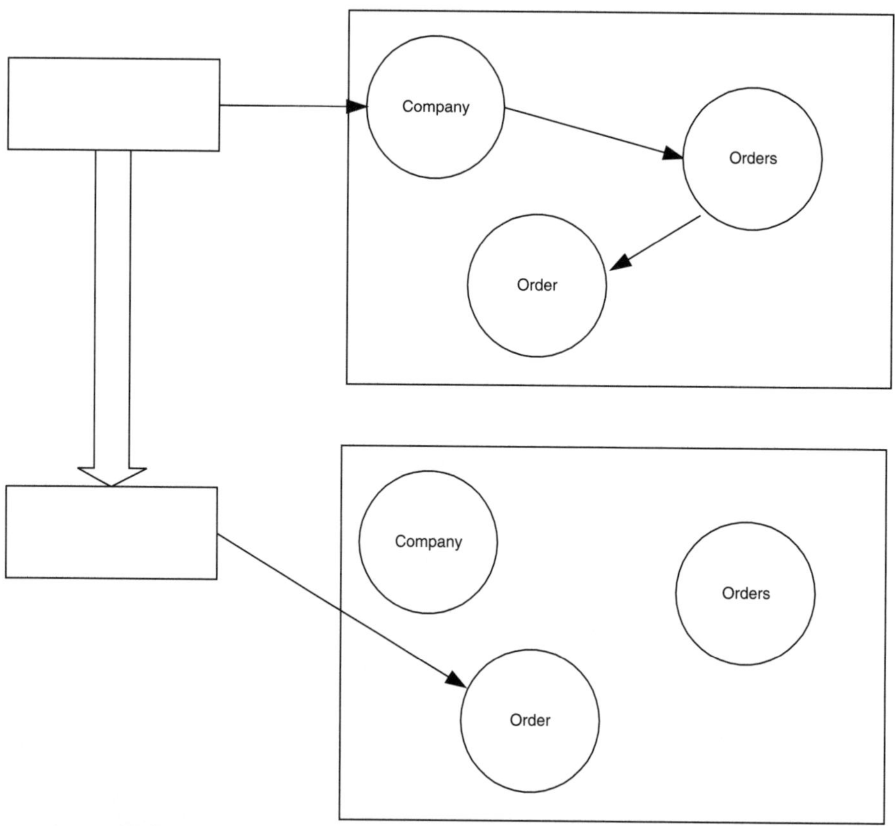

Figure 6–14 *A client accessing the Orders object through the Company object to retrieve an Order object.*

```
Public Function Item(index As Variant)
Dim ord As Order
If VarType(index) = vbString Then
    rec.Find "OrderId = '" & index & "'"
    If rec.EOF Then
      Err.Raise 381
    End If
Else
    If index > rec.RecordCount Then
      Err.Raise 381
    End If
    rec.AbsolutePosition = index
End If
Set ord = New Order
ord.Id = rec("Orderld")
Set Item = ord
End Function
```

The Add procedure can be simple, if you assume that creating an Order object adds a new record to the system, as is the case in the WholesaleManagement component (the CreateOrder method of the Product object is used to add new orders). If not, the Add method of your collection will have to include whatever code is required to create a new record in the database. In the WholesaleManagement component, the Add method just requeries the Recordset in order to ensure that it includes the newly added order:

```
Public Sub Add(OrderIn As Order)
    rec.Requery
End Sub
```

For the Remove method, the bulk of the work is delegated to the Order object. The Orders object's Remove method first finds the appropriate record, then creates an Order object for it, and finally calls the object's Delete method. The Recordset must also be requeried to reflect the changes in the database:

```
Public Sub Remove(Index As Variant)
Dim ord As Order
If VarType(Index) = vbString Then
    rec.Find "Orderld = '" & Index & "'"
Else
    rec.AbsolutePosition = Index
End If

Set ord = New Order
ord.Id = rec(″Orderld″)
ord.Delete
Set ord = Nothing
rec.Requery
End Sub
```

It's not possible to implement the For Each...Next structure for the collection object when a Recordset is used. The For Each...Next structure calls the NewEnum method only once, when the For Each loop first starts. At that point, the For Each structure retrieves the number of objects in the collection (ignoring any objects added in the NewEnum method). So, unless you have a collection with as many objects in it as there are records in the Recordset, the For Each...Next structure won't work (and if you had a collection with that many objects, it would defeat the purpose of using the Recordset).

▲ Case Study: Callbacks

Events provide a way for objects to communicate with clients. However, events are a relatively inefficient way to communicate with another program. One way to look at events is that events are the object's way of calling a method of the client. In this view, the client's event procedure is a method that it exposes for components to execute. Since the client doesn't have a type library, and the component wouldn't have access to it at compile time anyway, every RaiseEvent is really a late bound call to a method on the client. As with any late bound call, there are a lot of inefficiencies built into the process of locating the client's routine, validating it, and executing it. An alternative to Events is to use a callback object. Creating a callback involves more cooperation between the client and the component than using an event does. However, callbacks do provide an example of how useful the techniques that I've discussed in this chapter can be.

A callback is an object created by the client from a Class module in the client project. The client then passes a reference to the callback object to the component (see Figure 6–15). Once it accepts a reference to the callback object, the component can call the methods or set and read the properties of the callback object. Since the callback object's Class module exists in the client program, the callback object's code can call routines in the client program and access Public variables in the client. The result is that the component, by using the callback object given to it by the client, can communicate with the client.

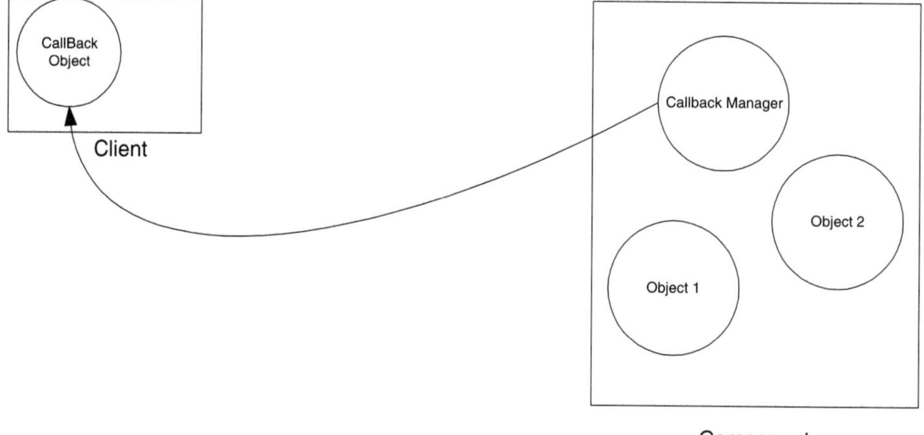

Figure 6–15 *A callback object is passed by the client to the component for the component to use to communicate with the client.*

For the callback object to be useful, though, it must meet the communication needs of the component, not the client. In the same way that the component defines the events that it fires, the component must define the callback object that it will use. To ensure that the callback object exposes the methods and properties that the component requires, the component contains the definition of the component. The component defines the callback object that it needs by including an interface module with the routines for the methods and properties of the callback object. A client that wants to use the callback object to receive messages from the component must implement a Class module with the interface defined by the component.

From a design point of view, you would say that using a callback object causes the client and the component to be "closely coupled"—they both have to know a great deal about each other in order to work together. Using events leaves the client and the component "loosely coupled." In general, the more closely coupled two items must be, then the more expensive it is to maintain them. Your costs go up because the more closely coupled a component is with its clients, the more likely it is that a change to the component will require a change to all of its clients.

The component must also have an object that can accept the callback object when the client passes it to the component. At runtime, the client will create an instance of the callback object and pass the object either to a property of the component or as a parameter to a method or event. The component can then call the methods and properties of the callback object to communicate with the client.

The simplest possible callback object contains a single method that allows the object to pass a variant to the client. The callback object's definition in the component would look like this (I've assumed that the Class module containing this code is called ICallback):

```
Public Sub Message (msg As Variant)
End Sub
```

The simplest mechanism to pass the callback object to the component is for one of the objects in the component to have a property that accepts a Callback object. A Public variable of type ICallBack meets the need nicely.

Now that the component has an object that can accept a reference to the Callback object, the other objects in the component need some way to make use of the Callback object. Again, the simplest possible version is to add a method to the object that accepts the callback and, in the routine, invoke the Message method of the callback object received from the client. Since the method will be used only by other objects in the component, it should be declared as Friend. It might be tempting to set the Instancing property of the object that accepts the Callback reference to Private, but that won't work. Since the client needs to see the object that accepts the callback, the object can't be declared Private.

Here's the code for the object in the component that receives the CallBack object and provides a method for calling the Callback object's Message method (I'll assume the code is in a Class module called CallManager):

```
Public clb As ICallback

Friend Sub SendMessage(strMessage As String)
    clb.Message strMessage
End Sub
```

In the client, the developer will have to add a Class module that implements the ICallback interface. The Class module will then have to implement the Message method:

```
Implements ICallBack
Private Sub ICallBack_Message(msg As Variant)
MsgBox.msg
End Sub
```

At runtime, the client will need to create the callback object and pass it to the component by setting the clb property of the appropriate object in the component. Assuming that the component is called Component, the code in the client to pass the callback object would look like this:

```
Dim ccl As Component.CallManager
Dim ccb As ICallBack

Set ccl = New Component.CallManager
Set ccb = New ClientCallback
Set ccl.clb = ccb
```

Now, when the object's SendMessage method is called by another object in the component, the Message method in the callback object created by the Client will be run. In this case, all that happens is that the message that is passed to the callback object is displayed, but you could add any code that you wanted.

Summary

This chapter reviewed the techniques that you can use to tailor the interface for your component. You saw how you can implement multiple interfaces in a single Class module and design the interface of your component so that you can enhance it over time. You also saw how to hide methods, properties, and events (or even whole Classes) from the clients using your component.

In addition to looking at how your component interacts with clients, this chapter gave you the tools to tailor the way that your component interacts with Windows, the Object Browser, and the end user. These tools included using the Procedure Attributes dialog, defining collections, and allowing your component to run as a standalone program.

At this point, you should consider going back to some of the earlier components that you have designed. You may well find that there is some functionality in the component that shouldn't be available to the client. The design of your component may lead you to define objects that are Private to the component. You may also have objects that should have some of their methods declared as Friend. The most important change that you should make is to create a set of interface classes that will allow you to upgrade your component without disrupting your component's users.

With your component ready for production, you now have to start thinking about how you are going to deploy it. In the next chapter I'll look at those issues. Some of the decisions that you will make in compiling your component will have a significant impact on its client's performance, for instance.

When it comes to discussing interfaces, nobody does it better than Deborah Kurata in *Doing Objects in Microsoft Visual Basic 6* from Sams Press.

Also, now that you know how to create objects, you'll want to know how you deliver those objects to the developers that will use them. In the next chapter, I look at the tools that come with Visual Basic that allow you to deploy your components. I also discuss some of the performance issues involved in working with components. You'll also learn about Visual Component Manager, a tool provided by Microsoft to help you manage and re-use the code that you develop for your applications.

S E V E N

Deploying

This chapter goes into the issues that raise their ugly heads after you've designed your component and started looking ahead to releasing it into the world. For instance, now you're going to have to think about ensuring that your component has the appropriate performance for the environment that it's going to execute in.

In this chapter I look at the efficiency issues that are important to component development (along with a discussion of "efficiency" in general). This includes a discussion of in-process and out-of-process components, which wraps up the criteria on deciding between creating an ActiveX DLL or an ActiveX EXE. As you move toward deployment, I show you how to manage the internal names that identify your component to other programs and the strategies that you can follow in issuing new releases. The chapter wraps up by looking at some of the tools that Microsoft provides to help support reusing your perfected components, and at the deployment process itself.

Performance Matters

Throughout this book I've emphasized the importance of getting your design right. If the structure of your component is correct, maintaining and enhancing it will be easy. If the interface for your component matches the needs of the developers who will be using it, your component will be easy to develop with.

I've seen more bugs introduced because of a misguided attempt to improve performance than almost any other cause. To quote Kernighan and Plauger in *The Elements of Programming Style* (McGraw-Hill) "If a program doesn't work, it doesn't matter how fast it runs."

One of my favorite examples of misguided efficiency is a program that did a search on a sorted array that contained, at most, 100 items. The search found the item in the middle of the range, then checked to see if the search item was greater or lesser than the array item. If the search item was less, the code calculated the mid-point between the start of the array and the item just checked, and compared that array item to the search item. This is a standard binary search and is guaranteed to find the search item in a 100 position array in seven tries.

The programmer had "enhanced" the routine to not only compare the search item to the mid-point in the range, but also to the array items on either side of the mid-point. If the search item was in one of these two positions, the search could be abandoned at that point.

I thought about this for awhile. With a binary search, worst case scenario, the code was going to access the array seven times. With the additional checks against the item on either side of the mid-point, the programmer had added fourteen more accesses into the array. Effectively, then, I could expect the routine to take three times longer unless one of those extra checks found the search item. The programmer had added fourteen more checks, so the odds of getting an early hit were 100/14, or one chance in seven. And that includes getting a hit on the last access into the array when there would be little or no time left to be saved. So to save between one and six accesses to the array the programmer added fourteen accesses compared to the original version.

I assume that this enhancement had been made before the program was run because, while the program was too slow, this code didn't really make any difference to the application's performance. The performance of the program was actually controlled by another routine that sorted two thousand items in an array. The code sorted the data by taking the last item in the array and reading through the array until it found the first item greater than the selected item. The routine then moved every subsequent item in the array down one, and inserted the new item. The code then repeated this process until a pass through the array found no items to move. Not only would a simple bubble sort have cut the run time of this routine by an order of magnitude, it turned out that writing the data out to disk, calling a standard sort routine, and reading the data back in took half the time. Had the programmer run the application before enhancing it, he would have noticed where the real bottleneck was and made the enhancements there.

Having said all that, practical considerations around the performance of your component are important. No matter how elegant your design is, if your code takes too long to perform typical tasks, your component will not be used. The techniques that are recommended for speeding up Visual Basic programs, in general, apply here also. In this section I restrict myself to discussing those techniques that apply to ActiveX components.

Performance Costs

You'll often run across recommendations to improve the performance of your component by using API calls or building your own string functions. It's often easy to lose track of what costs and benefits are actually associated with any technique that is supposed to speed up your application. Many speed enhancements come at a cost that may not offset the performance gains that they supply. Remember that API calls make it more likely that your application will abend, that using your own string handling functions allow you to add new bugs to your program, and that clever code is harder to read, maintain, and enhance.

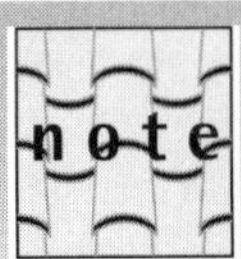

It has been estimated that for each dollar spent in development, you can expect to spend six dollars in maintenance. That estimate was made at a time when the estimated life span of a computer application was six years. The Year 2000 crisis has suggested that computer systems last considerably longer than that. In 1997, for instance, I was invited back to work on a Y2K project for a system that I had worked on in 1984 and which is still running today.

Maintenance is not just bug fixes. Maintenance tasks can be classified as follows:

SUPPORT: • This category includes regularly performed activities that are required to keep the system running. Also in this category is handling requests like: Can you explain how this work?, Can you re-run this report for me?, We're thinking of enhancing this application... . It's estimated that these kinds of activities take 25% of the time spent on maintenance.

ADAPTIVE CHANGES: • These are changes required by changes in the way that the company does business. Typical activities in this area range from updating reports to reflect a new company name to major revisions based on new tax laws. You can assume that 20% of your maintenance time is spent on these activities.

BUG FIXES: • These are changes to programs to get them to perform as specified, estimated at 15% or less of maintenance time spent.

ENHANCEMENTS: • This is the only category where the tasks are optional, but it is also the category that has the greatest chance of delivering real value to an application's users. In most shops these tasks absorb 40% of the maintenance budget.

As Figure 7–1 shows, if you work out the total cost of ownership over the lifetime of an application, the resulting percentages are (listed in order of percentage of dollars spent):

Enhancements: 33%
Support: 20%
Development: 16%
Adaptive changes: 17%
Bug fixes: 13%

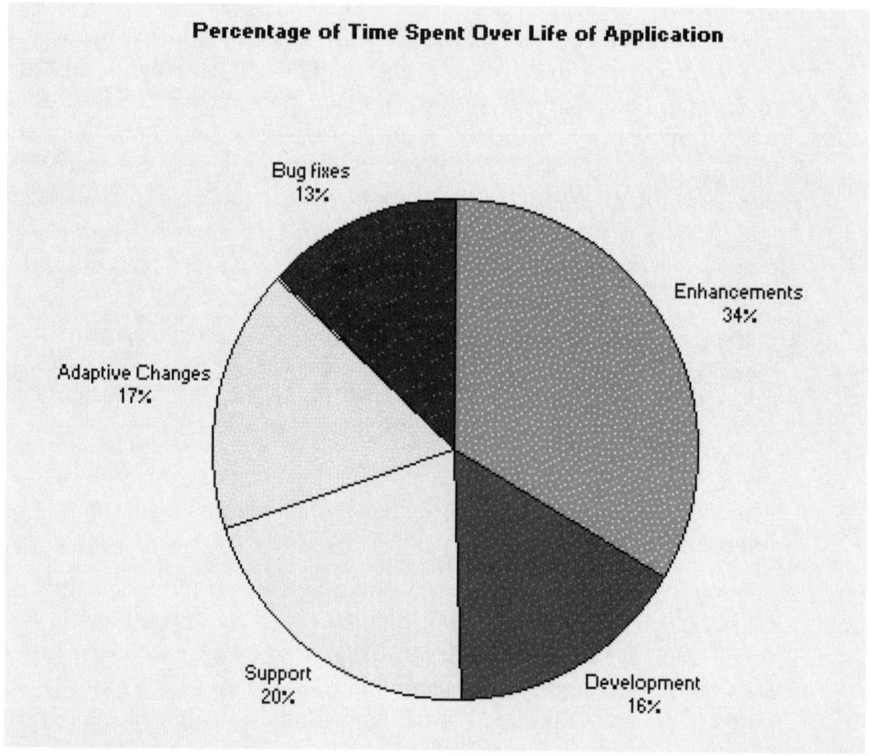

Figure 7–1 *Dollars/Time spent over an application's life.*

Given those numbers, your focus should always be on practices that lower the cost of maintaining your program. Your focus should always be on how you can reduce the need for support, make changes easier, and, yes, reduce the chances for bugs.

What's my point? Any change you make purely to improve performance should be balanced against the costs that will be incurred over the life of the application. If you are not making a significant improvement in response time (i.e., one that will be noticed by your users), the change is probably not worth making.

My second point is that these enhancements frequently don't give you much improvement, anyway. Typically, the sample code that comes with these recommendations executes a single function thousands of times to save a quarter of a second. It's unlikely that a typical client will call one of your objects' methods thousands of times between the time that the user presses the Enter key and the application's form is redisplayed.

The one exception where small gains in performance may be worth making is when a component is executing on a shared resource. This occurs when a component is placed on a server and accessed by many users, either on a network or over the Internet. In these situations, a millisecond saved here and there can add up to significant savings. Even here, the benefits only occur when many users are sharing the resource simultaneously and the server is operating at capacity. Given the cost of extra processors and memory, you may be better advised to upgrade your server than to incur the costs of creating an application that will be difficult and expensive to maintain.

Improving Performance

In the following discussion, I use the general concept of "expense" when discussing the kinds of changes that you make to improve your component's performance. I will say that one technique is more "expensive" than another if it takes longer to execute or, occasionally, if it uses more of some fixed resource (typically, random access memory). How much more expensive one technique is over another will vary from one computer system to another—on a very fast computer with a lot of free physical memory the difference between two techniques might turn out to be milliseconds. In this section I make recommendations about what you can do to make your component "cheaper" to use.

Throughout this book, I've provided benchmarks that compared different examples of code by discussing how many milliseconds it takes to execute the operation 1000 times. How relevant those examples are to your case is up to you decide. How valuable the difference is also up to you. A technique that takes hours to implement, makes your application more expensive to maintain, and saves you only a few milliseconds is probably not worth following up. It's not worthwhile to spend time implementing enhancements that provide a performance gain that your users won't notice.

The only sure way to get a significant improvement in the performance of any application is to reduce the application's reads and writes to the hard disk. Effective ways of reducing your costs are using SQL (as opposed to record-by-record processing) and calling stored procedures. Redefining your design to reduce data accesses will improve performance more than any other suggestion in this chapter.

TALKING TO OBJECTS

For components, the best thing that you can do is to reduce the number of calls that an application makes to the methods and properties of an object (see Figure 7–2). In general, clients will have the lowest costs when they can perform the maximum work with the minimum calls. In fact, if a client is going to call your object over a network using DCOM, then minimizing the number of calls to your component isn't just "icing on the cake," it's essential. With current network technology, each call to an object executing on a remote server can add seconds to your application's response time.

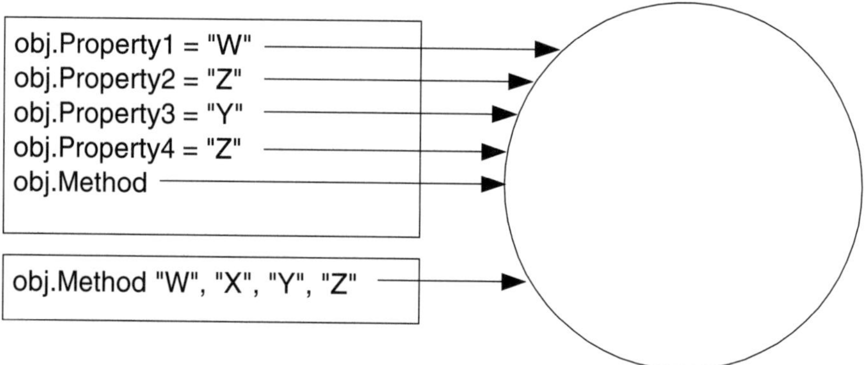

Figure 7–2 *Using parameters and properties with a method.*

This isn't purely a performance issue, either. Ideally, the interface for your application should be designed so that simple tasks can be done simply. I designed one object that required setting four or five properties and then calling a method to perform a single, frequently performed task. Not only did this slow down every application that used the object, it was also a pain in the keyboard for the developers using the object (who I heard from).

Where information must be provided to perform an activity, it's cheaper to allow the developer to pass that information as parameters to the method. Supplying multiple parameters to a method isn't a problem for programmers if you give your parameters meaningful names. Visual Basic's IntelliSense support and the ability to use named parameters makes calling methods with many parameters easy to do. I redesigned the interface for my object so that a single method call that accepted a number of parameters would do the whole job.

While I just referred to passing parameters to methods, remember that you can pass multiple parameters to properties also. While multiple parameter properties aren't common, there are situations where they will be the right choice for your interface.

In Process and Out-of-Process

There are a number of considerations that will cause you to decide whether to compile your application as an ActiveX DLL or as an ActiveX EXE. For instance, as discussed in the chapter on objects, an EXE can be shared among multiple programs running on the same computer. EXEs can also be run on a standalone basis (as discussed in the chapter on interfaces). If you want to have your component execute under the supervision of Microsoft Transaction Server, you will have to compile it as an ActiveX DLL. However, if, after looking at those issues, you have not been driven to choose whether your application is to be an EXE or a DLL, there are some performance implications that you should consider.

ADDRESS SPACES

Every Windows 95 program thinks that it is running on a computer with four gigabytes of real, physical memory. Each application also thinks that it has the whole computer to itself, sharing memory only with the DLLs that it calls. This illusion is created by the Windows operating system to ensure that each application operates in its own address space (see Figure 7–3), isolated from the other applications executing on the same computer.

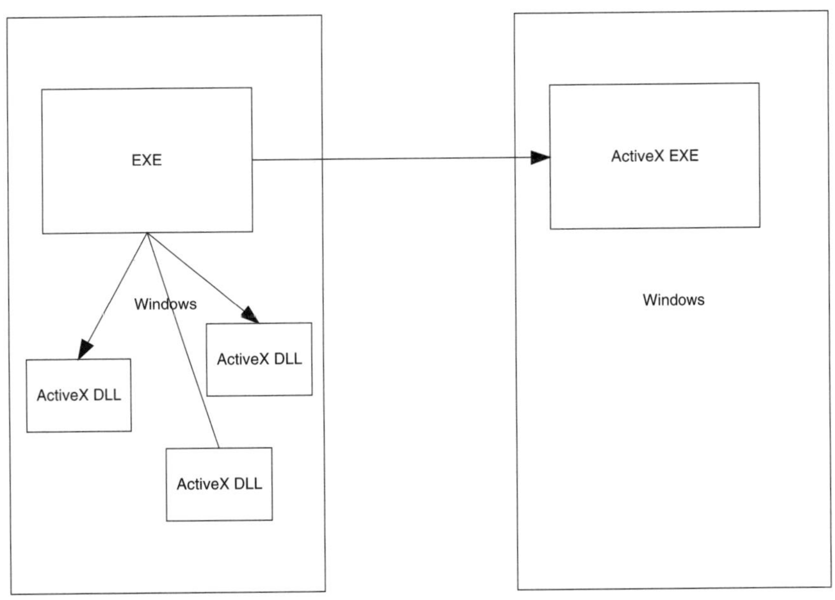

Figure 7–3 *The relationship between EXEs and DLLs under Windows 95.*

When an object runs in the same address space of its client it is said to be an "in-process" component. An object that runs outside of the client's address space is said to be an "out-of-process" component. In general, communication with out-of-process components will be more expensive than with in-process components.

When two programs communicate, they have to share address space. One application must put information into a memory location that the program it wants to communicate with can access. This process is simple if the two programs share a single address space. Once a location in memory is settled on as the place to post messages, the two programs can write directly to that location. Some locking scheme may be required to ensure that one application doesn't read information while the other is still trying to write it, but the process is straightforward.

If two programs are running in separate address spaces, the communication process is more expensive. When program A writes to a memory location, that location is in program A's address space. As a result, that memory location is unavailable to program B that's running in its own memory space and is the program that is supposed to read the message. For the message to be made available to program B, Windows must copy the data to program B's address space and place it in some appropriate location.

If, rather than just passing data, program A calls a procedure in program B, then costs go up again. Normally, to execute a function, the calling program just transfers execution to the location in memory where the function starts. Where the two programs are in different address spaces, the transfer to the start of the function the process is more complicated. In this situation, Windows must intercept and convert the call to a different memory location in a different address space. If parameters are being passed, that parameter data must also be made available in the other address space. If the called routine returns a value, that returned data must be copied back to the original address space.

EXEs

When you compile a component as an ActiveX EXE, you cause it to be run in a separate address space from the application that called it. As a result, the interaction between a client and a component compiled as an EXE will incur the overhead of translating between two address spaces. While this process is more expensive than using an in-process component, there are benefits. Since an ActiveX EXE component runs in a separate address space, it does not have access to its client's memory and so cannot corrupt the calling program's memory.

There's one other benefit to using an EXE: A 16-bit ActiveX EXE can be used by both 32- and 16-bit clients. If you are distributing an application to both 32- and 16-bit environments, creating a 16-bit ActiveX EXE might be an excellent choice to reduce the number of versions of your application.

Components compiled as ActiveX EXEs are out-of-process components that will generally have poorer performance than in-process components. ActiveX EXEs will also be more robust than in-process components because they cannot corrupt their client's memory (or have their memory corrupted by the client).

While it won't be the deciding factor in selecting an EXE over a DLL, starting another process does require about half a megabyte of memory. The more processes that you start, then, the more demands you will make on your computer's memory.

DLLs

When a component is compiled as a DLL and run on the same computer as the client, it runs in the same address space as the client. The costs of calling a method of a component in the same address space as the client is small (in fact, only marginally more expensive than calling a procedure within the client itself). There are costs associated with in-process components, though. With in-process components, since the component is in the same address space as the client, they can corrupt each other's memory.

Components compiled as ActiveX DLLs are in-process components that will generally have better performance than out-of-process components. They will be less robust than out-of-process components because of the possibility of memory corruption.

If your component displays a modeless form (a form that can be displayed without stopping you from working on another form), you may have to compile your application as an EXE. You can't, for instance, open a modeless form from an ActiveX Control used in Internet Explorer. The App object's NonModalAllowed property will be true when your component is executing in an environment that allows Modeless dialogs.

DCOM AND REMOTE OBJECTS

Any component, regardless of how it's compiled, if run on a separate computer than the client, functions as an out-of-process component. And, for remote objects, the time required to communicate over a network and the variation in response time is so large that it swamps the time difference between in-process and out-of-process calls.

Benchmark: Internal Procedures, In-Process, Out-of-Process

Throughout this book I've advocated designing your application as a set of interacting objects and, by implication, compiling these objects as reusable components. The question comes up of what kind of performance burden this design strategy will impose. This set of benchmarks compares calling functions and subroutines in an application to calling functions and subroutines (exposed as methods) in an in-process and out-of-process component.

The calls to an internal subroutine took 3 milliseconds on my test computer and calls to a method defined as a subroutine in an in-process object also took 3 milliseconds. However, calling an identical routine on an out-of-process component shot the processing time up to 990 milliseconds, adding almost a full second to the time it took to perform 1,000 calls.

Calling a function in the program took about as long as calling a subroutine in the program (3 milliseconds) but calling an identical function in an in-process DLL took twice as long (7 milliseconds). The time to call a function in the out-of-process component took about as long as the call to the subroutine in the out-of-process component (880 milliseconds).

The lesson to take away is that defining your application as a set of interacting objects (as long as the objects are part of an in-process component) imposes no real performance burden, though subroutine based methods are faster.

LOAD POINTS

Before any program can be executed, it must be loaded into some location in memory. Most components will contain calls to procedures within the component. Most components will also include code that reads and writes variables. When the component is compiled, the calls to the procedures are replaced with transfers of control to the memory location containing the procedure. Similarly, reads and writes of variables become accesses to particular memory locations. When the component is compiled, all of these memory locations are assigned based on the assumption that the component will reside at a specific location in memory.

Out-of-process components, because they are loaded into an address space of their own, are always loaded to the same location in memory. In-process components, however, are not. When an in-process component is loaded into memory, Windows must load the component to a location not already occupied either by the client or some other component. If this is the same location that was used when the component was compiled, the component's compiled code can now be executed. However, if that space is already occupied, the component is loaded to a different location in a process called rebasing. Since the component is in a different location than was assumed during the compile, rebasing includes a "fix up" or adjustment of all of the memory locations in the component's code (see Figure 7–4).

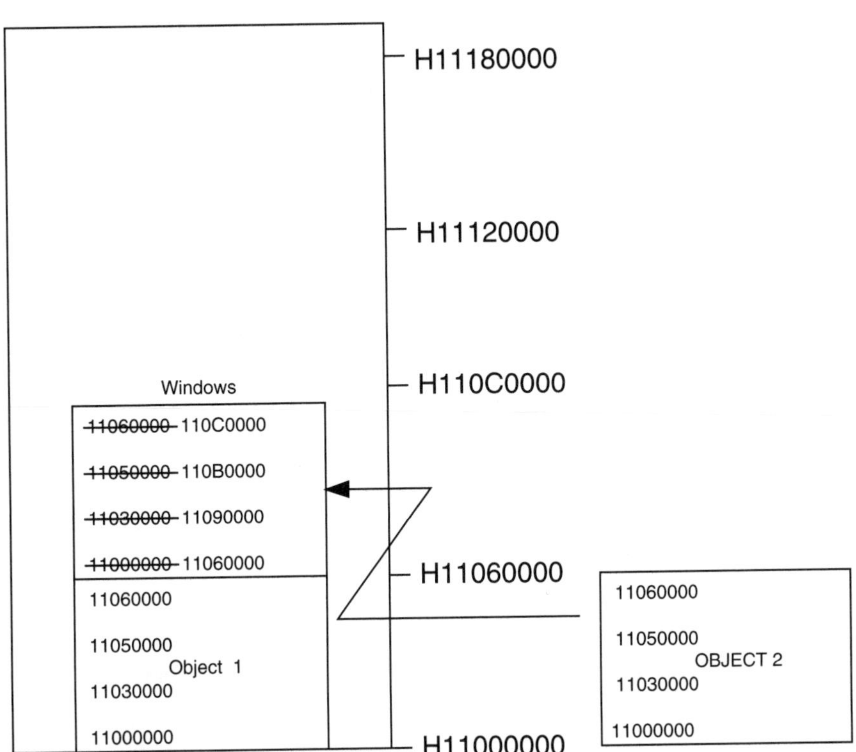

Figure 7–4 *Relocating a DLL to an empty load point.*

There are two expenses associated with a fix-up operation. The first, and most obvious, is the time spent performing the fix-up operation. The second expense is that rebasing can cause multiple copies of the same component to be loaded. Once the fix-up process has been performed, the code has been tailored to run at a specific location in memory. Should another client attempt to use the same component, the component will be loaded again rather than shared with the second client.

You can reduce these expenses by eliminating rebasing and the subsequent fix up. In Visual Basic, you do this by specifying the location in memory to which your in-process component is to be loaded. This is set in the DLL Base Address text box on the Compile tab of the Project Properties dialog. Microsoft recommends setting this hexadecimal number to multiples of 64K between &H11000000 and &H80000000. Typical memory addresses are &H11060000, &H110C0000, &H11120000 (note that the last four positions are always zero).

There are three strategies that you can follow in dealing with the DLL load point:

1. Plan and set the DLL Base Addresses for your components.
2. Ignore the setting.
3. Pick a random number.

The first strategy assumes that have a clear idea of what components are going to be loaded into memory by a client so that you can set the DLL Base Address to ensure that no two components will load to the same location. You will also have to take into account the size of your components—simply setting this number to positions 64K apart won't work. If you have a 128K component loading at address &H11000000, it will occupy all the positions from &H11000000 to &H11020000. This strategy makes sense if the costs saved in avoiding fix ups offset the costs of this planning effort.

Ignoring the DLL Base Address setting assumes that you will not be able to predict which addresses will be available at load time, so a fix up operation will always be required anyway. Your attitude here is that cost reduction in avoiding fix ups does not offset the time spent in carefully setting the property.

The final strategy, pick a random number, assumes that if there is sufficient variety in DLL Base Addresses you will, on most occasions, have most of your components load to free locations and not be rebased.

The one thing that you can be sure of is that if you never change the Base DLL Address and a client loads two of your components, the client will pay for a fix up.

My strategy is a variation of option 3. I generated a list in an Access database of addresses, 64K apart, starting at &H112C000. When I create a component, I take a number from this list and check it off. Should I ever use all of these numbers (there are several thousand of them), I will erase my check marks and start over. The cost to me is small and, I believe, I avoid a fix up on most of my components most of the time.

BYVAL AND BYREF, METHODS AND FUNCTIONS

For in-process components, passing ByRef parameters will have the least cost. For a ByRef parameter, all that is passed is the address to the location of the parameter's data. ByVal parameters are more expensive since a copy of the data must be made before a reference to the new copy is passed to the routine. This additional cost is largest for strings, and increases with the size of the string. For data types that are roughly the size of an address (e.g., the numerics and object references) the cost of passing a value ByVal can be zero. Of course, as I discussed in the chapter on coding objects, with ByRef parameters there is a danger that the called routine may inadvertently update the data passed to it.

Benchmark: ByVal and ByRef in In-Process and Out-of-Process

Parameters can be passed to methods either ByVal or ByRef. My previous tests with components have all used ByRef (the default). Changing the passing mechanism to ByVal from ByRef added 2 Milliseconds when passing a string in an in-process component. Changing from ByVal to ByRef when passing a string to an out-of-process component added a little more (12 Milliseconds). With integer variables, the difference between ByVal and ByRef is virtually 0 for in-process but adds 40 milliseconds out of process, and object references actually process faster when passed ByVal in-process.

Passing objects to an out-of-process component is even more expensive than passing data. If the passed object is in the client's address space, then each call in the component to the object will have to be translated into an access to memory back in the client's address space. This cost is worth bearing in mind if you are considering using callbacks in place of events for an out-of-process component.

The same sort of discussion applies when deciding whether to implement a method as a subroutine or a function. Since, like a ByRef parameter, a function can return a value, functions are more expensive in an out-of-process component than subroutines.

In general, parameters that use object variables should be restricted to in-process components. Out-of-process components should use ByVal with object parameters, and in-process components should use ByRef. Out-of-process components should, wherever possible, implement methods as subroutines rather than functions.

Benchmark: Returning Data In-Process and Out-of-Proccess

Returning values from methods are affected by whether the component is in-process or out-of-process, and the data type of the returned value. For in-process components, the difference between data types is small (ranging from 1 millisecond for an integer through 4 milliseconds for a string to 7 milliseconds for an object). The values for an out-of-process component are much larger and show greater variation: 890 milliseconds for an integer, 948 milliseconds for a string, and 1657 milliseconds for an object.

A Final Warning

I'm repeating myself but, once again, these recommendations are important only if performance is your primary concern. On your equipment or for your application, the performance gains that these recommendations give you might be too small to be worthwhile. My definition of "fine tuning an application" is "the belief that small, insignificant changes will result in something other than small, insignificant improvements."

Before altering your design to make these kinds of optimizations, let me remind you that converting an ActiveX DLL to an ActiveX EXE is a matter of setting a few compile options and recompiling the program. If you modify your design to control how parameters are declared or eliminate methods that return values because you've compiled the component as an ActiveX EXE, any benefits that result from your work could be wiped out with a single recompile of your component. Even without recompiling your program, moving a DLL from the client's computer to a server converts it from an in-process server to an out-of-process server and may make all your work useless.

You'll get the best performance if you get the design right, provide the ability to perform most tasks with a single call, and make the most efficient use of data access.

Threading

Threading probably causes more confusion than any other single topic in creating components. In this section, I tackle the topic and suggest some strategies that you can follow when developing your components.

THREAD BASICS

First things first: What is a thread? Every EXE (ActiveX or otherwise) is said to run inside a process. Threads are created inside a process, so every EXE has its own process and one or more threads within that process. Within a process, a thread is a path of execution through the component. The more threads that you have available to your component, the more paths that can be followed. If only one thread is available to your component, then only one path can be followed. This means that with one thread only one client can execute any instructions in your component and that client can follow only one path through the component at a time. If a component has multiple threads, then multiple sets of instructions can be processed at any one time. With multiple threads, several clients can execute a shared, multi-threaded component at the same time, or one client could have several methods executing simultaneously.

Next point: Why do you care? The problem is that a component that has only one thread available to it can process only one request from one client at a time. If a client calls a method in a component, then any other attempt to execute the component's code will be blocked until the already executing client request finishes. In a situation where many clients will be executing a component simultaneously, all clients have to wait until the client currently using the component is finished.

You should also realize that threads are allocated on a component by component basis. If a component is compiled as an ActiveX DLL, then every client gets their own copy of the component. Unless the client is multi-threaded or you have implemented asynchronous processing, only one method can be called at a time anyway. If you've designed your ActiveX EXE components with a SingleUse object as the entry point for the component, then every client will also get their own copy of the component. In this situation also, multiple threads are useful only if the client can issue an asynchronous call to the component, or the client itself is multithreaded.

Since an ActiveX EXE runs in its own process and so gets a thread of its own, a component can mimic multithreading by launching another ActiveX EXE component.

Finally, if your component is executing on a computer with a single processor, only one thread executes at a time. You should remember that assigning multiple threads to a component will not add additional computing power to your computer.

THREAD BENEFITS AND COSTS

Threads have a cost. Starting a new thread is not free. While you may set your component up with multiple threads, there comes a point where starting a new thread doesn't provide benefits that outweigh the costs. Among other costs, when a thread is created, a copy of all of the global data for the component is made. If your object has a Sub Main procedure, that routine will be re-executed. An object with lots of global data and a long-running Sub Main is not a good choice for a multiple-threaded component. In addition, since the Global data area is copied for each thread, objects may not be able to communicate because they no longer share the Global data. Figure 7–5 shows the relationship between components, processes, threads, and global data.

On a single processor computer, extra threads may not give you any benefits at all. Since threads are related to the execution of the program, threads require control of a CPU in order to be useful. In a single processor computer, multiple threads are less useful than in a multiprocessor computer because any threads must wait until the currently executing thread frees up the processor. In addition, as you add multiple threads to a single processor CPU, response time degrades. This is because the operating system has to spend more time switching the CPU between the various threads and performing the necessary bookkeeping to keep track of each.

Typically, on a single processor computer, you will want to use multiple threads only where you have some methods that run significantly longer than other methods. If you have a method that takes a minute to complete, while

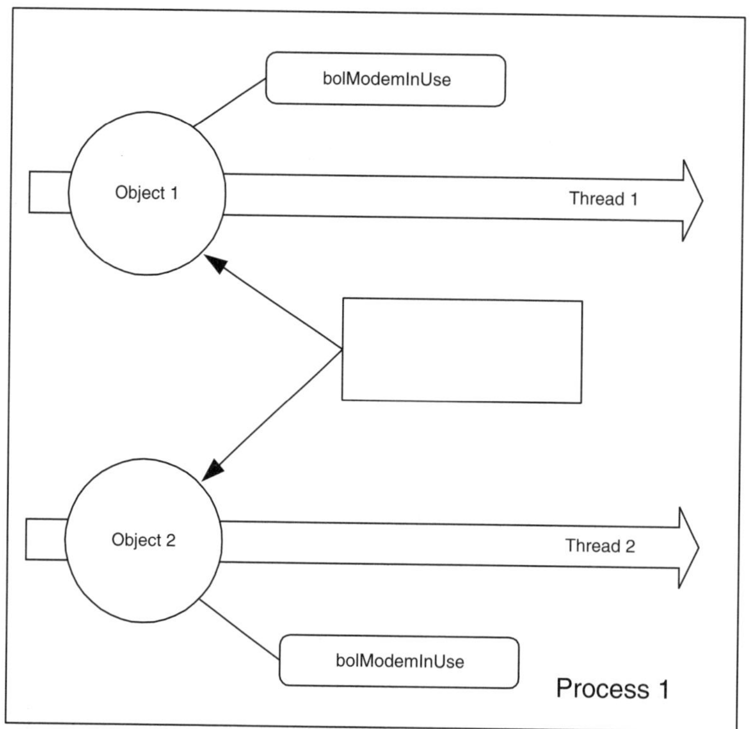

Figure 7–5 *Components, clients, threads, processes, and global data.*

other methods take only a few seconds, adding additional threads may be an excellent design decision.

As an example, I had an ActiveX EXE component with one method that took a full minute to complete (it was doing some data analysis on a several large tables). Almost every other method on the same component took, at most, a second or two. Originally, I had made the component single-threaded because it would be used only on single processor computers. However, if a client called my long-running method, the component was unusable until the data analysis was complete and method reached completion. If one client called my analysis method and another client called one of the component's other methods, the second client wouldn't see its method complete for one minute and a couple of seconds. One minute was spent waiting for the first client's data analysis to complete, the last two seconds were spent waiting for the second client's method to complete (see Figure 7–6).

I switched the component over to being multithreaded because it would change the way that multiple requests like this would be handled. When the second client called the shorter-running method, that method would start to execute while the longer-running method was still executing. Since I was still running on a single processor computer, my object incurred the costs of starting the second thread and switching between the two threads. These costs did lengthen the time it took to execute both processes. However, the shorter running method still returned considerably sooner than if it had waited for the longer-running method to complete.

Notice that the longer-running method also took longer to execute than if it had run by itself. The net result was that the longer-running method returned slightly later and the shorter running method returned considerably sooner. Since both methods took longer, the average processing time for both methods increased. On a multiple processor computer, the increase in run time would have been minimal, as the new thread would have been assigned to a separate processor and no thread switching would have taken place.

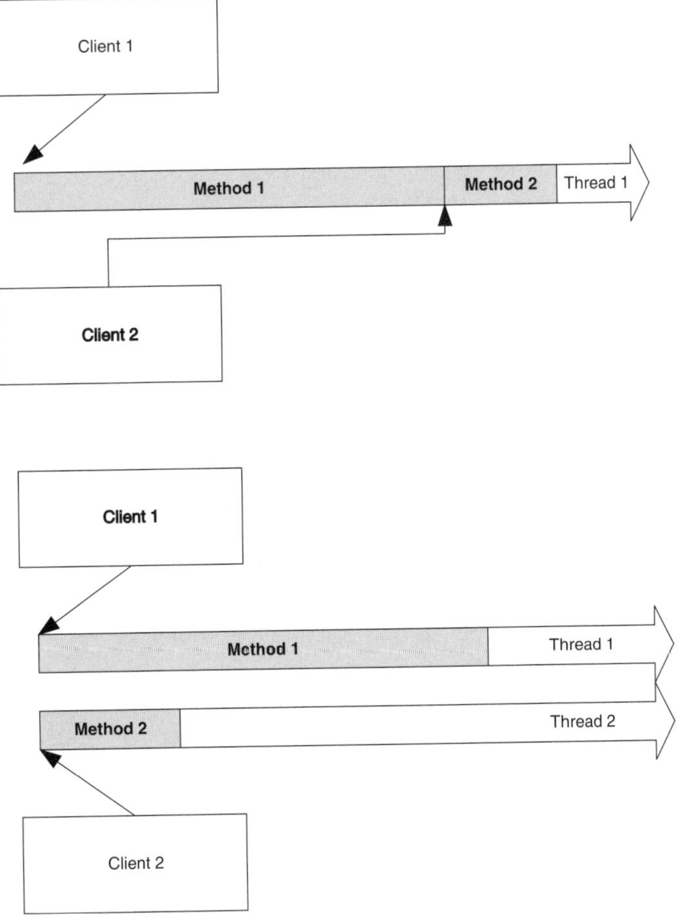

Figure 7–6 *Single threading versus multiple threading.*

The rule to remember when a multithreaded component object executes on a single processor machine is "The more threads that are available, the more responsive the component will be, though average response time for the component will increase."

THREADING DANGERS

There are dangers to creating a component with multiple threads. Since a component shares all of its Global data (e.g., Forms, Public variables declared in standard Modules), multiple threads can result in different routines in the same object trying to update the same data at the same time. This code, which adds 1 to the public variable x, looks perfectly safe:

```
x = x + 1
```

In an ActiveX EXE with multiple threads that has this line in two different routines, you could easily have two clients executing this line at the same time. Assuming that x contains the number 2, the client that executes this line first will read the value 2 out of the variable x and add 1 to it. During that time, the second client could read the value 2 out of x and add 1 to it. The first client puts the newly calculated value 3 back in x and, a microsecond later, so does the second client. If the variable x is supposed to keep a count of the number of times that it was updated, the value in x is now wrong: It's 3 when it should be 4.

Another problem occurs if one or more object methods are asynchronous, that is, if a method returns control to the client while continuing to execute code in the component. Once control is returned to the client, the client can call another method of an object in the same component. Normally, the second call will have to wait until the code triggered by the first call finishes executing. However, it is possible for the first method call to give up control, allowing the second method to start executing. If a client ends up executing multiple sets of code in the component at the same time, the situation is referred to as reentrancy.

Reentrancy can occur when you write a routine that:

- Uses DoEvents
- Calls a method or sets a property on an object in another thread
- Triggers an event handler on an object in another thread
- Shows a form

Once you perform one of these activities, your routine gives up control of the processor and allows other requests to be processed.

As an example, a client could call Method1 of Object1. This method returns control to the client when its code displays a Form. The client could then call Method2 of Object1 while the Form is being displayed. This would cause the client to reenter the component, executing Method2 before the code in Method1 finished executing. In this situation, Method2 could actually completely finish executing before Method1 does. Changes to shared data made by the call to Object2 could create problems for the code still to be executed in Object1.

I'm not suggesting that you shouldn't use Forms or DoEvents in your object. I am suggesting that you must be careful how you share data between the code used by these methods. If you have implemented multithreading and have common data, you may want to set up semaphores in the routines that update that data to make sure that only one routine writes at a time.

You cannot convert an object from single-threaded to multithreaded if it contains a single-threaded ActiveX control or an MDI form. You cannot call Friend routines on an object executing on another thread, so if you convert a component to multithreaded you may find that calls between two objects work on some occasions and fail on others, depending on whether two objects are on the same thread. In Visual Basic 5, if you want to use multithreading you must remove all forms from your project and mark it as Unattended Execution.

THREADS AND ACTIVEX DLLs

Thread options are set on the General tab of the Project | Properties dialog (see Figure 7–7). Threading is really only an issue with ActiveX EXEs. An ActiveX DLL, since it runs in the same process as the client, cannot create any new threads (creating threads are the responsibility of the client.)

With ActiveX DLLs, the default setting of Apartment Threaded makes the component multithreaded. Apartment Threading allows each object in the component to run on its client's threads (see Figure 7–8). If you have three objects in the component, then each can execute on the thread provided by their client, improving the responsiveness of your component. In addition, since the communication between a multithreaded component and a multithreaded client is generally faster, you should leave this setting at its default of Apartment Threaded if your component might ever be used by a multithreaded client.

The other ActiveX DLL choice, single threaded, is really just present to support legacy clients that cannot communicate efficiently (or at all) with multithreaded clients.

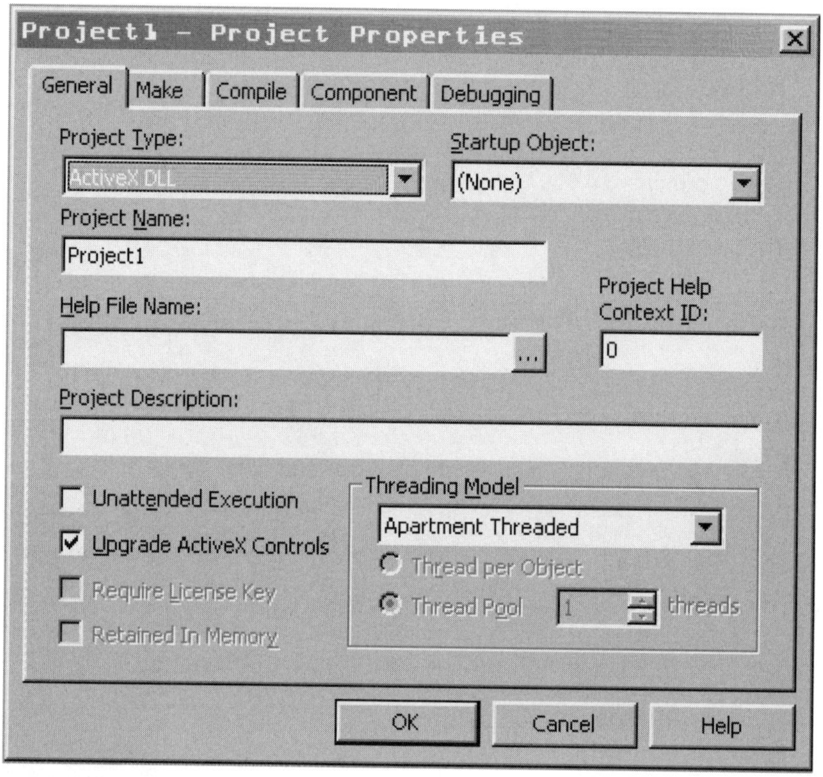

Figure 7–7 *The General tab.*

THREADS AND ACTIVEX EXEs

If your component is an ActiveX EXE, then, because it is a separate program running in its own process, it can actually create new threads. So, while there are only two threading options for an ActiveX EXE (thread per object and thread pool) the implications are more significant than with an ActiveX DLL.

Thread per object causes each new instance of an object in the component to run on a separate thread. If three different objects are created, then there will be three threads executing, regardless of how many clients are calling the objects. If a second instance of an already created object is created, a new thread is created also (see Figure 7–9).

With the thread pool option you can put a cap on the number of new threads that are created. When you select thread pool, each new instance of an object starts a new thread, up to the limit specified in the thread pool option (the default is 1, which causes the component to be single-threaded).

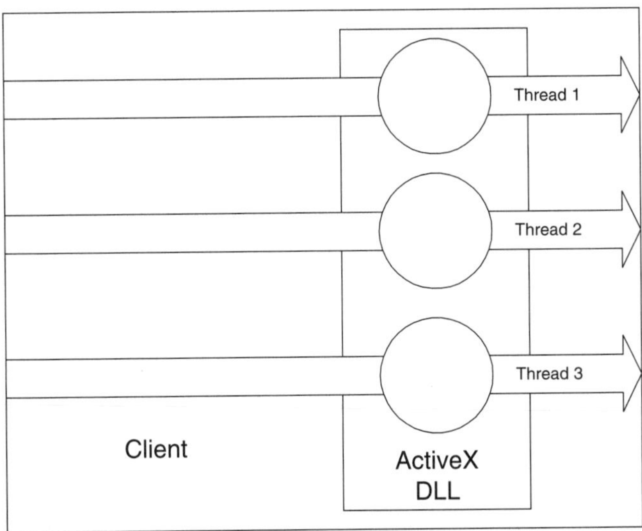

Figure 7–8 *Apartment threaded ActiveX DLLs.*

If more objects are requested than there are threads in the pool, new objects will be assigned to an already existing thread.

With the thread pool option, objects are assigned to threads on a round robin basis and no attempt is made to do any load balancing (see Figure 7–10). As an example, suppose a component has a thread pool setting of 3 and

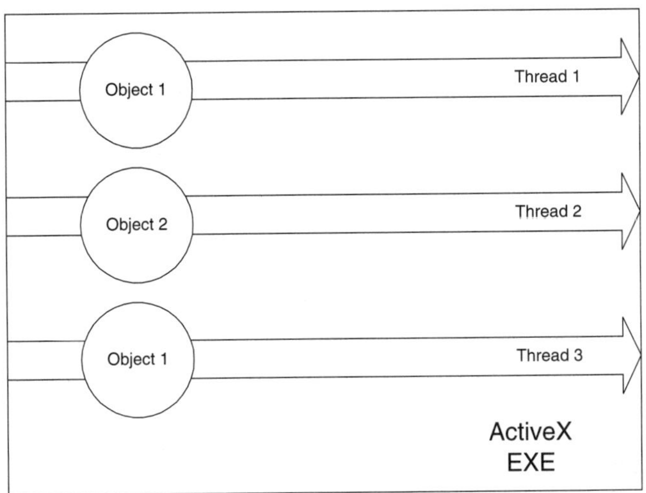

Figure 7–9 *Thread per object ActiveX DLL.*

five objects have been created. Using a simple round robin process of assigning threads, the first object would have gone on thread 1, the second object on thread 2, and the third object on thread 3. When the fourth object was created, it would have been assigned to thread 1, as the next thread in the rotation. The fifth object will be assigned to thread 2. Now, assume that at this point both of the objects on thread 1 are destroyed, leaving the thread that they were on unused. The sixth object created will still go on thread 3 because thread 3 is the next thread that comes up in the rotation.

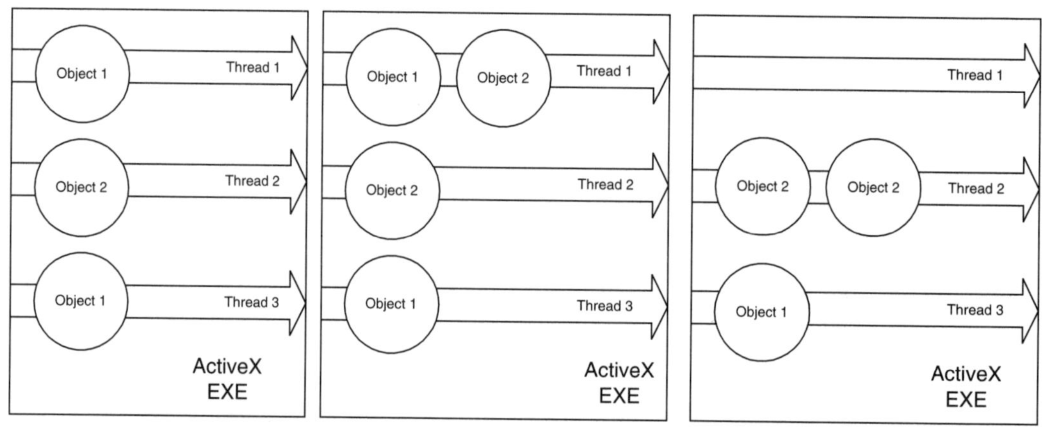

Figure 7–10 *Assigning threads to objects in an ActiveX EXE with the thread pool option set to 3.*

THREAD DECISIONS

So what's the appropriate setting for multithreading on an ActiveX EXE? If your component will be executing on a multiple-processor computer, then a thread for each processor is appropriate. Use thread pool and set the cap to match the number of processors.

If your component will execute on a single-processor computer, multiple threads will give you a benefit only when you have a combination of long-running and short-running routines. A low thread pool setting of two or three is appropriate here (remember, no matter how many threads you have, there's still only one processor so only one thread will actually be executing at any time). Thread per object should probably be used only when you have a clear idea of the number of objects that will be in use simultaneously and that number is in the same range that you would set the thread pool to.

INTERNAL CREATES

The preceding discussion assumed that the objects were created by the component's client. When objects are created by other objects in the same component, no new threads are created. New objects created by other objects in the same component go on the same thread as the object that created them. This means that Private and PublicNotCreateable objects will always be on the same thread as the object that created them and will block calls to that object.

As with the Instancing property, CreateObject requests are always treated as an external request and can generate new threads. So, objects created from other objects in the same component with CreateObject will be on different threads and will not block calls to each other.

I've suggested in the previous discussion that an object can call methods on another object running on a separate thread. To do so, however, the calling object will have to be passed a reference to the object on the other thread by the client since objects on separate threads don't share Public variables. The only other mechanism to get a reference to an object on another thread is to use CreateObject. Calls made to objects running on other threads are about as expensive as a call to an out-of-process component.

When I've had a multithreaded object start behaving in a way that I didn't expect, I have found the ThreadId property of the App object useful in debugging. This property returns the identifier for the thread that the object is currently executing on and lets me determine when two objects share or don't share a thread. This value is also written to the log file so I can have it displayed just by using the App object's logging methods.

Identifiers

Within Windows, components, objects, and interfaces are all known by a unique identifier. When you add a reference to a component to your Visual Basic project, you pick up the identifiers for the objects and interfaces that make up that component. When you compile your application, the identifiers from the type library replace the names of those objects and interfaces. Even when you use CreateObject with a progid to create an object, Windows just uses the progid to look up the appropriate identifier for the object and uses that.

When you compile your component, Visual Basic assigns identifiers to your components, objects, and interfaces. These identifiers are Globally Unique Identifiers (GUIDs), a 32-byte string that is guaranteed to be unique. As part of compiling your component or installing it on a computer, the GUID is added to the computer's Windows registry with the necessary information to find the file that the GUID belongs to.

As you can imagine, then, controlling the identifiers assigned to your component is very important. Since clients actually use GUIDs to find your component, if your component is assigned new identifiers, clients will be unable to find your component. The only way for a client to pick up your component's new identifiers is for the client to be recompiled so that it can pick up the new identifiers. Visual Basic provides you with a set of tools that allows you to manage when a new GUID is generated. Before describing those tools I'll outline the cases when you want to change your GUIDs.

Generating GUIDs

When you compile your component, you can have a new set of GUIDs generated for your application. In addition to changing your GUIDs, you can also change the file name that you compile your component to. Control of your component's GUID and file name allows you to handle distribution of upgrades to developers using your component.

Scenario 1: Upgrade or First Release

In the typical upgrade/first release scenario you want to make a new version of your component available, replacing any old versions, if they exist. For an upgrade, you do not want to force any clients to be recompiled. In this scenario, you don't want to change either the file name for your component or its identifiers. You want the file name to stay the same so that the new version of your program will be installed over top of the previous version. Any changes to the registry will be just to record the addition of new interfaces (see the chapter on interfaces for a discussion of handling version upgrades). Existing clients will be able to continue to use your component without recompiling because the identifiers for the interfaces that they use will not have changed.

Scenario 2: New Version—Replacement

In the new version scenario, you want to replace an existing version of your application, prevent developers from using the old version, and force a recompile of any clients that use your component. This scenario is appropriate when you discover a bug or some other problem that makes it undesirable to continue using the old version of the program and you want to completely replace it. This is also the situation that you get into if you don't use interfaces to handle versioning.

In this scenario you will generate new identifiers for your application but will not change the name of the file that you compile to. When your component is installed on a computer, any clients that use it will have to be recompiled. Clients will have to be recompiled in order to pick up the new identifiers for your component because you will have overwritten the existing file with the version with the new identifiers.

Scenario 3: New Version—Enhancement

In this scenario, you want to provide a new version of your component but allow the old version to continue to be used. This option requires you to change both the component's file name (so that your new version doesn't override the existing file) and the component's identifiers (so that new registry entries that are made do not overwrite the existing entries). Clients that want to use the new version must be recompiled, but clients that aren't recompiled can continue to use the old version. Developers will also be able to choose to use either the old or the new version. This scenario is appropriate when the new version of a component involves sufficient changes that using interface versioning to handle the upgrade isn't appropriate.

Table 7.1 summarizes the three scenarios.

Table 7.1 Upgrade Scenarios

Scenario	GUIDs	File Name
Upgrade/First Release	No Change	No Change
New Version—Replacement	Change	No Change
New Version—Enhancement	Change	Change

A potential fourth scenario is to change the file name but not change the GUIDs. While certainly an option, it's difficult to imagine a situation where you'd want to do this. Effectively, programs would be redirected to the new version of the program without having to be recompiled. However, because the file name wasn't changed, the old version's file wouldn't be overwritten. This option should be taken when you, for some reason, want to keep the old file on the user's computer but have clients use the new version of the component.

Changing GUIDs

You can change your file name when you compile your component. You force a change to your component's GUIDs by picking a Version Compatibility option from the Component tab of the Project | Properties menu (see Figure 7–11). The three options there are No Compatibility, Binary Compatibility, and Project Compatibility.

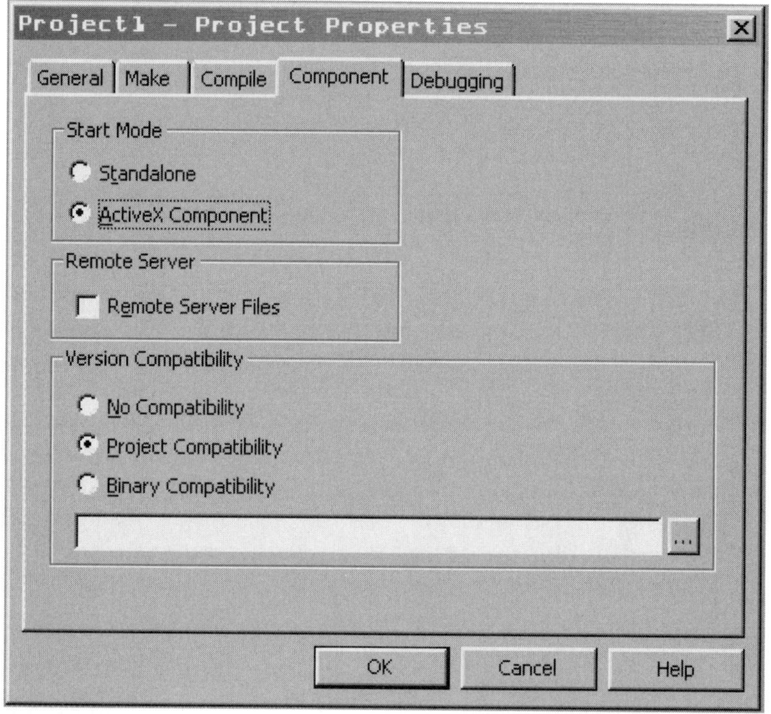

Figure 7–11 *The Component tab.*

NO COMPATIBILITY

For either of the New Version options, you will want to select No Compatibility. No Compatibility causes Visual Basic to assign new identifiers for your component, all of its objects, and all of the interfaces within the component.

BINARY COMPATIBILITY

The Upgrade scenario is the usual situation that you will find yourself in. For an upgrade, either no changes have been made to any of the component's interfaces or the changes have been handled by supplying new interfaces. In this situation, you want Visual Basic to use the same identifiers as were used the last time the component was compiled. The Binary Compatibility option is designed to support those scenarios. However, Visual Basic will not let you maintain your identifiers if you have broken one or more interfaces in your application.

In order to maintain identifiers you must supply Visual Basic with a reference version of your component. As part of preparing a component for release I always compile a copy of the program to some safe directory. In this case "safe" means some directory where I won't overwrite or delete the file (something that I'm prone to do if I'm not careful). I also change the name of the file and the project when I create the reference copy for reasons that I discuss shortly. With that reference copy created, I select the Binary Compatibility options and set the text box at the bottom of the tab to the full path name of my reference copy of the component.

When you select Binary Compatibility, Visual Basic compares the current version of the program to the reference version. If there are differences between the interfaces of the two versions, then Visual Basic will notify you that the new version of the component is different from the old version.

With Binary Compatibility, depending on the severity of the differences, Visual Basic will give you two choices when it finds a difference. One choice, Break Compatibility, generates new identifiers for all objects and interfaces. The other choice, Preserve Compatibility, generates new identifiers only for the actual differences between the current version of the component and the reference version. Once you select the Break Compatibility option you can no longer select Preserve Compatibility, though you will continue to be notified of each discrepancy. If you do choose Break Compatibility, Visual Basic will force you to give your project a different name and file name from the reference copy of the component (which is why I change the file and project names on my reference copy).

With Binary Compatibility, if you have chosen to break your component's interface, then you should choose Break Compatibility to completely replace all of your component's identifiers. If you pick Preserve Compatibility, clients that use your component have to be recompiled anyway, to pick up the changed identifiers. As a result, minimizing the number of new identifiers through Preserve Compatibility doesn't save any time for developers who use your component.

Only if you know that the changed identifiers are limited to objects or interfaces used by only a few clients should you choose Preserve Compatibility. In this situation, only those clients that use the items with changed identifiers will need to be recompiled and the rest of the clients can continue to use your component without being recompiled.

PROJECT COMPATIBILITY

Project compatibility is appropriate during the development process when you are frequently making changes to your component. As long as a Class Module or interface continues to exist, Visual Basic will maintain its identifier. As methods or properties are added or removed, new identifiers are silently assigned to them. By reducing the number of times that new identifiers are generated, you can reduce the number of times that your test bed applications have to be recompiled.

It is essential that you switch to Binary Compatibility for components that have been released for use by other developers. Without the notice generated by Binary Compatibility you may think that you are releasing an upgrade that does not require a recompile by developers when, in fact, you are generating a new version.

Version Numbers

While it has no effect on the behavior of your component except during installation, it's also a good idea to turn on the Auto Increment option on the Make tab of the Project | Properties menu choice (see Figure 7–12). This option will automatically increment the version number that is displayed on this tab each time that you compile your component. There is no intelligence built into this feature. The Major and Minor version numbers, for instance, will not increment automatically if you break compatibility.

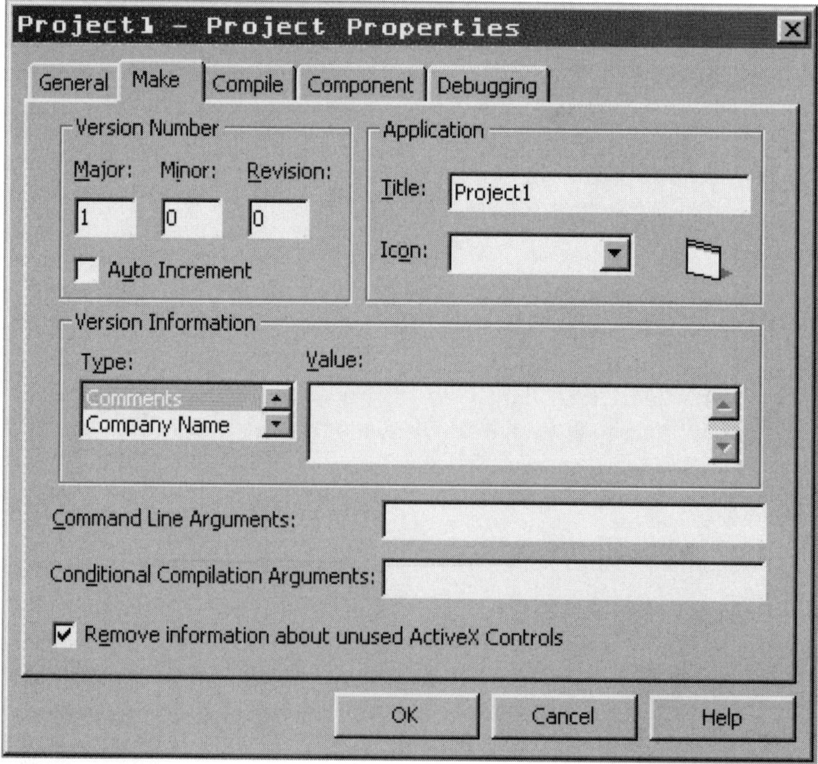

Figure 7–12 *The Make tab.*

This version information is stored in a standard location in the compiled version of your component. As a result, the version number is available to a number of utilities, including the property window of Windows Explorer. Version numbers can be a tremendous help when you're trying to determine if the version of the component installed on some computer was created from the source that you have on your development computer.

If you use one of the many setup programs on the market (including the Package and Deployment Wizard that comes with Visual Basic), they will take advantage of this version number information. When a setup program copies files to a computer's hard disk as part of installing your component, the setup program will check the version number information before replacing any existing files. By automatically incrementing your version number with each compile, you provide a relatively reliable way for the setup program to determine if your user has an earlier or later version of your component. When a file with a lower version number is going to be copied over a file with a higher version number, the setup program will notify the user and let the user decide what action to take.

You can retrieve the version number for your compiled component using the Application object's Major and Minor properties. If your component has a visible user interface, you might want to display the version number somewhere on the form. This code moves the version number to a label:

```
lblVersion = App.Major & "." & App.Minor
```

Where you don't have a visible user interface, you might want to add a version number property of your own:

```
Public Property Get VersionNumber() As String
    VersionNumber = App.Major & "." & App.Minor
End Property
```

Installing Components

Once you've written your component, it's time to distribute it. Installing your component on a target computer has two parts: copying the necessary files to the computer and updating the Windows registry. The process of making the necessary registry entries is known as registering your component. The registry information that you add is used by Windows when a client requests your component. The information includes, for instance, the location of the component's compiled code file so that Windows can locate it and load it into memory.

Generally, there are four different scenarios under which you may send out your component:

1. The component is to be used by other developers and needs to be installed on their computer so that they can develop with it and later distribute it themselves.
2. Your component is to be installed on a user's computer to become part of an application.
3. Your component is to be installed on a server and used by a client running on a computer somewhere on the same network.
4. The component is to be downloaded over the Internet and installed on a user's computer by Internet Explorer.

From an installation point of view, scenarios one and two are identical: The files are copied to the user or developer's computer and the necessary registry entries are made on the same computer.

For scenario three, where the component is installed on a server, the files are copied to the server and the necessary registry entries are made. In addition, the registry entries must also be made on the client computer. The registry must be made on the client so that Windows can redirect requests made at the client to the server. Basically, in this scenario the registry entries help fool the client program into thinking that the component is installed on the client computer.

The Internet download scenario doesn't require you to install the component at all. Instead, you only need to create the package that will be downloaded and executed on the client computer. The installation package is then copied to a Web server where it can be requested by users using Internet Explorer.

Tools

There are at least a few situations where getting your component's registry entries made is easy. When you compile your component, the necessary registry entries are automatically made on the computer that the component is compiled on. ActiveX EXEs are also easily registered: An ActiveX EXE makes its registry entries the first time that it is run.

ActiveX DLLs can't be run like EXEs, but you can register them by using the Regsvr32 utility. Passed the full path name to a DLL, Regsvr32 will update the registry by pulling all the necessary information out of the DLL file. This command, entered from Windows 95/98's Start | Run menu choice would register the WholesaleComponent.DLL file found in the root directory of drive C:

```
Regsvr32 C:\WholesaleComponent.DLL
```

REMOTE SERVER FILES AND CLIREG

Where a client uses DCOM to access a component running on a server, only the component's registry entries must be made on the client. Visual Basic supports this through the option on the Component tab in the Project | Properties dialog called Remote Server Files.

When you select the Remote Server Files option, compiling your component will produce, in addition to the EXE or DLL, a file with the type VBR. You can then use the CliReg32 program to read this file and make the necessary registry entries for a client computer. Clireg32.EXE can be found in your C:\Program Files\Microsoft Visual Studio\Common\Tools\ClirReg\ directory. When you run CliReg32, it pops up a dialog that lets you set the communication protocol, the name of the server that the component has been installed on, and the network protocol (see Figure 7–13). Unless you are running on Windows 95 without DCOM installed, you should always pick the DCOM option.

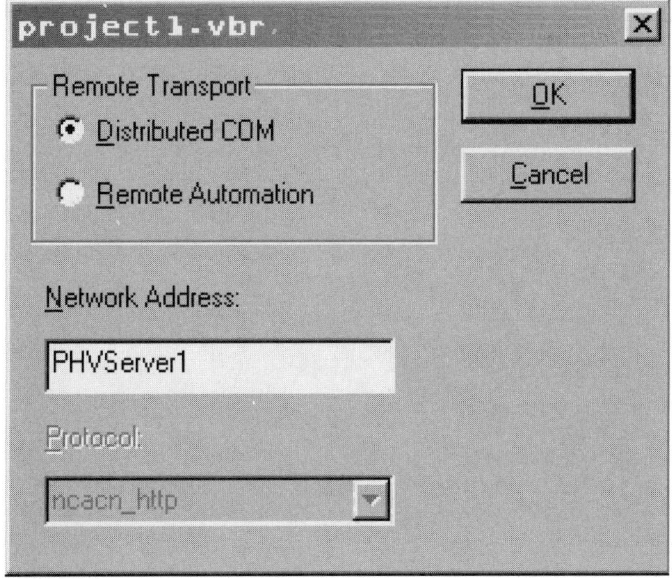

Figure 7–13 *The CliReg32 dialog.*

DCOM AND DCOMCNFG

Once a component is registered on a computer, you can access the component from any computer on the network using Distributed COM (DCOM). You don't have to make any changes to your component to have it used under DCOM. Let me repeat that: You don't have to make any changes to your component to have it used under DCOM. Nor are any changes required to the client. Windows will make it appear to clients that your component is running locally. Windows will also convince the component that all the requests that are coming to it are from a local client. In many ways, then, using DCOM is an installation issue rather than a development issue.

The items on program efficiency discussed earlier in this chapter do become more important when a component is being accessed over DCOM. Because network traffic is inherently slow, you want to make sure that your component can be used with the minimum number of calls to its methods and properties.

To make your component available over the network, you use the DCOM Configuration utility, DCOMCNFG.EXE, to configure the component (see Figure 7–14). The DCOMCNFG utility is used

- on the server, to set the security for the component.
- on the client, to modify the component's registry entries so that requests for the component are redirected to the server.

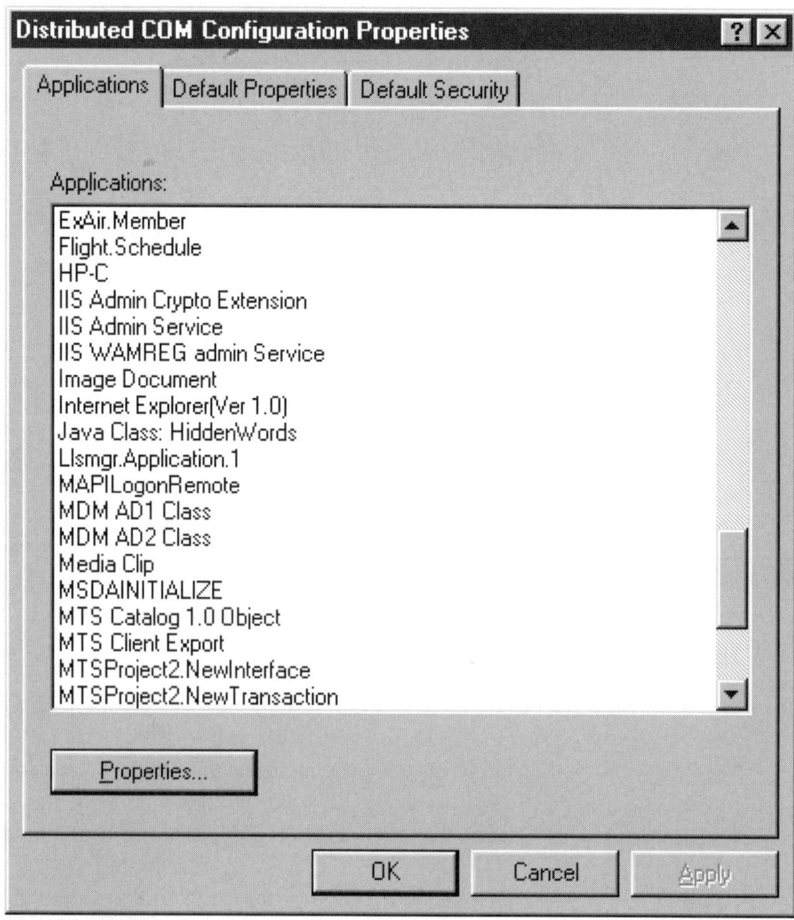

Figure 7–14 *The DCOM Configuration utility's initial form.*

Server-side Configuration • On the computer with the component, you start DCOMCNFG which will present you with a list of objects registered on your server. You select the object that you want to make available over the network and click on the Properties button. Of the four tabs that make up the Properties dialog, on the server you are only interested in the Security and Identity tabs (see Figure 7–15).

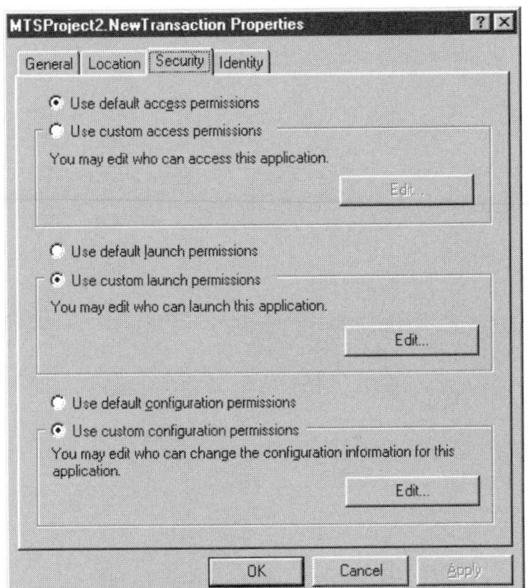

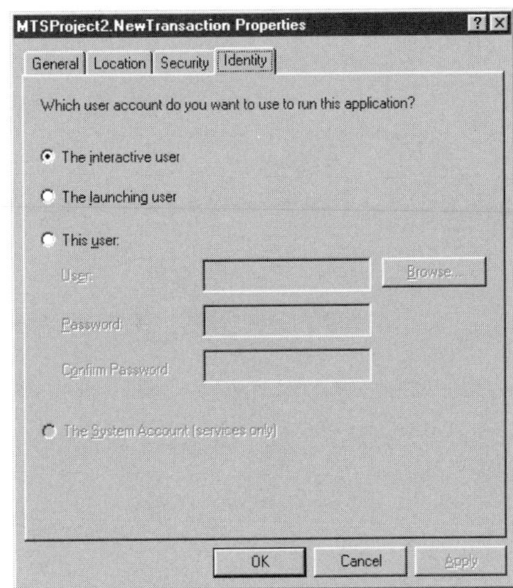

Figure 7–15 *DCOMCNFG's Security and Identity tabs.*

On the Security tab, you can accept the default security settings (set from the initial DCOMCNFG screen) or tailor the permissions for this component. You can set permissions that control who is allowed to launch the component, who is allowed to call its methods and properties, and who is allowed to configure the component (as you are doing now with DCOMCNFG).

On the Identity tab you control what security the component uses while executing. The default setting, the Launching User, causes the component to use the security of the user who requested the component to be run. If users with different permissions request the component, Windows will load one copy of the component for every different security setting.

The first choice on the Identity tab, the Interactive User, gives the component the permissions of whoever is currently logged onto the server. This means that, depending on who's logged on when the component is requested, it could pick up the security of the server administrator or the operator who manages the backups.

The most appropriate choice is the last one: This User. In this option you enter the user id and password for any user on the system. This allows you to establish a user id with the appropriate security for the component.

As I discovered, it's important that the user that you set up be configured so that their password never expires. I had components in several different systems fail simultaneously when the clock ran out on the password of the user id that they shared.

CLIENT-SIDE CHANGES • On the client computer, you also run DCOMCNFG which, again, presents you with a list of objects registered on the computer. Not all of these objects may actually be installed on your computer (i.e., if CliReg32 was used to register but not install the component). Once you select the object, clicking on the Properties button displays and selecting the Location tab lets you set how requests for this object are to be handled (see Figure 7–16).

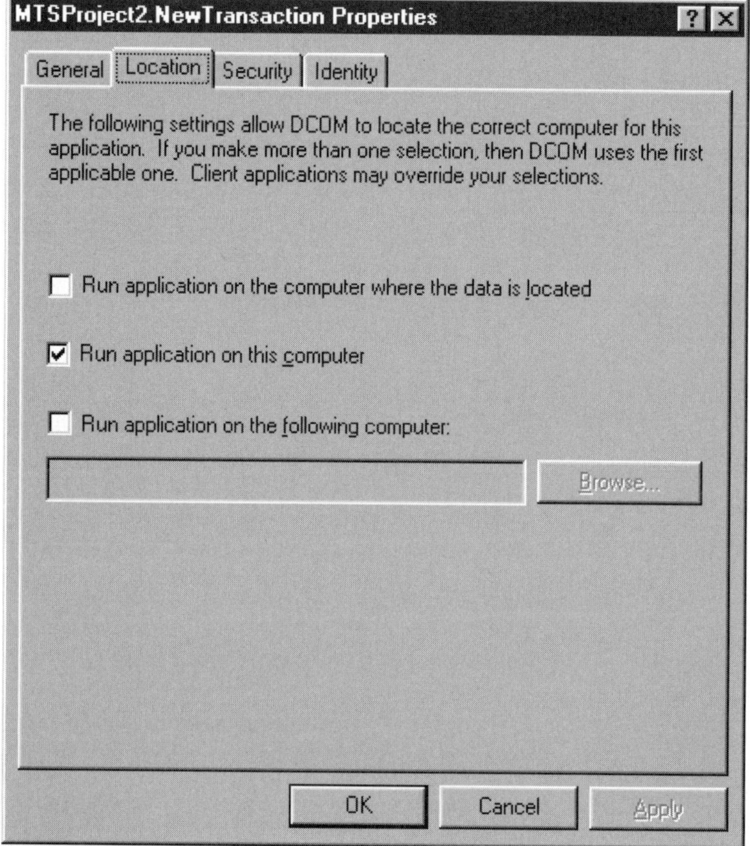

Figure 7–16 *DCOMCNFG's location tab.*

The location tab is typically the only tab that you use on the client computer. The tab gives you three choices:

- Run application on the computer where the data is located
- Run application on this computer
- Run application on the following computer

The default setting, Run application on this computer, causes requests for the component to load the compiled file into the client's memory and execute the component on the client's CPU. The other two options cause any requests for this component to be routed to some other computer. When the request is received on the remote computer, the component (if it is installed on that computer) will be loaded into the remote computer's memory and execute on the remote computer's CPU. The first choice, Run application on the computer where the data is located, requires you to provide a data file for the server.

To redirect all requests for a component to another computer, you need only select the last option, Run application on the following computer, and enter the name of the computer that the component is installed on.

DEPENDENCIES

The problem with copying files and making the registry entries yourself is that you may not copy and register all of the files that your component requires. Visual Basic requires a number of support files to be installed on any computer that a Visual Basic program runs on. If you used other objects (e.g., ActiveX Data Objects for data access) or ActiveX Controls that aren't intrinsic to Windows, they must be present, also. In turn, any files that these objects or Controls require must also be installed for your component to work.

All Visual Basic components need the MSVBVM60.DLL file installed, among others. This library contains a number of common routines that are used by all Visual Basic components and is included in all Visual Basic installs by default. There is a set of libraries called the COM helper libraries that contain standard COM routines, and some of those are also included by default. If the target computer has had a Visual Basic program installed on it, then it will already have these files.

All of these related files are said to be dependencies of your component. You can find what most of the dependencies are by using the program Depends.EXE. Depends is a tool that comes with Visual Basic that analyzes an ActiveX EXE or DLL to determine what files the component requires to run.

The first time that you run Depends, it adds a new item to the context menu for DLL and EXE files. After running Depends once, when you right-mouse click on an EXE or DLL, one of the choices that appear on the menu is View Dependencies. Selecting this choice runs Depends for the selected file and displays the form shown in Figure 7–17. The Module File View at the bottom of the Depends form lists the files that the component depends on. Once you know what's on your component's dependency list, you can insure that the dependent items are installed with your component (or hope that they're already installed on the target computers).

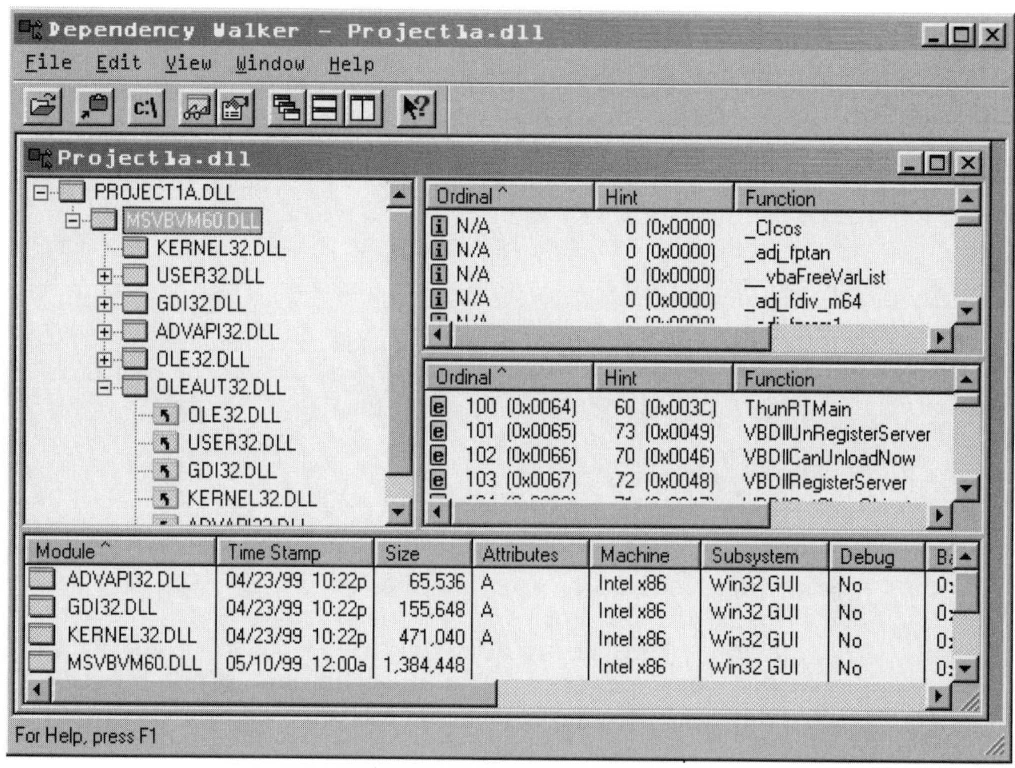

Figure 7–17 *Depends showing the dependencies for a minimal ActiveX project.*

Uninstall

The information that's written to the registry includes the location of the file containing the compiled code for the component. As a result, moving your component to another location after it is registered can cause the programs that use it to fail.

If you do need to move a component to another location, you should first uninstall it in order to remove all of the component's registry entries. After the uninstall has cleaned up the registry you can then install the component again into the new location. Many install packages automatically generate uninstall routines that delete your component's files and remove registry entries.

If you remove a component from your computer, it's also probably a good idea to uninstall the component. Removing unnecessary entries from your registry reduces the size of the registry, speeding up all processing associated with it. At one point, I had been experimenting with an application that wrote entries to the registry. When I was done, my registry had ballooned to almost 10 megabytes in size and my computer took 45 minutes to boot.

You can also uninstall by hand. Deleting the application files isn't very difficult, though it can be time consuming, and can be done with Windows Explorer. To remove the registry entries for an ActiveX DLL, you can use the Regsvr32 utility. Passed the switch /u along with the full path name of the file, Regsvr32 will use the information in the DLL to find and remove its registry entries. This command line removes the entries for the DLL that I installed earlier in this section:

```
Regsvr32 /u C:\WholesaleComponent.DLL
```

Similarly, ActiveX EXEs can be unregistered by running the EXE and passing the /u switch on the command line. This command will unregister the component MyEXE.EXE:

```
C:\Program Files\MyEXE.EXE /u
```

The order of operation matters here. Since Regsvr32 needs the information in the DLL file to determine what registry entries to delete, you should unregister your component before deleting the files.

Package and Deployment Wizard

While it is possible to register your component by hand using Depends and Regsvr32, it's not recommended for the faint of heart. I use these tools only when I'm debugging with installed components that aren't behaving the way I expected. When you need to install a component on a client or a server, use a good install package creation program.

Visual Basic 6 comes with the Package and Deployment Wizard (Figure 7–18). Unlike the flaky Setup Wizard of previous versions of Visual Basic, the Package and Deployment Wizard actually creates reliable setup programs. Running the Wizard will create one or more CAB files containing compressed versions of all of the programs that are required by your component (and the component itself). Also generated by the Wizard are an INF file which describes how to unpack the CAB file and a SetUp.EXE program which users can run to install your component. All you need to do is copy the Wizard's output to floppy disks or a shared network directory so that it can be run on the target computers.

In this section, I don't walk you through the Wizard (the Wizard does an effective job of that). What I do is describe the effect of the various choices that the Wizard provides.

While the Package and Deployment Wizard is a considerable improvement over the old Setup Wizard, there are also a number of third-party packages available. I've noticed, for instance, that a number of Microsoft packages have used InstallShield from the InstallShield Software Corporation to create their setup programs.

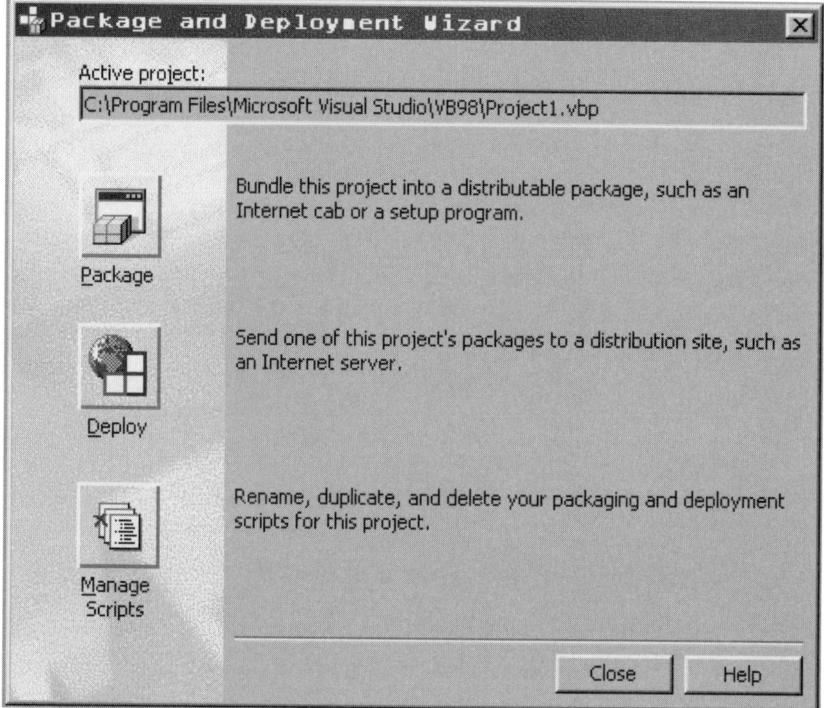

Figure 7–18 *Visual Basic's Package and Deployment Wizard.*

To use the Wizard, you must first add it to your Add-Ins menu. To do this, select Add-Ins | Add-In Manager. In this dialog box, select Package and Deployment Wizard and then click on the Loaded/Unloaded option in the lower right corner of the dialog to give it a check mark. If you want the Wizard to appear on your menu the next time you load Visual Basic, check the Load on Startup option.

Once the Wizard has been added to your Add-Ins menu, you can start it by selecting Add-Ins | Package and Deployment Wizard. Unless you have just saved your project, the Wizard will offer to save your project again. If it does, select Yes.

CREATING PACKAGES

The Wizard gives you three choices:

- Package: This creates a setup package.
- Deploy: Use this to copy a package to somewhere else on your computer or network.
- Manage Scripts: Work with the scripts created as part of running the other two options.

If you pick Package, the Wizard will offer to recompile your program, unless you just recompiled it.

The only way to avoid having to respond to the Wizard's dialogs to save and recompile your project is tc save the project and then compile it just before opening the Wizard. Reversing the order, compile and then save, will skip the first dialog but not the first.

After you've selected Package, you are given a list of the kinds of packages currently available to the Wizard (see Figure 7–19). The Standard Setup Package creates a setup program that could be used to distribute the component to developers or clients. The Internet Package creates a setup routine that could be downloaded and installed by Internet Explorer. The last choice, Dependency File, is used to update existing setup programs. Since it's included in the other two choices, I'll discuss it first.

DEPENDENCY FILE • The Dependency File option just analyzes your project for its dependencies and writes them to a DEP file. The dependency file is used by the Wizard when your component is to be included in another component's installation. Since the Wizard only examines the current Visual Basic project it can only determine the dependencies for other components in the install by reading their DEP files.

The initial form in this process lets you select or create a directory for the several files generated by this Wizard. However, if you select a directory that doesn't have the compiled program in it, the Wizard will complain. Furthermore, when the Wizard goes to add the component to an installation package, it won't find the DEP file unless it is in the same directory as the compiled component. So, while you have a choice here, there's really only one place to put the file: the directory containing theEXE or DLL.

The Wizard will then ask you if you want to include the necessary files to support Remote Automation. Unless you know that you will be using Remote Automation, select No. Since Remote Automation was a stopgap technology provided with Visual Basic 4 to fill in until DCOM was ready, you probably won't be using it.

The next form in the Wizard lists all the dependencies that could be found by analyzing your project. In this list, only the checked files will be

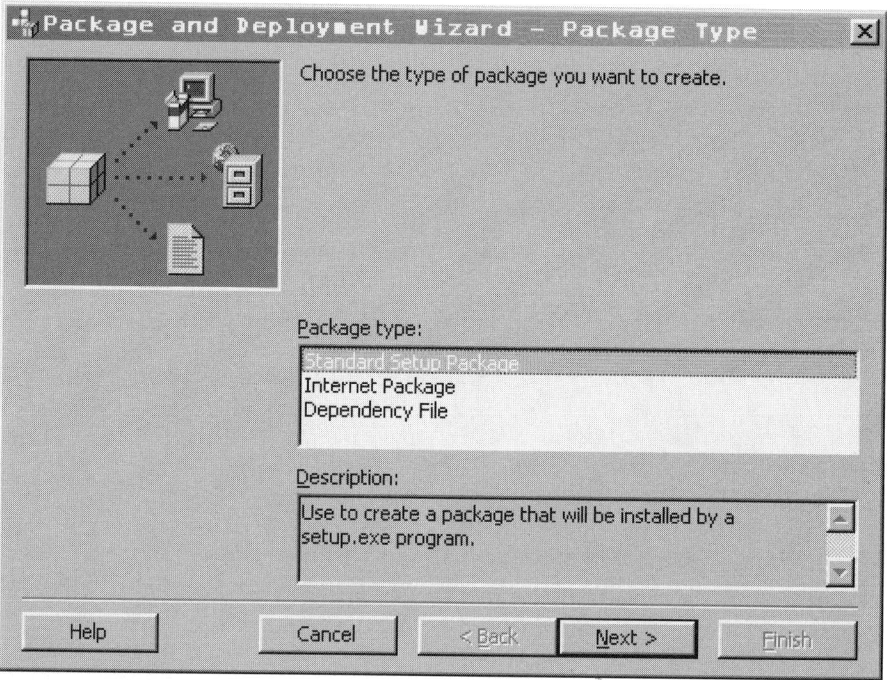

Figure 7–19 *The built in Wizard packages.*

written to the DEP file. Since many of the dependency files are already present on most of the computers running Windows, a lot of the files in the list won't be checked.

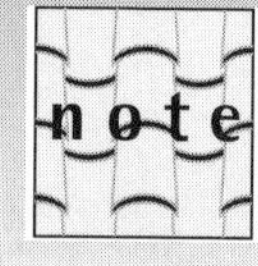

Depending on how paranoid you are feeling, you can choose to check off some or all of these files. The only penalty for checking off additional files is a larger setup program.

The Add button on this form lets you include files that you know your component requires but are not included in the list. Your component might, for instance, include an MDB file to store information in and you will want to include that in the dependency list.

The next form in the Wizard allows you to insert the DEP file into a CAB file. CAB files are Microsoft's format for compressed files and hold the items to be installed by the setup program. You can also provide the name for the INF file which contains the information used to unpack the CAB files. The URL text box on this form allows you to download an existing CAB file to update, otherwise the Wizard creates a new file. If you are updating an existing installation program, you will want to select the CAB file generated for that install.

The Wizard next allows you to specify on what directory to install the files that you've selected. On this form you specify the directory by selecting from a list of pre-defined constants. These constants (or macros as the form refers to them) and the directory that they represent include:

```
$(WinSysPath): the Windows\Systems directory
$(ProgramFiles): the Program Files directory
$(AppPath): the directory specified by the user when running
the setup program
```

You can add subdirectories to the ends of these constants. If you wanted your files to be put in a subdirectory called MyApp in the Program Files directory, you would set the Install Location to $(ProgramFiles)\MyApp.

STANDARD SETUP PACKAGE • The Standard Setup Package choice creates a setup program for your application. Many of the forms in this part of the Wizard duplicate the process of creating a dependency file. You are given additional choices, including the size of the CAB files that you want to create, the title to display on the setup program's splash screen, where to place the component in the Start menu, and so on. The form that allows you to update the Start menu also lets you add menu items to the Start menu to link to other files (use the form's Items button to add these shortcuts).

The Standard Setup Package routine creates a new directory to hold all of the files for your install program. The routine also adds a Support subdirectory to the directory containing your Setup program. Support contains all the files that are compressed into the CAB files for your install program. Support will also contain a BAT file that, when run, will recreate your CAB file. This batch file is useful when you recompile your program because you this batch file is faster than the Wizard. Provided that you haven't broken your interfaces or changed your dependencies, then you won't have to rerun the whole Package and Deployment Wizard.

The Standard Setup Package registers your component and installs all the necessary files and their dependencies on the target computer. For a component that's to be used on a server and accessed via DCOM, this is more of an install than is required by the client. Since all the client needs is the appropriate registry entries, CliReg32may be a more appropriate tool. Alternatively, Microsoft's system administration tools will let you update a client's registry over the network.

INTERNET PACKAGE • Like the Standard Setup Package, this option creates a setup program. The package that's created, however, is designed to be downloaded over the Internet and installed by Internet Explorer. Because of that, you are given the option to have some of the dependencies download in separate files, as necessary, from some other site. You must also mark the objects in your component as being safe for scripting and/or initialization (a topic that I return to in the chapter on ActiveX Controls). Typically, this option is used only with ActiveX Controls.

SCRIPT FILES

When you are finished running any of the Package options, the Wizard lets you give that series of actions a name and save it as a script. The next time that you select Package, you will be able to select one of the scripts that you have created. That script effectively provides a new set of default values for the steps that the Wizard walks you through. From the Manage Scripts choice in the Wizard you can rename, delete, and create copies of the scripts, but you can't edit their content in any way.

DEPLOY

The Scripts are also used by the Deploy choice in the Wizard. The Deploy button leads you through a series of forms that let you copy the results of a Package operation to a folder on your computer or on the network. You can also move the files to a Web server using either HTTP or FTP. If you pick the Web publishing option, make sure that you enter the full name of the server, including the protocol (e.g., ftp://MyServer, not just MyServer).

If you use the Web posting option, you must have Microsoft's posting acceptor component installed on the Web server. This is part of the Visual Studio Server Installation.

Visual Component Manager

Visual Component Manager (VCM) provides a graphical interface to the Microsoft Repository. Microsoft Repository is a database of saved program components (including Visual Modeler diagrams) kept in a Jet or SQL Server database. VCM lets you maintain multiple repositories and switch among them. Shared databases (like SQL Server) can be used to store components that will be used by multiple developers. In VCM, components refer not only to ActiveX items but any part of a Visual Basic project.

VCM, like Visual Modeler and the Package and Deployment Wizard, must be loaded from the Add-Ins | Add-In Manager dialog. Once it is loaded, it appears on Visual Basic's View menu. When you first start VCM, it offers to load a set of templates. This option is worth taking as it adds all of the template items that come with Visual Basic to the repository. VCM also includes a set of pre-defined folders for organizing your components. These range from a place to keep source code, to menus, to Forms, and all the rest of the items that make up a Visual Basic project. VCM refers to all of these items as components, which is a broader definition than I use in the rest of this book.

Working with VCM

The VCM interface consists of three panes (see Figure 7–20). The left pane has an Explorer-type list of all of the repositories and the folders within each repository. The upper right pane (the Contents window) shows the contents of the currently selected item in the Explorer window (either a set of folders or a set of components). The lower right pane (the Properties windows) shows information about the item selected in the Contents Window.

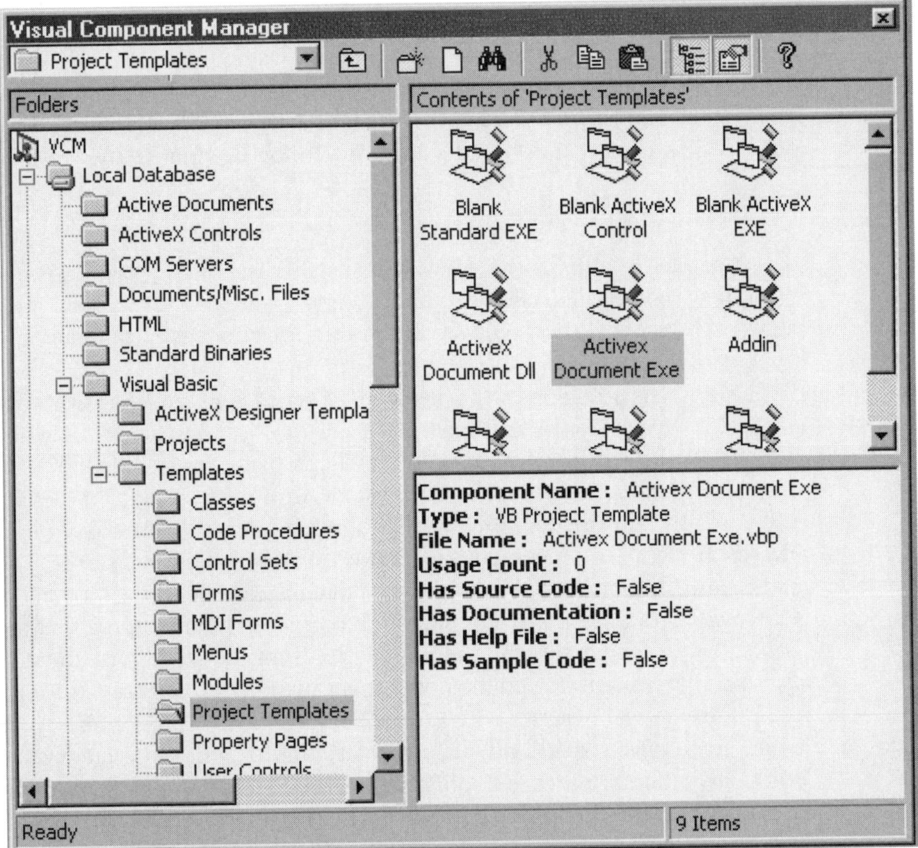

Figure 7–20 *Visual Component Manager.*

RETRIEVING A COMPONENT

To add an item from VCM to your project, you just navigate through folders in the Explorer window to the folder containing the component that you want. The component itself will appear in the Contents window. The Properties Window will provide information on the item currently selected in the Contents window, including the item's Name, Usage Count, whether or not it has associated help files, and other data. To add an item from the Contents pane to your project, just right-mouse click on the item and select Add to project. The only problem that you might have is when the currently selected item in your project isn't appropriate for the component that you are adding. If, for instance, you are adding a menu, you must have a form selected because menus can only appear on forms. Since the VCM form is modeless, you can switch back and forth between it and your project without difficulty.

The Find dialog, which is reached by clicking on the binoculars on the toolbar, lets you search for components without navigating through the folders. You can search by most of the characteristics of the component including keyword, name, when the component was last published, and description. The resulting list of files looks very much like the Find utility from the Windows Start menu. Once the list of matching components is presented, you can double-click on a component to display it in the Contents pane.

PUBLISHING A COMPONENT

You can add an item to the repository (or Publish it) two ways. From within VCM, you right-mouse click on the Contents pane and select New | Component. A wizard will then guide you through the process of publishing a component.

The wizard begins by having you select the primary file in the component. VCM will automatically pick up some of the related files. If you pick a Visual Basic Project, for instance, VCM will automatically include the files in that project as part of the component. A later form in the wizard will let you add additional files to the component. With the file selected, you classify it (a Class file can be either a Document or a VB Class Template, for instance), give it a name, and indicate if the component includes sample code, documentation, source code, or a Help file. In addition to providing information about the component to programmers who are selecting it from the repository, these choices also make it easier to locate the component with the Find tool.

Subsequent forms in the wizard let you add a description, assign keywords from a list (or add new keywords to the list), and indicate if any of the components require registration. Provided you include all the necessary dependency files in the component and flag the items that require registration, VCM will do a minimal install when you add items from it to your project.

You can also add items to the repository from within Visual Basic, provided that you have saved them (VCM works with files rather than objects in memory). Simply right-mouse click on the item in the Project Explorer window and select Publish Component from the context menu. The initial form in this wizard has you select a repository and a folder within the repository. Once you've done that, you work with the same wizard that VCM used to add your component.

Since multiple developers can be updating a shared repository, VCM includes a Refresh option on its pop-up menus that redisplays the current contents of the repository.

CHANGING A COMPONENT

If you are unhappy with the choices that you made when you published your component, you can repeat the process by selecting Republish... from the item's context menu. This takes you back through the wizard, allowing you to change any of the settings for the component.

Selecting Properties from an item's context menu lets you change the description and keywords for the item. You can also drag and drop (or cut and paste) an item from one folder to another.

VCM Issues

The presence of Visual Component Manager creates the possibility of developing objects for the repository rather than for any specific application. As someone who has built two separate source code management systems, it concerns me that VCM does not integrate with a source control tool (e.g., Microsoft's Visual Source Safe). The code in VCM is not monitored in any way to prevent multiple developers working on it at the same time, for instance. If you are building a component to be placed in VCM for use by others, then you still need to manage your component's source code. Nor does VCM prevent the proliferation of multiple objects that basically do the same thing.

VCM doesn't necessarily support reuse, either. VCM does support component based reuse: You can use VCM to hold ActiveX components and have them installed on developer machines when added to a project. But VCM also supports storing and retrieving ordinary source code. While having a library of common, useful routines isn't a bad thing, it's a minimal form of code reuse. Every developer who takes source code out of VCM gets their own private copy of the routine. Over time, these copies will change into different code as developers modify their programs. More important, changes/fixes/enhancements made to the original code will not affect the copies that the developers have taken. True component reuse allows you to update all the applications that use a component just by reinstalling the component.

VCM also doesn't keep track of who has used what item from the repository. If you discover some horrible bug in one of your common, useful routines, you won't get any support from VCM in finding where it has been used. The closest that VCM comes to supporting this is the usage count, which tells you how many times the item has been retrieved. Of course, if you have found a horrible bug and the item's usage count is very high, that information may just depress you.

And, as an especially annoying "feature," once you add VCM to be opened when Visual Basic is loaded, it isn't treated as a standard window in the Visual Basic IDE. VCM will appear on the screen every time you open Visual Basic. Neither minimizing nor closing VCM before closing Visual Basic will prevent it from occupying screen space the next time that you start Visual Basic.

Summary

This chapter covered the issues around moving your component out of development and into the real world of production. I discussed performance issues and what you can do to speed up your components. I also outlined the difference between in-process and out-of-process components and the results of selecting one over the other. You got an introduction to the issues around thread management in multithreaded components and saw how to move your components into a DCOM environment. I also outlined the three strategies that you can follow in managing the load points for your DLLs.

I then outlined the three strategies that you can follow when releasing your component and how Visual Basic's various compatibility options can be used. That led to a description of the tools available for distributing your component, with an emphasis on Visual Basic's Package and Deployment Wizard. I concluded by describing how you can use Microsoft's Visual Component Manager as your front end to the Microsoft Repository where you can keep track of the components available for you to use.

When it comes to distributing your applications and using Visual Component Manager, Microsoft's Visual Basic documentation covers these topics best. For more information on Microsoft Repository, your best source is Microsoft's Web site: msdn.microsoft.com/repository. The VCM entry point is a ridiculously long URL—you're better off to use the MSDN table of contents and look for VCM under Component, Design, and Analysis tools in the Visual Studio Documentation. On DCOM issues, the book for Visual Basic programmers that goes into the topic best is Ted Pattison's *Programming Distributed Application with COM and Microsoft Visual Basic 6.0* from Microsoft Press. For performance tips, your best source is the various magazines and newsletters. The magazine that I recommend is *Visual Basic Programmer's Journal* from Fawcette Press. The newsletter that I like best is *Visual Basic Developer* from Pinnacle Press which, among other features, has a monthly column by one of the gurus of component development, Dan Appleman. I should point out my conflict of interest here: I have had articles published in both journals and edit the *Smart Access* newsletter, which is also published by Pinnacle.

PART THREE

Integrating

In This Part

Objects can be used in a variety of environments ranging from creating ADO data providers to integrating with Microsoft Transaction Server to building Design Time Controls for Visual InterDev. This section shows what you must do as a developer to use your components in these environments. For each environment, the code required, the capabilities supported, the object's life cycle, and the debugging support available are described.

EIGHT

ActiveX Controls

The legend is that when Visual Basic's original developers brought their product in to show Bill Gates, he was very impressed. He especially liked the ability to drag items from the toolbox and add them to a form to give a program increased functionality. As the story goes, Bill Gates was so impressed with this feature that he asked if he, as a developer, could add new items to the toolbox. He was told that no, only Microsoft would be able to that. In the story Bill then sends the developers back to the lab with instructions not to return until other developers could add new items to the toolbox. This, reputedly, was the origin of the VBX specification. Through many twists and turns that specification has evolved to give us ActiveX Controls.

The ability to add new items to Visual Basic's toolbox has been the cornerstone of the product's success. While Visual Basic is a terrific development environment, it's the ability to extend it that has made Visual Basic into a powerful tool for delivering solutions for almost any situation. While, initially, only C++ developers could create ActiveX Controls, version 5.0 gave Visual Basic developers the ability to create ActiveX Controls, too.

You already know most of what you need to know to create an ActiveX Control. Properties, methods, and events are all created the same way in an ActiveX Control as they are in an ActiveX Component. There are some differences, though, which is what this chapter is all about. An ActiveX Control has some additional events, for instance, that fire over the course of its life. I also return to the Procedure Attributes dialog to discuss some options there that are only relevant to an ActiveX Control. You'll also see how to create and code a set of Property Pages to support a control with complicated properties to set.

Most of this chapter revolves around understanding the methods and properties of the UserControl. In the same way that most Visual Basic programs begin with a form, an ActiveX Control project begins with a UserControl. You'll find the UserControl object very similar to the standard Form object, but it has some additional capabilities that will let your ActiveX Control do anything a control developed in any other language can.

Introducing ActiveX Controls

Make no mistake about it, ActiveX Controls are a peculiar kind of object. Unlike true components, controls can't be created with the New command or the CreateObject/GetObject functions. In Figure 8–1 you can see the position of ActiveX Controls in relation to other COM components. Until Visual Basic 6, the only way to create a control was to drag it onto a Visual Basic form from the toolbox at design time. At run time all that could be done was to create copies of an existing control in a control array. While Visual Basic 6 has extended the Load command so that a new control can be added to a form at run time, it's still an awkward process. ActiveX Controls remain the objects that are created at design time in the process of developing an application.

Even with these restrictions, ActiveX Controls provide the best way to solve a number of problems. If you want to package up functionality with a user interface that is to be integrated into the user interface of a number of different forms, ActiveX Controls are for you. ActiveX Controls can also be downloaded and installed silently (or as silently as your user will permit) over the Internet, allowing you to distribute applications over an intranet. If you're interested in selling programs developed in Visual Basic, the ActiveX Control market is one of the largest in the programming world.

Whenever anyone comments that Visual Basic isn't a true object-oriented programming tool, I concede that may be so. But I also point out that the Visual Basic Control market is the only commercial, wide--spread success story in object-oriented development.

A Typical ActiveX Control

My first ActiveX Control was for an order entry system. Because of the legacy data that the system was to use, retrieving customer information was a nightmare. For instance, to retrieve a customer's billing address, a program would first go to the customer table. If the address there was flagged as a billing address, that was the address to use. If it was not, the program would then have

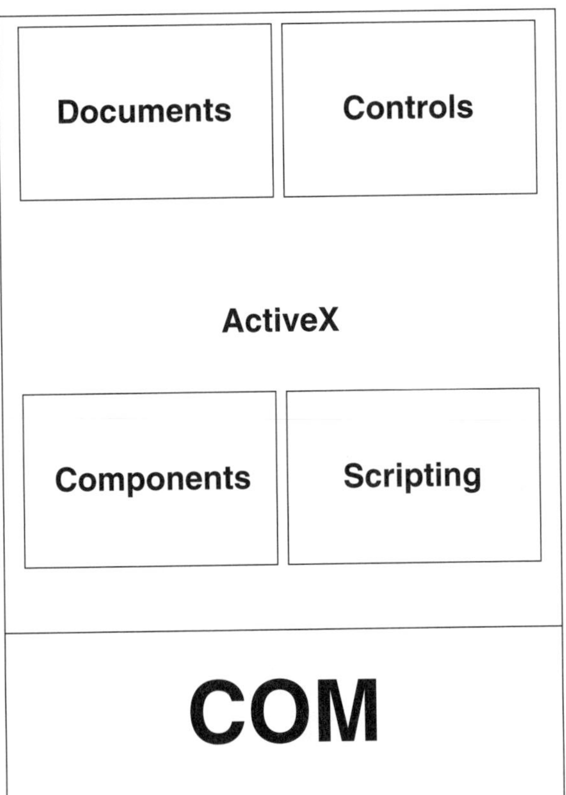

Figure 8–1 *The COM hierarchy including ActiveX Controls.*

to read the invoice table (unless the customer was flagged as an employee, in which case the program read the employee records table before reading the invoice table). An address in the invoice table could be used, provided it was from an invoice that was: a) paid and b) less than two years old. If an invoice like that couldn't be found, an address from the payments table could be used (provided the payment was less than one year old). If, at this point, the program still didn't have a valid address, it could use the original address found in the customer table. Updating the customer address had even more rules around it. And that was just one of the fields that made up the customer information.

Since customer information would have to be retrieved and displayed on many different forms, repeating this code on every form would only have compounded an already messy situation. Adding a standalone form to the project to handle customer information wouldn't have helped since the information needed to be integrated into the display of other forms in the system. Creating an ActiveX Control that included all of the appropriate functionality was the best answer.

To create the control, I launched an ActiveX Control project and dropped a series of controls onto the UserControl object that was included in the default version of the project. Most of the development of the control was no different from the development of the equivalent Visual Basic form. The major difference was that my code exposed a number of methods, properties, and events that allowed the container that the control was on to manipulate the control. Controls added to a UserControl are referred to as "constituent controls."

For instance, each of the TextBoxes on the UserControl had a property that allowed the code in the container to read and update the TextBox. The control had a CustomerName property that made the contents of the txtCustName TextBox available to the container's code. The relevant routines looked like this:

```
Public Property Get CustomerName() As String
    CustomerName = Me.txtCustName
End Property
Public Property Let CustomerName(CustName As String)
    Me.txtCustName = CustName
End Property
```

I gave the control three methods. The Read method, passed a customer number, loaded the various text boxes on the control with information from the system's database. Calling the Validate method caused all the edit checks on the data to be performed. Finally, the Update method would write the data in the control back to the database. To notify the client that something had gone wrong during the Read method, the control would fire the ReadFail event and pass an error code with the name of the field that was being read. Similarly, the WriteFail event fired if there was a problem while updating the database.

There were various other features built into the control. The AllData property, for instance, returned a UDT containing all the information displayed on the control. A ValidField property accepted a parameter consisting of a field name and returned an error code if the field failed its edit checks.

You can consider the creation of an ActiveX Control the equivalent of defining a small, reusable form that contains methods, properties, and events. Your code will have the same access to the controls on your UserControl object as your code has to controls on an ordinary Form object.

ActiveX Control Projects

In the same way that a Visual Basic project begins with a form, an ActiveX Control begins with a UserControl. Working with a UserControl is very much like working with a form. The first ActiveX Control that I created, in fact, looked very much like a standard Visual Basic form.

Your UserControl's code is saved in .CTL files. The compiled version of the control goes into a file with a .OCX extension, though the format of the file is identical to a DLL. Any developer that uses your ActiveX Control as part of an application must distribute its OCX with the application.

Your ActiveX Control project can contain as many ActiveX Controls as you want (see Figure 8–2). Each UserControl object that you add to your project defines another control. In effect, you can create a kind of "control component." As with a component, loading one member of the component loads the whole component into memory. As a result, when a developer adds your ActiveX Controls to their toolbox, any other controls in the same OCX file will also be added.

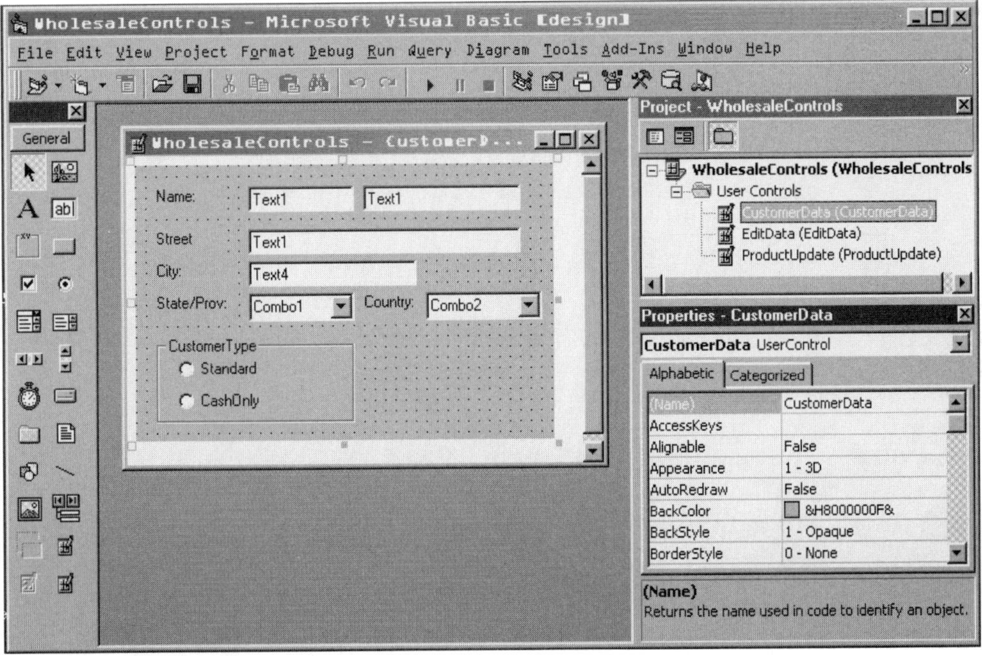

Figure 8–2 *An ActiveX Control project with multiple controls defined.*

Putting multiple controls in the same project makes sense where the controls share code. The common code can be put in standard modules and called from all the UserControls in the project. However, the more controls there are in a project, the larger the resulting OCX that must be distributed with any application that uses any of the controls. And, of course, at run time the whole component will be loaded into memory even if the application is using just one of the controls.

You can add other Visual Basic modules to your ActiveX project. Class modules, for instance, can make the development of an ActiveX Control easier, just as they can with a standard application. While an ActiveX Control that pops up a form at run time is certainly unusual, there's no reason that you couldn't write one.

You can add ActiveX Controls to the other Visual Basic project types (e.g., ActiveX DLL, Standard EXE). However, the control will be usable only to be used on Forms within the project.

Debugging an ActiveX Control

If the ActiveX Control project is the only one loaded (or is set as the startup project), pressing the Run button has some unusual results. When you run an ActiveX Control project, Visual Basic will create an HTML page that uses the control and then start Internet Explorer to have it load and display the page. If this is an effective strategy for you, you can create an HTML page that exercises the control and have Visual Basic use it. You can set the name of the page to call on the Project | Properties | Debug menu choice.

Normally, you will debug a UserControl like an ActiveX DLL. The steps to follow are:

1. Add a Standard EXE project to your Visual Basic session.
2. Set the new project as the startup project.
3. Drag your ActiveX Control from your toolbox onto the form in the new project.

You will not be able to test your control if its code won't compile or it's open in its designer (though you can leave the control's code window open). Some changes to your ActiveX Control will require you to delete the control and drag it onto the form again. All of these conditions are signaled by your ActiveX Control appearing with black diagonal lines across it on the test form.

ActiveX Controls and Visual Basic

Even if you never intend to create an ActiveX Control, the time spent learning how they work is well invested. For instance, until I started creating ActiveX Controls, I had no idea that a control's code was actually executing at design time. Of course, this should have been obvious to me since the controls responded when I changed their properties. As you'll see in a later chapter, Design Time Controls take this one step farther and run only at design time.

I never understood siting issues until I started working with ActiveX Controls. An ActiveX Control only runs within a container. As a result, until the ActiveX Control is fully loaded and located in the container, it's not fully functional. This process of positioning the control in the container is called *siting*. Once a control is sited, it has access to information about the container; prior to being sited, the control does not. One of the side effects of siting is that, should something go wrong with the control before it is sited, it may produce no error messages or the error messages may not be accurate. Only after a control has successfully finished siting can it be used safely.

I also assumed that the Visual Basic Integrated Development Environment (IDE) and an ActiveX Control must have a complex relationship that coupled the two of them closely together. In fact, ActiveX Controls and the Visual Basic IDE are very loosely coupled. When a control is added to a form, the IDE sweeps through all the properties for the control and adds them to Visual Basic's Property List. To display the control's properties, the Property List then reads the value for each property in the same way that any other program would. When a developer changes a value in the Property List, the Property List sets the value of the property just like any other client would.

The ActiveX Control's relationship with the Visual Basic IDE—or any other development environment—is the secret of its simplicity and flexibility. From the ActiveX Control's point of view, Visual Basic is just another program that sets and reads its properties. No special handling is involved.

UserControl Lifecycle Events

The events fired by the UserControl duplicate the events fired by the Visual Basic Form object. Some of the events fired by an ActiveX Control fire both at design time and run time. The Resize and Show events, for instance, fire in both environments. Other events normally fire only at runtime—the Click event, as an example. Later in this section you'll see how to activate those events at design time, also.

Any code that uses the RaiseEvent keyword is always ignored at design time.

There are a number of events that an ActiveX Control has that a Visual Basic form does not. I discuss them in this chapter in context of the properties or methods that they relate to. However, there are three events that are central to creating an ActiveX Control. They are InitProperties, ReadProperties, and WriteProperties. All of these events fire both at design time and run time.

The Life Cycle of an ActiveX Control

To understand why these three events are special, you need to understand the life cycle of an ActiveX Control (see Figure 8–3). In this section, I describe the life of an ActiveX Control after you've finished creating it, have compiled it, and it has been released to the world for developers to use.

An ActiveX Control begins its life when a developer draws it on a Visual Basic form or other ActiveX container. Once the control has been created, the control's properties can be read and set by the container's design time environment. The developer then works with the control, through the IDE, to tailor it for the application that it will be part of.

The next important milestone in the control's life occurs when the container is closed and removed from memory at the end of a design session. This causes the control to also be removed from memory. The problem is that, while the control was in memory, the developer using it will have set some of the control's properties. Since the developer expects those property settings to be maintained for the next design session, the control must store that information before it is removed from memory.

The next step in the control's life occurs when the container is reopened for further development activities and the control is loaded back into memory. At this point, the control must recover and reload any information stored when it was removed from memory. Depending on how many times the container is modified, this process of unloading and reloading the control in the design environment can be repeated many times.

Eventually, however, the control's container is compiled into an executable program and distributed to the application's end users. The control now continues to be loaded into memory as the application is invoked by its users. There is a slight difference: No design time activities take place and the control will now exhibit its run time behavior. When users finish working with the application, the control is removed from memory when the program is shut down.

INITPROPERTIES

The InitProperties event is fired when the ActiveX Control is added to the container. Since this is the beginning of life for your ActiveX Control, this is where you should perform any initialization tasks. Typically, this routine is used to set the default values for the properties that the control exposes. The standard for ActiveX Controls is to set default values for all the properties on the control. Providing default values for your properties is a real boon for developers, especially for controls that have a large number of properties. I know that on most of the controls I use, I set very few of the available properties and take the default values for most of them.

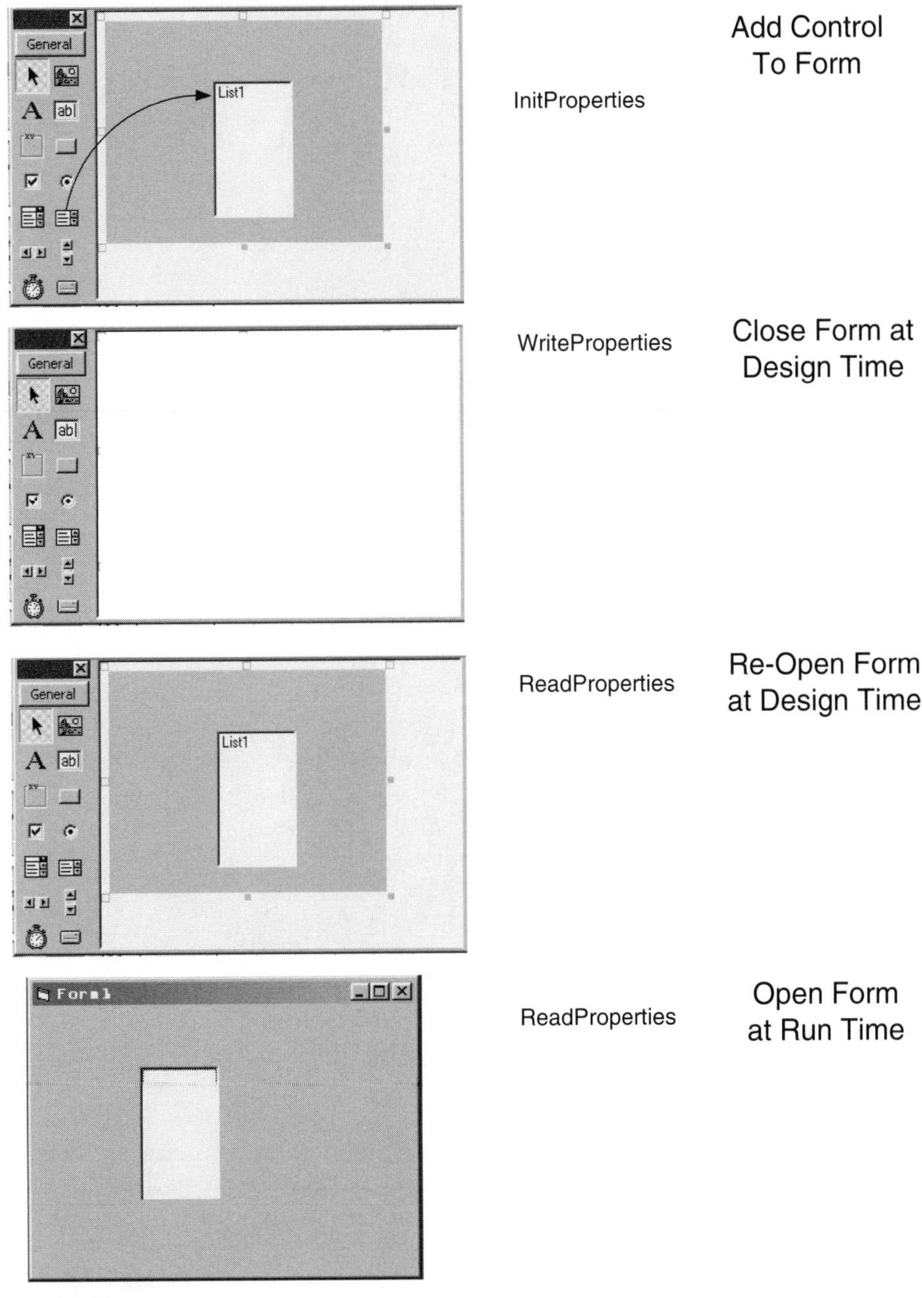

Figure 8–3 *The life cycle of an ActiveX Control.*

A typical InitProperties event will contain code that sets the values of the control's member variables. This code sets the value for the m_Caption variable:

```
Dim m_Caption As String

Private Sub UserControl_InitProperties()
m_Caption = "My Control"
End Sub
```

While you could use the control's Initialize event to set these values, the Initialize event fires each time that the control is loaded into memory. The InitProperties event fires only when the control is first created. As the control is reloaded into memory either at design time or run time, the InitProperties event will not fire again.

WRITEPROPERTIES

The WriteProperties event fires during design time, just before the container that the control is on is removed from memory. During the time that the container was open, the developer will have configured your ActiveX Control by setting its properties in Visual Basic's Property List. Since your control is about to be removed from memory, all record of those settings are in danger of being lost. The WriteProperties event provides you with a chance to write the value of those properties in a PropertyBag. I introduced the WriteProperties event and the PropertyBag object in the chapter on objects, and I return to them now primarily to look at the methods of the PropertyBag in more depth.

In the chapter on objects, you saw how the PropertyBag provided a way for a client to store a persistable object. As a result of a client calling the WriteProperty method of a PropertyBag to store an object, the object being stored received a WriteProperties event and a reference to the PropertyBag it was being stored in. In the same way, ActiveX Control containers are expected to provide a PropertyBag for the control to store data in. As with a persistable object, your control's code is not responsible for where the PropertyBag is stored; you are just responsible for putting the data that you need in the bag.

The PropertyBag object is still created by the client (in this case the container holding the control) and a reference to the PropertyBag is passed into the WriteProperties event that the control receives. At development time, the Visual Basic IDE will participate in providing the PropertyBag. At run time, the container alone is responsible for retrieving the PropertyBag. There are rules around when the container calls the WriteProperty method to store your ActiveX Control. For instance, an ActiveX container does not call the WriteProperty method as the container is removed from memory at run time. While an ActiveX Control is expected to remember what was done to it during design time, changes made at run time are discarded.

As an example, the following code saves the current value of the m_Caption variable under the name ControlCaption. The code also passes a default value of "My Control" as the third parameter to the WriteProperty method. As you can see, there's no difference between the WriteProperties event in an ActiveX Control and a persistable object:

```
Private Sub UserControl_WriteProperties _
(PropBag As PropertyBag)
 PropBag.WriteProperty "ControlCaption", m_Caption, _
"My Control"
End Sub
```

The default value in the third parameter controls whether anything is actually written to the PropertyBag. If the value in the m_Caption variable matches the default value in the third parameter (in this case, "My Control"), nothing is added to the PropertyBag. If there is already an entry in the PropertyBag under the name ControlCaption, then that entry will be removed rather than rewritten to the value of m_Caption. Since most properties on most controls are never changed from their default values, not writing to the PropertyBag when a property is at its default value can substantially reduce the amount of data put in the bag.

You must call the PropertyChanged method for at least one property on your control to have the WriteProperties event fire. If the container believes that no properties have changed, it will skip calling the WriteProperty method that triggers your control's WriteProperties method.

READPROPERTIES

The ReadProperties event fires when the control's container is loaded back into memory and your ActiveX Control is reactivated. A PropertyBag containing all the entries added in the WriteProperties event is passed into the event. As with a persistable object, this event is where you should pull any data out of the PropertyBag and restore your member variables to their previous state.

The following code retrieves the value stored under the ControlCaption name from the PropertyBag object passed to the event and passes it to the m_Caption variable. A default value of "My Control" is passed to the method as its second parameter.

```
Private Sub UserControl_ReadProperties _
(PropBag As PropertyBag)
m_Caption = PropBag.ReadProperty("ControlCaption", _
            "My Control")
End Sub
```

In the ReadProperty method, if an entry for the name is not found in the PropertyBag, then the default value in the second parameter is returned by the ReadProperty method. In the previous example, if no entry for "Control-Caption" is found in the ReadProperty method, the value "My Control" will be returned by the method.

It's essential you make sure that the value used as the default in the Read and Write operations is the same value. You should consider defining a Constant to hold the default value. While it isn't essential that the initial value used in the InitProperties match this default value, it usually turns out that it does.

UserControl Properties

The UserControl provides a number of properties that a standard Form object does not. Simply setting these properties allows your control to duplicate the behavior of ActiveX Controls. In this section I describe properties, more or less in alphabetical order. Some related properties (like the Backstyle and MaskPicture properties) are discussed together. I also defer the discussion of the various data-related properties until the next chapter, as they deserve a chapter to themselves.

AccessKeys

A shortcut key allows a user to activate a control by pressing the Alt key and a letter on the keyboard. A CommandButton with the caption Exit can be clicked by pressing Alt_X. Your control can duplicate this functionality by setting the AccessKeys property to the letter or letters that you want to be shortcuts for your control. This code, for instance, will cause your control to get focus when the Alt_A or Alt_F keys are pressed:

```
UserControl.AccessKeys = "af"
```

Where the focus will go within your control can be complicated. For instance, if there are controls on the form, the focus will go to the first control in the Tab order. This topic is discussed more fully under the CanGetFocus property.

If you are going to use the AccessKey property you will need to write a Property Procedure that allows the developer working with your control to set the AccessKeys property. This code shows a caption property that checks for an ampersand in the string passed to it and sets the AccessKeys property to the letter following the ampersand:

```
Public Property Let Caption (ControlCaption As String)
Dim intPos As Integer
```

```
    intPos = Instr(ControlCaption, "&")
    If intPos > 0 Then
      UserControl.AccessKeys = Mid(ControlCaption, _
                                   intPos + 1, 1)
    End If
End Property
```

A developer using a control with this code would set the shortcut key for the control like this:

```
UserControl11.Caption = "E&xit"
```

THE ACCESSKEYPRESS EVENT

The UserControl fires an AccessKeyPress event when one of the keys in the AccessKeys property is pressed even if the focus is already on your ActiveX Control. This is different from the GotFocus event, which will not fire if the control already has the focus. The KeyAscii parameter passed into the AccessKeyPress event allows you to determine which key fired the event. For some sample code, see the DefaultCancel property.

The AccessKeyPress event does not fire if a shortcut key for one of your ActiveX Control's constituent controls is pressed.

CONSTITUENT CONTROLS

Constituent controls on your ActiveX Control may also have shortcut keys. Any shortcut keys that you set up on your constituent controls will be treated as if they were listed in the UserControl's AccessKeys property. When a user presses the shortcut key for one of the constituent controls on your ActiveX Control, focus will shift to that constituent control. The event that fires when the focus shifts to the constituent control will vary, though. For instance, a CommandButton that has its access key pressed will fire a Click event before any other event.

Alignable

The Alignable property can be set to True or False (the default) to signal to the container whether or not the content of your control can be aligned. Setting the Alignable property has no effect on the appearance or position of your ActiveX Control. Setting this property to True will cause the PropertyList to display an Align property when a developer is using your control. The developer can set this property to one of the available values (in Visual Basic these are Left, Right, Top, and Bottom). In some containers, like Visual Basic, setting the Align property will cause the container to adjust the location of your control (see Figure 8–4).

While setting the Alignable property has no effect on your control, you may want to write code to respond to changes in the Align property. You might, for instance, want to adjust the location of your constituent controls to

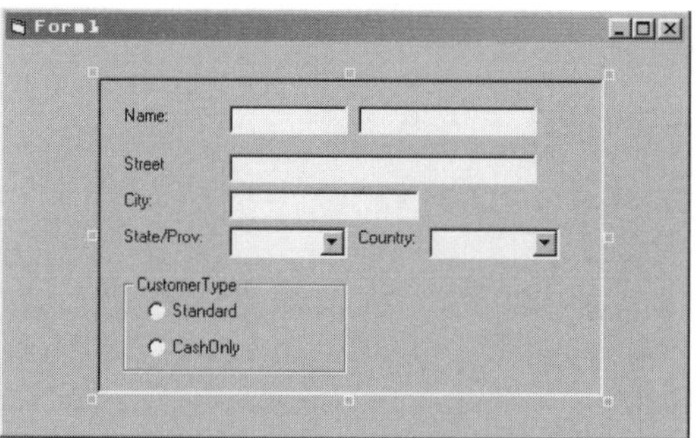

AlignNone

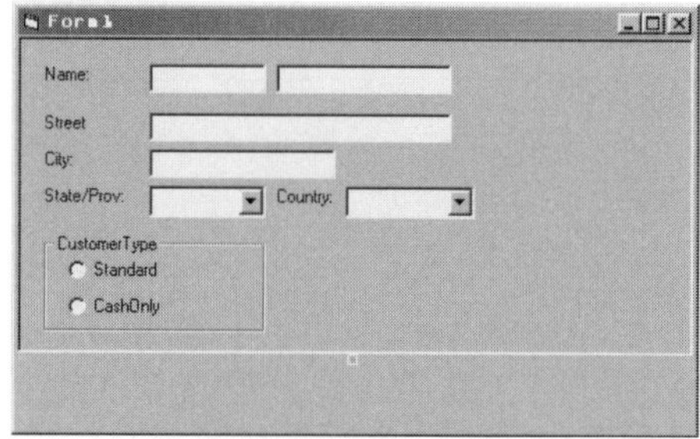

AlignTop

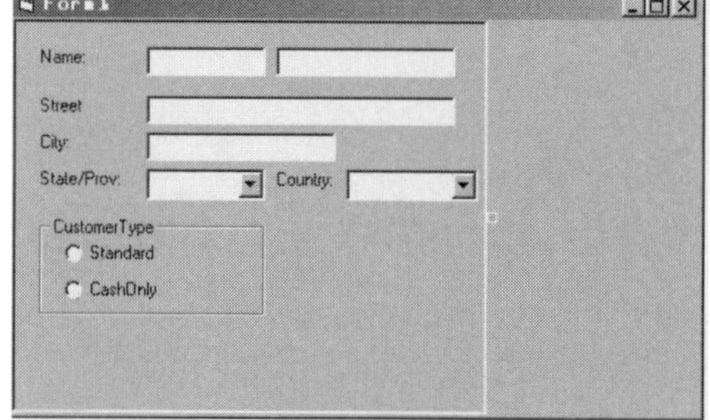

AlignLeft

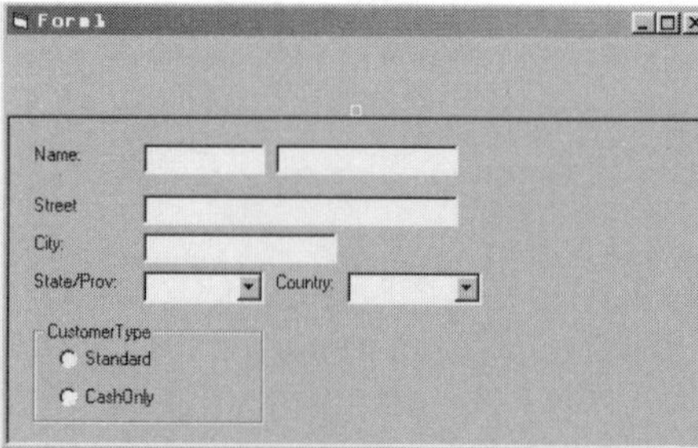

AlignBottom

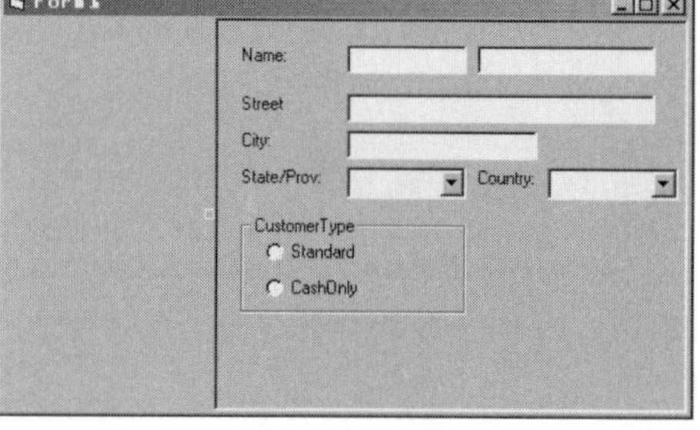

AlignRight

Figure 8–4 *A control aligned Left, Right, Top, and Bottom in Visual Basic.*

match the way that your ActiveX Control has been aligned. Later in this section, under the discussion of the Extender object, I show you how you can determine how your control is aligned.

Align is different from Alignment. Alignment refers to how characters are justified in text (left, right, center, or full). Align describes the way that controls relate to each other. Lining up all the text boxes on the form so that their right or left edges match is an example of using Align.

BackStyle

Setting a UserControl's BackStyle property to Transparent causes any controls placed underneath your ActiveX Control to "show through." Ignoring the MaskPicture and MaskColor properties, which I discuss later, the only areas of your control that will be opaque are:

- where there are constituent controls
- where you've drawn or printed on the surface of the control (i.e., using the Print, Line, or Circle methods)

In addition, run time mouse events will be passed through the transparent areas to other controls that the developer places underneath your control or to the container itself. This ability to "pass through" events requires Visual Basic to determine which of a series of controls that are stacked on top of each other should receive a mouse event. If all of the controls have their Windowless property set to False, the first control with an opaque area underneath the mouse will get the event. I discuss the Windowless property in more detail later in this chapter, but it seems appropriate to discuss its effect on events now.

Before you start reading this next section, you should consider whether you are interested at all. I describe how to handle mouse events when a developer stacks a set of transparent, windowless controls on top of each other. If you never intend to create a transparent, windowless control, you can skip down to the next property entry.

WINDOWLESS CONTROLS

Assigning events to a set of controls placed on top of each other gets complicated if the controls have their Windowless property set to True. When a mouse event, like MouseOver or Click, occurs over a set of stacked controls, Visual Basic will make up to three passes through the stack of controls to decide which one should get the event. The first control in the stack that has a non-transparent area under the mouse will get the event. Failing to find a control that meets that condition, Visual Basic will next look for a control where the mouse event was close to a non-transparent part of the control. If that also fails, Visual Basic will pass the event to the topmost control where the mouse event took place inside of the control's area.

CLIPBEHAVIOR

On windowless controls that have their BackStyle property set to Transparent, the ClipBehavior property controls where non-transparent areas appear. Setting ClipBehavior to vbClipRegion causes graphics that you draw on your UserControl to appear only if drawn on a non-transparent area. Setting ClipBehavior to vbClipNone allows the graphics to display regardless of the state of the UserControl area that they are drawn on.

If you set ClipBehaviour to vbClipRegion, then you will have to use the MaskPicture and MaskColor properties to make some of your control non-transparent. Figure 8–5 shows the result of switching the ClipBehavior property from Region to None.

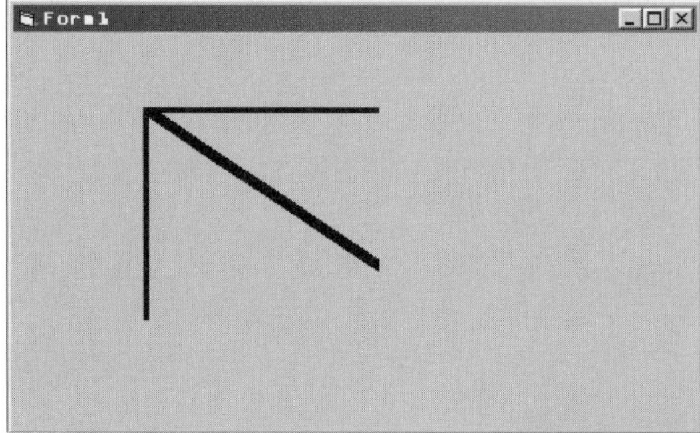

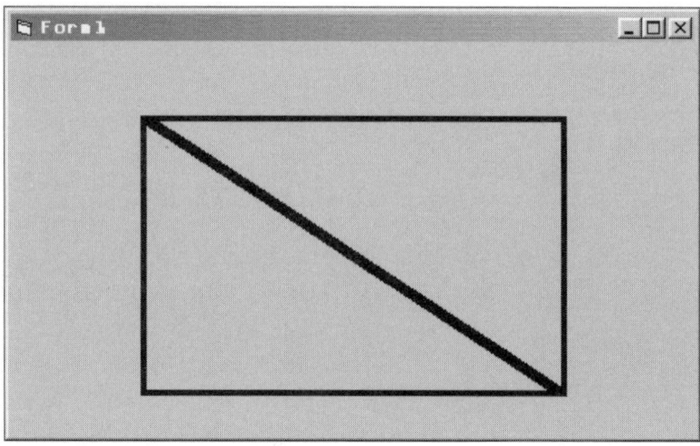

Figure 8–5 *The same control with and without clipping.*

MASKPICTURE AND MASKCOLOR

The MaskPicture and MaskColor properties are used to create non-transparent areas of the control. Unlike the Picture property, the MaskPicture property does not cause the UserControl to display a picture. Instead, when the UserControl's BackStyle property is set to Transparent, the MaskPicture and the MaskColor properties define a pattern of transparent and non-transparent areas on the UserControl. Loading the MaskPicture property with a bitmap overlays the UserControl with the picture. The areas of the MaskPicture that are the same color as the MaskColor property will be transparent. The areas of the MaskPicture that do not match the MaskColor property will display the UserControl's BackColor. The MaskPicture itself is not actually displayed (see Figure 8–6 for an example).

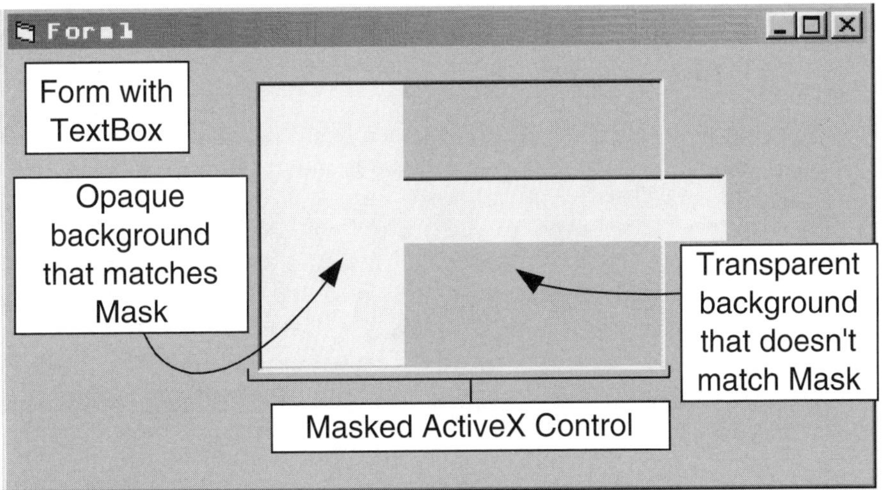

Figure 8–6 *A control with a MaskPicture loaded and MaskColor set to black.*

Like the Form object's Picture property, you can set the MaskPicture property either at design time or at run time. If you set the property at run time, you can either copy it from the picture property of some other control or load a picture from a file using the LoadPicture function. This code demonstrates both techniques:

```
UserControl.MaskPicture = Image1.Picture
UserControl.MaskPicture = LoadPicture ("C:\MyMask.JPG")
```

Only black and white work reliably for the MaskPicture/MaskColor operations.

The MaskPicture is not resized to fit the control, so you will probably need to fix the size of your ActiveX Control (see the InvisibleAtRuntime property for the code to do that).

To sum up: If the UserControl's ClipBehavior property is set to None, then graphics, MaskColor/MaskPicture areas, and constituent controls form non-transparent areas. If ClipBehavior is set to Region, then only the MaskPicture and MaskColor properties control transparency.

THE HITTEST EVENT

Now that your stacked, transparent, windowless controls have some non-transparent areas, you can start controlling which controls get the mouse events. As Visual Basic processes a stack of controls, you can use the UserControl's HitTest event to determine if your control should receive the event. The HitTest event will fire before any other event in the control. When the HitTest event is fired, your control is passed the *x* and *y* coordinates of the mouse and a "HitResult" parameter. The HitResult parameter will have one of two values:

0: indicates that the mouse was clicked over a transparent area of the control

3: indicates that the mouse was clicked over a constituent control or an area of the UserControl that has been drawn on

You can leave the HitResult parameter alone or change it to any value from 0 to 3. Leaving or setting the value to 0 indicates that you do not want your control to receive the mouse event. A value of 3 indicates that you want to receive the event unless some control higher in the stack also returns a 3.

You can also change HitResult to 1 or 2. A 2 indicates that you feel that the mouse was clicked close to a non-transparent area on your control (how you determine what "close" means is up to you). You won't get the mouse event unless no other control returns a 3 and no control higher in the stack also returns a 2. A 1 indicates that the mouse event occurred within your control (again, how you determine that is up to you) but not close to a non-transparent area. You will get the event unless some control higher in the stack returns a 1 or any control returns a 2 or 3.

A HITTEST EXAMPLE

The following example shows the kind of code that you can write to determine if a hit is "close" or "inside." This code assumes that the control is a 500 by 500 units square and has its BackStyle property set to Transparent. At the center of the square is a hollow box, 100 units on a side (i.e., the box runs from 200, 200 to 200, 300 on the control). The sides of the box are 5 units wide, so the transparent center of the box runs from 205, 205 to 295, 295. Only the area actually occupied by the lines of the square will be recognized as non-transparent by Visual Basic (see Figure 8–7).

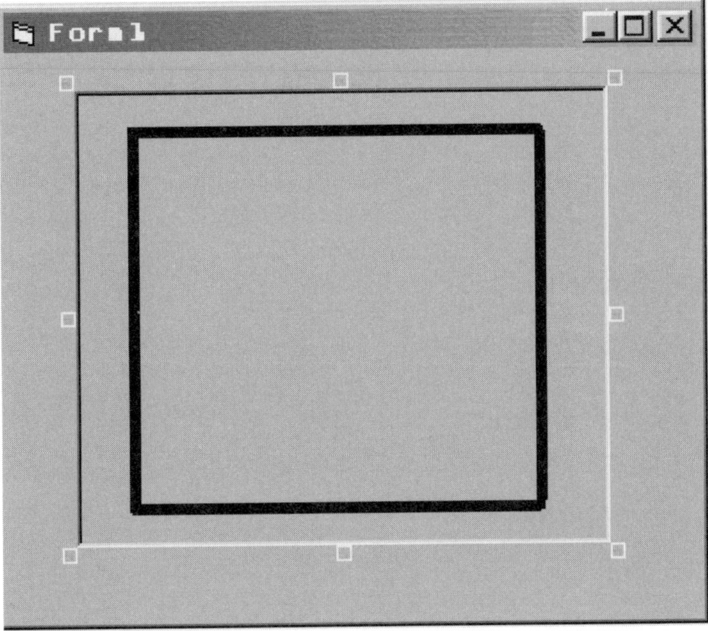

Figure 8–7 *A control with a set of hit regions defined.*

The non-transparent box could have been created three different ways:

- ClipBehavior is set to None and the box was drawn with the Line method
- ClipBehavior is set to None and the box is a constituent control
- Clipbehavior is set to region and the box is the result of using MaskPicture/MaskColor

If the mouse event occurs over one of the lines that make up the box, the HitTest event will be passed a 3. A mouse event over any other part of the control will receive a 0. To improve the chances of the user hitting the box, the HitTest event contains code to promote the HitResult of 0 to 2 for any event that occurs inside the box. An event outside the box, but within 10 units of it (i.e., from 195, 195 to 315, 315) is promoted from a 0 to a 1:

```
Private Sub UserControl_HitTest(X As Single, Y As Single, _
                                HitResult As Integer)
If HitResult = 0 Then
    If X > 205 And X < 295 And _
      Y > 205 And Y < 295 Then
    'mouse co-ordinates inside the box
      HitResult = 2
    ElseIf X > 195 And X < 315 And _
      Y > 195 And Y < 315 Then
      'mouse co-ordinates within 10 units of the box
      HitResult = 1
    End If
End If
End Sub
```

To use the terms from the Visual Basic documentation, a 3 indicates that the event took place in the control's "Mask" area and a 0 indicates the event is in the control's "Outside" area. The 2 is said to be in the "Close" area and the 1 indicates the "Transparent" area.

Since mouse events fire at design time, you may want to check the Usermode before taking any action. If you don't, this event's processing will occur every time the developer drags the mouse over the control code.

HITBEHAVIOR

The HitBehavior property can be set to vbUseRegion (the default), vbHitBehaviorNone, or vbHitBehaviorUsePaint. Using vbHitBehaviorNone means that the HitTest event will always be passed a 0 (though you can set it in the HitTest event to whatever value you want to return). Some performance gains are made by Visual Basic, which does less testing before calling the HitTest event.

The default setting of vbHitBehaviorUseRegion causes the HitTest event to receive a 3 if a mouse event occurs over a non-transparent area of the mask (i.e., any area of the MaskPicture that matches the color of MaskColor). Performance is slower than with vbHitBehaviorNone.

Setting the property vbHitBeviorUsePaint reduces performance again but causes the HitTest routine to pass a 3 only where a mouse event occurs directly over a graphic. As an example, this setting is required when you have graphics drawn on the UserControl with the Line and Circle methods and want the HitTest event to pass you a 3 when they are clicked on. This was the setting that I assumed for the preceding example.

CanGetFocus

Not all controls can get the focus (i.e., be clicked on or tabbed to). A Label control cannot get the focus, for instance. If you want your control to behave this way, just set the UserControl CanGetFocus property to False (the default is True). When this property is set to False, then your ActiveX Control can't have any constituent controls that can get the focus.

When building an ActiveX Control, if you set UserControl's CanGetFocus property to False, Visual Basic will gray out all the controls on the toolbox that can accept focus. This effectively highlights the only controls that can still be added to the UserControl

Even if your UserControl has CanGetFocus set to True, the UserControl will not get the focus if it has any constituent controls that can get the focus. When focus is moved to your ActiveX Control, the focus will actually be received by the first control in the tab order that can accept focus (i.e., is not a Label Control). Only if none of the constituent controls are controls that can accept focus will a UserControl with constituent controls fire a GotFocus event.

It's your responsibility to alter the appearance of your ActiveX Control to indicate that it has received the focus. If you have constituent controls, this will be taken care of automatically: The control receiving the focus will automatically redraw itself. A CommandButton, for instance, will draw a box around its caption when it gets the focus.

If your control has no constituent controls that can receive focus, then you will have to add the code yourself to indicate that your control has the focus. The following code sets the UserControl's BorderStyle to Fixed Single when the control gets focus and to None when it loses focus:

```
Private Sub UserControl_GotFocus()
    UserControl.BorderStyle = 1
End Sub

Private Sub UserControl_LostFocus()
    UserControl.BorderStyle = 0
End Sub
```

ControlContainer

A ControlContainer is a control that a developer can place other controls on. ActiveX Controls that a developer places on a ContainerControl cannot be dragged off the container. When the developer moves the ContainerControl, any controls that have been placed on it move with it. If a container's Visible Property is set to False, the controls placed on it are also made invisible. If the

ContainerControl is disabled, all the contained controls are also disabled. Visual Basic's Panel is an example of a ControlContainer. A control container provides a window that the contained controls are displayed in. In Figure 8–8 you can see a control container with one of its contained controls only partially displayed at the bottom.

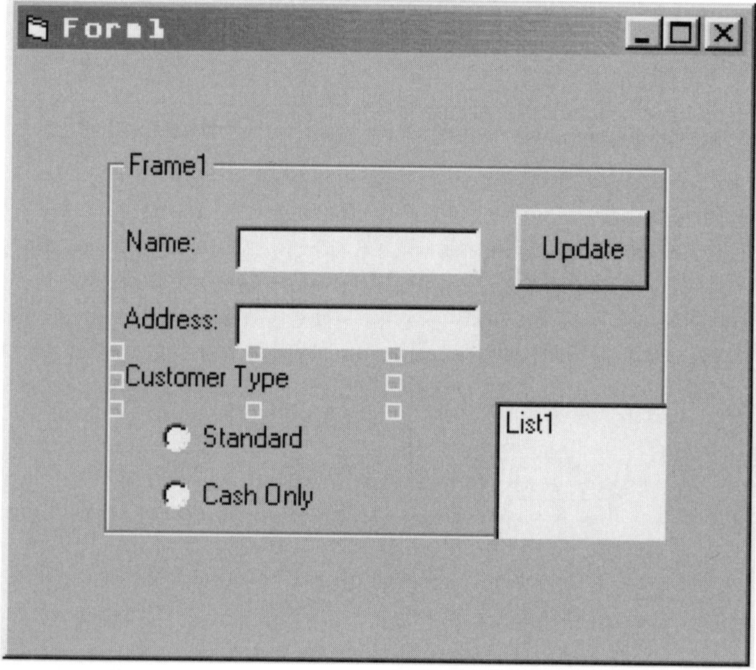

Figure 8–8 *A control container.*

Contained controls are a different concept from constituent controls. You add constituent controls to your ActiveX Control as part of creating it. After you compile and distribute an ActiveX Control with its ContainerControl property set to True, a developer can draw your control on a form, and then place other controls on it. They do not become constituent controls but can be managed by your ActiveX Control. If you take advantage of Visual Basic 6's ability to load new controls at run time with the Load command, those controls are also constituent controls.

If you set your UserControl's BackStyle to Transparent, any controls placed on a transparent area of your control will disappear.

Container controls require that the container they are placed on support some specific ActiveX interfaces. The Visual Basic Form does, but the Access 97 Form object does not. A ContainerControl placed on an Access 97 form will work, but any controls that the developer places on it will be disabled.

CONTAINEDCONTROLS

The ContainedControls collection lets you manipulate the controls that a developer has placed on your ContainerControl. This code, for instance, loops through all the controls on the container setting any text boxes to a zero length string:

```
Dim ctl As Control
For Each ctl In UserControl.ContainedControls
    If TypeOf ctl Is TextBox Then
      ctl.Value = ""
    End If
Next
```

ContainerHwnd

While the name of this property might make you think that it is related to creating a ContainerControl, you'd be wrong. This property returns a reference to the window of the container that your control has been drawn on. If your ActiveX Control has been placed on a Visual Basic form, this property contains a reference to the form's window.

DefaultCancel

Some controls can be set up as the Default or Cancel control for a form. A CommandButton, for instance, has a Default property and a Cancel property. Setting a CommandButton's Default property to True will cause the CommandButton's Click event to fire when the user presses the Enter key. Setting the Cancel property to True will cause the CommandButton's Click event to fire when the Escape key is pressed.

You can give your ActiveX Control the same ability by setting the UserControl's DefaultCancel property to True. This will automatically add the Default and Cancel properties to your control—you don't have to write any code to implement these properties. If a developer sets either of these properties to True, your control's AccessKeyPress event will be fired when the user presses the Enter or Escape key. Again, you don't have to add any code to make this happen. All you need to do is put the code you want to run in the AccessKeyPress event.

If you also let developers assign shortcut keys to your control using the AccessKey property, you may want to distinguish between when the Access-

KeyPress event is fired by a shortcut key or by the Enter/Escape key. You can do this with the KeyAscii parameter passed into the event:

The AccessKeyPress event fires if the UserControl has the focus and the user presses the Enter key, regardless of the setting of the Default property.

```
Private Sub UserControl_AccessKeyPress(KeyAscii As Integer)

Select Case KeyAscii
Case vbKeyReturn
      'Enter key pressed
    Case vbKeyEscape
      'Escape key pressed
    Case Else
      'other shortcut keys
End Select

End Sub
```

Only one control on a form can have its Default property set to True. When you set a control's Default property to True, any other controls have their Default property set to False. The same is true for the Cancel property. This is also taken care of for you.

The Windows standard is for the Default control to display differently from the other controls on the form. A CommandButton that is the Default control for the form will display a thick black border. It is your responsibility to determine whether you are the Default control and alter your control's appearance. You can determine if you are the Default control by checking the Extender object (I discuss the Extender object later in this chapter).

You can't set the Default or Cancel properties for any constituent controls unless the UserControl's DefaultCancel property is set to True.

EditAtDesignTime

Setting this property to True allows the developer to put your control into a run time state while working with it at design time. This means that the UserControl events that normally don't fire at design time (like the Click event or events for your constituent controls) will now fire. To turn on this ability, the developer must right-click on your ActiveX Control and select Edit from the popup menu (see Figure 8–9). The control will stay in this run time mode until the developer shifts the focus to another control.

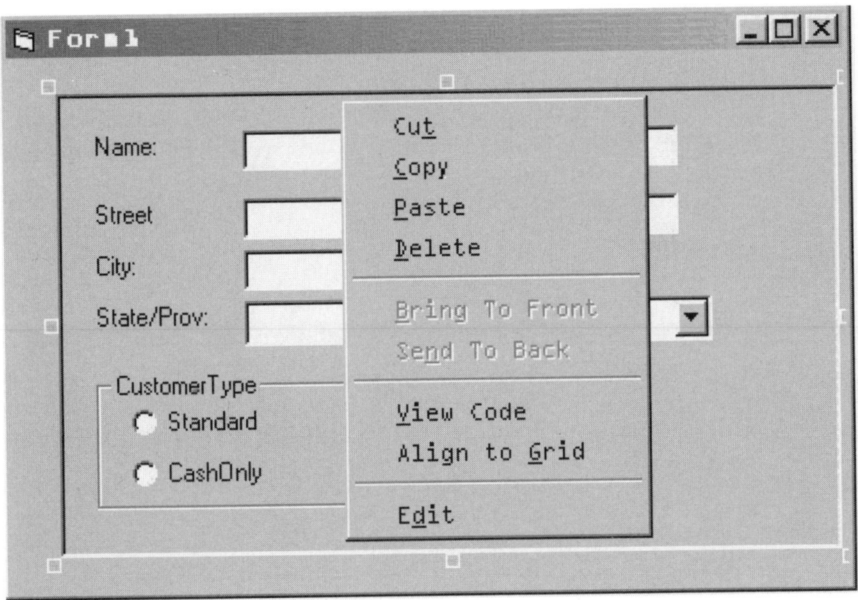

Figure 8–9 *A control's popup menu, showing the Edit command.*

While the code is in the run time state, the developer will not be able to move the control. Once in the run time state, clicking on the control will fire the UserControl's Click event instead of selecting the control.

EventsFrozen

When EventsFrozen property is True, it indicates that the container will not respond to any events that you raise from your control. Since the container isn't responding to any events, you can use this property to decide to skip raising events or defer them until later:

```
If UserControl.EventsFrozen = True Then
    bolFireWarningEvent = True
End If
If UserControl.EventsFrozen = False Then
    RaiseEvent WarningEvent
End If
```

ForwardFocus

Some controls, when they receive the focus, automatically move the focus to the next control in the tab order. The Visual Basic Label control, for instance, has this behavior. You can give your ActiveX Control the same behavior by setting the ForwardFocus property to True.

If ForwardFocus is set to False, your control can receive the focus but only if the control's CanGetFocus property is also set to True. The setting of CanGetFocus is irrelevant if ForwardFocus is True.

Hyperlink

If your control is being used on a container that can request Web pages, you can use this property to retrieve a Hyperlink object. The Hyperlink object lets you issue commands to the container. The Hyperlink object's NavigateTo method lets you tell the container to request a new Web page. This code, for instance, causes the container (if it supports Hyperlink navigation) to request the default page from the Microsoft site:

```
UserControl.Hyperlink.NavigateTo _
          "http://www.microsoft.com"
```

InvisibleAtRunTime

The name says it all. A control with this property set to True will not be visible at run time on any form that it is placed on when the form is running (though the control will be visible when the form is in design mode).

Typically, a control that's invisible at run time will have a fixed size. The simplest way to ensure that happens is to use this code in the UserControl's Resize event:

```
Private Sub UserControl_Resize()
    Me.Height = 500
    Me.Width = 500
End Sub
```

The InvisibleAtRunTime process actually prevents your control from being placed on the form at run time. As a result, some properties (like the Extender properties discussed later in this chapter) are not supported.

Not all containers support the InvisibleAtRunTime property, so your control may display even if you set this property to True. In the section on UserControl Events, I discuss how to handle this.

Parent

This property returns a reference to the container that your ActiveX Control is being used on. You use the Parent property to access the methods and properties of the control's container. This code, for instance, displays the caption of the form that the control is situated on:

```
MsgBox UserControl.Parent.Caption
```

Some care has to be taken when using the Parent property because different containers have different methods and properties. You should always put in error checking to handle situations when the property or method that you are trying to access isn't supported by the control's Parent. This code displays the message "No Caption Available" if the control's container doesn't have a caption property:

```
Dim strCaption As String

On Error Resume Next
strCaption = UserControl.Parent.Caption
If Err.Number > 0 Then
    strCaption = "No Caption Available"
End If
Msgbox strCaption
```

The Parent property (and related properties that provide information about the container) cannot be used until the control is sited. As a result, you shouldn't access this property any earlier than the Show event. Using this property in the Initialize or InitProperties event will prevent your control from loading.

PARENTCONTROLS

ParentControls is a collection that provides access to all of the controls in the container that your ActiveX Control is being used on. On a Visual Basic Form, this collection includes the Form itself. In addition to giving you access to the container's controls, the ParentControls collection has a Count property that returns the number of controls in the collection.

Since the ParentControls collection is available at design time, you can, by setting the EditAtDesignTime property to True, create an ActiveX Control that supports development activities. An ActiveX Control, added to a form, could write out a documentation file for the form it sits on, as an example.

The following code demonstrates the ParentControls collection by loading an array with the name and current value of each text box on the container. The routine begins by declaring a variable to refer to each item in the collection. Since the collection includes controls and the form itself, the variable has to be declared as Object. The routine then uses the collection's Count property to dimension an array called strText. The array is made large enough to hold one entry for each control on the container. With the array dimensioned properly, the code uses a For...Next loop to process each control in the collection:

```
Dim obj As Object
Dim strText() As String
Dim intCount As Integer

ReDim strText(1,UserControl.ParentControls.Count - 1)

For Each obj In ParentControls
     If TypeOf obj Is TextBox Then
       strText(0,intCount) = obj.Name
       strText(1,intCount) = obj.Text
       intCount = intCount + 1
End If
Next
```

In the ParentControls collection, which of the controls' properties can be accessed will vary from container to container. Some containers will provide the Extender properties, other containers will not (I discuss the Extender properties later in this chapter). As an example, the Visual Basic Form object does provide the Extender properties, while Internet Explorer does not.

You can determine whether the container provides the Extender properties by checking the ParentControls collection's ParentControlsType property. If ParentControlsType is equal to vbExtender, then the Extender properties of the controls in the collection can be used. If the property is equal to vbNoExtender, then the properties will not be available.

This code sets the Left property (an Extender property) of every text box to 0, but only if the container makes Extender properties available:

```
Dim obj As Object

If UserControl.ParentControls.ParentControlType = _
              vbExtender Then
    For Each obj In ParentControls
      If TypeOf obj Is TextBox Then
        obj.Left = 0
      End If
    Next
End If
```

Public

You can set the Public property of a UserControl to False if you want to prevent it from being accessed by clients outside of your ActiveX Control Component.

ToolboxBitmap

Set this property to the icon you want to display in the toolbox to represent your ActiveX Control. This should be a bitmap 16 pixels high × 15 pixels wide. If you provide a bitmap with a different size, it will be stretched or compressed to fit. In Figure 8–10 you can see the results of compressing a bitmap that was larger than 16 × 15 pixels.

Figure 8–10 *A 32 X 32 pixel bitmap compressed to a Toolbox Bitmap.*

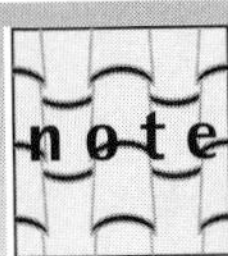

Your control will also get a Tooltip to display in the toolbox. When a developer hovers the mouse over your control's icon in the toolbox, the UserControl's Name property will be displayed.

Windowless

You can create a lightweight ActiveX Control by setting the UserControl's Windowless property to True. Windowless controls use fewer system resources than standard ActiveX Controls and generally run faster. They accomplish this by not exposing a reference to a window that a control is normally displayed in (which is why they are referred to as "windowless"). Both Visual Basic's Label and Image controls are lightweight controls.

Windowless controls have some restrictions compared to normal ActiveX Controls. You can only use other lightweight ActiveX Controls as constituent controls on a windowless ActiveX Control. You can't use the BorderStyle property of the UserControl to indicate when your control has focus—without a window you don't have a border. The EditAtDesignTime property is also disabled. You cannot set the ControlContainer property to True.

You won't be able to make API calls from your lightweight control if the call requires that you to pass a reference to your window. If you do need to make an API call that requires a reference to the window for your control, you can try using the UserControl's ContainerHwnd property. While this property is a reference to the window of the container that your control is on, rather than to your control's window, it sometimes works. Developers who use API calls that require a reference to a control's window won't be able to use those calls with your lightweight control.

While some containers don't support lightweight controls, developers should still be able to use your control in those environments—the container will just create a window for your control.

Setting ClipBehavior to vbUseRegion will have no effect in contaainers that don't support windowless controls because they display your control in a window.

The Extender Object

As you've added controls to Visual Basic forms, you've probably noticed that there are some properties that are shared by all ActiveX Controls: Top, Left, Tag, etc. Now that you're thinking about creating your own ActiveX Controls, you may also have noticed that some of these properties don't really make sense until you add the control to a container. What does a Top property, for instance, mean until the control is placed on a container? And, if the Top property changes, how could you write code to safely relocate your control in the container anyway?

These properties are not, in fact, properties of the ActiveX Control. So, the good news is that you don't have to write any code for them. They are, instead, properties of the container that the control is being used in.

You could look at these properties, like Top and Left, as properties of the form that are used to describe where each control on the form is located. When you change the Top value, it's the form that relocates the associated control. Rather than present these properties in a long list associated with the form, they are presented as part of the Property List for the control that they are associated with.

To be technically accurate, the Property List is actually showing you the properties for the Extender object that Visual Basic wraps around all ActiveX Controls. The Extender object exposes all of the properties of the ActiveX Control that it contains along with its own properties.

USING THE EXTENDER OBJECT

You can gain access to these properties through the Extender object that Visual Basic creates for your control. The Extender object is available through the Extender property of the UserControl object. As an example, this code displays the Top property for the control:

```
MsgBox UserControl.Extender.Top
```

A more useful example is the following code. The code displays an error message but uses the Extender's Name property. The Extender's Name property is the name given to the control by the developer when the control is added to the container:

```
Msgbox "Invalid Condition in control " & _
       UserControl.Extender.Name
```

The Extender properties are available at design time, allowing you to modify what's done to your control. This code, for instance, ensures that the control always relocates itself to the upper left corner of the container that it's in:

```
Private Sub UserControl_WriteProperties _
          (PropBag As PropertyBag)
     UserControl.Extender.Top = 0
     UserControl.Extender.Left = 0

End Sub
```

Microsoft advises against setting the Extender properties as those properties are the responsibility of the developer using the control.

EXTENDER LIMITATIONS

Not all containers support all possible Extender properties. Of the properties that are available, some of them are available only some of the time. The Align property, for instance, is available only if the UserControl's Alignable property is set to True. Unless you are tying your control to a specific container, you should always include error handling code around any use of the Extender property to handle the situation where the property isn't available.

The following code checks to see if the container has an Align property. If it does, the control moves all of the controls to the appropriate edge of the control:

```
Dim ctl As Control

On Error Resume Next
If err.Number = 0 Then
    Select Case UserControl.Extender.Align
      Case vbAlignLeft
        For Each ctl In UserControl.Controls
          ctl.Left = 0
        Next
      Case vbAlignRight
        For Each ctl In UserControl.Controls
          ctl.Left = _
                     UserControl.Width - ctl.width
        Next
    Case vbAlignTop
        For Each ctl In UserControl.Controls
          ctl.Top = 0
        Next
    Case vbAlignRight
        For Each ctl In UserControl.Controls
          ctl.Top = _
                    UserControl.Height - ctl.Height
        Next
    End Select
End If
```

Table 8.1 lists the properties that are supposed to be supplied by any Extender object. However, if you want your control to run in the largest number of containers, you shouldn't assume that these properties are present either.

Table 8.1 The Recommend Extender Properties

Property Name	Data Type	Read/ Write	Description
Name	String	R	The name the user assigns to the control instance.
Visible	Boolean	RW	Indicates whether the control is visible.
Parent	Object	R	Returns the object which contains the control, such as a Visual Basic form.
Cancel	Boolean	R	True if the control is the cancel button for the container.
Default	Boolean	R	True if the control is the default button for the container.

Extender properties are late bound, so accessing them is slow. You should try to minimize the number of times that you use the Extender object.

DUPLICATING NAMES

If you create a property that duplicates an Extender property for the container, things can get awkward for the developers using your control. If, for instance, you defined a property called Fred, your code will not be accessed if the container's Extender has also has a Fred property. If the developer wants to access your control's Fred property, they must use this syntax:

```
UserControl.Object.Fred = 4
```

The Visual Basic form actually wraps your ActiveX Control inside another object which duplicates all of your control's methods and properties. This wrapper has the Object property which the developer can use to access your control directly, as the prerceding code does.

The Ambient Object

Like the Extender object, the Ambient object gives you access to information about your control's container. The Ambient control provides information about the container. Particularly, the Ambient object provides access to properties about the appearance of the container. These properties allow you to add code to your control to integrate it more completely into your container's appearance. Figure 8–11 shows the results of building a control that doesn't integrate with its container.

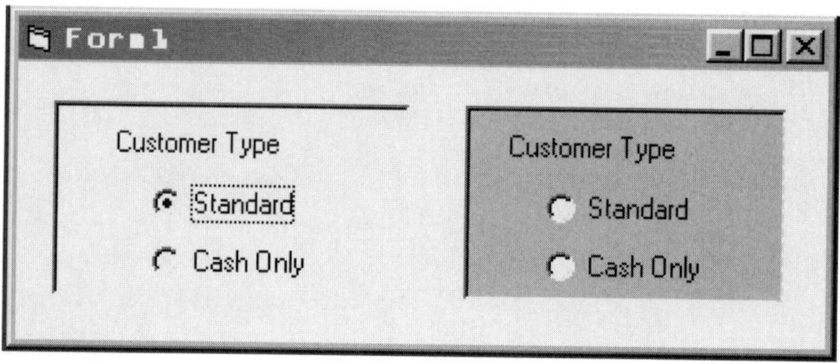

Figure 8–11 *The control on the left is using the ambient object to match the container's background color.*

As an example, this code makes sure that the UserControl's BackColor matches the color of its container:

```
UserControl.BackColor = UserControl.Ambient.BackColor
```

This code draws a black line around the UserControl if it is the Default control for the form:

```
If UserControl.Ambient.DisplayAsDefault = True Then
     UserControl.Line (0,0)-(UserControl.Extender.Width, _
                              UserControl.Extender.Height)
End If
```

One of the more useful Ambient properties is UserMode. When this property is False, it indicates that the control is being used in design mode. A value of True indicates that the control is in run time or that the property isn't supported by the container. UserMode allows you to have properties behave one way at design time and another way at run time. For instance, a property that is read-only at design time but read-write at run time, could be written to return a zero length string at design time:

```
Public Property Get ReadAtRunTime() As String
     If UserControl.Ambient.UserMode = False Then
       ReadAtDesignTime = ""
     Else
       ..run time processing...
     End If
End Property
```

Table 8.2 lists the recommended Ambient properties that every container is expected to provide. Again, like the Extender object, you shouldn't count on any particular property being available unless you are writing your control to be used in only one container.

Table 8.2 Recommended Ambient Properties

Property Name	Description
LocaleID	Provides a code indicating the conventions around displaying dates, currency, and other regional settings.
UserMode	Indicates if the container is in design time or run time.
DisplayAsDefault	True when the control is the Default control for the form.

AMBIENTCHANGED EVENT

If you intend to use the Ambient object to integrate your control into your container, then you also need to know when the ambient properties change. The AmbientChanged event meets this need by firing whenever an ambient property is changed in the container. The event is passed the name of the property that changed as a parameter.

Typical code in the AmbientChanged event uses a Select structure and the PropertyName parameter to determine what action to take. The following code handles two properties. If the container's BackColor changes, the code changes the UserControl's BackColor to match. If the Default property is changed, then the code checks to see if the property is now True or False. If the control has become the Default control, the code draws a black line around the control. If the control is no longer the Default control, the code draws a line the same color as the BackColor around the control:

```
Private Sub UserControl_AmbientChanged _
(PropertyName As String)

Select Case PropertyName
  Case _BackColor_
    UserControl.BackColor = _
      UserControl.Ambient.BackColor
  Case _DisplayAsDefault_
    If UserControl.Ambient.DisplayAsDefault = _
            True Then
      UserControl.Line _
        (0,0)-(UserControl.Extender.Width, _
        UserControl.Extender.Height), , B
    Else
      UserControl.Line _
        (0,0)-(UserControl.Extender.Width,
        UserControl.Extender.Height), _
        UserControl.BackColor, B
    End If
End Select

End Sub
```

Unlike Extender properties, Ambient properties can be early or late bound, so the costs of accessing the Ambient object are minimized.

Ambient and Extender properties aren't available during the Initialize and Terminate events of the UserControl object.

UserControl Events

Most of the events that are peculiar to the UserControl are discussed with related properties or methods. In this section I discuss the events that the UserControl fires as it gains and loses focus, the Show and Hide events, and what to do if the InvisibleAtRunTime isn't supported by the container that your control is being used in.

EnterFocus, ExitFocus

The EnterFocus event fires when the UserControl (or any of its constituent controls) gets the focus. The ExitFocus event fires when the focus shifts to another control in the same application. Since the UserControl doesn't support Activate, Deactivate, you can use these events instead to perform processing when the user enters or leaves your control. You can also create a Boolean variable to track when your control has the focus:

```
Dim bolInFocus As Boolean

Private Sub UserControl_EnterFocus()
    bolInFocus = True
End Sub

Private Sub UserControl_ExitFocus()
    bolInFocus = False
End Sub
```

Hide

The Hide event fires when control is removed from the screen. This event occurs as the control is deleted from a container at design time, as the container is unloaded from memory at design time or run time, and when the control's Extender visible property is changed from True to False.

Show

The Show event fires as a control is made visible within the container. This event occurs as the control is added to a container at design time, as the container is loaded into memory at run time, and when the control's Extender visible property is changed from False to True.

SUPPORTING INVISIBLEATRUNTIME

To ensure that your control does not display, even in a container that doesn't support InvisibleAtRunTime, you can add this code to the Show event:

```
Private Sub UserControl_Show()
    UserControl.Extender.Visible = False
End Sub
```

Of course, this assumes that the container's Extender object has a Visible property.

If the control has its InvisibleAtRunTime property set to True, then the Show and Hide events do not occur.

UserControl Methods

As with the discussion of properties and events, I ignore those methods that the UserControl has in common with the Form object to concentrate on the ones that are special to the UserControl object.

AsyncRead

The AsyncRead method allows you to download data from a file or URL. Calling the AsyncRead begins the process of transferring data either to an array of bytes, to a file on your hard disk, or to a picture. The picture format is compatible with the Picture property of controls like the Image control or the output of the LoadPicture function. It is your responsibility to provide the code to read the file or byte array that the data is loaded to if you choose those options.

After calling the AsyncRead method, the code in your control continues to execute while the read operation occurs in the background. The AsyncReadProgress event fires repeatedly during the course of the read to give you the opportunity to monitor the operation's progress. The AsyncReadComplete event fires when the read is complete. Both events are passed the AsyncProp parameter, which is a reference to an AsyncProperty object. This object contains the results of the read operation in its Value property: the picture, the byte array, or the name of the file containing the data (depending on which read option was used).

When you start an AsyncRead, you assign the operation a name. You can use that name with the CancelAsyncRead method to end the read operation prematurely.

A SAMPLE ASYNCREAD

This code reads a picture from the Website *www.phvis.com*. The second parameter passed to this method specifies how the read is to occur (in this case, to create a Picture). The read operation is assigned the name GetPicture:

```
UserControl.AsyncRead "http://www.phvis.com/phv.jpg", _
                       vbAsyncTypePicture, "GetPicture"
```

A button on the form lets the user cancel the operation using the name assigned to it by the AsyncRead method:

```
UserControl.CancelAsyncRead "GetPicture"
```

In the AsyncReadProgress method, the code uses the AsyncProp object to determine how many bytes of the maximum to download have been read:

```
Private Sub UserControl_AsyncReadProgress _
          (AsyncProp As AsyncProperty)
Dim dblPercentComplete

If AsyncProp.BytesMax > 0 Then
    dblPercentComplete = _
          AsyncProp.BytesRead/AsyncProp.BytesMax
End If

End Sub
```

Like all events, the AsyncReadProgress event is synchronous: Processing on the read stops until the code in the event procedure completes. As a result, using this event can slow down your AsyncRead operation.

In the AsyncReadComplete event the Value of the downloaded object is moved into an Image control on the form:

```
Private Sub UserControl_AsyncReadComplete _
                         (AsyncProp As AsyncProperty)
    Image1.Picture = AsyncProp.Value
End Sub
```

PropertyChanged

This method notifies the design environment that a property has been changed. The method accepts one parameter, the name of the property that has been changed. PropertyChanged should be called from the Let routine of every property that can be changed at design time. Typical code looks like this, which notifies the design environment that a property named Caption has changed:

```
Public Property Let Caption (ControlCaption As String)
    m_Caption = ControlCaption
    UserControl.PropertyChanged "Caption"
End Property
```

Notifying the Visual Basic IDE that a property has changed seemed like wasted effort to me until I realized that the Visual Basic IDE has no special relationship with the ActiveX Controls on the form. If a property is changed through Visual Basic's Property List, then the List will display the current value. However, if the property is changed through some other mechanism (like the PropertyPages described below), then the IDE has no way of knowing that it is no longer displaying the current value. The PropertyChanged method lets the IDE know that it should update the Property List.

PropertyChanged is also important in creating data bound controls and is discussed in that chapter.

In the example above, the PropertyChanged method is used to notify the IDE that the Caption property has changed. Once notified, the Property List can then read the control's Caption property to get the current value and display it.

The WriteProperties event is controlled by the container—in this case the Visual Basic IDE. If Visual Basic doesn't think any properties have changed, it may not fire the WriteProperties event. Using PropertyChanged helps ensure that the event is fired.

Procedure Attributes

I discussed the Procedure Attributes dialog briefly in the chapter on Interfaces. Many of the dialog's features, however, make sense only in the context of an ActiveX Control, so I finish the discussion of the dialog here.

After pressing the Advanced button, you can set a number of attributes for the event, property, or method that you select in the combo box at the top of the dialog (see Figure 8–12 to review the layout of the Property Attributes dialog).

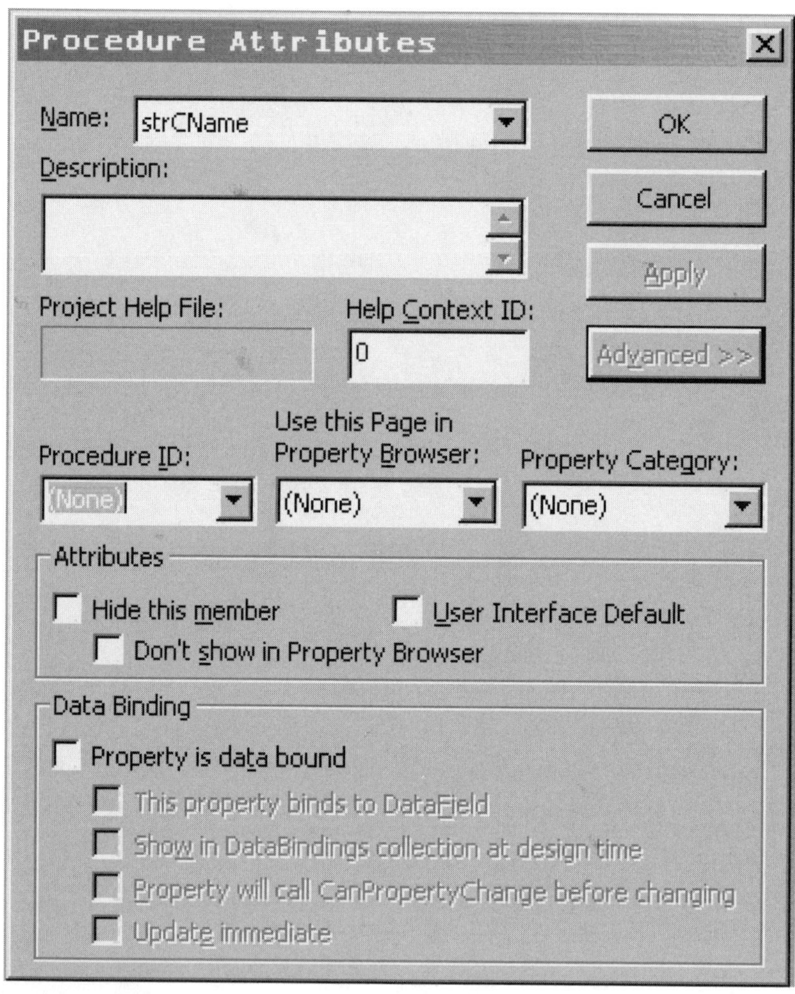

Figure 8–12 *The Property Attributes Dialog.*

Procedure ID

As discussed in the chapter on components, this combo box allows you to assign specific IDs to methods and properties. Assigning a predefined ID signals to the container that this method or property is to get the special processing. The various ID's are listed by the methods or properties that they are associated with.

ABOUTBOX

Assigning the AboutBox ID to a method causes an About entry to be added to the Property List for the control. When the developer clicks on the builder button beside this entry, it causes the method assigned the ID to execute. This method should display an "about box"—a fixed size dialog displaying copyright and version information about the control.

ENABLED

The Enabled ID should be assigned to a property that returns a Boolean (True/False) value. Assigning this ID to a property causes an Enabled property to be added to the Property List. When the developer sets or reads the Enabled entry in the Property List, your property's Let or Get procedures will be called. When passed a False, the routine should set all the Enabled properties of all of the constituent controls to False.

The following code shows the typical code required to support the Enabled property. As the code in the Property Let shows, you must also set the Enabled property of the UserControl itself:

```
Option Explicit
Dim m_Enabled As Boolean

Private Sub UserControl_Initialize()
    m_Enabled = True
End Sub

Public Property Let Enabled(EnableSetting As Boolean)
Dim ctl As Control
    For Each ctl In UserControl.Controls
      ctl.Enabled = EnableSetting
    Next
    UserControl.Enabled = EnableSetting

    m_Enabled = EnableSetting
End Property
Public Property Get Enabled() As Boolean
    Enabled = m_Enabled
End Property
```

While you can call the property anything that you want, it's simpler to call the property Enabled. Among other benefits, it means that run time code will use the same name as the Property List.

TEXT AND CAPTION

Assigning the Text or Caption IDs to a property causes the Property Let routine to be called by the Property List on every key stroke. Normally, a value is passed to the control from the Property List only when the developer finishes entering a value and presses the Enter key. For a property with the Text or Caption ID, the value in the Property List is sent to the control with every keystroke entered into the Property List. This is the facility that lets the Visual Basic form update its Caption with each character that you enter into the Property List.

Don't Show in Property Browser

Selecting this option in the Attributes area allows you to prevent a property from appearing in property browsers like Visual Basic's Property List. Unlike the Hide This Member choice, this has no effect on IntelliSense support or the Object Browser. You should use this option to remove any property that can't be used at design time from the Property List or appears only in a Property Page.

Property Category

Entering (or selecting) a value in the Property Category combo box assigns a property to a category in the Categorized listing in Visual Basic's Property List (or any other property browser that takes advantage of property categories). If you don't assign a value in the Property Category, the property will be categorized as "Misc."

User Interface Default

Checking this box causes the selected property or event to become the default item at design time. When the developer adds your control to a form, the property flagged as the User Interface Default should be the property initially selected in the Property List. When the developer double-clicks on your control to open the code window, the procedure for the event marked as the User Interface Default will be written automatically. This option is different from the Default option in Procedure Id, which controls what method or property will be invoked when code accesses the object without specifying a method or property at run time.

Property Pages

A PropertyPage is a form that you can use to help developers set the properties for your control. You may want to add a PropertyPage to your project when you have

- a property that's hard to set. A property that requires a full pathname to a file would benefit from a PropertyPage that lets the developer use the Windows standard File Open dialog to find the file.
- several interrelated properties that must be set. A PropertyPage can display the properties together and do cross edits among them.
- a control that would require a large number of properties to be exposed at design time. Instead of filling the Property List with all those Properties, you could use a PropertyPage that interacts with a method or Friendly property on the control.
- a control that you want to work in development environments that don't have a built-in Property List.
- a property that can be set at design time, but that returns an Object type.

Like the UserControl, a PropertyPage looks very much like the Visual Basic Form object but has some special methods, properties, and events to support its special function.

A set of Property Pages is shown in Figure 8–13. You are responsible for creating only the portion of the form that's displayed on each tab. Visual Basic will take care of adding tabs to your form, layering the tabs on top of each other, and providing the three buttons at the bottom of the dialog.

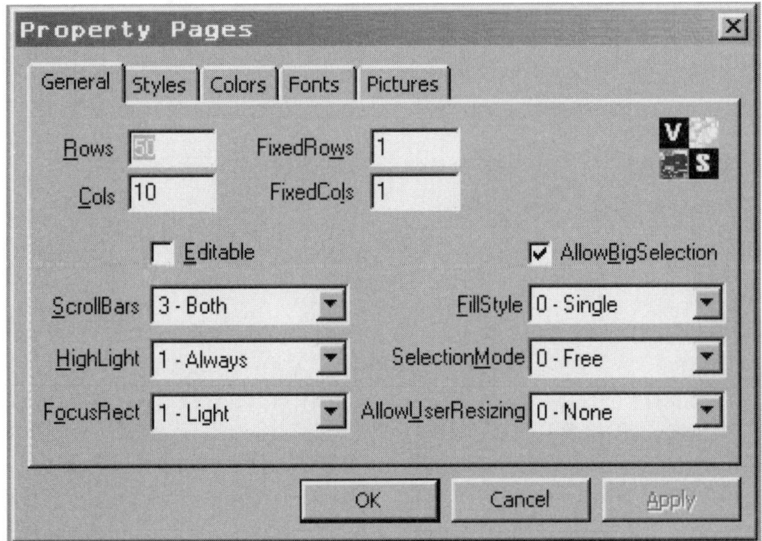

Figure 8–13 *A set of Property Pages for an ActiveX Control*

Associating a Property Page With a Control

Adding a PropertyPage to a project doesn't associate it with any UserControl or Property that you've designed. Since you can have multiple UserControls in a single project, you can associate your PropertyPage with several controls.

There are two ways to associate a Property Page with a control. Both methods require that you add the PropertyPage that you are going to use before assigning it. The first way is to use the Procedure Attributes box. After selecting a Property in the Name combo box and clicking on the Advanced button, you'll find a combo box labeled Use This Page in Property Browser. Clicking on the down arrows for this box displays a list of Property Pages available to the project. In addition to any PropertyPages that you've created, you'll also find four standard Pages: Font, Color, Format, and Picture. These are four standard dialogs that are built into Windows itself (see Figure 8–14)

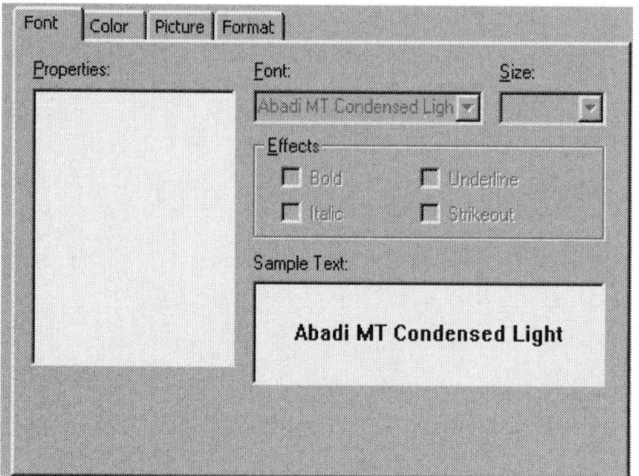

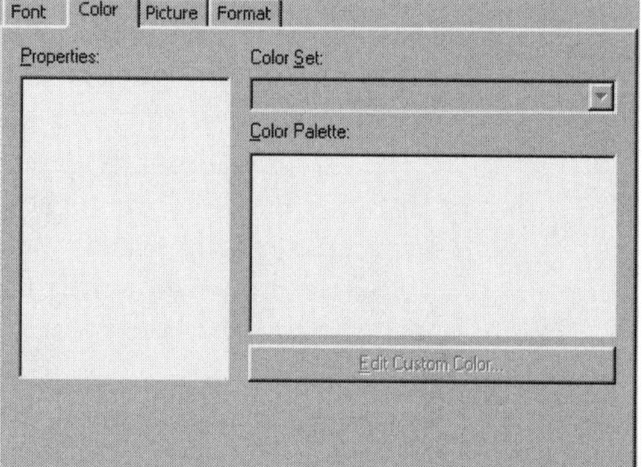

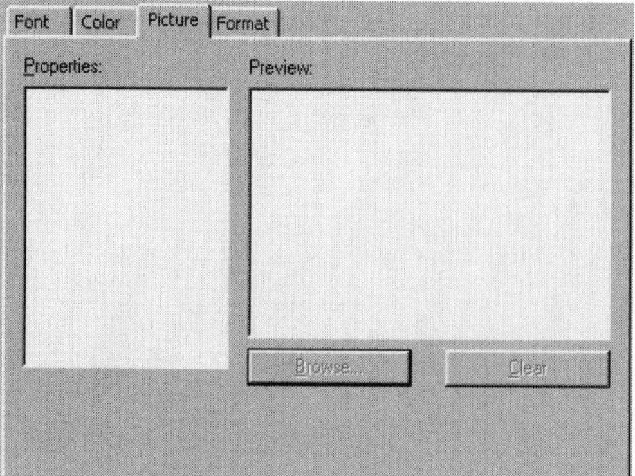

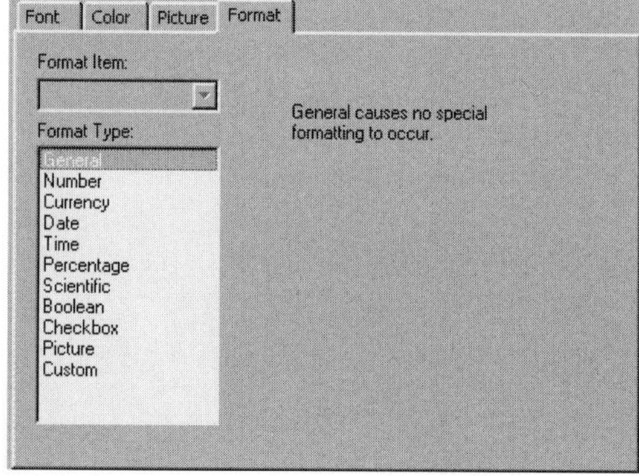

Figure 8–14 *The four standard property pages.*

Selecting one of the Pages from the Procedure Attributes dialog box will associate the Page with the property displayed in the dialog. When your control is used on a form, a builder button (the little gray button with the three dots) will be displayed beside the property that you assigned the page to in the Property List. This is the best way to go if the page's sole purpose is to help the user set the value for that single property.

Frequently, however, the reason that you add a PropertyPage to a project is to help the developer set several properties that are interrelated. You could assign the Page to each of the properties involved. However, in this situation it makes more sense to associate the Page with the control as a whole, rather than with any particular property. To do this, in Visual Basic's Property List, click on the PropertyPages property for the UserControl object. A builder button will appear and, when you click on it, you will be taken to the dialog that lists all of the PropertyPages in the Project (see Figure 8–15). Each page that you check off in this list will be available to the control.

When you use this second process, a developer using your ActiveX Control will find a property called (Custom) at the top of your control's Property List. Clicking on the builder button for this property displays the tabbed dialog of all of the PropertyPages associated with the control.

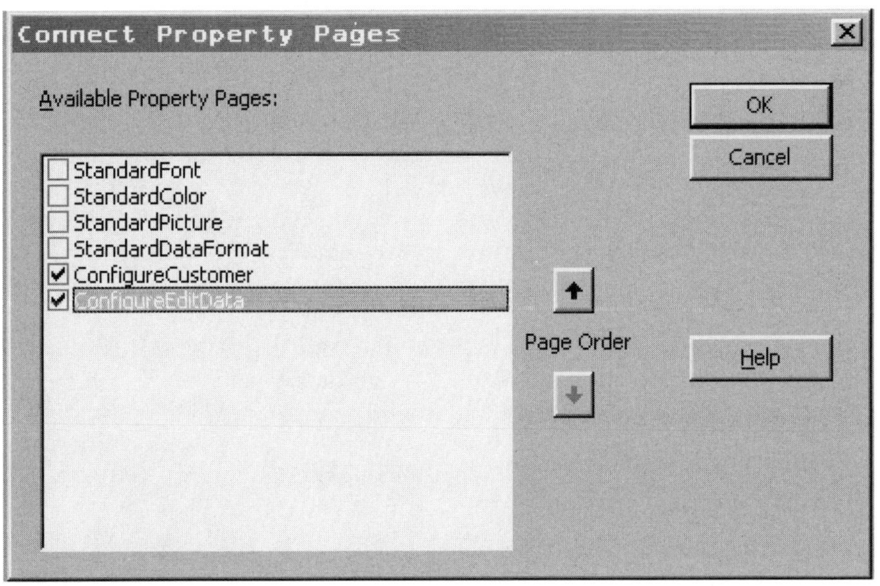

Figure 8–15 *The Connect Property Pages Dialog.*

The Life of a PropertyPage

One key thing to remember about PropertyPages is that they're not modal. That is to say, while a the Property Page dialog is displayed, the developer has the ability to return to the form and make additional changes to it. This was one of the benefits that I got from learning to create ActiveX Controls: I had always assumed that the dialog was modal and that I had to close it before I could go back to work on my form.

A PropertyPage first comes into existence when it is opened from Visual Basic's Property List. One or more controls may be selected when the Page is displayed. As it opens, the Page needs to gather and display all of the appropriate information about the controls that it is supposed to help update. At the very least, this will mean displaying the current values of the properties that the Page updates. Initially, the Apply button on the dialog will be grayed out.

The developer can then work with the Page to set your control's properties. Once the developer has made a change, the Apply button should become enabled. The developer can then click on the Apply button to update the relevant properties on the selected controls updated with the changes made in the PropertyPage. Alternatively, the developer can click on the OK button to apply changes and close the dialog. The Cancel button closes the dialog without applying the changes.

It is your responsibility to write the code that displays and updates the property values for the selected controls. Visual Basic will ensure that only controls that the Page is associated with will be selected when your page is displayed (and that the controls are all the same class).

Object Type Properties

A property that returns an object is difficult to use with the Property List because the Property List will only display properties that return non-object values (e.g., String, Variant, etc.). If the property can be modified at design time, the simplest solution is to create a PropertyPage to set the object-type property and assign the Page to the control. Developers who want to set the object property at design time can click on the (Custom) property to display the PropertyPage.

The alternative is to declare the property as Variant so that it will integrate with the Property List. At design time you'll need to return and retrieve some place holder text that the Property List can display (at run time you'll want to return and retrieve the object). As a result, you'll need to use the Ambient object's UserMode property to check if the property is being called at run time or design time. The benefit is that the developer will be able to click on the property to get a builder button that displays the property's PropertyPage.

You'll still need to have a Property Page to update the control at design time. The Page won't be able to update the property directly because the

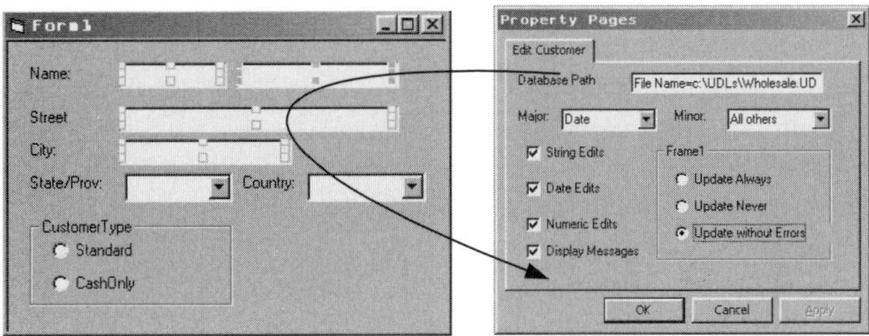

EditChange, SelectionChanged Events:
Gather Information

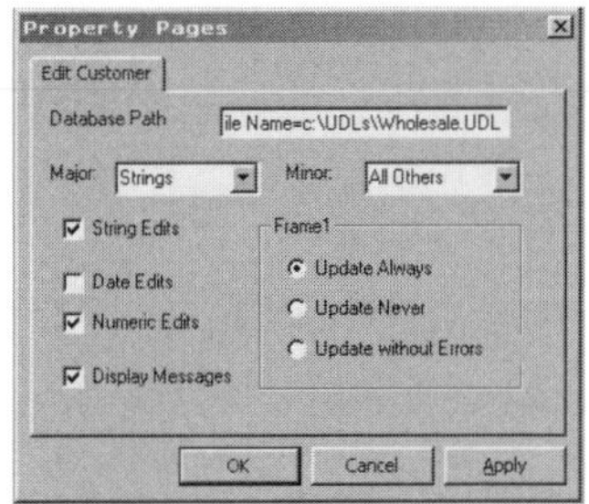

Edit data, set Changed property

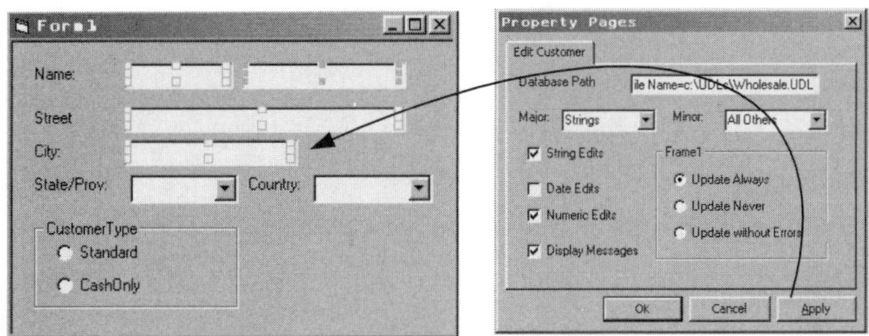

ApplyChanges Event:
Update Controls

Figure 8–16 *The Life of a Property Page. First, the page displays information about the selected controls. After editing, the page updates the selected controls*

UserMode testing added to the Property Procedure will prevent changes at design time. So you'll have to provide a method or property for the PropertyPage to work through. This method or property should be declared as Friend so that the control's clients can't call it at run time.

Since the Property List only works with Lets and Gets, if you want developers to use the Set syntax with your property you'll also have to provide a Property Set routine. You'll need to add error handling around the Property

Let in case developers inadvertently use it at run time. With the property declared as variant, you'll need to add error handling code to catch bad values passed at run time. Developers will get no IntelliSense support or design time checking of parameters since the property is declared as variant. The lack of compile time parameter checking opens the door to more run time errors in the application using the control because a bad parameter won't be noticed until the code is executing.

The benefit of all this work is that the property will appear on the Property List and developers will be able to bring up the Property Page by clicking on a builder button by the property's name. If you feel that the costs incurred are worth the benefit, go ahead. Otherwise, just associate the page that will manage this property with the control and have the developer access it through the (Custom) property.

PropertyPage Properties

THE STANDARDSIZE PROPERTY

A PropertyPage has only one unique property at design time: the StandardSize property. You can set this to one of three values: Custom (make the Page any size at all), Small (the Page is wide and short), or large (the page is taller). Interestingly enough, Microsoft encourages you not to use the predefined sizes but to stick with the default setting: Custom.

THE CHANGED PROPERTY

The Changed Property allows you to signal to the PropertyPages dialog that contains your page that the user has made a change that will require updates to control properties. When you set this property to True, it should cause the dialog's Apply button (which is initially grayed out) to be enabled. Typical code in the Change event for a text box might look like this:

```
Private Sub Text1_Change()
    PropertyPage.Changed = True
End Sub
```

SELECTEDCONTROLS AND SELECTIONCHANGED

The SelectedControls property holds a collection with a reference to every control currently selected. You can use this collection to determine which controls should have their properties displayed on the PropertyPage and which controls should be updated when the Apply button is clicked. The SelectionChanged event fires each time the membership of the collection changes, including when it is first loaded.

The following code will update a text box on the Page with the value of the Caption property for the controls in the SelectedControls collection. The standard in the Windows world is to display the property's value if only one control is selected. If multiple controls are selected, the value of the property is displayed only if all the controls have the same value for the property. If the controls have different values, then no value should be displayed. The code demonstrates one way of achieving that for string properties:

```
Private Sub PropertyPage_SelectionChanged()
Dim myc As MyControl
    For Each myc in PropertyPage.SelectedControls
      If IsEmpty(txtMyProperty) Then
        txtMyProperty = myc.Caption
      ElseIf txtMyProperty <> myc.Caption
        TxtMyProperty = ""
      End If
    Next
End Sub
```

The sample code cycles through the SelectedControls property. As it retrieves each control, the code checks to see if the txtMyProperty text box on the form is empty, indicating that this is the first time through the loop. If the text box is empty, the code moves the value of the control's Caption property into the text box. If the text box isn't empty, it indicates that this is the second time through the loop. In this situation, the routine checks to see if the value in the text box matches the Caption property of the current control. If it does, nothing is done. If the values are different, the text box is set to a zero length string. As a result, the text box will display blank when the selected controls have different values.

The Name property of the PropertyPage is used as the text for the Page's tab in the PropertyPage dialog.

PropertyPage Events

Having already discussed the SelectionChanged event, there are only two events on the PropertyPage left to discuss.

APPLYCHANGES

The ApplyChanges event fires when the user clicks on the Apply button or the OK button when the Changed property is True. In this event routine your code should sweep through the controls in the SelectedControls collection, setting them to the values entered on the PropertyPage. This code does that with the Caption property:

```
Private Sub PropertyPage_ApplyChanges()
Dim myc As MyControl
    For Each myc in PropertyPage.SelectedControls
      myc.Caption = txtMyProperty
    Next
End Sub
```

EDITPROPERTY

This event fires when the PropertyPage is opened from a single property in the Property List rather than from the (Custom) property. The event fires even if the Page is already displayed. If multiple PropertyPages are currently displayed, all of the Pages except for the one requested are removed. You can use this event to give developers a chance to save their changes before switching Pages.

Distributing

With your ActiveX Control is designed, built, and debugged, you are ready to distribute it. The process described in the chapter on Deploying also applies to ActiveX Controls. In this section, I concentrate on the issues special to distributing ActiveX Controls.

Internet Downloads

One special feature of ActiveX Components is that they can be downloaded and installed by Internet Explorer. Since an ActiveX Component is a compiled Windows program, users have some concerns about what a rogue control could do to their computer. Microsoft developed the Authenticode standard to try to relieve those concerns.

AUTHENTICODE

Authenticode attempts to convert the process of downloading a control into an experience equivalent to buying software at a store. To do this, Authenticode requires that you buy a digital signature from a third-party source. To purchase this signature, you must supply enough information about yourself or your company that a disgruntled recipient of your control could find you. The digital signature functions like the company name and address on the box of software at the store.

The signing process also generates a digital key, whose value is dependent on both the signature and the bytes that make up the control. Should anyone modify either the signature or the control after the signing process is complete, this key will no longer match the ActiveX Control. This key is intended to perform the same function as the shrinkwrap around a box in a store: It assures you that the product has not been tampered with since it left the factory.

The general consensus is that Authenticode has not been successful at reassuring users that it's all right to download ActiveX Controls from the Internet Web sites they visit. This has limited the use of ActiveX Controls to a means of distributing software and Web-based applications to company employees over an intranet.

To use Authenticode, you'll need to download Microsoft's Internet Software Development kit.

SAFETY

If you are going to download and install your control using Internet Explorer, you must also mark your control as being Safe for Scripting and Safe for Initialization. Marking your control as Safe for Scripting means that you believe that there is no way that the events, methods, and properties of your control could ever be manipulated to do harm to the user's computer or gain access to private information. Marking your control as Safe for Initialization means that you believe that there is no way that the initial PARAM tags fed to your control could cause your control to do harm or invade the user's privacy.

Since the settings of the Safety flags are purely the judgment call of the control's developers, it's questionable how accurately they represent the control's "safeness."

The easiest way to mark your code as Safe for Scripting or Initialization is to run the Package and Deployment Wizard. The fifth form in the "Internet Package" choice gives you an opportunity to mark your controls (see Figure 8–16). This causes registry entries to be made for your control, indicating how safe it is.

IOBJECTSAFETY

You can also indicate your control's safety level by adding the IObjectSafety interface to your control. The methods and properties of this interface allow the control's client to determine if the control is safe by calling the GetInterfaceSafetyOptions method. This method is generally faster than reading the registry and allows you to include code that indicates if your code is safe under one set of circumstances and not safe under another. For instance, you might make your control safe for scripting by allowing the client to disable certain features of your control.

To use the IObjectSafety interface, you must first set a reference to the VB6-IObjectSafety Interface in your Project | References list. You then need to add this line to the top of each UserControl that will be using the IObject-Safety methods:

```
Implements IObjectSafety
```

Your code must then implement the following methods:

```
Private Sub IObjectSafety_GetInterfaceSafetyOptions _
    (ByVal riid As Long, pdwSupportedOptions As Long, _
    pdwEnabledOptions As Long)
End Sub
Private Sub IObjectSafety_SetInterfaceSafetyOptions _
    (ByVal riid As Long, ByVal dwOptionsSetMask As Long, _
    ByVal dwEnabledOptions As Long)
End Sub
```

If your control is unsafe under any conditions for both scripting and initialization, you only need to raise an error condition and return the hex value &H80004005.

```
Err.Raise &H80004005
```

If your control is safe for scripting then you'll add code to the GetInterfaceSafetyOptions to return a value in the pdwSupportedOptions parameter. Here's the code that returns the necessary values:

```
'control is safe for initialization
pdwSupportedOptions = &H2
'control is safe for scripting
pdwSupportedOptions = &H1
'control is safe for both scripting and initialization
pdwSupportedOptions = &H1 Or &H2
```

More sophisticated use of this interface can be made. The riid parameter that is passed to both routines contains the identifier for a specific interface. You can use this parameter to determine which interfaces the client is questioning the safety. This is particularly important in SetSafetyInterfaceOptions, which the client will use to request that an interface be disabled so that the object can be made safe.

Testing for interface code requires a number of Windows API calls to extract CLSIDs, so I refer you to the sample code on the MSDN disks that come with Visual Studio. You can find the sample project in Samples\VB98\Iobjsafe. The necessary API calls and a routine that uses them to return CLSIDs are in the standard module modSubMain.

The sample program also declares Constants for the various values that are to be returned. Copying these to your program allows you to avoid having to remember the correct hexadecimal values.

Licensing

Any developer who uses your control is going to have to distribute it with their application to the people who will be using that application—the end users. If you do not want the end users to be able to develop new applications with your control, then you need some way to limit the ways that your control is used. You want to allow the developer to use the control both in run time and design time but, when the developer distributes your control, you want end users to be restricted to run time use only.

Licensing support in ActiveX Controls is supported through the VBL (Visual Basic License) file that you can distribute with your control. Visual Basic will generate a VBL if you select "Require License Key" on the General tab of the Project | Properties menu choice. The VBL file should be included in your setup program when you are distributing the control with design time rights. The VBL should not be distributed when you want to limit the control's use to run time (i.e., with applications that use your control).

This would be a wonderful solution if it actually worked. Unfortunately, a number of containers don't discriminate between design and run time. Those containers require the license to use your ActiveX Control under any circumstances. The Microsoft Office applications and ActiveX Documents, for instance, check for licensing information whenever they use a control.

Internet Explorer has the same problem, but also provides a workaround. After you have created an Internet package to download and install all the controls on a Web page, you can use LPK_Tool.exe. The program lists all the ActiveX Controls on your computer and allows you to select one or more of them. LPK_Tool then creates an LPK file that contains all the license keys for the selected controls. With the file created, you can add it to your Website and have Internet Explorer download it by adding this tag to the Web page:

```
<OBJECT
 CLASSID="clsid:5220CB21-C88D-11cf-B347-00AA00A28331">
    <PARAM NAME="LPKPath" VALUE="/mysite/lpks/myctls.lpk">
</OBJECT>
```

Internet Explorer will use the information in the LPK file to authorize using the controls on the current Web page, but will not store the license information permanently on the computer.

When your control is being used in design time, any constituent controls are also in design time. So, if you are distributing your control to other developers, you must also include the licenses for any constituent controls that your control uses and that you have the right to distribute.

Summary

In this chapter I've looked at the first of several special kinds of ActiveX objects and components. ActiveX Controls have a number of features that aren't shared with other ActiveX objects. After describing ActiveX Controls and how to create an ActiveX Control project, I looked at the UserControl form. I described all of the elements that make a UserControl different from a Form and you saw how to use those elements in constructing an ActiveX Control. This included learning about the ActiveX Control life cycle and how the Ambient and Extender objects allow your control to interact with its container.

You next saw how to use the Procedure Attributes dialog to have Visual Basic give your controls special processing options. PropertyPages were introduced as a way of providing support for developers using your control. Finally, I looked at the issues around distributing an ActiveX Control.

There a number of books that discuss creating ActiveX Controls. One of the best is Daniel Appleman's *Developing COM/ActiveX Components with Visual Basic 6: A Guide to the Perplexed* (Sams). I have the great good fortune to teach a course for Learning Tree International on COM and Visual Basic that was developed by Guy Eddon. His book (written with this father, Henry Eddon), *Programming Components with Microsoft Visual Basic* (Microsoft Press) covers ActiveX Controls very effectively.

The next step is yours: creating your own ActiveX Control. One place to begin is the sample ActiveX Control that I described in the section "A Typical ActiveX Control." After building this control, you should develop at least one form that uses the control. Only by both building and using a control will you begin to understand how to develop them effectively.

N I N E

Data Binding, Providers, Consumers, and RDS

Most business applications are database applications. Microsoft's new data access strategy, ActiveX Data Objects (ADO), was designed from the ground up to be a COM-compliant technology.

In this chapter I look at a variety of ways that you can use objects in conjunction with data. First, I show you how to create data bound ActiveX Components and Controls. You'll then see how to create both ActiveX and OLE DB data providers that integrate into the ADO framework. With those building blocks in place, I discuss the ADO "consumer and provider" architecture and how you can build complex applications by joining together data aware objects. Finally, I show you how to create "custom data factories" that can send data interactively over the Web to be manipulated by scripts running in Internet Explorer.

Data Bound Controls

Many ActiveX Controls are data bound controls. Data bound controls can work with one of the Data controls that have shipped with Visual Basic since version 3.0. The Data control (in the Jet, RDO, and ADO versions) retrieves a collection of records from a database and then processes the collection one record at a time. A data bound control can work with the Data control by displaying and/or updating one or more fields from the records in the collection.

One example of a data bound control is the text box, which can be bound to a field in the records retrieved the Data control. As the Data control moves from record to record, the text box bound to it will automatically display the current value for the field that it is bound to. If the user changes the contents of the text box, the new data is passed to the Data control, which updates the database with the new value. Figure 9–1 shows a typical Visual Basic form with two Data controls and a number of data bound controls.

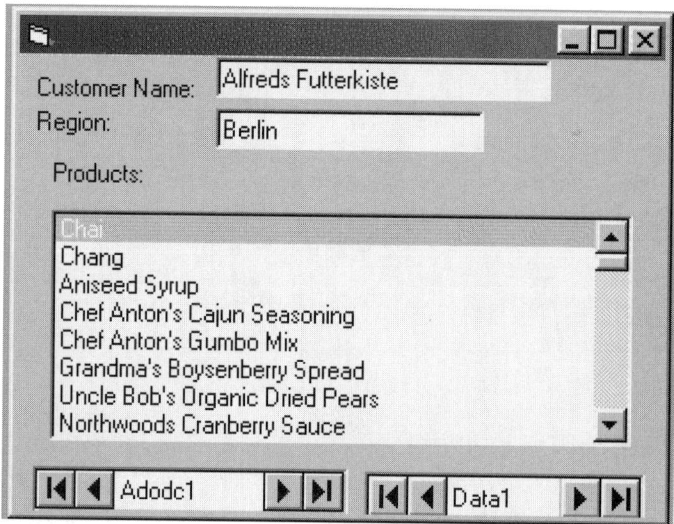

Figure 9–1 *A Visual Basic form with two data controls (the VCR-style objects) and several data bound controls.*

A Data control is a kind of data source or, in ADO terms, a "data provider." A data aware object that accepts data from a provider is called a "data consumer."

Turning an ordinary object into a data aware object just means opening the Procedure Attributes dialog, selecting one of the object's properties, and checking off the Property as data bound option (see Figure 9–2). With an ActiveX Control, whatever properties you mark in this fashion are added to the DataBindings collection of any container that the control is used in.

Developers working with a form can use the form's DataBindings collection to bind your control to a data provider. As the data provider retrieves records, it will use the information in the DataBindings collection to find any data consumers, like your control, that are bound to it. When the provider finds a data bound control, it will pass the requested field from the record to the data bound property on the control.

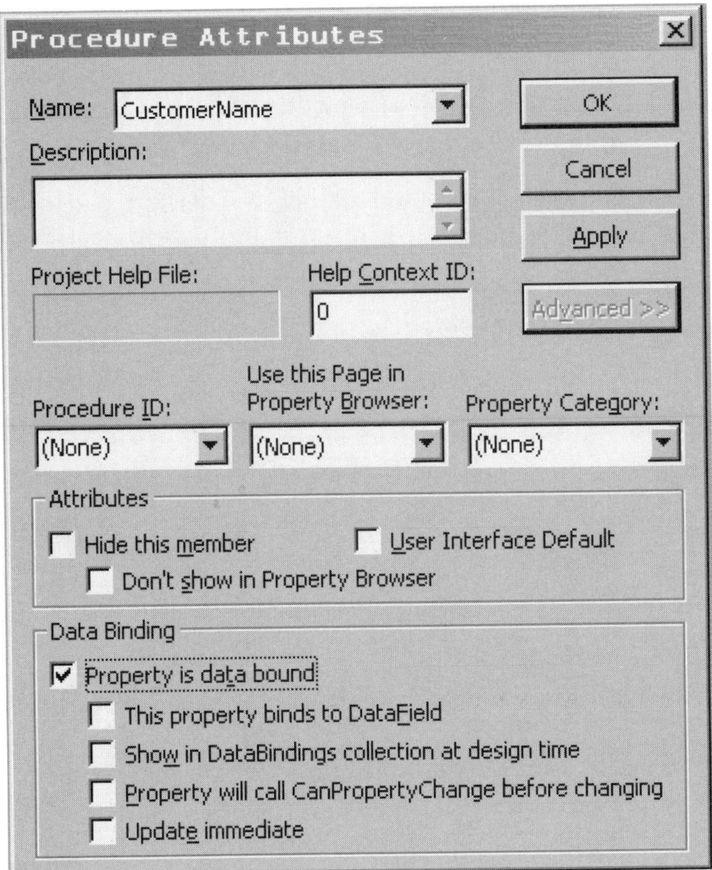

Figure 9–2 *The Procedure Attributes dialog showing the data binding options.*

ActiveX components can also be data bound. Since, unlike ActiveX Controls, components aren't part of a container, you have to create a BindingCollection object to hold the information about which objects are bound to which providers. I'll show that technique later in this chapter when I discuss creating data consumers.

Very little code is required on your part to make your objects data bound. Your Property Let procedures will be run as the value of the field is passed to your object's property by the data provider. Similarly, when data is to be returned from your object to the data source, your Property Get procedure executes as the provider retrieves the current value of the data bound property. From your control's point of view there is nothing special happening: The provider reads and writes the data bound property like any other client.

There are a number of other data-binding related options in the Procedure Attributes dialog. I discuss them here.

DataField Binding

In an ActiveX Control, checking off the Property Binds to DataField option implements the form of data binding that is easiest for developers to use when working with your control. With this option checked off, developers using your control will find four new items in your control's Property List: DataField, DataSource, DataFormat, and DataMember (see Figure 9–3). You don't need to write any code to implement these properties.

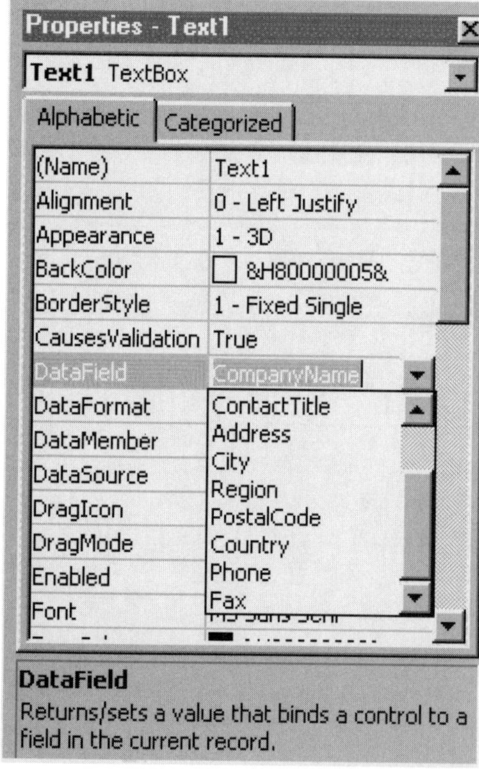

Figure 9–3 *A control's Property List displaying the DataField properties.*

With these properties available, a developer can bind your control just by setting the DataSource and DataField properties. The developer must set your control's DataSource property to the name of a Data control on the form. Your object's DataField property must be set to the name of one of the fields being retrieved by the Data control. If your control just displays data, the only thing that you had to do to make all this possible was to check off the Property is data bound and Property binds to DataField options.

If you want your control to also update the data that it displays, then you have to add some code to your control. It is your control's responsibility to notify the provider when the user changes the data in the control. Without this notification, the provider won't call your Property Get to retrieve the latest value of the property that the provider is bound to. To notify the control that the data has changed, you must call the UserControl's PropertyChanaged method and pass it the name of your property.

As an example, the ActiveX customer information control that I built had a CustomerNumber property that was marked as data bound to the DataField property. The Property Let and Get routines for the CustomerNumber property moved data in and out of the txtCNumber text box on the UserControl. In order to signal that the CustomerNumber property had been updated on the screen, I just called the PropertyChanged method from the Change event of the txtCNumber text box. If the user typed anything in the txtCNumber text box, the PropertyChanged method would ensure that the provider was notified so that the new value would be retrieved through the CustomerNumber Property Get. The code looked like this:

```
Public Property Get CustomerNumber() As String
    CustomerNumber = txtCNumber
End Property

Public Property Let CustomerNumber(CustNumb As String)
    txtCNumber = CustNumb
End Property

Private Sub txtCNumber_Change()
    UserControl.PropertyChanged "CustomerNumber"
End Sub
```

The PropertyChanged method is also available in ActiveX components where it is a method of the Class object rather than the UserControl object: Class.PropertyChanged.

Other Options

Selecting the Show in DataBindings Collection option at design time adds the DataBindings property to your control's Property List. Developers who click on this property in the Property List at design time will bring up a dialog that lets them assign your data aware properties to data sources they've placed on the form (see Figure 9–4). This option is essential if your Control has more than one property that can be data bound and you want developers to be able to assign data source to it at design time without writing code.

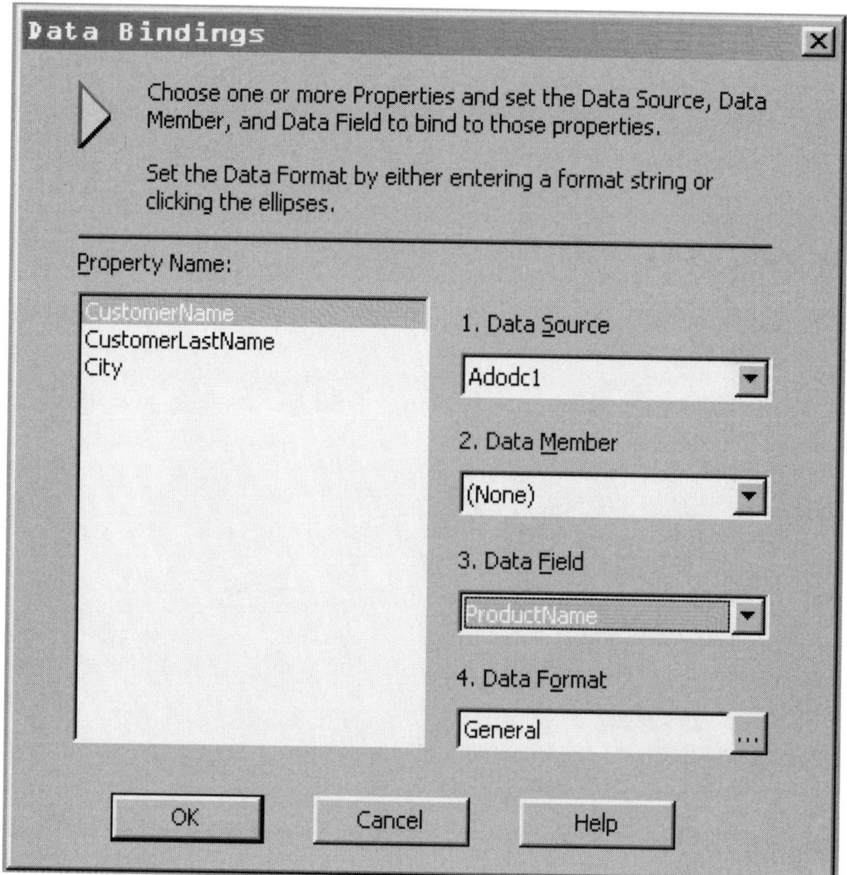

Figure 9–4 *The DataBindings dialog.*

The Update Immediately in the Procedure Attributes dialog option is supposed to cause the control to update the database with every change made to the control. Normally, the data is updated only when you move to a new record. However, I could not discover any difference in the behavior of my ActiveX Controls and Components when I set this option on.

The option Property will call CanPropertyChange before changing signals to clients using your object that you intend to avoid trying to update read-only data. The UserControl's CanPropertyChange method is supposed to check to see if the data that your property is bound to is updateable. If it is not (i.e., the provider that your control is bound to is in read-only mode), the CanProperty-Change method will return False. By calling the CanPropertyChange method, you can check to see if you can return updates to the provider.

If you check off the Property will call CanPropertyChange option, then you are signaling to Visual Basic that you intend to call the CanProperty-Change method before any update activity. Presumably, you are also promising that if CanPropertyChange returns False, then you will not attempt to update the data. You might, for instance, lock the corresponding text box to prevent changes to the data if the method returns False or not call the PropertyChanged method. Modifying the sample code from my CustomerAddress control, I could have written the text box event code to check that the CustomerNumber property is bound to updateable data:

```
Private Sub txtCNumber_Change()
    If UserControl.CanPropertyChange("CustomerNumber") = _
                                                False Then
    PropertyChanged "CustomerNumber"
End Sub
```

When your control is used in Visual Basic, CanPropertyChange is an exercise in futility because the method always returns True. Visual Basic simply ignores attempts to update read-only data and doesn't generate any errors. However, if you expect developers to use your control in containers other than Visual Basic, or you want to prepare for the day when CanProperty-Change does something useful in Visual Basic, you should make use of this method. If you are consistent about using the CanPropertyChange method, then you can inform your control's clients by checking off the Property will call CanPropertyChange before changing option.

ActiveX Data Providers

Microsoft's latest data strategy revolves around a technology called OLE DB, which provides a COM-based way to access data. Previous data access methods like DAO and RDO were object-oriented wrappers around a set of C-based function calls. OLE DB is designed from the ground up to create and interact with COM objects.

The OLE DB architecture is shown in Figure 9–5. A Visual Basic program issues its data requests through the objects that make up the ADO model. These objects pass those requests to the OLE DB middleware. OLE DB, in turn, interacts with an OLE DB provider, which actually retrieves the data.

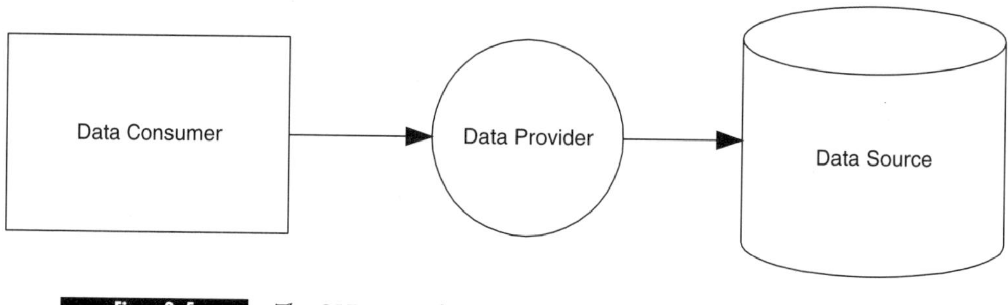

Figure 9–5 *The OLE DB architecture.*

A data provider is a COM component that accepts requests from OLE DB and returns a Recordset. How the Recordset is generated is entirely up to the provider. While Microsoft urges you to create providers that accept data requests in the form of SQL commands, the provider can define any data access language that it wants. Data providers that accept SQL exist for a large number of databases, including Microsoft's SQL Server and Oracle's database management systems (DBMS). A provider also exists for Microsoft's search engine, Index Server, which accepts commands in a form of SQL. On the other hand, the OLE DB provider for directory services accepts commands as a series of parameters that bear no relation to SQL.

As the variety of OLE DB providers suggests, one of the benefits of OLE DB is that, in theory, it allows your programs to use ADO to interact with any data source that has a data provider. One data provider is ODBC, the basis for Microsoft's earlier data access methodologies. Since almost every relational DBMS from Oracle to Unidata is ODBC compatible (and so are several non-relational data sources like text files and Excel spreadsheets), OLE DB allows you to access all your existing data sources.

What I find exciting about this strategy is that I can create my own OLE DB providers in Visual Basic. If you have data stored in some proprietary format, you could create a provider for that data that would integrate into the OLE DB framework. Your data would become accessible from any ADO-compliant tool—and any COM-compliant tool is ready to use ADO. If you want to control access to the database or hide the details of retrieving a complicated set of data, you might even create an OLE DB provider where your data is stored in a relational database.

I'll begin by showing you how to create a data provider to which you can bind data aware controls. After that, you'll see how to create a provider that can be used directly from ADO.

Data Providers

Both ActiveX Components and Controls can act as data providers. The first step is to set the Class or UserControl's DataSourceBehavior property to vbDataSource. Setting the DataSourceBehavior property identifies your object as a data provider. It also adds a new event—the GetDataMember event—to the module.

You should use an ActiveX Control instead of a component when you want your provider to have a user interface that integrates with the application's interface.

THE GETDATAMEMBER EVENT

The next step in creating a provider is to write code for the object's GetDataMember event. The GetDataMember event is fired when it's time for your provider to return its Recordset to the consumers that are bound to it. The event is passed two parameters: DataMember and Data. Your code must return an ADO Recordset in the Data parameter. The string passed in the DataMember event will contain information that you can use to determine what Recordset you create. Here's a sample GetDataMember routine that returns a Recordset (the Recordset itself is created in the Class's Initialize event):

```
Dim rs As Recordset

Private Sub Class_GetDataMember(DataMember As String, _
                               Data As Object)
    Set Data = rs
End Sub

Private Sub Class_Initialize()
    Set rs = New Recordset
    rs.CursorType = adOpenStatic
    rs.LockType = adLockOptimistic
    rs.Open "Select author from authors", _
            "file name=c:/windows/desktop/sample.udl"
End Sub
```

The GetDataMember event is fired on a number of occasions. For instance, when a developer is working with a data aware ActiveX Control, one of the available properties is called DataField. Clicking on the down arrow in this property displays a list of fields that the developer can use. Visual Basic provides this list by firing the DataMember event for your control and retrieving your Recordset. With the Recordset in hand, Visual Basic can then determine what fields it includes and display them in the DataField's dropdown list.

DATAMEMBER

The DataMember parameter is blank when Visual Basic fires the DataMember event to retrieve the field names at design time. At run time, the DataMember event in your ActiveX control will be called once without a DataMember parameter, and then once for each control that it is bound to. On the call made for each ActiveX Control, the DataMember parameter holds the value that the consumer has set for the control's DataMember property.

The GetDataMember event is fired only once at design time, no matter how many controls on the form bind to your ActiveX Control.

The initial call with the DataMember set to blank allows the container to determine the number of columns in the Recordset and other information that the container needs to work with the Recordset. If you require your clients to use a DataMember to access your provider, then you can process requests where the DataMember is blank differently from true data calls. Where the DataMember is blank, you can return a Recordset with all of the necessary columns, but you don't need to actually retrieve any data. This can improve your object's responsiveness both at design and run time by shortening the time spent to retrieve Recordset information.

In the following example of the GetDataMember event, I've used the DataMember parameter to control which records are included in the Recordset:

```
Dim rs As Recordset

Private Sub Class_Initialize()
    Set rs = New Recordset
    rs.Open "Select * From Employees"
End Sub

Private Sub UserControl_GetDataMember _
    (DataMember As String, Data As Object)
Select DataMember
    Case "Salary"
      rs.Filter = "Salary = True"
    Case "Hourly"
      rs.Filter = "Salary = False"
    Case Else
      rs.Filter = ""
End Select
Set rs = Data
End Sub
```

You can provide your object's users with a list of available DataMembers by appending a string to the DataMembers collection of your object. Visual Basic will query this collection and use it to report to the consumer what the valid DataMember options are for your provider (see Figure 9–6). To support the two DataMember options for the preceding sample code, I would use this code:

```
UserControl.DataMembers.Add "Hourly"
UserControl.DataMembers.Add "Salary"
```

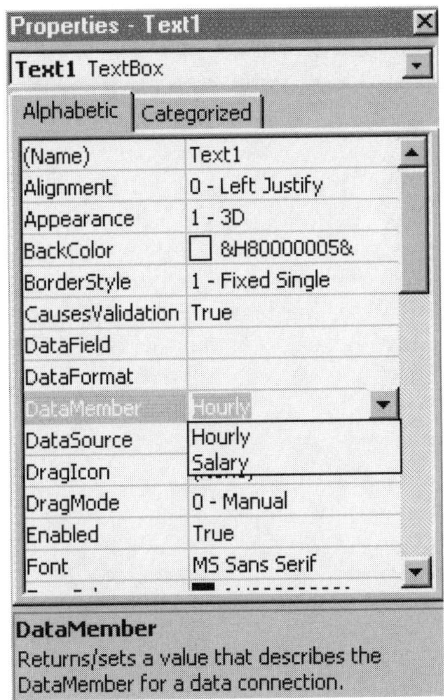

Figure 9–6 *An ActiveX Control's property list, displaying the DataMember property.*

You should also warn consumers if the Recordset that you are returning changes. You do this by calling the DataMemberChanged method and passing the name of the DataMember affected.

This code, for instance, stores the value passed in the GetDataMember method event in a module level variable. In this example, I assume that the Recordset is dynamic. With a dynamic Recordset, the query that retrieves the records is reexecuted on each MoveNext, ensuring that the Recordset always reflects the latest data. The code in the Provider's MoveNext method keeps track of the record count on the Recordset, and fires a DataMemberChanged should the number of records in the Recordset change:

```
Dim m_DataMember As String

Private Sub Class_GetDataMember(DataMember As String, _
                               Data As Object)
    m_DataMember = DataMember
    Set Data = rs
End Sub

Public Sub MoveNext()
Dim lngRecordCount As Long

    lngRecordCount = rs.RecordCount
    rs.MoveNext
    If lngRecordCount <> rs.RecordCount Then
      UserControl.DataMemberChanged m_DataMember
    End If

End Sub
```

PROVIDER METHODS

Most data providers include some methods for manipulating the records in the Recordset. The following code, for instance, implements MoveFirst and MoveLast methods for the object by calling the equivalent function of the object's internal Recordset:

```
Public Sub MoveFirst()
    rs.MoveFirst
End Sub
Public Sub MoveLast()
    rs.MoveLast
End Sub
```

OLE DB Providers

Now I move beyond creating data sources for data bound controls to creating a true OLE DB provider. An OLE DB provider is an object that can be called from ADO to return a Recordset. For instance, to retrieve data from an Access database, I would use code like this:

```
Dim rs As ADODB.Recordset
Set rs = New ADODB.Recordset
rs.Open "Select * From Authors", _
    "Provider=Microsoft.Jet.OLEDB.4.0;" & _
    "Data Source=C:\MyDB.MDB;Persist Security Info=False"
```

The string beginning "Provider=" is the connection string that provides all the information that ADO needs to connect to the database. The object specified in the Provider parameter (Microsoft.Jet.OLEDB.4.0) is the OLE DB provider that extracts the data from the Access database and passes it to ADO.

You can create providers of your own that can be called from ADO in exactly the same way:

```
rs.Open "Select * From Authors", _
    "Provider=PetersOLEDBProvider;"
```

CREATING THE PROVIDER

You begin creating an ADO provider by adding a reference to the Microsoft OLE DB Simple Provider 1.5 Library to your Project | References list. With that reference added, you need to implement the OLE DB Simple Provider interface:

```
Implements OLEDBSimpleProvider
```

With that line added, you'll have to add routines for all of the methods that make up the OLE DB Simple Provider interface. How many of these routines you actually implement is up to you. In order to create a read only provider, you must return values for getColumnCount, getRowCount, and getVariant. The names and purpose of the methods that make up the interface are summarized in Table 9.1.

Table 9.1 Methods of an OLE DB Simple Provider

Method Name	Description
AddOLEDBSimpleProviderListener	Passes an OLE DB listener to your object to fire.
DeleteRows	Passed a position in the array of records and a number, delete the number of rows specified, beginning at the position specified.
Find	Passed a starting position, a column number, and a value, find the specified value and return the row number.
GetColumnCount	Return the number of columns in the array.
GetEstimatedRows	Return the number of rows in the array, or your best guess.
GetLocale	Return the locale id for the text strings in the array.
GetRowCount	Return the number of rows currently in the array.

Table 9.1 Methods of an OLE DB Simple Provider (Continued)

Method Name	Description
GetRWStatus	Passed a column number and a row number, return whether the value can be updated. If either the column or the row are -1, return the status for the whole row or column.
GetVariant	Passed a row, a column, and a format, return the value at that position in the array.
InsertRows	Passed a position in the array and a number of rows, add the number of blank rows specified after the position specified.
IsAsync	Return a True if control will be returned to the client while the array is being built.
RemoveOLEDBSimpleProviderListener	Passes a listener to be removed.
SetVariant	Passed a row number, a column number, a format, and a value, update the position in the array with the value.
StopTransfer	Stop adding rows to the array.

For this chapter I created a provider that simply gives access to an array of prime numbers. I began by creating a class called clsPrimes with this code to initialize the array:

```
Implements OLEDBSimpleProvider
Dim intPrimes(3) As Integer

Private Sub Class_Initialize()
    intPrimes(1) = "2"
    intPrimes(2) = "3"
    intPrimes(3) = "5"
End Sub
```

How you retrieve the data and respond to request for the data is entirely up to you. I've chosen to store my data in an array. Since the methods of the SimpleProvider interface pass a row number and a column number, responding to these requests is relatively straight forward: I just return the cell in the array that corresponds to the row and column number passed. In this provider, because the array has only one column, the process is even simpler as I can ignore the column number passed.

```
Private Function OLEDBSimpleProvider_getColumnCount() _
```

```
                        As Long
    OLEDBSimpleProvider_getColumnCount = 1
End Function

Private Function OLEDBSimpleProvider_getEstimatedRows() _
                        As Long
    OLEDBSimpleProvider_getEstimatedRows = 3
End Function

Private Function OLEDBSimpleProvider_getRowCount() _
                        As Long
    OLEDBSimpleProvider_getRowCount = 3
End Function

Private Function OLEDBSimpleProvider_getVariant _
        (ByVal iRow As Long, ByVal iColumn As Long, _
         ByVal format As std.OSPFORMAT) As Variant
    OLEDBSimpleProvider_getVariant = intPrimes(iRow)
End Function
```

The iRow parameter that's passed to your getVariant routine will vary from 1 to the number you return in getRow-Count.

With the provider built, you now need to create an interface class that will manage access to your provider. This interface class is an ActiveX provider object like the ones that you saw you in the previous section of this chapter. As with any ActiveX provider, the Class module must have its DataSourceBehavior set to vbDataSource and implement a GetDataMember routine. The Class's GetDataMember routine will look like this:

```
Private Sub Class_GetDataMember(DataMember As String, _
                                    Data As Object)
    Set Data = New clsPrimes
End Sub
```

As you can see, not much has really changed. Where, before, the GetDataMember routine set the Data parameter to a Recordset object, it now sets the Data parameter to my clsPrimes object. Figure 9–7 shows the relationship among all of these components.

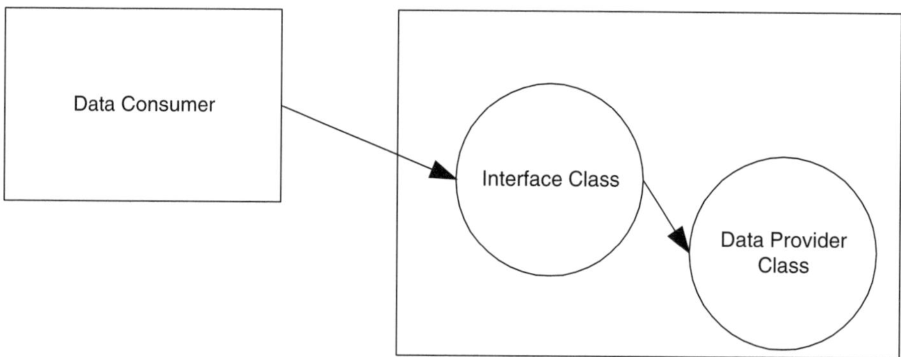

Figure 9–7 *An ADO provider, interface class, and client.*

The next steps require you to step out of Visual Basic. To have your class treated as an ADO provider, you need to generate a GUID and create a bunch of registry entries that identify your provider to ADO.

To generate a GUID, you can use either of two Microsoft-supplied tools. The first, and less convenient, is UUIDGen.EXE. You can find it in C:/Program Files/Microsoft Visual Studio/common/tools. UUIDGen is a DOS command-line utility, so to run it you can either open a DOS window or execute it from the Start menu's Run option. I pass the utility two switches:

- /i This switch produces a short text file containing a new GUID.
- /o This switch should be followed by the file name where the text file should be placed.

This command line, for instance, generates the text file in c:\myguid.txt:

```
uuidgen.exe /i /oc:\myguid.txt
```

The resulting file will look something like this:

```
[
uuid(bcde9140-5068-11d3-a8c8-00107a901a5f),
version(1.0)
]
interface INTERFACENAME
{

}
```

The only part that you need from the file is the GUID (in this case, bcde9140-5068-11d3-a8c8-00107a901a5f).

The other tool is GUIDGEN.EXE. Unlike UUIDGEN, this is a Windows utility. Running the program produces the dialog shown in Figure 9–8. You should select option 4 (Registry Format) and click on the New GUID button to generate your GUID, which will be displayed in the Result section of the dialog. Clicking on the Copy button will copy the GUID to the Windows clipboard and, from there, you can paste it anywhere that you like. You can download GUIDGEN from the MSDN Web site at *msdn.microsoft.com*.

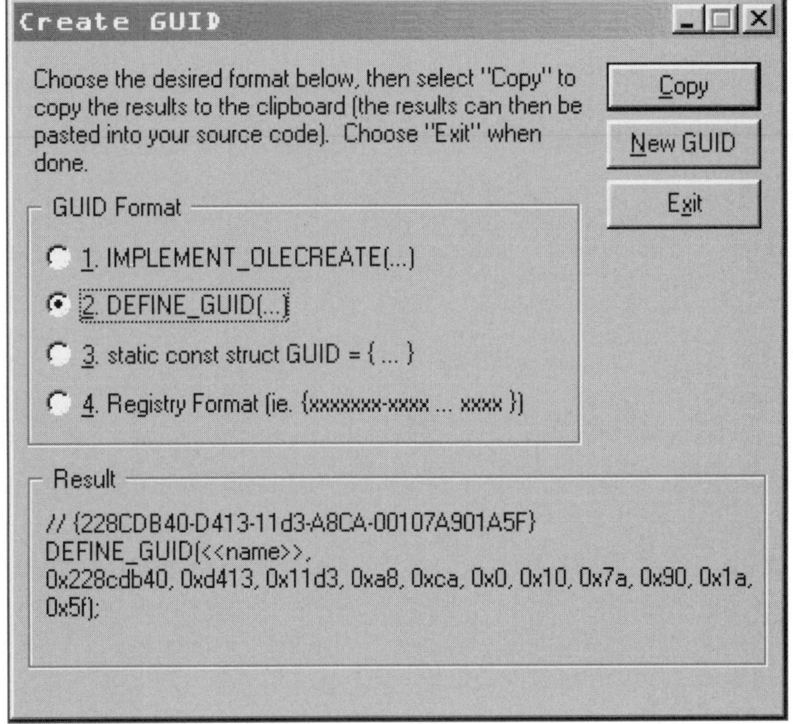

Figure 9–8 *The GUIDGEN.EXE utility.*

For the registry entries, I've borrowed the following template from a fellow Learning Tree instructor, Robert Macdonald. I keep the template text in a file on my hard disk and update it in Notepad with the entries appropriate for my provider. After saving the file to my hard disk with a file extension of .REG, I double click on the file in Windows Explorer to cause RegEdit to read the file's entries and update my Windows registry. I then store the file someplace safe to distribute with the setup routine for the component.

To modify the template for your provider, you'll need to make the following changes:

1. Replace **GUID** with the GUID that you generated with UUIDGEN.
2. Replace **Full Name** with any descriptive text (just make sure that you use the same text in both places that the full name is required).
3. Replace **Component** with the name of your Visual Basic project from the Project | Properties menu choice.
4. Replace **Connection** with the progid of your interface class (that's the Class with its DataSourceBehavior set to vbDataSource). The progid will be the project name and the class name, separated by a period.

Here's the template:

```
REGEDIT4

[HKEY_CLASSES_ROOT\**Component**]
@="**FullName**"

[HKEY_CLASSES_ROOT\**Component**\CLSID]
@="{**GUID**}"

[HKEY_CLASSES_ROOT\CLSID\{**GUID**}]
@="**Component**"

[HKEY_CLASSES_ROOT\CLSID\{**GUID**}\InprocServer32]
@="c:\\ProgramFiles\\CommonFiles\\System\\OLEDB\\MSDAOSP.DLL"
"ThreadingModel"="Both"

[HKEY_CLASSES_ROOT\CLSID\{**GUID**}\ProgID]
@="**Component**.1"

[HKEY_CLASSES_ROOT\CLSID\{**GUID**}\VersionIndependentProgID]
@="**Component**"

[HKEY_CLASSES_ROOT\CLSID\{**GUID**}\OLE DB Provider]
@="**FullName**"

[HKEY_CLASSES_ROOT\CLSID\{**GUID**}\OSP Data Object]
@="**Connection**"
```

The following text is an example of what a typical set of entries would look like. In this case, my Visual Basic project was called DataBinding and the interface class was called clsPrimeI. I gave the provider the arbitrary name "Peters OLE DB". I used the GUID from the UUIDGen example:

```
REGEDIT4

[HKEY_CLASSES_ROOT\Databinding]
@="Peters OLE DB"

[HKEY_CLASSES_ROOT\Databinding\CLSID]
@="{bcde9140-5068-11d3-a8c8-00107a901a5f}"
```

```
[HKEY_CLASSES_ROOT\CLSID\{bcde9140-5068-11d3-a8c8-00107a901a5f}]
@="Databinding"

[HKEY_CLASSES_ROOT\CLSID\{bcde9140-5068-11d3-a8c8-00107a901a5f}\InprocServer32]
@="c:\\Program Files\\Common Files\\System\\OLE DB\\MSDAOSP.DLL"
"ThreadingModel"="Both"

[HKEY_CLASSES_ROOT\CLSID\{bcde9140-5068-11d3-a8c8-00107a901a5f}\ProgID]
@="Databinding.1"

[HKEY_CLASSES_ROOT\CLSID\{bcde9140-5068-11d3-a8c8-00107a901a5f}\VersionIndependentProgID]
@="Databinding"

[HKEY_CLASSES_ROOT\CLSID\{bcde9140-5068-11d3-a8c8-00107a901a5f}\OLE DB Provider]
@="Peters OLE DB"

[HKEY_CLASSES_ROOT\CLSID\{bcde9140-5068-11d3-a8c8-00107a901a5f}\OSP Data Object]
@="Databinding.clsPrimeI"
```

Figure 9–9 shows some of the resulting entries in the registry.

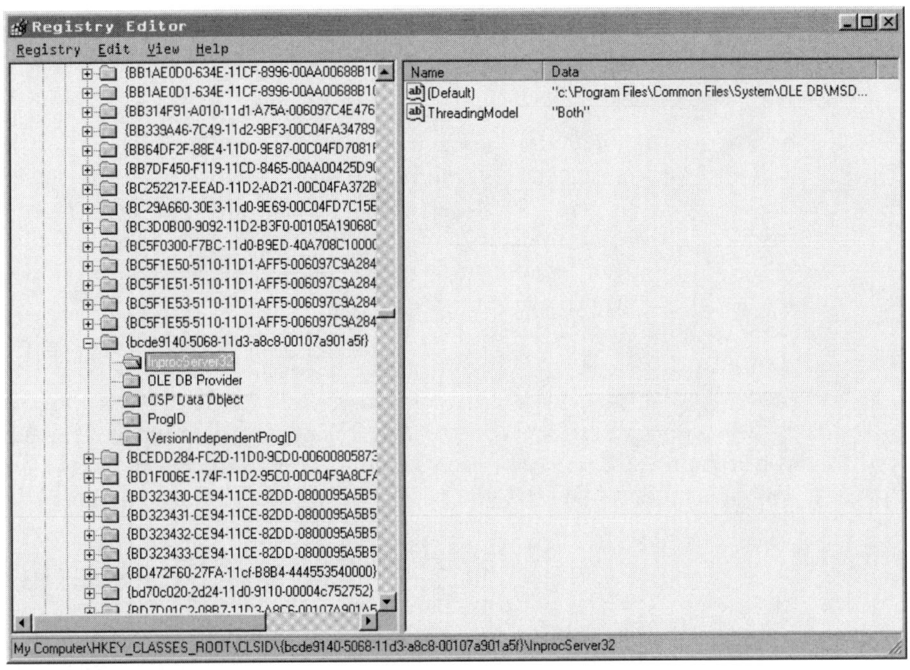

Figure 9–9 *The required entries to support an ADO provider.*

To use your ADO provider, the developer sets the provider attribute in a connection string to the name of your Visual Basic project. This code, for instance, displays all of the prime numbers in my clsPrimes class using my ADO provider (you don't have to write the methods and properties for the standard Recordset object):

```
Dim rs As ADODB.Recordset
Dim intPrime As Integer
Set rs = New ADODB.Recordset

rs.Open "", "Provider=Databinding;"
Do Until rs.EOF
    MsgBox rs.rec(0)
    rs.MoveNext
Loop
```

UPDATES

The first thing that you will probably want to add to your provider is the ability to perform updates. To do that you must indicate to ADO that the records are updateable by using the getRWStatus method:

```
Private Function OLEDBSimpleProvider_getRWStatus _
        (ByVal iRow As Long, _
        ByVal iColumn As Long) As MSDAOSP.OSPRW
    OLEDBSimpleProvider_getRWStatus = OSPRW_READWRITE
End Function
```

This method will be passed a row and column number and you must return one of the four enumerated values given in Table 9.2. If the row parameter is –1, you should return a value that indicates the updateability of the specified column for all the rows that you are returning; if the column parameter is –1, the updateability of all columns for the specified row should be returned; if both values are –1, then you should return the updateability for the whole Recordset.

With the read/write status of the array flagged, you can write the routine to update your data. ADO will call the setVariant routine when an update is made, passing the row and column number of the field to be updated, along with the new value. It's your responsibility to update whatever data source you drew the information from. For the Primes data provider, the only data source is my internal array, so its setVariant routine looks like this:

```
Private Sub OLEDBSimpleProvider_setVariant _
         (ByVal iRow As Long, ByVal iColumn As Long, _
         ByVal format As MSDAOSP.OSPFORMAT, _
         ByVal Var As Variant)

    Primes(iRow) = Var
End Sub
```

Table 9.2 Values to be Returned by the getRWStatus Method

Update Status Return Values	Description
OSPRW_DEFAULT	Updates allowed
OSPRW_MIXED	Update status not known, or a combination of updateable and non-updateable (i.e., when the column or row parameter is set to -1 and some rows/columns can be updated and others cannot)
OSPRW_READONLY	Updates not allowed
OSPRW_READWRITE	Updates allowed

COMMANDS

You will also want to give your data provider the ability to accept commands. I gave my clsPrimes provider the ability to accept a command that told it where to start the list of prime numbers. Taking the easy way out, I made the syntax for my provider as simple as possible: The developer must pass me the number to start the prime numbers list at. A developer using my provider would write this code to have the provider start the prime number list at 11:

```
rs.Open "11", "Provider=Databinding;"
```

Any commands given to your provider will be passed to your interface class in the DataMember property of its GetDataMember event. The code in your GetDataMember event can then manipulate the provider object to get the results that the developer wants.

As an example, for my prime number provider, I added a property called StartNumber to the provider Class module clsPrimes. This property adjusted the list of prime numbers returned by the provider so that they began at the value passed to StartNumber. In the interface class clsPrimeI, I had the GetDataMember code set the StartNumber property to the command passed in the DataMember parameter. With that done, I returned my object through the Data parameter:

```
Private Sub Class_GetDataMember(DataMember As String, _
                                Data As Object)
Dim clp As clsPrimes

    Set clp = New clsPrimes
    clp.StartNumber = DataMember
    Set Data = clp
End Sub
```

EVENTS

ADO Recordsets can fire events. A client, for instance, can declare a Recordset using the WithEvents keyword and then write code to respond to events fired by the Recordset. This code, for instance, will execute before any updates occur in the Recordset:

```
Dim WithEvents rs As Recordset

Private Sub rs_WillChangeField(ByVal cFields As Long, _
       ByVal Fields As Variant, _
       adStatus As ADODB.EventStatusEnum, _
       ByVal pRecordset As ADODB.Recordset)
     'pre-update processing
End Sub
```

In your code, you can use the OLEDBSimpleProviderListener object to fire events back to the clients using your provider. As each client connects to your provider, the addOLEDBSimpleProviderListener event will fire in your provider and pass you a reference to an OLEDBSimpleProviderListener object. As each client disconnects, the removeOLEDBSimpleProviderListener event will fire. The OLE Listener object is your connection to the clients using your provider.

In the add event, you can take a reference to the Listener object passed in. With that reference to the Listener object, you can use its methods to notify your clients of the actions that your provider is taking or is about to take. Each method of the Listener object causes a corresponding event to fire in the client using the provider. This code, for instance, fires events before and after any update to the Primes array:

```
Dim iosp As OLEDBSimpleProviderListener

Private Sub _
    OLEDBSimpleProvider_addOLEDBSimpleProviderListener _
        (ByVal pospIListener As _
        MSDAOSP.OLEDBSimpleProviderListener)
Set iosp = pospIListener
End Sub

Private Sub OLEDBSimpleProvider_setVariant _
        (ByVal iRow As Long, ByVal iColumn As Long, _
         ByVal format As MSDAOSP.OSPFORMAT, _
         ByVal Var As Variant)
    iosp.aboutToChangeCell iRow, iColumn
    Primes(iRow) = Var
    iosp.cellChanged iRow, iColumn
End Sub

Private Sub _
```

```
OLEDBSimpleProvider_removeOLEDBSimpleProviderListener _
      (ByVal pospIListener As _
        MSDAOSP.OLEDBSimpleProviderListener)
    Set iosp = Nothing
End Sub
```

When the provider calls the aboutToChangeCell method, the client receives the WillChangeField event; calling the cellChanged method fires the FieldChangeComplete event in the client using the provider.

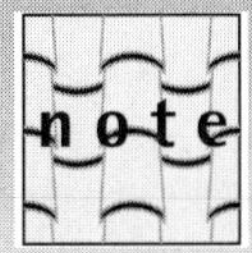

There doesn't seem to be any way to respond to the client setting the adStatus variable that's passed to the client in the event that results from calling the Listener's methods.

If your provider can be used by multiple clients, you'll need to keep a reference to all of the Listener objects that are passed to you. A collection is an excellent choice for holding those references. This version of the add Listener method adds each Listener object to a collection:

```
Dim colListeners As Collection

Private Sub Class_Initialize()
    Set colListeners = New Collection
End Sub

Private Sub _
    OLEDBSimpleProvider_addOLEDBSimpleProviderListener _
        (ByVal pospIListener As _
        MSDAOSP.OLEDBSimpleProviderListener)

    If Not (pospIListener Is Nothing) Then
      colListeners.Add pospIListener
    End If

End Sub
```

As the code in your provider executes and you want to fire events back to your clients, you'll need to loop through the collection, firing the appropriate methods:

```
Private Sub OLEDBSimpleProvider_setVariant _
        (ByVal iRow As Long, ByVal iColumn As Long, _
         ByVal format As MSDAOSP.OSPFORMAT, _
         ByVal Var As Variant)
    Dim iosp As MSDAOSP.OLEDBSimpleProviderListener

    For Each isop In colListeners
```

```
      iosp.aboutToChangeCell iRow, iColumn
    Next
    Primes(iRow) = Var

    For Each isop In colListeners
      iosp.cellChanged iRow, iColumn
    Next
End Sub
```

The remove Listener event will fire as each client disconnects from your provider. In the remove event, you'll have to find the Listener object in the collection that's associated with the client who's disconnecting. The remove event is passed a reference to the Listener for the disconnecting client, so it's just a matter of finding the matching object in the collection and then removing it:

```
Private Sub _
    OLEDBSimpleProvider_removeOLEDBSimpleProviderListener _
    (ByVal pospIListener As _
      MSDAOSP.OLEDBSimpleProviderListener)
    Dim iosp As MSDAOSP.OLEDBSimpleProviderListener
    Dim intColPos As Integer

    intColPos = 0
    For Each isop In colListeners
      intColPos = intColPos + 1
      If iosp Is pospIListener Then
        ColListeners.Remove intColPos
        Exit Sub
      End If
    Next

    End Sub
```

Data Consumers

In addition to creating OLE DB providers, you can also create OLE DB consumers with Visual Basic. OLE DB data consumers are objects that bind to a data provider to process the records provided. It's possible in Visual Basic to create consumers that not only accept data but also pass the results to another data consumer.

As a developer, you can build OLE DB consumers and providers that each perform some activity on the Recordset that's passed to them. With a set of these objects available to you, it's possible for you to build applications just by connecting the appropriate objects together. The initial provider in the chain can extract data and pass it to the consumer that it is bound to. The consumer can perform some activity on the data and then pass it to the next consumer in the chain, and so on, until the data has been transformed to meet your needs.

Simple Data Consumer

A simple data consumer binds just one of its properties to just one field. The first step in creating a simple data consumer is to set the Class or UserControl's DataBindingBehavior to vbSimpleBound. This property identifies your object as a consumer. You then need to create the property that will work with the data provider. The simplest property just accepts data and updates a variable private to the object:

```
Dim m_DataHold As String

Public Property Get DataProperty() As String
    DataProperty = m_DataHold
End Property

Public Property Let DataProperty(InputData As String)
    M_DataHold = InputData
End Property
```

The DataBindingBehavior property can also be set to vbComplexBound. Complex bound consumers work with objects created by the Data Environment in Visual Basic and bind to an entire row in a Recordset rather than just one field. Because of their relationship with the Data Environment, complex bound consumers don't fit into the kind of data manipulation object model that I discuss in this chapter.

BINDINGCOLLECTION

As I said earlier in the chapter, for ActiveX Components a developer must use a BindingCollection object to tie a consumer to a provider. Binding means the same thing with consumers as it did with data aware controls: As the provider moves from record to record, the provider will automatically pass the record's data to the consumer object.

To use the BindingCollection, the developer must add the Microsoft Data Binding Collection to the Project | References list. The developer must then create the provider and consumer objects that are to be bound together. I'll assume that the provider object is called DProvider and that the consumer is called DConsumer. Creating the objects doesn't look different from creating any other pair of objects:

```
Dim dpr As DProvider
Dim dcon As DConsumer

Set dpr = New DProvider
Set dcon = New DConsumer
```

With the two objects created, the developer then creates a BindingCollection to bind the objects together. Once the BindingCollection object is created, the developer sets its DataSource property to the object that will provide the data, DProvider in this case:

```
Dim bnd As BindingCollection
Set bnd = New BindingCollection
Set bnd.DataSource = dpr
```

The next step is to add to the collection the object that will consume the output of the BindingCollection's data source. In this case, that's the DConsumer object. Adding a consumer to the BindingCollection object requires three parameters:

1. A reference to the object
2. The name of the consumer's property to be updated
3. The field from the provider's Recordset that is to update the property.

An optional fourth parameter lets you supply a name to refer to this object in the collection.

The following code adds the dcon object to the BindingCollection that has dpr as its data source. In this code, I'm binding the field called "EmployeeName" from dpr's Recordset to the property of the dcon object called "EName":

```
bnd.Add dcon, "EName", "EmployeeName"
```

With that code, the developer's work in transferring data from the provider to the source is done. Using the methods and properties of the provider object, the developer can move through the records that the provider retrieves. As the provider moves from record to record, the consumer's bound property (EName) will automatically receive the current value of the field (EmployeeName) that it is bound to.

You're not limited to binding your fields to properties that you've defined or to ones normally considered as "data" properties. This code, for instance, binds EmployeeDescription to the ToolTipText property of an object:

```
bnd.Add dcon, "ToolTipText", "EmployeeDescription"
```

If multiple consumers are to be provided by a single data source, the developer can add more consumers to the BindingCollection object:

```
Dim dcon2 As DConsumer
Set dcon2 = New DConsumer
bnd.Add dcon2, "DataProperty", "FieldName"
```

Figure 9–10 shows the structure of consumers, providers, and BindingC-ollections.

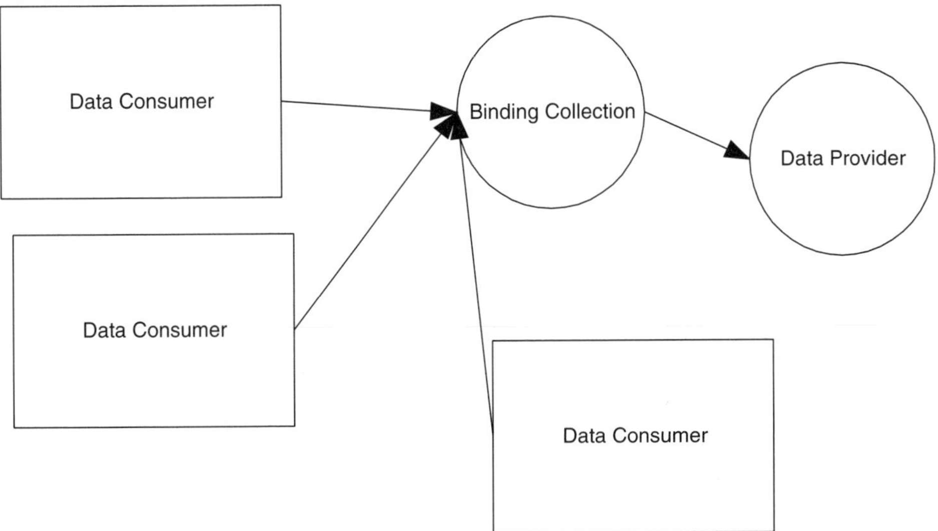

Figure 9–10 *A typical consumer-provider relationship using a BindingCollection.*

If you've created a provider that accepts commands through the Data-Member parameter, you can set the BindingCollection's DataMember before assigning the data source. The value that you set the DataMember property to will be passed to the provider in the DataMember parameter of the GetData-Member event:

```
Dim bnd As BindingCollection
Set bnd = New BindingCollection
bnd.DataMember = "Customer"
Set bnd.DataSource = dpr
bnd.Add dcon, "DataProperty", "FieldName"
```

You can remove a consumer from a BindingCollection by using the collection's Remove method and passing it the name used in the fourth parameter of the Add method. This code, for instance, first adds dcon to the BindingCollection and then removes it:

```
bnd.Add dcon, "DataProperty", "FieldName", "First"
bnd.Remove "First"
```

PROPERTYCHANGED

For a read-only consumer, the code you've seen above using the BindingCollection is all that you need. You don't even have to use the data bound options of the Procedure Attributes dialog. However, if you want your consumer to pass data back to the provider to have the provider update the data source, two more steps are required.

First, the property in the consumer that is going to be bound must be flagged as data bound in the Procedure Attributes dialog. Second, as with the ActiveX data aware controls discussed earlier, the consumer must also signal that the data needs to be returned to the provider by using the Property-Changed method.

Service Provider Objects

There's no reason that a consumer can't, in turn, be a data provider: All you have to do is set a Class module's DataBindingBehavior and the DataSource-Behavior properties to values other than vbNone. By creating an object that is simultaneously a provider and a consumer, you can link several predefined objects together to perform standard processing activities. This kind of object is called a service provider because, while it doesn't extract the initial data, it provides a service by manipulating the data.

You can create a library of objects that perform a set of standard operations on the contents of a Recordset. Since each provider produces a Recordset, this means that you can create any combination of providers, service providers, and consumers that you need. For instance, you could have an object that accepts data and wraps it in a set of XML tags. Another object might, when provided a Recordset of XML strings, add XSL statements to the Recordset. As shown in Figure 9–11, a developer could link together a data provider, the XML service provider, and the XSL consumer to create a complete XML application.

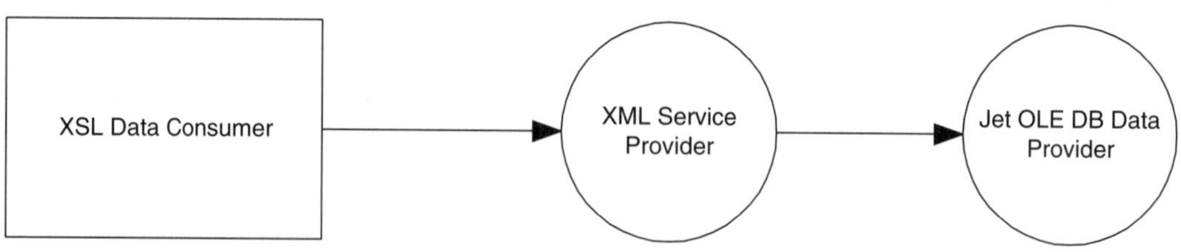

Figure 9–11 *Linking together providers, consumers, and service providers.*

DEFINING A SERVICE PROVIDER

A service provider object is an object that can be bound to a provider but that also returns a Recordset. These two features allow the object to appear anywhere in a chain of data manipulating objects (except at the start of the chain, which must be a provider).

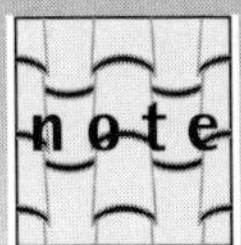

A chain with a service provider that you create will be read-only. Changes made to the properties of the consumer at the head of the chain will not be propagated down through the service provider to the provider at the other end.

When an object appears in the middle of the chain it must accept any data passed to it, just like an ordinary consumer. In order to also act as a provider, the object must also prepare a Recordset to pass to the next consumer, higher in the chain. Not surprisingly, then, code for a service provider combines features of both providers and consumers. Like a provider, a service provider has a GetDataMember event to return a Recordset. Like a consumer, a service provider has a data bound property. Combining them can give code that might look like this:

```
Dim rs As Recordset

Private Sub Class_Initialize()
    Set rs = New Recordset
    rs.Fields.Append "MyData", adChar, 50
    rs.CursorType = adOpenStatic
    rs.LockType = adLockOptimistic
    rs.Open
    rs.AddNew
    rs.Update
End Sub

Public Property Let DataIn(InValue As String)
    m_localData = InValue
    rs("MyData") = m_localData
    PropertyChanged "DataIn"
End Property

Private Sub Class_GetDataMember(DataMember As String, _
                                Data As Object)
    Set Data = rs
End Sub
```

In the Initialize event, the object's code creates a Recordset with a field called "MyData". The code adds a single record to the Recordset. Like a consumer, the service provider has a data bound property—in this case, DataIn. In the DataIn routine, the data passed to the object is used to update the single field in the Recordset. The GetDataMember event returns the Recordset to the consumer higher in the chain. By updating the field in the Recordset, the data is made available to the next consumer in the chain. This code, coupled with setting both the DataBindingBehavior and DataSourceBehavior properties, creates a service provider object that can appear anywhere in the chain (except at the provider end).

If the service provider modifies the data that it receives before passing it on, it should do so in the data bound property (in this case, DataIn).

BUILDING A CHAIN

When building a chain of consumers, providers, and consumer providers, the application that builds the chain could bind all of the objects. The code to build a chain consisting of a single provider, service provider, and consumer would look like this :

```
Dim con As clsConsumer
Dim spv As clsServiceProvider
Dim prv As clsProvider
Dim bnd As BindingCollection
Dim bnd2 As BindingCollection

Set con = New clsConsumer
Set spv = New clsServiceProvider
Set prv = New clsProvider

Set bnd = New BindingCollection
Set bnd.DataSource = prv
bnd.Add spv, "DataProperty", "FieldName"

Set bnd2 = New BindingCollection
Set bnd2.DataSource = spv
bnd2.Add con, "DataProperty2", "DataFieldName"
```

However, you can reduce the demands on the developer who uses your service providers by placing code in each object to bind the object to its provider.

The first step in creating this routine is to realize that a consumer can use the BindingCollection's Add method to bind itself to a provider. The code that will cause a consumer (or service provider) to bind itself to a provider (or another service provider) looks like this:

```
Set cpv = clsProvider
Set bnd = New BindingCollection
Set bnd.DataSource = cpv
bnd.Add Me, "DataProperty", "FieldName"
```

Using this technique, you can write a Bind method for your service providers that causes the object to bind itself to the previous data provider in the chain. The routine will consist of the code first shown, so the only question left to answer is: What sort of information must be passed to the Bind method?

Basically, the Bind method will need most of the parameters that the BindingCollection's Add method requires. For instance, the routine will need a reference to the provider (or service provider) that it will bind itself to. The routine will also need the name of the field from the provider that the object is to bind to. You don't, however, need to pass the name of the property that will be updated with the data from the provider.

While the BindingCollection's Add method requires that you specify the name of the property to be updated along with the field in the provider's Recordset, you will know the property name when you write the Bind method code. Remember that the Bind method code will be put in the consumer object's Class module, which is where the code for the data bound property can also be found. As a result, you will know the name of the property that you are binding because it is part of the same object as the Bind method. The field name from the provider, on the other hand, will vary depending on what provider you are binding to.

So, the Bind method will accept two parameters: the data provider object to bind to and the field to accept from the provider object. Here's some sample code from a service provider showing the data bound property and the Bind method:

```
Dim m_dtb As BindingCollection

Public Property Let DataIn (InValue As String)
    m_LocalData = InValue
End Property

Public Property Get DataIn() As String
    DataIn = m_LocalData
End Property

Public Sub Bind(ProvIn As Object, strField As String)
    Set m_dtb = New BindingCollection
    Set m_dtb.DataSource = ProvIn
    m_dtb.Add Me, "DataIn", strField
End Sub
```

The Bind method allows the consumer object to bind itself to any provider or data provider. This means that a variety of objects can be passed in to the routine through the routine's ProvIn parameter. As a result, the ProvIn parameter has to be declared as an Object to accept any provider.

An enhancement to the Bind method would allow the field name passed to the routine to be optional. If the provider returns a Recordset with only one field (as is the case in my example), the provider could expose a FieldName property that supplies that name. The Bind method code could look like this:

```
Public Sub bind(ProvIn As Object, _
              Optional strField As String = "")
Dim strFieldName As String

    If strField = "" Then
      strFieldName = ProvIn.FieldName
    Else
      strFieldName = strField
    End If

    Set m_dtb = New BindingCollection
    Set m_dtb.DataSource = ProvIn
    m_dtb.Add Me, "DataIn", strFielName
End Sub
```

A SAMPLE CHAIN

A chain might consist of a data provider (clsProvider) that provides data to a service provider (clsSP1) which, in turn, provides data to another service provider (clsSP2), which passes its data to the consumer at the head of the chain (clsConsumer). To build a chain using these objects, the developer begins by declaring and creating the objects that are to be used:

```
Dim P As Provider
Dim SP1 As clsSP1
Dim SP2 As clsSP2
Dim C As clsConsumer

Set P = New clsProvider
Set SP1 = New clsSP1
Set SP2 = New clsSP2
Set C = New clsConsumer
```

Now, the routine calls the Bind methods of the various objects to build the chain (I've assumed that I have to tell the Bind method which field in the provider's Recordset to bind to):

```
C.Bind SP2, "FinalField"
SP2.Bind SP1, "MiddleField"
SP1.Bind P, "DataField"
```

The chain is now built. The developer can use the methods of the provider at the end of the chain to move through the Recordset, and use the properties of the consumer at the other end of the chain to extract the results of the chain's processing.

Remote Data Services

One of the givens in the Internet/intranet development world is that there is client-side development and there is server-side development. In this world, data access is done on the server because that's where the data is. Remote Data Services (RDS) makes this definition obsolete. With RDS, you can reach back to the client from the Web browser and execute components to retrieve data. The resulting Recordsets are passed down to the browser for processing there. As a result, you can integrate the client and the server to a greater degree than ever before.

RDS solves a variety of problems with Web applications:

- The browser can access and update data back on the server without a round trip to the server.
- Since RDS allows scripts to execute components on the Server, proprietary code doesn't have to be included in the page downloaded to the client.
- Scalability is improved because much of your data manipulation can be done at the client.
- Components executing on the server can be compiled code, with corresponding gains in performance.

RDS makes all this possible by returning Recordsets to the client where script code can manipulate and update the data.

In the following examples, I haven't made any attempt to create classes in my client-side code. Prior to IE 5 and the release of VBScript 5, it wasn't possible to create classes with VBScript so the examples in this section show user interface code directly manipulating data.

With IIS 4.0, Microsoft has provided a set of tools that lets you get up and running with RDS quickly. In this section I show you how to use RDS and also how to build a component that will execute on your server to extend RDS's capabilities.

An RDS Case Study

My first significant application with RDS was built for one of Canada's major banks. The application had to be finished in six weeks and deployed across Canada. Given the tight schedule and wide deployment, the bank turned to the current hot Rapid Application Design tool: The Internet. The bank had standardized on Internet Explorer as their browser so that they could make use of all of Microsoft's Web application development tools. I was brought in because of my expertise in developing intranet applications using those Microsoft tools. Thanks to RDS, we were able to implement a client-server application running over the company's intranet well before the delivery date.

RDS Architecture

The RDS architecture is simple. From the browser, an ActiveX Control—the DataSpace—communicates with the server to create an ActiveX Component. The DataSpace control hands back to the script a reference to the server component. The script in the browser can then call the component's methods to have it return ADO Recordsets to the client.

The DataSpace ActiveX Control comes with IE 4.0 and later. The default server component (called the DataFactory) comes with IIS 3.0 and later.

To make the DataSpace control available to the script in your Web page, you add this tag to the page:

```
<OBJECT
classid=clsid:BD96C556-65A3-11D0-983A-00C04FC29E36
height=1 width=1 name=dsp id=dsp>
</OBJECT>
```

The DataSpace control can be used to create a DataFactory on the server which can return Recordsets to the script executing in the browser. Once the Recordset object has been retrieved, client-side script can make changes to the data, delete records, and even add new records. You can then return the Recordset to the server for updates. Figure 9–12 shows the basic architecture of RDS.

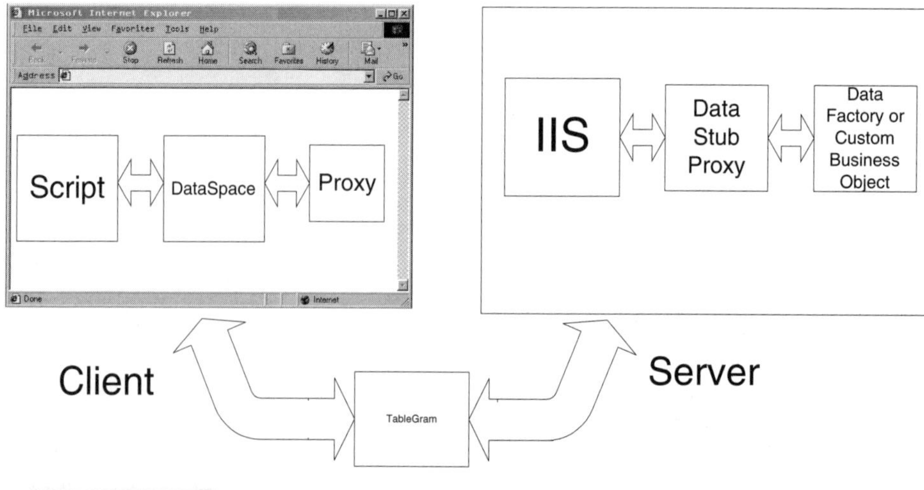

Figure 9–12 *The architecture of RDS.*

The diagram also looks under the hood of the RDS architecture to show some objects that you can't interact with directly. As the diagram shows, data is sent back and forth between the client and the server over HTTP through a set of MIME-type tablegrams. More important, your client-side code does not interact directly with the server component. Instead, your script is actually issuing calls against a proxy that stands in for the server-side component. On the server, the DataFactory interacts with another RDS proxy that marshals the returned Recordset into the tablegrams.

The Default DataFactory

IIS ships with a default DataFactory that allows you to issue queries against OLE DB data sources on the server and return a Recordset to your client-side script. This script code creates the default DataFactory object on the server phvserver1. It then uses the DataFactory's Query method to retrieve a Recordset of all of the records in the Customer table:

```
Set dtf = dsp.CreateObject("RDSServer.DataFactory", _
                              "HTTP://phvserver1")
Set rec = dtf.Query("File Name=MyUDL.UDL", _
                       "Select * From Customers")
```

To update the data back on the server, you use the default DataFactory's SubmitChanges method. The SubmitChanges method accepts two parameters: A connection string and the Recordset to be sent back for processing. This code adds a new record to the Recordset (using the standard Recordset methods) and then sends the Recordset back to the server for updating:

```
rec.AddNew
rec("CompanyName") = "First National"
rec("City") = "Goderich"
rec.Update
dtf.SubmitChanges "File Name=MyUDL.UDL", rec
```

Custom DataFactories

The default DataFactory is a useful, but limited, tool. Often, you will want to move some of your data processing to the server to reduce the amount of code in your Web page. The simplest way to do this is to create a custom RDS business object whose methods and properties you can tailor to meet your specific needs.

The DataFactory is a security hole in the IIS architecture. With the DataFactory installed on your server, if hackers can provide the connection information for a data source on the server, then they can issue commands to the DataFactory. All they need to do is load a page into any Web browser with the appropriate script code to create the DataFactory. Microsoft has identified the security issues as follows:

"The RDS DataFactory object, a component of Microsoft Data Access Components (MDAC), exposes unsafe methods. When installed on a system running Internet Information Server 3.0 or 4.0, the DataFactory object may permit an otherwise unauthorized Web user to perform privileged actions, including:

Allowing unauthorized users to execute shell commands on the IIS system as a privileged user.

On a multi-homed Internet-connected IIS system, using MDAC to tunnel SQL and other ODBC data requests through the public connection to a private back-end network.

Allowing unauthorized accessing to secured, non-published files on the IIS system."

An RDS business object has no special interfaces or required methods. The major design consideration is that the object must return a specific kind of ADO Recordset. The object must also be completely stateless. An RDS business object is created on the server and kept in memory for exactly as long as it takes to execute a method. The object is destroyed as soon as the method finishes executing. From the client, though, this is hidden from your script. As Figure 9–12 showed, your script actually executes the methods of a proxy in the browser. The proxy isn't destroyed unless you set your client-side object variable to Nothing (or let the variable that refers to the proxy go out of scope).

In the bank application, one of the functions was to find records that met a particular set of criteria. Determining which records met the criteria meant issuing a series of SQL calls to retrieve data from a variety of tables. Rather than implement all this code on the client, I created a custom business object that accepted a set of parameters, did all the necessary processing, and returned only the required records.

I already had a number of server-side objects written for this project and implemented in a Visual Basic 6.0 project called Bank. To create a customer RDS business object, I added another Class module to the Bank project, called it DataSearch, and put this the following code in it:

```
Public Sub FindRecords (ParamArray strParms())As Recordset
Dim rec As RecordSet
Set rec = New Recordset
rec.CursorLocation = adUseClient
rec.CursorType = adOpenStatic
rec.LockType = adLockBatchOptimistic
…processing to find records…
Set FindRecords = rec
End Sub
```

The code shows the properties that must be set for the Recordset that's to be returned to the client. Since the Recordset will be managed at the client, the CursorLocation property must be set to adUseClient. The cursor must be a Static cursor so that all the data for all of the records is loaded into the Recordset when it's opened. If you intend to do updates with the Recordset, you must also set the CursorType to support batch updating.

With the object installed on the server, the script code in the Web page to call the object from the client looked like this:

```
Set bds = dsp.CreateObject("Bank.DataSearch", _
    "HTTP://www.phvserver1.com")
Set rec = bds.FindRecords (strParm1, strParm2, strParm2)
```

Since the object is launched by the RDS proxy on the server, you need to add your object to the list of objects that the proxy can launch. This means adding the object's progid to a list in the server's registry under this key (see Figure 9–13):

```
HKEY_LOCAL_MACHINE\SYSTEM\CURRENTCONTROLSET\
            Services\W3SVC\Parameters\ADCLaunch
```

Your client-side script, in addition to accepting Recordsets, can also pass a Recordset back to a business object on the server. Once your custom DataFactory receives the Recordset, it can make the necessary updates to the data source.

Summary

In this chapter, I looked at a variety of ways that you can integrate COM components with data. I began by returning to ActiveX Controls and showed how you can convert the controls that you've developed into data bound controls. From there, you saw how to make ActiveX components that integrate into the ADO architecture. I began with simple ActiveX data providers and went on to create true OLE DB providers. Custom data providers can allow you to access data in proprietary formats or hide details of complicated data accesses. You also saw how to create data consumers and hybrid consumer/providers that could be strung together to handle complicated processing tasks. Finally, I looked at RDS, an OLE DB technology designed for the Internet. You learned how to create a custom business object that could be called from the client to return data from the server.

You could begin working with these tools by taking an existing ActiveX control and making it data aware. As I said in the chapter on ActiveX Controls, you won't really appreciate what you've done until you use that control to build an application. Another task worth trying is building a data provider and a couple of data consumers that work with it. A provider that could read

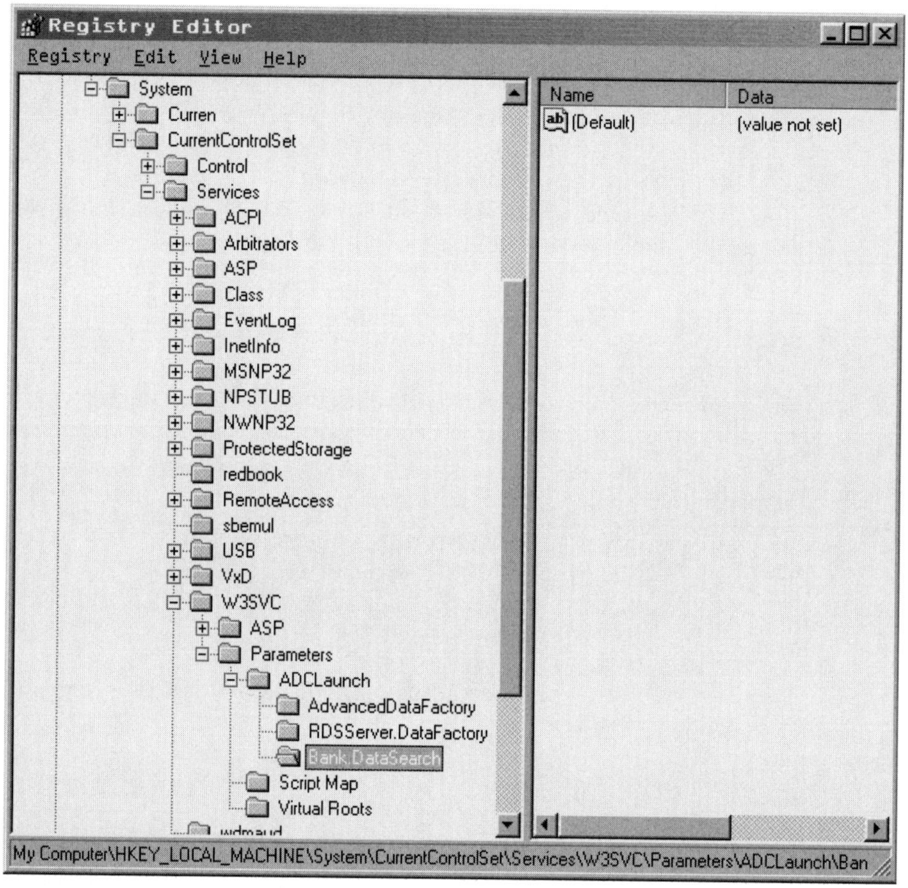

Figure 9–13 *Registry entries to support a custom business object.*

lines out of a text file could be useful. A service provider that would convert a Recordset into a set of comma delimited records might also come in handy, as would a consumer that converts its input into an HTML table. With a provider and two consumers built, you could try linking them together to see how well they cooperate. Finally, you could convert your data provider into a DataFactory compatible with RDS and deliver to the Web.

Creating ADO consumers and providers in Visual Basic is relatively easy. The critical portion is how you create the Recordset that your data provider returns. To understand the nuances of the Recordset object, the only reference that you need is a good book on ADO. One that I like very much is called *VB Developer's Guide to ADO*, by Michael Gunderloy from Sybex. The best article that I've read on creating OLE DB Providers is by Rob Macdonald and was originally published in the Visual Basic Developer newsletter from Pinnacle Publishing. You can find it on the MSDN disks in the periodicals section. The Registry template file in the ADO provider section is straight from Rob's article. Rob's Web site at *www.salterton.com/hill* contains a variety of useful Visual Basic articles.

T E N

Design Time Controls

With Visual InterDev 1.0, Microsoft introduced a new kind of ActiveX Control—the Design Time Control (DTC). DTCs offer a new way to speed development and to distribute development tools. Unlike a standard ActiveX control, a DTC can write to its container. A DTC control interacts with its container by implementing an interface that contains methods that the container calls to add text to itself. While this may sound like a particularly limited ability, it is the key to creating development tools that are independent of the development environment that they are used in. A DTC can operate in any ActiveX hospitable environment and support any design activity that depends on generating code.

In this chapter I show you how to create a design time control. I create a DTC that will add the necessary code and HTML to implement Remote Data Services in a W'eb page. As discussed in a previous chapter, Remote Data Services (RDS) is a service built on ADO that allows a browser to access data back on the server. Figure 10–1 shows a Web page that uses RDS to display a grid full of data. What's remarkable is that the data being displayed was requested from a script executing in the browser and the data is being cached at the browser. Since the data is stored in the browser, it can be sorted or filtered without a trip to the server, all thanks to RDS. RDS allows you to build a responsive, flexible user interface while reducing network traffic.

Using RDS is a great way to deliver data to your users, but coding it can be time consuming. This chapter creates a DTC that will generate all the standard code needed to work with an RDS datasource.

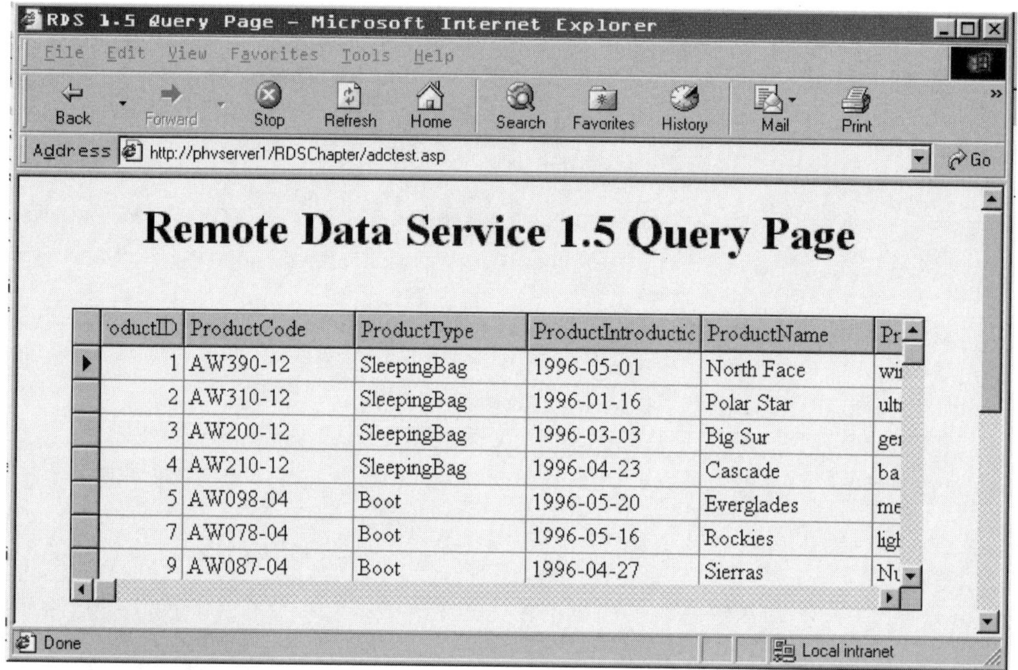

Figure 10–1 *This Web page contains an invisible RDS control which retrieved and cached on the client the data required by the Grid control.*

In order to build DTCs with Visual Basic 5.0 you'll have to download the Design-Time Control Software Development Kit. You can find the file (DTCSDK60.EXE) at Microsoft's Visual InterDev site (*http://msdn.microsoft.com/vinterdev*) in the Downloads section under Code Samples. In addition to providing the type libraries and other support that you will need to create sophisticated DTCs, the kit also includes the DTC help file and Choice Inspector. The Choice Inspector lets you review the current topics and the postings that have been made to them for any environment where you are using your DTCs.

Before using any of the Choices functionality, you'll need to add references to your Visual Basic project to DTC60.TLB and WEBDC.TLB. Installing the DTC SDK does not add the necessary type libraries to your registry entries, so when you go to your Project | References list you won't find the DTC SDK listed. To get the necessary references, you'll have to click on the References' Browse button and navigate to the files containing the type libraries. If you've taken the defaults when installing the SDK, you'll find the necessary files in C:\Program Files\DTCSDK60\INCLUDE. Selecting the DTC60.TLB and WEBDC.TLB files will add the libraries to your References list and also select them.

With Visual Basic 6.0, the necessary interfaces are included with Visual Basic and you need only check off 'Microsoft DTC FrameWork' in your References list.

Introducing DTC

As I mentioned in the last chapter, when I created my first ActiveX Control using Visual Basic, I was surprised to discover that the control was running both at design time and run time. On reflection, this should have been obvious. After all, there had to be some mechanism to redraw a control as it was resized or to alter the visual interface of the control as the values in the property list changed.

At design time, a control's properties are displayed in Visual Basic's property list. To get the values to display that property list, Visual Basic reads the control's properties in the same way that your program reads the control's properties. As the developer makes changes in the entries in the property list, Visual Basic sets the control's properties. So, from the control's point of view, Visual Basic is just another COM application that sets and reads the control's properties. The Visual InterDev environment works with controls in the same way.

It's a natural extension of this model to have the executing control make changes to the container based on the changes being made to the control's properties. Unfortunately, the ActiveX Control specification does not provide for a Control to change the container that displays it. The Design Time Control specification was developed to permit the container to be modified from the control.

As the name implies, DTCs are intended to be used only at design time. At design time DTCs behave like any other ActiveX control: they redraw themselves, respond to mouse clicks, display popup menus, and invoke property pages. Unlike Wizards and Add-ins, which are intimately bound up with the object model of the tool that they are part of, a DTC adds to its environment without invoking the specific object model of the container that it is running in.

Unlike a Wizard, a DTC can be rerun without losing the results of the previous session with the DTC.

When requested by the container, a DTC takes the information that the developer entered and writes out text to the container. This defines the processing cycle for a DTC: gather information from the developer during the design session and write out text when requested.

Designing a Simple DTC

The DTC specification has changed since it was first introduced. I begin with the simplest possible DTC—one that could be created in Visual Basic 5 and used in Visual InterDev 1.0. Once I've demonstrated how that control works, I go on to a control that takes advantage of the new features of the DTC specification. This control could also be developed in Visual Basic 6.0 and used in Visual InterDev 6.0.

A DTC has a simple visual interface that acts as a placeholder when the control is activated during an editing session. Your DTC's visual interface doesn't have to look like anything. The DTC that I'm developing initially has as its user interface a rectangular form with a single label on it.

If the result of the text that the DTC creates will have a specific appearance, it helps the developer if the DTC mimics that appearance. For instance, the VID 6.0 DTC that is used to generate the HTML to create a form button itself resembles a button.

RDS

To use RDS, you must create an RDS.DataControl object in the browser. This DataControl object passes a SQL string back to a server running IIS 4.0. On receipt of the request, IIS 4.0 creates an RDSServer.DataFactory object which handles the requests from the browser (see Figure 10–2).

The DataFactory handles communication with the database, issuing requests for data and receiving records in return. The DataFactory sends the data it gets from the server back to the browser. The RDS.DataControl object caches all the data sent to it by the DataFactory.

The asynchronous nature of the transfer allows the browser to start displaying the data as soon as the first records show up. Once the data is received and cached, the browser can sort or filter it without having to return to the server. Updates can be made within the browser and submitted to the server as a single batch for asynchronous processing. ActiveX controls and Dynamic HTML can be bound to the DataControl so that they automatically display the data received.

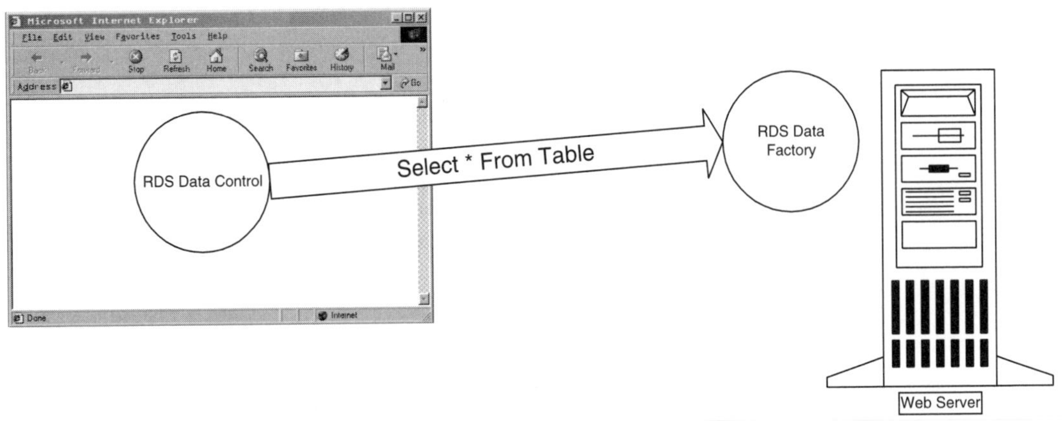

Figure 10–2 *The RDSControl causes the creation of the RDSDataFactory on the server by requesting data.*

The DTCRDS Specification

The DTC that I developed writes out the necessary HTML and client side script to add Remote Data Services to a browser-based application. For want of a better name, I call this control the DTCRDS.

The text that the DTCRDS control will generate consists of

- an object tag to invoke a data bound control (in this case, the Sheridan Grid Control that ships with RDS)
- an object tag to create an RDS.DataControl
- a script that provides the necessary code to load the grid with data when the page is displayed.

An ActiveX Control

The initial stages of creating a DTC are identical to the processes involved in creating a standard ActiveX control. These steps include defining properties, saving property values, and integrating with the development environment. With a DTC, though, the control will be built in Visual Basic but the design-time environment it will run in will be Visual InterDev. The DTC specification hides the differences between the Visual Basic and Visual InterDev environments from the designer.

Defining Properties

To begin creating a DTC, I started up Visual Basic and selected 'ActiveX Control' from the initial menu. I placed a label on the default UserControl with a caption that read 'RDS DTC' and sized the form to fit the label. I changed the name of the form to RDSDTCUI and set the project's name to DTCRDS.

The first routine that I added to my control was the UserControl_InitProperties. I used this routine to set the default values of the control's properties. For this DTC, I set up three properties:

Server	the server that the page is to get its data from
DSN	the DSN on the server that the control will use
SQL	the SQL command that is to be passed to the DSN

Setting default values for all properties is an important part of creating a robust DTC. It's impossible for the DTC to predict when the container will request that the DTC write text to the container. It's entirely possible that the container may request the DTC to write text before the developer has had a chance to set the control's properties. By providing default values, you guarantee that no matter when a request comes to add text, the resulting text will be complete and syntactically correct.

The code for the DTCRDS's InitProperties looks like this:

```
Private Sub UserControl_InitProperties()
'set initial values for properties
  strDSN = "ServerDSN"
  strSQL = "Select * From Table;"
  strServer = "ServerName"
End Sub
```

I could have added a number of other properties for this control: the height and width of the grid control's display, the name of the RDS and Grid controls, and so on. However, the point of this chapter is how to create a DTC, and these three properties provide all the examples that I need.

With the default values for the control's properties set, I added Property procedures for each of the properties defined for the control:

```
Dim strSQL As String
Dim strServer As String
Dim strDSN As String

Public Property Let SQL(SQLString As String)
  strSQL = SQLString
  UserControl.PropertyChanged "SQL"
End Property

Public Property Get SQL() As String
  SQL = strSQL
End Property

Public Property Let Server(ServerName As String)
  strServer = ServerName
  UserControl.PropertyChanged "Server"
```

```
  End Property

Public Property Get Server() As String
  Server = strServer
End Property

Public Property Let DSN(DSNName As String)
  strDSN = DSNName
  UserControl.PropertyChanged "DSN"
End Property

Public Property Get DSN() As String
  DSN = strDSN
End Property
```

While I've used property procedures, these properties could have just as easily been implemented as public variables. The processing cycle of the DTC ensures that the properties won't be used until the text is going to be written out. You can defer any validation of the properties until the control writes out its text to the container.

As with any ActiveX control, it's better practice to validate property settings as soon as they are made. Like any other user, developers appreciate immediate feedback. Providing a PropertyPage where the settings are complex is also appreciated.

Persisting Properties

The next step in developing a DTC is to create the routines to persist and retrieve the values of the properties. Like a standard ActiveX control, this is done through the ReadProperties and WriteProperties events:

```
Private Sub _
  UserControl_ReadProperties(PropBag As PropertyBag)
'Retrieve property values
 strDSN = _
  PropBag.ReadProperty("DSN", "ServerDSN")
 strSQL =  _
  PropBag.ReadProperty("SQL", "Select * from Table;")
 strServer =  _
  PropBag.ReadProperty("Server", "ServerName")
End Sub

Private Sub _
  UserControl_WriteProperties(PropBag As PropertyBag)
'Save property values
PropBag.WriteProperty "DSN", strDSN, "ServerDSN"
PropBag.WriteProperty "SQL", strSQL, _
```

```
    "Select * from Table;"
PropBag.WriteProperty "Server", strServer,  _
"ServerName"

End Sub
```

As with a standard ActiveX control, you save and retrieve a DTC's properties through the PropertyBag object. In Visual InterDev, adding to the PropertyBag causes Visual InterDev to write an HTML Param tag to the Web page for each property of the control. It's the presence of these Param tags that allows the DTC to be rerun.

There is a 1K limit to the value parameter of a Param tag, so a really big property might have to be spread across several Param tags.

A developer will drag a DTC into a container, set some of the control's properties and move on to some other task. The container will ask the DTC to generate its text and add that text to the container. The container will also store the control's properties.

Later, the developer might decide to change the DTC's settings. When the developer reactivates the DTC control, the code in the control's ReadProperties event will reload the properties from the last session. The developer will review the property settings and make the necessary changes. After the developer has changed the control's properties, the container will request that the control regenerate its text. Once the container receives the new version of the control's text, the container replaces the old text with the new.

One of the results of this process is that changes to the values of the Param tags made outside the DTC are honored by the DTC (provided they are valid and consistent, of course). Changes to the text generated by the DTC, however, will be lost when a DTC is reactivated because the container deletes it before requesting the new text.

The Design Time Control Interface

The routines that I've shown so far are typical of any ActiveX control. Converting this ActiveX control to a Design Time Control consists of implementing the IProvideRuntimeText interface and adding a GetRunTimeText method to the control. The GetRuntimeText method is the method that the container will invoke to add text to the container.

The GetRunTimeText Method

The following code is the GetRuntimeText method for the RDSDTC. The code isn't very easy to read but is relatively straightforward. The function builds a string of HTML, incorporating the settings the developer has made in the control's properties.

Some of the code is the HTML that will invoke the Grid control when the page is downloaded to the browser:

```
"<OBJECT id=""Grid"" Width=400 Height=100 " & _
  "DATASRC=""#RDS"" " & vbCrLf & _
```

In the code, the vbCrLf is used to start the following text on a new line in the container. The line feeds are added primarily to make the code easier to read should the developer want to look at the text that the control produced. HTML, in general, doesn't require that its text be written on separate lines. Instead HTML uses <BR> tags to create line breaks when the text is displayed. Of course, line feeds also make the code easier to read when you are debugging your control's output.

One of the places where you must insert line feeds is in script code. Most scripting languages require that each statement appear on a separate line. When the GetRuntimeText creates the script code, it inserts line feeds between the statements in the script:

```
"<SCRIPT LANGUAGE=""VBSCRIPT"">" & vbCrLf & _
  "Sub Window_OnLoad" & vbCrLf & _
  "RDS.Connect = ""DSN=" & strDSN & ";""" & vbCrLf & _
```

As the last code example shows, with the strDSN variable the GetRuntimeText also concatenates the internal variables that hold the property settings into the text that the method writes out.

The resulting string is put in the variable strOutputString. As with any function, the value of the function is returned to the client (in this case, Visual InterDev) by setting the name of the function to the variable holding the result:

```
strOutputString = "<OBJECT id=""RDS"" " & …
IProvideRuntimeText_GetRunTimeText = strOutputString
```

Here's the complete version of the GetRuntimeText method:

```
Implements IProvideRuntimeText

Public Function IProvideRuntimeText_GetRunTimeText() As String
Dim strOutputString As String

 strOutputString = "<OBJECT id=""RDS"" " & _
  "CLASSID=" &
 """clsid:BD96C556-65A3-11D0-983A-00C04FC29E33"">" & _
```

```
    "</OBJECT>" & vbCrLf & _
    "<OBJECT id=""Grid"" Width=400 Height=100 " & _
    "DATASRC=""#RDS"" " & vbCrLf & _
    "CLASSID=" &
    """clsid:AC05DC80-7DF1-11d0-839E-00A024A94B3A""" & _
    vbCrLf & _
    "CODEBASE=""http://" & strServer & _
   "/MSADC/Samples/ssdatb32.cab"">" & _
    "</OBJECT>" & vbCrLf & _
    "<SCRIPT LANGUAGE=""VBSCRIPT"">" & vbCrLf & _
    "Sub Window_OnLoad" & vbCrLf & _
    "RDS.Connect = ""DSN=" & strDSN & ";""" & vbCrLf & _
    "RDS.SQL =""" & strSQL & """" & vbCrLf & _
    "RDS.Server = ""http://" & strServer & """" & _
    vbCrLf & _
    "RDS.ExecuteOptions = 2" & vbCrLf & _
    "RDS.FetchOptions = 4" & vbCrLf & _
    "RDS.Refresh" & vbCrLf & _
    "Grid.Rebind" & vbCrLf & _
    "End Sub" & vbCrLf & _
    "</SCRIPT>" & vbCrLf

 IProvideRuntimeText_GetRunTimeText = strOutputString
End Function
```

DTC Output

The easiest way to understand the output from the DTCRDS control is to look at the text that it creates:

```
<!--METADATA TYPE="DesignerControl" startspan
<OBJECT ID="RDSDTCUI1" WIDTH=127 HEIGHT=40
 CLASSID="CLSID:9E580C7D-0FEA-11D2-BA56-0000B4400C76">
<PARAM NAME="_ExtentX" VALUE="3360">
<PARAM NAME="_ExtentY" VALUE="1058">
<PARAM NAME="DSN" VALUE="pubs">
<PARAM NAME="SQL" VALUE="Select * From authors;">
<PARAM NAME="Server" VALUE="phvserver1">
 </OBJECT>
-->
<OBJECT id="RDS"
CLASSID="clsid:BD96C556-65A3-11D0-983A-00C04FC29E33">
</OBJECT>
<OBJECT id="Grid" Width=400 Height=100 DATASRC="#RDS"
CLASSID="clsid:AC05DC80-7DF1-11d0-839E-00A024A94B3A"
CODEBASE="http://phvserver1/MSADC/Samples/ssdatb32.cab">
</OBJECT>
<SCRIPT LANGUAGE="VBSCRIPT">
Sub Window_OnLoad
RDS.Connect = "DSN=pubs;"
```

```
RDS.SQL ="Select * From authors;"
RDS.Server = "http://phvserver1"
RDS.ExecuteOptions = 2
RDS.FetchOptions = 4
RDS.Refresh
Grid.Rebind
End Sub
</SCRIPT>

<!--METADATA TYPE="DesignerControl" endspan-->
```

The material from the <OBJECT id="RDS" line to the </SCRIPT> tag was produced by the control. The rest of the text that you see was added by the control's container, Visual InterDev. To begin with, Visual InterDev enclosed the DTC's text in HTML comment:

```
<!--METADATA TYPE="DesignerControl" startspan
<!--METADATA TYPE="DesignerControl" endspan-->
```

In the opening startspan comment tag, Visual InterDev inserted an <OBJECT> tag which contains the CLSID of the DTC that generated the text. Visual InterDev uses the information in the Object tag to invoke the DTC if the developer wants to make changes to the generated text:

```
<OBJECT ID="RDSDTCUI1" WIDTH=127 HEIGHT=40
 CLASSID="CLSID:9E580C7D-0FEA-11D2-BA56-0000B4400C76">
```

The MetaData and Object tags let Visual InterDev recognize text generated by the DTC. If the MrtaData tags are deleted, the text generated by the DTC will remain but the DTC itself will disappear from your page.

Following the Object tag, Visual InterDev inserts the Param tags for the properties that the control defined. Closing off the list of Params and marking the end of the information about the DTC is an </OBJECT> tag:

```
<PARAM NAME="_ExtentX" VALUE="3360">
<PARAM NAME="_ExtentY" VALUE="1058">
<PARAM NAME="DSN" VALUE="pubs">
<PARAM NAME="SQL" VALUE="Select * From authors;">
<PARAM NAME="Server" VALUE="phvserver1">
</OBJECT>
```

Following the </OBJECT> tag that marks the end of the information about the RDSDTC, you can see the actual text written out by the DTC:

```
<SCRIPT LANGUAGE="VBSCRIPT">
Sub Window_OnLoad
```

```
RDS.Connect = "DSN=pubs;"
RDS.SQL ="Select * From authors;"
RDS.Server = "http://phvserver1"
RDS.ExecuteOptions = 2
RDS.FetchOptions = 4
RDS.Refresh
Grid.Rebind
End Sub
</SCRIPT>
```

The code in the GetRunTimeText routine can be hard to read. It's a good idea to create a sample of the text that your DTC will create and test it thoroughly before creating your GetRunTimeText function. Trying to debug your code from within the DTC is frustrating. You're far better off to copy code that you know works into the DTC GetRuntimeText routine and then wrap the necessary Visual Basic around it.

Registering the DTC

Like any other ActiveX control, you must register your DTC by adding an entry for it in the Windows registry. This enables the containers that support the DTC specification to find the control. You must also add a key under the control's CLSID entry in the registry to indicate that this control is a Design Time Control.

Containers determine whether a control is a DTC by checking to see if there is a CATID_WebDesignTimeControl key under the control's CLSID. Once you have registered your control, you can create this additional entry by running the Regsvrdc utility, passing the ProgId of your DTC. Assuming that you took the defaults when installing the SDK, you can find Regsvrdc.exe in c:\program files\DTCSDK60\Tools\.

For this example, the Visual Basic project was called DTCRDS and the control itself was called DTCRDSUI. so Visual Basic will generate a ProgId of DTCRDS.DTCRDSUI for this control. I can flag the control as a Design Time Control with the command

```
c:\program files\DTCSDK60\Tools\Regsvrdc DTCRDS.DTCRDSUI.
```

Using the Simple DTC

Using this Design Time Control is simple. In Visual InterDev you must first add the control to your toolbox. In Visual InterDev 6.0, you'll do this by right-mouse clicking on your Design-Time Controls toolbox tab and selecting "Customize Toolbox". Find your DTC on the Design Time Control tab and click on it to select it. When you close the Customize Toolbox dialog, you'll find the control in your toolbox. To use the control, just open a Web page and drag the control from the toolbox to the page.

Once placed on the page, the control will display its visual interface (Figure 10–3 shows DTC Grid in place). Clicking on the control will bring up its properties in Visual InterDev's property list. Once you've set the properties, the control is ready to generate the text when requested. In VID 1.0, you'll have to preview the page in Internet Explorer to see if you've set your properties correctly. In VID 6.0, you need only switch to the QuickView tab.

To convert to just the text generated by the control, right-mouse click on the control in Source View and select 'Always View as Text'.

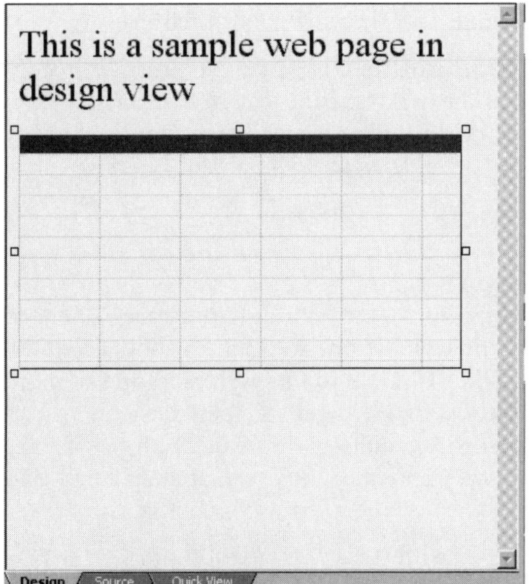

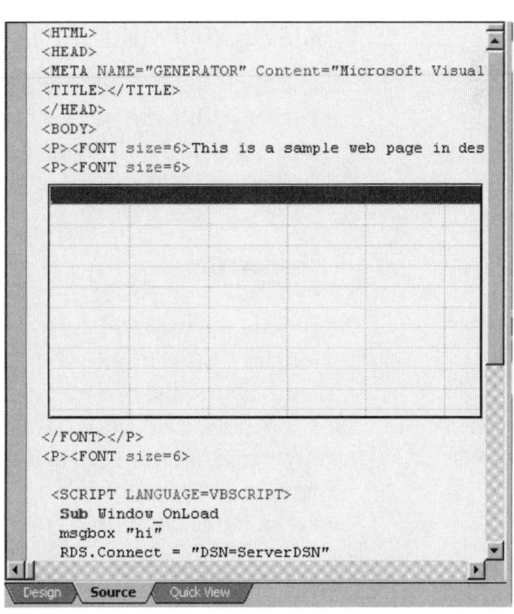

Figure 10–3 *In Visual InterDev 6.0. in both the Source and Design views, the control's form is displayed.*

Integrating Design-Time Controls

As you can see, creating a simple DTC isn't hard to do. However, you will frequently find that the DTCs in a container need to interact with each other. In this section I show you how a DTC can make information about itself available to other DTCs in the same container, and to the container itself.

The sample control that I've built would be more useful if it was split into two DTCs: one to generate the RDS control and another to generate the grid. Breaking the control up this way would let me add multiple grids to a form, all driven from the same RDS control. In fact, it would be a small step to create additional controls to generate lists, combo boxes, and other user interface widgets.

Splitting the control that I've designed into two controls isn't hard to do. However, the new grid control can't really operate without the RDS control. When adding the grid DTC to a container, the developer would want the control to be aware of the data source DTCs already in the container. In fact, it would be convenient for the grid DTC to provide a drop-down list of the available data sources in the container that the grid could connect to. And, once you've connected the grid DTC to a specific data source control, you should get a list of available data fields that the data control retrieves.

By now, if you've worked with Visual InterDev, you've probably recognized that this description matches the way that the data aware DTCs available in Visual InterDev actually work. In this section, I show you how to get DTCs to work together just like the ones delivered with Visual InterDev.

Choices

DTCs work together by participating in a "publish and subscribe" environment. A DTC can publish a list of choices that provides information about the control. To subscribe to a choice, other DTCs bind themselves to one or more of the published choices. For DTCs to work together, their designers need only agree on the way that choices will identify themselves. With that agreement in place, subscribing DTCs can find the choices that they need and extract information from them.

In this section I implement a RDS and a ComboBox control. The RDS control will, when it's added to the container, publish its name to identify itself as an available datasource. The ComboBox control will, when added to the container, bind to the choice published by the RDS control. Once the ComboBox control is associated with a data source's Choice object, the control will get, from the Choice object, the name of the control and the list of fields that is being retrieved. The ComboBox control will use this information to write out the HTML for a DropDown List object, the HTML equivalent of a ComboBox. To create the DropDown List object, the ComboBox's output would add to the container an HTML Input tag with its Type attribute set to Select.

All of this publishing and subscribing is managed by the ChoicesEngine that runs in the container that the DTCs are being used in. The ChoicesEngine is provided automatically by DTC-compliant containers. Your control must provide the methods and properties that the ChoicesEngine depends on so that it can interact with your controls.

PUBLISHING A CHOICE

You invoke the interfaces that publishing and subscribing require with this line:

```
Implements IDesignTimeControlSite
```

The IDesignTimeControl interface gives you access to the site object associated with your control. The site object is created by the ChoicesEngine when it finds your DTC and provides the channel for your controls to communicate with the ChoicesEngine (see Figure 10–4). Adding this interface will require you to write routines to implement the following Property Procedures:

- Get for DesignTimeControlSet — No code is required for this routine
- Set for DesignTimeControlSite — The container will use this property to pass your control a reference to the DTC's site object.
- Get for DesignTimeControlSite — Not required, but should be used to return the reference to the site object acquired in the Set Property Procedure.

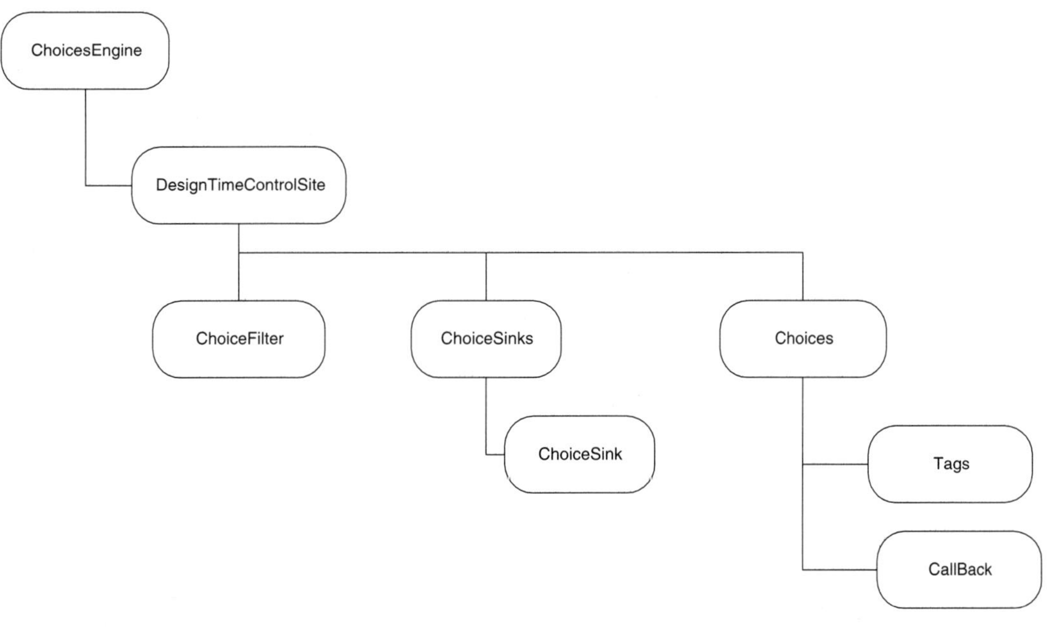

Figure 10–4 *The Choices object model*

You'll also have to put in the declarations to support the methods that the ChoicesEngine requires. The ChoicesEngine calls these methods at specific points in its processing cycle:

While the names of these methods follow the standard for event names (they all begin with "On"), they are written as methods. On the other hand, you won't go far wrong in thinking of them as events. This kind of relationship between methods and events demonstrates how closely related they really are.

- OnChoiceChange — Used to react to changes in the Choice objects that the control is bound to.
- OnRebind — Called during Rebinding to allow processing of the Choices collection
- OnGetChoices — Used to create dynamic choices.
- OnHostingChange — This method is called when the container requests that the object be destroyed.
- OnChoiceConflict — Fired when two Choice objects with identical Text properties (and TextMustBeUnique properties set to True) are published. Also fired when the conflict is resolved.

You must declare an object variable that you will use to access your DTC's site object. You set that variable to the parameter passed to the Property Set routine for your DesignTimeControlSite property. You'll need to access the control's site object throughout the life of the control, so the object variable must be declared at the module level:

```
Dim dts As IdesignTimeControlSite
Private Property Set _
      designTimeControl_DesignTimeControlSite _
          (ByVal RHS As IDesignTimeControlSite)
Set dts = RHS
End Property
```

The site object maintains a collection of Choice objects in its Choices collection. You can publish a new object to the collection by using the collection's AddChoice method. This method returns a Choice object that you can use to work with the ChoicesEngine. The AddChoice method accepts the parameters shown in Table 10.1.

Table 10.1 Parameters Required by the AddChoice Method

Parameter Name	Data Type	Description	Required?
Category	Variant	Reserved for future use. Currently this must be set to Nothing.	Yes
Description	String	This sets the Description property of the Choice object returned by the method.	Yes

Table 10.1 Parameters Required by the AddChoice Method (Continued)

Parameter Name	Data Type	Description	Required?
Type	String	This categorizes the Choice objects by type so that subscribers can filter Choice objects.	Yes
Text	String	Defaults to the object's description. Once the Choice object is created, changes to the Description and Type property are independent of each other. Typically, the Text property contains information useful to the subscribing DTC.	No
Interest	Long	Reserved for future use. Defaults to 100.	No
Sequential	Boolean	When set to True, the DTC's Choice objects are only available to other DTCs that follow it in the container. When set to False, this DTC's Choice objects are available to any other DTCs in the container.	No
Tag	Variant	Adds an entry to the objects Tags collection.	No

Similar to the AddChoice method is the AddPopupChoices method which creates a Choice object with a callback object for accepting user input (see Callbacks and Popups, later in this chapter).

To notify other DTCs that it's available for use, my RDS control will publish a Choice with a Type property of DataSources. I begin by declaring an object variable to refer to the Choice object that I'm about to create. When I create the object with the AddChoice method, I set the object's Type as 'DataSources'. I'll set the object's Description to a unique value (in this case, the name of the control in the container—RDSDTCUI1).

Setting the Description property to a unique value lets you distinguish among your controls when you have several copies of the same DTC in a container.

Since the DisplayName property isn't available at the time this property routine is set, I've used a dummy value of "RDS Control" when using the AddChoice method. Here's the resulting code:

```
Dim dts As IdesignTimeControlSite
Dim chcDataSource As Choice
```

```
Private Property Set _
    JDesignTimeControl_DesignTimeControlSite _
        (ByVal RHS As IDesignTimeControlSite)
Set dts = RHS
Set chcDataSource = dts.Choices.AddChoice(Nothing, _
                    "RDS Control", "DataSources")
End Property
```

You can change the control's properties after it is created. In this code, I set the control's description property to the DTC's DisplayName as part of the control's Show Event:

```
Private Sub UserControl_Show()
    chcDataSource.Description = _
        UserControl.Ambient.DisplayName
End Sub
```

SUBSCRIBING TO A CHOICE

Now that the RDS control has published a Choice that indicates that it is available for use, the ComboBox DTC can subscribe to that Choice. To subscribe, the ComboBox DTC must create a ChoiceSink object in the DesignTimeControlSite Property Set routine. ChoiceSinks are created by adding a new object to the site object's ChoiceSinks collection using the collection's AddChoiceSink method. The AddChoiceSink method accepts the two parameters shown in Table 10.2.

Table 10.2 Parameters Required by the AddChoiceSink Method

Parameter Name	Data type	Description	Required?
Type	String	Restricts the Choice objects recognized to Choice objects whose Type property matches this value.	Yes
Text	String	Sets the Text property of the resulting ChoiceSink object.	No

The ChoiceSink object that is created will bind to one Choice object with a matching Type property. If multiple Choice objects with the same value in their Type property exist (i.e., if multiple RDS controls have published DataSources Choice objects), the control will bind to only one.

```
Dim dts As IDesignTimeControlSite
Dim chsDataSource As ChoiceSink
```

```
Private Property Set _
    JDesignTimeControl_DesignTimeControlSite _
        (ByVal RHS As IDesignTimeControlSite)
Set dts = RHS
Set chsDataSource = _
            dts.ChoiceSinks.AddChoiceSink("DataSources")
End Property
```

Once a ChoiceSink object is created, you can use its BoundChoice property to get a reference to the Choice object to which it is bound. The following code allows the ComboBox control to access the bound RDS control's Description property and add it to a list box:

```
ListBox1.AddItem chsDataSource.BoundChoice.Description
```

Once you've added the code to bind to a Choice, you add code to the methods of your control that IDesignTimeControlSite requires. To begin with, you will probably want to implement the OnChoiceChange method. The ChoicesEngine calls your OnChoiceChange method to allow you to respond to changes in the Choice object that your DTC is bound to. Some of the occasions that will trigger a call to the OnChoiceChange method are:

1. some property of the bound Choice object changes
2. the ChoicesEngine changes the Choice object bound to the ChoiceSink
3. you first bind to a Choice.

As you probably noticed, item 2 in the list suggests that you can find yourself bound to a new object without any action on your part. A new Choice object may be bound under a number of situations. Here are a few:

- Initially no choice object was available (i.e., the developer added the ComboBox control before adding the RDS control) and now one is available (the developer has added an RDS Control).
- There were two RDS controls on the form and the one that you bound to has been deleted. The ChoicesEngine will automatically bind you to the other Choice object.
- The RDS control has had its Enabled property set to False and is no longer available for use.
- The Choice has been removed from the Choices collection through the collection's Revoke method.
- The Choice object that you were bound to has been deleted and your control is no longer bound to any object.

The OnChoiceChange method is passed two parameters. The first is a reference to the ChoiceSink object that your control is now bound to (if you are no longer bound, this parameter will be set to Nothing). The second parameter indicates the nature of the change (the values for the Change parameter are listed in Table 10.3). A typical OnChoiceChange event will include a Select statement that will do the appropriate processing for each of the changes.

Since the same event fires for every ChoiceSink that the DTC uses, you will need to check the Type property of the ChoiceSink's BoundChoice object to determine what processing to take. Here's a typical example of an OnChoiceChange event:

```
Private Sub IDesignTimeControl_OnChoiceChange _
(ByVal ChoiceSink As ChoiceSink, _
 ByVal Change As dtcChoiceChange)
Select Case Change
  Case dtcChoiceChangeNewChoice
    If ChoiceSink Is Nothing Then
      ...processing for unbound state...
    ElseIf ChoiceSink.BoundChoice.Type = "DataSource" Then
      ...processing for DataSource choice...
    End If
  Case dtcChoiceChangeText
  ...processing for remaining change types...
End Select
End Sub
```

Since there will be times that your ChoiceSink isn't bound to any Choice, you should never use a ChoiceSink object without checking to see that it is not set to Nothing. If your control attempts to work with an unbound ChoiceSink, in Visual InterDev at least, you get an "object not set method", your DTC locks up, and you can't delete it from your page.

Table 10.3 Values for the OnChoiceChange Event

Constant	Description
dtcChoiceChangeNewChoice	New Choice object bound or the object has lost its binding
dtcChoiceChangeText	Choice object's Text property changed
dtcChoiceChangeDescription	Choice object's Description property changed
dtcChoiceChangeEnabled	The Choice's enable property has been changed
dtcChoiceChangeTag	A member of the Choice object's Tags object has changed
dtcChoiceChangeType	Choice object's Type property has changed
dtcChoiceChangeSequential	Choice object's Sequential property has changed (presently not supported)

REBINDING

DTC compliant containers are constantly performing rebinding operations to associate Choices with ChoiceSinks. It's during the rebinding process that the OnChoiceChange event for subscribing objects will fire, for instance. Rebinds are normally done asynchronously during idle time. You can force a synchronous or immediate rebind. If a significant property of a DTC Choices object changes (the control's name, for instance), you may want to force synchronous rebinding so that the developer is looking at the latest data.

Calling the Rebind method of your site object enables you to control whether a change is posted synchronously or asynchronously (or, to look at another way, to ensure that you are picking up the latest data). You control the type of rebind by passing one of two parameters to the method: dtcRebindNow for a synchronous (immediate) rebind, dtcRebindWhenPossible for an asynchronous rebind. Here's what that method looks like:

```
dts.Rebind dtcRebindNow         'synchronous rebind
dts.Rebind dtcRebindWhenPossible'asynchronous rebind
```

SELECTING A CHOICE OBJECT

All this works fine as long as I have only one RDS control available. However, I could easily have two RDS controls in the container, each retrieving data from a different source. In this situation, when I add a ComboBox DTC to the container, I will want the ComboBox to display a list of available data source DTCs so that the developer can select one of them to bind to the ComboBox. There are two operations involved here: getting the list of DataSources controls and binding to the selected control.

To get a list of available Choice objects, you need to browse the Choices collection itself. Two of the methods that are part of IDesignTimeControlSite interface are passed a refernence to the Choices collection when the methods are called: OnRebind and OnGetChoices. Both methods are called by the ChoicesEngine during the Rebind process.

To display the list of available RDS data source controls, you apply a filter to the Choices collection in the OnRebind method. The Filter method of the Choices collection returns a new Choices collection containing only the objects that match the filter. You define a filter by creating a ChoiceFilter object using the site object's CreateChoiceFilter method. Once you've created the ChoiceFilter, you set its properties to indicate the kind of object that you are looking for (a ChoiceFilter's properties duplicate many of the Choice object's properties). Finally, you pass the filter to the Filter method of the Choices collection.

To create a collection of Choice objects whose Type property is set to "DataSources", I create a ChoiceFilter object and set its Type property to "DataSources". I then pass the ChoiceFilter to the Choices Filter method and retrieve a private Choices collection (the real Choices collection is not affected by the filter). Once I have this new collection, I can display the Description properties of the Choice objects in it. The code in my control's OnRebind method would look like this:

```
Private Sub IDesignTimeControl_OnRebind
                       (ByVal Choices As Choices)
Dim ccl As Choices
Dim chf As ChoiceFilter
Dim chc As Choice

Set chf = dts.CreateChoiceFilter
chf.Type = "DataSources"
Set ccl = Choices.Filter(chf)
ListBox1.Clear
For Each chc In ccl
  ListBox1.AddItem chc.Text
Next
End Sub
```

If you set the Invert property of a ChoiceFilter to True, then you will select Choices that don't match your ChoiceFilter settings. The ChoiceFilter's Reset method restores the ChoiceFilter to where it will match any Choice object and sets Invert to False.

The actual code that you will put in the OnRebind method will be more complicated than this sample. This code that I've shown here will add every valid Choice object to the ListBox each time the OnRebind method is called. This means that each Choice object will appear in the ListBox many times because the OnRebind method is called so frequently. To handle this, in the OnRebind method you must loop through entries already displayed to make sure that they are still part of the Choices collection. If they are not, you will have to remove them from the display. Conversely, any Choice items that are not part of the display will need to be added to the display.

Now that I've presented a list of available Choice objects to the developer, I can let them select a control to bind to. This process also uses a filter, but this time it is passed to the Filter method of a ChoiceSink object. Passing a ChoiceFilter to a ChoiceSink limits the number of objects that it can bind to.

Once the developer has selected one of the DTCs displayed in the ListBox, I create a new ChoiceFilter object and use it with the current control's ChoiceSink to bind to a new control. Unfortunately, you cannot filter on the Description property. Fortunately, in my previous code, I added the Text property to the ListBox and you can filter on the Text property. The result is code like the following in either the Click event of a button on the control or in the DoubleClick event of the ListBox itself:

```
Set chsDataSource = dts.ChoiceSinks.AddChoiceSink
chsDataSource.ChoiceFilter.Text = _
  ListBox1.ListData(ListBox1.Text)
```

TAGS

Normally, the Text property of the Choice object is used to hold the information associated with the control. For the RDSControl, the Text property might contain the list of fields that the control will be retrieving. This would be useful information for a ComboBox DTC because it would let developers select the fields they want the ComboBox to display. However, in order to put the list of field names in the Text property, you'd have to store the list as a single string with the individual field names separated by delimiters. This can be awkward to work with.

The Tags collection of the Choice object provides a more flexible way of storing multiple data values. A Tag belongs to a Tags collection of some Choice object and consists of a name and a value. You use the AddTag method of the Choice object to add a new Tag to the Choice object's Tags collection. The AddTag method accepts two parameters: the name of the tag and the tag's value (the name parameter can be omitted).

This code creates a Choice object and then adds a Tag called "SQL" with the value "Select * From DistinctRow" as a dummy statement:

```
Private Property Set _
          designTimeControl_DesignTimeControlSite _
            (ByVal RHS As IDesignTimeControlSite)
Set dts = RHS
Set chcDataSource = dts.Choices.AddChoice(Nothing, _
        "RDS Control", "DataSources")
chcDataSource.AddTag "SQL", "Select * From DistinctRow"
End Property
```

You can remove a tag with either the DeleteTag or DeleteTags method. The DeleteTag method accepts the name of a single Tag and deletes it. The DeleteTags method accepts two parameters: the index number of the first tag to delete and the number of tags to remove. In the following code, the DeleteTag method deletes the "SQL" tag. The DeleteTags method deletes the second tag and the two tags following it in the collection:

```
chcDataSource.DeleteTag "SQL"
chcDataSource.DeleteTags 2, 3
```

Each entry in the Tag collection has both a Name and an Item property. To read a tag, you can provide the name of the tag, the number of the tag's position in the collection, or use a For...Each loop to process the whole Tags collection. You can only access the Tags collection from the Choice objects passed in the Choices collection to the OnRebind method.

All of these code snippets would retrieve the "SQL" tag into the strSQL variable for the first object in the Choices collection:

```
Dim chc As Choice
Dim ing As Integer
```

```
Dim strSQL As String

Set chc = Choices(1) 'get reference to first Choice
'get reference by name
strSQL = chc.Tags.Item("SQL")

'assumes SQL is first in collection
strSQL = chc.Tags.Item(1)

'finds reference by searching
For ing = 1 to chc.Tags.Count
  If chc.Tags.Name(ing) = "SQL" Then
    strSQL = chc.Tags.Item(ing)
  End If
Next
```

What makes the Tags collection especially useful is that you can filter Choice objects based on what tags they have and what value they are set to. You can filter using Tags just by adding to a ChoiceFilter object the Tag that you want to match. This code, for instance, binds a DTC's ChoiceSink to the first Choice object with a tag called "SQL" that is set to "Select * From DistinctRow":

```
Set chsDataSource = dts.ChoiceSinks.AddChoiceSink
chsDataSource.ChoiceFilter.AddTag("SQL", _
  "Select * From DistinctRow")
```

Since you can filter Choice objects based on what Tag objects they have, Tags can be a flexible way for DTCs to identify themselves to developers. A DTC could create a Tag called 'Identity' with a value of the control's DisplayName. In the OnRebind method, other DTCs could retrieve the Identity tag and display it to the developer to allow the developer to select the desired control. When the developer selects one of the Choices, the DTC could filter the Choice objects to bind to the one with the Tag value that the developer selected. This gets around the inability to filter based on a Choice's Description property.

If you add multiple tags to a ChoiceFilter, all the tags must match in order to bind to a Choice. The AddSpecialTag method lets you add a tag where any combination of tags can make a match.

You can also manipulate the value of the first item in a Choice object's Tags collection by setting or reading the object's Tag property.

User Interface

Providing the developer with the ability to select a Choice object also means providing the developer with an interface. You could, of course, create a set of Property Procedures that the developer could access through the control's Property List. This can be awkward, though, especially for properties that are best displayed as lists.

You can also let the UserControl itself be your interface. Since a DTC does not appear at run time, you can use the control's interface to display the design time options available to your developers as the control in Figure 10–5 does. Unfortunately, not all potential DTC containers are guaranteed to support the display of a DTC's interface (though Visual InterDev does).

To ensure that your DTC will work in all possible containers, you should use Property Pages as the primary mechanism for letting developers interact with your control.

The DTC specification also provides two other mechanisms for interacting with developers using your control: Callbacks and PopUps.

CALLBACKS AND POPUPS

You can create a callback object that interacts with the developer to retrieve information to update a Choice's Text property. A callback object is created using a standard Class module, and can contain any code that you want. The only requirement for the object is that it must implement this method:

```
Public Sub ProcessPopUpChoice(ByVal c as Choice, _
  ByVal text as ChoiceSink, s as String, cancel as Boolean)
```

You should find the process of creating a DTC Callback very similar to the process described in the chapter on Interfaces for creating callbacks.

The Class module's ProcessPopUpChoice method will be called whenever a DTC's code attempts to read the Text property of a Choice object. In the ProcessPopUpChoice method, you can perform any processing that you want. You use the method's parameters as follows:

c • A ref this to True to indicate that the developer cancelled entering information. Reference to the choice that called the method.

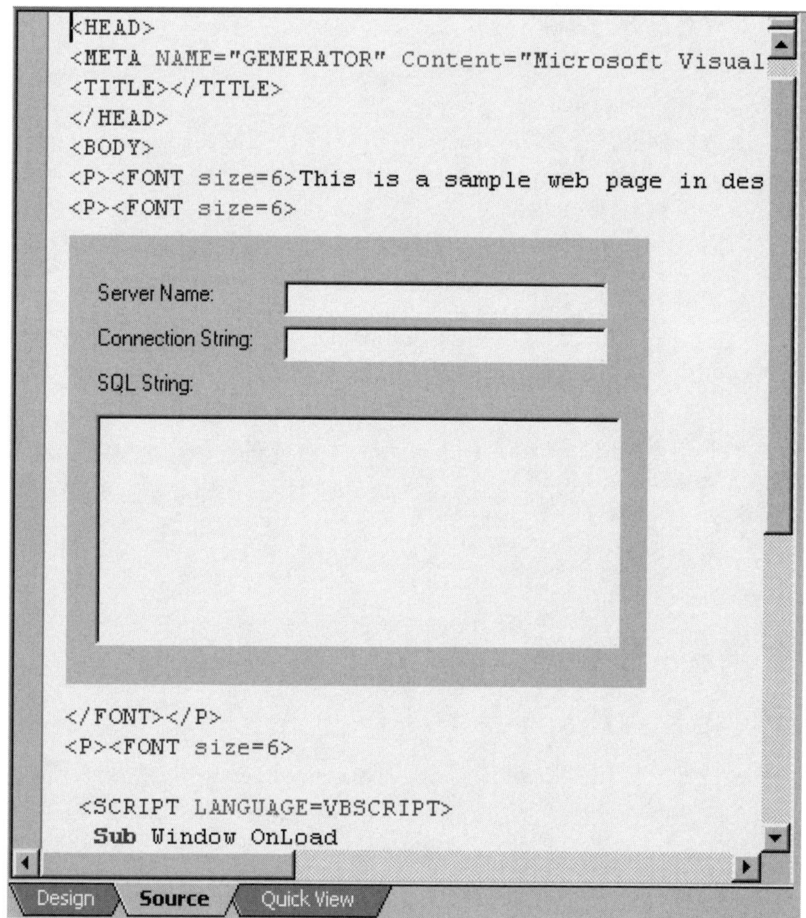

Figure 10–5 *A DTC using the UserControl as its interface.*

TEXT • The name of a choice sink.

S • Set this parameter to the value that you want to return to the Choice object's Text property.

CANCEL • Set this to True to indicate that the developer cancelled entering information.

To associate a callback object with a Choice object, you must set the Choice's Callback property to refer to an instance of the object. In this example, I've created a Class module called MyCallBackObject containing code to collect a Choice's Text property. This code instantiates the object and sets a Choice's Callback property to point to the object:

```
Dim clb As MyCallBackObject
Set clb = New MyCallBackObject
Set chcDataSource.CallBack = clb
```

The simplest callback object would contain just the ProcessPopUpChoice method, and that method would consist of nothing but an InputBox:

```
Public Sub ProcessPopUpChoice(ByVal c as Choice, _
  ByVal text as ChoiceSink, s as String,_
                          cancel as Boolean)
  Dim strInput As String
  strInput = InputBox("Please enter a value",
                    "Enter a value")
  If strInput = "" Then
    cancel = True
  Else
    s = strInput
    cancel = False
  End If
End Sub
```

You can determine if a Choice object has a callback object associated with it by checking the Choice's Popup property. This property returns a reference to the Choice's callback object, if one exists.

Dynamic Choices

The Choice objects that I have discussed so far have been static Choices. Once added to the Choices collection, these objects will remain available until they are removed (using the Collections Revoke method) or the DTC that created them is deleted.

In addition to static Choice object, you can also create dynamic Choice objects. A dynamic choice is added to the Choices collection during a Rebind operation. If no DTC subscribes to the Choice object during the Rebind operation, the Choice object is discarded. You add a dynamic choice to the collection in your DTC's OnGetChoices method. This method is called by the ChoicesEngine during Rebinds and passes a temporary Choices collection as one of the parameters to the method. Choice objects added to the collection in this routine will be deleted from the collection if no DTC binds to them.

Here's a sample OnGetChoices event that adds the DataSources Choice as a dynamic, rather than static, choice. Note that the code for adding the Choice object is identical to the code used when adding the static choice, only the method that the code is in has changed:

```
Private Sub IDesignTimeControl_OnGetChoices _
      (ByVal Choices As DTC60.Choices)
```

```
Set chcDataSource = dts.Choices.AddChoice(Nothing, _
      "RDS Control", "DataSources")

End Sub
```

Rebinding is a very frequent occurrence in the life of a DTC, so you shouldn't have much going on in the OnGetChoices method because it will slow down Visual InterDev's user interface. The same is true of the Rebind method.

Destroying the Object

Visual InterDev allows the developer to replace a DTC with the text that it will generate. Once a DTC is removed, of course, all of the Choice objects that it published will be destroyed. This may cause problems for the object subscribing to these objects, depending on how they have persisted information from the object. When your DTC is about to be destroyed, the OnHostingChange method is called, passing two parameters.

The first parameter indicates the type of change (dtcHostingChangeReplaceWithRunTimeText or dtcHostingChangeViewAsText). The 'replace with runtime text' option completely destroys the DTC, including the information necessary to reload it. The 'view as text' option leaves the information to reload the object in place so that it can be recreated. Figure 10–6 shows the options as they are presented in Visual InterDev.

The second parameter allows you to Cancel the operation by setting it to True. Depending on how you've built your DTCs you may choose to prevent the operation, allow the operation, or warn the developer and allow them to cancel the operation. In this sample code, I've chosen to warn the developer and allow them to back out:

```
Private Sub IDesignTimeControl_OnHostingChange _
      (ByVal Change As DTC60.dtcHostingChange, _
      Cancel As Boolean)
Dim lngResponse As Long
lngResponse = _
  Msgbox("This is a horrible mistake. Proceed?", _
      vbYesNo+vbDefaultButton1, _
      "Warning, Warning, Will Robinson")
If lngResponse = vbNo Then
    Cancel = True
End If

End Sub
```

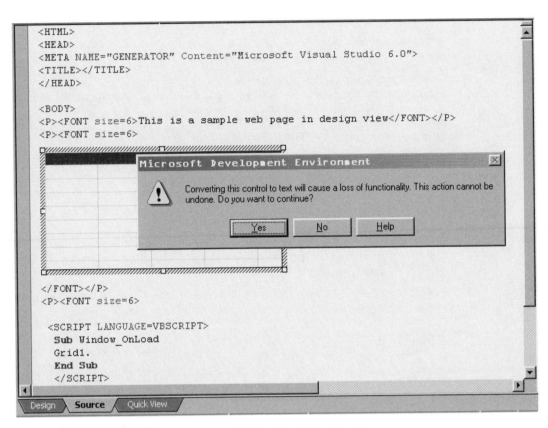

```
<HTML>
<HEAD>
<META NAME="GENERATOR" Content="Microsoft Visual Studio 6.0">
<TITLE></TITLE>
</HEAD>

<BODY>
<P><FONT size=6>This is a sample web page in design view</FONT></P>
<P><FONT size=6>
```

Microsoft Development Environment

Converting this control to text will cause a loss of functionality. This action cannot be undone. Do you want to continue?

Yes | No | Help

```
</FONT></P>
<P><FONT size=6>

 <SCRIPT LANGUAGE=VBSCRIPT>
  Sub Window_OnLoad
  Grid1.
  End Sub
  </SCRIPT>
```

Design | Source | Quick View

Figure 10–6 *Destroying a DTC in Visual InterDev 6.0.*

Persisting the Object

As with any values in an ActiveX control, you'll need to save the values of your Choices from one invocation of your DTC to another. The PropertyBag routines that the UserControl supports let you write and read the information that will allow you to recreate your Choice objects when your DTC starts up again.

Also, you can't count on the Choice object always being present when your DTC generates its runtime text. You should always save your Choice information to local variables, read and write those values to the control's PropertyBag, and use those internal variables when creating your runtime text.

If you want the data that you used to select the Choice objects to be available at design time for developers to change from the Property sheet, you'll also have to establish properties that expose that information.

For the ComboBox control, the net effect of all of those requirements generates the following code. First, I establish Property Procedures that identify the Choice object that the control is bound to:

```
Dim m_DataSourceName As String
Public Property Let DataSource(DataSourceName As String)
  m_DataSourceName = DataSourceName
End Property
Public Property Get DataSource()
  DataSource = m_DataSourceName
End Property
```

In the PropertyBag routines, I write and save both the information provided by the Choice and the information that I need to find that Choice object again. Since each RDS control has a unique name, I just need to write out the m_RDSControl variable holding the Control's name. I also save all of the Choice's information to local variables and use the WriteProperties to write that information out also:

```
Private Sub _
 UserControl_WriteProperties(PropBag As PropertyBag)

PropBag.WriteProperty "RDSControl", m_DataSource, "RDS1"
PropBag.WriteProperty "Field", m_FieldName

End Sub
```

In the ReadProperties routine, I can read in the name of the RDSControl and the data that I received from it:

```
Private Sub _
 UserControl_ReadProperties(PropBag As PropertyBag)

m_DataSource = _
              PropBag.ReadProperty("RDSControl", "RDS1")
m_FieldName = _
              PropBag.ReadProperty("Field")

End Sub
```

In the DesignTime Set, I check to see if I have a value for the control name. If I do, I bind to that Choice using a ChangeFilter. If not, I bind to the first control of the correct Type:

```
Private Property Set _
              IdesignTimeControl_DesignTimeControlSite _
                    (ByVal RHS As IDesignTimeControlSite)
Set dts = RHS
If m_DataSource = "" Then
Set chsDataSource = dts.ChoiceSinks.AddChoiceSink
```

```
chsDataSource.ChoiceFilter.AddTag("Identity", m_DataSource)
Else
Set chsDataSource = _
dts.ChoiceSinks.AddChoiceSink("DataSources")
End If
End Property
```

In my GetRuntimeText method, I check to see if I have a Choice object. If I do, I use the information from it. If the object isn't available, I use the information retrieved from the PropertyBag:

```
Implements IProvideRuntimeText

Public Function IProvideRuntimeText_GetRunTimeText() As String
Dim strOutputString As String

If chsDataSource Is Nothing Then
  ...build text with m_FieldName ...
Else
  ...build text using chsDataSource...
End If

 IProvideRuntimeText_GetRunTimeText = strOutputString
End Function
```

Debugging

Debugging a DTC is a pain. Once you drag a DTC into a container (like a Visual InterDev Web page), the control is considered to be in use and you may not able to recompile it back to its old file name. Closing the object's container (i.e., the Web page in Visual InterDev) frequently frees up the DTC's OCX file so that the control can be recompiled. If you can't replace the file, you can either change the file name or shut down and restart the program (i.e., Visual InterDev).

Based on my experience, renaming the file on each compile seems the most reliable method. I append a number to the end of the file name for my DTCs (e.g., MyDTC2.OCX) and just change it when necessary.

When first creating your DTC, here are the steps that you should follow to handle versioning during the testing and debugging phase:

1. Create a version of the control with all of its methods, properties, and events defined but no code in the routines.
2. Compile this version of your DTC as the "reference copy" of the program.

3. In the project's Properties, on the Component tab, set the project's compatibility mode to Binary.
4. Also on the Component tab, select the version of the program that you compiled in step 2 as your reference.
5. Compile the program to a different file name.
6. Run Regsvr32, passing it the name you used in the second compile of the program in step 5.
7. Use Regsvrdc to register the objects in your project.
8. Start Visual InterDev, open a project, click on the Design-Time Control bar, right click on the Toolbox, and select Customize Toolbox.
9. In the Customize Toolbox on the Design-Time Control tab, select your controls.

Following these steps should prevent you from having to reselect the DTC from Visual InterDev's Customize ToolBox setting after every compile. You shouldn't have to rerun Regsvrdc, either—at least as long as you don't break compatibility. All you should have to do, after compiling the program to a new name, is run Regsvr32 passing the new file name of your DTC component.

Despite following the process that I've just outlined, I've sometimes found that I had to cycle Visual InterDev to pick up the new version of my Design Time Controls.

If you do break compatibility, the smart thing to do is:

1. Recompile the project, replacing the reference copy you created in step 2 of the previous list.
2. Recompile the project to the current name of the program
3. Rerun Regsvr32, using the reference version of the program that you created in step 1.
4. Rerun Regsvrdc for each object.
5. Cycle the container (i.e., shut down and restart Visual InterDev).
6. Reselect your controls from the Customize Toolbox dialog.

As you can see, it makes life a lot easier when you get your interface right before you start coding, and then stay compatible.

CHOICE INSPECTOR

With the DTC SDK, you get the Choice Inspector, a handy control for use in debugging your DTCs (see Figure 10–7). The Choice Inspector is itself a DTC and must be registered using these commands (assuming that you've taken all the defaults in installing the SDK):

```
Regsvr32 c:\program files\DTCSDK60\Tools\CInspect.DLL
Regedit c:\program files\DTCSDK60\Tools\Cinspect.DLL
```

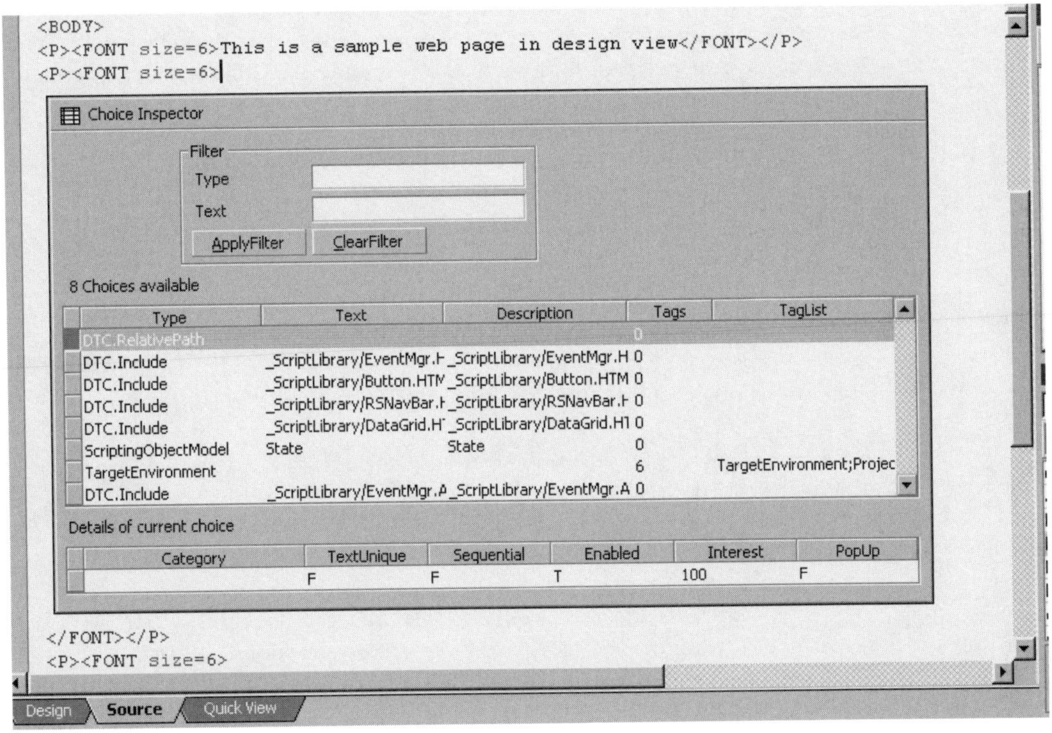

Figure 10–7 *The Choice Inspector.*

Once added to a container, the Choice Inspector provides a list of all the DTCs on the page, the current values for their properties, and a list of all of their tags' names. It's a good check on whether or not you're publishing what you think you are. You can use the Choice Inspector's filtering capabilities to limit the objects displayed to objects with a specific Type or Text value.

Publishing an Object Model

Your DTC may generate text that defines an object. The ComboBox DTC, for instance, adds text to the page that defines an HTML DropDown list. If your code generates JavaScript (or VBScript, version 5.x) code, then the code that the DTC produces may also define objects. However, none of these objects are available to the developer at design time. As a result, the container can't be aware of the objects defined by your DTC or provide IntelliSense support for the developer that wants to use them.

The DTC SDK provides an interface that allows you to publish an object model that describes the object that your DTC generates. The container will treat this description as if the object was actually present in the container.

To begin publishing an object model, you need to add the RCIA and RCIP type libraries to your project's References list. Once you've added those References, you need to implement the IRuntimeClassInfoProvider interface:

```
Implements IRuntimeClassInfoProvider
```

With this interface added, you must create procedures for the GetRunTimeClassInfo and the GetSupportedScenarios.

SCENARIOS

An object model is relevant only in certain scenarios. For this example, I'm going to publish part of the object model for the HTML DropDown List that the ComboBox DTC generates. A ComboBox is useful only in client-side coding, so this object model will be associated with the "client" scenario.

Different containers will support different scenarios, and the container's documentation will tell you what they are. The client scenario, for instance, is available in Visual InterDev.HTM and .HTML files.

You signal to the development system what scenarios your DTC supports by returning one or more scenario names (separated by commas) in the GetSupportedScenarios method. This is the appropriate routine for the ComboBox control:

```
Private Function _
  IRuntimeClassInfoProvider_GetSupportedScenarios() _
                                                  As String
  IRuntimeClassInfoProvider_GetSupportedScenarios = "client"
End Function
```

BUILDING A MODEL

I created just a subset of an HTML DropDown List's object model: the onFocus event, the Focus method, and the Value property. I put the code that defines this model in my control's GetRuntimeClassInfo method. The container uses this method to request object model information. The GetRuntimeClassInfo method is passed two parameters, but only one is useful. The first parameter passed is the name of the current scenario. The second parameter is a Long variable which is currently reserved for future use and is set to zero.

The routine defines the object model using two RuntimeClassInfoAuthor objects and returns one of them to the container. In this sample code, the routine starts by checking to see if it's being called in the correct scenario. If it is, the routine then creates a RunTimeClassInfo object:

```
Private Function _
    IRuntimeClassInfoProvider_GetRuntimeClassInfo _
      (ByVal bstrScenario As String, _
       ByVal dwReserved As Long) As Variant
Dim rcaObject As RuntimeClassInfoAuthor
If bstrScenario = "client" Then
Set rcaObject = New RuntimeClassInfoAuthor
```

With the rcaObject created, the routine now adds information about the object that is being created by the ComboBox DTC. There are three methods used to add items to the object model, as listed in Table 10.4. Each method accepts a number of parameters which give the name of the DTCs method, the names of the parameters it expects to be passed, and some descriptive text. You could think of this as creating type library information on the fly.

Table 10.4 Methods of RuntimeClassInfo Object

Method Name	Adds Information About	Parameters
ShowEvent	Event	Name of the event Comma-delimited list of parameters The number of optional parameters A text description of the event
ShowMethod	Method	Name of the method Comma-delimited list of parameters Number of optional parameters A text description of the method
ShowProperty	Property	Name of the property A text description of the property
ShowGroup	Object	A RuntimeClassInfo Object

As an example, in order to declare an event called "GetOrder" with three parameters (OrderNumber, CustomerName, and Status), the last two of which are optional, I would use:

```
rcaObject.ShowMethod "GetOrder", _
"OrderNumber, CustomerName, Status", 2, "Gets an order"
```

To publish the three items of object model for the DropDown List that I selected, I would use these three lines of code:

```
rcaObject.ShowMethod "Focus", , , _
  "Moves focus to the control"
rcaObject.ShowProperty "Value", _
  "Current data for the control"
```

```
rcaObject.ShowEvent "onFocus", , , _
  "Fires when control gets focus"
```

With the interface for the object defined, the next step is to create a new RuntimeClassInfoAuthor to publish the object model. In publishing the object model, I have to give it a name that the developer can use to write code with.

Typically, I use the same name for the object generated by the DTC as I do for DTC itself: the DTC's DisplayName. It's just one thing less to remember.

Publishing the object model consists of calling the new RuntimeClassInfoAuthor object's ShowObjectProperty method, passing the name that I want to use and the RuntimeClassInfo object that I defined the interface with:

```
Dim rcaModel As RuntimeClassInfoAuthor
Set rcaModel = New RuntimeClassInfoAuthor
rcaModel.ShowObjectProperty _
  UserControl.Ambient.DisplayName, rcaObject
```

At this point all that's left to do is return the second RuntimeClassInfoAuthor object from the GetRuntimeClassInfo method. However, Visual InterDev expects the returned object to be of the type IUnknown. So I have to assign the second RuntimeClassInfoAuthor object to some variable declared as IUnknown and return that:

```
Dim iun As IUnknown
Set iun = rcaModel
Set IRuntimeClassInfoProvider_GetRuntimeClassInfo = iun
```

The GetRuntimeClassInfo routine, like the OnRebind and OnGetChoices methods, is a method that you will want to make as fast as possible. This routine is called very frequently by the container.

Figure 10–8 shows the IntellSense support that the developer using your control will get. In addition, in Visual InterDev, the objects defined by your DTC appear in the script outline with other objects that fire events.

Other Options

There is a set of features that allows a DTC to interact with its container rather than just with other controls. The ability to call on services provided by the container allows the DTC to use parts of the development system as components. Within Visual InterDev, for instance, a DTC could call on Visual InterDev's Query Builder to help developers construct SQL statements (this is the

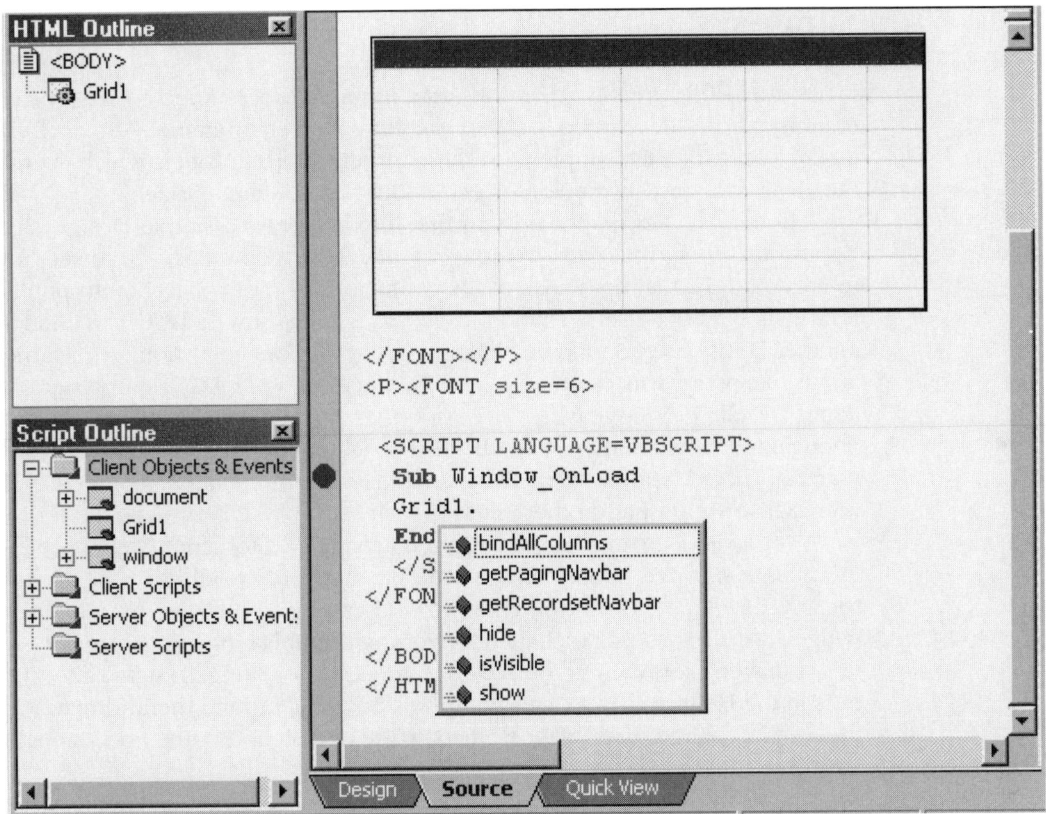

Figure 10–8 *Intellisense support for the DTC. Notice that the object also appears in the ScriptOutline.*

example included with the DTC SDK documentation). You can also, from your DTC, access any data resources that the developer has created using Visual InterDev's data environment. Since these features are container specific, I won't discuss them here.

The DTC Framework that comes with Visual Basic 6.0 includes a number of other objects that Microsoft currently provides no documentation on or has indicated aren't yet implemented. I'm always hesitant to count on undocumented items working correctly or, if they do work in some fashion, that they will continue to work that way in later versions so I skip them also. Should they ever get documented, I'll include them in a later edition of this book.

Summary

DTCs can fulfill a multitude of tasks and, in the future, I expect to see a proliferation of DTCs developed for the Visual InterDev environment. Microsoft has already used them to implement the Scripting Object Model, which merges the client-side and server-side object models into a single model.

In this chapter, I showed you first how to create a simple Design Time Control that would add text to a page. From there, you moved on to see how to create a DTC that made use of the container's Choices collection to publish information about itself. That topic led to seeing how a DTC can bind to another DTC, based on the information in the Choices collection. You learned about the options in creating a user interface for your DTC: properties, the control itself, PropertyPages, and Popups. I introduced you to the pain of debugging DTCs and the Choice Inspector debugging tool. You also saw how your DTC could publish an object model that the container could use for IntelliSense support and other features.

You could develop a DTC to generate HTML for your Web pages. A DTC that supported your company's design standards would be a handy tool for any developer. Developing the RDS Control and a set of user interface widgets would give you a chance to work with publishing and subscribing.

I haven't found any complete references to creating Design Time Controls in the Help file that comes with the DTC SDK. I found the information in the version that I used vague, incomplete, ambiguous, and, occasionally, wrong.

My only regret with design-time controls is that they are not yet supported as a development tool within VB 6.0. I hope, Microsoft's migration to HTML and DHTML as the standard for all user interfaces will enable DTCs to be used in more environments. When that happens, DTCs will become the most powerful tool in the VB/VBA developer's arsenal.

E L E V E N

ActiveX Documents

The ActiveX Documents specification remains the ActiveX technology that has yet to catch on. In many ways, ActiveX Documents are a natural extension of Object Linking and Embedding, an important part of the Windows environment. Yet ActiveX Documents remain the guest at the wedding: always a bridesmaid, never a bride. They look like a really good idea but nobody seems to be building production systems with them. ActiveX Documents are a great way to deliver Visual Basic applications and Office documents over the Web. Yet, at least as of this writing, not many developers seem to be creating ActiveX Document applications.

In this chapter I introduce you to ActiveX Documents: what they are, how they work, and how to use them effectively. I show you how to create applications using the technology and how to deliver those applications using a Web browser or other ActiveX container. You may well find that this is just the tool that you need to solve a problem that you face. If so, this chapter tells you everything that you need to know. On the other hand, you may agree that ActiveX Documents are just an interesting footnote in the history of ActiveX technologies.

What Is an ActiveX Document?

I think that part of the problem with ActiveX Documents is that it's a really poor name for the technology. An ActiveX Document is, in theory, a file that can be viewed inside another application. This sounds suspiciously like Object Linking and Embedding (OLE), the major difference being the level of control exercised by the document.

Microsoft Word documents are ActiveX Documents and provide a handy example of what the technology looks like. In Figure 11–1 you can see a Microsoft Word document displayed inside Internet Explorer. To make this happen, I just typed the file name for the Word file into Internet Explorer's address box.

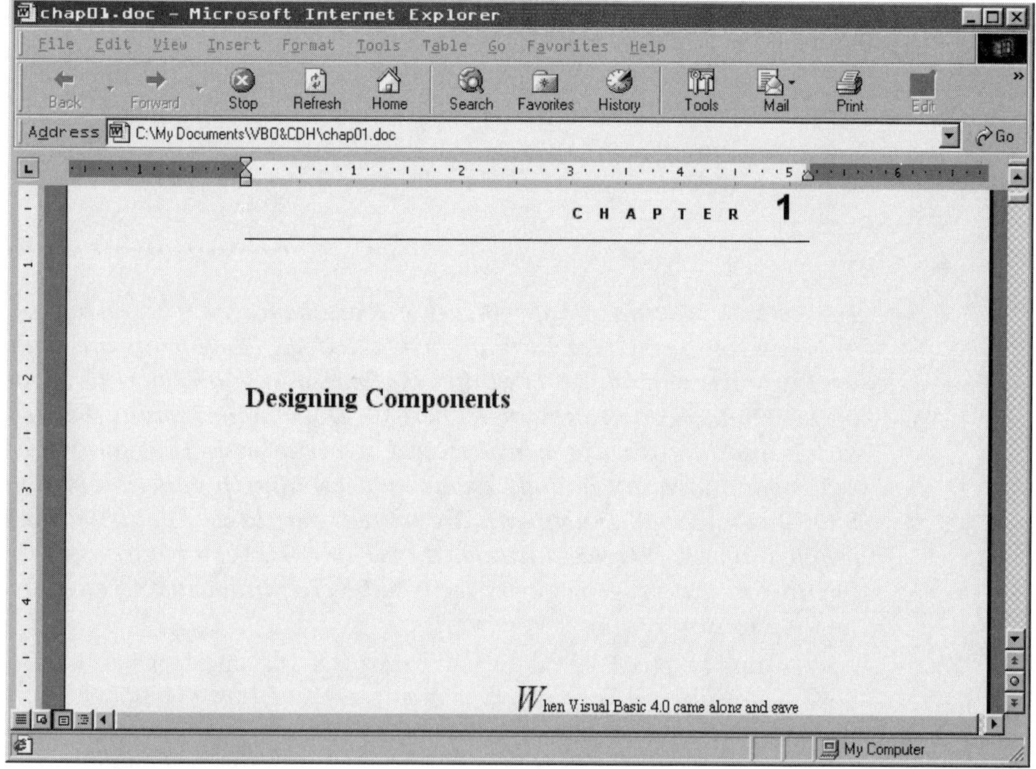

Figure 11–1 *ActiveX Documents in action: Internet Explorer displaying Microsoft Word.*

If you look closely, you can see how an ActiveX Document differs from an OLE embedded document. You can see that the scroll bars along the bottom aren't Internet Explorer's; they're Microsoft Word's. Unlike OLE, which displays the data inside a window within the container application, an ActiveX Document actually merges its window with the window of the document's container. The menu in the figure shows a combination of Word (Table, Insert) and Internet Explorer (Go, Favorite) items.

Of course, there's nothing special about the Word document that's being displayed, which is why ActiveX Documents is such an unfortunate name. The file or document doesn't have any special abilities that make it an ActiveX item. Instead, it's the displaying program (in this case, Microsoft Word) and the container application (Internet Explorer) that create the result that you see in Figure 11–1.

The ActiveX Document specification describes how to build ActiveX Document servers. An ActiveX Document server is a program that, when called by a compliant container, will display a document inside the container's window. When you start an ActiveX Document Project in Visual Basic, you are really creating an ActiveX Document server.

The Life Cycle of an ActiveX Document

At this point, it's a good idea to take a first look at the life cycle of an ActiveX Document. The process begins with an end user working with some container. In the process of using that container application, the user requests some document (see Figure 11–2). The container recognizes that this document has an ActiveX Document server associated with it. The container invokes the server, passing it the contents of the document. The server and the container merge their user interfaces and the user begins to work with the contents of the document using the services provided by the ActiveX Document server.

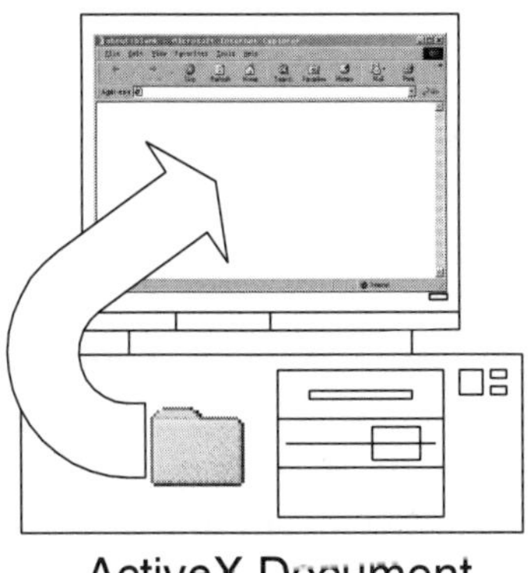

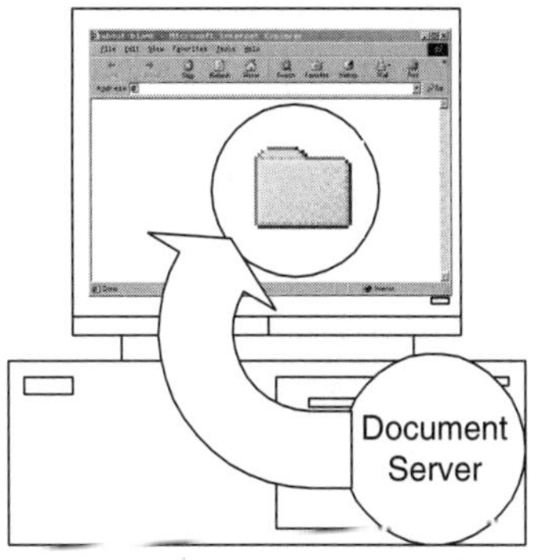

Figure 11–2 *The life cycle of an ActiveX Document.*

Ideally, the invocation of the server by the container is so seamless that the user isn't aware that they are working with a container. From the user's point of view it appears that they are working with a tool that provides specialized handling for a wide variety of data. Internet Explorer, for instance, is that kind of container. With Internet Explorer you can move from HTML pages to Word documents to Excel spreadsheets, with the appropriate server invoked automatically. Of course, given the size of the Word and Excel servers, you need a very fast computer to make it all look seamless. In Figure 11–1 it's Internet Explorer, acting as a container, that has invoked Word as a document server.

Developing

Visual Basic allows you to create applications that conform to the ActiveX Document specification. When you package your application for distribution, one of the items that Visual Basic produces is a file with the extension VBD. This VBD file contains a pointer to the Visual Basic server that you created. A user will load your VBD file into an ActiveX container. This will cause the container to invoke your Visual Basic program. From your program you can embed information in the VBD file to be read by your program the next time it is invoked.

Which brings me back to why "ActiveX Documents" is such a terrible name for the technology. You create an ActiveX Document server, not a document. Instead, in this chapter I don't always refer to your Visual Basic program as an "ActiveX Document server" (it's quite a mouthful). So, when I refer to building your ActiveX Document, remember that you're really building a document server and that the document (the VBD file) will be generated for you.

You can choose to compile your server as either a DLL or an EXE file. Regardless of whether you choose to compile your application as an in-process (DLL) or out-of-process component (EXE), your document and server must be downloaded to the computer that the container is running on before they will start to execute. As a result, installing an ActiveX Document application has three parts: installing the container, the server, and the VBD file, as I discuss later in this chapter.

Containers Matter

Since an ActiveX Document server is always displayed inside a container, your application will be limited by the container that hosts your document. In this chapter I draw examples from three containers: Internet Explorer, Microsoft Office Binder, and the Visual Basic Development Environment (see Figure 11–3).

INTERNET EXPLORER

Internet Explorer is probably the container that you are most familiar with. You can load a Word document (or a VBD file) just by typing its file name into the Address box. If a hyperlink in a Web page points to a Word document, Internet Explorer will download the file and load Word as the server.

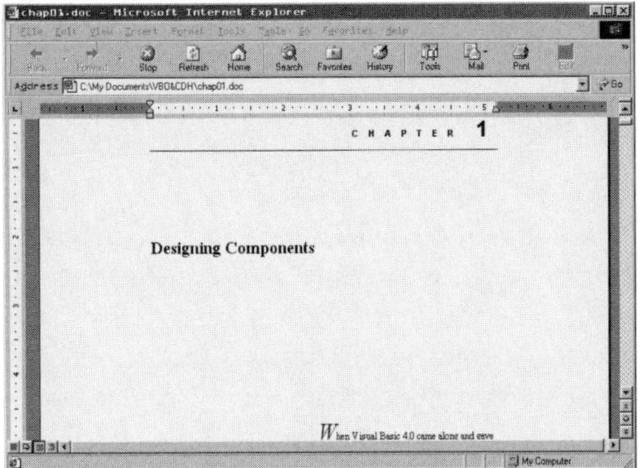

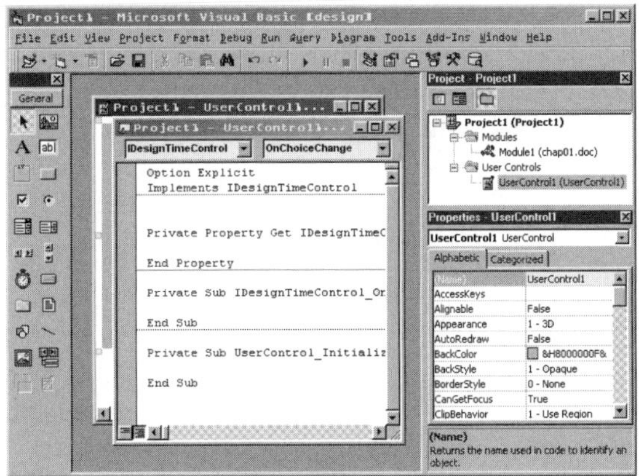

Figure 11-3 *The three ActiveX containers.*

MICROSOFT OFFICE BINDER

The Office Binder is distributed with Microsoft Office. Binder allows you to load several documents into one Binder file. Within the Binder you can select documents that are contained in the file and the appropriate server will be automatically loaded. Binder provides some options to consolidate the documents. If you print all the documents in the Binder, for instance, the pages of the various documents will be numbered consecutively.

VISUAL BASIC IDE

The Visual Basic IDE is itself an ActiveX container. Each file type that's supported by Visual Basic (e.g., FRM, BAS, CLS) has an editor associated with it. Double clicking on a file in Project Explorer opens the file in the associated editor. Effectively, in the development environment, FRM, BAS, and CLS files act as ActiveX Documents.

CONTAINER DIFFERENCES

The three environments, Internet Explorer, Microsoft Office Binder, and Visual Basic, enforce very different behaviors on the server that works with them. In Internet Explorer, to fetch a new document into the browser you must have Internet Explorer request a new URL. Within the Visual Basic environment, you will open a new window to display the object. With the Microsoft Office Binder, you open documents by adding and removing sections from the Binder.

Since Internet Explorer is the most ubiquitous container, most of my examples in this chapter come from Internet Explorer, though I have some examples that draw on the other two containers. I look at creating ActiveX Documents in Visual Basic in some depth in the chapter on Visual Basic add-ins.

As you'll see, because of the differences among containers, when you build an ActiveX Document server you will either have to target your application for a specific container or test to see what container your server is running in. Because these containers are so different, it's unlikely that you will create an ActiveX Document that will work in multiple containers. That doesn't necessarily mean that your documents are limited. To begin with, your container could be Internet Explorer, which would allow your server to become part of a Web-based application. To look at it another way, it wouldn't make sense to design a server that's useful to Visual Basic programmers to work anywhere other than in the Visual Basic IDE.

The Viewport

You'll find the creation of the user interface for your ActiveX Document server very similar to the process that you follow when working with a Visual Basic Form or UserControl. There is one unique characteristic of an ActiveX Document, however. An ActiveX Document displays inside a window made available to the server by the container application. This window is referred to as the viewport.

When you design an ActiveX Document server, you will lay out its user interface in much the same way as you would design a Visual Basic form. Unlike a Form, however, the window that displays your user interface isn't under the control of your application. Instead, the containing application provides a viewport that will display some (or all) of your user interface.

You can use all of the controls from the Visual Basic toolbox on your ActiveX Document except for the OLE control.

Internet Explorer provides a familiar example of how the viewport works. When you open a Word document in Internet Explorer, you can only see as much of the page as Internet Explorer's window allows. The page being displayed is not resized to fit into the space made available by Internet Explorer. If the page is too big to display in the window, scroll bars appear in the container window that allow the user to roll up and down or back and forth to view the whole page. The page that is being displayed cannot expand or contract Internet Explorer's window—that is under the sole control of the user.

All ActiveX Documents follow this convention: The container and the user control the viewport. Many of the ActiveX Documents features that are unique to this technology are designed to help you manage the viewport. As you will see, you can find out how big the viewport is, provide hints to the container on how and when scroll bars should be displayed, and control what part of your user interface is displayed in the viewport.

ActiveX Documents Applications

You should consider using ActiveX Documents wherever you are trying to integrate compiled applications with an ActiveX Document container. Since it's not possible to create ActiveX Document containers with Visual Basic, you have to design your application around existing containers. The most general-purpose of ActiveX Document containers is Internet Explorer. More specialized containers like the Office Binder and Visual Basic imply certain kinds of applications. Office Binder's interface and inherent functionality imply a document management kind of application (in particular, an application that bundles documents together). An Office Binder application that performed some other function would be difficult for your users to understand. (not to mention how odd your users would find it to start up Visual Basic in order to use an ActiveX Document-based order entry system).

Since Internet Explorer can download ActiveX Documents from a Web site, ActiveX Documents have been lumped in with other Internet technologies. Certainly, ActiveX Documents provide you with a way of delivering form-based applications using Internet Explorer, but that doesn't mean that ActiveX Documents make sense only on the Web. On the other hand, it's not clear that ActiveX Documents are necessary anywhere.

Getting Started

You begin creating your ActiveX Document by selecting either ActiveX Document DLL or ActiveX Document EXE. This opens a project containing a single UserDocument object. Like a Form (or a UserControl) the UserDocument is the base from which you build your ActiveX Document server. When you save your project, the UserControl is saved to a DOB file.

EXE OR DLL

The decision between choosing to compile your ActiveX Document server as an EXE or a DLL will be made on the same criteria as for any other component. For instance, as with other components, a DLL will run in the same memory space as the container and give you the fastest performance. One consideration peculiar to ActiveX Documents concerns modeless forms and DLLs. Depending on the container, you may not be able to open a modeless form from a DLL. If you are in a container that supports having multiple forms open (i.e., the Visual Basic IDE but not Internet Explorer), your users will not be able to work on any other form until they close your form.

Since an ActiveX Document application is always downloaded to the container's computer, ActiveX Document servers cannot run on a remote server using DCOM.

UserDocument Events

Like a UserControl, a UserDocument fires Initialize, Terminate, ReadProperties, and WriteProperties events. The ReadProperties and WriteProperties events accept a property bag from the container. While it has no effect on your code, the PropertyBag is implemented differently by different containers. Internet Explorer stores the PropertyBag information in the VBD file that it read to invoke your server. The Office Binder stores the information in to the ODB file that the VBD file is part of. For a more complete discussion of the PropertyBag events, see the chapters on components and on ActiveX Controls.

While the three containers referred to in this chapter fire all of the events listed here, the Property-related events are not guaranteed by the ActiveX Document specification. You should ensure that the containers that are targeting your server do fire these events before taking advantage of them.

Like the UserControl, the UserDocument supports AsyncReadProgress and ASyncReadComplete, which allow you to perform asynchronous downloads. Again, see the chapter on ActiveX Controls for a discussion on using these events.

The UserDocument also fires a Resize event. Unlike a Visual Basic Form, which fires this event when the Form is resized, in a UserControl this event is fired when the container is resized.

STARTUP AND TERMINATION EVENTS

Like a UserControl, the UserDocument doesn't fire Load, Unload, Activate, or Deactivate events, but it does have Show, Hide, EnterFocus and ExitFocus events.

The EnterFocus fires when the UserDocument or any control on it gets the focus. The ExitFocus event fires when the focus switches to some object other than the UserDocument within the same application. In Internet Explorer, for instance, the ExitFocus event fires when the user moves to another page. The Hide event fires when the UserDocument is no longer displayed. The order of events in the life-cycle of an ActiveX Documents is shown in Figure 11–4.

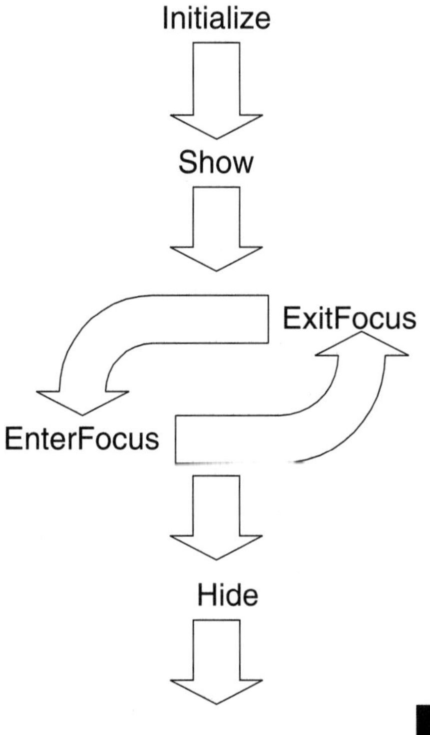

Figure 11–4 *The order of events during the startup and shutdown of an ActiveX Document.*

The Terminate and Initialize events occur before the document is sited, which means that the Show and Hide events are the ones you should use for any initialization or termination activities related to the user interface.

The WriteProperties and ReadProperties events, even when supported, are not guaranteed. If the PropertyChanged method isn't called, then the WriteProperties method won't be fired. If there is no data in the PropertyBag, the Read-Properties event won't be called.

SCROLL EVENT

The only event unique to the UserDocument is the Scroll event. This event will fire when the user scrolls moves through your document using a scroll-bar. This does not mean that you need to write any code to implement scroll-ing. The container will take care of repositioning your user interface in the viewport as the user adjusts the scrollbar. This event is purely to notify you that the viewport is changing.

In most containers, the viewport is not repositioned if the user tabs to a control that is outside the viewport. Tabbing from a textbox displayed in the viewport to one outside the container's window will not bring the textbox into view. As I discuss later in this chapter, you can write code to reposition the viewport but this code will not also fire the Scroll event.

If the user moves the scrollbar by dragging on the thumb, when the Scroll event will fire is controlled by the UserDocument's ContinuousScroll property. If you set the ContinuousScroll property to False, the Scroll event will fire only when the user releases the scroll bar and your user interface is repositioned. If the ContinuousScroll property is set to True, the event will fire as the user moves the thumb on the scroll bar. Setting the ContinuousScroll property also affects how scrolling is handled. If the ContinuousScroll prop-erty is set to False, then the UserDocument will not be repositioned until the thumb is released. When the property is set to True, the UserDocument is redrawn as the thumb is moved.

The ContinuousScroll property has no effect on scrolling that is initiated by clicking on the arrows at either end of the scrollbar, or clicking in the scrollbar above or below the thumb. In both of these cases, the Scroll event fires after your user interface is repositioned.

UserDocument Methods

As with the UserControl object, the UserDocument supports the AsyncRead and CancelAsyncRead methods to allow you to download from a URL. The PropertyChanged method is also supported by the UserDocument as it is with the UserControl The only method unique to the userDocument is the Set-Viewport method.

POSITIONING THE VIEWPORT

The SetViewport method is used to control where the viewport is positioned over your UserDocument. The method accepts two parameters that specify the location of the left side and top of the viewport within the document. This code moves the viewport to a position 20 twips in from the left edge of the document and 1000 twips down from the top:

```
UserDocument.SetViewport 20, 1000
```

One use for the SetViewport method is to provide a button that allows your users to return to the top of your form:

```
Private Sub cmdStart_Click()
  UserDocument.SetViewport 0, 0
End Sub
```

If your document is broken up into sections, you can use SetViewport to relocate the viewport relative to your document. The UserDocument's ScaleWidth and ScaleHeight properties can be useful here because they allow you to control your form's coordinate system. While your UserDocument might be 6360 pixels high and 5760 pixels wide, you can change the coordinate system to 100 by 100 units with these two lines of code:

```
UserDocument.ScaleHeight = 100
UserDocument.ScaleWidth = 100
```

With the UserDocument's height and width both set to 100, this line of code would now relocate the upper left corner of the viewport halfway down and halfway across the form:

```
UserDocument.SetViewport 50, 50
```

When teaching, I'm often asked what unit of measure is being used after you set the ScaleHeight and ScaleWidth properties: pixels, inches, twips, whatever? I used to explain that the coordinate system is simply in "units" that don't correspond to any existing measuring scheme. Lately, I've taken to humbly suggesting that the resulting measurement unit be referred to as "vogels."

If your form is broken up into ten horizontal sections of equal height, then each section will be 10 units high if the UserDocument's ScaleHeight is set to 100. A command button that would reposition the viewport so that the third section was displayed would look like this:

```
Private Sub cmdThird_Click()
  UserDocument.SetViewport 0, 20
End Sub
```

As I mentioned, you can use the SetViewPort method to ensure that a control on your form is displayed when the user tabs to it. This code, in the

GotFocus event of a textbox, moves the Viewport to display the upper left corner of the control:

```
Private Sub Text2_GotFocus()
  UserDocument.SetViewport 720, 3840
End Sub
```

Using the SetViewport method will not necessarily reposition the viewport. If moving the viewport would cause the viewport to extend beyond the top or bottom of your document, the container may not respond to the SetViewport method. No error will be raised if the viewport is not moved.

UserDocument Properties

The properties that are unique to the UserDocument are related to managing the Viewport or scrolling.

HSMALLSCROLLCHANGE, VSMALLSCROLLCHANGE

These two properties control how far the viewport will move when the user clicks on the arrows at either end of the scrollbar. HSmallScrollChange sets the distance for the horizontal scrollbar, while VSmallScrollChange controls the distance of the vertical scrollbar. The distance is in twips, unless the Scale-Height and ScaleWidth properties have been set. Changing the ScaleWidth and ScaleHeight after setting HSmallScrollChange or VSmallScrollChange has no effect on how far the thumb will move.

For instance, assume that the form is 6000 twips tall. Setting VSmall-ScrollChange to 2000 will cause the thumb of the scrollbar to move a third of the height of the UserDocument each time one of the arrows on the scrollbar is clicked. Changing the ScaleHeight after setting VSmallScrollChange will not change this.

```
UserDocument.VSmallScrollChange = 2000
UserDocument.ScaleHeight = 4000
```

However, setting the ScaleHeight before setting VSmallScrollChange does have an effect. Reversing the two previous lines will set the height of the document to 4000 units. As a result, a VSmallScrollChange of 2000 will cause the scroll bar to move half the height of the form when the arrow at the top or bottom of the scroll bar is clicked.

```
UserDocument.ScaleHeight = 4000
UserDocument.VSmallScrollChange = 2000
```

When a user clicks in the area above or below the thumb, the thumb moves a "LargeScrollChange" amount. You cannot set this value—the container sets the LargeScrollChange value to the current height and width of the viewport.

SCROLLBARS

The Scrollbars property can be set at design time to control which scrollbars are displayed on the form. You can set the Scrollbars property to any one of the values in Table 11.1 to ensure that when the container adds scrollbars, that you get only the ones you want.

Table 11.1 Settings for the UserDocument Scrollbars Property

Constant	Setting	Description
vbSBNone	0	No scrollbars
vbHorizontal	1	Horizontal scrollbars only
vbVertical	2	Vertical scrollbars only
vbBoth	3	Both horizontal and vertical (default)

At run time, the property is read only and reports the setting made at design time (not which scrollbars are currently displayed).

MINHEIGHT, MINWIDTH

The MinHeight and MinWidth properties let you tell the container when to display scrollbars (provided that the Scrollbars property is set to something other than vbSBNone). If you don't set these properties, the container will add scrollbars to its window whenever the viewport is smaller than the total size of your UserDocument. If you want scrollbars added at some size smaller than your UserDocument, you can set these properties to that smaller size.

For instance, if you have a UserDocument that is 6000 twips high, then, as soon as the viewport is less than 6000 twips high, the container will add scrollbars to its window. However, if this particular UserDocument has all of the user entry fields in the top 4000 twips and a graphic in the bottom 2000 twips, accepting the default might be a poor design decision. If the graphic is one that, quite frankly, your users don't need to see, you may choose not to have scrollbars display until the viewport is less than 4000 twips. If so, you would use this code:

```
Private Sub UserDocument_Initialize()
  UserDocument.MinHeight = 4000
End Sub
```

As with VSmallScrollChange, MinHeight and MinWidth are set in the current units for ScaleHeight and ScaleWidth.

VIEWPORTHEIGHT, VIEWPORTWIDTH, VIEWPORTLEFT, VIEWPORTTOP

The ViewportHeight, ViewportWidth, ViewportLeft, and ViewportTop properties are read only. Using them, you can determine what part of your UserDocument is being displayed in the viewport. The ViewportTop and ViewportLeft properties report how far the viewport is from the top and left side of the UserDocument (see Figure 11–5).

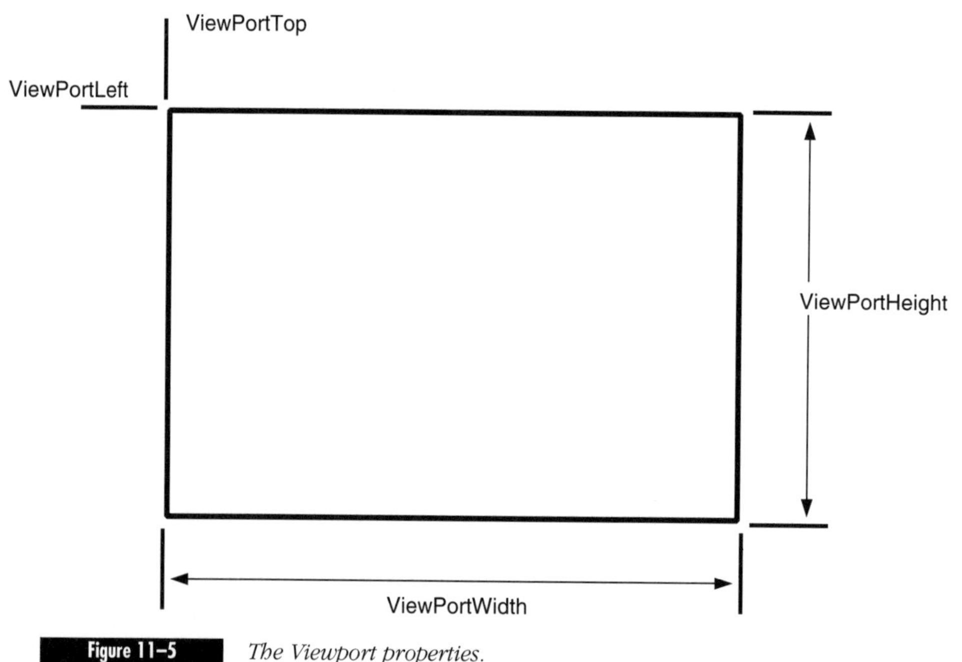

Figure 11–5 *The Viewport properties.*

ViewportHeight and ViewportWidth give the height and width of the viewport. They are also the distance that the window will scroll if the user clicks in the scrollbar area above or below the thumb. The unit of measure is twips, unless ScaleHeight and ScaleWidth have been set.

Debugging ActiveX Documents

When you debug an ActiveX Document application, Visual Basic creates a VBD that will invoke your server for the container to load. The first time that you debug your application, the Debugging dialog will pop up to allow you to select which of the documents in your application you want to debug. After you've selected a UserDocument in the Start Component combo box, Visual Basic will create the VBD file.

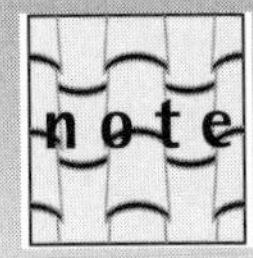

If you later want to change which UserDocument is initially displayed, you can change it on the Debugging tab from the Project | Properties menu choice.

Debugging an ActiveX Document that uses Internet Explorer as its container is easy to do: Just click on the Run button. Visual Basic will call Internet Explorer and have it display the VBD file.

If your document requires a different container than Internet Explorer, you can use one of the other three choices on the Debugging tab (see Figure 11–6):

- Wait for component to be created: Visual Basic will create the VBD file and then wait for you to use the VBD file. You can load the VBD file using the container of your choice to start the debugging session.
- Start Program: With this option, you specify the full pathname to the container that you want to use to load your document. Visual Basic will start the container for you and have it display the VBD file.
- Start browser with URL: Here you must specify the full path to the VBD file that Visual Basic will create. This option has the same effect as just clicking on the Run button.

When you have finished a debugging session, shutting down your container (typically, Internet Explorer) doesn't stop Visual Basic. You'll have to press the Stop button in Visual Basic before you can edit your code. Pressing the Stop button before shutting down your test container may or not be a problem—it all depends on the container. With Internet Explorer 5.0, when I was finished testing my server I would switch to Visual Basic and stop the server from running. An annoying message would pop up warning me that this could create problems, but I just clicked on the Yes button to shut down my debugging session anyway. After making my edits, I would start up my application and it would cause Internet Explorer to reload the page and carry on.

When testing your ActiveX Document over the Web, remember that your server must be downloaded to your computer in order to execute. To prevent problems during this download you must make sure that Internet

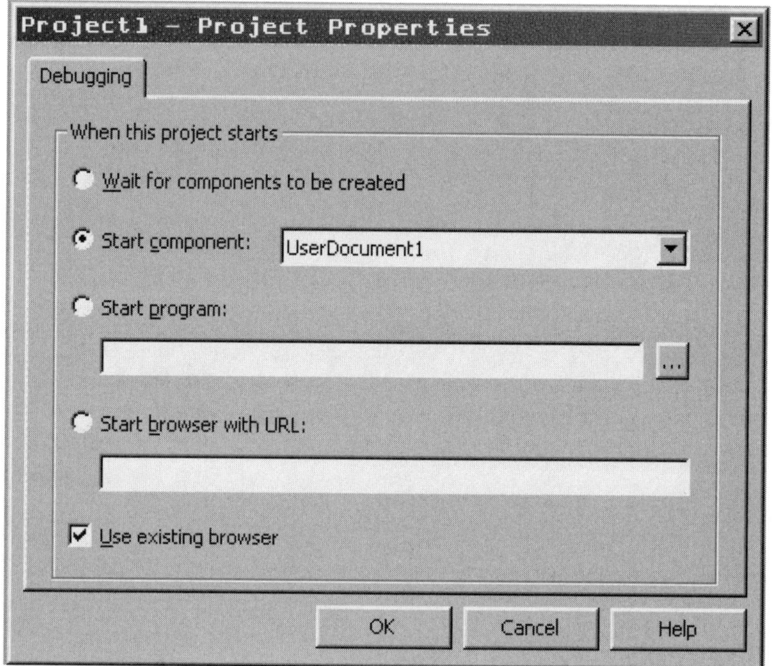

Figure 11–6 *The Debugging options for an ActiveX Document.*

Explorer's security is set to something other than High. You must also have enough disk space on your test computer for the server and whatever support files are bundled with it. Also, check that you don't have an old copy of the program in either the Occache or Downloaded Program Files folders.

You must also manage GUIDs with your ActiveX Document. If the VBD file that you are using doesn't have the same classid as the server that you are testing, your server won't be invoked.

Menu Negotiation

When a container displays an ActiveX Document, it merges the server's menus with its own. In Figure 11–1 you saw how Internet Explorer merged its menus with Microsoft Word's. The Go and Favorites menu were Internet Explorer's, but the Table and Insert menus belonged to Microsoft Word.

The final decision on where the menus go rests with the container. However, when you place menus on your ActiveX Document, you can indicate where you would like the document's container to put your menus. When you use Visual Basic's menu editor to create a menu, you can set the menu's NegotiatePosition property to one of four settings (see Figure 11–7):

0 - None
1 - Left
2 - Center
3 - Right

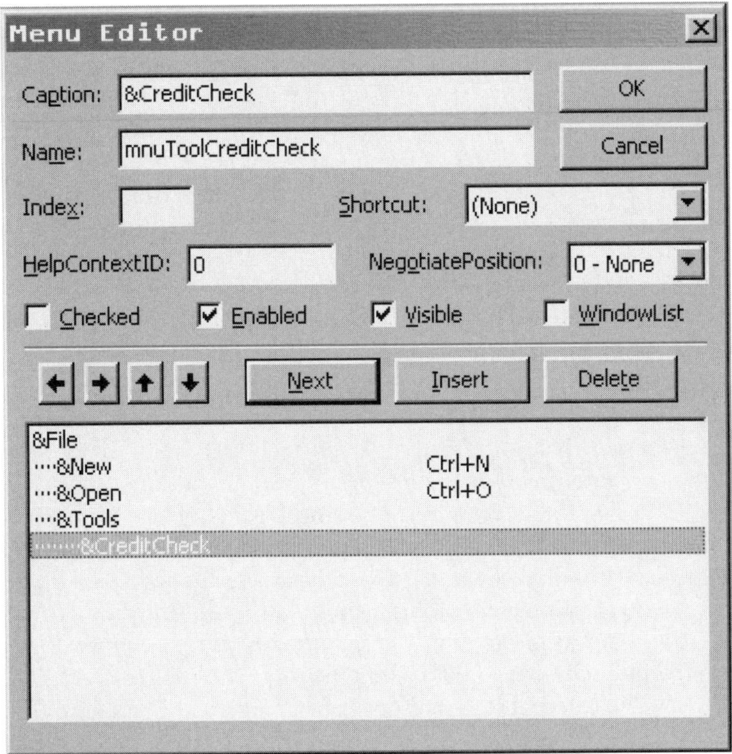

Figure 11–7 *The Visual Basic menu editor.*

A menu whose NegotiatePosition is set to zero will not be added to the container's menus. When NegotiatePosition is set to Center, it indicates that the menu is to be displayed somewhere on the menu bar. If NegotiatePosition is set to Right, a menu item will be added to the bottom of the container's Help menu. Clicking on this item will display the ActiveX Document menu as a submenu of the container's Help menu.

Setting NegotiatePosition to Left indicates that you want your menu displayed as close to the File menu as possible. Your ActiveX Document's menus can never be the leftmost menu on the container's menu bar. This is reserved for the File menu of the container because it is the container that controls opening and closing the ActiveX document.

Implementing and Distributing

As I mentioned at the start of this chapter, there are three parts to distributing an ActiveX Document: the container, the server, and the VBD file. For this chapter, I assume that the container is already installed on the client computer.

With the container installed, you must install the server (your Visual Basic program) to display the document. In the same way that a user must have Microsoft Word installed on his or her computer to display a Word document, the user must have your ActiveX Document server installed on their computer to display your VBD file. Like any other component, an ActiveX Document has a classid that is written to the registry. Other programs—like ActiveX Document containers—invoke the server by using the classid that they find in the VBD file.

The second part of distributing the application involves the document that will invoke your server. The user must request the document that requires your server. This document is the VBD file produced by compiling the UserDocument. The VBD contains the classid of the ActiveX Documentation server that you created. When the VBD file is opened by the container, the container invokes the server associated with the classid.

When you run the Package and Deployment Wizard for an ActiveX Document project you can create either a Standard Setup Package or an Internet Package. With the Standard Package, a setup program that will install the server will be created, along with one or more CAB files. You can then distribute this setup package to the users who will be using your application. The VBD file will be created in the directory with the program.

The Internet Package option will create a CAB file, the VBD file, and an HTML file. The HTML file contains sample code to download and install your server. The following HTML will, when added to a Web page, install a server called SampleDocServer:

```
<OBJECT ID="SampleDocServer"
CLASSID="CLSID:EBF3FB44-6837-11D3-A8CA-00107A901A5F"
CODEBASE="\\www.server.com\Project1a.CAB#version=1,0,0,0">
</OBJECT>
```

When the page containing this HTML is read by Internet Explorer, the Object tag will cause Internet Explorer to download the CAB file that contains the server from the location *www.server.com*. Internet Explorer will then extract and install the server on the user's computer, making all the necessary registry entries. The next time the user visits this page, Internet Explorer will use the Object tag's classid attribute to check the registry to see if the server is already installed. If the classid is found, the CAB files will not be downloaded again.

As part of generating the CAB file, you can choose to include the support files that ActiveX Documents require. Including all of these files will make your CAB file significantly larger. Provided your target users already have those files installed, you can leave them out of your install. Of course, if your users don't have those files, your application won't run.

With your ActiveX Document server now installed, your user can access the document that will invoke the server. Sample code that you would add to a Web page to load the VBD file would look like this (see Figure 11–8):

```
<a href=UserDocument1.VBD>UserDocument1.VBD</a>
```

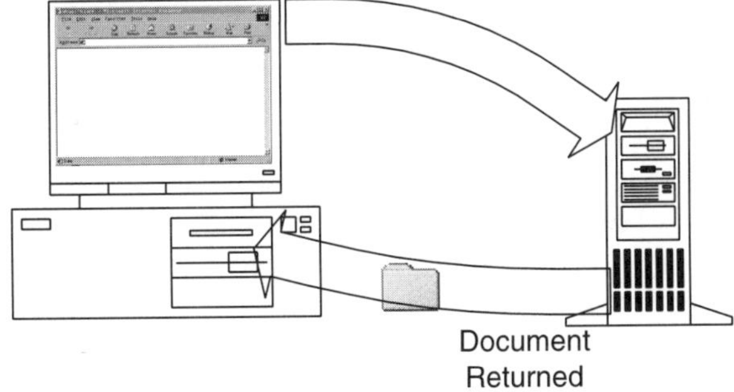

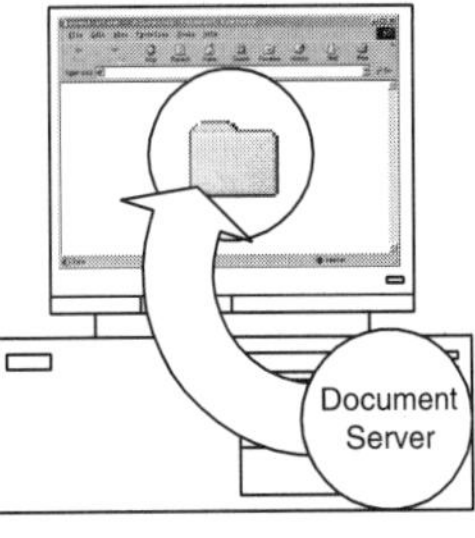

Figure 11–8 *Downloading and installing an ActiveX Document server and invoking a VBD file.*

You can combine different methods of installing your ActiveX Document server and requesting your page. You could have a Web page that, when visited by your users, would install your document server. Your users could then invoke the VBD file from Office Binder or the Visual Basic IDE (assuming that the filepath to the VBD file was available to the user). Alternatively, you could use a setup program to install your server (thereby avoiding the download time) but have your users request the VBD file over the Net to run your application in Internet Explorer.

If, when downloading or opening an ActiveX Document, you get the message "Opening file *DocumentName*.VBD. What would you like to do with this file? Open it or save it to disk?", the most likely cause is that the Microsoft Virtual Machine hasn't been installed. You'll need to rerun the package and deployment wizard and add this option to your package.

Issues in ActiveX Document Development

There are some special challenges in creating ActiveX Document applications with multiple UserDocuments. Like an ActiveX Component, all the parts of an ActiveX Document application are loaded at the same time, though typically only one of the ActiveX Documents in the application will be displayed at any time. Making sure that the documents display in the right order and work together effectively requires some special techniques. You'll also need to know what container your server is executing in so that you don't execute code that won't work in that container.

Managing State

Which of your UserDocuments is displayed is controlled by which VBD the user chooses to open. Since the container opens and closes all UserDocuments, your ActiveX Document server can't control, for instance, which UserDocument is displayed first. Even after the first server is loaded, while you may have code to control which document displays next, there is nothing stopping the user from requesting some other VBD file.

If your application is made up of independent pages, this isn't a problem. On the other hand, if it's important that users go through the servers in a particular order, you'll have to manage your application's state. For instance, if your application has two servers (UserDoc1 and UserDoc2) and it matters that UserDoc1 display first, you can use a global variable to control the order in which documents are displayed.

For this example, I define a Public Integer variable called intAppState. Initially, this variable will have a value of zero:

```
Public intAppState As Integer
```

In UserDoc1, the button cmdUpdate performs all the updates required by the page and signals that processing for that page is complete. In the click event for that button, I set the variable intAppState to 1 to indicate that UserDoc1 is complete and the user can now safely load UserDoc2:

```
Sub cmdUpdate_Click()
  …update processing…
  intStateApp = 1
End Sub
```

In UserDoc2's Show event, I check the intStateApp variable. If it is 0, then it indicates that UserDoc1 hasn't been processed. In that case, the code navigates to UserDoc1:

```
Sub UserDocument_Show()
  If intAppState = 0 Then
    Document.Hyperlink.NavigateTo "C:\UserDoc1.VBD"
  End if
End Sub
```

Determining the Container

In order to determine what container your application is running in, you can use the TypeName function, passing it the UserDocument's Parent property (the Parent property returns a reference to the UserDocument's container). The return values for the three ActiveX Document containers discussed in this chapter are listed in Table 11.2.

Table 11.2 Return Values for TypeName Function

Document Container	TypeName Return Value
Internet Explorer	IwebBrowserApp
Microsoft Binder	Section
Visual Basic	Window

In Internet Explorer, to move form one document to another you use the Navigate method of the Hyperlink object. In the Microsoft Binder, you add a new section. To create an ActiveX Document that would work in both environments, you would need to use code like this:

```
Select Case TypeName(UserDocument.Parent)
  Case "Internet Explorer"
    Document.Hyperlink.NavigateTo "C:\NextPage.VBD"
  Case "Section"
    UserDocument.Parent.Parent.Sections. _
      Add ,"c:\NextPage.vbd"
  Case Else
    Msgbox "Unable to call next page in this container."
End Select
```

Using NavigateTo from a container other than Internet Explorer will start Internet Explorer and load your server into it.

Exploiting VBD Files

In addition to some special challenges, ActiveX Documents also present special opportunities. Since an ActiveX Document server is invoked by a VBD file, you can take advantage of the information in the file as part of your application's design. Internet Explorer, for instance, stores the PropertyBag in the VBD file. As a result, you can create files that contain particular property settings and use those to control the behavior of your server. You can also set up your application so that users can load new blank VBD files or files with property settings already made. Loading a blank VBD would start a new entry in the application, while loading with property settings would let the user work with an existing entry.

As an example, an Order Entry system might be based around a series of ActiveX Documents (as shown in Figure 11–9). Users could download from the Web server a VBD file that contains no information. When the user enters a customer number, that information (along with the sales order number) could be written to the PropertyBag and saved in the VBD file. Since the VBD file that user works with is downloaded to the user's computer, the VBD file on the server remains data free and can be used to create new orders. When the VBD file is reloaded from the user's hard disk, the UserDocument's ReadProperties event will fire, allowing the application's code to retrieve the customer id and sales order number from the PropertyBag.

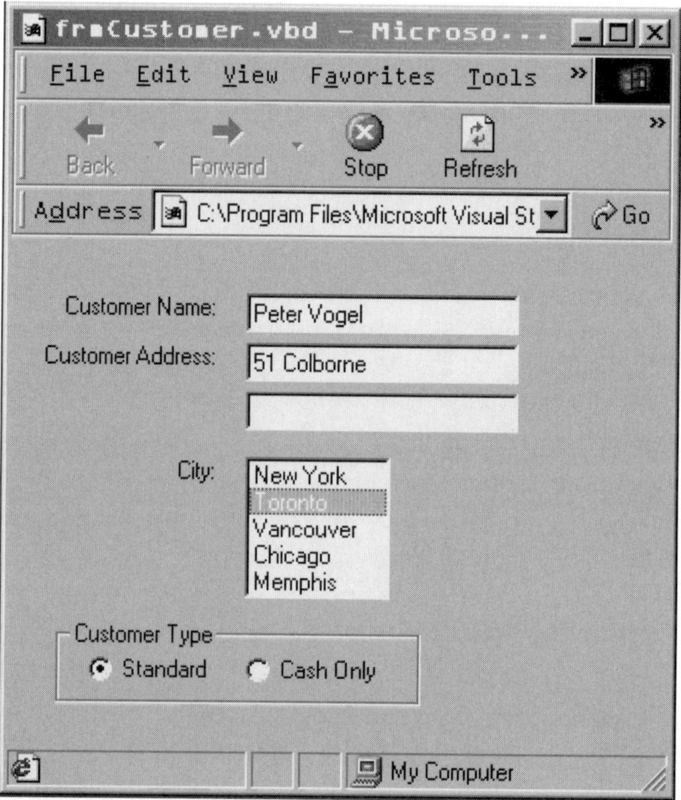

Figure 11–9 *A VBD-based application.*

Unfortunately, there is no built-in way to manage VBD files. The only way to prevent the updated VBD file from being overwritten the next time the file is downloaded is to use Visual Basic's file handling commands to copy the file to a new location or change its name.

Cooperating UserDocuments

As with any ActiveX Component, all members of the application are loaded when any UserDocument in the application is requested. You can add methods and properties to your UserDocument and call them from other UserDocuments in the same application. However, there are two problems: The UserDocument whose properties and methods you are calling must be instantiated, and a reference to the document has to be available to the UserDocument that is calling the methods.

The only way to instantiate a document is to have the container load the document. Since a UserDocument can't load another UserDocument the only way to pass a reference from one to another to is use Public variables. A UserDocument can set a Public variable to refer to itself and then instantiate a second UserDocument by navigating to it, as shown here:

```
Public usd As UserDoc1
Sub cmdNextPage_Click()
  Set usd = Me
End Sub
```

The second UserDocument can then retrieve the reference from the Public variable and use it to access any methods or properties defined in the first UserDocument. The first UserDocument will remain instantiated as long as there is a reference to it.

You must make sure that you set all references to other UserDocuments to Nothing in order to ensure that your application will terminate appropriately.

ActiveX Documents and Visual Basic Applications

One of the attractive concepts of ActiveX is that it can be used to deliver Visual Basic programs over the Web. When ActiveX Documents came out, the functionality of these applications was limited because there was no way for the code in the document server to access data back on the Web server. While the server could be downloaded over the Internet or an intranet, the code could only access data on the local network. Thanks to Remote Data Services (discussed in the chapter on Data Binding) that's no longer true: Your ActiveX Document can read and write data on servers on the Internet, your local intranet, or your network.

Microsoft provides the ActiveX Document Migration Wizard to aid in converting a standard Visual Basic application into an ActiveX Document application (see Figure 11–10). Effectively, what the Wizard does is transfer your property settings, code, and controls from your Form objects to a set of UserDocument objects.

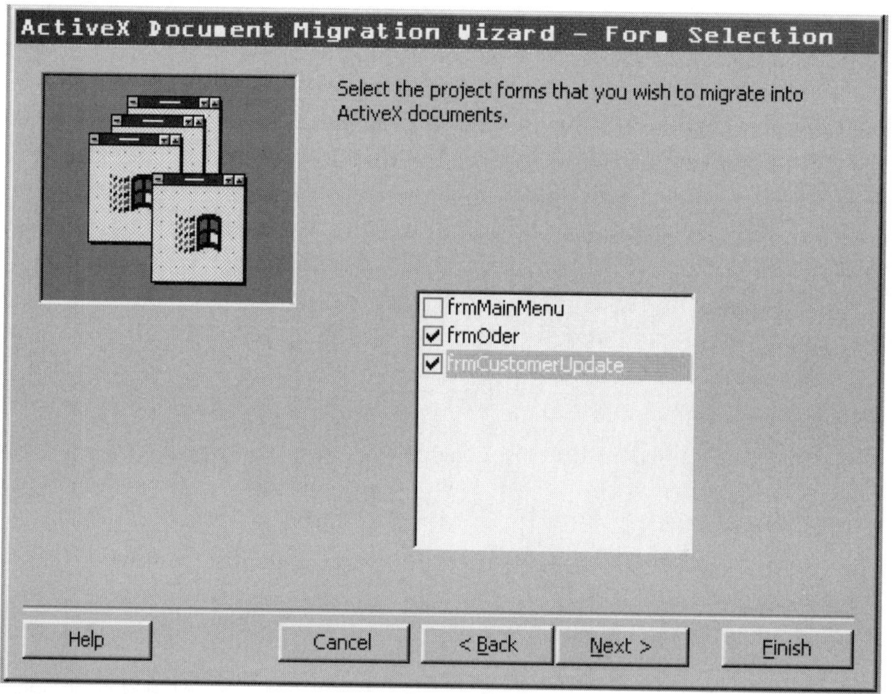

Figure 11–10 *The ActiveX Document Migration Wizard.*

However, there's only so much that the Wizard can do. It can't do anything with code in the Form Load and Unload events, for instance, because a UserDocument doesn't have those events. Nor can the Wizard re-create the navigation among the forms in the application since an ActiveX Document's navigation depends on the container that it is displaying in. The Wizard will leave in place the application's original Form navigation methods (Show, Load, and Hide) but will comment them out. It's your responsibility to replace these commented-out events with the appropriate container-based code.

Summary

In this chapter you've learned how to create ActiveX Document applications and how to deliver those applications using a Web browser or other ActiveX container. You may well have found yourself saying that this is the perfect answer for a problem that you've been dealing with. Or, you may just file this knowledge away in case you ever need it someday.

The only real references for this technology is the material in the Visual Studio Help files. The two major references are the entry on the UserDocument object and Building ActiveX Documents. So, when it comes to building ActiveX Documents, your best reference is probably experimenting with the technology itself. You might want to try re-creating one of your Visual Basic applications as an ActiveX Document that can be downloaded over the Web, for instance.

TWELVE

Microsoft Transaction Server Objects

Microsoft Transaction Server is the foundation on which you can build scalable, reliable n-tier applications. I know that sounds like marketing hype but, in the Windows world, it's true. Microsoft Transaction Server (MTS) will take care of ensuring that your objects cooperate to maintain the integrity of your data. MTS will manage your components so that they place the minimum load on your server. MTS will also ensure that access to your objects is limited to only those users who should be using those objects. MTS isn't just for DCOM applications, either. MTS runs on Windows 98 and can be used to manage components running on the same computer as their client. The services provided by MTS are so important that, with Windows 2000, MTS becomes part of the operating system under the name Component Services.

In this chapter I give you an introduction to the services that MTS provides and why you want to use them. As you'll see, you can take advantage of some of the MTS services without making any changes to COM component that you have already built. However, as you'll also see, you can improve the integration of your component with MTS and capture even more of the benefits that MTS provides.

MTS Architecture

MTS provides its services through a process called interception. Interception begins when a client program creates an object and Windows goes to the Registry to retrieve the pathname to the executable file that will satisfy the request. Normally, what Windows finds is the full pathname to a an EXE or DLL file that holds the component that the object is part of. With DCOM, Windows finds the name of the computer on the network that the request is to be routed to. With MTS, the Registry entries for a component's objects are rewritten so that all requests for the objects in a component are routed to Microsoft Transaction Server. This puts MTS in a position to control your objects on behalf of the clients who request them.

One of the noteworthy features of MTS is how little it changes what you've learned in previous chapters. No change is required to clients when the components that they use are put under the control of MTS. For instance, when a client accesses an MTS-controlled object on a remote server, it's still DCOM that handles the communication between the client and the remote server (see Figure 12–1).

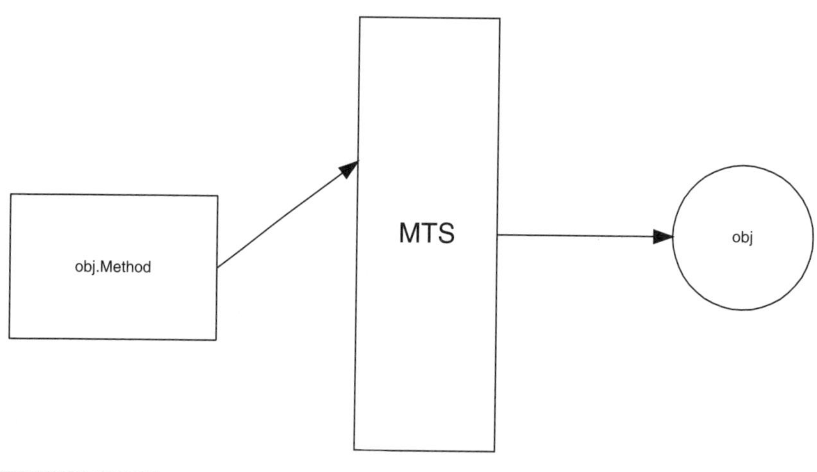

Figure 12–1 *MTS intercepts all client requests.*

For a component to work with MTS, it must be compiled as a DLL and all objects must have their instancing property set to MultiUse.

Creating a Package

You put a component under the control of MTS by using Microsoft Transaction Server Explorer. MTS Explorer lets you set up packages that contain one or more components. To do this, MTS Explorer has you create a package and then add components to it. When you add a component to a package, MTS rewrites the registry entries for all of the objects in the component so that any request for those objects turns into a call to MTS.

If you reinstall or recompile a component that is part of a package, the MTS's registry entries for that object may be overwritten. MTS Explorer's Refresh function restores the MTS settings for a single package or all of the packages installed on a computer.

To put a component under the control of MTS, you must first create a package to hold the component. The steps to create a package are:

1. On the computer that the component is to run on, start Transaction Server Explorer.
2. Select the computer that you want to create the package on from the Computers folder.
3. Right-mouse click on the Packages Installed folder and select New | Package.
4. Click on the Create Empty Package button.
5. Enter a name for the package and click on the button.
6. Set the security to be applied to the package and click on the Finish button.

With an empty package created, you can add components to it:

1. In the left pane of MTS Explorer, click on the package to reveal the Components folder underneath it (see Figure 12–2).
2. Right-mouse click on the Components folder and select New | Component.
3. Click on either the Install New Components or Import Components that are Already Registered button.
4. If you picked the Install New Components button, click on the Add Files button and browse to the file that contains your component. Click on the file to select it. Click on the Open button to add your component to the package.
5. If you picked the Import Components button, select a component from the list and click on the Finish button.

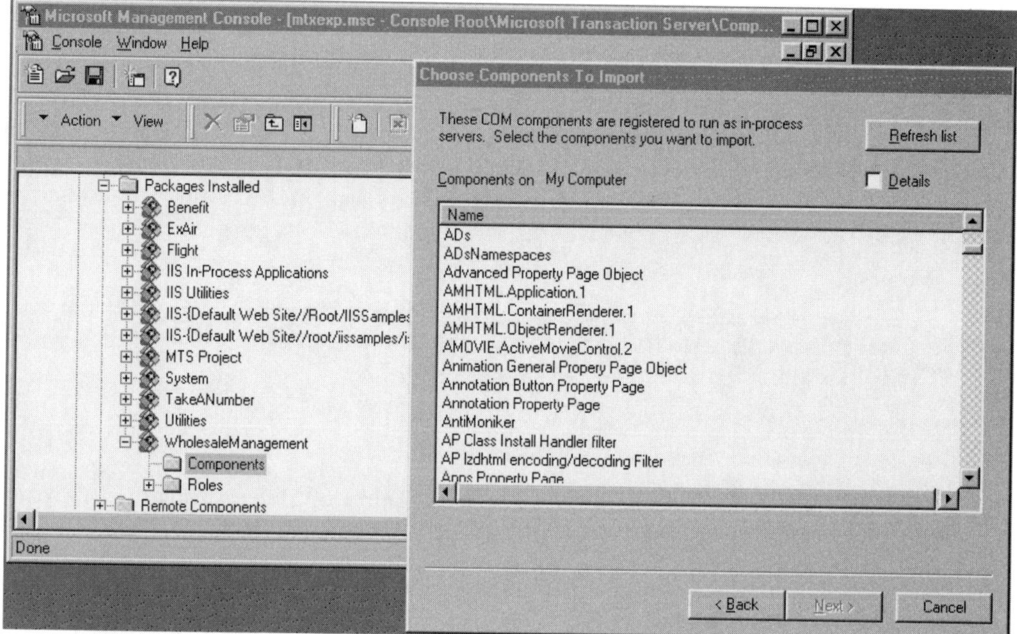

Figure 12-2 *Adding a component to an empty package.*

The settings for MTSTransactionMode for your objects are ignored if you use Import Components. You will have to use the Transaction tab of the object's Properties dialog in MTSExplorer to set the transaction mode for the objects in the component.

Configuring the Package

With the package created, the package's Properties dialog lets you set options for the package. The dialog's Activation tab includes an option that affects the performance of your component. On this tab you can set whether the package is to be a Library or Server package (Server is the default). Selecting Server causes your package to run as an out-of-process component, while Library causes your package to run in-process.

A remoted object is always out-of-process, so if your component is being run from a client on another computer you shouldn't take the Library option. Further, when a component runs as a Library package, MTS does not provide the automatic security that it can provide for a Server package. Performance, however, will be better with Library packages then Server packages and should be considered when the client executes on the same computer as the component.

The ObjectContext Object

When a component is managed by MTS, the client no longer interacts directly with it. Instead, MTS creates a proxy for the client to work with. From the client program's point of view, it appears that the object is created on demand in response to the client's request. In fact, the client interacts with an ObjectContext object created by MTS to stand in for the object that the client requested. This proxy object allows MTS to intercept and manage the client's interaction with the object (see Figure 12–3).

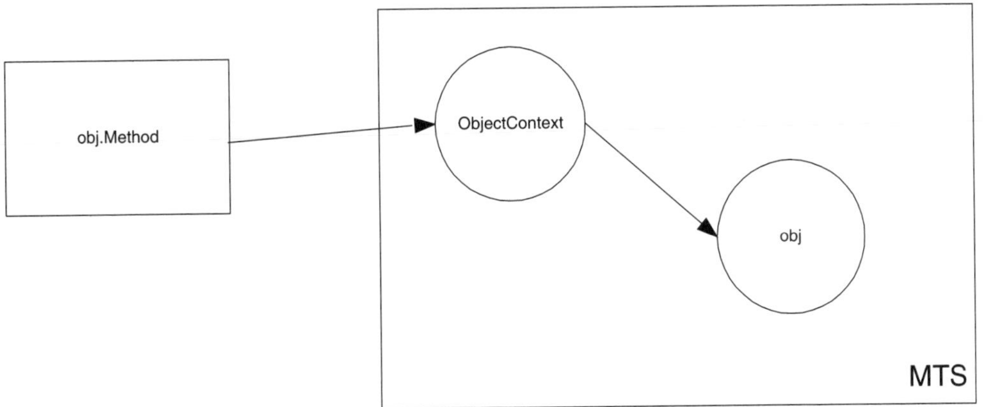

Figure 12–3 *Clients, objects, and the ObjectContext.*

One benefit of using a proxy occurs when a client uses the New command or the CreateObject function to create an object. MTS does not create the object when the client issues the New or CreateObject statement. MTS does return a reference to the requested interface to the client so that the client doesn't realize that the object hasn't been created.

MTS will not actually create the requested object until the client uses some method or property of the object. This is referred to as "Just-In-Time" activation. The effect is to reduce the load on the server by deferring the creation of the object until it's actually required. And, of course, if the client never uses a method or property of the object, MTS will never create the object.

In addition to acting as a stand-in for your object, the ObjectContext object also provides a set of methods that allows you to integrate your component with MTS. In the following section I look at the services provided by MTS and discuss the changes that you can make to your component to take advantage of MTS services.

By using the ObjectContext's methods, your object can interact with MTS. You must first add the Microsoft Transaction Server Type library to your project's References list. This reference adds a Global object called AppServer to your project. You can then retrieve a reference to your object's ObjectContext object by using the AppServer's GetObjectContext method. This code, for instance, returns a reference to the ObjectContext object that is acting as the object's stand in:

```
Dim ctx As ObjectContext
Set ctx = AppServer.GetObjectContext
```

MTS Services

Microsoft Transaction Server provides four services to the components that it controls:

- *Management:* With MTS you can manage the inventory of objects installed on a computer through MTS Explorer. For instance, MTS Explorer, lets you view the statistics generated by the objects under MTS's control, view and resolve transaction problems, and set up security for packages. I won't spend much time on MTS Explorer, except where it's part of creating an object to work with MTS.
- *Transaction Management:* This service allows you to ensure that all of the data updates performed by a group of objects are either made or rejected as a group. Without this service there is the possibility that some of a client's updates could be made while others are not made because one object abends.
- *Scalability:* MTS will manage the creation and termination of the objects under its control to reduce the overall load on the server.
- *Security:* By using MTS's security services, you can control which users are allowed to use your objects.

You can take advantage of many of these services by simply setting properties for your object rather than writing code, a technique referred to as declarative programming. With declarative programming you don't have to write any code in order to take advantage of MTS's services.

In the following sections I look at each of the services that MTS provides. In each section I describe why the service is important to you and then show you what changes you would need to make to a component to take full advantage of that server. I begin with the transaction management services.

Transaction Management

A common problem with many applications is that they have to update more than one datasource. I worked for one company where all the accounting information was kept in a DB2 database running on an AS/400, while all the inventory and manufacturing information was stored in the RDB database management system (DBMS) on a VAX 11/780. Making a change on the VAX in the quantity on hand in the inventory system required a corresponding change in the inventory accounts on the AS/400. Every once in a while, an update on the AS/400 would succeed while the corresponding update on the VAX would fail. Tracking down and correcting these discrepancies was a time consuming process.

It's not that we didn't have transaction management code in place. With both databases we could invoke the three essential functions required by transaction management. We could:

- *Start a transaction:* This command signals to the DBMS that all subsequent updates are to be treated as a group.
- *Commit a transaction:* Issued after a transaction is started, this command tells the DBMS that all updates since the transaction started should be written to the database.
- *Abort a transaction:* Issued after a transaction was started, this command tells the DBMS that something has gone wrong and that all the updates since the start of the transaction should be discarded.

Before starting to update the database on the VAX, our programs would start a transaction. When all the updates had been passed to the DBMS, our programs issued a command to write the updates to the database. If the program abended before it issued its commit transaction command, the DBMS would do an automatic rollback. This handled some of our problems.

For instance, if a program recorded the transfer of inventory from one warehouse to another, it would use two steps. In the first step, the program would reduce the inventory in one warehouse. In the second step, the program would add the corresponding amount to the inventory in the other warehouse. Letting the first update succeed while the second one failed would "lose" the inventory that was being transferred. Transaction management ensured that either the inventory was successfully transferred or it was left where it was.

The problem was that each DBMS managed its transactions separate from the other database. While each DBMS would ensure that all of the updates against it were completed or abandoned, there was no central control to ensure that one DBMS wouldn't accept updates when the other database management system rejected its updates.

Microsoft's strategy is to provide tools to help you manage working with multiple databases—a good strategy for a company whose DBMS has a relatively small share of the market. Oracle, on the other hand, has the largest share of the market and urges developers to put all of their data in one database—Oracle.

MTS TRANSACTION MANAGEMENT

When you put an object under the control of Microsoft Transaction Server and access a data source, MTS monitors your object's activity. Provided that the DBMS supports one of the transaction protocols that MTS uses, MTS can signal to the DBMS that it should start transaction management for the object's updates. Should your application abend without completing its transaction, MTS will also notify the DBMS to back out any updates that your objects performed. The number of databases involved doesn't matter: MTS will manage a package's updates across all the databases involved.

MTS supports the major transaction industry standard protocol, XA. Microsoft's Distributed Transaction Control (DTC) package must also be running on the computer with MTS since it's the DTC that actually manages transactions for MTS.

MTS effectively issues all three of the transaction commands (start, commit, and abort) on behalf of the objects under its completion. Should an object run to completion successfully, MTS notifies all the participating DBMSs that the updates performed since the transaction began should be committed. If the application abends, MTS notifies the DBMSs that all the updates should be discarded. This functionality is provided for any component under MTS's control without the addition of any additional code.

STARTING A TRANSACTION

In Visual Basic 6, you can control when MTS notifies the DBMS that a transaction has begun for an object by setting the MTSTransactionMode property on your class module. The four available settings are:

- *NoTransactions:* The updates made by this object are never discarded.
- *RequiresNewTransaction:* MTS will notify the DBMSs involved that a transaction has begun.
- *UsesTransactions:* No start of transaction message will be issued but this object's updates can be discarded if it is called from another object as part of a transaction.
- *RequiresTransaction:* If the DBMSs have not been notified that a transaction has begun, they will be notified.

You can also set the transaction requirements for a component from the Transaction tab of an object's Properties dialog in MTS Explorer. This is your only option for Visual Basic 5 components.

The differences between the various settings may seem subtle. However, these four choices will cover all the transaction management situations that you will run into. As an example of the ways that you can use these settings, I use an object that updates a log file of activity in the system: the Audit object. The audit object is called by other objects in the system to record the activity performed by the calling object. Audit adds records to a table in the application database to provide a history of the activity in the system. Depending on how important it is to have a complete audit log, you might pick any one of the four transaction settings (see Figure 12–4).

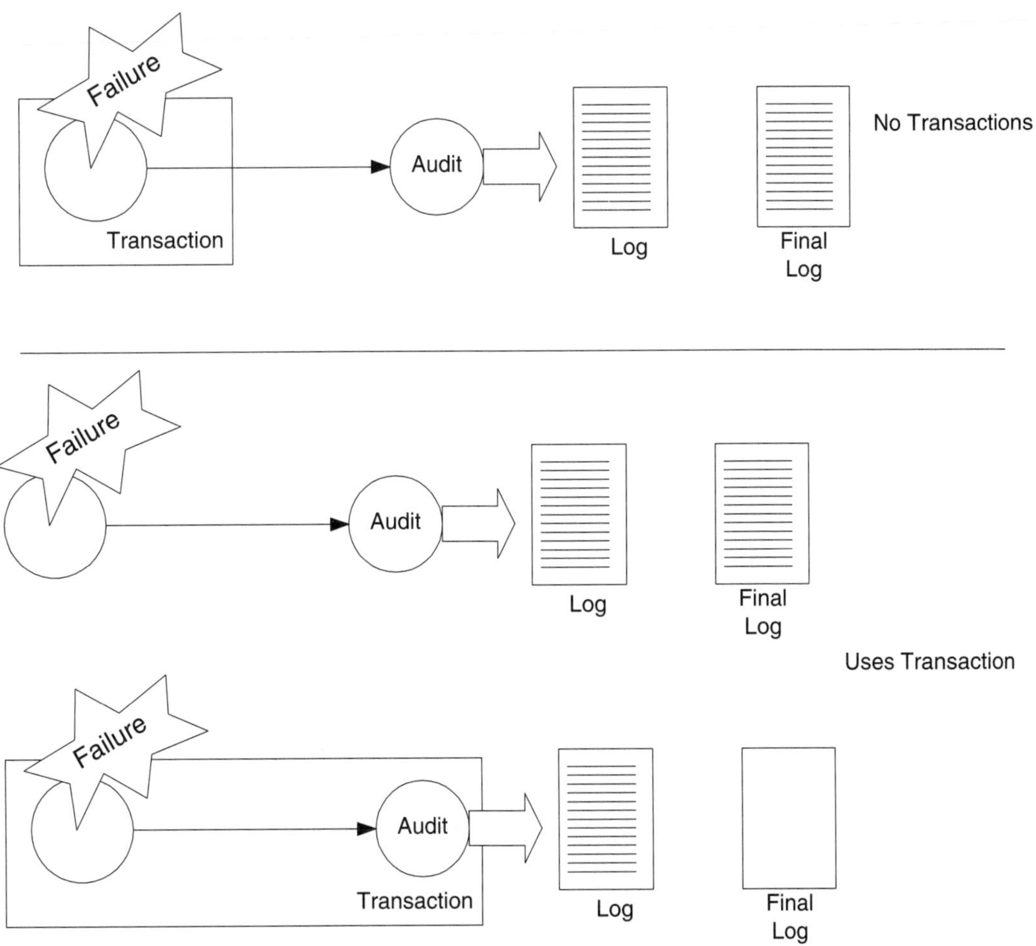

Figure 12–4 *Using the Audit object in four different transaction modes.*

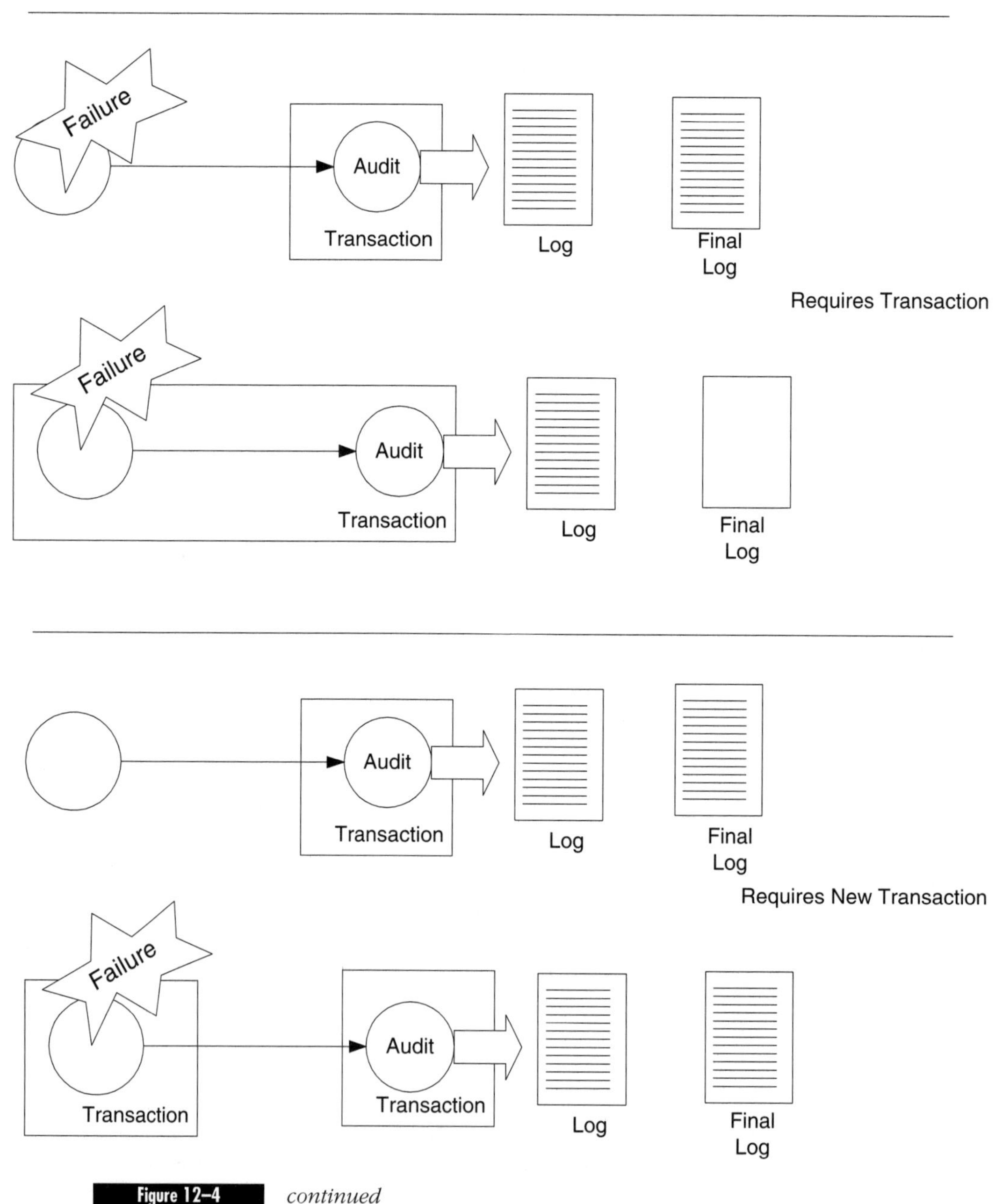

Figure 12–4 *continued*

For instance, you might want Audit to record every activity in the system, even the when the resulting updates are discarded. In this scenario, you would set the object's MTSTransactionMode to NoTransactions. By making this setting you guarantee that no audit records will ever be lost. MTS will not start a transaction for the Audit object and, as a result, its updates will never be lost. If a transaction has been started when Audit is started, the updates made by the Audit object will not be part of it.

In a different scenario, you might want the Audit object to take its direction from the object that it is called from. If the object that calls Audit is running in a transaction, you might want Audit to run in a transaction also. In this scenario, if the calling object abends and its updates are discarded, you want the Audit updates discarded also. In this scenario the assumption is that if the calling object's updates get backed out, there's no point in keeping the audit log for those discarded updates. On the other hand, if the audit log is called from an object that isn't using transactions (which means that its updates will never be discarded), you want Audit to also run in a non-transaction mode so that audit records are never lost. The UsesTransaction setting would give you that behavior. MTS will never issue a start transaction message for the object but, if the calling object is in a transaction, Audit will participate in that transaction.

In the third scenario, the audit log is regarded as a useful but not essential feature. If something goes wrong while creating the audit records, it's all right to lose the audit records. However, you don't want the updates made by the calling object to be discarded just because the Audit object blew up. The RequiresNewTransaction settings causes MTS to issue a start transaction message when Audit starts running. Should the Audit object abend, all the updates made by the Audit object will be discarded. However, the updates made by the calling object will be untouched. Audit would have a transaction inside of the transaction that it is called from.

A transaction inside another transaction is called a "nested transaction."

Finally, you might want your Audit object to always run in a transaction, even if it's called from an object that doesn't use transactions. In this scenario, you're concerned that if something goes wrong with Audit's updates, then Audit's record of the system's activity won't be accurate. You want Audit's records either to be completely accurate or discarded. If Audit is called from an object that is in a transaction, then you want Audit to be part of that transaction so that if the calling object's updates are discarded Audit's record will also be discarded. However, if Audit is called from an object that doesn't use transactions, in this scenario, you still want Audit's updates to be in a transaction. You've decided that Audit's updates should be backed out if something goes wrong, even if the calling object's updates are not. The RequiresTransaction setting would give you this behavior. With RequiresTransaction, MTS will not send a start transaction message if a transaction has already been started (in that way, this setting is like UsesTransactions). However, MTS will send a start transaction message if there isn't a transaction running (unlike UsesTransaction). Table 12.1 summarizes the four settings.

Table 12.1 MTSTransactionMode Settings

Setting	Description
RequiresNewTransaction	Always start a transaction, nested if necessary. Updates can be discarded.
RequiresTransaction	Start a transaction if one hasn't been started. Updates can be discarded.
UsesTransaction	Never start a transaction, but participate in any existing transactions. Updates may or may not be discarded.
NoTransactions	Never start a transaction. Updates are never discarded.

With MTS you cannot start a transaction using code. MTS will issue the start transaction command based on the declarative transaction requirements for the component.

INTEGRATING TRANSACTION MANAGEMENT

You can further integrate your object with MTS by using the methods that the ObjectContext object provides for working with transactions. Two of the methods (EnableCommit and DisableCommit) signal the status of your updates to MTS. The IsInTransaction method returns True if your object is running in a Transaction. Finally, CreateInstance allows you to start another object and have it be part of your transaction.

If you have provided sufficient error handling in your object, it's entirely possible that something could go horribly wrong with your object's updates, but your code might not abend. In this case, MTS will assume that it's all right to have your updates written to the database.

Typically, you issue the ObjectContext object's DisableCommit method as part of your error handling in order to signal to MTS that something is not right with the updates your component has made. When MTS gets a Disable-Commit message from any object in a transaction, MTS will discard all the updates made in the transaction, regardless of which object made them. The ObjectContext object also has an EnableCommit method that indicates to MTS that the updates made by your object have gone well.

Using the EnableCommit method does not guarantee that your object's updates will be committed. Only if none of the objects in a transaction issue a DisableCommit will MTS guarantee that the updates will be made.

The following code, for instance, gets a reference to the ObjectContext object. Once that reference is retrieved, the code creates an error handler that transfers control to error handling code at the bottom of the routine if anything goes wrong. In the error handling code, the routine uses the Disable-Commit method to indicate to MTS that updates that have been performed should be discarded. If no error occurs, however, the code will finish with an EnableCommit before exiting the routine.

```
Dim ctx As ObjectContext
Set ctx = AppServer.GetObjectContext

On Error GoTo BadUpdates

'updates to multiple databases
ctx.EnableCommit

ExitLabel:
  Exit Sub

BadUpdates:
  ctx.DisableCommit
  Resume ExitLabel
```

Not all MTS objects are in transactions. MTS will never run a library package in a transaction, for instance. An object with an MTSTransactionMode of UsesTransactions may or may not be in a transaction, depending on how it was called. EnableCommits and DisableCommits are unnecessary when the object isn't in a transaction. You may also want to take some special action if your code isn't executing in a transaction. The ObjectContext object's IsIn-Transaction method allows you to check whether you are in a transaction and skip calling the two commit methods. The method returns True when the object is in a transaction and False when the object is not. Rewriting the error handled from the previous example to take advantage of IsInTransaction would give you this code:

```
BadUpdates:
  If ctx.IsInTransacton = True Then
    ctx.DisableCommit
  End If
  Resume ExitLabel
```

COORDINATING UPDATES

EnableCommit and DisableCommit make it very easy for you to create transactions that use multiple objects, all of which make updates. Normally, you would have to add the code to each object to have it start a transaction. You would then have to work out some way to check that each object succeeded in all of its updates. When you had that confirmation, you could then call each object to have it finish its transaction. Without this kind of code, you couldn't be sure that one object had not discarded all of its updates while the other objects wrote their updates to the database.

Under Microsoft Transaction Server, either all objects in a transaction complete successfully, or none do. If any one of the objects in the transaction issues a DisableCommit, then all of the updates for all of the objects in the transaction will be discarded. No code to coordinate updates among the objects is required in order to ensure that transaction management is maintained.

The essential phrase in the previous paragraph is "all objects in a transaction." If an object under the control of MTS creates another object using either New or CreateObject, that new object will be in a different transaction. In order to create a new object in the same transaction, you must use the CreateInstance method of ObjectContext object to create the object. This code, for instance, creates an object with a progid of MyComponent.MyObject in the same transaction as itself:

```
Dim ctx As ObjectContext
Dim myo As MyComponent.MyObject


Set ctx = AppServer.GetObjectContext
Set myo = ctx.CreateInstance("MyComponent.MyObject")
```

Since CreateInstance was used to create MyObject, it will be part of the object's transaction (unless its Transaction mode is set to NoTransactions or RequiresNewTransactions). Should either the object that uses this code or MyObject, issue a DisableCommit, the updates for both objects will be discarded (see Figure 12–5).

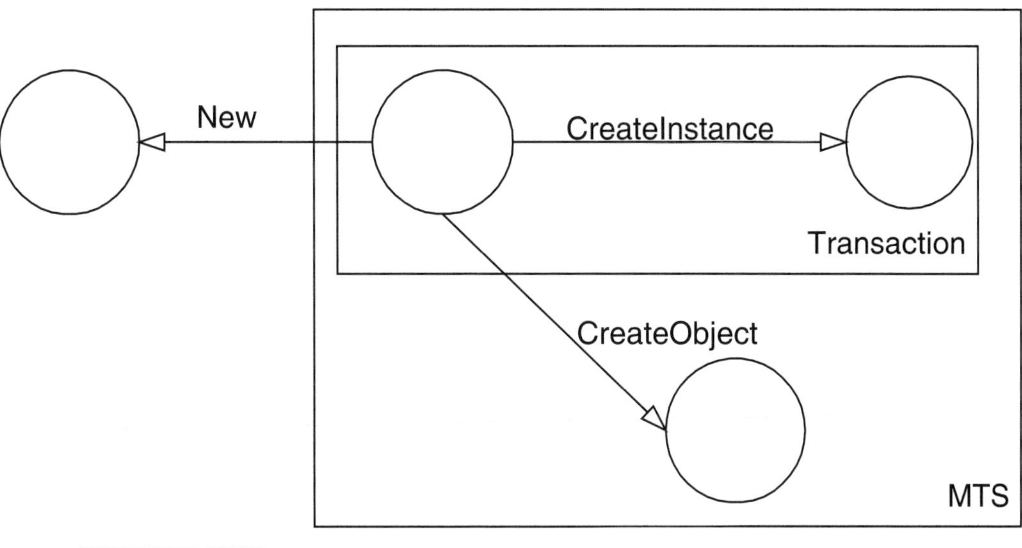

Figure 12–5 *CreateInstance, New, and CreateObject.*

warning

If the object being created is not under the control of MTS, then CreateInstance functions like CreateObject and the object will not be part of your object's transaction. If you use New instead of CreateInstance, the object will be created outside of MTS and will also not be part of your object's transaction.

While I've concentrated on database management systems in this discussion, you can use ActiveX Data Objects to read and write a wide variety of data sources. If those data sources support any of the transaction protocols that MTS supports, those data sources can also participate in MTS transactions.

Security

Microsoft Transaction Server implements security through roles. Using MTS Explorer, you can establish a set of roles for your package during the devel opment of your component. Once your roles have been created, you can assign them to the interfaces in the package. At implementation time you can finally assign users or groups from the NT file system to the roles. With MTS security enabled for a package, only users in one of the roles assigned to an interface will be able to use the interface. A single interface can be assigned multiple roles and a single user can be assigned to multiple roles. This declarative approach to security eliminates most of the security code that you would otherwise have had to write. As long as you design your interfaces so that they contain all and only the methods required by a specific set of users, declarative security will handle all of your security needs.

Roles are enforced only when a client requests an object within a package. Roles are not enforced when an object in a package uses another object in the package. For instance, ObjectM might have been assigned the Manager role while ObjectC was assigned the Clerk role. Only users with the Manager role can start ObjectM and only users with the Clerk role can start ObjectC. However, if ObjectM starts ObjectC, no error is raised because security is checked only for the object directly interacting with the client. On the other hand, if ObjectM returns a reference to ObjectC to the client, the client will not be able to use the reference unless the client is in the Clerk role.

PROGRAMMATIC SECURITY

However, in addition to the declarative security managed through MTS Explorer, MTS provides a set of methods with the ObjectContext object that allow you to build your own, custom security. The first method to use is IsSecurityEnabled, which lets you check to see whether security checking is available. The IsSecurityEnabled method returns True if security checking is being performed. Security checking isn't available if the object is running in a Library package or under MTS in Windows 98.

Programmatic security can be used in conjunction with MTS declarative, role-based security. While you may allow your object to be used by several different roles, there may be some methods or properties that should be available to only some of the roles that can access the object. Ideally, you would segregate those methods or properties to separate interfaces, but as the number of interfaces on your object multiplies, it becomes more difficult for clients to work with your object. The IsCallerInRole method allows you to check to see if the user who has requested your object is in a specific role. Passed the name of a role, this method returns True if the caller is in the specified role.

Don't ever delete a role that's referenced in your component. Passing IsCallerInRole the name of a role that doesn't exist in your package causes your object to abend.

In the following code, the routine checks to see if security is enabled. If it is, the code checks to see if the user accessing this routine is in the 'Manager' role. If the user isn't in the Manager role, the code exits the subroutine:

```
Dim ctx As ObjectContext
Set ctx = AppServer.GetObjectContext
  If ctx.IsSecurityEnabled = True Then
    If ctx.IsCallerInRole("Manager") <> True Then
      Exit Sub
  End If
End If
```

A user may be assigned to multiple roles and, since IsCallerInRole returns True for all the roles that a user has been assigned to, you shouldn't reject a user because they are in a specific role. For instance, a user assigned to the Manager role might also be assigned to the Clerk role so that the user could access other objects in the package. While the Clerk role isn't allowed to use this routine, the Manager role is. As the code above shows, the correct practice is to check to see if the user is a member of the permitted group and then allow them to run the routine. Had the code checked if the user was a member of the Clerk group and then rejected the user, valid users would not be able to run the routine since some Managers are also Clerks.

Roles are not used if the client creates the object with CreateObject rather than the New keyword. So, once roles have been assigned to the object and security enabled in MTS Explorer, the client will not be able to use your object with CreateObject.

In some cases, role-based security may not be appropriate because you want to know the identity of the person who created or called the object. In addition, it is possible for the client who calls the current method to be different from the client that created the object. As an example, a client could create an object and pass a reference to the object to another application being run by another user. Role based security does not distinguish between the client who created the object and the client who is currently using it. MTS's SecurityProperty object allows you to write code that returns the name of either the user calling a method or the name of the user who created the object.

You can retrieve the SecurityProperty object from the SecurityProperty property of the ObjectContext object. This code, for instance, checks to see if the person who called the object is "Peter Vogel" and exits the routine if it is not:

```
Dim ctx As ObjectContext
Dim scp As SecurityProperty

Set ctx = AppServer.GetObjectContext
Set scp = ctx.SecurityProperty
If csp.GetOriginalCallerName = "Peter Vogel" Then
  Exit Sub
End If
```

The four properties of the SecurityProperty object are listed in Table 12.2.

Table 12.2 The SecurityProperty Object's Properties

Property Name	Description
GetDirectCallerName	Returns the userid of the user who called the object.
GetDirectCreatorName	Returns the userid of the user who created the object.
GetOriginalCallerName	Returns the userid of the user who called the original object that resulted in this object having its method or property called.
GetOriginalCreatorName	Returns the userid of the user who created the original object that resulted in this object having its method or property called.

Scalability

My feeling is that the term "scalable" gets tossed around a lot with nobody really understanding what it means. Some more naive developers seem to use "scalable" to mean that an unlimited number of users can be added to an application without any degradation in performance.

If the word "scalable" means anything anymore, it means that the performance of your application will degrade gracefully as the load increases. In other words, if you double the number of users, response time will—at worst—double. A non-scalable system is one that "walks over a cliff" when a certain number of users is reached. With a non-scalable application, adding one more user can cause your response time to increase catastrophically. All applications become unusable when the load gets large enough. Technically, no application is "scalable," but an application can be more or less scalable.

Microsoft Transaction Server attempts to improve the scalability of your application by reducing the load on the computer running your components. MTS does this by reducing the copies of your code loaded at any one time.

LOADING AND UNLOADING

I've already discussed Just-In-Time activation where MTS defers creating your object until the client actually uses one of its methods and properties. This feature is provided to every component that is under the control of MTS without you having to add any code to your component.

You can, however, further integrate your component with MTS by using some additional methods of the ObjectContext object. The SetComplete and SetAbort methods perform the same function as EnableCommit and Disablecommit, but go beyond them to support improved scalability. In addition to indicating the state of your updates, SetComplete and SetAbort also indicate to

MTS that your object has completed all of its work and can be removed from memory. You can substitute SetComplete and SetAbort for EnableCommit and DisableCommit in your component, provided that you understand the impact that this will have on your component's state management.

When your code calls the ObjectContext's SetComplete or SetAbort methods, MTS uses this to determine if the package's updates should be discarded, just as it does for EnableCommit and DisableCommit. As with DisableCommit, if one object issues a SetAbort, all of the updates in the transaction, by any of the objects involved in the transaction, will be discarded.

In addition, with SetComplete and SetAbort, MTS also deactivates your component, reducing its demands on the server's resources. When the client calls another method or property for your object, MTS activates your component to service the client's request. Windows will not call your object's Intialize and Terminate events when MTS activates and deactivates your component.

The client remains unaware of the object being activated and deactivated. The client continues to interact with the ObjectContext object, which remains in memory at all times. The ObjectContext object makes it appear to the client that the object that it created is always available (see Figure 12–6).

STATE MANAGEMENT

One of the side affects of deactivating your object is that all the data in your object's internal variables is lost. Effectively, your object has no way of knowing what action it performed last because it can't use module level variables to store information from one method or property call to another. Your object is said to be stateless, a condition which has its own set of problems.

I illustrate what I mean by looking at the problem from the client's point of view. Typically, object that manages customer information might be used like this:

```
Dim cst As Customer
Set cst = New Customer
cst.ID = "Peter Vogel"
MsgBox cst.StreetAddress
cst.StreetAddress = txtNewAddress
```

The last four lines of this routine, presumably, would display and update the address for the customer "Peter Vogel." The object is assumed to maintain its state between the times that its properties are used. When the StreetAddress property is used by the client, the object remembers that the ID property was set to "Peter Vogel" in the previous call and retrieves the StreetAddress for "Peter Vogel." The object is stateful because it knows what it did last.

A stateless object, on the other hand, has no way of keeping track of what happened the last time that it was called. As a result, when the StreetAddress

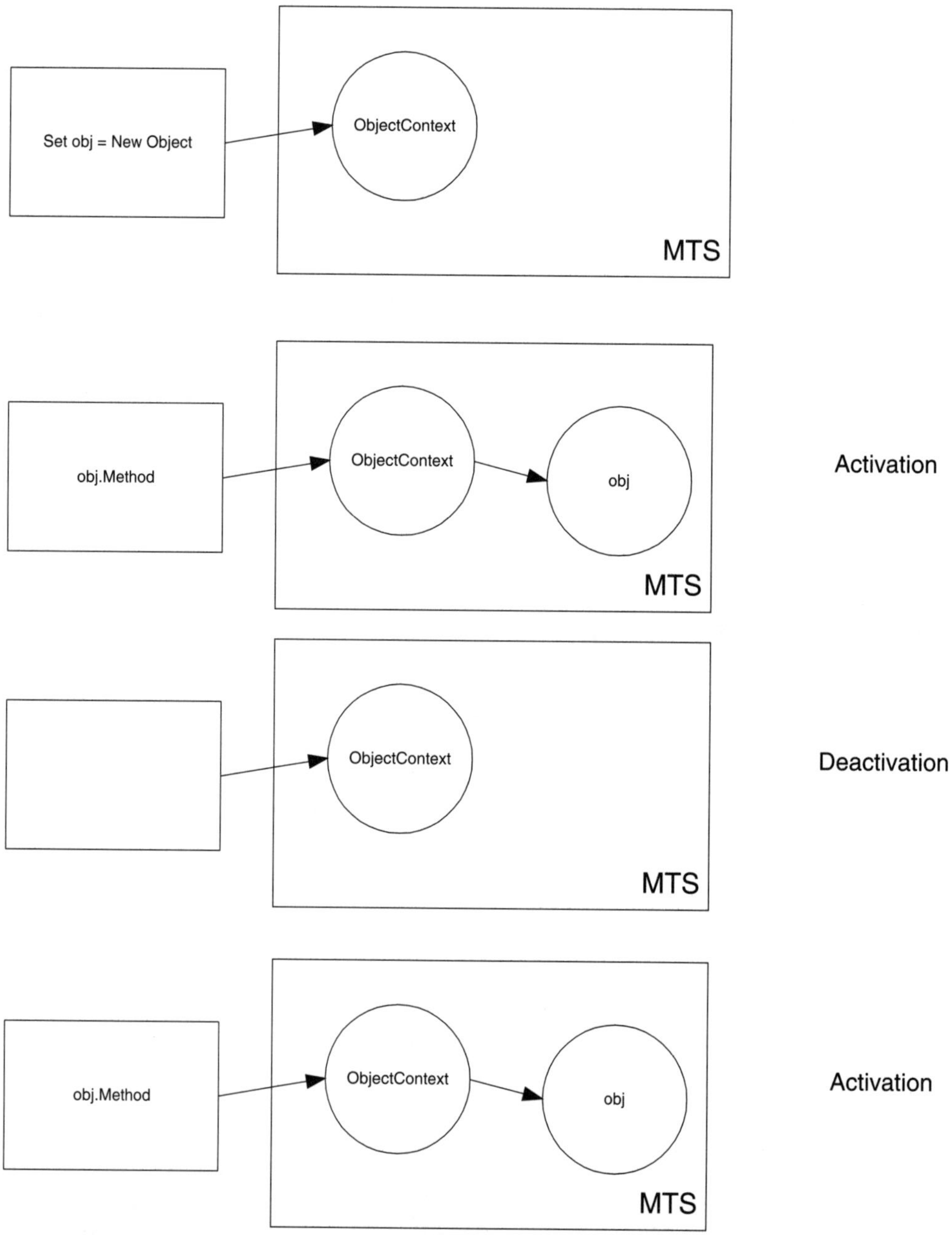

Figure 12–6 *Activation and deactivation.*

property is used, the code in the object has no way of determining which record to retrieve to get the customer address. The object doesn't remember what customer it was working with in the previous call. This is what would occur if the object's code called the SetComplete or SetAbort methods at the end of ID property routine. Those methods would signal to MTS that the Customer object could be deactivated, making the object stateless.

Using SetComplete and SetAbort improves the scalability of applications that use your component by making them stateless. If you want to use SetComplete and SetAbort, then you must either create a stateless object or store your state in some convenient place.

It may well be that your object is stateless by design. For instance, if the methods and properties that make up your object are unrelated to each other, then they may not need to share data. This is the situation when your object is really just a library of useful routines to be called by the client.

You can also create a stateless client by having the client pass all the necessary information to your object each time that the client calls a method on the object. One way to rewrite my previous example to demonstrate this technique would have me convert the address properties to methods and have the client pass the Customer ID on each call:

```
Dim cst As Customer
Set cst = New Customer
MsgBox cst.StreetAddress("Peter Vogel")
cst.ChangeStreetAddress("Peter Vogel", txtNewAddress)
```

In this code, the StreetAddress Property Let has become the StreetAddress function which, when passed a customer ID, returns the customer's address. The StreetAddress Property Get becomes the ChangeStreetAddress subroutine, which accepts the ID of the customer to change and the new address. If you take advantage of Visual Basic's ability to pass multiple parameters to an object's property (as discussed in the chapter on objects), then you don't even have to convert the methods to properties.

```
Dim cst As Customer
Set cst = New Customer
MsgBox cst.Address("Peter Vogel")
cst.Address("Peter Vogel") = txtNewAddress
```

While rewriting the code wouldn't be a tremendously difficult task, the result is an object that is more difficult for your clients to use. Instead of just calling your object's methods or properties, the client is now also responsible for keeping track of the necessary state information and passing it to your object as needed.

Your second alternative is for your object to store its state information somewhere more permanent than its internal variables. Your object could, for instance, store enough information to recover its state in a database. This isn't a complete solution. At any one time, multiple copies of your object may be active. Each copy of the object will need some way to keep track of the primary key for the record that it wrote to the database. If your object doesn't know which record to read from the database, then the object can't retrieve the data it wrote to the database. Reading and writing a database will also slow down your object as it will now be limited by the speed of the hard disk that the DBMS is storing its data on.

THE SHARED PROPERTY MANAGER

Microsoft has provided the Shared Property Manager (SPM) as a place where objects can store information (Figure 12–7 shows the object model for the SPM). The Shared Property Manager stores your data in memory and so does not slow down your application the way that writing to a DBMS would. In many ways, the SPM functions like an ActiveX Control's Property Bag. Unlike a PropertyBag, the SPM allows you to organize your properties into groups, rather than treating each property individually.

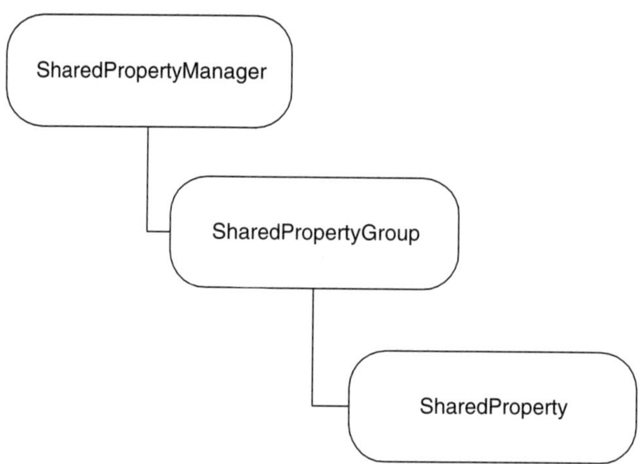

Figure 12–7 *The SharedPropertyManager object model.*

To use the Shared Property Manager, you must first add a reference to the Shared Property Manager Type Library to your Visual Basic project. Your components must then create a SharedPropertyGroupManager from this component using either CreateObject or CreateInstance from the components. In this code, I've used CreateInstance:

```
Dim ctx As ObjectContext
Dim pgm As SharedPropertyGroupManager
Dim spg As PropertyGroup

Set ctx = AppServer.GetObjectContext
```

```
Set pgm = _
  ctx.CreateInstance("MTxSPM.SharePropertyGroupManager.1")
```

Don't create or manipulate any SPM objects from your object's Initialize or Terminate events. The Initialize and Terminate events can occur before the ObjectContext is created and before the SharedPropertyGroupManager is ready for use with your package.

Once created, the Group Manager lets you create new groups of Shared-Property objects or retrieve existing groups. To retrieve a Group, you use the Manager's Group method. This code retrieves a group of properties called MyProperties:

```
Dim ctx As ObjectContext
Dim pgm As SharedPropertyGroupManager
Dim spg As PropertyGroup

Set ctx = AppServer.GetObjectContext
Set pgm = _
  ctx.CreateInstance("MTxSPM.SharePropertyGroupManager.1")
Set spg = pgm.Group("MyProperties")
```

Before any object in a package can retrieve a group, some object in the package must create it using the Group Manager's CreatePropertyGroup method. When you create a Group Manager, you specify what happens when two objects access the same property in a Group and when the Group will be destroyed. The CreatePropertyGroup method accepts four parameters: name of the group, lock type, persistence type, and an existence flag.

Naming the Group • The first parameter of the CreatePropertyGroup method allows you to give the PropertyGroup a name. If the PropertyGroup doesn't already exist, the method will create the group and return a reference to it.

If the PropertyGroup does already exist, the method returns a reference to the existing group and sets its last parameter (the existence flag) to True. Any settings that you specified in the second or third parameters of the method are ignored if the PropertyGroup already exists. Instead, the second and third parameters will be set to whatever value the already existing group has.

Since the last three parameters of the CreatePropertyGroup method can be used to return values, you should always use variables for those three parameters.

Locking the PropertyGroup • The second parameter of the CreatePropertyGroup method allows you to set the Group's isolation level or lock type. The isolation level controls how multiple clients will be allowed to access the properties in the Group. Passing the predefined constant LockSetGet in the method's second parameter sets the lowest level of locking. LockSetGet specifies that properties in the newly created Group are to be locked only while they are being read or written. This setting prevents two objects from updating the same property at the same time but doesn't prevent clients from accessing other properties in the Group while one property is being read or written. Also, with this setting, a property is locked only for as long as it takes to read or write it.

Alternatively, you can set the isolation level to LockMethod to specify that the whole Group is to be locked for as long as a method reading or writing any property in the Group is executing. You need the LockMethod option in two situations:

- When you need to change or read several properties as a group and it's important for the values in these properties to stay consistent while they are read
- When you retrieve a value from a property and use its value to update a property in the group

A counter provides the simplest example of when you need to use the LockMethod setting. With a counter, the code in an object retrieves the counter's current value from a property, adds 1 to it, and puts the resulting value back in the property. Without LockMethod, two objects might read the property sequentially and, as a result, get the same value. Both objects would then add 1 to the value that they had retrieved and put the result back in the property. The net effect is that the property would now understate the number of times it has been updated.

If the PropertyGroup's isolation level had been set to LockMethod, then, when the object reads the counter property, the Group would be locked. This would prevent any other object from changing the property until the update method finishes executing. The object that read the property could add 1 to the counter value, update the property, and finish, confident that all other objects would be locked out until its processing was finished. When the counter update method finished executing, other objects could access properties in the Group.

The LockMethod setting can slow down the responsiveness of clients using your objects as they wait for access to a property that is locked by another object.

PERSISTING THE GROUP • The third parameter passed to the CreatePropertyGroup method allows you to control when the group is to be destroyed. Passing Standard to this parameter indicates that the Group object is to be destroyed as soon as there is no variable pointing to the Group. This works well for clients that aren't activated and deactivated (i.e., aren't issuing SetAborts and SetCompletes). However, if the object that is using a Group is deactivated, all of the object's variables (including variables pointing to the Group) are destroyed. With the variables that refer to the Group destroyed, the Group will, as a result, be discarded.

A setting of Process for this parameter ensures that the Group will be around as long as the client continues to use the object. This is the setting that you should use when you are intending to use the SPM to maintain state in a stateless object.

The following code creates a PropertyGroup called "UnlockedProperties." Since the release mode parameter is set to Process, the PropertyGroup will not be destroyed until the client is through with the package. Updates to properties in this group are not based on the values in other properties, so the LockMethod setting is not required. The isolation level has been set to LockSetGet to prevent any object having to wait for another object to release a property. If the object already exists, the method's third parameter will be set to True and the method will return a reference to the already created UnlockedProperties Group:

```
Dim ctx As ObjectContext
Dim pgm As SharedPropertyGroupManager
Dim spg As PropertyGroup
Dim bolExists As Boolean
Dim lngIsolationLevel As Long
Dim lngReleaseMode As Long

Set ctx = AppServer.GetObjectContext
Set pgm = _
  ctx.CreateInstance("MTxSPM.SharePropertyGroupManager.1")
lngIsolationLevel = LockSetGet
lngReleaseMode = Process
Set spg = pgm.CreatePropertyGroup("UnlockedProperties", _
        lngIsolationLevel, lngReleaseMode, bolExists)
```

This code retrieves a reference to an existing PropertyGroup:

```
Dim ctx As ObjectContext
Dim pgm As SharedPropertyGroupManager
Dim spg As SharedPropertyGroup

Set ctx = AppServer.GetObjectContext
Set pgm = _
  ctx.CreateInstance("MTxSPM.SharedPropertyGroupManager.1")
Set spg = pgm.Group("UnlockedProperties")
```

CREATING PROPERTIES • Once a SharedPropertyGroup has been created, you can add SharedProperty objects to it to hold data for you. A SharedProperty is a variant, which means it can hold any data that you want, from numbers to dates, from arrays to object references. The PropertyGroup object provides two Create methods for adding SharedProperty objects: CreateProperty for creating named properties and CreatePropertyByPosition for numbered properties.

The CreateProperty method accepts two parameters: a name to identify the property that you wish to create and a flag that the SharedPropertyManager uses to tell you if a property with that name already exists. The CreatePropertyByPosition method also accepts two parameters: the number used to identify the property and a flag to indicate if that number has already been used. You can use 0 as the first property number. If the SharedProperty object already exists, the Create methods return a reference to that object.

This code uses the CreateProperty method to create a SharedProperty object called Savings. The code checks the bolExists parameter after the method executes to determine if the property already exists and, if it does, sets the property to zero:

```
Dim sp As SharedProperty
Dim bolExists As Boolean
Set sp = spg.CreateProperty("Savings", bolExists)
If bolExists = True Then
  spg.Property("Savings") = 0
End If
```

This code uses CreatePropertyByPosition method to create a SharedProperty object numbered 0. The code checks the bolExists parameter after the method executes to determine if the property already exists and, if it does, sets the property to zero:

```
Dim sp As SharedProperty
Dim bolExists As Boolean
Set sp = spg.CreatePropertyByPosition(0, bolExists)
If bolExists = True Then
  spg.PropertyByPosition(0) = 0
End If
```

To retrieve a named property, you use the PropertyGroup object's Property property. To retrieve a numbered property you must use PropertyByPosition property.

Using numbered properties will give you the fastest code, but creating properties with names makes your code easier to read. With this code, for instance, it's hard to determine what is actually being accomplished:

```
spg.PropertyByPosition(0) = spg.PropertyByPosition(0) - 25
spg.PropertyByPosition(1) = spg.PropertyByPosition(1) + 25
```

This code, using named properties, is clearer:

```
spg.Property("Savings") = spg.Property("Savings") - 25
spg.Property("Checking") = spg.Property("Checking") + 25
```

The Property and PropertyByPosition properties both return a reference to a SharedProperty object. In turn, the SharedProperty object's Value property returns the value held in the SharedProperty. You could rewrite the code that initializes the Savings property like this:

```
Set sp = pg.Property("Savings")
sp.Value = 0
```

However, there's no performance gain to rewriting the code this way and most programmers would probably consider the rewritten version harder to read than the original.

A Property Group should be shared only among objects in the same DLL. Since the Shared Property Manager associates data with the package, trying to share properties among DLLs can be risky. If your object passes information between DLLs in the same package by having them read the same property group, your code will fail if the DLLs are later moved into separate packages.

When an object in another DLL is accessed, shared information should be passed in a method or property call. The object in the second DLL can then save the information in its own property group if it needs to.

MAINTAINING STATE • While the SPM gives you an efficient way to store information, the Property Groups that your objects create are associated with the Package that the object is part of. Every user that accesses the package will share the same properties. If you want to use the SPM to maintain state, then you'll need some way to separate the state information for one client from state information from another.

One way is to create a separate Property Group for each client. To make this work you'll need some way to identify which Group belongs to each client. One way is to generate an identifier for each client and return that value to the client. On each call, the client will need to pass that identifier back to your object so that you can retrieve the state information. You will need a method or property that the client will use when it starts to interact with your object. In this method or property you will generate the ID and return it to the client.

The Customer object that I used at the start of this chapter would be an example of this approach. The Customer ID could be used to identify the state information for a particular customer. Each subsequent call to the Customer object would have to include the Customer ID to allow the object to retrieve the appropriate SharedProperty objects. While the Customer object might have to use multiple SharedProperty objects in order to maintain state, the Customer object's clients would only have to keep track of the Customer ID.

This approach is quite flexible as it allows a single client to work with several clients simultaneously just by requesting multiple Customer IDs. However, you have to consider what will happen if multiple clients are working with the same customer. Since the Customer ID is being used to identify the PropertyGroup, two clients working with the same customer will be working with the same PropertyGroup. This may or may not be a problem, depending on how your component is written.

Another alternative is to use a value provided by the client to create a PropertyGroup for each client. As I discussed in the section on Security services, it is possible to retrieve the name of the client from the ObjectContext object. This technique doesn't require the client to explicitly pass an identifier to your routine since MTS provides the caller name automatically. However, in an n-tier distributed system, your object may be created by a package executing on another server. In this situation, GetDirectCallerName returns the name of the server, not the ultimate user. As a result, many objects might share the same direct caller name, as they are all accessed by packages running on the other server.

ACTIVATION AND DEACTIVATION

If you want to save and restore state you are going to have to add code to perform those activities to your object. You could place code to retrieve state at the start of each method or property, and code to save state at the end of each routine. This approach would allow you to retrieve only the values required by the specific routine and save only those values that changed by the routine. While very efficient, this would also result in a lot of duplicated code as many methods and properties would save and retrieve the same values.

MTS provides you with two methods that you can use to eliminate this duplicated code. These methods are part of the ObjectControl interface which you can choose to implement in your object.

The ObjectControl method requires you to write an Activate and a Deactivate method for your object (and the CanBePooled method, which I discuss later). MTS will call the Activate method just after activating your object and before running the method or property requested by the client that triggered your object's reactivation. The Deactivate method will be called after the method completes and before your object is deactivated. Typically, the Activate method is used to read state information from the Shared Property Manager and the Deactivate method is used to write to it. These methods can be used to perform any activity that you need to have done as your object is activated and deactivated.

In this code, I use the ID property to create a SharedPropertyGroup named after direct caller, and initialize some values in it. In the Activate method, I retrieve the Group and move the property values into internal variables. Finally, in the Deactivate method, I move the variables back into the SPM:

```
Implements ObjectControl
Dim ctx As ObjectContext
Dim pgm As SharedPropertyGroupManager
Dim spg As SharedPropertyGroup

Dim bolStatus As Boolean
Dim curBalance As Currency

Public Property Let ID(CustId As String)
Dim bolExists As Boolean
Dim lngIsolationLevel As Long
Dim lngReleaseMode As Long
Dim sp As SharedProperty

Set ctx = AppServer.GetObjectContext
Set pgm =
  ctx.CreateInstance("MTxSPM.SharedPropertyGroupManager.1")
lngIsolationLevel = LockSetGet
lngReleaseMode = Process
Set spg = _
  pgm.CreatePropertyGroup(ctx.Security.GetDirectCallerName,
     lngIsolationLevel, lngReleaseMode, bolExists)
Set sp = spg.CreateProperty("Status", bolExists)
Set sp = spg.CreateProperty("Balance", bolExists)
spg.Property("Status") = False
spg.Property("Balance") = 0
End Property

Private Sub ObjectControl_Activate()

Set ctx = AppServer.GetObjectContext
Set pgm =
  ctx.CreateInstance("MTxSPM.SharedPropertyGroupManager.1")
Set spg = pgm.Group(ctx.Security.GetDirectCallerName)
bolStatus = spg.Property("Status")
curBalance = spg.Property("Balance")

End Sub

Private Sub ObjectControl Deactivate()
spg.Property("Status") = bolStatus
spg.Property("Balance") = curBalance
End Sub
```

POOLING OBJECTS

Under Windows 2000 and COM+, Microsoft Transaction Server implements object pooling. With object pooling, if an object loaded into memory is not currently being used by its client, MTS will let another client use the object. This reduces the load on the server by reducing the number of copies of the object required to satisfy all clients. Instead of having one copy of the object for every client that requested it, MTS keeps only enough copies to satisfy the clients that are currently using the object. If an object is used by a large number of clients that call its methods infrequently, pooling can reduce the number of objects that must be kept in memory (see Figure 12–8).

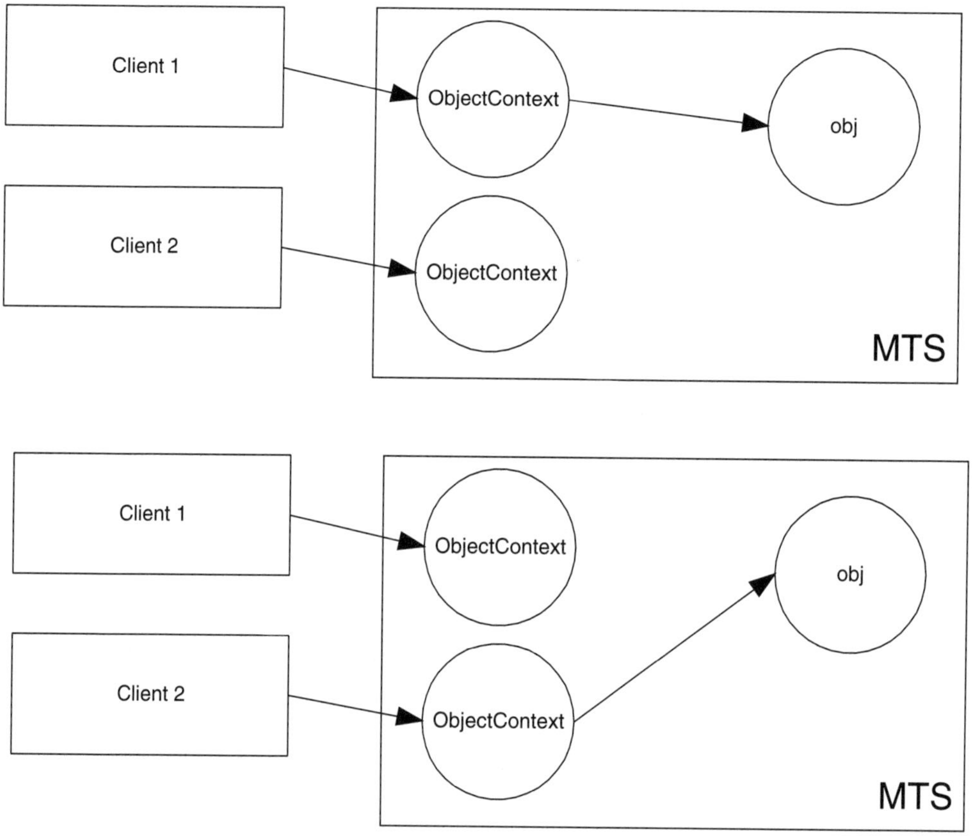

Client 1
ObjectContext
obj
Client 2
ObjectContext
MTS

Client 1
ObjectContext
obj
Client 2
ObjectContext
MTS

Figure 12–8 *Object Pooling.*

MTS under Windows NT 4.0 doesn't implement pooling. Under Windows 2000, Visual Basic components cannot be pooled because of the way that Visual Basic threads are handled.

If you have added the ObjectControl interface to your application, MTS will call the CanBePooled method for your object just after the Deactivate method. If this method returns True, MTS can share the object among all clients requesting it. Since MTS will assume that your object can't be pooled, you only need to add code to this routine if your object can be pooled. A typical CanBePooled routine (for an object that can be pooled) looks like this:

```
Private Function ObjectControl_CanBePooled() As Boolean
  ObjectControl_CanBePooled = True
End Function
```

Pooling makes sense when the Initialize code for an object performs a lot of time consuming non-client specific activities. By pooling an object, the number of times that the Initialize routine is called is reduced because a new object is not created.

Even though pooling isn't implemented in NT 4.0 and isn't available for Visual Basic 6.0 programs under Windows 2000, it's still a good idea to consider whether your object can be pooled. Microsoft introduced a new threading model with Windows 2000 and it's not impossible that the next version of Visual Basic will support it. If so, your objects could participate in pooling, provided that you have designed your object with pooling in mind.

RETURNING REFERENCES

On occasion, you may return a reference to your object to the client. This Property Get, for instance, returns a reference to the object that the routine is part of by using the Me keyword:

```
Public Property Get MeRef() As MyObject
  Set MeRef = Me
End Sub
```

Since a client interacts with an ObjectContext object rather than the object itself, you must never return a reference to your object to your client. Returning a reference to your object to the client would allow the client to bypass MTS. In fact, your reference may not even be valid if your object is currently deactivated. Your clients should always interact with your object through MTS's ObjectContext object. To handle this, the AppServer object provides the SafeRef method which returns a reference to your object that can be passed to a client. The SafeRef method converts a reference to your object into a reference that will not bypass the ObjectContext object. Rewriting the previous code to use SafeRef would give you this code:

```
Public Property Get MeRef() As MyObject
  Set MeRef = AppServer.SafeRef(Me)
End Sub
```

A more typical example is when your object creates another object and returns a reference to that object to the client. Here again, you must use SafeRef to return the object. This code creates a NewTransaction object and uses SafeRef to return a reference to the object to the client:

```
Public Function GetNextObject() As New.Transaction
Dim nobj As NewTransaction
Dim ctx As ObjectContext

Set ctx = AppServer.GetObjectContext
Set nobj = ctx.CreateInstance("New.Transaction")
Set GetNextObject = AppServer.SafeRef(nobj)
End Function
```

Distributing

If there's one process that I regularly get wrong when creating remote components, it's deploying the clients and components. I will forget to generate the remote server files when I compile the component but not realize this until I've installed the component on the server. So, I'll have to recompile the component to generate the remote server files for the client-side install. I then usually reinstall the component on the server just in case, somehow, the GUID's assigned to the component have somehow changed. Even with the remote server files in hand, I have to install them on all the client computers. As part of the client install, I must run DCOMCNFG to redirect all requests for the component to the server that the component is installed on.

Microsoft Transaction server simplifies this processes through the creation of PAK files. After creating a package in Transaction Server Explorer, you can right-click on the package and select Export. In the Export Package dialog that appears, you provide the name of the package to be created (see Figure 12–9). MTS will create a PAK file containing all of the information necessary to install your package under MTS. Setting the Save Windows NT Ids option on this dialog cause MTS to include the specific user ids that are assigned to each role in the PAK file. The Export function also copies all of the DLLs that make up the package into the directory that you create the PAK file in.

You can now install your package on any other computer running MTS. After selecting New | Package in MTS, you click on the Install Pre-Built Packages button and browse to the directory with your PAK file. MTS will read the PAK file, set up the package, and install all of the components that make up the package.

The Export operation also creates a Clients folder in the directory with the PAK file. This folder will contain an EXE file with the name you assigned to the PAK file. Running this executable on the client machine will make all the necessary registry entries on the client (including the entries that DCOMCNFG would make to redirect requests for the component to the server).

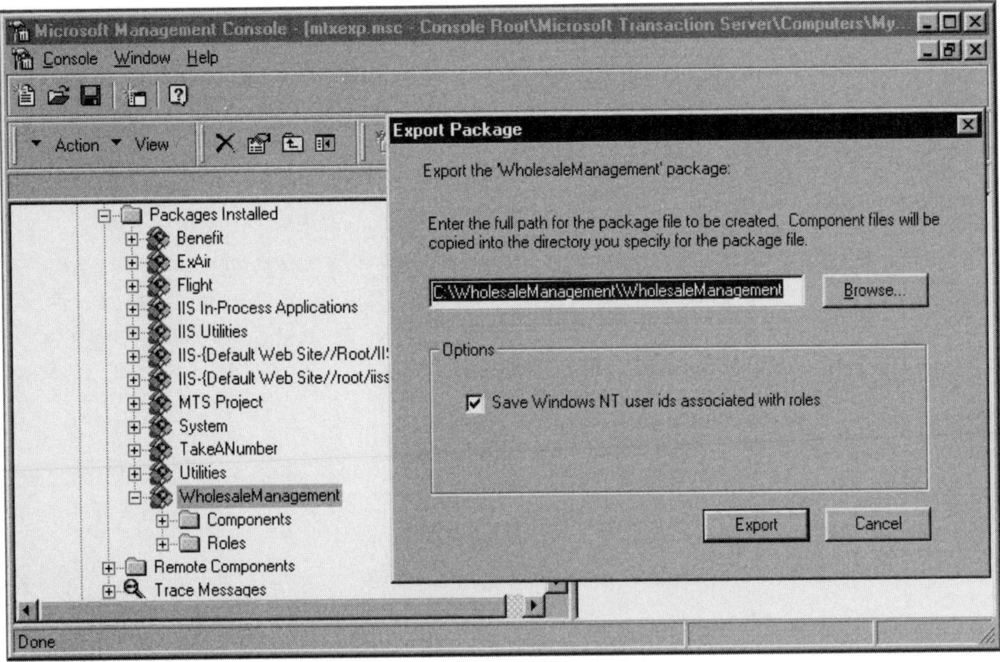

Figure 12–9 *Creating a PAK file using MTS Export feature.*

A copy of the component is also copied on the client (it's put in to the Program Files\Remote Applications directory in a subdirectory with the component's GUID).

Debugging

Debugging Microsoft Transaction Server components can be awkward. To make sure that your client is picking up the latest version of your component, you must

1. Recompile the component.
2. Delete and re-create the package.
3. Export the package.
4. On the client computer, run the Export's client EXE file.
5. In the client program, remove the object from the references list and re-add it.

With Visual Basic 6, Microsoft has provided a better way, provided that you are using Visual Basic on a Windows NT computer with MTS, and Service Pack 4 or later installed. You don't even have to put your object under the control of MTS, either: Simply setting the MTSTransactionMode is enough to cause Visual Basic to put your component under MTS's control when you start to debug.

There are a bunch of things that you can and can't do, though:

- You must set the project's compatibility options to Binary Compatibility.
- You cannot debug multiple components or use multiple clients.
- You cannot set watches on variables that should use SafeRef (e.g., references to objects created by CreateInstance, GetObjectContext, or SafeRef itself).
- You cannot debug code in either the Initialize or Terminate events.
- You cannot test security because the package is treated as a Library package. Your calls to IsSecurityEnabled will return False and IsCallerInRole will return True.

With Visual Basic 5.0, you can't fully debug your MTS modules from within the Visual Basic IDE. Your only alternative is to compile your program with the Create Symbolic Debug Info option set. This allows you to use the Symbolic Debugger that ships with Visual Studio and is normally used with compiled C or C++ programs.

If this seems like too much trouble, you can do some limited debugging of MTS components in Visual Basic 5. The Microsoft Knowledge Base article Q188919 describes how to add a registry key that will enable the ObjectContext object without the presence of MTS. The ObjectContext's transaction oriented methods (SetComplete, EnableCommit, etc.) have no effect in this environment. The ObjectContext's security methods mimic a Library package (i.e., IsSecurityEnabled and IsInTransaction return False, while IsCallerInRole returns True). CreateInstance will start an instance of the requested object.

When you're debugging security, changes that you make to roles and their assignments are not applied until the package finishes running. By default, MTS packages are left running for three minutes after the last method or property call to an object in the package.

Summary

In this chapter you've been introduced to the services that Microsoft Transaction Server can provide to your components. You've seen how MTS can make transaction management simpler, improve the scalability of the applications that use your components, and implement a flexible security system. You can get many of those benefits without tailoring your component to MTS at all.

I also showed you how you could improve your object's integration with MTS. By adding calls to EnableCommit and DisableCommit, you can signal the state of your updates to MTS. Using SetComplete and SetAbort, you can signal not only whether your updates should be committed, but also whether your object needed to be retained in memory (though at the cost of becoming stateless). Adding the three methods that make up the ObjectControl interface allows you to maintain state as your object is activated and deactivated. Finally, by designing your interfaces with the security needs of your application's users in mind, you can eliminate the need for any security-related code. You also saw how you would have to convert some of your existing code that uses New or CreateObject to use the CreateInstance method.

The Microsoft Help information on MTS is very complete. The book that I would recommend for more information on MTS is Scott Hillier's and Dan Mezick's *MTS Programming with Visual Basic* (Sams). The book goes beyond what you need to do with your objects to work with MTS and discusses a methodology for creating distributed applications. You'll also find more information on MTS's user interface, MTS Explorer.

At this point you need to start working with MTS. The technology behind MTS is essential to building and managing distributed components. I would begin by taking an existing component and adding it to a new MTS package. You could then create a PAK file by exporting the package, and run the resulting client EXE to make the package available to an application on another computer. This would give you a MTS component that takes advantage of the minimum sets of services provided by MTS. The next step is to integrate your objects with MTS by using the ObjectContext object and the ObjectControl interface. You'll probably be pleasantly surprised by how easy it is to build an MTS-compliant component.

THIRTEEN

Internet Components

*The Internet has created the possibility of building applications that can reach every breathing entity in the known universe. This opportunity has swept the development world like a firestorm. In front of the storm, the developers untouched by the Internet wait and worry; behind the firestorm, the landscape is changed forever. Within companies, the prevalence of Internet-based tools has triggered the development of intranet applications designed to run on local networks using Internet protocols. Programmers find no safe haven as the Internet based technologies burn their way into intranet applications that are used within the business. The term "i*net" was invented just to cover tools and application strategies used in both the Internet and intranet environments.*

Microsoft has camps on both sides of the firestorm's front. Prior to Visual Basic 6, there were a handful of ActiveX Controls that developers could add to their forms to gain access to the Internet. With Visual Basic 6, IIS and DHTML Applications explicitly provide a way to create Web based applications without leaving the Visual Basic environment.

Yet Visual Basic has always had a place in the i*net world, with or without these new additions. My personal explanation for why IIS and DHTML Applications were created is that the Visual Basic development team was told to get the word "Internet" onto the box that Visual Basic ships in any way that they could. Like ActiveX Documents, these two technologies are a good news–bad news story: Some of the technology is very useful, some of it is useful only in specific niches.

In this chapter, I'll introduce you to creating Web-based applications using Visual Basic. I'll outline how you can use Visual Basic in i*net development and why you'd want to. You'll see not only how to create and use the Web-oriented classes that come with Visual Basic 6, but the other ways that Visual Basic can be used to create Web-based applications.

I*Net Applications

I do quite a bit of i*net development. A lot of the tools and techniques that I use are the same ones that I use in non-internet client/server application development. However, the i*net world is very different from the ordinary world of client/server. So, before discussing how to use Visual Basic in Web development, I'm going to review the fundamentals of Web application development using Microsoft's tools.

The Internet is a network with the potential to include every computer in the world. To achieve this goal, the Internet uses a number of protocols that, effectively, define the Internet. The fundamental protocol is TCP/IP, which describes how messages are routed between computers and how computers identify themselves on the network.

Riding on top of TCP/IP are the protocols that define the various services that the Internet provides. These include POP/SMTP for electronic mail, FTP for transferring files, and HTTP for the World Wide Web. It's the Web that is currently the target for most application development, primarily because the Web allows you to deliver a user interface to any computer/operating system that has a Web browser.

Client/Server Development on the Web

Developing for the Web retains much of the structure of client/server development. The user runs some client program that makes requests to the server. The server supplies services to the client. The Web-based services are very clearly defined: The client (typically a browser) requests a page of text and the Web server responds by sending the requested page (or a standard error message) (see Figure 13–1).

The browser's request for a page is formatted as a Uniform Resource Locator or URL. The first part of the URL specifies the protocol to use to format the request. For Web activity, this defaults to HTTP. The next part of the URL specifies the server that the request is to be routed to and the port on the server to use (the default for the port is 80). The remainder of the URL specifies the full name of the file being requested. If the URL doesn't include the file name, the server will usually respond with a default file. You can also append data to the end of the URL to send to the server. Typically, the file that the browser requests contains plain text, but the request can also be the

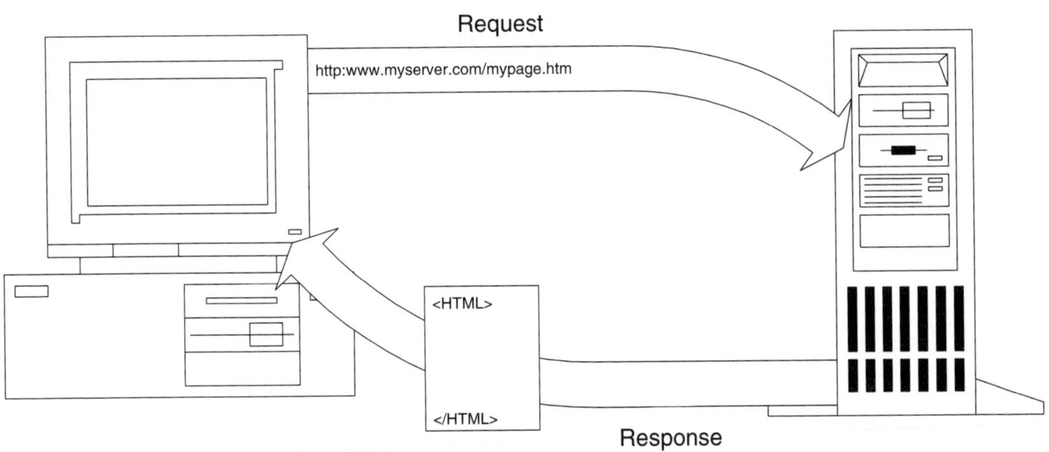

Figure 13–1 *The Request/Response cycle defines Web-based applications.*

name of a program to execute. However, even when the browser requests a program to run, the program must produce a text page to be sent back to the browser.

The browser that issues the request for the page also adds some information to the request for the file that contains the page. This additional information includes

- the address of the computer that sent the request (so that the page can be routed back to the browser).
- the name and version of the browser making the request.
- data entered into the page by the user while the page was displayed.
- information stored on the client computer the last time that a page was requested from the server.

The Web server receives this request and makes the information sent along with the request available to the processes running on the server computer. The server also retrieves the requested file and performs any processing on the file's contents prior to sending it to the browser. The result of the processing is a Web page that is sent back to the server. The page that is sent consists of nothing but text, formatted according the HTML specification. Like the browser, the server can include some additional information along with the page that's sent to the browser, including data to be stored on the client's computer. Once the page is sent to the client, the Web server goes on to service the next request for a page and loses all interest in the previous client.

When the client receives the page that it requested from the server, the browser begins to parse and display the HTML text that makes up the page. This text consists of two things: text to be displayed (content) and tags (formatting instructions). Tags are identified by being enclosed in less than and greater than characters (< and >) and are not displayed. Instead, the tags are used by the browser to control how the page's content is to be displayed. Some tags trigger further requests to Web servers. The <IMG> tag, for instance, causes the browser to request a graphic file from a Web server while the <OBJECT> and <APPLET> tags cause the browser to request a program to be downloaded from a server to be run on the client.

There are two interesting features about this process. I'm using the term "features" here in the same sense that it is used in the sentence, "That's not a bug, that's a feature." One feature is that the Web server sees each request for a page (or image, or program) as a separate activity. The Web server has no sense of an ongoing "conversation" between the client and the server. Web applications are stateless.

The second feature is that there are really two completely divorced development environments in the Web world. The browser is the host for your client-side development. On receiving a page, the browser will do whatever the page tells it to do. You can target some of the functionality of your application to be client-side processing by controlling what text you place in the page sent to the browser. You can, for instance, embed client-side script code or have the browser request the download of other programs.

The other development environment is the Web server. When a page is requested, the server can use the data that accompanies the request for a page using server-side code. On the server, you can also prepare the page that is to be sent to satisfy the browser's request.

HTML AND DHTML ELEMENTS

From the developer's point of view, a page is made up of elements. An HTML element is any object defined by an HTML tag that has a Name attribute. This tag, for instance, defines a H1 element because it has a Name attribute:

```
<H1 Name=MyHeading>
```

Once you assign a name to a tag, you can manipulate the element from the script code on the page. I can retrieve the Name property of the element in my previous example with code like this:

```
strName = window.document.MyHeading.Name
```

An HTML element has its methods, properties, and events defined by the World Wide Web Consortium (W3C) as part of the Document Object Model specification (the W3C is also the body responsible for the HTML specification). Of course, browser vendors can extend the Document Object Model specification in their browsers.

A DHTML element is any tag with an Id attribute. This code defines an H1 tag as a Dynamic HTML (DHTML) element:

```
<H1 Id=MyHeading>
```

Once assigned an Id attribute, the element has all the methods, properties, and events specified in the DHTML object model. However, the object model for DHTML is not yet completely defined. The draft W3C specifications do seem to resemble the implementation found in Internet Explorer 4 and 5. There are a number of differences between the Document Object Model and the DHTML model, but the chief is that DHTML allows far more control over the elements of a page than DOM.

A tag can be both an HTML and DHTML element by having both Name and Id attributes.

The Microsoft Tools

Microsoft offers tools to create Web applications for both the client and server-side environments. On the client, Microsoft's tool of choice is the Internet Explorer Web browser. Two of Internet Explorer's features are important to these Web development classes. First, in addition to downloading and displaying Web pages, Internet Explorer supports downloading, installing, and executing fully compiled ActiveX Controls. Internet Explorer also supports DHTML. DHTML allows programs executing in the browser to completely change display of the page currently being viewed in the browser.

Not all browsers support the same capabilities. In the section on DHTML Applications, I concentrate on Internet Explorer because it is the only browser that supports ActiveX Controls and the version of DHTML used by DHTML Applications. This effectively limits DHTML Applications to intranet development.

On the server, Microsoft offers Active Server Pages (ASP) running on Microsoft's Web server, Internet Information Server (IIS). ASP provides a way for developers to generate the page to be sent to the browser when the page is requested. ASP allows the developer to embed code in their Web pages and, as the page is sent to the browser, have ASP execute the code in the page. The executing code can process the data sent with the request and modify the page before it is sent to the client.

Microsoft's tools support the Web development paradigm. On the server side, you can modify the page that is being sent to the browser. Some of the features of this Web based technology can seem to blur this distinction, so you need to bear it in mind to understand what is happening when you develop Web applications using Visual Basic.

Web Development With Visual Basic

So how do Visual Basic's Web-oriented classes fit into the model of Web application development that I've sketched out here? Visual Basic's development tools include two different kinds of tools: DHTML Applications and IIS Applications.

DHTML Applications allow you to create ActiveX Controls that the browser can download to the user's computer (provided that the user is using Internet Explorer). These ActiveX Controls can access the DHTML-enabled tags in your Web page to modify the page after it is received in the browser.

IIS Applications allow you to create ActiveX components that will run on the Web server and use objects from the ASP environment. IIS Application components allow you to create and modify Web pages after they are requested by the user and before they are sent to the browser.

The two kinds of Web application development tools that Microsoft provides in Visual Basic, then, give support for development on the client and on the server: DHTML for client-side development, IIS Applications for server-side development. But it's also important that you realize that you don't need to use DHTML or IIS applications to integrate Visual Basic with Web development. You can use DHTML to manipulate a Web page by using script code embedded within the page itself, for instance, without creating a DHTML Application. In addition, any ActiveX Control that you create can be used as part of a Web page without it having to be explicitly designated a DHTML application. You also can create pages with server-side ASP code that call ActiveX components with creating IIS Applications. However, all of these other solutions require you to use some tool in addition to Visual Basic. What Visual Basic 6 allows you to do is create Web-based applications without ever leaving the familiar interface of Visual Basic.

ActiveX Designers

Visual Basic 6 also makes explicit the concept of using a designer, but designers really aren't new to Visual Basic. As a Visual Basic programmer, you know that you get one kind of window when you're editing a module and a different kind of window when you're editing a form. The Code window and the Form Design window were two different editors that shipped with Visual Basic.

An ActiveX Designer is a tool to help you create an object. An ActiveX Designer will provide an environment that supports the creation of a specific kind of object. An ActiveX Designer will provide you with specific properties, methods, and events that you require for the object. The UserControl designer, for instance, provides support for creating ActiveX Controls. ActiveX Designers typically include a run-time component that must either be distributed with your object or compiled into your DLL or EXE.

With Visual Basic 6 you can add additional ActiveX Designers to your development environment. You add a new designer to a Visual Basic project the same way that you would add an ActiveX Control, by selecting Components from the Project menu. Once the Component dialog displays, click on Designers tab (see Figure 13–2), which presents you with a list of ActiveX Designers installed on your computer. Any Designers that you check off will be added to your Project menu with the entry "Add *designer*" where *designer* is the name of the ActiveX Designer that you selected. When the Project menu gets full, new designers appear on the More Designers submenu.

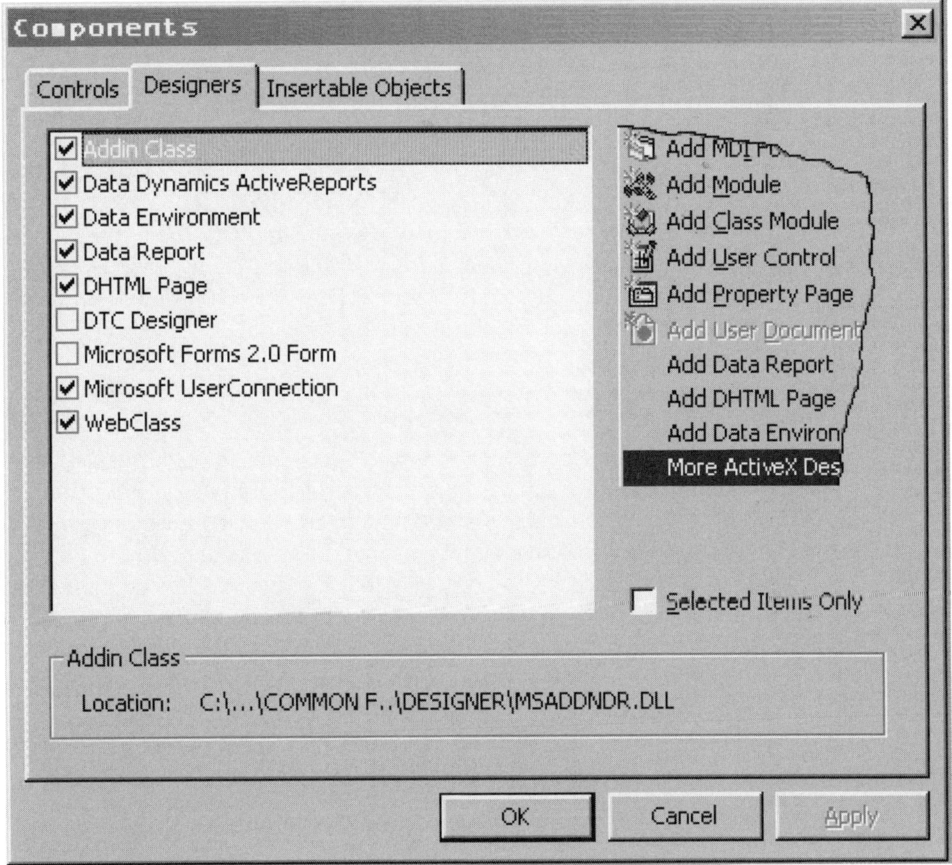

Figure 13–2 *The Designer tab of the Components dialog.*

USING AN ACTIVEX DESIGNER

To use an ActiveX designer to add a new object to your project, you just select the appropriate Add Designer option from the Project menu. The designer is added to your Project Explorer window. To work with a designer once it has been added to your project, just double click on it in the Project Explorer window. Visual Basic will open the appropriate designer for you to use to modify the object associated with it.

Currently, designers can only be created using C++. Ideally, Microsoft (or some third party) will create a designer for creating ActiveX Designers.

This is exactly the process that you follow with the other designers that ship with Visual Basic. For instance, when you double click on a form, Visual Basic starts up a copy of the Form designer and displays your form in it. If you want to work on two forms at once, you open two copies of the Form designer, each in its own window.

The designers for Visual Basic's Web-based classes work the same way. When you double click on a DHTMLPage in the Project Explorer window, Visual Basic displays the file in a DHTML Designer. To create two DHTMLPages, you would add two designers to your project.

There are a couple of limitations to ActiveX Designers. They can only produce Class modules, for instance. The Class modules produced by ActiveX Designers are normally private—you can't create objects that can be used outside of your component using an ActiveX Designer unless the designer provides you with a way of changing its Instancing setting (most designers don't).

The files generated by an ActiveX Designer might not be added to Visual SourceSafe (or whatever source control tool that you are using) as you add them to your project. If, when creating the file, you are not prompted to add the file to Visual SourceSafe, you'll need to explicitly add the file by using the Project | Add File menu choice. You'll need to check the Add as Related Document on this dialog and add the file that the ActiveX designer stores its results in.

DHTML Applications

Dynamic HTML Applications are the more restrictive of the two Web application development classes. The result of creating a DHTML application is an ActiveX Control, which can only be used in a browser that supports ActiveX Controls, that is, Internet Explorer. There is a plug-in for Netscape Navigator that supports ActiveX Controls but that's only useful if you can get your users to install it. In addition, ActiveX Controls run only on the Windows/Intel platform.

For Internet-based applications, unless you are going to reject users with Netscape Navigator or users who are browsing from platforms other than Windows/Intel computers, restricting yourself to Internet Explorer probably isn't a valid option. If you do decide to use DHTML Applications in an Internet application and not reject users, you will have to build two versions of your page: One for Internet Explorer and one for every other browser. This is time consuming, expensive to test, and hard to maintain as you must keep the two different versions of your site synchronized.

For intranet based applications, however, ActiveX Controls can make a lot of sense. ActiveX Controls are downloaded and installed on the user's computer by Internet Explorer the first time that the user displays the page. The second time that the user requests the Web page, the ActiveX Control is run from the user's hard disk—no download is required. As a result, ActiveX Controls can provide a simple way of distributing software to your users.

Creating a DHTML Project

To create a DHTML Project, you begin by selecting DHTML Application from the Visual Basic New Project dialog. This creates a project with a DHTML Designer and a single standard Module.

THE DHTML DESIGNER

The designer that you get when you double click on a DHTMLPage is called the DHTML Designer. The DHTML Designer is a low-end HTML editor that consists of two panes (see Figure 13–3). The pane on the right is a What You See Is What You Get editor that allows you to drag and drop HTML elements, enter text, define tables, and generally create a Web page. The pane on the left gives you a tree view of all of the HTML elements that you've added to your Web page.

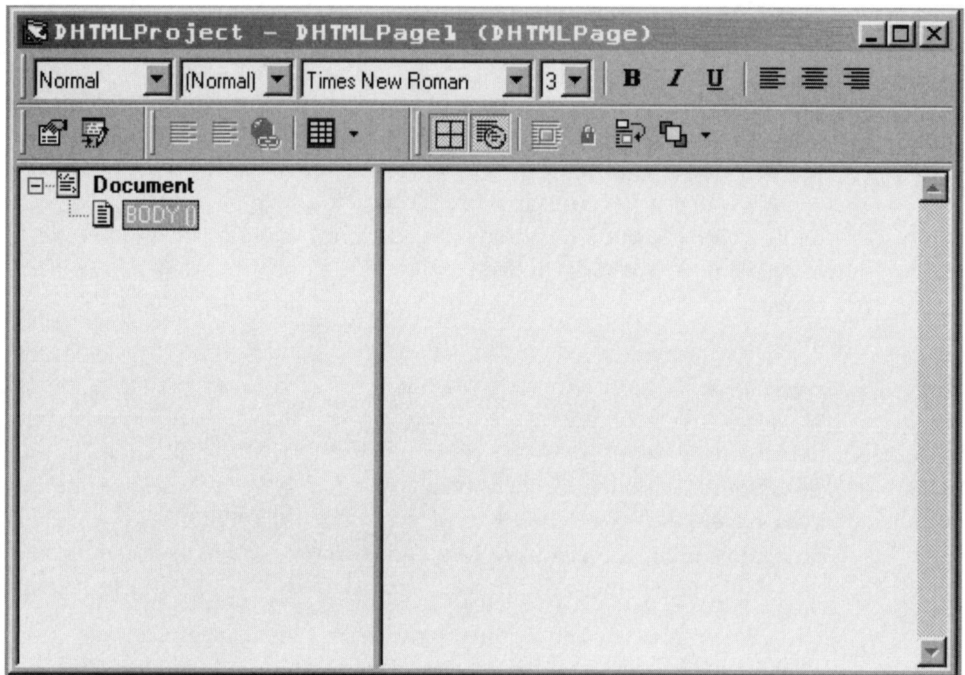

Figure 13–3 *The DHTML Designer.*

If you have any experience with any other HTML editors, you will probably be disappointed with the DHTML Designer. In fact, Microsoft urges you to create your Web page in some other editor and then import it into the DHTML Designer.

You can import an existing Web page into the designer by clicking on the first button on the designer toolbar (DHTML Page Designer Properties). On the Properties dialog that appears, select the Save HTML in an External File option (see Figure 13–4). With the option selected, you can either enter the pathname to the file that you want into the dialog's text box or click on the Open button and use the standard Windows File Open dialog to find the file. If you use the Open button, Visual Basic will fill in the text box on the dialog. You can also click on the New button and enter the name of a page to create a new file.

Regardless of how you create your Web page, when you close your project, the DHTML Designer must save your Web page to your hard disk. The default is to save your Web page in a file with the extension DCA in the same directory as your application. Visual Basic will keep track of this file as it

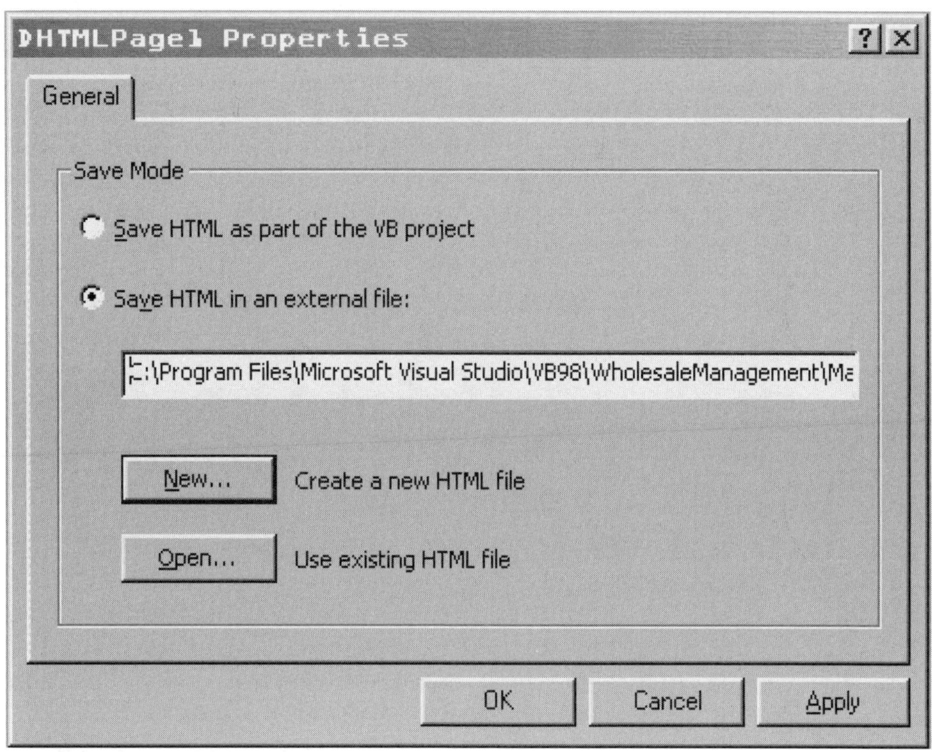

Figure 13–4 *The Properties dialog of the DHTML Designer.*

does for any of the other files that make up your Visual Basic project. Copying your project from computer to computer will be simpler if you take this option.

If you want to make changes to your HTML using some other editor, however, you must save your page in an external file. You do this by clicking on the DHTML Page Designer Properties button, selecting the Save HTML in an External File option and then clicking on the New button. This brings up the Create HTML file dialog, where you can enter the file name that you want to use.

When you save your Web page as an external file, the name appears in the Designer's SourceFile property. You can also change the external file name just by updating the Source File property in Visual Basic's Property Window. If you enter a file name in the Source File property in the DHTMLPage's Property List, a File Open Dialog will open but the file you select in this dialog will be ignored in favor of the value you enter in the Property window.

If you choose to save your Web page as an external file, you can use any editor that you want to make changes to it. You can even invoke an external editor by clicking on the second button on the designer's tool bar (Launch Editor). Unfortunately, the editor that starts up is Notepad. You can change the editor by entering the full path name to the editor's executable file on the Advanced tab of the Tools | Options menu choice. You can also edit your page outside Visual Basic using another editor. After saving your file in the external editor and returning to Visual Basic, you'll need to right-mouse click on the Template and select Refresh HTML Template to update the Web-Class designers display.

One standard format for Web pages is to use frames to display multiple pages simultaneously. While you can create the individual pages that appear in frames using the DHTML Designer, you will have to create the frameset page which defines the frames using some other tool.

When you compile your application, regardless of how you managed your Web page during development, a separate HTML file will be generated. You can specify the file's name by setting the BuildFile property of the DHTML Designer. If you don't specify the name, Visual Basic will generate a name for you based on the Designer and project names.

As you would when you create a standard Visual Basic form, you add items to the Web page by dragging them from the toolbox. With the DHTML designer, however, rather than dragging ActiveX controls, you are dragging HTML elements. These elements are defined by the HTML specification as defined by the World Wide Web Consortium (the W3C). Many of the typical Windows controls (like TextBoxes and CommandButtons) have equivalent HTML elements. The properties and events for an HTML element are also different from the properties and events that you are accustomed to using from ActiveX Controls on a Visual Basic Form. In addition, there is no Label control in HTML. Instead, you just type your text in the right-side pane of the designer.

In order to work with an element you must assign a value to its ID property. Any elements with values assigned to their ID properties appear in bold in the DHTML Designer. From within your code you refer to elements of the page by the value assigned to their Id property.

The DHTMLPage designer requires that each ID be unique. This is different from the DHTML model, where duplicate Ids are treated like an array. As a result, when you import your page into Visual Basic, duplicate IDs get numbers appended to their values (e.g., two controls with their ID properties set to MyControl will be accessed from your code as MyControl1 and MyControl2).

By right-clicking on the toolbar and selecting Components, you can add ActiveX controls to the HTML toolbox. Once the control is added to the toolbox you can drag the control onto your Web page. However, the HTML <OBJECT> tag that's added when you drag the control onto the form doesn't include either the Codebase or Cabbase attributes which specify the package to download and install the control. Unless you expect the controls to be already installed on your user's computer, you will have to create a download package for the control and copy it to your Web server. Once you've created a download package and placed it on your server, you can update the HTML with the location of your package.

The DHTMLPage Object

Once you've created your page using the designer, you can start adding code to your ActiveX Control. Double-clicking on any of the elements on your page opens a window that lets you add code to the events associated with the element. Figure 13–5 shows the DHTML Designer's code window. Many of the event procedures that are called by the DHTML page are defined as Boolean Functions. If the Function doesn't return a True value, the event is cancelled. In the following code, after displaying the message "Hello World", the code sets the Function to True to ensure that the event is recognized

```
Private Function TextField1_onClick() As Boolean
  MsgBox "Hello World"
  TextField1_onclick = True
End Function
```

As with any other Visual Basic project, you will build your application by interacting with a series of objects. The DHTMLPage object provided by the designer represents your ActiveX Control and provides access to the page that the control is placed on. Through the DHTMLPage's properties, you can retrieve the BaseWindow object (which corresponds to the DHTML Window object) and the Document object (which matches the DHTML Document object).

For instance, to set the value of a text box in a form on your page, you would use the following code. This line of code uses the DHTMLPage object's Document property to retrieve the Document object that represents the page that the control is part of. The code then uses the Document object's All method to find an element that has its ID property set to TextBox and set its Value property to "Hello World":

```
DHTMLPage.Document.all.MyTextBox.Value ="Hello World"
```

Discussing the large and powerful DHTML model is beyond the scope of this chapter. Your best reference for the DHTML objects is a book on the DHTML object model itself, as implemented in Internet Explorer 4.0 or 5.0. What I discuss here are the features that are part of the DHTMLPage object.

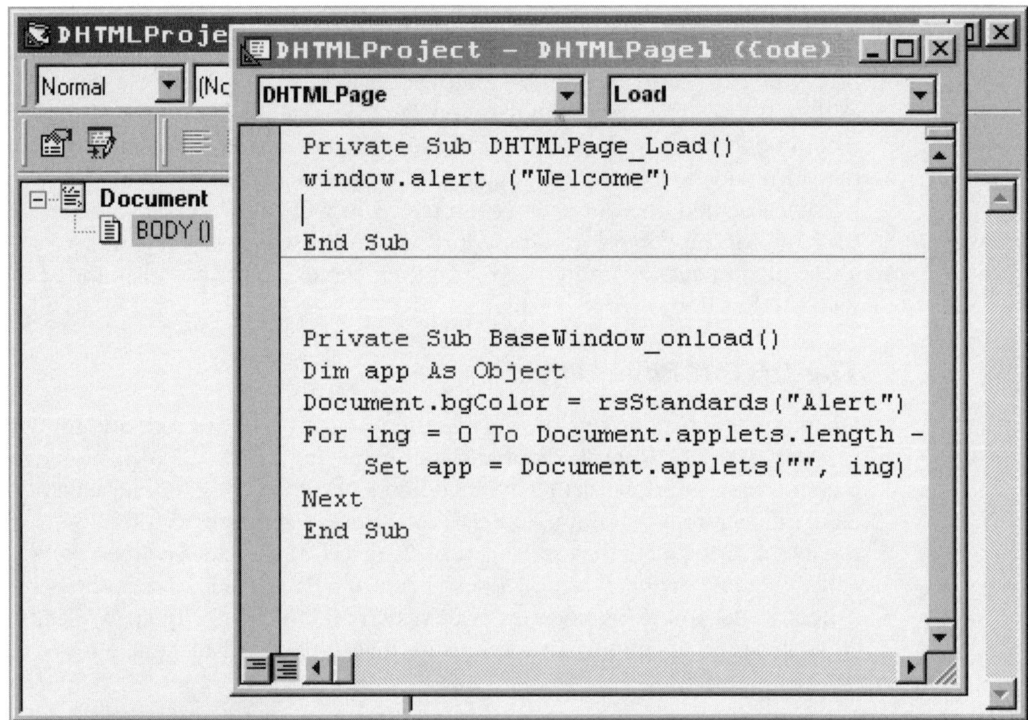
DHTMLProject - DHTMLPage1 (Code)
Normal
DHTMLPage
Load
Document
BODY ()
Private Sub DHTMLPage_Load()
window.alert ("Welcome")
End Sub
Private Sub BaseWindow_onload()
Dim app As Object
Document.bgColor = rsStandards("Alert")
For ing = 0 To Document.applets.length -
Set app = Document.applets("", ing)
Next
End Sub

Figure 13–5 *The DHTML Designer's code window, which allows you to add code to events associated with elements on your page.*

The DHTMLPage object fires two events that aren't part of the DHTML model. Like any ActiveX Control, a DHTMLPage fires Initialize and Terminate events as the control is created and destroyed. The DHTMLPage object also fires Load and Unload events. The Load event fires as the page containing the control is loaded while the Unload event fires when the user requests another page. The events that make up the DHTML model will fire between the DHTMPage's Load and Unload events.

The Unload event is relatively straightforward and should be used for any "end of page" processing. When the Unload event fires, all the elements of the page are still available and can be accessed from your code in this event (something that's not true of the object's Terminate event). Unlike a Form's Unload event, there is no corresponding QueryUnload event that allows you to cancel the request for the new page (though that can be done using the DHTML object model).

The Load event is slightly more complicated than the Unload event. The DHMTLPage's AsyncLoad property controls when this event fires. When the AsyncLoad is set to True, the Load event fires as soon as the first element on the page is displayed—provided, of course, that your ActiveX control is downloaded and installed. With AsyncLoad set to False, the Load event fires as soon as the last element on the page is displayed and is ready for use (i.e., when the control and page are fully sited). You would set AsyncLoad to True when you want to carry out some processing as your page is displayed.

State Management

In the Web world, your forms will be stateless—Public variables are not shared among the DHTMLPages in a project due to the way that your Controls are processed. When the browser requests a page from your server, it receives a page that contains tags to download, install, and run your ActiveX Control. The browser can then request another page, to receive a second control. By the time that the second page with its control is downloaded, the first control has been destroyed. Each DHTMLPage is a separate Web page requested from your Web server and cannot communicate with other controls on other pages.

To pass data between pages, you'll need to use one of the techniques typical of Web applications: the query string, hidden fields, and so on. Again, these techniques require a full understanding of how to create Web-based applications and I refer you to the books that I list at the end of the chapter.

The DHTML Application project does provide support for maintaining state by using cookies. As defined by the HTML specification, cookies are data stored on the client at the request of the Web page. As each page is brought down to the browser, it can pick up the cookies left by an earlier page (see Figure 13–6).

Cookies are not without problems, however, as many users feel that they are invasion of privacy. Users can choose to turn off their browser's ability to work with cookies. In addition, some browsers do not support working with cookies (though Internet Explorer and Netscape Navigator have since version 3).

Only pages retrieved from the same Windows domain (URL) can share cookies. You can keep only 20 cookies per site, no more than 4K worth of data can be saved in a single cookie, and Internet Explorer imposes a limit of 300 current cookies.

As part of every DHTML Project, Microsoft provides two routines that can read and write cookies for you. These routines can be found in the modDHTML module in your project and are called PutProperty and GetProperty.

To use the PutProperty subroutine you must pass it a reference to the HTMLDocument that your control resides in, the name of the cookie that you wish to write, and the value to write to the cookie. This call creates a cookie called UserState to hold the value "Beginning":

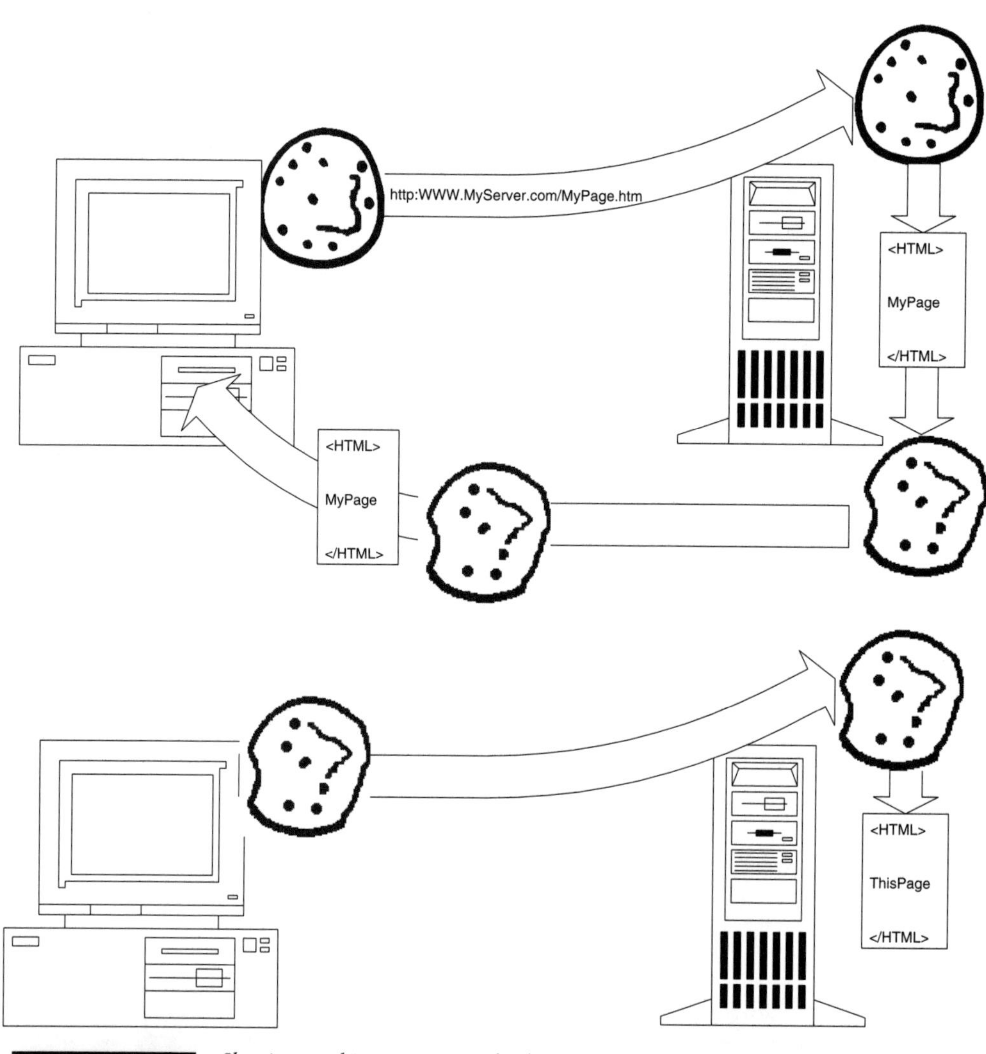

Figure 13–6 *Sharing cookies among multiple pages. In the first diagram the cookie is sent to the server with a request for the page. A cookie is returned with page. Later the page sends the cookie back to the server.*

```
PutProperty DHTMLPage.Document, "UserState", _
                    "Beginning"
```

To retrieve a value from a cookie, you call the GetProperty function, passing only a reference to the document and the name of the cookie that you want to read. The function will return the value of the cookie (or a zero length string if the cookie doesn't exist). This code retrieves the value of the UserState cookie into the variable strState:

```
strState = GetProperty(DHTMLPage.Document, _
                    "UserState")
```

Cookies written like this will be kept only until the user shuts down the browser. You can, however, write out a cookie that is kept around even after the browser is shut down, allowing you to store information from one browser session to another. To do this, you must pass an expiry date for your cookie as the last parameter to the PutProperty subroutine. The cookie will be available until the date that you specify. The following code, for instance, ensures that the cookie will be kept for the next 30 days. The code does this by using Visual Basic's DateAdd function to add thirty days to today's date to generate the date that controls how long to save the cookie:

```
PutProperty DHTMLPage.Document, "UserState", _
                    "Beginning", DateAdd("d",30, Date())
```

Remember that cookies are stored on the user's computer. If the user accesses your application from a computer at work, then any cookies that you write will be stored on the user's work computer. If your user then goes home and requests the same page, the cookies that you wrote to the user's work computer won't be available to your code when it executes on the user's home computer.

Debugging and Deploying

When you press the F5 key to debug your program, Visual Basic will

1. start your control.
2. make the necessary registry entries to allow any program that uses the control to find it.
3. start Internet Explorer.
4. have Internet Explorer load the page specified in the BuildFile property of the DHTML Designer specified in the Start Component option of the Debugging tab.

In order to have the page download and use your control, Visual Basic adds an <OBJECT> tag to your page to invoke your ActiveX Control. A typical tag looks like this (the value of the clsid attribute will vary from control to control):

```
<!--METADATA TYPE="MsHtmlPageDesigner" startspan-->
<object id="DHTMLPage1"
classid="clsid:5600217A-8A42-11D3-A8CA-00107A901A5F"
width=0 height=0>
</object>
<!--METADATA TYPE="MsHtmlPageDesigner" endspan-->
```

You may not want to start your debugging with one of the pages in your project. If, for instance, you are using frames, then you may want to open the page that defines your frames. To do this you should select the Start Browser with URL option on the Debugging tab and give the name of the page that you want to start with.

When you choose the Make option on the File menu, Visual Basic generates an ActiveX Control and an HTML page for each DHTML Designer in your project. The HTML page will contain the <OBJECT> tag necessary to download your control and install it on the user's computer. The HTML page will have the name that you specify in the SourceFile property for the DHTMLPage designer.

You will still need to use the Package and Deployment Wizard to create the CAB files for your application. Once the package is created, you'll need to copy the HTML pages and CAB files to your Website. Finally, you must update the <OBJECT> tags for your ActiveX controls with the location of your CAB files. Once all of this is done, clients can start requesting your Web page with its associated control.

IIS Applications

Unlike DHTML Applications, IIS Applications are not browser dependent, which makes them the more useful of the two Web development technologies. With IIS Applications you are creating ActiveX components that run on your Web server and do not interact directly with the user's browser. Instead, your IIS Application will generate a Web page that will be sent to the user's browser. Provided that the code in your ActiveX component doesn't generate any HTML that the user's Web browser can't digest, then your IIS Application should be able to work with any browser.

The Life Cycle of an IIS Application

Every Web application begins with the user requesting a page. When you compile or debug your IIS Application, Visual Basic creates a Web page whose server-side script code that will create and run your ActiveX component. I call this your ASP page for the purposes of this discussion.

When your ASP page is requested by a browser, the script code uses a component called WebManager to start your component running. The code in your ActiveX component then creates a Web page that is returned to the browser that requested the page. I call this page the "returned page."

Normally, the page that Visual Basic will generate to invoke your component will have the same name your Designer used to create the Class that generates the page. However, you can give the page a different name by setting the Designer's NameInURL property to the name that you want to use.

When the page that your IIS Applications generated is received by the browser, the HTML that your component wrote to the page will be processed and displayed to the user. After working with the returned page, the user will request your ASP page from the server, beginning the cycle all over again.

Effectively, your IIS Application is a page that, when delivered to the browser, requests itself from the server when the user asks for a new page. Each time that your ASP page is requested, the code in your ActiveX component will have access to information the user entered on the returned page while it was displayed in the browser. Your server-side ActiveX component will be able to use that data to make updates to databases or do whatever other processing is required. You can also use that information to control what HTML goes back down to the user's browser in the returned page (see Figure 13–7).

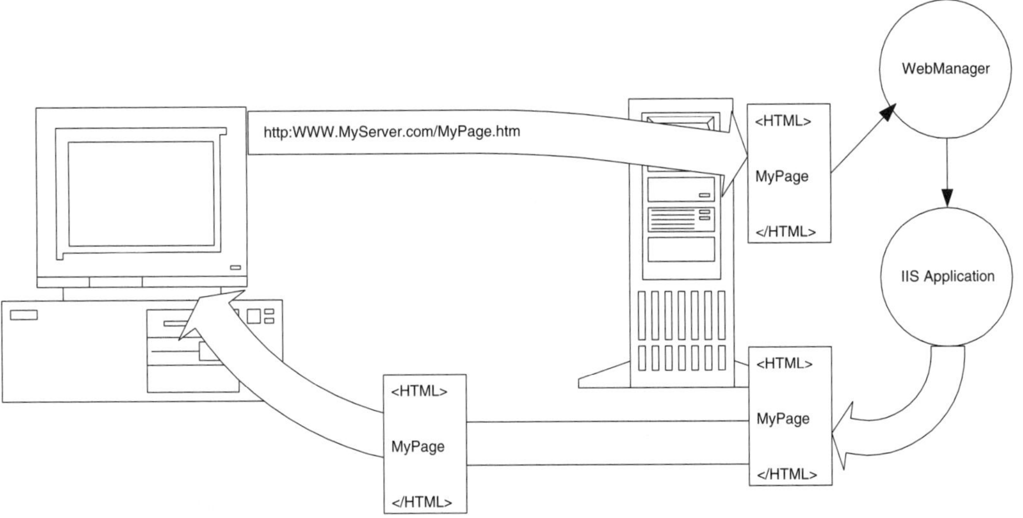

Figure 13–7 *The life cycle of an IIS Application. A user requests your page, the page calls WebManager, WebManager calls your component, and you generate a page to return tothe browser.*

Creating an IIS Application

Creating an IIS Application begins by selecting IIS Application from the opening Visual Basic dialog. This creates a project with a single WebClass ActiveX Designer in it. Double-clicking on the WebClass designer opens the editing window shown in Figure 13–8.

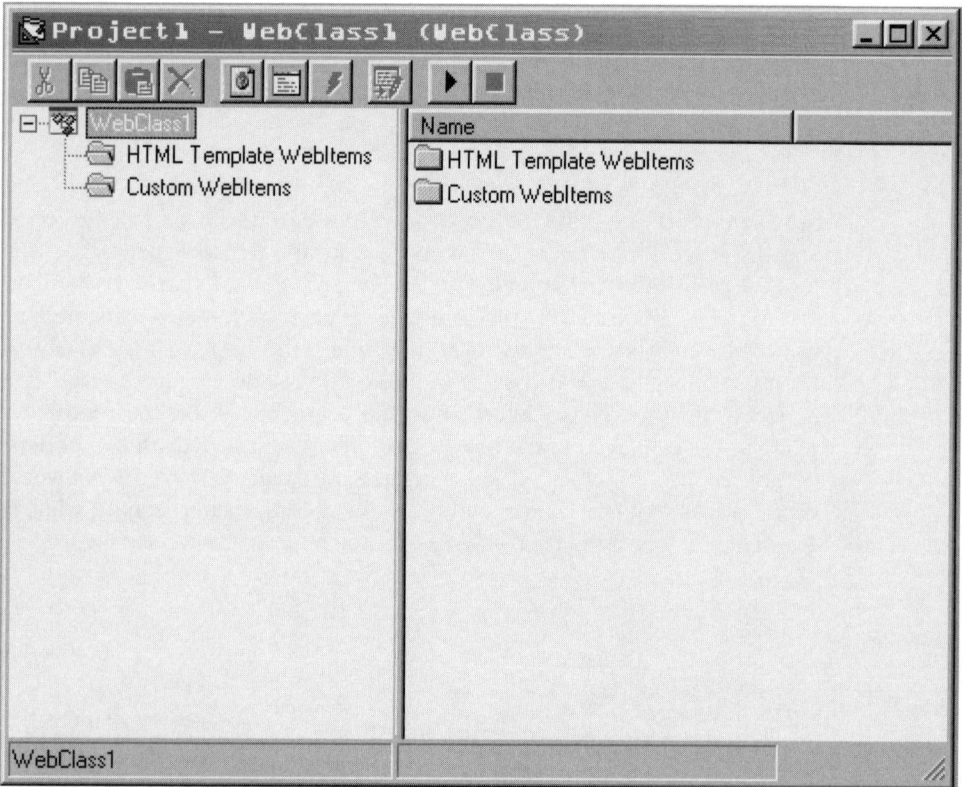

Figure 13–8 *The IIS Application designer.*

THE IIS APPLICATION DESIGNER

Each WebClass designer allows you to create one object within the ActiveX component that Visual Basic will generate from your project. Within each Designer you can add WebItems and Templates. WebItems are code that execute on the server to create a Web page that is returned to the client's Web browser. You add new WebItems by clicking on the Add Custom WebItem button on the Designer's toolbar. Think of WebItems as the Web equivalent of a code module.

A Template is an HTML page that you can send to the browser from your IIS Application. You will create your Templates with some HTML development tool (e.g., Front Page), and then add them to your project by clicking on the Add HTML Template WebItem button on the Designer's toolbar. You can also add code to your Template to modify its contents or process data sent with the returned page. Think of Templates as the HTML equivalent of a Visual Basic form with its code module.

Technically, what I call a Template in this chapter is a WebItem with an associated Template. However, it simplifies the discussion if I can refer to "Templates" and "WebItems" rather than "WebItems with an associated Template" and "WebItems without associated Templates."

From a programmer's point of view, the difference between WebItems and Templates is primarily one of convenience. From the code in a WebItem you can write any text that you want to create the returned page. However, most Web pages contain a lot of text—which can require a lot of code to be generated. Templates, on the other hand, are pages containing most of the HTML that you want to send to the browser. Since the Template contains most of your HTML, all you have to do from within your code is modify selected portions of the Template before it goes to the browser.

One thing to bear in mind with WebItems is that the page that you send to the browser doesn't exist anywhere on your hard disk. Instead, the page is generated from your WebItem's code on demand. As a result, the content of your WebItem generated pages can't be indexed and these pages will be invisible to search engines. Templates let you store the static parts of your page in files on your server where they can be indexed and found by search engines.

USING TEMPLATES

To send a Template to the client that requested your WebClass's page, you use the Template or WebItem's WriteTemplate method. When the WriteTemplate method is called from a Template without a parameter, the method sends the specified Template to the browser. Alternatively, you can specify a Template file as the parameter to the WriteTemplate method. You can't call a Template from a WebItem without specifying a Template file.

The following code, for instance, sends the file behind the OrderRequest template to the browser. The method is being called from a WebItem named wbiHandleOrder:

```
wbiHandleOrder.WriteTemplate "OrderRequest.HTM"
```

You may find that you can't add HTML Template items immediately after creating a project. If so, you will need to shut down and reopen Visual Basic after creating your project before attempting to add a Template.

If your application uses a Template, then you will typically want to modify selected portions of the page before it goes to the browser. You mark the areas of the page that you want to modify with a set of tags that begin with a special set of characters. The default set of characters is "WC@" but you can control which characters are used by setting the TagPrefix property of your Template. A typical set of tags to define an area of the page that you want to rewrite would look like this:

```
<WC@OrderNumber> Order Number Goes Here </WC@OrderNumber>
```

The tag is made up of the prefix (WC@) followed by the TagName (in this case, OrderNumber). The area between the opening and closing tag is referred to as the TagContents (in the example, the area occupied by "Order Number Goes Here").

Once you issue the WriteTemplate method, the Template's ProcessTag routine will be called for every set of WC@ tags in the template. The ProcessTag routine will be passed the full tag (prefix and name), the TagContents, and a flag called SendTags. Your code will check the TagName to determine which tag triggered the routine and, armed with that information, update the TagContents variable appropriately. The SendTags flag controls whether the WC@ tags are left in the page when the page is sent to the browser.

This code, for instance, replaces the TagContents with the value of the strOrderNumber variable, but only if the TagName is OrderNumber:

```
Sub FeedbackPage_ProcessTag(ByVal TagName as String, _
TagContents as String, SendTags as Boolean)
  If TagName = "WC@OrderNumber" Then
    TagContents = strOrderNumber
  EndIf
  SendTags = True
End Sub
```

Since the code sets SendTags to True, the WC@ tags will be left in the page when it is returned to the browser. Assuming that the strOrderNumber contained the value "798341", the HTML page would look like this after the TagContents are replaced:

```
<WC@OrderNumber> 798341 </WC@OrderNumber>
```

Setting the SendTags flag to False causes your WC@ tags to be removed from the page before it is sent to the browser. Sending or leaving the WC@ tags should make no difference to the display of the page. Since the WC@ tags aren't valid HTML tags, they should be ignored by the browser.

If you write text that contains WC@ tags to the TagContents, then you will need to have your page processed again after you write your tags so that you can process the inserted tags. To make this happen, you must set the Template's ReScanReplacement property to True. With this property set to True, the page will be processed repeatedly until no WC@ tags are found.

USING THE ASP OBJECTS

From within your WebItems and Templates you can also work with the six objects that make up the ASP object model: Application, Session, Response, Write, Server, and Error. The WebClass object has a property for each of these objects that you can use to retrieve a reference to the ASP object. For instance, you can use the WebClass's Response property to retrieve a reference to the ASP Response object. You can then use the Response object's Write Method to write text to the returned page. This code, for instance, writes the order number to the Web page, surrounded by bold tags:

```
WebClass.Response.Write "<B>" & strOrderNumber & "</B>"
```

You can also access one of the optional objects that ships with ASP but isn't part of the ASP object model. This is the BrowserType object, which provides a convenient way of determining what functionality that the browser you are sending the page to supports. The WebClass's BrowserType property returns a reference to this object.

This code, for instance, checks to see if the browser supports cookies and, if the browser does, uses the ASP Response object to send a cookie to the browser:

```
If Webclass.BrowserType.Cookies = True Then
  WebClass.Response.Cookies("OrderNumber") = _
                               strOrderNumber
End If
```

Like DHTML, discussing the ASP object model is outside of the scope of this chapter. The references at the end of this chapter include books on the ASP object model and Web development.

IIS Events

When working with IIS Applications, it's important to understand what events in your ActiveX component will fire and when. Some events are built into the WebClass object. The events that are unique to the WebClass object are BeginRequest, EndRequest, Start, and FatalErrorResponse. Each WebItem or Template can also fire Respond, ProcessTag, and UserEvent events (I discussed the ProcessTag event in the section on using Templates).

The WebClass Object fires the FatalErrorResponse event. When the WebClass is "terminated due to an error," to quote the Visual Basic documentation. A Web page will still be returned to the browser even if your class abends, so you could use this routine to write information to the page before it goes back to the client in the event of an error.

WEBCLASS PROCESSING CYCLE

When the user requests your ASP page, the code in the page will activate your ActiveX component. Your WebClass object will, like any ActiveX component, fire an Initialize event. Immediately after that, the WebClass's BeginRequest will fire. EndRequest will fire after all other processing is completed, just before the Web page is sent to the browser. Your ActiveX component's Terminate event may or may not fire after the EndRequest event, depending on the setting of the StateManagement property (see Figure 13–9 for a chart of the event cycle).

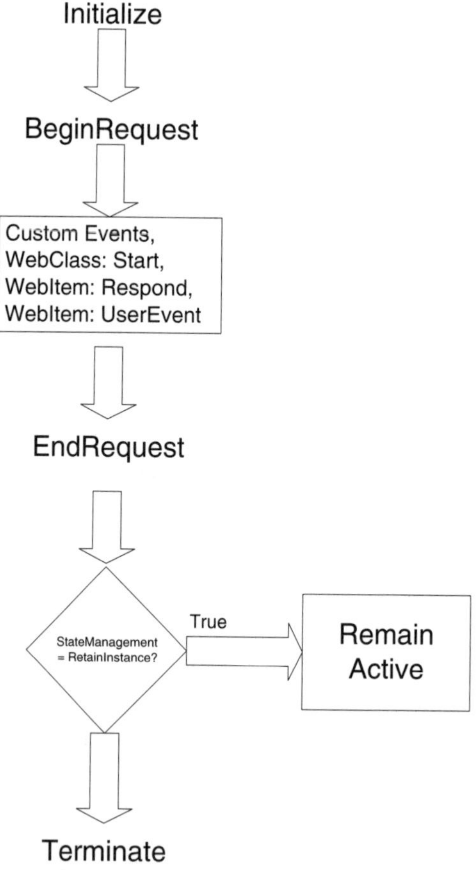

Figure 13–9 *The WebClass event cycle.*

Typically, you will use the BeginRequest event for any processing that is common to all the pages that might be returned to the browser (e.g., opening a database). The EndRequest event is also normally used for any processing that is common to all the pages (e.g., writing a copyright notice to the bottom of the page or closing a database).

After the BeginRequest, the event that fires next depends on how your ASP page is requested. You have the ability to have the returned page call your ASP page and request a specific WebItem, Template, or routine in your component. I'll begin by discussing how to add routines to your component that can be called from the returned page as part of requesting your ASP page.

CUSTOM EVENTS

The IIS Designer allows you to add custom events to Templates or WebItems by right-mouse clicking on the Template or WebItem and selecting Add Custom Event. Custom Events are simply routines in your ActiveX component that can be called when your ASP page is requested from the browser. It's your responsibility to add HTML to your Web page that will invoke your code as part of requesting your ASP page. Since your routines are called as part of requesting your routine, you must associate the call to your routine with an HTML tag that can be used to request your ASP page (e.g., a <FORM> tag or an <A> tag).

In a Template, you can associate your Custom Event routine with HTML tags already in the Template. The IIS Designer lists in its right window all the tags in the Template that can request your page. You can have these tags call one of your routines by right-mouse clicking on the tag and selecting Connect to Custom Event. You can also select Connect to WebItem from the tag's popup menu to have the HTML tag request a specific WebItem or Template, rather than one of your Custom Event routines. The IIS Designer will take care of updating the Template's HTML tag so that it will call your routine.

You can also use code to write text to the Web page to create a tag that will request a Custom Event. The Write method of the ASP Response object lets you write text (including HTML tags) to your Web page. The WebClass's URLFor method will generate the text to request a WebItem or Template with a Custom Event. You pass the URLFor method the name of a WebItem or Template with a routine name and the method returns the HTML that will request that routine in the specified WebItem or Template.

This code, for instance, writes an Anchor tag with an Action attribute that will call the Template wtmOrderPage and run the routine called OrderComplete:

```
Response.Write "<A HREF=""" & _
  WebClass.URLFor(wtmOrderPage,"OrderComplete") & _
  """>Click Here to Request the Page</A>"
```

The resulting HTML will look like this:

```
<A
HREF="WebClass1.ASP?WCI=wtmOrderPage&WCE=OrderComplete">
Click Here to Request the Page</A>
```

As you can see, the tag's HREF attribute will call the page that invokes your control (in this case, WebClass1.ASP). Following the "?" there is information that the WebClassManager component that invokes your component will use to control which routine will be called. This information includes the name of the WebItem (wtmOrderPage) and the name of the routine (OrderComplete).

During processing, after you add tags that call your ASP page to the returned page, the page will be sent to the client. When the user activates the appropriate tag (e.g., by clicking on "Click Here to Request the Page" inside the <A> tags), a request for your ASP page—and possibly a WebItem or Template with a Custom Event—will be sent to the server. When the request is received, your ActiveX component will be activated by the WebClassManager and the appropriate WebItem, Template, or Custom Event invoked.

Putting all that together, the request for the page that invokes your IIS Application can consist of any one of three possibilities:

1. Just the name of your page
2. The name of your page and a Template or WebItem
3. The name of your page, a Template or WebItem, and a Custom Event routine

If the request for your ASP page is just the name of the page, the Start event of your WebClass will be run. This is the event that will normally be run the first time that a user requests your page because that request typically just includes the name of the page.

When you add a WebClass to your application, the Start routine for the WebClass will contain code to write a minimal Web page.

If the request for your page specifies a Template or a WebItem but no event, the Respond event for the Template or WebItem will fire. For instance, the Respond event is the event that will fire if a tag has been connected just to a WebItem or Template but not to a Custom Event.

If a Template and a Custom Event is specified but the event routine can't be found, the Template or WebItem's UserEvent will fire. The UserEvent will be passed the name of the routine that was requested. This code checks the name of the routine that was requested and, if it is "DeleteOrder," deletes the order whose number is in strOrderNumber.

```
Private Sub WebItem1_UserEvent(ByVal EventName As String)
Dim conn As Connection
  If EventName = "DeleteOrder" Then
    Set conn = New Connection
    conn.Execute "Delete * From tblOrders " & _
      "Where OrderNo = '" & strOrderNumber & "'"
  End If
End Sub
```

Typically, you will use URLFor to write out text that will call the User-Event routine.

Finally, if the request for your page includes the name of a Template or WebItem and the name of a valid event, then that routine will be executed.

Using the NextItem Property

Once your WebClass's code starts processing, there are three mechanisms that you can use to control which page is sent to the browser. Two of them have already been discussed: Writing to the returned page directly using the ASP objects or using the WriteTemplate method to send a Template.

You can also control which page is sent to the browser by setting the WebClass's NextItem property to one of the WebItems or Templates in the project. This code, for instance, sets the NextItem property to a Template named wbtOrderRequest:

```
Set WebClass.NextItem = wbtOrderRequest
```

When the event that this code is part of finishes processing, the Respond event of the specified WebItem or Template will fire (in this case, wbtOrderRequest). If you set the NextItem property to a Template (rather than a WebItem), then you must issue the WriteTemplate method from the Respond event in order to actually write the Template file. This code in the Respond event of the wbtOrderRequest Template completes the process begun with the previous code:

```
WbtOrderRequest.WriteTemplate
```

Typically, the page that you will want to send to the browser will depend on what page you sent last time and the information that the user entered on that page. So, in order to determine the next page, you will have to keep track of what page was last sent, which brings me to the topic of maintaining state.

Maintaining State

You have a couple of choices when it comes to maintaining state with IIS applications. Since the ActiveX Component resides on the server and is called repeatedly by the client, you can choose to keep the component active between requests. If you do keep your component active, you can maintain state by setting Public variables in your component.

To keep your component active between requests, all you need to do is set the WebClass's StateManagement property to the predefined constant wcRetainInstance at design time. You can terminate your component and remove it from memory by using the WebClass's ReleaseInstance method:

```
WebClass.ReleaseInstance
```

If your user doesn't request a page for twenty minutes, your component will automatically be destroyed.

The twenty minute timeout value is the default value for IIS and can be changed either from the IIS manager or from within your code.

There are a couple of watchouts here, though. The ability to keep your object in memory is dependent on the ASP Session object. The Session object requires that the user's browser support cookies and that the browser have its cookie facility turned on. Your client's browser must, at the very least, accept undated cookies in order for StateManagement to work.

While you can check if the user's browser supports cookies by using the WebClass' BrowserType property, that doesn't tell you if the facility is turned on. The only way to check that StateManagement is working is to set a Public variable to some value, use the Response object's Redirect method to request a routine in your WebClass and, in that routine, check the value of the Public variable. If the variable isn't set to the correct value, your client isn't accepting cookies.

Another way to manage state is to append state data to any URL in the returned page through the WebClass's URLData property (see Figure 13–10). Any tag in your returned page that will request your ASP page will include a URL that refers to your ASP page. Information added to those URLs will be available to your component when your ASP page is requested. You can retrieve this data by passing the name "URLData" to the ASP Request object's QueryString.

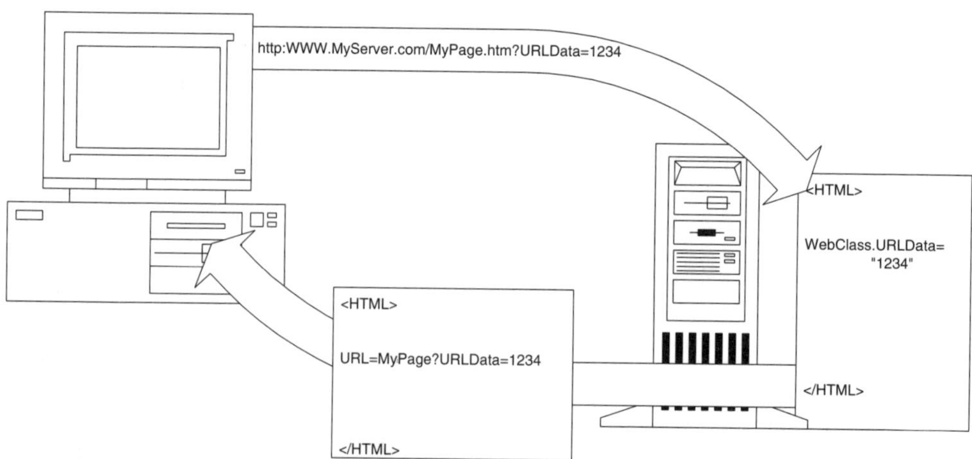

Figure 13–10 *Maintaining state through the URLData property. Along the bottom, the page sent includes URLData. When the page is again requested (along the top) the URLData is sent back to the server.*

This code, for instance, sets the URLData property to the order number:

```
WebClass.URLData = strOrderNumber
```

This code retrieves the value from the Request object's QueryString collection:

```
StrOrderNumber = WebClass.Request.QueryString("URLData")
```

Controlling Form Flow

In this section, I'd like to pull all of the preceding information together to show how you would use it to control the user's progress through the forms that make up your application. The following discussion assumes that the user keeps requesting your page. Should the user enter the address for another page, or use the browser's Back or Next buttons, or select an item from the Favorites list, the IIS Application cycle will be broken.

Generally, when the user requests your page for the first time, the request will simply include the page name. As a result, the WebClass's Start event will fire. From that event you can either write to the page that will be returned using the ASP Response object, use the NextItem property to call a WebItem or Template, or use the WriteTemplate method of one of your Templates to send a Template to the browser.

If control is transferred to a Template or WebItem through the NextItem property, the object's Respond event will fire. From the Respond event in a WebItem you can write to the page. In a Template, you would use the object's WriteTemplate method to add the Template to the page being sent to the browser. If your Template includes WC@ tags, the ProcessTag event will fire for each tag. If you use the WriteTemplate method of a Template in your WebClass's Start event to invoke a Template, however, the Template's Respond event will not fire, though its ProcessTag event will.

The text in the Template or the text that you write to the page must include some tags that request your page. You may have those tags included in the Template and associated with a WebItem or Template and a Custom Event. Alternatively, you might write the tag out using the URLFor method. If you need to hold on to some information to use when your page is requested again, you can write it to the URLData property.

The user must use one of the returned page's tags to request your page. If the tag includes the name of a WebItem or Template, then, when the user requests your page, the Respond event of that object will fire. A WriteTemplate method can then be used to send either the current Template or another one to the browser.

Why You Don't Need IIS Applications

Before discussing debugging and distributing your WebClass, I repeat here what I said at the start of this chapter: You don't need IIS Applications to use

Visual Basic to build Web applications. From an ASP page you can use ActiveX components that you create with Visual Basic. This ASP script code uses the Server object's CreateObject method to create an object called Order.CommitOrder and then invoke its UpdateOrder method:

```
<%
Set objCMOrder = Server.CreateObject("Order.CommitOrder")
objCMOrder.UpdateOrder
%>
```

You can also access the objects that make up the ASP object model from within Visual Basic components without using IIS Application. To make this happen, you must set references both to the MTS object library and to the ASP object library in your Visual Basic project. The reference to the MTS object library will let you use the Item method of the ObjectContext object to retrieve references to the ASP objects. The reference to the ASP object library lets you declare variables that can point to ASP objects that you retrieve. This code, for instance, gets a reference to the ASP Request object from the ObjectContext object and then uses the Response object's Write method to add text to the page going back to the browser:

```
Dim rsp As Response
Dim obc As ObjectContext

Set obc = AppServer.GetObjectContext()
Set rsp = obc.Item("Response")
rsp.Write "<Form Method=Post Action=MyPage.ASP>"
```

There are some details to be careful of, though:

- You should never store a reference to a Visual Basic object in an Application or Session object. Doing so in code will generate a run time error. Doing it in the Global.ASA with an <OBJECT> tag will avoid the error message, but cause all calls on all pages to the object to be serialized (i.e., executed in order, one after another) which reduces the scalability of your application.
- In general, you shouldn't use the ASP objects within your component (it limits the usefulness of your component by binding it to the ASP environment). You should, however, use Server.CreateObject in your Visual Basic code rather than New or CreateObject to create any new objects. This allows ASP to recognize your component's threading model, ensures that the objects that you create can participate in transactions that include the ASP page, and allows you to access the ASP objects from your component.
- Don't use GetSetting or SaveSetting to read and write the registry as they access keys under the HKey_Current_User hive, which isn't available to IIS.
- Because of type conversion issues, parameters passed to methods should be declared as Variant if you want them to be passed ByRef from VBScript.

Debugging IIS Applications

When you press the F5 key to debug your project, Visual Basic will make all the necessary entries to register the component created from your Webclass. Visual Basic will also create pages to call each of your WebClasses and then call Internet Explorer to display one of them. The first page requested by Internet Explorer will be the WebClass specified in the Start Component option on the Debugging tab of the Project | Properties menu choice. If you want Internet Explorer to request a different page, you can specify that page in the Start browser with URL option, also on the Debugging tab.

In order to process the server-side page that invokes your component, your page must be served up by a Web server. Visual Basic will use Personal Web Server to serve up your page, so it must be installed on your computer. Personal Web Server must be configured to run ASP pages out-of-process in order for debugging to take place. If you don't have this option set, Visual Basic will offer to set it as part of starting the debugging session (see Figure 13–11).

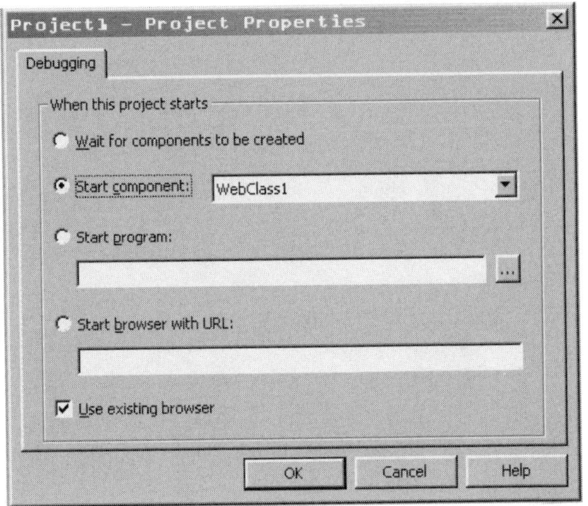

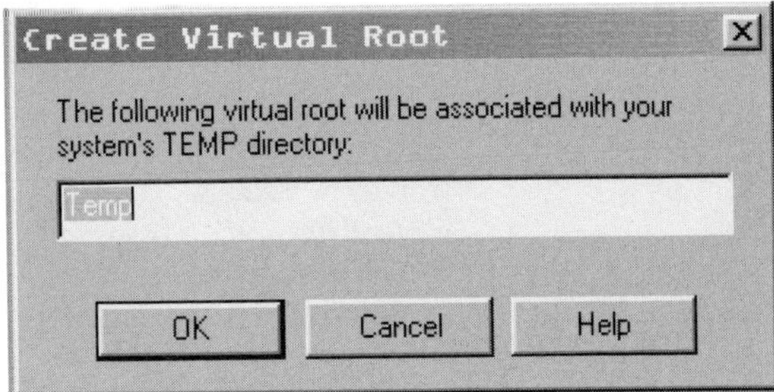

Figure 13–11 *Messages generated by the initial debugging session.*

Internet Explorer can only request pages from a virtual directory on a Web server. So, Personal Web Server must set up a virtual directory from which to request your Web files. Since Visual Basic will have created your ASP page in whatever directory you have been saving your project files in, that directory will be the basis for the virtual directory that Personal Web Server creates. By default, Personal Web Server will give the virtual directory the same name as your project, but you will have an opportunity to change this at the start of the first debugging session.

When you have finished a debugging session you don't have to shut down Internet Explorer—provided you have set StateManagement to wcNoState (the default). In this situation, you can simply stop Visual Basic and start it again to continue debugging. However, if you set StateManagement to wcRetainInstance, you'll have to shut down the browser at the end of each debugging session in addition to stopping Visual Basic.

There are some significant differences between the way that your application behaves in debugging mode and when it is compiled and executing on your Web server. On the Web server, your application will be multithreaded with the problems and issues described in the chapter on Deploying. When debugging, however, your component will be run as a single-threaded object. The Unattended Execution option for your project will be set on by default, so all messages from your component will be written to the Windows NT application log. In debugging mode, however, you'll get the standard Visual Basic MsgBox displays.

Deploying IIS Applications

When you pick Make from the File menu, Visual Basic will create an ActiveX component for your project. Visual Basic will also create a Web page (with the extension .ASP) for each WebClass. Each of these pages will contain the server-side code to activate one of your WebClasses.

For instance, if you created a WebClass called OrdEntry in a project called OrdManage, Visual Basic would create a Web page called OrdEntry.ASP. The script code that it contained would look something like this:

```
<%
Response.Buffer=True
Response.Expires=0

If (VarType(Application("~WC~WebClassManager")) = 0) Then
    Application.Lock
  If (VarType(Application("~WC~WebClassManager")) = 0) Then
    Set Application("~WC~WebClassManager") = _
      Server.CreateObject("WebClassRuntime.WebClassManager")
  End If
  Application.UnLock
```

```
End If

Application("~WC~WebClassManager").ProcessNoStateWebClass _
  "OrdManage.OrdEntry", _
    Server, _
    Application, _
    Session, _
    Request, _
    Response
%>
```

The code in the If block checks to see if a reference to the Visual Basic supplied object WebClassRunTime.WebClassManager exists. If it doesn't, the code creates the object and stores it in the ASP Application object under the name ~WC~WebClassManager. With that object created, the bottom part of the code passes the name of your object (OrdManage.OrdEntry) to the WebClassManager's ProcessNoStateWebClass method, along with references to five of the ASP objects. If you have set the WebClass's StateManagement property to wcRetainInstance, the WebClassManager's ProcessRetainInstanceWebClass method will be used instead of ProcessNoStateWebClass. Somewhere after that point, your object will be created and its processing will begin.

You will need to create a package to install your IIS application on your server. This will need to include the WebClassRuntime component, but the Package and Deployment Wizard will ensure the component is included. If an IIS Application has already been installed on the server, you can choose to remove the WebClassRuntime component from your package.

You must also include in your installation the ASP pages generated by Visual Basic and any other Web pages that you used as Templates.

Summary

In this chapter you were introduced to the IIS and DHTML applications and how they can be used to create applications that run over the World Wide Web from within Visual Basic. You also got a peek at the first ActiveX Designers that can be added to Visual Basic.

I began by showing you how to create DHTML Applications. DHTML Applications are really ActiveX Controls that you can add to a Web page in order to interact with the page's elements. I discussed how to use the DHTMLPage Designer and outlined how to use the object's methods and properties. DHTML Applications can only be used in Internet Explorer 4.0 or greater.

You then learned how to build IIS Applications. IIS Applications are a combination of ActiveX components that execute on your Web server and Web pages containing the ASP code to call your component. You learned how to generate Web pages that go to the browser and that would, in turn, request your page from the server. You also saw the various techniques that are available to you to call the routines in your component from HTML tags in your Web page. Finally, from IIS Applications, you can access the objects that make up the ASP object model.

Before you start working with these tools you should become familiar with the special problems with creating Web applications. A good overview of the Microsoft technologies can be found in *Microsoft Official Web Commerce Solutions Web Technologies* by Micro Modeling Associates. For more detail on the DHTML object model itself, I'd recommend *IE5 Dynamic HTML Programmer's Reference* by Brian Francis, Alex Homer, and Chris Ullman from Wrox as a good combination of tutorial and reference. To really exploit IIS Applications, you'll need to become familiar with the ASP object model. An excellent reference is *Professional Active Server Pages 3.0* by various authors, also from Wrox. Finally, after becoming familiar with ASP, DHTML, and Web development, look at the article "Design Considerations for IIS Applications" in the MSDN disks that ship with Visual Studio.

A useful exercise at this point would be to take an existing Visual Basic control and convert it into a Web-based application using the technologies. To do this you'll have to move your database access to an IIS Application and tie the various update activities back to HTML tags on your form. Any data validation that requires database access will also have to be done by your IIS Application. Your User Interface, on the other hand will have to be implemented through a DHTML Application that will respond to events triggered in the browser by the user interacting with your application.

F O U R T E E N

Script Components

All of the objects that I've discussed so far have one thing in common: They've been compiled. Microsoft's Scripting technologies go one step further and lets you create objects with nothing more complicated than Notepad. You can use these objects from your Windows desktop, from within Internet Explorer, and from any COM application (including ASP). With Scripting you can write code that executes in your Web browser and reaches back through the Internet to execute objects on your server. Scripting allows Web Developers to use the same technologies that you use to build your applications (Script, HTML, and DHTML) to build the components that your application uses. For the Windows power user, script finally provides a missing part of the Windows operations System: Script provides a batch language for Windows.

This chapter describes a technology that Microsoft originally called ActiveX Scripting but now just refers to as Scripting. ActiveX Scripting first appeared as a way for developers to switch among different languages when writing code to execute in Internet Explorer or ASP. Since then the technology has spread everywhere. In this chapter I provide an introduction to Scripting and where you can use it (everywhere from the Windows Desktop to Office 2000). You'll begin by seeing how to create both client-side and server-side Scriptlet objects, which don't need to be registered. Then I show you how to create components using script that you can register and call from any COM-compliant language, a technique that involves combining XML with Script code. DHTML and ASP will appear again as environments where you can use scripting components. Finally, I list some of the tools that Microsoft has provided for working with script.

Introducing Scripting

The term "scripting" does not have a clear definition. Generally, a language is called a scripting language because the vendor slapped that label on it, so the term means different things to different people. In general, the term refers to languages that are

- *Hosted:* the language must execute in some environment and can't be compiled to run standalone.
- *Interpreted:* the language is read and executed on a line-by-line basis rather than converted completely into machine code for execution.
- *Limited:* the language is missing some key features that prevent it from being a full-fledged development tool.

I should point out that none of these definitions are very satisfactory. Every program executes in some container, if only the operating system of the computer that it is running on. With Microsoft's scripting languages, the whole script is compiled (at least to a pseudo-code state) before any part of it is executed. And every language is missing features that another development language supports.

The underlying metaphor for scripting languages is that the program exists just to coordinate the activities of objects. Like a script for a cast of actors, a scripting program makes sure that every person (object) involved plays their part at the right time. Yet, as I've tried to suggest in this book, that's the trend for every language in the modern "object-oriented" world.

More and more of the functionality that would have been embedded in a language back when I started programming has been moved out to a set of objects. The languages that are to be used to create objects need to be full-featured development tools, capable of accessing every feature of the operating system and computer. However, the languages that build applications out of objects may need only the ability to stitch together the necessary objects and manipulate the user interface. Scripting languages may, in fact, be the future of application development.

ActiveX Scripting

ActiveX Scripting was Microsoft's original term for the ability to swap in different language engines on demand. Available language engines include implementations of JavaScript/ECMAScript, VBA, and PERLE, among others. In a Web page, using scripting, a programmer could enter this code:

```
<Script Language=VBScript>
Dim intMyValue
Function Increment(intIn)
  Increment = intIn + 1
End Function
</Script>

<Script Language=JScript>
  var Answer = Increment(intMyValue)
</Script>
```

The example shows some of the flexibility of Microsoft's Scripting technology. The first script block contains code written in VBScript while the second block contains JScript (JScript is Microsoft's implementation of ECMAScript, the equivalent of Netscape's JavaScript). The language-neutral basis of the ActiveX specification means that the JScript code in the second block can call the VBScript routines defined in the first block. Variables are freely shared between the two scripts, despite the differences in the languages.

The code in either script block can access the objects made available by the environment that they are executing in. In my example, the code executes inside of Internet Explorer and so would be able to manipulate the object in the Document Object Model (DOM) or the DHTML object model.

Mixing scripting languages on the same page does impose a performance burden on your application: It will take longer to process your page than if you used only one language.

VBScript

Since this book is about Visual Basic, I'm going to use VBScript to demonstrate how to create components in script. The VBScript interpreter is distributed with Internet Explorer, Windows 98, and IIS (as is JScript). You can also get other interpreters (a script version of PERLE, for instance) from vendors other than Microsoft.

It's appropriate, then, to begin this chapter with a look at the VBScript language. You could think of VBScript as the Visual Basic for Applications (VBA) language with a prefrontal lobotomy: all the dangerous and complicated stuff removed.

VBA is the language engine underlying all of Microsoft's "VB*" tools (except VBScript). When you buy Microsoft Word, Excel, Access, or Visual Basic, you get VBA. With the Microsoft Word product you get a hosted editor for creating VBA programs plus a set of document management and creation objects. With the Visual Basic product you get a standalone editor and a compiler. I'm told that the Microsoft Word product also includes free word processor along with VBA and its document objects, but how good can anything you get for free really be?

VBScript was designed to be a language whose engine used the minimum amount of memory and operated "in the sandbox." A language is said to be "in the sandbox" when it can't interact with any of the persistent features of the computer that it is operating on. VBScript, for instance, includes no keywords for:

- Loading and executing objects (e.g., New, CreateObject, GetObject)
- Working with the file system (e.g., Open, Kill)
- Directly accessing the operating system (e.g., Declare)

If your application needs these abilities, then you will have to augment your VBScript program with objects that provide those facilities. Since VBScript doesn't include any keywords to load an object, the objects will have to be provided by the Script's host environment. For instance, for server-side Web-based applications, script code has access to the Server object, which includes a CreateObject method. By using the Server object's CreateObject method, ASP hosted script code can load and execute objects.

The VBScript language was also designed to be small so that its language engine could be easily downloaded and installed. To achieve this goal, some VBA language features were removed to reduce the size of the language engine. In the initial version of VBScript, for instance, the Select statement was absent. Many features have since crept back in (the Select statement is supported by the latest version of VBScript). On the other hand, the very useful VBA Format function is still not part of the VBScript language.

However, it would be a mistake to think of the VBScript language as just a subset of the Visual Basic for Applications language. When the Format function was removed, for instance, it was replaced by a set of more efficient (though more limited) functions: FormatDateTime, FormatCurrancy, FormatNumber, and so on. These functions have since made their way to VBA. Since the release schedules for VBA and VBScript aren't synchronized, VBA generally includes all the capabilities of the last version of VBScript but may not include features from a more recent version of VBScript.

In general, new releases of VBA tend to be synchronized with release of Visual Basic (which is released with Visual Studio) while new versions of VBScript tend to come out with new releases of Internet Explorer or Internet Information Server. Currently, VBA 6.0 includes all the language features of VBScript 4.0. However, after the release of Visual Studio 6.0 and VBA 6.0, new versions of Internet Explorer and VBScript were released. The current version of VBScript (5.0) includes Execute and Eval, which aren't part of VBA. These statements allow you to create a string variable containing VBScript commands and then have those commands executed by passing the string to either Eval function or the Execute statement. This is a feature that may never be available in compiled versions of the language, since its functionality is normally restricted to interpreted execution environments. These two commands, however, do give VBScript parity with JavaScript, which has always had equivalent functionality.

Scripting Hosts

The original hosts for Scripting were ASP and Internet Explorer. Microsoft has since provided the Windows Script Host as part of the Windows operating system.

A scripting host performs two functions. First, it loads the script that's to be executed, identifies the language engine to invoke, and begins processing of the script. Second, the scripting host provides a set of objects for the scripting language to access. Since a scripting language is limited to running "in the sandbox," the objects that the host makes available to the script have a significant impact on what a script can and can't do.

A script running in Internet Explorer, for instance, has no access to any object that allows the script to load a new object. So, in the Internet Explorer environment, the browser must load all objects that the script can use. In the ASP and Windows Script Host environments, on the other hand, there are objects available that allow a script to load and execute new objects. In ASP a script can use the Server object's CreateObject method, while under the Windows Script Host you would use WScript object's CreateObject method.

In Office 2000, you can add scripts to your Word, Excel, and PowerPoint documents. However, the scripts will only execute when the documents are saved in HTML/XML format and viewed in Internet Explorer.

WINDOWS SCRIPT HOST

The Windows Script Host for Windows provides the hosting environment for scripts that are run in the Windows. With the Script Host, Windows finally acquires a native batch language. The great thing about the Windows Script Host is that it loads very quickly, making it a good choice when creating small procedures like batch files.

Since this is a book on building objects, complete coverage of the Windows Script Host would be inappropriate. In this section I provide enough information on the Windows Script Host to enable you to use Script components from a Windows Script Host application.

The Windows Script Host comes with Windows 98 and Windows 2000. It is a download add-on to Windows 95 and Windows NT.

You can run scripts in any of three different ways:

1. Associate a file extension with the scripting host interpreter (WScript.EXE). On my computer, I've associated .vbs (for VBScript) with WScript.EXE, so that double clicking on a file ending with vbs causes the scripting engine to read the file and start executing it. With this association made, I can also execute a script file by entering its name in the Start | Run dialog.
2. Run the interpreter engine, WScript, passing the name of the file containing the VBScript program (e.g., WScript c:\sample.vbs). This method allows you to pass one or more of the command line switches listed in Table 14.1 to the scripting engine. The syntax for using the engine is

```
Wscript filename options arguments
```

3. Run a file with the extension .wsh. A wsh files contains a set of parameters for the scripting host, specifying the file containing the script and which command line parameters are to be applied. This method gives you all the benefits of double clicking a file to execute a script with all the flexibility of setting command line parameters. A wsh file can be created for a vbs file by right-mouse clicking on a vbs file, selecting Properties, and then clicking the Script tab on the resulting dialog (see Figure 14–1). Here's a sample wsh file that runs the Sample.VBS file with the options //I //T:10 //logo:

```
[ScriptFile]
  Path=C:\Sample.VBS

  [Options]
  Timeout=10
  DisplayLogo=1
  BatchMode=0
```

Table 14.1 The Windows Script Host Command Line Options

Option	Description	Default
//B	Suppresses errors and prompts (effectively runs the script in batch mode)	
//H:CScript	Invokes the console (DOS-based) scripting engine	
//H:Wscript	Invokes the Windows scripting engine	Yes
//I	Allows errors and prompts (opposite of //B)	Yes
//logo	Displays logo	Yes
//nologo	No banner displayed	
//S	Makes current settings the default	
//T:nn	Sets maximum time for script execution to nn second	

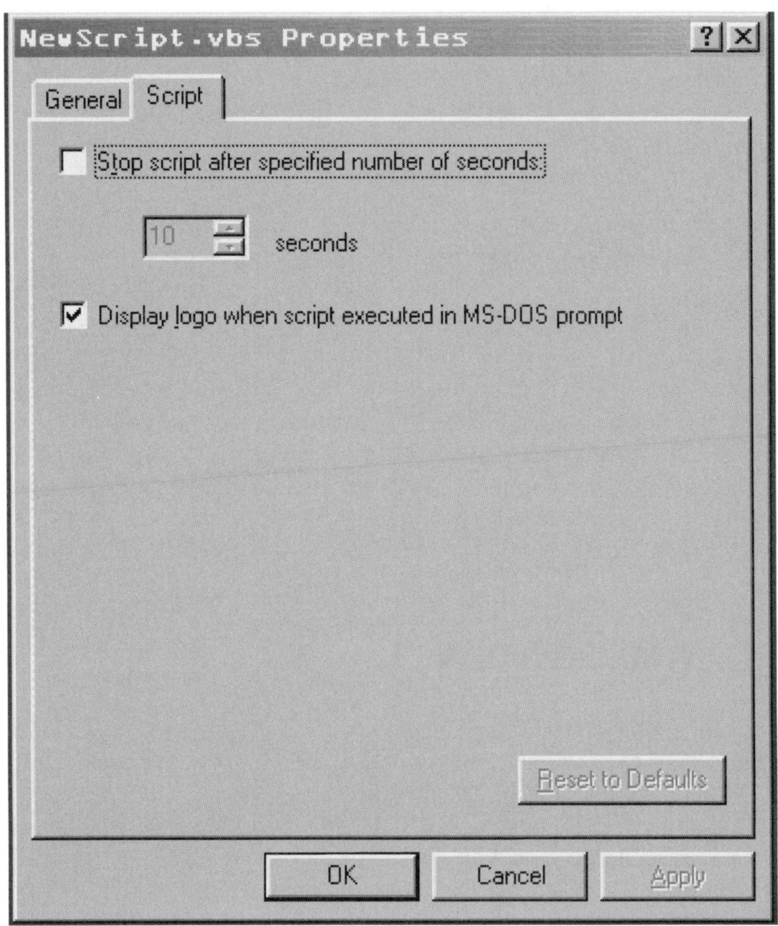

Figure 14–1 *The properties page for a Windows Script Host Script.*

USING OBJECTS FROM THE WINDOWS SCRIPT HOST

The Windows Script Host provides the WScript object, which has some very useful methods and properties. The relevant method for this book is CreateObject, which allows you to invoke other objects so that you can use their methods and properties. This code, for instance, starts up Word and adds a blank page:

```
Set wrd = WScript.CreateObject("Word.Application")
wrd.Documents.Add
wrd.Visible = True
```

The Wscript's CreateObject method also accepts a second parameter that allows you to specify a prefix that's used to define subroutines to catch events fired by the object. In the following code, for instance, CreateObject is used to instantiate an object and catch its events. The object (in this case, Project.Object) fires a Load event that the script catches in the CatchEvent_Load routine:

```
Set obj = _
  WScript.CreateObject("Project.Object","CatchEvent")

Sub CatchEvent_Load
  obj.Visible = True
End Sub
```

When you're finished with an object that you've invoked to catch events, before setting the object to Nothing, you should disconnect it from the scripting host using the Disconnect method:

```
WScript.DisconnectObject obj
Set obj = Nothing
```

DHTML Scriptlets

The simplest objects to create with Script are the DHTML Scriptlets used in Internet Explorer 4.0 and up. A DHTML Scriptlet is a text file that includes a combination of HTML, DHTML, and script. You can choose to expose some or all of the script routines as public methods or properties. The result is a file that, when included in a Web page, produces an object. If the text file includes HTML, then the object also has a user interface that will be incorporated into the Web page that uses the Scriptlet (see Figure 14–2). You might think of a Scriptlet as a kind of ActiveX Control created from Script and HTML.

Creating a DHTML Scriptlet Object

This code defines a simple Scriptlet containing a text box, a command button, and some code to validate the contents of the text box:

```
<HTML>
<BODY>

<INPUT Type=Text Name=txtEMailAddress Id=txtEMailAddress>
<INPUT Type=Button Name=cmdValidate Id=cmdValidate
  Value="Check Data" onClick=CheckEMailAddress()>

<Script Language=VBScript>
Function CheckEMailAddress()
  CheckEMailAddress = True
```

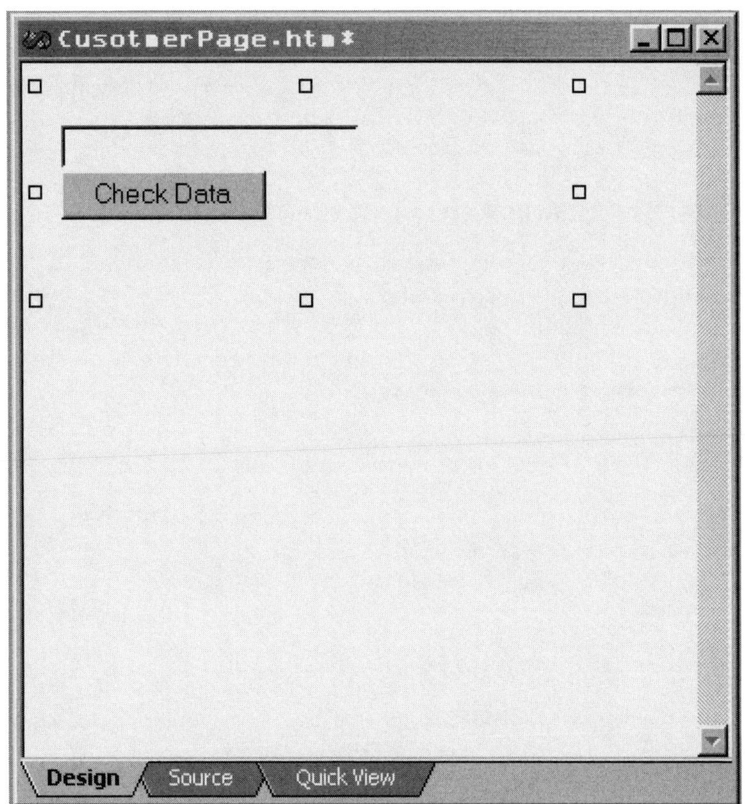

Figure 14–2 *A Web page displaying a Scriptlet.*

```
  If Instr(document.all.txtEMailAddress.value, "@") = 0 Then
    MsgBox "Bad E-Mail address."
    CheckEMailAddress = False
  End If
End Function
</Script>

</BODY>
</HTML>
```

To add this Scriptlet to a Web page, you would use this HTML tag:

```
<OBJECT Id=GetEMail Type=text/x-Scriptlet
  Style="HEIGHT: 100px;LEFT: 0px; TOP: 0px; WIDTH: 100px">
    <PARAM Name="URL"
      Value="http://MyServer/MySite/MyScriptlet.HTM">
</OBJECT>
```

The <OBJECT> tag is used to cause the browser to download a program—in this case, your Scriptlet. The tag's Type attribute indicates that the object to be downloaded is a Scriptlet. The Param tag provides the browser with the information on where to find the Scriptlet to be downloaded. The <OBJECT> tag also assigns the DHTML Id GetEMail to this object.

METHODS, PROPERTIES, AND EVENTS

My previous example showed a completely self-contained Script. However, Scriptlets can also expose methods and properties, and fire events. To expose any routine as a method, you only need to add the prefix "public_" to the function name. Rewriting the preceding Scriptlet to expose the CheckEMail-Address method would look like this:

```
<Script Language=VBScript>
Function Public_CheckEMailAddress()
  Public_CheckEMailAddress = True
  If Instr(document.all.txtEMailAddress, "@") = 0 Then
    MsgBox "Bad E-Mail address."
    Public_CheckEMailAddress = False
  End If
End Function
</Script>
```

Since the <OBJECT> tag that invoked the Scriptlet assigned it the name GetEMail, I can call the CheckEMailAddress function from the page that is hosting the Scriptlet like this:

```
bolResult = document.all.GetEMail.CheckEMailAddress()
```

There is no need to use New or CreateObject to load the object—the <OBJECT> tag takes care of creating the object. Effectively, the <OBJECT> tag creates an object from the text in the HTML page MyScriptlet.HTM.

To create a property, you add the prefixes "Public_Get_" and "Public_Put_" to the name of the property to create Get and Put routines (Puts are the equivalent of a Property Let routine). This code, for instance, creates an EMail property that retrieves and updates the value of the Scriptlets txtEMailAddress TextBox:

```
Sub Public_Put_EMail(strAddress)
  Document.all.txtEMailAddress.Value = strAddress
End Sub
Sub Public_Get_EMail()
  Public_Get_EMail = Document.all.txtEMailAddress.Value
End Sub
```

The EMail property could be used from code on the hosting page like this:

```
document.all.GetEMail.EMail = "peter.vogel@phvis.com"
Msgbox document.all.GetEmail.Email
```

In addition to simple data types like strings and numerics, you can use the Get and Put routines to return and accept objects from your Scriptlet.

Events can be raised by using the RaiseEvent method of the External object. The External object is provided by Internet Explorer and is accessed through the External property of the Document Object Model's Document object. The RaiseEvent method accepts two parameters: the name of the event and a reference to an object (typically, the object that triggered the event).

The following code inside a Scriplet would fire an event when the edit on txtEMailAddress fails. The code passes a name for the event (BadEMail) and a reference to the EmailAddress TextBox to the hosting page:

```
<Script Language=VBScript>
Function Public_CheckEMailAddress()
  Public_CheckEMailAddress = True
  If Instr(document.all.txtEMailAddress, "@") = 0 Then
    Window.External.RaiseEvent "BadEMail",
      document.all.txtEMailAddress
    Public_CheckEMailAddress = False
  End If
End Sub
</Script>
```

To catch the events fired by RaiseEvent, the hosting page must implement an OnScriptletEvent routine. This routine will be called for all of the events fired by the RaiseEvent method. In a page that hosts a Scriptlet, you would add this code to catch events from the Scriptlet GetEMail:

```
Sub GetEMail_onScriptletEvent(strEName, objEObject)
  If strEName = "BadEMail" Then
    MsgBox objEObject.Value & _
      " must have a @ sign to be a valid address."
  End If
End Sub
```

The name of the routine consists of the Id attribute of the Scriptlet's <OBJECT> tag followed by the name of the event joined by an underscore. The two parameters passed to the routine are the same ones passed by the RaiseEvent method: the name of the event and a reference to the object that fired the event. In this example, the code checks the name of the event and, if it is "BadEMail", displays the current value of the TextBox and a message.

You can also pass events fired by elements within the Scriptlet out to the page that is hosting the Scriptlet through "event bubbling." If a DHTML element fires an event and no routine exists to process that event, then the event will fire for the next element up in the HTML hierarchy (see Figure 14–3).

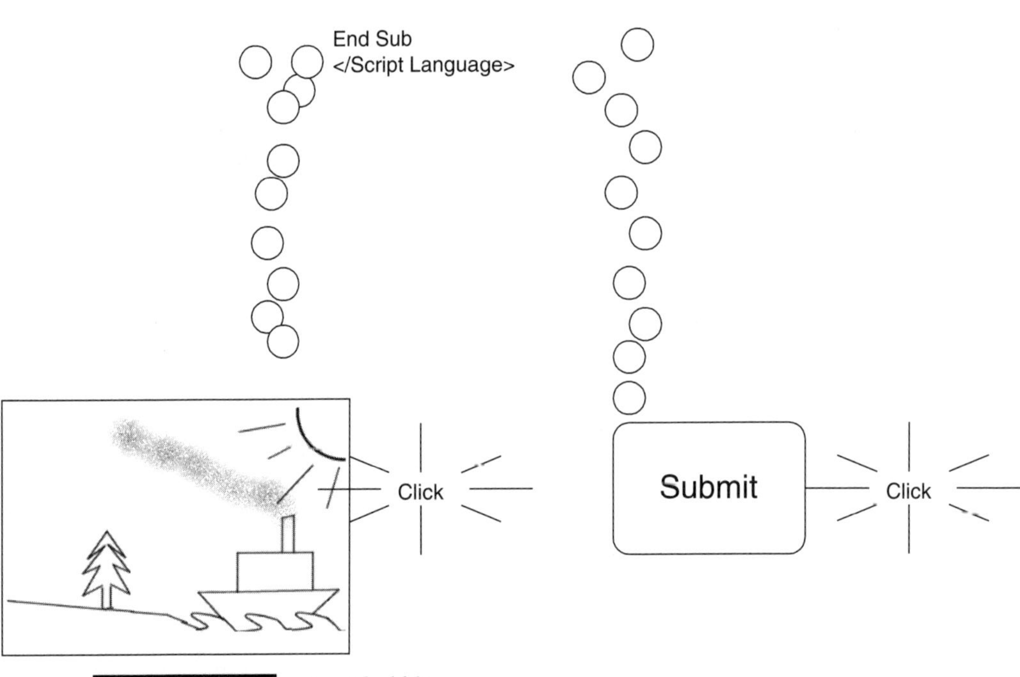

Figure 14–3 *Event bubbling.*

A TextBox in a Form on a Web page provides a simple example. If the user clicks on the TextBox, the TextBox will fire an onClick event. If no onClick event routine exists for the TextBox, the Form that the TextBox is part of will fire an onClick event, and so on right up to the Document object. The event "bubbles up" through the elements on the page until it is processed.

Only the onClick, onDblClick, onKeyDown, onKeyUp, onKeyPress, onMouseDown, onMouseUp, and onMouseMove events can be bubbled. This code, for instance, bubbles any onClick event in the Scriptlet that isn't handled within the Scriptlet out to the hosting page:

```
Sub Window_onClick()
  Window.External.BubbleEvent()
End Sub
```

The hosting page handles this onClick event as it would any event fired by an object on the page. This code would be used to catch the onClick event for the GetEMail object:

```
Sub GetEMail_onClick()
  ...code to process the event
End Sub
```

Scriptlets can contain anything that a Web page can—including an object tag for another Scriptlet.

Remote Scripting and ASP Remote Objects

Remote Scripting allows you to write code to execute in Internet Explorer that reaches back through the Web to execute objects on the server. This gives your client-side code access to server-side resources without making the user wait through a roundtrip to the server (see Figure 14–4).

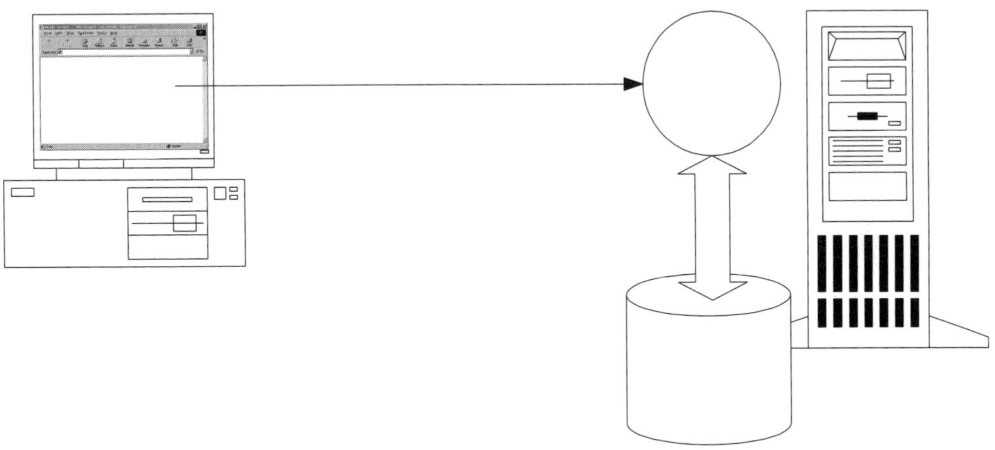

Figure 14–4 *Remote scripting.*

To use Remote Scripting as described here, you must be using IIS 4.0 or later as your Web server. However, you should be able to use any browser with Remote Scripting because the underlying technology is implemented using a Java applet. Having said that, if you intend your client-side code to run in a browser other than Internet Explorer, you should write your script in JavaScript. I stick to VBScript for the examples in this chapter.

You can download the necessary updates to IIS that are required to support Remote Scripting from the Microsoft scripting site (*www.microsoft.com/scripting*). This package also includes a set of files that you will need to use in developing your application:

- RS.HTM: standard client-side routines
- RS.ASP: standard server-side routines
- RSProxy.class: a Java applet which the routines in RS.HTM will download to your client and which handles communication with the server.

The following examples assume that these files have been placed in a directory called ScriptLibrary immediately under the root directory for your Website. If you're using Visual InterDev as your development tool, this directory is automatically created for you as part of starting a new Web project.

ON THE SERVER

Once you have set up the directory and placed the standard files in it, you can create a file to hold your server-side object. Your server-side object must be in a file with an ASP extension. Since this file never goes to the browser, it doesn't need to include any HTML. The file must, however, include the following entries which incorporate some standard routines into your file and then run the Remote Scripting initialization routine:

```
<%@ Language=JScript %>
<!--#INCLUDE FILE="../_ScriptLibrary/RS.ASP"-->
```

You can then add any functions or subroutines that you want to use to define methods. The process of defining methods is slightly more complicated than with DHTML Scriptlets. First, you must create a Class using VBScript 5.0's Class statement. You then place your routines inside the Class declaration.

With the class defined, you must then make it available to the clients that call your object. You do this by creating a variable called public_description and setting it to a new instance of your Class. Finally, you must initialize remote scripting by calling the RSDispatch routine from RS.ASP. This sample code creates an object called DBManager with a method called MakeConnection:

```
<Script Language=VBScript RunAt=Server>

Class DBManager
  Public Sub MakeConnection()
    Set conn = _
      Server.CreateObject("ADODB.Connection")
    conn.Open "File Name=c:\MyDatabase.UDL"
    Set Session("Connection") = conn
  End Sub
End Class

Set public_description = new DBManager
RSDispatch

</Script>
```

Parameters passed to a server-side method must be passed as strings. The object can return both objects and variants.

ON THE CLIENT

The Web page that will use your server-side object needs to initialize Remote Scripting by adding the following entries to the page. You must first add this script block to have the routines in RS.HTM included in your Web page:

```
<SCRIPT Language="JavaScript"
  src="../_ScriptLibrary/RS.HTM">
</SCRIPT>
```

Your next script block must call the RSEnableRemoteScripting routine in the RS.HTM page to initialize Remote Scripting on the client:

```
<SCRIPT LANGUAGE="javascript">
   RSEnableRemoteScripting("../_ScriptLibrary");
</SCRIPT>
```

With those entries made, the client-side program can then create the server-side object using the RSGetASPObject function. The RSGetASPObject accepts a single parameter, the URL to the ASP page. After the object has been created, calling its methods and properties looks like any other object. This code would create a server-side object from a file called MyObject.ASP and call its MakeConnection method:

```
Set objConn = RSGetASPObject("MyObject.ASP")
objConn.MakeConnection
```

If the method returns a value, then you must accept an object from your server-side object. This object is referred to as the Call object and its return_value property will contain the value returned from the server-side method. This code accepts a Call object from the GetCustomerName method and displays the result:

```
Set objCall = objConn.GetCustomerName(strCustomerNumber)
Msgbox "The customer name is " & objCall.return_value
```

THE CALL OBJECT

In addition to result_value, the Call object has a number of useful properties:

- Status: You should check this after each RSExecute call. A value of –1 indicates that the call failed, while 0 indicates successful completion.

- Message: This property contains either "Completed" for successful calls or an error message for unsuccessful calls.
- Data: Contains XML information from the object about any error condition.

Other properties and methods relate to calling objects asynchronously, which can only be done using JScript.

Defining Script Components

With DHTML Scriptlets there was no need to register your object because the <OBJECT> tag provided all the information that the hosting page needs to invoke your object. The same is true of remote scripting because the RSGetASPObject function simply accepted the URL for your object. However, to use a Script object from any other environment you'll need to register your Script object so that it can be loaded using CreateObject or New. Fortunately, Scripting also allows you to create Script components that can be registered and so found by any other application. Table 14.2 shows the relationships among clients and objects with the three scripting technologies that I've discussed so far.

Table 14.2 Script components location and registration requirements.

	Client	Server	Registration Required?
DHTML Scriptlets	Yes		
Remote Scripting	Joint	Joint	
Script Components	Yes	Yes	Yes

The following discussion assumes that you've got the current version of the Microsoft scripting components installed on your computer. The latest version can be downloaded from the Microsoft scripting site (*msdn.microsoft.com/scripting*).

To create a "registerable" Script object, you must add XML tags to your Script file that contain the information required for registration. The XML tags also allow you to generate a type library for your component to support other COM applications. These two features (registration and type library generation) together give you the ability to create true components using Scripting.

In Script, the term Component always refers to a single class. You can't, in Script, create a component that contains multiple objects. Instead, you create multiple components that are part of a package instead of objects that are part of a component.

XML

A brief introduction to XML is probably in order at this point. XML is a language for defining tags. This is very different from HTML, which is a collection of specific tags. XML, instead of being a list of tags, specifies the rules for creating tags. Microsoft has used XML to define a set of tags to be used with Script components.

Another difference between XML and HTML is the way that the tags in the two systems are typically used. HTML tags are normally used to control the appearance of the text in a Web page. XML tags, however, are normally used to define the data that the tags are used with. As an example, Microsoft's XML tags for use with Scriptlets define a registration tag that holds all the registration information for a Scriptlet:

```
<registration
  Description="A registered Scriptlet."
  ProgID="RegisteredScriptlet.Object1"
  Version="1.00"
  ClassID="{af1303fr-fb20-3405-d278-8ee2945300af}"
/>
```

The registration tag's attributes provide all the information that is needed to register your component. Unlike an HTML tag, none of the attributes are concerned with how the material is to be displayed.

The last major difference between XML and HTML is the way that the syntax rules are enforced. With syntax checking turned on, your code must adhere strictly to the rules of XML. For instance, the name of the registration tag includes no capital letters. XML will accept "registration" but will not recognize "Registration" as a valid tag in the Script environment.

Creating a Script Component

To create a Script component, you begin by creating a text file with the extension WSC. You then enter a combination of XML and Script to define your component. The XML required to define a Script component is wordy, but relatively straightforward. These tags define all the required information:

- package: Wraps multiple components.
- component: Wraps one component.
- public: Defines the exposed methods, properties, and events.

- implements: Defines the interfaces that can be used by the component.
- registration: Provides all the information required to register the component.
- object: Loads an object and assigns it an id to use from within your code.
- reference: Provides information about other objects used by the component (equivalent to adding a reference to the Visual Basic references list).
- resource: Defines constants and other values to be used in the component.
- comment: Wraps all comments.
- script: Wraps all code.

The file to create a Script component that would open and name a new Word document might look like this:

```
<package>
  <comment>
        Author: Peter Vogel
    Date: 99/01/04
  </comment>

  <component id="MyScriptComponent">
    <registration
      progid="MyScriptComponent.OpenDocument"
         description="A sample object"
         version="1.0"
         clsid="{bcde9140-5068-11d3-a8c8-00107a901a5f}"/>

  <reference guid="000209FF-0000-0000-C000-000000000046"/>

    <public>
       <property name="DocumentName"/>
       <method name="OpenFile"/>
       <event name="FileOpen"/>
    </public>

    <script language="VBScript">
    dim DocumentName
    Function OpenFile()
     Set wrd = WScript.CreateObject(GetResource("MSWord"))
    wrd.Documents.Add
    wrd.SaveAs FileName "MyDocument.DOC", wdFormatRTF
    FireEvent "FileOpen"

    End Function
    </script>
```

```
   <resource id="MSWord">Word.Application</resource>
</component>
</package>
```

PACKAGE AND COMPONENT TAGS

The package tag is required only if there is more than one component in the file. Since my example includes only one component, I could have been omitted the package tag. The two parts of the package tag (<package> and </package>) must enclose all the components in the file.

The component tag encloses one script component. The id attribute assigns the component a class name.

Components in the same file can invoke each other using the Create-Component function. If my example file had included a component called CreateWord with a method called StartWord, I could have used the component like this:

```
Set cwo = CreateComponent("CreateWord")
cwo.StartWord
```

REFERENCE, RESOURCE, AND OBJECT TAGS

The reference tag allows you to pick up type libraries to use within your component, allowing you to use the predefined constants defined in the library in your script. In my example, I've used the reference tag to load a reference to the Word.Application type library. The reference tag's attributes allow you to add a reference using either object's ProgId or GUID. This reference tag uses a progid to retrieve type information for the ADODB Connection object:

```
<reference object="ADODB.Connection.2.0"/>
```

You can also specify a version number using the reference tag's version attribute:

```
<reference object="ADODB.Connection" Version="2.0"/>
```

Any tag that isn't a paired tag (like the reference, event, and method tags) must end with "/>" instead of just ">".

The object tag allows you to load another object. This tag, for instance, loads Microsoft Word and assigns it to the object variable wrd:

```
<object id=wrd progid="Word.Application"/>
```

The resource tag gives you the ability to define constants to be used in your component. This resource tag defines the constant ScriptName and assigns it the value MyScriptComponent.WSC:

```
<resource id="ScriptName">MyScriptComponent.WSC</resource>
```

You retrieve resources using the GetResource function. This code uses the ScriptName resource in an error message:

```
MsgBox GetResource("ScriptName")
```

COMMENT TAGS

You can use the comment tag inside any other tags. In this example, I've used it inside the Script tag:

```
<script language="VBScript">
 <comment>
 This component opens a new Word file and saves it
 under the name specified in the first argument passed to
 the script
 </comment>
Dim varName
```

THE REGISTRATION TAG

The registration tag's attributes provide most of the information that's required by the Window's registry. All of the registration's attributes (progid, classid, version, description, remotable) are optional. You must, however, provide one of the classid or progid attributes.

You can use GUIDGen.EXE or UUIDGen.EXE to generate the ClassId. See the chapter on data providers for a discussion of how to use these tools.

Though I've provided both the classid and progid attributes (and that's the best practice, as I discuss here) in my example, I could have omitted one or the other. If you omit the progid attribute, no progid is created for your object and you'll have to access the object exclusively by its classid. Since the progid is the most convenient way for you to refer to your component, if you're only going to provide one then you will probably want to provide the progid and omit the classid.

If you omit the classid, one will be generated for your object. Providing the classid, however, reduces the changes in the component's registration information each time you register it. If you omit the classid, it will be generated during the registration process. This means that your component will have a different classid on every computer on which it is registered. It also means that you will have to recompile any programs that use your component if you reregister your component. As I said, the best practice is to include both the classid and the progid.

The remotable attribute indicates whether the component can be accessed from another computer on the network using DCOM. This example of the registration tag creates a remotable component:

```
<registration
  progid="MyScript.MyObject"
  remotable="true"/>
```

This component could now be accessed using the version of the CreateObject function that accepts a server name, like this:

```
Dim obj As Object
Set obj = _
  CreateObject("MyScript.MyObject", "PHVServer")
```

Finally, if you set up the registration tag as a paired tag, you will be able to include a script block between the start and end tags. This block can contain a routine called Register to run when the component is registered and a routine called Unregister to be run when the component is unregistered. In this example, the component displays a simple message during these two events:

```
<registration
  progid="MyScriptComponent.OpenDocument"
    clsid="{bcde9140-5068-11d3-a8c8-00107a901a5f}">
    <script language="VBScript">
  Function Register()
    MsgBox "Registered"
  End Function
  Function Unregister()
    MsgBox "Unregistered"
  End Function
    </script>
    </registration>
```

I use registration scripts for two purposes. As I discuss later, the Register function can be used to generate a type library for your component when it is registered. I also use the function to provide feedback to me on which version of my component is being registered. To do this, I display a message from the Register routine using the MsgBox statement. I update the message displayed from the Register routine whenever I find that I'm making changes to my component that don't seem to be having any effect on the way it runs. A typical Register routine for me looks like this:

```
Function Register()
  MsgBox "Version 3.2"
End Function
```

The message "Version 3.2" will now be displayed when I register my component, assuring me that I am registering the version of the component that I just finished making changes to. On at least a few occasions, I have found that the file that I've been registering hasn't been the file that I've been changing.

EVENT TAG

The public tag contains tags for each property, method, and event that you want your component to expose. While your component may contain many routines, only the ones listed between the public tags will be available to clients using your component.

The event tag allows you to define an event and assign it a dispid. Just like assigning a dispid to an event in an ActiveX Control, this feature allows you to have your event be treated like one of the events defined in the ActiveX specification (e.g., the NewEnum method that lets a collection participate in a For Each...Next loop). Assigning a dispid also reduces the changes in the component's interface definition when you generate your component's type library. Without the dispid attribute, your event could get a new dispid each time it is registered.

This event tag defines the event CustomerNotFound and gives it the dispid 126:

```
<public>
  <event name="CustomerNotFound" dispid="126">
</public>
```

The fireEvent method allows you to raise the events that you define in the event tag. The fireEvent method has the same syntax as the RaiseEvent method discussed earlier in this chapter under DHTML Scriptlets. However, the client using your object can treat an event fired by the fireEvent method like any other object's event. This is different from RaiseEvent, which required the containing page to create an onScriptletEvent routine.

This code fires an event called BadEMail and passes a reference to the txtEMailAddress TextBox:

```
fireEvent("BadEmail", txtEMailAddress)
```

To catch this event, the client using your object would include a routine like this (assuming that the name of the object firing the event is GetEMail):

```
Sub GetEMail_BadEMail(EObject)
  MsgBox EObject.Value & _
    " is not a valid e-mail address."
End Sub
```

If the amount of XML that I discuss here is starting to seem daunting, don't be dismayed. Microsoft provides the Script Component Wizard which will generate most of these entries for you (see Figure 14–5).

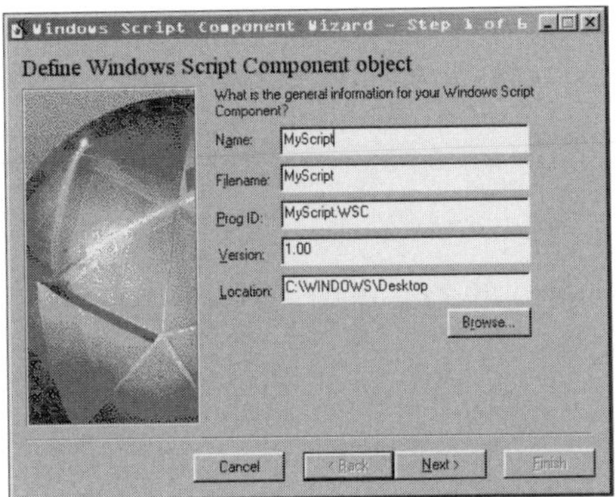

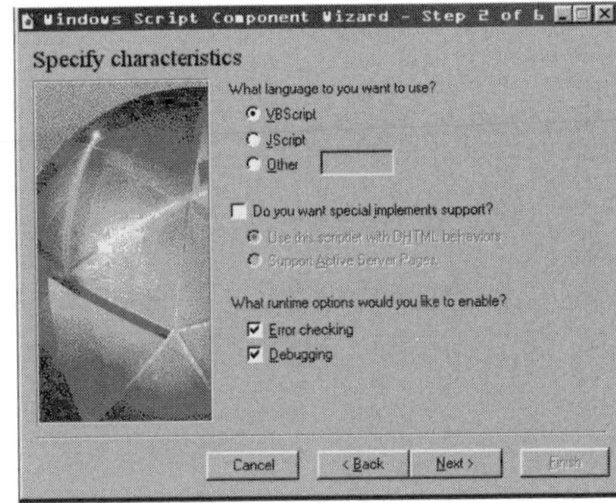

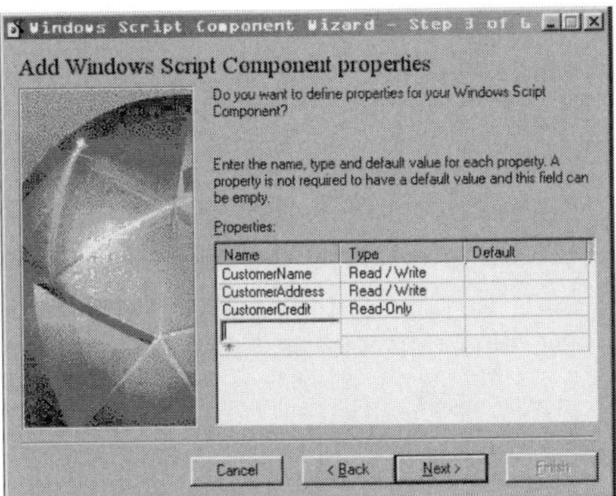

Figure 14–5 *The Script Component Wizard.*

PROPERTY TAG

The simplest version of the property tag lets you establish one of the public variables in your script code as a property of your component. These property tags, for instance, turn the CustomerName and CustomerNumber variables into properties of the component:

```
<public>
  <property name="CustomerName"/>
  <property name="CustomerNumber"/>
</public>

<script language="VBScript">
Dim CustomerName
Dim CustomerNumber
</script>
```

You can also create property procedures to implement your properties. To indicate that the routine uses property procedures, you can add get and put attributes to the property tag. This property tag defines a property called EMailName that will be implemented with property procedures:

```
<public>
  <property name="EMailName"get put />
</public>
```

You can also use the paired version of the property tag to indicate that your property is implemented through property procedures. This tag also indicates that the EMailName property is implemented with property procedures:

```
<public>
  <property name="EMailName">
  <get />
  <put />
  </property>
</public>
```

Having indicated that you are using property procedures to implement your property, you must write the routines. The property procedure's names will be made up of the property name, prefixed by either "get_" or "put_". This code implements the get and put routines for the EMailName property:

```
<script language="VBScript">
Function get_EMailName()
...script code
End Function
Sub put_EMailName(EMailAddress)
...script code
End Sub
</script>
```

The property tag also supports an internalname attribute, which frees your code from having to use the name of the property in your script. For instance, if you implement your property by using a variable, you don't have to give your variable the same name as your property. The internalname attribute lets you assign variables to properties in any combination that you want. This property tag, for instance, uses the strEMail variable to implement the EMailName property:

```
<public>
  <property name="EMailName" internalname="strEMail"/>
</public>

<script language="VBScript">
Dim strEMail
</script>
```

The Get and Put tags also support an internalname attribute. These tags, for instance, create a property called EMailName that uses two routines (EMailIn and EMailOut) to implement the property:

```
<public>
  <property name="EMailName">
    <get internalname="EMailOut">
    <put internalname="EMailIn">
  </property>
</public>

<script language="VBScript">
Function EMailOut()
...script code
End Function
Sub EMailIn(EMailAddress)
...script code
End Sub
</script>
```

The put routine is restricted to a single parameter, so you can't create properties that accept indexes.

The single tag version of the property tag can also be used to define property procedures with names that don't depend on the name of the property. The equivalent single tag version of the previous example would look like this:

```
<property name="EMailName" get="EMailOut"
                           put="EMailIn"/>
```

Omitting the get creates a write-only property, while omitting the put creates a read-only property. This single tag version creates a read only EMailName property:

```
<public>
  <property name="EMailName" get />
</public>
<script language="VBScript">
Function get_EMailName()
...script code
End Function
</script>
```

METHOD TAG

The method tag lets you define methods for your component. The simplest form of the method tag provides the name of the method and commits you to writing a subroutine or function with the same name. This tag establishes a method called SendMail for the component:

```
<public>
  <method name="SendMail" />
</public>

<script language="VBScript">
Sub SendMail()
…script code
End Sub
</script>
```

As with the property tag, you can assign a routine with a different name to a method by using the method tag's internalname attribute. This tag assigns the routine EMailProcess to be run when the component's SendMail method is called:

```
<public>
  <method name="SendMail" internalname="EmailProcess" />
</public>

<script language="VBScript">
Sub EMailProcess()
…script code
End Sub
</script>
```

And, as with the event tag, you can assign a dispid to a method:

```
<method name="SendMail" dispid="126" />
```

While your functions and subroutines defined with the method tag will be able to accept parameters, no information about those parameters will be included in your component's type library. If you want to include parameter information about your method's parameters in your type library then you'll need to use the paired version of the method tag. The paired version of the method tag allows you to include parameter tags that name your parameters between the opening and closing method tags. This example declares that the SendMail method accepts two parameters called Address and Message:

```
<method name="SendMail">
  <parameter name="Address" />
  <parameter name="Message" />
</method>
```

THE COMPONENT, XML, AND CDATA DIRECTIVES

You can also add the component directive tag to your Script file. This tag lets you define whether your component can be debugged and how errors are handled. A typical component directive looks like this:

```
<?component error="true" debug="true" ?>
```

Setting the error attribute to true causes the component to display error messages if it abends; if the attribute is set to false or omitted the object will just fail silently. Setting debug to true allows you to debug your component with the Script debugger. The default for both of the attributes is false, so omitting the directive creates a silent, undebuggable component.

I could also have included the XML directive in my component definition file. The XML directive looks like this:

```
<?XML version="1.0"?>
```

The XML directive enforces stricter syntax checking on your tags. For instance, with the directive added, all values supplied to an attribute must be quoted. You should add the directive if you are going to use an XML editor like Microsoft's XML Notepad to work with your Script component. You'll have be diligent about your XML syntax; XML is very fussy: script must be spelt with a lower-case "s," for instance.

The XML directive has the following attributes:

- version: the version of XML used in the file (must be "1.0")
- standalone: Always set to True as no formal definition exists for these tags. Can be omitted
- encoding: the character set used. This can be set to any of the character sets supported by Internet Explorer.

If you use the XML directive, it can't be preceded by anything, including white space. The "<" that begins the directive must be the first character in the file.

If you use the XML directive, you should also enclose any script blocks in a CDATA block. Here's an example of a script enclosed in a CDATA block:

```
<script language="VBScript">
<![CDATA[
 dim DocumentName
 Function OpenFile()
  Set wrd = WScript.CreateObject(MSWord)
DocumentName = Wscript.Arguments(0)
wrd.Documents.Add
wrd.SaveAs FileName WScript.Arguments(0), wdFormatRTF
FireEvent "FileOpen"
End Function
]]>
</script>
```

Without the CDATA block, XML will attempt to parse your script. Any characters that are part of the XML tag language (e.g., "<" and ">") will trigger XML syntax errors and prevent your object from registering. Using CDATA is said to make the text within it "opaque" to XML.

IMPLEMENTS

The implements tag is used when you are creating a component that will be used with interfaces other than the standard Automation interface. When you omit the implements tag, as I did in my example component, you are creating a component that can be used from other COM objects using CreateObject or New. However, Scripting comes with two other interfaces that allow you to create Script components that work in other environments.

Setting the implements tag's id attribute to ASP allows you to create a component that can access the ASP objects when the component is run from a Web page. Setting the attribute to Behavior is supposed to allow you to write code that will respond events fired from your Web page and interact with DHTML elements. In many ways, these options allow your Script component to function like a Visual Basic IIS or DHTML Application. This tag implements the ASP interface:

```
<implements id="ASP" />
```

If you have implemented the ASP interface in your component, you will be able to refer to the ASP objects (Response, Request, Application, Session, Server, and Error) from within your component. This code, for instance, uses the ASP Response object to write a message to the Web page before it is sent to the browser:

```
<implements id="ASP" />
<script language=VBScript>
  Response.Write "Hello World"
</script>
```

The name attribute in the implements tag assigns a prefix to the objects in the interface to prevent conflicts between identical names in different interfaces. Setting the default attribute indicates that if a method doesn't have a prefix, the prefix in this tag should be assumed.

In between the <implements> and </implements> tag, you place any tags required by the interface. The ASP interface and the default Automation interface require no tags. I'll discuss the tags required by the Behavior interface in the section on DHTML Behaviors.

Registering Script Components

Assuming that you've installed Internet Explorer 5.0, registering your Script Component is easy: Right-mouse click on the WSC file and select Register Component from the popup menu (see Figure 14–6). Once your component is registered, you can use it from any COM compliant development tool using New, CreateObject, or GetObject. You can download the necessary support files from the Microsoft Scripting technologies site (*msdn.microsoft.com/scripting*), if you don't want to install Internet Explorer.

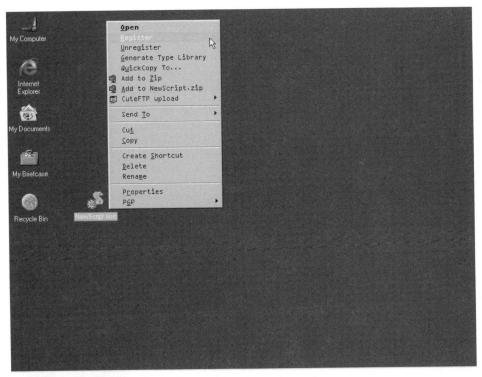

Figure 14–6 *Registering a script component from its popup menu.*

One of the benefits of registering your components is that the syntax of your XML tags will be checked, provided that you've begun your file with the XML directive.

You can also register a component using the version of Regsvr32.exe that ships with the script component package. This version of Regsver32 will accept a URL that points to your component:

```
regsvr32 file:\\c:\WordOpen.wsc
```

If you are installing your component on a computer that doesn't have the appropriate version of Regsver32, you can register your component through the scripting runtime dll (which must be registered on the computer for your component to work). This example registers the scripting runtime and then uses it to register the component:

```
regsvr32 scrobj.dll
regsvr32 scrobj.dll /n /i: file:\\c:\WordOpen.wsc
```

There's no facility to create the remote server files necessary to register a component on a client that is going to access your component using DCOM. Microsoft suggests the following process:

1. Register the component on the server.
2. Using Regedit.exe, locate the HKEY_CLASSES_ROOT\component-ProgID entry for your component and select it.
3. From the Registry menu, choose Export Registry File to create a .REG file
4. Copy the .REG file to the client computer.
5. Double-click on the .REG to have the client registry updated with the information in the file.

To unregister your Script component you can right-click on the WSC file and select Unregister or run Regsvr32.exe with the parameters listed above and the -u flag.

TYPE LIBRARIES

The simplest way to create a type library for your component is to right-mouse click on the WSC file and select Generate Type Library from the popup menu. This will create a file called Scriptlet.tlb, which you should rename to match your WSC file.

You can also generate a type library from within your Script component by using the Scriptlet TypeLib object. You can create the object using this code:

```
set gtl = CreateObject("Scriptlet.TypeLib")
```

The Scripting documentation continuously refers to this object as either Scriptlet.GenerateTypeLib or Component.GenerateTypeLib. Neither is correct. The code shown here actually works.

With the TypeLib object created, you can then use its methods and properties to generate your type library. The object's Path property lets you specify where the file is to be created. The TypeLib object's GUID property allows you to specify a GUID for the type library, which is different from the GUID for the component. The Name property lets you assign a name to your library. The object's Major and Minor version number properties cannot be set from VBScript. After setting the properties that you can, you call the object's Write method to create your type library.

This code, for instance, generates a type library file c:\MyScriptComponent.tlb:

```
set gtl = CreateObject("Scriptlet.TypeLib")
gtl.Path = "c:\MyScriptComponent.tlb"
gtl.GUID = "{a1e1e3e0-a252-11d1-9fa1-00a0c90fffc0}"
gtl.Name = "WordManager"
gtl.Write
```

The best place to put this code is in the Register function inside the registration tags. This will cause your type library to be generated as part of registering your component.

You can include multiple components in the same type library by using the TypeLib object's AddURL method. This method accepts the path name to a WSC file and will cause the type information for that file to be included in the type library generated by the Write method. This code, in a Windows Script Host VBS file, generates a type library that includes information about three Script Components (see Figure 14–7):

```
set gtl = CreateObject("Scriptlet.TypeLib")
gtl.AddURL "c:\Component1.WSC"
gtl.AddURL "c:\Component2.WSC"
gtl.AddURL "c:\Component3.WSC"
gtl.Path = "c:\MyScriptComponents.tlb"
gtl.GUID = "{a1e1e3e0-a252-11d1-9fa1-00a0c90fffc0}"
gtl.Name = "ScriptComponents"
gtl.Write
```

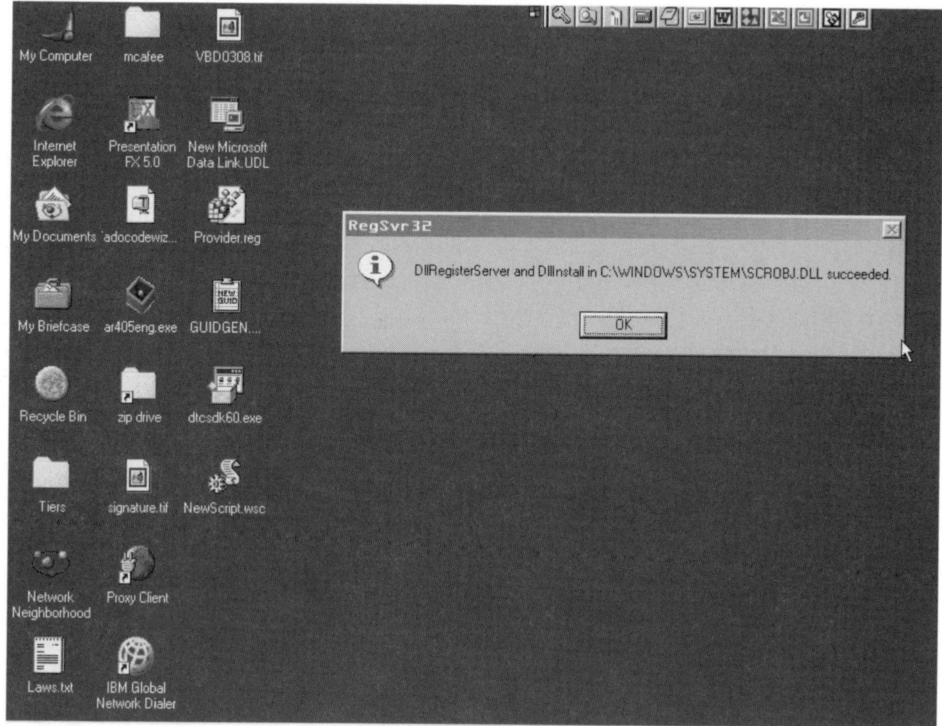

Figure 14–7 *This message indicates successful registration of your component.*

The gtl Reset method clears out the URLs added through the AddURL method. If you are creating a second type library from within the same Register routine, you should call the Reset method immediately after the Write method that creates the first type library.

Using a Scripting Component

A registered component can be used from any COM compliant language. In the following examples, I use Visual Basic (with brief mentions of ASP and the Windows Script Host).

Visual Basic

In general, in Visual Basic you can treat your Script component like any other COM object, though there are a couple of frustrating limitations. You start the component using the CreateObject function as you would any COM object:

```
Dim obj As Object
Set obj = CreateObject("MyScriptComponent.OpenDocument")
```

Since this code declares the object variable as type Object, you'll get no IntelliSense support or any of the other benefits of early binding. You can get some of those benefits, though, by generating a type library for your component. You can then add this type library to your Visual Basic project's References list using the Browse button on the Project | References dialog. No matter what you name your TLB file, the entry in your References list will always be "Scriptlet Type Library."

You won't be able to regenerate your type library as long as any running program, including the Visual Basic development environment, is referring to the library. If you want to re-create the type library, you'll have to remove the reference to it in your Visual Basic project (or exit the project).

If you want to declare an object variable to point to your component, you must use the value you declared in the component tag (the class name). However, the CreateObject function requires that you pass it the progid from the registration tag. The resulting code would look something like this:

```
Dim mys As MyScriptComponent
Set mys = CreateObject("MyScriptComponent.OpenDocument")
```

When you try to run this code, however, you get a type mismatch error because your object variable is declared as one type (MyScriptComponent) but CreateObject is returning another type (MyScriptComponent.OpenDocument). Also, for the same reason, you can't use the New command with your Scriptlet or declare your component using WithEvents.

My practice is to declare my object variable using my Script component's class to get the IntelliSense drop-down lists during development. I then switch my declaration over to use Object before running my application.

Microsoft's documentation on this point suggests that you can declare your object variable using the progid value from your Script component's registration tag. Microsoft's documentation then goes on to show how, by declaring your object variable using WithEvents, you can catch events fired by your Script object. As of this writing, this isn't possible since you can't declare your object variable with the component's progid.

You can also start your Script component by using the GetObject function. With GetObject, you must identify your object as a Script object and pass the full path name to the WSC file that defines it, like this:

```
Set obj = GetObject("script:c:\MyScriptComponent.WSC")
```

With GetObject, if your WSC file contains more than one object, then you must specify which one you want. You do that by following the file name with a pound sign (#) and the name of the object.

```
Set obj = _
  GetObject("script:c:\MyScriptComponent.WSC#OpenDocument")
```

The Window Script Host and ASP

In ASP, you start your Script component as you would any other component, using the CreateObject method of the Server object:

```
Set obj = _
   Server.CreateObject("MyScriptComponent.OpenDocument")
```

In the Window Scripting Host, you would use the CreateObject method of the WScript object to load your Script component:

```
Set obj = _
  WScript.CreateObject("MyScriptComponent.OpenDocument")
```

The DHTML Behavior Interface

DHTML Behaviors allow you to extend the behavior of a tag on your page by attaching code to the element that the tag defines. Once assigned to an HTML element, a Behavior extends the element's functionality in these ways:

- The Behavior can respond to events fired by the element.
- Properties defined in the Behavior will appear as properties of the element.
- Events fired by the behavior will appear as events for the element
- Methods defined in the behavior become methods of the element

If the method or property that you define in your Behavior has the same name as an existing property or method of the element that it is assigned to, your Behavior code will override the built-in property or method. Effectively, then, DHTML Behaviors let you define an object with methods, properties, and events, and then associate that object with some element on your web page. That element will acquire a combination of whatever native methods and properties that it has in the DHTML object model and the ones that you define in your Behavior. In the long run, DHTML Behaviors will probably replace the DHTML Scriptlets technology.

Defining a Behavior uses tags and code almost identical to defining a Script component so, since you're already familiar with how to create a Script component, I'll begin this section by looking at how to assign your Behavior to elements on your Web page. In Figure 14–8 for instance, the onMouse-

Open event of a text box has been used to display a message. After that, I look at specific features of DHTML Behavior components.

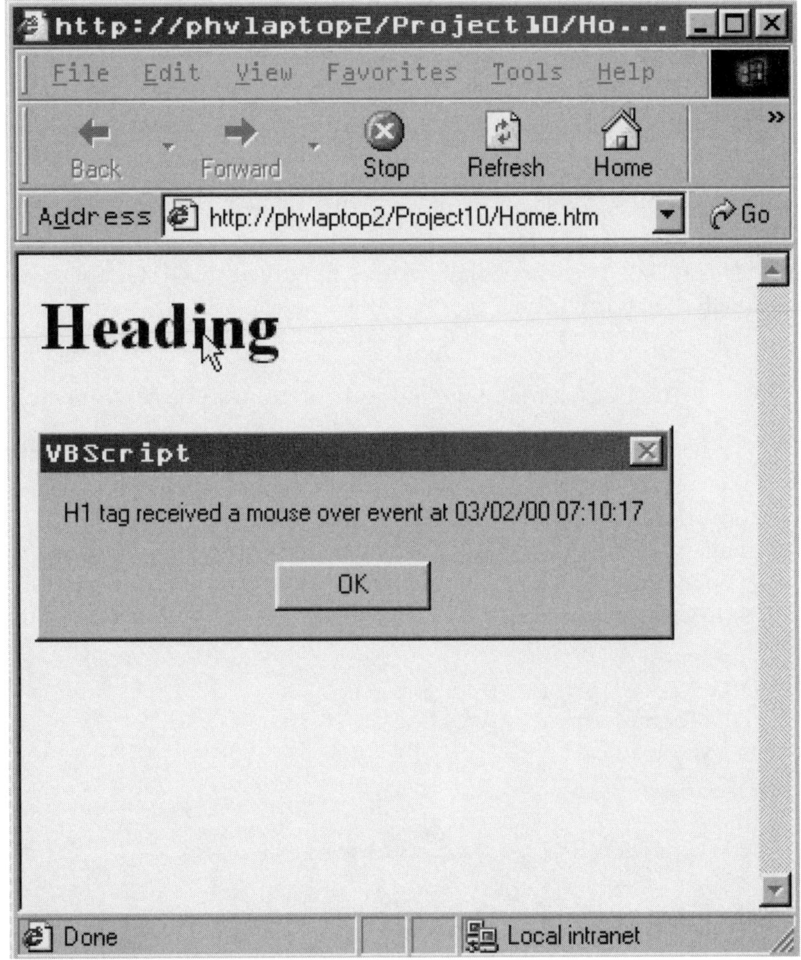

Figure 14–8 *A DHTML Behavior in action, displaying a message box from the onMouseOver event of a text box.*

Assigning Behaviors

There are a number of ways that you can assign your Script component to an element in your Web page to make it a DHTML Behavior. You can apply a behavior to an element on a page from the Script code on the page by using the addBehavior method. This code assigns the MyDHTML.htc file to the an element called txtName:

```
document.all.txtName.addBehavior("MyDHTML.htc")
```

If the behavior has already been added to the element, it's not added again and no error is raised.

The removeBehavior lets you remove a behavior from an element:

```
document.all.txtName.removeBehavior("MyDHTML.htc")
```

Microsoft has proposed a new style attribute for elements, as part of the Cascading Stylesheet specification. This new attribute, named "behavior" lets you assign a DHTML Behavior to an element as part of the element's style. This HTML, for instance, picks up a file called MyDHTML.htc and associates it with the Style attribute of a text box:

```
<INPUT Id=txtName Style="behavior:url(MyDHTML.htc)">
```

The behavior attribute of the style can also be set from code:

```
document.all.txtName.style.behavior = "url(MyDHTML.htc)"
```

Using the Style attribute lets you assign a behavior to all elements that are defined with a specific HTML tag. To do this, you use Style tags in your page to list the tags that you want to assign behaviors to. For each tag name, you specify the URL for the behavior that you want to assign to the tag. This HTML, for instance, assigns behaviors to the H1 and LI tags on the page:

```
<STYLE>
H1 {behavior:url(MyDHTML.htc)}
LI {behavior:url(MyOtherDHTML.htc)}
</STLE>
```

Behaviors, as described here, are only fully implemented in Internet Explorer 5.

You can assign multiple behaviors to a single element or tag. DHTML will execute each of the relevant behaviors in the order that they were assigned to the tag using addBehavior. If the Style attribute is used to assign the behavior, the rules for Cascading Stylesheets apply to control which assignment is used. However, you can assign multiple behaviors in a single Style, like this:

```
<STYLE>
H1 {behavior:url(MyDHTML.htc), url(MyOtherDHTML.htc)}
</STLE>
```

You can also use the Style tag to assign a behavior to an HTML class. With the Class defined, you can then assign elements of the page to the class and then call the behavior's methods as needed for each member of the class.

The following set of Style tags associates a behavior file with a class called MyBehavior. The MyDHTML file contains a Disappear method, so any elements assigned to the class will acquire that method:

```
<STYLE>
  .MyBehavior {behavior:url(MyDHTML.htc)}
</STYLE>
```

Within the page, I can assign any elements on the page to the class by using the tag's Class attribute. The Class attribute accepts the name of the class that you established in the Style tag.

As an example, the following HTML assigns a textbox to the MyBehavior class. The Id attribute of the Input tag gives this member of the class the name txtName. As a result, the txtName element is now a member of the MyBehavior class and acquires all the methods and properties defined in the MyDHTML.htc file:

```
<INPUT Type=Text Class=MyBehavior Id=txtName>
```

I can now call the methods in the behavior for any member of the class. The following HTML, when the onClick method of the button is fired, calls on the txtName element's Disappear method. The element txtName acquired the Disappear method by being a member of the class that was assigned the MyDHTML.htc behavior:

```
<INPUT Type=button onClick=txtName.Disappear>
```

You don't need to register a DHTML behavior, so you can omit the registration tag from a DHTML behavior component.

Defining the DHTML Behavior

Microsoft's documentation suggests that you can use the implements tag to flag your component as implementing the Behavior interface. I never was able to get this to work. However, giving the file containing your Behavior code an extension of .HTC, which identifies the file as a "text/x-component", does enable you to add Behaviors to your web pages. In this section, I will review how to create methods, properties, and events within the DHTML Behaviors that you will assign to your page's elements. Much of the process is identical to the way that the XML tags are used in Script Components. Before that, however, there is one case where a tag within the HTC file is used to bind the Behavior to the element.

ATTACHING EVENTS

You use a Behavior's attach tag to associate your object's routines with events fired by tags on the page. The onevent attribute of the tag allows you to specify which routine in your Behavior to run when the element receives an event. The following attach tag, for instance, will cause the Behavior's DisplayMessage method to be run on the onMouseOver event for the tag or element that the Behavior is attached to:

```
<attach event="onMouseOver" onevent="DisplayMessage"/>
```

The special case I that I mentioned earlier occurs when you want to associate your routine with an event fired by the two objects that have no tags: the Window and the Document objects. The attach tag's for attribute can contain "window", "document", or "element" (the default, "element", assigns the Behavior to the element that you've associated the Behavior with). The settings "window" and "document" assign the Behavior to events fired by the Window and Document objects. As an example, this attach tag runs the DisplayMessage routine when the Window's onLoad event fires:

```
<attach event="onLoad" onevent="DisplayMessage"
for="Window" />
```

EVENT TAG

The event tag in a DHTML Behavior can be used to define new events for the element. Events fired from a DHTML Behavior by using an Event's Fire method are treated like any other event raised by an element in the page.

The following code, for instance, in a file called MyDHTML.HTC defines an event called onAttention and gives it an Id of Att. The code also uses the attach tag to have a routine called NoticeMe run during the element's onmouseover event. The NoticeMe routine uses the onAttention event's Fire method to raise this event for the element that the Behavior is assigned to (Figure 14–9 shows the order of events):

```
<event name="onAttention"  id="Att" />
<attach event="onmouseover" onevent="NoticeMe"/>

<script language="VBScript">
Sub NoticeMe
  Att.Fire
End Sub
</script>
```

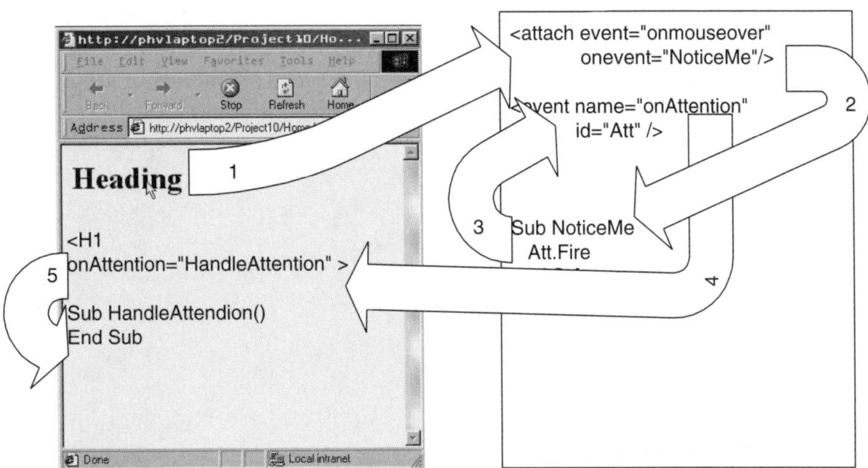

Figure 14–9 *The flow of control in the attach event example. The H1's onMouseOver event runs the NoticeMe routine, which fires the onAttenton event which runds the HandleAttention routine.*

The following code associates the MyDHTML Behavior component with all of the H1 tags on the page. The H1 tag shown in the example uses the onAttention event fired by the Behvior to run a routine called HandleAttention:

```
<STYLE>
H1 {behavior:url(MyDHTML.htc)}
</STYLE>

<H1 onAttention="HandleAttention()" Id=H1Note>
  This Topic
</H1>
<Script Language=VBScript>
Sub HandleAttention()
  Msgbox "H1 tag got a mouse over event"
End Sub
</Script>
```

You must use the Event name as an attribute in the tag that the Behavior is assigned to in order to catch an event fired in a behavior. I could not, in the previous example, have simply used a VBScript routine named H1Note_onDisappear to catch the onDisappear event fired by the H1Note element. I had to use "onAttention=HandleAttention()" in the tag itself.

The end result is that when the user moves the mouse over this H1 element, the element's onMouseOver event will cause the NoticeMe routine of the MyDHTML.htc behavior to execute. This will cause the onAttention event to be fired for the element. For the H1 tag that will cause the HandleAttention routine on the page to be run.

The Fire method of an event can be used to pass an Event object back to the element that the Behavior is assigned to. This code used the CreateEventObject (discussed later) method to create an Event object. It then sets the event object's ReturnValue property to the current date and time, and returns the event object through the Fire method that raises the event:

```
<script language="VBScript">
Sub onAttention(objEvent)
  Set evt = CreateEventObject()
  evt.ReturnValue = Now()
  Att.Fire(evt)
End Sub
</script>
```

The routine that catches this event can then retrieve the value from the Window's Event object:

```
<STYLE>
H1 {behavior:url(MyDHTML.htc)}
</STYLE>

<H1 onAttention=HandleAttention() Id=H1Note>This Topic</H1>
<Script Language=VBScript>
Sub HandleAttention()
  Msgbox "H1 tag received a mouse over event at " &
    Window.Event.returnValue
End Sub
</Script>
```

PROPERTY AND METHOD TAGS

You can create properties and methods for your DHTML Behavior component the same way as you would for a script component, by using the property and method tags. This code, in an HTC file, creates a new property called ETag and a new method called DisplayMessage:

```
<property name="ETag" get="GetTag" put="PutTag" />
<method name="DisplayMessage" internalname="Display" />
<script Language="VBScript">
Dim m_Tag
Function GetTag()
  GetTag = m_Tag
End Function
Sub PutTag(inValue)
  m_Tag = inValue
End Sub
Sub Display
  Msgbox "Hello, World."
End Sub
</script>
```

With the Behavior created and stored in my MyDHTML.HTC file, I can associate with an element on the page and use my new property as if it were an intrinsic property of the tag. I can also call my new method:

```
<STYLE>
H1 {behavior:url(MyDHTML.htc)}
</STYLE>
<H1 Id=H1Note>This Topic</H1>

<Script Language=VBScript>
Sub HandleAttention()
  Document.all.H1Note.ETag = "Special Tag"
  Document.all.H1Note.DisplayMessage
End Sub
</Script>
```

If you specify a Put routine in the Property tag, the element's onPropertyChange event won't fire when your property is updated. You must fire the onPropertyChanged event for the element yourself using the property's FireChange method:

```
<property Name="ETag" Get="GetTag" Put="PutTag"
        id="ETag"/>
<Script Language="VBScript">
Sub PutTag(inValue)
  m_Tag = inValue
  ETag.FireChange
End Sub
</Script>
```

You can capture this event by using the tag's onPropertyChange event:

```
<H1 Id=H1Note onPropertyChange="PropertyRoutine">
  This Topic</H1>
<Script Language=VBScript>
  Sub PropertyRoutine
    MsgBox "H1Note ETag property updated"
  End Sub
</Script>
```

Behavior Methods and Properties

The Behavior interface also supports the element property and the attachNotification, and createEventObject methods.

ELEMENT PROPERTY

The element property returns a reference to the object that caused the object's method to execute. This code, for instance, uses the element's Visibility property to make the element (and anything contained between the element's start and end tags) disappear:

```
Sub HandleDisappear()
  element.Visibility = "hidden"
End Sub
```

In DHTML code, the "this" keyword normally returns a reference to the element that the code is associated with. With behaviors, however, "this" refers to the function that called the behavior.

CREATEEVENTOBJECT

You can use the createEventObject method to create an Event object that can be used as the second parameter of the fireEvent method. The createEvent-Object method creates an Event object whose properties you can set before using it as the object returned by the fireEvent method.

Passing an Event object to the client that uses your component standardizes the way that you communicate with your client. Instead of the client receiving a variety of objects in event procedures, routines that accept your script component events will always get an Event object. The Event object's properties are defined by the DHTML specification, which also reduces the amount of documentation that you have to supply.

You can add new properties (expando properties) to an Event object if you use JScript to define your component.

As an example, this code creates an Event object and sets its Result property to the value of the txtEMailAddress element. The code then uses the fireEvent method to fire an event and uses the Event object as the second parameter to the method:

```
Set EObject = createEventObject
EObject.Result = txtEMailAddress.Value
fireEvent("BadEMail", EObject)
```

The BadEMail event routine that catches this event would have to be written to accept an Event object as a parameter. A typical example might look like this (assuming that this behavior is attached to an object called txtE-Mail):

```
Sub txtEMail_BadEMail(objEvent)
  Msgbox objEvent.Result & " is not a valid entry."
End Sub
</script>
```

Tools

Microsoft has provided a variety of tools for working with Script, all of them available from Microsoft's Scripting Web site. The Script Debugger is also installed with Internet Explorer and Internet Information Server (see Figure 14–10) and the debugging support it provides is one of the nicer features of the Script environment. Within the Script Debugger, you can step through your code, examine and change variables, skip or reexecute lines of code and execute script statements in immediate mode. You can't modify your code from within the debugger, though. You can invoke the debugger from within your script by inserting a Stop statement.

The Script Control is an ActiveX Control that you can add to your Visual Basic program (or any other development tool that supports ActiveX controls) to incorporate Scriptlets as part of your program's user interface. The Script Encoder will encrypt your Script code to make it more difficult for end users to read (though it won't stop anyone determined to crack your code).

New versions of the various hosts and the VBScript language are constantly being released. VBScript 5.0 added the ability to create Class modules to the language, for instance. New versions of the Windows Script Host expose more of the Windows operating system as a set of objects that you can manipulate from your scripts. More of Microsoft's tools make use of scripts (Microsoft Transaction Server came with a set of Windows Script Host routines for managing MTS, for instance).

Summary

In this chapter you were introduced to Scripting and how to create objects and components using Script. After introducing you to some of the technologies involved (Scripting itself and the various scripting hosts, among other topics), you saw how to create DHTML Scriptlets and Remote Scripting objects. From there, you learned how to create script components by adding XML that allowed you to register your component and generate type libraries.

Once you saw how to create a script component, I showed you how to incorporate it into COM applications and client-side Web applications as a DHTML Behavior. I also covered the issues around registering your component and took a brief look at the tools that are available.

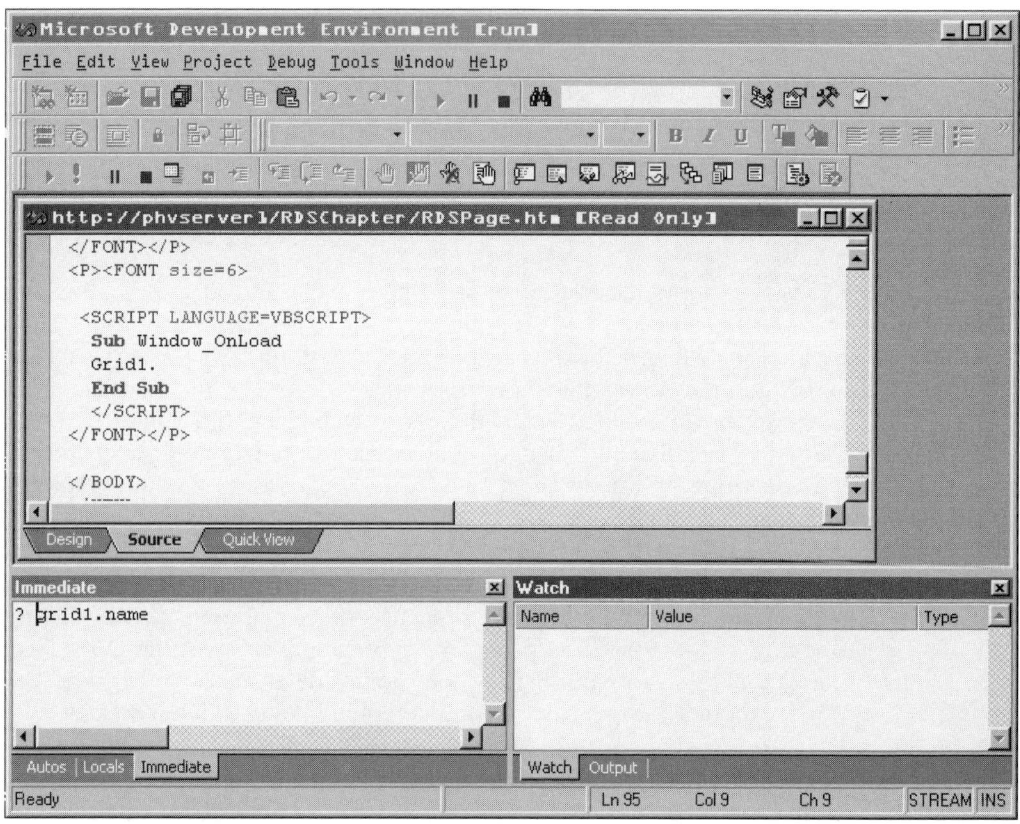

Figure 14–10 *The Script Debugger.*

When it comes to getting more information on the Scripting technologies, one reference is the many articles written by Dino Esposito. He has published numerous articles on Scripting in *Microsoft Internet Developer*, among other magazines. Several of those articles appear in the MSDN library and on the MSDN site (*msdn.microsoft.com*). All of them are worth reading. He also has two books on Scripting. The more comprehensive is *Instant DHTML Scriptlets,* which covers all of the Scripting technologies. Unfortunately, the technology has moved so fast that the book, published in 1998, no longer reflects the state of the art. The other book is narrower in focus and concentrates on the Windows Script Host. It's called *Windows Script Host Programmer's Reference*. More recent is *VBScript Programmer's Reference* by a variety of authors (ISBN:1861002718) which is comprehensive and generally very good. All are from Wrox press. The Microsoft Scripting Website (*msdn.microsoft.script*) remains your best source for up-to-date news on the technology and related tools.

If you have a Web browser, you can start using DHTML Scriptlets right away. You could begin by converting the DHTML Application from the previous chapter into a Scriptlet. Portions of the object that are tied to specific events could be broken out into a script component and assigned as DHTML Behaviors. Your IIS Application could be converted into a script component that implements the ASP interface and be called from your ASP script code. With your client-side and server-side objects created, the next step would be to use remote scripting to have a DHTML Scriptlet access and run a Server Scriptlet.

F I F T E E N

COM Add-Ins

Add-ins let you extend the capability of Microsoft Office, the Visual Basic IDE, or Microsoft's Development Environment by adding your own components to these powerful applications. You can enhance any of these tools with your own code that will integrate with the tool and extend it.

In the past, it's been possible to extend both the Visual Basic IDE and the Microsoft Office components using Add-ins. However, each application handled Add-ins differently (Word even had its own peculiar DLL format for Add-ins). With COM Add-ins, a single mechanism is used for integrating with all applications that can use a COM Add-in (I'll refer to those applications as hosts). COM Add-ins break with the past by treating all hosts—Microsoft Office, the Visual Basic IDE and the Microsoft Development Environment (MDE)—the same. As a Visual Basic developer, you probably find the idea of adding new features to your development environment very attractive. Now, it's possible for you to use those techniques to extend any of your tools.

In this chapter I show you how to create a COM Add-in, how to configure it for, and how to integrate it with each of the hosting environments. To make your COM Add-in accessible from its host application (be it Office or Visual Basic), I show you how to work with the CommandBars component, which provides menus and toolbars for many of Microsoft's applications. You'll also find out how to use ActiveX Documents as part of your COM Add-in in Visual Basic. Finally, you'll also see how to integrate your COM Add-in with its host without using menus.

Truth in Marketing

Saying that COM Add-ins extend their hosts in the same way is something of an exaggeration. Any Add-in that you write will have to interact with the object model of the application that is hosting the Add-in. So, when creating any Add-in, you'll need to be familiar with the object model for the application that the Add-in is supposed to extend. While there are some objects that are shared among all of the environments (the objects that represent toolbars and menus, for instance), each environment has its own object model. An Add-in designed to extend Word will probably make use of the Document object, for instance, while an Excel Add-in would work with Worksheets. Once you add code to work with a specific host's objects, you've bound that Add-in to that host.

It's also not strictly true that a COM Add-in can be loaded by any of the potential environments. It's more accurate to say that you can configure your Add-in to work with as many of the hosting environments as you want. In this chapter I show you both how to set up your Add-in to work with any host and how to have one Add-in work with many hosts.

COM Add-ins and the Windows Registry

Prior to COM Add-ins, the mechanism for making host applications aware of the Add-ins that were available to them varied from host to host. The techniques in use included:

• Giving the Add-in a special file type (e.g., Access Add-ins have an MDA extension)

• Putting the Add-in in a predefined location (any MDA file in the Access directory would appear on Access's Add-ins menu)

• Some other mechanism (Visual Basic Add-ins had to be listed in the vbaddins.INI file).

With COM Add-ins and the latest versions of their hosts (Visual Basic 6.0, MDE 6.0, Office 2000), there is a common way for hosts to find COM Add-ins. Hosts now determine which Add-ins are available for them by reading a set of entries in the Windows registry. So, in addition to the normal entries for a component, a COM Add-in must also have entries in the Add-ins section of the registry for the host or hosts that will use it. For the Office components, that means an entry under the HKEY_CURRENT_USER\Software\Microsoft\Office\<application name>\AddIns key. For Visual Basic, a COM Add-in's entries would be placed in the section HKEY_CURRENT_USER\Software\Microsoft\Visual Basic\6.0\AddIns (see Figure 15–1). An Add-in that works with both Word and Visual Basic would have to be listed in both Access' and Visual Basic Add-ins section in the Windows Registry.

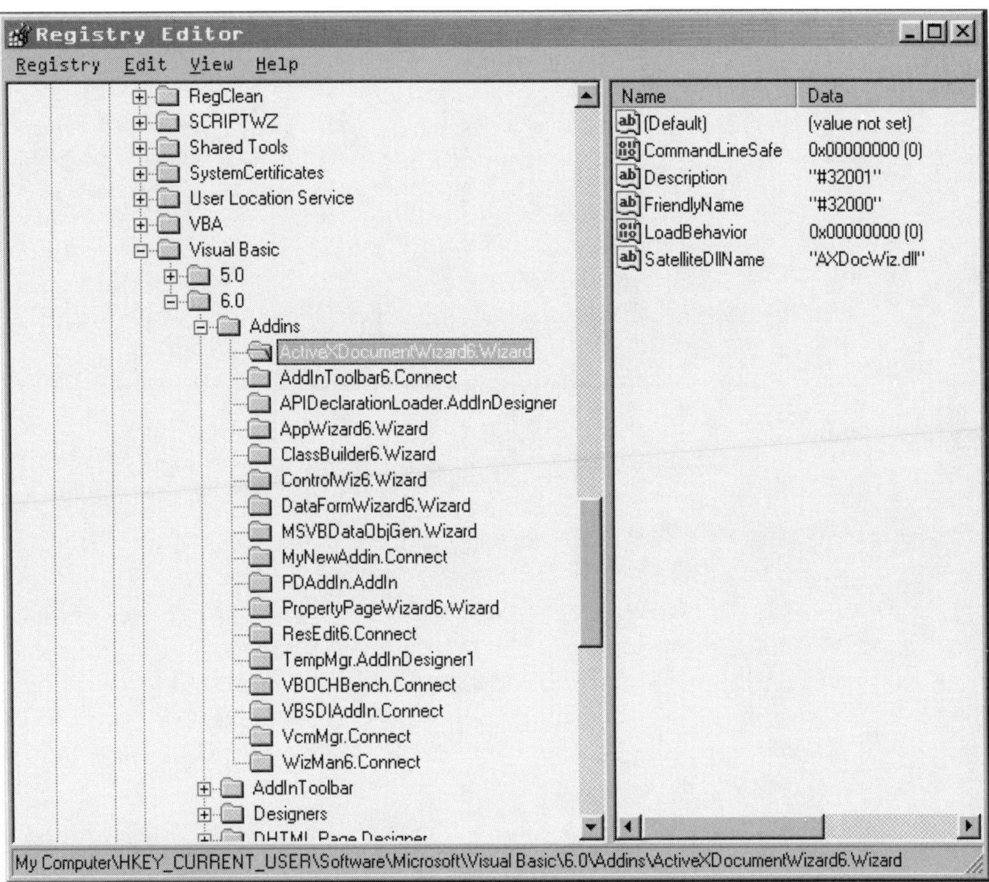

Figure 15–1 *Registry entries for Visual Basic.*

The key value for the registry entries is the progid for the Class module in your Add-in that contains the code to connect your Add in with its host. Under this key, you must add values indicating if the Add-in is safe to run from the Commandline (Visual Basic only), what LoadBehavior the Add-in is to follow, a Description for your Add-in, and a FriendlyName. The LoadBehavior setting controls when a host activates an Add-in (I discuss the effect of the LoadBehavior setting in the next section). The Description and FriendlyName are used by the References dialog and the Object Browser. The best strategy for creating the necessary entries is to copy the entries for an existing Add-in and modify them to match the need of your Add-in. The entries for a single Add-in are listed in Table 15.1.

Table 15.1 The Registry Entries Required Under the Add-ins Key

Value	Description
CommandLineSafe	When set to 0, provides a warning when the user specifies that the Add-in is to be used when Visual Basic is started from a command line.
Description	Text description of the Add-in. Used by the Add-in Manager.
FriendlyName	Text name for the Add-in
LoadBehavior	Numeric value

Users can get a list of all of the Add-ins in an application's Add-ins section by using the Add-ins Manager dialog, available from the Add-ins menu. The Add-ins menu choice is easy to use in both the MDE and Visual Basic because it appears on their standard menu bar.

The Add-ins menu for COM Add-ins is a little more difficult to get to in the Office because these applications must continue to support their old Add-in architecture. As a result, the Add-ins entry on the Office application's menus lists the old application-specific Add-ins rather than the new COM Add-ins. A new menu item does exists for COM Add-ins but it doesn't appear anywhere in the Office applications' standard menus.

Before being able to use the COM Add-ins Manager dialog (as opposed to the manager for application-specific Add-ins), you must add the COM Add-ins menu choice to their menu system. To do this, select Tools | Customize and click on the Commands tab to display a list of menu commands. The various commands are organized by the menus that they normally appear on, so you must click on the Tools entry in the Categories column to get the list of commands that includes COM Add-ins (see Figure 15–2). Once you've found the COM Add-ins choice, click and drag it to whichever menu or menu bar you want to use it from.

In the Office applications, a user can select an Add-in from the COM Add-ins menu to load it into an application. The Add-in will then be activated by the host using the LoadBehavior setting from the Add-in's registry entry to control how the Add-in is loaded. Visual Basic 6 and the MDE offer the user more control over how the Add-in is loaded. While you can set the LoadBehavior for your Add-in when you create it, Visual Basic and MDE users can override that option as part of adding the Add-in to their environment (see Figure 15–3).

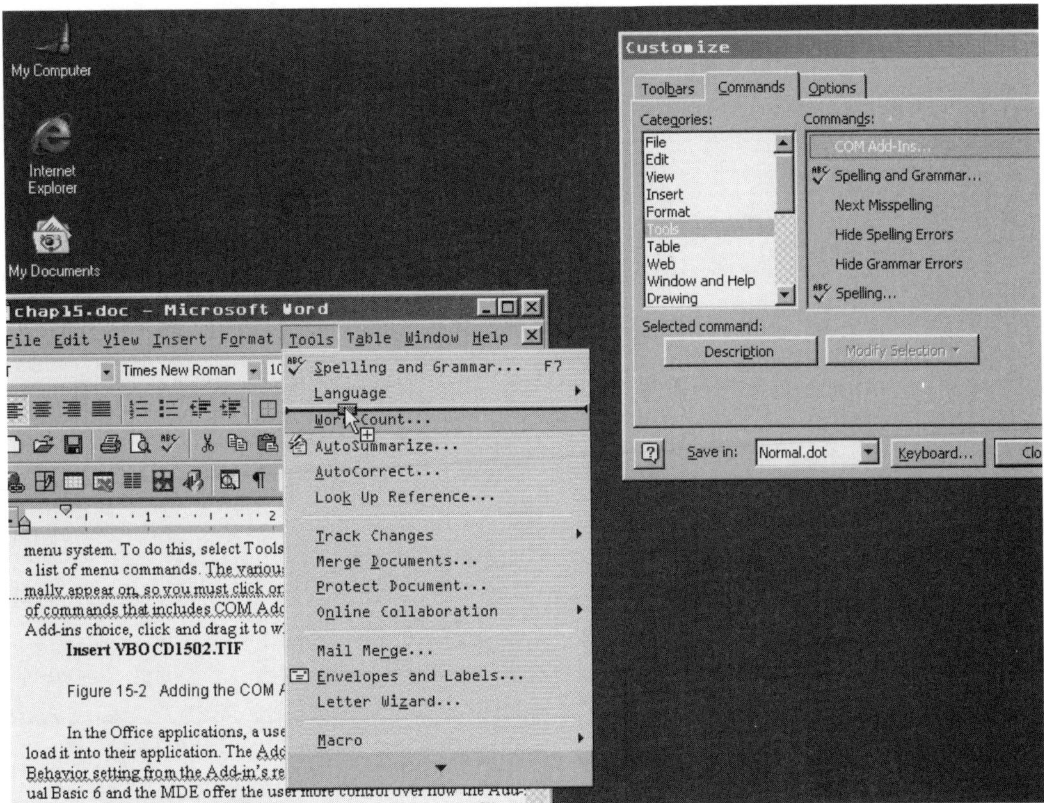

Figure 15–2 *Adding the COM Add-ins menu choice in Microsoft Word.*

Visual Basic 5

Visual Basic 5 can also use COM Add-ins but determines what Add-ins are available by reading the vbaddins.INI file. This is a standard INI file and can be updated either by using a text editor like Notepad or by calling the Windows API WritePrivateProfileString from an application. An entry for a COM Add-in called MyAddIn in the vbaddins.INI file would look like this:

```
[Add-Ins32]
MyAddIn.Connect=0
```

The entry in the Add-Ins32 consists of the progid for the Class in your Add-in that contains the code to connect your Add-in to Visual Basic plus the Add-in's LoadBehavior value. In the vbaddins.INI file, LoadBehavior can either be 0 (don't load) or 1 (load at startup).

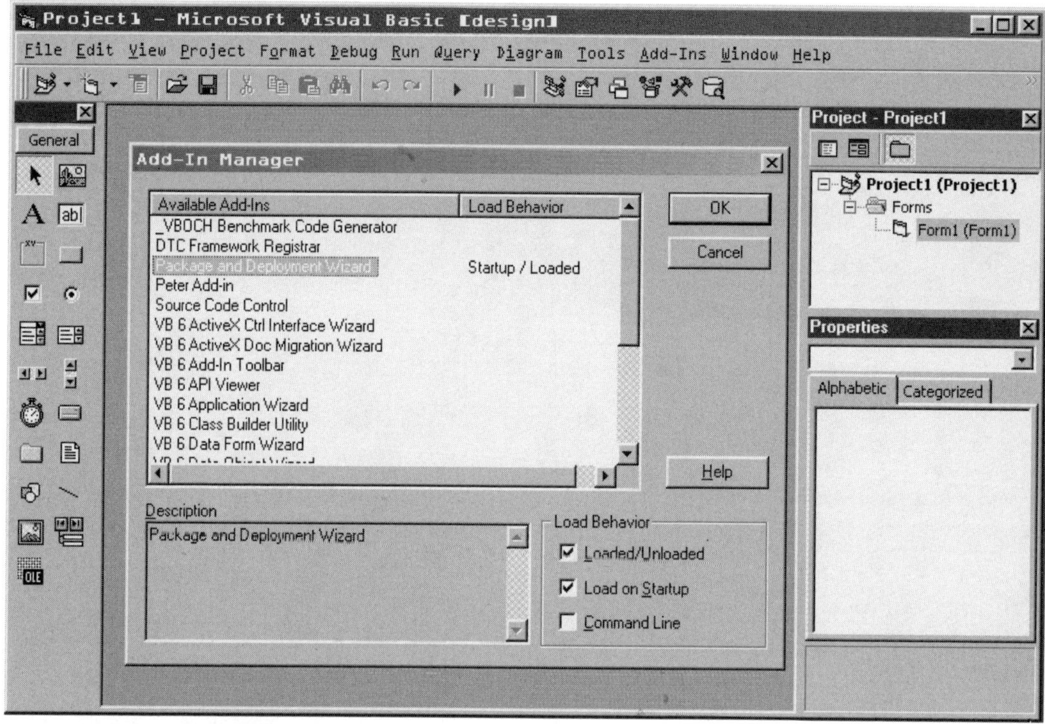

Figure 15–3 *Adding an Add-in in Visual Basic.*

You can set a friendly name for your Add-in in Visual Basic 5 by using the Object Browser. In your Add-in project, start the Object browser and select your Connect class. Right-mouse click on the Class and select properties. In the Member Options dialog that appears, enter a friendly name in the Description box and click on the OK button.

The Life Cycle of an Add-in

A COM Add-in only becomes active when it is loaded by a host. The host will first look for and run a routine called OnConnection in the Class used as the key for the Add-ins registry entries. This routine should contain whatever code is required to integrate your Add-in with the host. After running the OnConnection routine, the host will also call the following routines as it manages your Add-in.

- OnConnection: This method will be called when your Add-in is added to the host environment.

- OnDisconnection: This routine is called when your Add-in is removed from the host environment.
- OnStartupComplete: If your Add-in is loaded as part of the host's start up process, the host calls this routine when it finishes loading (including any initial documents or projects in the host).
- OnBeginShutdown If your Add-in is present when the host environment is being shut down, this routine will be called by the host as it starts to unload.
- OnAddinstUpdate: The host calls this routine when any Add-in is added or removed from the host environment.

When the methods are called by the host depends on how the host loads the Add-in. When a host reads the registry entries for its Add-ins, it uses the LoadBehavior entry for each Add-in to decide how to load the Add-in. The various settings for LoadBehavior and their descriptions are given in Table 15.2.

Table 15.2 LoadBehavior Settings

LoadBehavior Setting	Description
0	The Add-in is not loaded at all (the user must add it using the Add-ins manager).
2	The Add-in is loaded as the host starts up.
4	(Visual Basic only) The Add-in is loaded only when Visual Basic is run from the command line.
8	The Add-in's type library is loaded at startup, but the Add-in itself isn't loaded until explicitly requested (Load on Demand).
16	(Office only) The Add-in is loaded next time the host is started in order to allow the Add-in to configure the host, and then LoadBehavior is set to 8.

In addition to being loaded from the Add-ins dialog, an Add-in can be loaded from code in a macro running in the host or code in another Add-in. To load an Add-in programmatically, your code must access the host's AddIns (Visual Basic and the MDE) or COMAddins (Office) collection, find the Add-in to be loaded, set its Connect property to True, and then update the host's Addins/COMAddins collection. Normally, you will look for an Add-in using its human-readable description, but you can also look for an Add-in using its progid or GUID.

As an example, this code will work in any of the Office components to load an Add-in whose Description property is set to “MyAddIn”:

```
Sub Test()
Dim objCAddIn As COMAddIn

For Each objCAddIn In Application.COMAddIns
  If objCAddIn.Description = "MyAddIn" Then
    If objCAddIn.Connect = False Then
      objCAddIn.Connect = True
      COMAddIns.Update
      Exit Sub
    End If
  End If
Next
End Sub
```

Other properties of the COMAddIn objects in the COMAddIns collection are

- GUID: The GUID for the Add-In
- ProgId: The progid used to identify the Add-in in the registry
- Object: A reference to the Add-in

In the Office applications, the Addins collection (if it exists) refers to the old-style Add-ins, not to COMAdd-ins. You must use the COMAdd-ins collection in Office. In Visual Basic, on the other hand, the Add-ins collection refers to COM Add-ins.

Only the Office components offer the “load next time” LoadBehavior setting. This setting causes the Add-in to be loaded so that it can run its OnConnection routine and integrate itself with the host (e.g., add some required menu items). The Add-ins LoadBehavior setting is then changed to “Load on Demand.” The next time the user opens the host, only the Add-in's type library will load. The Add-in itself won't be loaded until it is requested.

CONNECTING AND DISCONNECTING

The key in the Windows Registry for an Add-in is the progid for one of the objects that the Add-in contains. The object whose progid you use as the registry key must implement the interface that the host uses to load your Add-in. Typically, the Class module for this object is called Connect and I'll assume that's the name that you use for the rest of this chapter. The Connect Class must expose one of the interfaces required by the Add-in specification and contain the routines that the host calls as part of working with your Add-in (e.g., OnConnection, OnStartupComplete, etc.).

The OnConnection routine will be called when the Add-in is first added to the host environment, whether the Add-in is loaded from the Add-in manager or from code. When the Add-in is added to the host, the OnConnection routine will be followed by a call to the AddInsUpdate routine as the host updates its Add-ins collection. The Add-in's OnConnection routine will also be run when the host reloads the Add-in as part of the host's startup process or, for Load on Demand, when the Add-in is requested.

If an Add-in is set to Load on Demand, disconnecting the Add-in counts as a "demand." If the user hasn't used your Add-in but goes to the Add-in Manager and removes your Add-in, your OnConnection routine will be called, followed by the AddInsUpdate routine, followed by the OnDisconnection routine.

Typically, the OnConnection routine will contain code to make the Add-in available to the host's user. For instance, an Add-in, as part of the OnConnection routine, could display a user interface for the user to interact with. Most Add-ins will create a menu item on the hosting application's menu system which can then be used to trigger code in the Add-in. There are other options which I discuss later in this chapter.

After its OnConnection routine is run, the next major event in the Add-in's life occurs when the host calls the OnDisconnection routine. This call signals that the Add-in is being removed from memory. The Add-in can be unloaded for two reasons:

1. The user has disconnected the Add-in (either by using the Add-in Manager or programmatically).
2. The host is shutting down.

You will normally put code in the OnDisconnection routine to undo any changes made to the host environment in the OnConnection routine.

Creating COM Add-ins

You can create COM add-ins from the VBA development environment that comes with Word, Excel and the other Office components, provided that you've installed Microsoft Office, Developer edition (MOD). MOD includes an ActiveX designer for creating the Class modules that make up your component (see Figure 15–4).

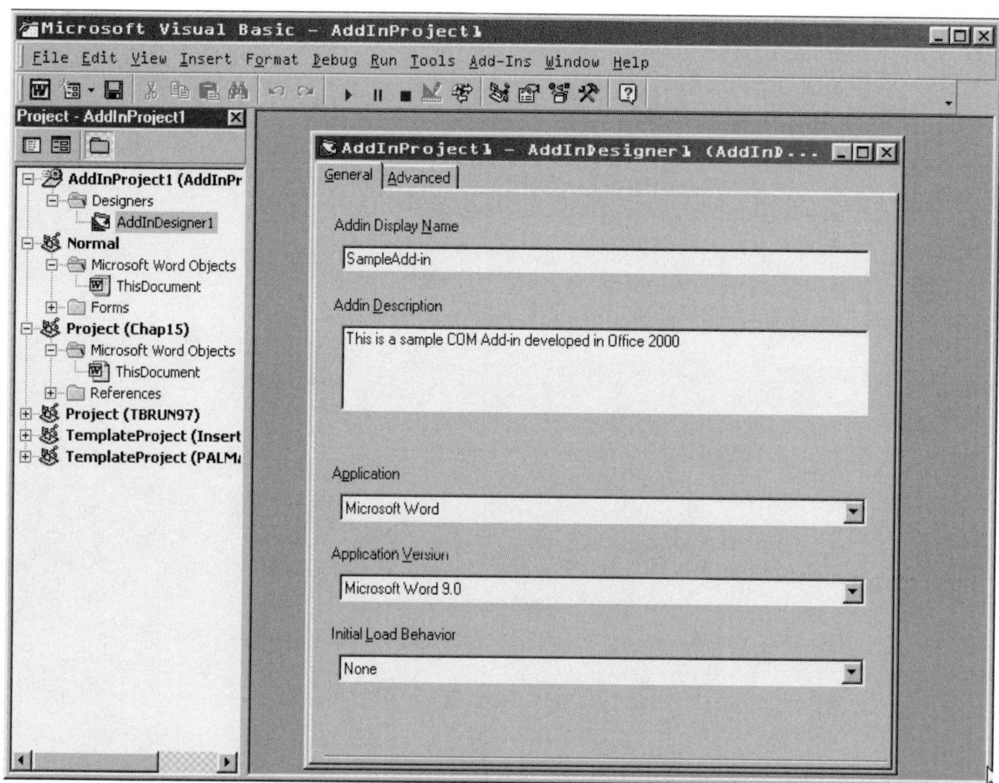

Figure 15-4 *Using the VBA Designer for Add-ins.*

However, there are a number of limitations to creating your COM Add-in using the Office environment. An Add-in created in VBA can't be compiled as an EXE, so you can't run your Add-in standalone or out-of-process. In the Office/VBA environment you can't, as part of your Add-in, create Property Pages or ActiveX Controls or ActiveX Documents. Visual Basic lets you do all of these things, providing you with a more powerful and flexible development environment to create your COM Add-in. The Addin ActiveX Designer that comes with MOD is also included with Visual Basic, so you can still use it even if you are developing with Visual Basic.

In this section, I show you how to build COM Add-ins using Visual Basic and ignoring the ActiveX Designer. By ignoring the Designer, I can give you a better look at how COM Add-ins actually work. However, the Designer gives you access to some features of the COM Add-in architecture that you can't get from pure Visual Basic code, so I also show you how to use it. Finally, the support for COM Add-ins has changed significantly from version 5 to version 6 of Visual Basic and I point out the differences between the versions.

Getting Started

After starting Visual Basic, you can choose to create your Add-in as an ActiveX EXE or DLL. The Visual Basic 6 New Project dialog also includes an Addin template, which will take care of some of the work for you. Picking the Addin template creates an ActiveX DLL project with a single form and a copy of the Addin ActiveX Designer named Connect.

The Addin Designer creates a Class module with the routines to connect your Add-in to one of the environments that can use COM Add-ins and make the necessary registry entries. You can still write your own code for the Connect class if you want different functionality than the Designer provides while letting the Designer take care of making the registry entries for you. The Designer's default code, for instance, works only if you are creating an Add-in to be hosted by the Visual Basic IDE.

In Visual Basic 5 and 6, if you choose not to use the Add-in project, you should create an ActiveX DLL or EXE project. With the project created, you'll need to implement the COM Add-in interface in the default Class module that's added to an ActiveX EXE or DLL project. As I said earlier, I assume that you call this Class module "Connect".

Since the Connect Class module will be accessed by the hosting application and multiple copies of the host may need to use it, you should leave the Class's Instancing property as MultiUse.

Once you've created the Class module, you must set a reference to the Visual Basic Extensibility library in your project (in Visual Basic 6, selecting Addin from the Visual Basic New Project dialog does this for you automatically). This gives you access to the interface that your Addin must implement. You should also add references to any object models that you want your Add-in to interact with. For instance, if you want to work with the host's menus and toolbars in Office, you should add a reference to the Microsoft Office Object Library. The Visual Basic IDE has its own set of objects for working with menus which duplicates the objects in Office, so you don't need to add a reference to the Office library to create menus in Visual Basic. If your application will work with the Word object model, you should set a reference to the Microsoft Word Object library (see Figure 15–5). Once you've set the references that you need, you can close the References dialog.

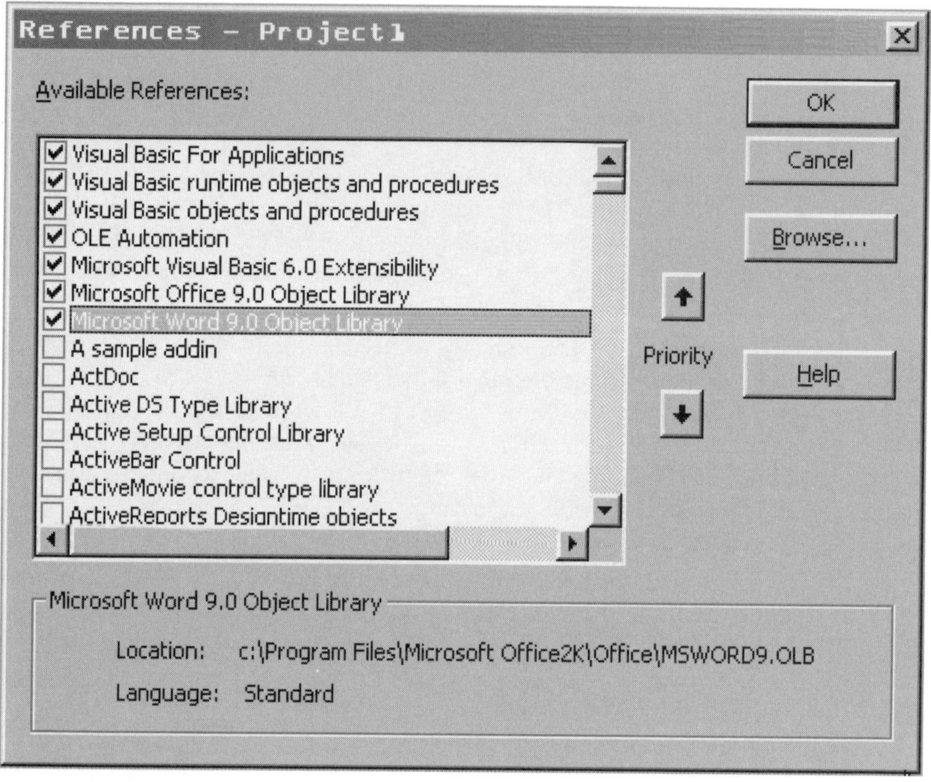

Figure 15–5 · *Typical References entries for a COM Add-in.*

You don't necessarily need to set an object reference to the application that will be hosting your Add-in. If you create a Word Add-in that will update the Outlook journal whenever it is run, you need a reference to the Outlook objects. If the Add-in never uses any of the Word objects, you don't need a reference to Microsoft Word. You only need a reference to the applications whose objects your Add-in will manipulate.

In the Connect Class module, you must implement either the IDTExtensibility interface (for Visual Basic 5) or the IDTExtensibility2 interface (for Visual Basic 6). With that interface added, you need to write the routines for the interface's methods listed earlier: OnConnection, OnDisconnection, OnStartupComplete, OnAddinstUpdate. In addition to those four, IDTExtensibility2 also requires that you write an OnBeginShutdown routine.

ONCONNECTION ROUTINE

As discussed earlier, the OnConnection routine is called in two situations. First, the routine is called when the user adds your Add-in to the host environment using the host's Add-in Manager. Second, the routine is called when the Add-in is loaded as part of the host's startup process.

The first parameter passed to the OnConnection method is a reference to the top-level object in the host environment (typically, the Application object). If other classes in your Add-in need access to the host's objects, then you'll need to set a Public variable to point to this object.

You don't need to worry that Public variables will appear as properties because your Add-in is not accessible from the host environment.

The second parameter passed is the ConnectMode. This flag provides you with information on when in the host's load process your Add-in was connected. The values that you will receive in this variable are:

- ext_cm_Startup — Add-in was started after the host was loaded but before any documents or projects are loaded.
- ext_cm_AfterStartup — Add-in was started after the host was loaded and after any documents were displayed.
- ext_cm_External — Add-in was invoked by a client.
- ext_cm_CommandLine: — Add-in was invoked when Visual Basic was started from a command line.

I check the ConnectMode and, if it is set to ext_cm_AfterStartup, I assume that the user has just selected my Add-in from the host's Add-in Manager dialog. In that situation, I perform any activities that integrate my Add-in with the host (e.g., adding menu items to call routines in the Add-in). I also display a reassuring message that the Add-in has loaded correctly and include the name of my Add-in in the message in case the user has selected my Add-in by mistake.

If the ConnectMode is ext_cm_Startup, I assume that the Add-in was added to the host in a previous session. In this situation, I assume that any activities to integrate the Add-in with the host were performed when the Add-in was first selected and don't reperform them. I don't, for instance, add any menu items that call the Add-in if the ConnectMode is set to ext_cm_Startup.

Don't perform any activities that assume that the host environment is fully loaded in the OnConnection routine. Instead, defer those activities to when the OnStartupComplete routine is called.

The third parameter for this method is a reference to your Add-in. Some of the object methods typically called by an Add-in require a reference to the Add-in itself. If you are going to use those methods (discussed later in this chapter), you should set a Public object variable to point to this object also.

The final parameter passed to the OnConnection method is an array of variants. This array is used by some hosts to pass information to the Add-in. The first entry in this array indicates how the hosting environment itself was loaded. The three values that this position can contain are listed in Table 15.3.

Table 15.3 Values for the First Position in the Custom Parameter

Custom(0) Values	Description
1	Host started as a standalone application.
2	Host is being embedded in another document.
3	Host started through Automation.

The second and third values of the custom array's first position require some explanation. The value 2 would be passed to an Excel Add-in if an Excel spreadsheet was being embedded in a Word document. The value 3 would be passed if a program was using Excel as component by starting it with New or CreateObject. In both situations you may not want your Add-in to be active (especially if it is a user interface enhancement). You may also want to disable any menu items that call your Add-in.

Here's a typical OnConnection method:

```
Implements IDTExtensibility2

Public bolInactive As Boolean
Public objHost As Object
Public objSelf As Object

Private Sub IDTExtensibility2_OnConnection _
   (ByVal Application As Object, _
  ByVal ConnectMode As _
       AddInDesignerObjects.ext_ConnectMode, _
  ByVal AddInInst As Object, _
  custom() As Variant)
```

```
On Error Resume Next
If custom(0) > 1 Then
  If Err.Number = 0 Then
    bolInactive = True
    Exit Sub
  Else
    Err.Clear
    On Error GoTo 0
  End If
End If

Set objHost = Application
Set objSelf = AddInInst
If ConnectMode = ext_cm_AfterStartup Then
  …perform integration activities…
  MsgBox "My Add-in successfully loaded."
End If
End Sub
```

This OnConnection routine first checks the custom array to see how the host application was started. Not all hosts pass this array to the routine, however, so you must test for its presence before using it. The mechanism that I show here (checking the first position and then checking for an error) is the only reliable method that I've found. If the Add-in is being started as part of being embedded or through Automation, I set a Boolean variable to flag to the other methods that they shouldn't execute and then exit the routine. Figure 15–6 shows a decision tree for the start up process.

If the routine is starting normally, then the code gets references to the Application and AddInInst objects. Finally, the code checks the ConnectMode property and, if the Add-in is just being added, performs any integration tasks (e.g., adding menu items) and displays a message indicating that the routine completed successfully.

ONDISCONNECTION PARAMETERS

The OnDisconnection routine is called when your Add-in is being unloaded. Your Add-in may be unloaded because the host is being shut down or because the user has decided to remove your Add-in in the Add-in Manager. The first parameter passed to the OnDisconnection method is RemoveMode, which tells you why your Add-in was removed from the host environment. There are two values passed in this parameter:

- ext_dm_HostShutdown: The host was shut down.
- ext_dm_UserClosed: The Add-in was removed from the Add-in manager.

Load Add-In

Process Custom array.

Automation?

Yes → Suppress User Interface unless host displayed. No Integration required.

No

Embedded?

Yes → User Interface Optional, No Integration required.

Standalone.

Load, continued

Load, continued

Process ConnectMode parameter.

CommandLine?

Yes → Suppress User Interface, assume all integration is done.

No

Startup?

Yes

No

AfterStartup?

Yes → Perform integration activites. User Interface display optional.

No

ConnectMode = External

Yes → No integration required. User Interface display optional.

Load Complete

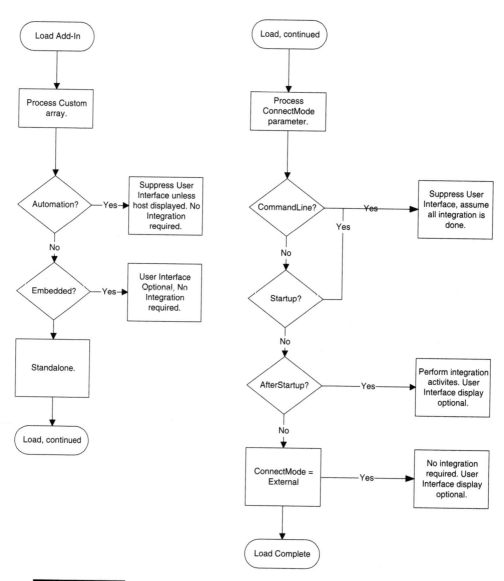

Figure 15–6 *Determining the start environment for an Add-in.*

The OnDisconnection routine is called after the OnBeginShutDown routine

In a typical OnDisconnection routine, I check the RemoveMode parameter to see if the Add-in is being removed because the user is unchecking the Add-in's entry in the Add-in manager. If so, I display a message indicating that the Add-in has been successfully removed and undo any integration changes made in the OnConnection routine (e.g., removing menu items). If the RemoveMode is ex_dm_HostShutdown, indicating that the Add-in is being removed from memory because the host is shutting down, I leave the OnConnection changes in place.

Here's a typical OnDisconnection routine that checks the RemoveMode to determine if it should back anything out of the host environment:

```
Private Sub AddinInstance_OnDisconnection _
  (ByVal RemoveMode As _
     AddInDesignerObjects.ext_DisconnectMode, _
  custom() As Variant)
If RemoveMode = ex_dm_UserClosed Then
  …disconnect activities…
  Msgbox "My Add-in has been unloaded."
End If
End Sub
```

The only other parameter passed to the OnDisconnection routine is the custom() array. The other four routines (OnStartupBegin, OnAddinstUpdate, OnBeginShutdown) are also only passed the custom() array.

SHARING CODE

If your Add-in is only going to be used by one host, you can early-bind the public object variable that points to the OnConnection routine's Application parameter by declaring it with the appropriate data type. In Microsoft Word, for instance, the object passed in the Application parameter is the Word.Application object, so the variable that is set to point to the parameter should be declared as Word.Application.

If the code that I used to demonstrate the OnConnection routine was only going to be used with Word, I would change the declaration for the objHost object variable to Word.Application to get the benefits of early binding (of course, after setting a reference to the Microsoft Word Object Library in my project):

```
Public objHost As Word.Application
```

If you want your Add-in to be used by multiple hosts, you have three options. You could, as I did in my OnConnection example, declare the variable that points to the Application parameter as Object. This will make your code late-bound, with all the attendant problems and costs.

Alternatively, you could create a Connect class for each host (this is what the Addin Designer does). As an example, if I wanted my Add-in to be used by both Word and Excel, I could create two classes called ConnectWord and ConnectExcel. Their OnConnection code would be very similar, but they would set different object variables to point to the OnConnection's Application parameter. The ConnectWord's OnConnection routine would look like this:

```
Public objWord As Word.Application

Private Sub IDTExtensibility2_OnConnection _
  (ByVal Application As Object, _
   ByVal ConnectMode As _
    AddInDesignerObjects.ext_ConnectMode, _
   ByVal AddInInst As Object, _
   custom() As Variant)

Set objWord = Application
```

ConnectExcel's OnConnection routine would be very similar but would use a variable declared to work with Excel:

```
Public objExcel As Excel.Application

Private Sub IDTExtensibility2_OnConnection _
  (ByVal Application As Object, _
   ByVal ConnectMode As _
      AddInDesignerObjects.ext_ConnectMode, _
   ByVal AddInInst As Object, _
   custom() As Variant)

Set objExcel = Application
```

In the Add-ins registry entries for Microsoft Word, I would add place all the entries for this Add-in under the progid for the ConnectWord object. The Excel AddIns registry entries would be placed under the ConnectExcel's progid. The result is that both applications would load the same Add-in component, but they would use different objects to connect the Add-in.

Because two different variables could be pointing to the host, the other routines in the Add-in would have to check to see which variable was set before using it:

```
If objWord Is Nothing Then
  ...Excel code
End If
If objExcel is Nothing Then
  ...Word code
End If
```

Your third option is to write a single OnConnection routine that checks the type of the Application parameter using TypeOf and then sets the appropriate object variable to point to the Application parameter. The code for the OnConnection routine in a combined Word/Excel Add-in might look like this:

```
Public objWord As Word.Application
Public objExcel As Excel.Application

Private Sub IDTExtensibility2_OnConnection _
  (ByVal Application As Object, _
   ByVal ConnectMode As _
    AddInDesignerObjects.ext_ConnectMode, _
   ByVal AddInInst As Object, _
   custom() As Variant)

If TypeOf Application is Word.Application Then
  Set objWord = Application
ElseIf TypeOf Application is Excel.Application Then
  Set objExcel = Application
Else
  Msgbox "This Add-in does not support this host."
End If

End Sub
```

Again, the code in the Add-in's routines would have to check to see which object variable was set before using it.

The Connection Designer

You can speed up the process of creating your Connect Class module by using the Addin ActiveX Designer. In addition to providing default code for the Connect object, the designer also frees you from updating your Add-in's registry entries.

While I don't find the default code all that useful, I heartily recommend using the Designer to save you fiddling with registry entries.

A default Addin Designer is added to your project when you create an Addin project (see Figure 15–7). You can add additional designers by selecting Add Addin Class from Visual Basic's Project menu. Each designer creates a Class module to handle connecting to one of the Add-in environments (Visual Basic IDE, Word, Excel, etc.).

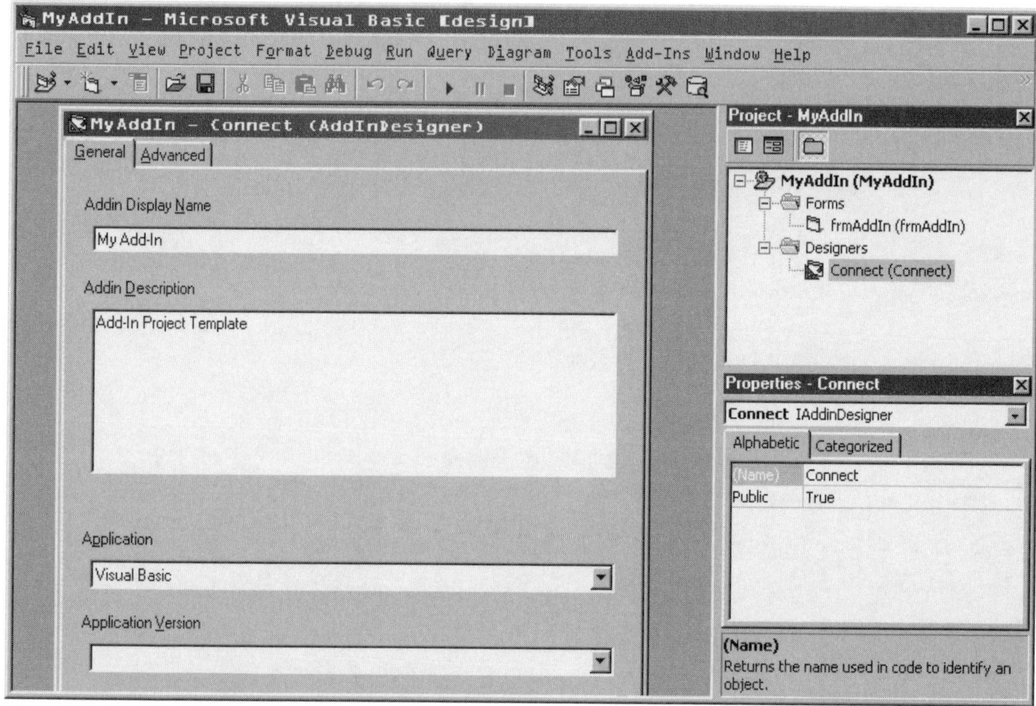

Figure 15–7 *The default Addin project.*

If you add additional Addin ActiveX Designers, you must set the designer's Public property to True before running your Add-in. With the designer's default setting of False, no host environment can find the object. You'll get an error message when you change this property, but you can ignore it.

The Addin Designer implements the AddinInstance interface. This interface is identical to the IDTExstensibility2 interface, except that

- The methods of the IDTExstensibility2 interface appear as events in the Designer
- The Class's Initialize and Terminate events are included as part of the AddinInstance interface.

You can use the AddinInstance interface only from an Addin Designer.

THE DEFAULT CODE

The default designer includes code for the OnConnection, OnDisconnection, and OnStartupComplete methods. The code also adds routines for three methods to the object: Show, Hide, and AddToAddInCommandBar. If you add additional ActiveX Designers, they do not include any default code.

The code in the default designer's Show routine displays a form called mfrmAddIn (the name of the default form added to the project when you create an Addin project). The Hide method hides the same form. The AddToCommandBar method creates an entry for your Add-in on the host application's Add-Ins menu, if it has one, and returns a reference to the new menu item. The object variable that points to this menu item is declared using WithEvents so that the events fired by the menu can be captured in the Add-in.

The AddToCommandBar routine is called from the OnConnection routine. The OnConnection method also sets a Public variable called VBInstance to refer to the host's Application object passed to the OnConnection routine.

The OnDisconnection routine's code keeps track of whether the default form is visible when the application shuts down and records that information in the registry using Visual Basic's SaveSetting command. In the OnConnection event, the routine retrieves the registry entry using GetSetting and restores the form to the state it was in when the host was shut down.

You can delete any of this code or replace it with your own version of these routines.

The OnStartupComplete routine is declared as part of the IDTExtensibility interface. It should have its name rewritten to make it part of the AddInstance interface.

The Addin Designer has two tabs. The first, the General tab, lets you set a number of values for your Class module (see Figure 15–8). You can also, from Visual Basic's Property Window, set a Public property which controls the Instancing property of the resulting Class module. First, I look at the settings available on the General tab.

APPLICATION, APPLICATION VERSION

These two entries allow you to determine which Add-ins section in the registry this Class will appear in. Selecting Word, for instance, will cause the Class module to be listed in the Add-ins section for Microsoft Word. You'll need to add an Addin Designer for each host that you want your Add-in to be available from.

LOADBEHAVIOR

The Designer lets you set the LoadName and LoadBehavior properties for the Class module and skip updating the registry yourself. The LoadName and LoadBehavior properties are set by selecting one of the choices in the Initial Load Behavior combo box on the Designer. You can choose among the options listed in Table 15.4, which duplicate the registry settings I listed earlier.

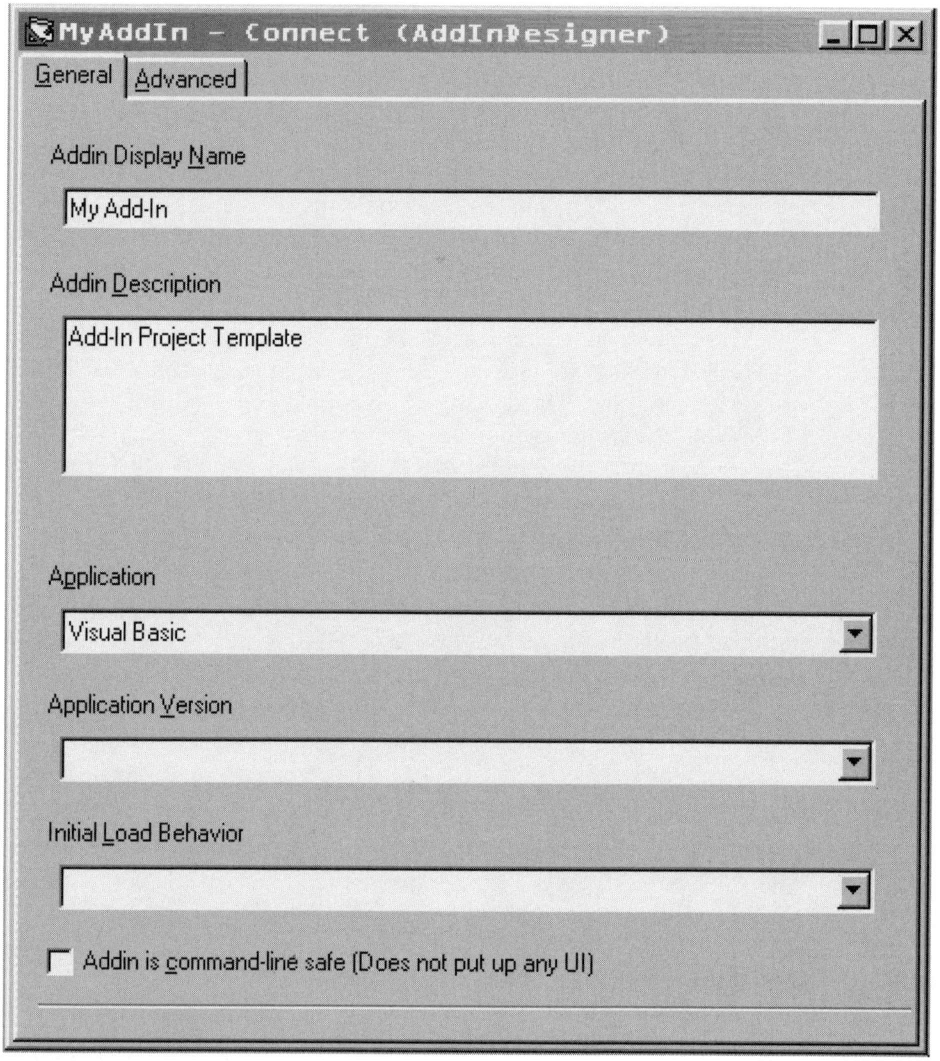

Figure 15–8 *The Visual Basic ActiveX Designer Add-in*

Table 15.4 Load Options Available Using the Addin ActiveX Designer

Load Option	Host	Description
Load on demand	Office	The Add-in will be loaded only when required.
Startup	Office/VB/MDE	The Add-in will be loaded with the hosting environment.
Load at next startup only	Office	The Add-in will be loaded with the hosting environment the next time the host is used and, after that, only when required.
Command line	VB/MDE	The Add-in will be loaded when the host is run from the command line.
None	All	The Add-in will appear in the Add-in Manager but will not be loaded.

DISPLAY NAME, DESCRIPTION, ADDIN IS COMMAND-LINE SAFE

These three options let you set the Description, FriendlyName, and CommandLineSafe entries in the registry for the Add-in. The value that you put in the Name property for the Addin Designer will be used as the name of the Class module that it creates. This means that the Name also sets the progid for the class. The progid for the resulting object will be a combination of the Add-in project's name and the Name property of the Addin Designer.

For Visual Basic and MDE Add-ins, the Designer includes a checkbox at the bottom of the dialog labeled Command line safe (if you can't see it, you need to resize the dialog). Setting the Command-line safe option indicates to Visual Basic or the MDE that your Add-in does not require user input. You should set this option when you know that your Add-in will not halt processing by asking for input when Visual Basic or the MDE is used from a command line to compile a program using the /run or /make switches.

Leaving the Command line safe setting blank doesn't prevent the user from setting your Add-in's Load Behavior in the Add-in manager to "Command Line." However, the user will get a warning message when this is done. If your Add-in has a visible user interface and you do set the Command-line safe option, then the user won't get a warning if your Add-in is set to be loaded when Visual Basic is run from the command-line. This will result in Visual Basic abending whenever the user tries to run it from the Command-line.

THE ADVANCED TAB

The second tab of the Designer, the Advanced tab, lets you enter two kinds of information (see Figure 15–9). First, it lets you associate a resource file with your Addin (resource files are typically used to support internationalization). This resource file must be in the same directory as your compiled Add-in file.

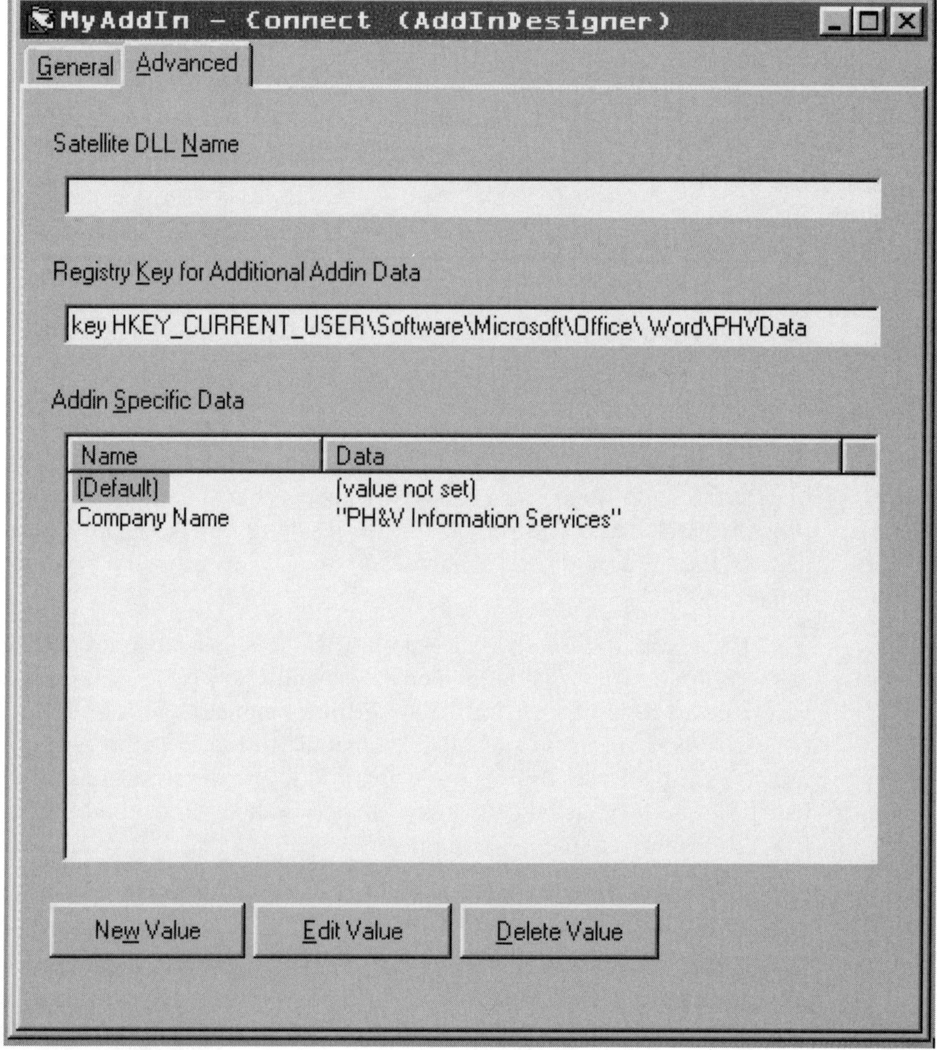

Figure 15–9 *The Addin Designer's Advanced tab.*

The Advanced tab can also be used to put some additional values in the Windows registry as part of installing your Add-in. In the text box labeled Registry Key for Additional Add-in Data you can specify the full name of a registry key that you want created or have entries added to. In the Addin Specific Data box, you can enter the name and data for the Values that you want stored under that key.

For instance, I typically store my company name in the registry with my Add-ins. Entering the key HKEY_CURRENT_USER\Software\Microsoft\Office\Word\PHVData, creates an entry under the same key as the Word Addins entry but called PHVData. Entering a value with the name "CompanyName" and value "PH&V Information Systems" stores my company information under my new key.

The additional registry entries that you create on the Advanced tab are also made if you start your Add-in for a debugging session.

Integrating Your Add-in and the Host

Once your COM Add-in is loaded, it can begin running. You may not need any further integration with your host's environment. You could, for instance, have your Add-in run as a background process using the techniques for creating asynchronous processing that I described in the chapter on Objects. More likely, though, your Add-in will not execute until the user requests it. There are four mechanisms that you can use to make your Add-in available to the host's user:

1. Display a form in the OnConnection routine for the user to interact with.
2. Open an ActiveX Document (Visual Basic only).
3. Respond to events fired by the host's objects.
4. Add a new menu item to the host's menu system.

In practice, these options are complementary. For instance, if you have your Add-in display a form for your user to interact with, your user may choose to close that form. In order to allow your user to redisplay the form, you'll have to add a menu item to the host's menu system. If you choose the third option and add an item to the host's menu system to activate your Add-in, you will find that you have to write code to respond to the menu item's events. Finally, even if you've set up your Add-in to run automatically when some event occurs in the host, you may want to provide a menu item that allows the user to turn this automatic processing off.

Displaying a Form

You can use the same tools in building a COM Add-in as you would when building a standalone application: Forms, Modules, UserDocuments, UserControls, and so on. One option that you can use in creating a COM Add-in is to have it display a Visual Basic Form complete with text boxes, command buttons, and whatever other controls are required by your Add-in. This has the benefit of allowing you to build your Add-in with the user interface techniques that you are familiar with from building Visual Basic applications. It's also the method implemented by the code in the default Add-in Designer in a Visual Basic Addin project (see Figure 15–10).

To display a Form from your Add-in, you use the same syntax as you would in any other Visual Basic program. This code, placed in the OnConnec-

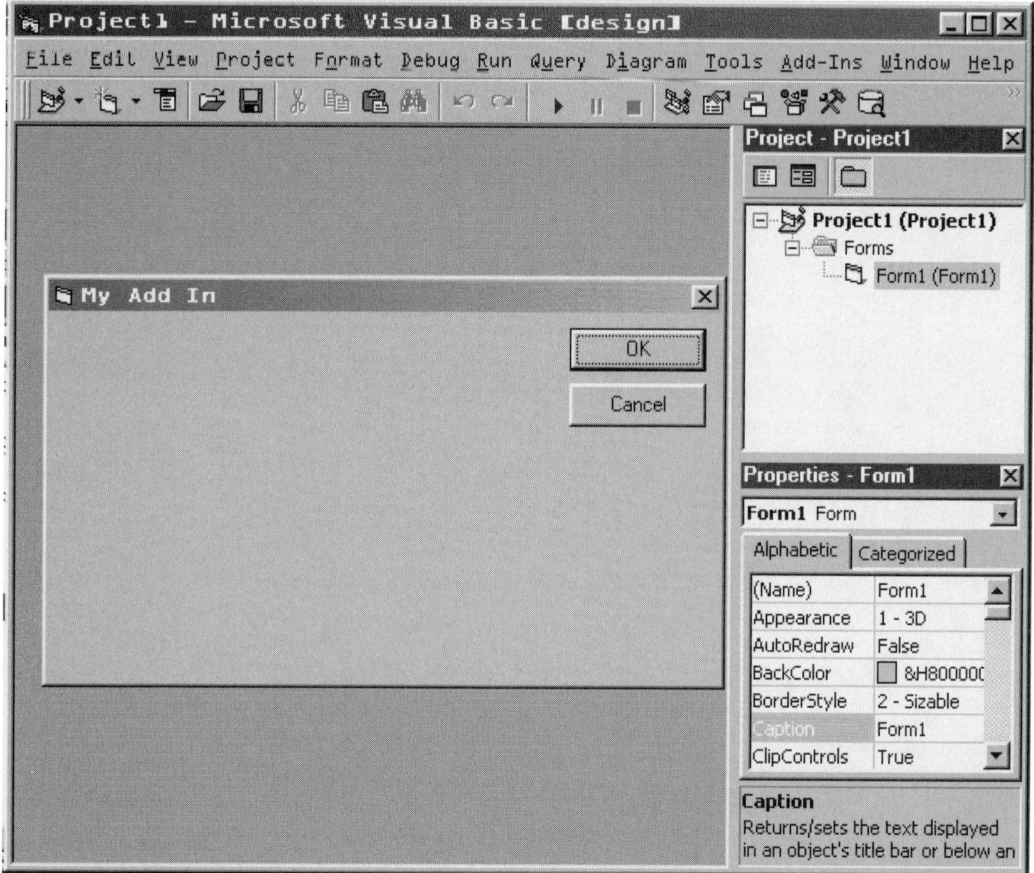

Figure 15–10 *The default Add-in project form displayed in a Visual Basic project.*

tion routine, would display frmAddinMain, the default Form added to an Add-in project:

```
frmAddin.Show
```

The Forms that you use as part of your Add-in can have all of the same controls and perform all of the same activities that a Form in a standard Visual Basic application would. The major difference is that when a user clicks on a button on your Add-in's form, the code behind the button will typically manipulate the object model of its host.

The following code, for instance, could be used from a Word Add-in to save all of the currently open documents. I've included the OnConnection routine from the Connect Class which sets the variable objWordApp to point to the Application parameter passed to the routine. With the objWordApp pointing to Word's Application object, the next routine (from the Click event of a button on a Form) uses the variable to loop through Word's Documents collection. For each document in the collection, the routine calls the Document object's Save method:

```
Public objWordApp As Word.Application

Private Sub IDTExtensibility2_OnConnection _
  (ByVal Application As Object, _
   ByVal ConnectMode As _
    AddInDesignerObjects.ext_ConnectMode, _
   ByVal AddInInst As Object, _
   custom() As Variant)

  Set objWordApp = Application
End Sub

Sub OKButton_Click
  Dim doc As Word.Document
  For Each doc In objWordApp.Documents
    doc.Save
  Next
End Sub
```

There are some problems with using a Form in an Add-in. To begin with, your Add-in's users won't be able to dock your Form or treat it like the other windows in the host application. Also, users expect that if a child window of an application is open when the application is shut down then, the next time that the application is started, the child window should display itself at startup. You expect, for instance, that Visual Basic will retain whatever configuration of toolbars and windows that you set up from one session to another. Left to its own devices a Form used in an Add-in won't do that. The code in the default Addin Designer includes code to save and retrieve information to the Windows registry just to duplicate this behavior.

Displaying an ActiveX Document

In Visual Basic 6, you can create an Add-in that does act like a typical child window of an application by using an ActiveX Document inside a ToolWindow. The Visual Basic Windows collection has a CreateToolWindow method that can be used to add a new window to be managed by Visual Basic. The ToolWindow can be docked and manipulated like any other window in the IDE. A ToolWindow's state at shutdown is automatically restored when Visual Basic is started again. The ActiveX Document inside the ToolWindow provides the user interface for your Add-in (Figure 15–11).

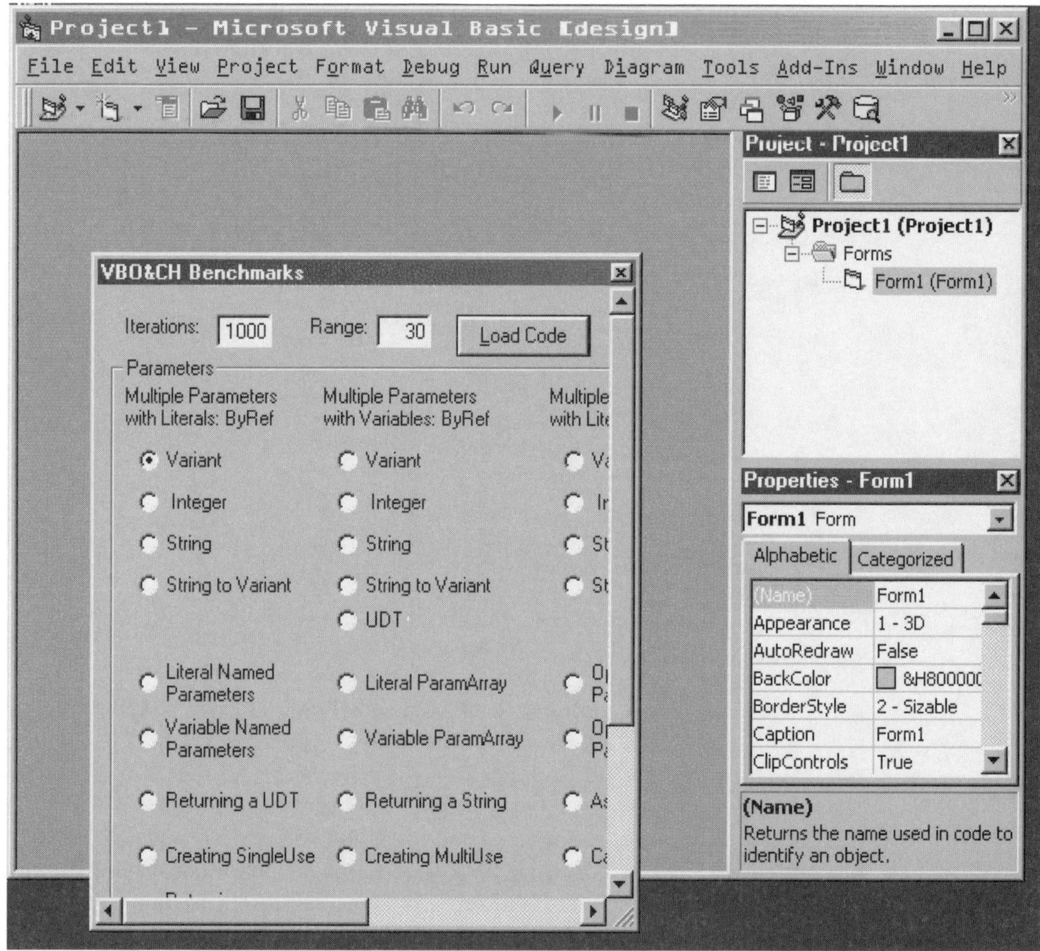

Figure 15–11 *Displaying an Addin ToolWindow in a Visual Basic project.*

The CreateToolWindow method accepts five parameters and returns a reference to the window that it creates. The first parameter is a reference to your Add-in. For this parameter, you should pass the AddInInst parameter that is passed to the OnConnection routine (or an object set to point to it).

The second parameter is the progid for your ActiveX Document. The first part of the progid will be your Add-in's Project Name (as set in Project | Properties) and the second part will be the UserDocument's name. Assuming that you selected Addin from the Visual Basic New Project dialog, your Add-in project will be called MyAddIn. If you add a UserDocument to your project and don't change its Name property, it will be called UserDocument1. As a result, the progid of the ActiveX Document would be MyAddIn.UserDocument1.

The third parameter that you pass to the CreateToolWindow method is the caption to be displayed in the ToolWindow's title bar. The fourth parameter is a GUID which you can generate using either UUIDGEN.EXE or GUIDGEN.EXE (see the discussion of these tools in the chapter on data providers). The CreateToolWindow returns a reference to your ActiveX Document in its fifth parameter, so that parameter should be an object variable declared as a reference to your ActiveX Document.

The GUID is used internally by Visual Basic to identify your window.

The CreateToolWindow method will create a ToolWindow object hosting the ActiveX Document whose progid is passed to it. The following OnConnecton routine creates a ToolWindow object from a User Document called UserDocument1:

```
Private Sub IDTExtensibility2_OnConnection _
  (ByVal Application As Object, _
   ByVal ConnectMode As _
      AddInDesignerObjects.ext_ConnectMode, _
   ByVal AddInInst As Object, _
  custom() As Variant)

Dim tlwMyWindow As Window
Dim objMyTool As UserDocument1

Set tlwMyWindow = _
  Application.Windows.CreateToolWindow(AddInInst, _
  "MyAddIn.UserDocument1", "My Tool", _
  "3a0b7e00-a017-11d3-a8ca-00107a901a5f",objMyTool)
End Sub
```

To call a method of your ActiveX Document you use the reference returned in the fifth parameter of the CreateToolWindow method. This code, for instance, uses the objMyTool reference returned in my previous example to call a method of the UserDocument1 object:

```
objMyTool.MyMethod
```

The object reference returned by the CreateToolWindow method points to the ToolWindow itself. You use the methods and properties of that ToolWindow object to manage the window that your ActiveX Document appears in. For instance, to make your document visible you would use the ToolWindow's Visible property and to close the ToolWindow you would use the ToolWindow's Close method:

```
tlwMyWindow.Visible = True
tlwMyWindow.Close
```

When you're finished using your ToolWindow, you should destroy both the ToolWindow and your ActiveX Document by setting their references to Nothing, like this:

```
Set objMyTool = Nothing
Set tlwMyWindow = Nothing
```

Responding to Events

You don't have to provide any user interface to your Add-in if the Add-in is designed simply to respond to events fired by the host environment. In many ways, having your Add-in respond to events provides the highest form of integration: Your Add-in simply extends the functionality of the host environment by performing additional tasks when the host signals the event.

To create an Add-in that responds to events, you begin by declaring an object reference using the WithEvents keyword. You then set that variable to point to an object in the host. With that done, you can write code that responds to the events fired by the Add-in's host. Effectively, you extend the host object's functionality without the user ever interacting directly with your Add-in.

As an example, the following code declares the objWordApp object using the WithEvents keyword. I then set the object variable to point to the Application object passed into the OnConnection routine. Now, when Word's Application object fires any events, code in the Add-in can be executed. In this sample, I've written code to execute when Word's Application object fires its Quit event to save all the open documents:

```
Public WithEvents objWordApp As Word.Application
Private Sub IDTExtensibility2_OnConnection _
   (ByVal Application As Object, _
    ByVal ConnectMode As _
       AddInDesignerObjects.ext_ConnectMode, _
```

```
    ByVal AddInInst As Object, _
    custom() As Variant)

  Set objWordApp = Application
End Sub

Private Sub objWordAdd_Quit()
  Dim doc As Word.Document
  For Each doc In objWordApp.Documents
    doc.Save
  Next
End Sub
```

Adding Your Add-in to a Menu

The most common method for integrating your Add-in into its host environment is to add an entry to the host's menu system. Fortunately, all of the hosting environments for COM Add-ins use the same component to manage their toolbars and menus. This means that menu management code that you create for your Add-in will work with any host.

The one exception to the CommandBars uniformity in all hosts is the way that they handle events. As I show later in this section, Visual Basic and the MDE handle events differently then Office.

The Office/Visual Basic/MDE menuing system consists of a series of menu bars. Each menu bar can contain one or more controls, including menus but also including buttons, text boxes, and combo boxes. Any menus that appear on a bar will contain menu selections. The standard menu bar consists of nothing but menu controls (File, Edit, etc.), each of which has several menu selections (e.g., the File menu has New, Open, Print). Figure 15–12 illustrates the various components of the menu system using Microsoft Word.

So, the complete process for adding a menu item consists of:

1. Adding a menu bar to the host
2. Populating that menu bar with items (including a menu proper)
3. Adding menu selections to any menus added in the previous step

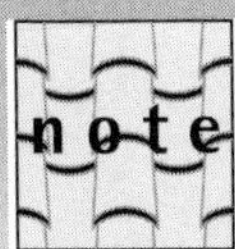

While the Windows user interface distinguishes between menus and toolbars, the object model allows you to mix menus, buttons, combo boxes, and text boxes on the same bar.

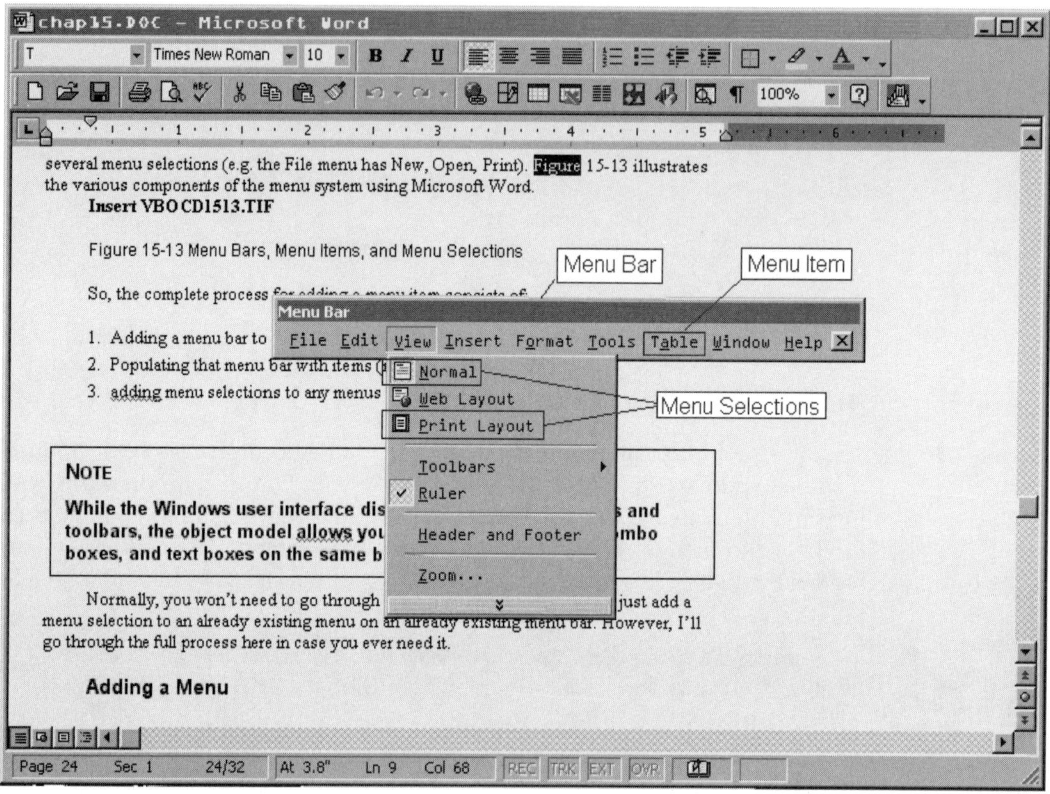
chap15.DOC - Microsoft Word
Times New Roman
10
100%
several menu selections (e.g. the File menu has New, Open, Print). Figure 15-13 illustrates the various components of the menu system using Microsoft Word.
Insert VBOCD1513.TIF
Figure 15-13 Menu Bars, Menu Items, and Menu Selections
Menu Bar
Menu Item
So, the complete process
Menu Bar
File Edit View Insert Format Tools Table Window Help
1. Adding a menu bar to
2. Populating that menu bar with items
3. adding menu selections to any menus
Normal
Web Layout
Print Layout
Menu Selections
Toolbars
Ruler
Header and Footer
Zoom...
NOTE
While the Windows user interface dis
toolbars, the object model allows you
boxes, and text boxes on the same b
and
mbo
Normally, you won't need to go through
just add a
menu selection to an already existing menu on
However, I'll
go through the full process here in case you ever need it.
Adding a Menu
Page 24 Sec 1 24/32 At 3.8" Ln 9 Col 68 REC TRK EXT OVR

Figure 15–12 *Menu Bars, Menu Items, and Menu Selections.*

Normally, you won't need to go through all these steps. Typically, you'll just add a menu selection to an already existing menu on an already existing menu bar. However, I go through the full process here in case you ever need it.

ADDING A MENU

You may want to create a menu bar for your Add-in in these situations:

- Your Add-in requires several menu entries and you want to make each of them available in a "tool-bar" like interface.
- Your Add-in requires several menus and you want to keep them on a bar of their own.
- You're going to use a text box, combo box, or drop down control in conjunction with your menu choices.

Menu bars are created by adding a menu bar item to the CommandBars collection using the collection's Add method. The CommandBars collection's Add method accepts four parameters:

1. Name: This is the name that your menu bar will have in the CommandBars collection.
2. Position: This parameter can have one of six settings. Four of the settings (msoBarLeft, msoBarRight, msoBarTop, msoBarBottom) will cause your new menu bar to appear docked on the left, right, top, or bottom of the host Window (see Figure 15–13). Using msoBarFloating will create a floating bar. The constant msoBarPopup will create the menu bar but not display it until you use the bar's ShowPopup method (Office only). Typically, you use msoBarPopup to create a context menu that you will display from a MouseDown event.
3. MenuBar: When set to True, the parameter causes the current active menu bar to be removed as part of adding your new bar.
4. Temporary: Your menu bar will be discarded when the user closes down the host application.

The Add method returns a reference to the menu bar that it creates. The object variable that holds the reference to your menu bar should be declared as CommandBar. Creating a menu bar doesn't cause it to be displayed so, after creating the menu bar, you'll need to set the bar's Visible property to True to make it visible.

As an example, the following code creates a menu bar and returns a reference to the bar. The code then uses the returned reference to display the menu bar. The parameters passed to the Add method in this sample code will cause the bar to first appear docked on the right side of the host's window and have the bar destroyed when the host shuts down. This menu bar could be retrieved from the CommandBars collection by using the name "MyBar":

```
Dim barMine As CommandBar

Set barMine = Application.CommandBars.Add("MyBar", _
            msoBarRight, False, True)
barMine.Visible = True
```

Normally, you shouldn't display your menu bar until after you've added any menu items to the bar. Not only does displaying a completed menu bar look more professional, the code that adds items to the bar runs faster if the bar isn't visible.

To destroy a menu bar, you must use its Delete method after retrieving the bar from the CommandBars collection. This code destroys the bar created by the previous control:

```
Application.CommandBars("MyBar").Delete
```

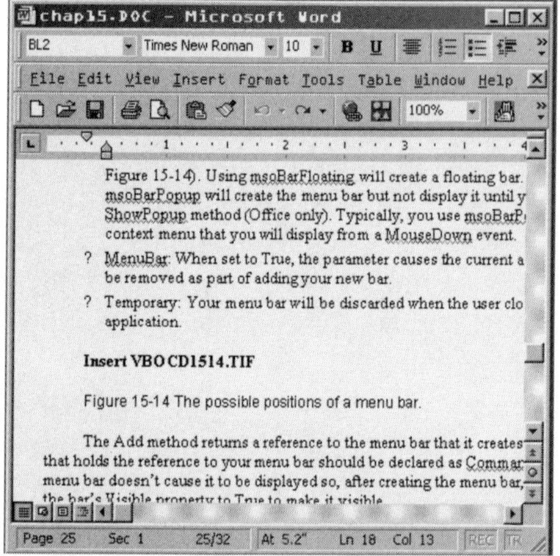

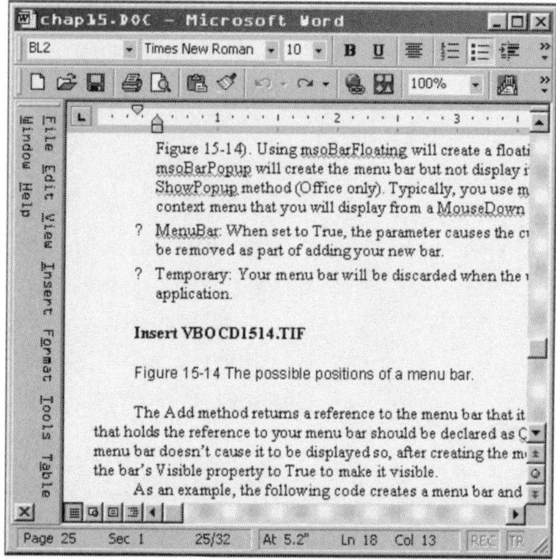

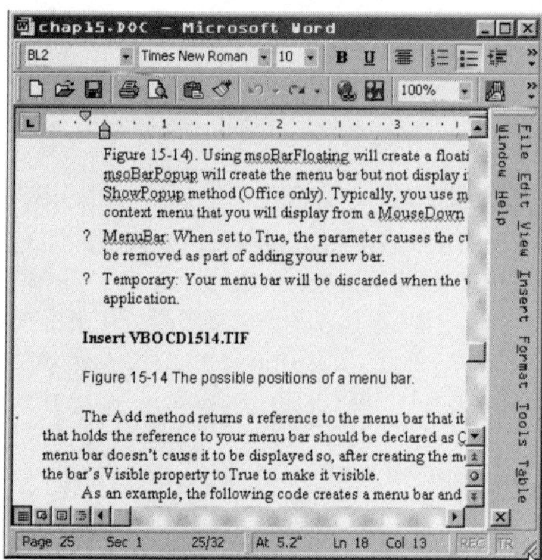

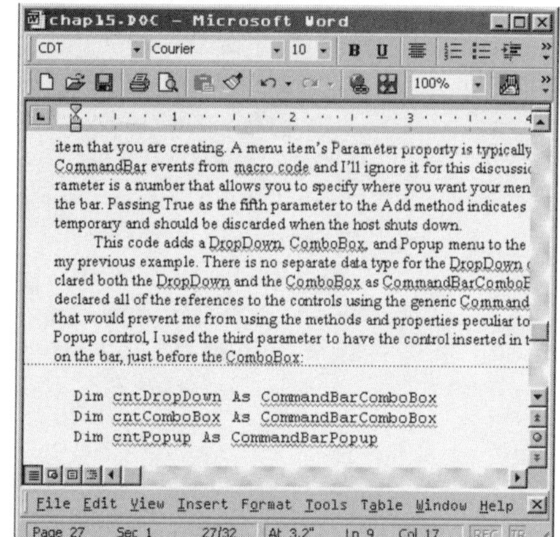

Figure 15–13 *The possible positions of a menu bar. Going clockwise from the upper left hand figure: top, right, bottom, and left.*

ADDING A MENU ITEM

The next step in integrating your COM Add-in by using the host's menu system is to add a menu item to your bar. You can add popup menus, buttons, text boxes, and combo/drop-down boxes to your menu bar. You add items to a menu bar by using the Add method of a menu bar's Controls collection. The Controls collection of a menu bar holds references to all of the items on the bar.

The CommandBar Add method accepts five parameters and returns a reference to the menu item that it creates. The first parameter specifies the kind of item that you want to add to your menu bar. For the examples in this chapter I stick to Popups (msoControlDropDown), ComboBoxes (msoControlComboBox), and Buttons (msoControlButton). For COM Add-ins, you can ignore the second parameter of the Add method.

You can also add text boxes (msoControlEditBox), but since they can't trigger an action in your Add-in, I'll pass over them.

The third parameter of the Add method allows you to set the Parameter property of the item that you are creating. A menu item's Parameter property is typically used in processing CommandBar events from macro code and I ignore it for this discussion. The fourth parameter is a number that allows you to specify where you want your menu item inserted on the bar. Passing True as the fifth parameter to the Add method indicates that the control is temporary and should be discarded when the host shuts down.

This code adds a DropDown, ComboBox, and Popup menu to the menu bar created in my previous example. There is no separate data type for the DropDown control, so, I've declared both the DropDown and the ComboBox as CommandBarComboBox. I could have declared all of the references to the controls using the generic CommandBarControl type but that would prevent me from using the methods and properties peculiar to each type. For the Popup control, I used the third parameter to have the control inserted in the second position on the bar, just before the ComboBox:

```
Dim cntDropDown As CommandBarComboBox
Dim cntComboBox As CommandBarComboBox
Dim cntPopup As CommandBarPopup

Set cntDropDown = _
  barMine.Controls.Add(msoControlDropDown)
Set cntComboBox = _
  barMine.Controls.Add(msoControlComboBox)
Set cntPopup = _
  barMine.Controls.Add(msoControlPopup, , 2)
```

Once your menu items are created, you'll want to set their properties (including Caption, Width, and ToolTip) to get the appearance that you want. For ComboBoxes and DropDowns, you'll also want to add items to their lists using their AddItem method. If you intend to use FindControl to locate the control later, you should also set the control's Tag property (more on FindControl in the next section). The result should look something like Figure 15–14.

Figure 15–14 *A menu bar with a menu, a button, a combo box, and a drop-down box.*

The difference between a ComboBox and a DropDown is that the user can type entries into the ComboBox but can only select items from the list of a DropDown.

You use the Popup menu control to add menus to your menu bar. Each Popup menu has a Controls collection of its very own with an Add method that lets you add menu items. You'll normally use a Popup menu's Controls collection to add CommandBarButtons to the menu. CommandBarButtons appear as the standard menu item that you click to make something happen. You can also add Popup menus to the Controls collection to create submenus.

This code adds a CommandBar button to the Popup menu that I created in the previous code:

```
Dim cntButton As CommandBarButton

Set cntButton = _
  cntPopup.Controls.Add(msoControlButton)
```

As I said, normally, you won't need all this code to have your Add-in invoked from a menu. For instance, in Visual Basic and the MDE, which have an Add-ins menu, the standard is to just add your menu entries to the Add-ins menu. The code to do that would look like this in Office:

```
Application.CommandBars( _
  "Add-Ins").Controls.Add(msoControlButton)
```

REMOVING A MENU ITEM

If you've retained a reference to a menu item, you can delete the menu item by using the item's Delete method. To remove the Popup control from the previous example, I could use this code:

```
cntPopup.Delete
```

If you didn't retain a reference to a control, but know what menu bar or popup menu it is on, you could loop through the item's Controls collection, checking the properties of the collection's members until you find the item that you want. This code searches the Controls collection of my Popup menu to find the control with the caption "Click Me":

```
Dim cnt As CommandBarButton

For Each cnt In cntPopup.Controls
  If cnt.Caption = "Click Me" Then
    cnt.Delete
  End If
Next
```

You can also use the FindControl method of the CommandBars collection, which will find a control anywhere in the menu system and return a reference to the control. Unfortunately, the only property that you can search for is the control's Tag property, which you pass as the third parameter to the method. This code, for instance, returns a reference to the control whose Tag property is set to "Find Me":

```
Set cntRef = _
  Application.CommandBars.FindControl( , , "Find Me")
```

RESPONDING TO EVENTS

Now that you've created your menu item, you can have it call your COM Add-in. For Visual Basic 6 and the Microsoft Development Environment, you must declare a CommandBarEvents object using the WithEvents keyword. When this object variable is set to point to a Visual Basic menu item, you can capture Click events from the CommandBarEvents object.

The following code declares a CommandBarEvents object and then associates it with the menu button that I created in my previous examples:

```
Dim WithEvents cbe As CommandBarEvents
Set cbe = Application.Events.CommandBarEvents(cntButton)
```

I can now write a Click event to process events from that menu item. The Click event will be passed three parameters by the Visual Basic IDE. The first parameter is a reference to the CommandBarControl that fired the event. The other two parameters passed to the Click event are relevant only if you are capturing events from one of the built-in Visual Basic menu items. These parameters are:

- Handled: A legacy item from Visual Basic 5. When set to True it indicates that event has been handled and should be skipped by any other objects responding to the event.
- CancelDefault: If your routine sets this parameter to True the normal activity performed by the menu item will be skipped.

The Handled parameter is present solely for compatibility with Visual Basic 5. Since it's impossible, in COM, to determine the order that clients will respond to an event, the results of setting the Handled property to True are unpredictable. You should not change the value of this parameter.

The Click routine declaration that would go with my previous sample code would look like this:

```
Private Sub cbe_Click( _
  ByVal CommandBarControl As Object, _
  handled As Boolean, CancelDefault As Boolean)

End Sub
```

For Office applications, the process of responding the menu events is simpler. You can declare both CommandBarButtons and CommandBarComboBoxes object variables using the WithEvents keyword. CommandBarButtons fire a Click event that receives the same parameters as the Click event in the Visual Basic IDE. The ComboBox fires a Change event that is passed one parameter, the reference to the ComboBox menu control that fired the event.

The DropDown control fires a Change event when a new value is selected from the DropDown's list. The same is true of a ComboBox. However, a ComboBox also fires an event when the user types an entry into the box. Unfortunately, the event is fired on the first character that's entered, not when the user finishes making the entry. As a result, there is no event that you can use to pick up the user's complete entry in the ComboBox.

Rewriting my previous code to use WithEvents means moving the declarations for the CommandBar Controls into the General Declarations area at the top of the Class module (WithEvents variables cannot be declared inside a procedure). With the event routines added for a CommandBarButton and a CommandBarComboBox, the resulting code in my Add-in looks like this:

```
Dim WithEvents cntButton As CommandBarButton
Dim WithEvents cntComboBox As CommandBarComboBox

Private Sub cntButton_Click( _
  ByVal Office.CommandBarControl As Object, _
  handled As Boolean, CancelDefault As Boolean)

End Sub
Private Sub cntComboBox_Change( _
  ByVal Office.CommandBarComboBox As Object)

End Sub
```

If you have Office 2000 co-existing with Office 97, the Office Object library is not always upgraded to 9.0. You must have the Office 9.0 Object library installed to use event routines for menu items. Everything except the WithEvents code will work with the Office 8.0 object library.

Debugging and Deploying

Debugging and deploying your Add-in is considerably easier if you use the ActiveX Designer. Without the Designer, after compiling your Add-in you'll have to make the necessary entries in the Windows registry in order for Visual Basic 6, Office, or the MDE to find your Add-in (for Visual Basic 5, you must make an entry to the vbaddins.INI file). As a result, if you don't use the

Designer, you won't be able to debug your Add-in interactively in the Visual Basic IDE because your Add-in must be compiled first.

If you use the Designer, on the other hand, the registry entries will be made for you when you compile your program. In addition, if you press F5 to start running your component in the IDE, a set of temporary entries will be made in the registry to allow your Add-in to be found. You can then start, for instance, a second copy of Visual Basic and find your Add-in listed in the Add-in Manager, ready to be tested.

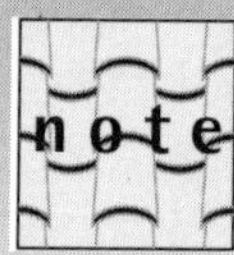

Generally, you will find that you can stop your Visual Basic Add-in project without affecting the Add-in's host. However, you will find that to resume debugging after restarting your Add-in, you must uncheck your Add-in in the Add-in Manager, exit the Manager, and reselect your Add-in in the Manager.

The most significant problem with debugging your Add-in is letting your Add-in disconnect. If you have a problem with your Add-in, you may be tempted to just stop it. While nothing bad will happen if you do, your OnDisconnection routine will not execute and any actions that are the responsibility of that routine (e.g., removing menus added in the OnConnection routine) will not be carried out. Depending on what's in your OnDisconnection routine, you may want to return to the host's Add-in manager and remove your add-in before stopping. This lets your onDisconnect event run. If you are testing your OnConnection event, it may be convenient in the Office hosts to move the COM Add-Ins menu item to your main menu bar where it's easy to call up.

When testing your Add-in, you'll probably find yourself continually returning to the Add-ins menu to check and uncheck your Add-in. At least during the testing phase for Add-ins targeted at the Visual Basic IDE, consider giving your Add-in a name that begins with a hyphen (e.g., _MyAddIn). This will sort your Add-in to the top of the Add-ins list where it will be selected as soon as you open the dialog. A simple ALT_L will then check (or uncheck) your Add-in.

In Visual Basic 6, if you used Designers to create your Connect classes, then the setup program that the Package and Deployment Wizard creates from your project will make the necessary entries in the Windows registry. If you don't use the Designers then you'll have to find some other way to add your Connect Class's progids to the appropriate Add-ins entries in the registry. In Visual Basic 5, no Designers are available and your Add-in can only be used with the Visual Basic IDE. Your setup routine will have to make the entry to the vbaddins.INI file that allows Visual Basic 5 to find your Add-in.

Summary

In this chapter I introduced you to COM Add-ins. You learned how to create an Add-in both with and without the Addin ActiveX Designer. I showed you how to set up your Add-in to connect to any of the COM Add-in hosts. You also saw how to create menus using the Commandbars objects common to virtually all of Microsoft's environments, and how you could integrate your Add-in with its host. While COM Add-ins provide a standard way of extending their hosts, you also saw the differences that do exist between Office and Visual Basic/MDE Add-ins.

You'll need to become familiar with the object model for any of the hosts that you want your Add-in to work with. Sybex has published an excellent series of books for each of the Office components under the general heading of "Macro & VBA Handbook" (e.g., *Word Macro and VBA Handbook*). For the Visual Basic IDE, O'Reilly has *Developing Visual Basic Add-ins* by Steven Roman. The first half of the book duplicates the material that I've covered here, but the back half investigates the Visual Basic IDE fairly thoroughly. For more information on CommandBars, I recommend "Command and Menu Bars" by Charlie Kindschi in the Visual Studio Help System.

If you are interested in a sample of what a Visual Basic Add-in looks like, you can download the Visual Basic IDE Add-in that generated all of this book's benchmark code from my company's Website at *www.phvis.com.*

Now you need to create an Add-in of your own. One that I've found useful (originally developed by Ken Getz) closes all the open windows in the Visual Basic IDE. Once you have that working, you could extend it to perform the same activity in Microsoft Word, or Excel.

PART FOUR

Windows 2000

While Windows 2000 is only slowly becoming a production environment for Visual Basic programmers, it will undoubtedly become the dominating environment in the next two to three years. While Visual Basic does not yet fully support Windows 2000, this section provides an overview of the capabilities of Windows 2000 that are relevant to component development and are supported by Visual Basic.

In This Part

SIXTEEN

Component Services

With Windows 2000, the world of COM undergoes some significant changes. Windows 2000 can be seen as the final triumph of COM because the Windows operating system is now based on a new version of COM (COM+) right from its foundations. COM+ is now a core technology for developing applications rather than a topic for the elite developer.

In Windows 2000, Microsoft Transaction Server (MTS) is gone, absorbed into the operating system and renamed Component Services. In addition to providing many of the management and control functions that used to be the responsibility of Microsoft Transaction Server, Component Services provides new features and capabilities to the component developer and resolves some problems that existed in COM.

The terminology also changes, of course. What was once an MTS package is now a COM+ Application, for instance. Some things haven't changed. Though Microsoft Transaction Server is gone, the ObjectContext object is still around and now provides your Visual Basic objects with access to information about the COM+ environment that they are running in.

In this chapter, I introduce you to the concepts behind Component Services and let you know what has (and hasn't) changed between Windows 95/98/NT and Windows 2000. From there, I go on to look at some of the new features available to the object and component developer.

Component Services Concepts

One of the key ideas in the world of Component Services is interception. With Microsoft Transaction Server, calls to a component were intercepted by MTS, which then managed the objects for the client. Component Services makes interception a core part of the client/server relationship. By taking control over the management of the interaction between a client and server, your objects can be controlled by just changing settings in the Component Services user interface (see Figure 16–1).

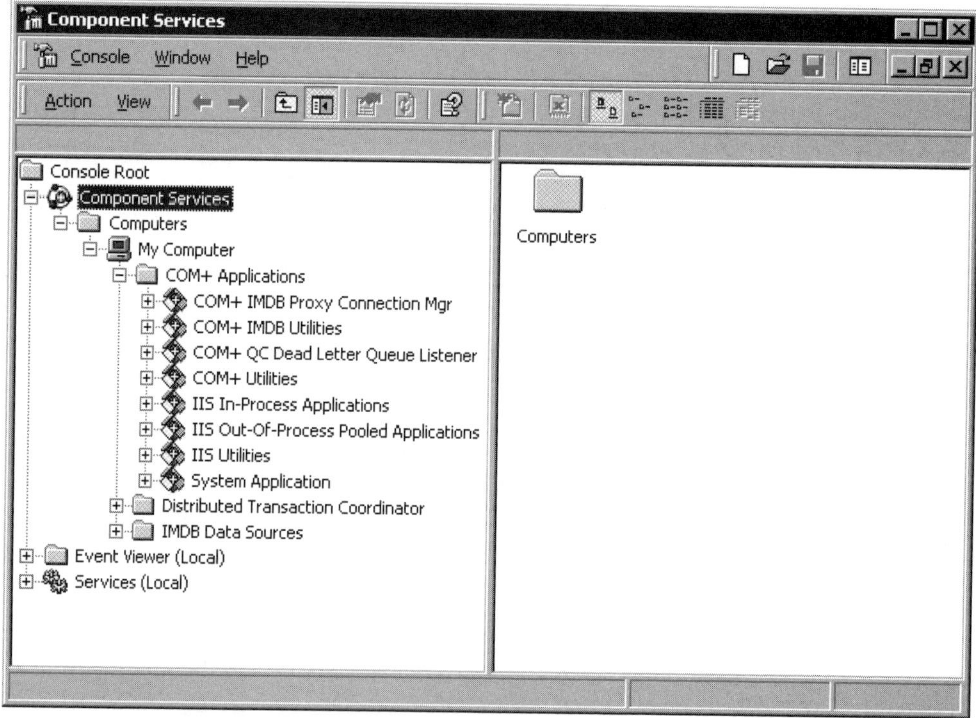

Figure 16–1 *Managing components with Component Services.*

Controlling your component's behavior by setting options in Component Services is another example of declarative programming. Declarative programming allows you to control the behavior of an object or component by setting properties instead of writing code. You've seen declarative programming before, in the chapter on MTS. In MTS you controlled the way that your component handled transactions by using declarative programming. Instead of writing code to manage transactions, you set options for the component: Requires a Transaction, Requires a New Transaction, and so on. With

Component Services, declarative programming is enhanced by providing you with more options to set for your component. Setting options is called configuring your application and the options that a component operates under is said to be its context.

Contexts and Configurations

It's interception that allows you to configure your components using Component Services. The configuration process lets you control the behavior of your component by right-mouse clicking on your component in the Component Services UI, selecting Properties, and then setting the options that you want. The resulting context for the component includes transaction options (participate in an existing transaction, start a new one, etc.), handling queued messages, threading (apartment threaded, not threaded, and so on), location of the component, and security.

One of the results of this configuration process is that when one COM object calls another, the two programs may not be configured similarly. COM+ compares the configurations of the client and the server components and either starts the new component in the client's context or creates a new context for the server that reflects the server's configuration. The relationships between client and server contexts can be complicated; even when a server component is created in its own context, the configuration of the client component can affect it. A client running in a transaction will force a component that supports transactions to become part of the client's transaction, for instance.

Calls between objects in separate contexts are intercepted by COM+, which performs any processing on the call required to handle the differences between the two contexts. Not surprising, then, you can take a performance hit when two objects have different contexts. Fortunately, one of the configuration options in Component Services is to configure a component so that it always runs in the same context in its client.

You can also have unconfigured components—components installed on the computer but not included in a COM+ application. COM+ provides a default context for these components. An unconfigured component will run in the context of the client that called it, provided they share the same threading model.

COM+ Features

COM+ offers some new features to the component developer. These include eliminating some of the more awkward features of COM, and providing new ways for components to interact (including Loosely Coupled Events and Queued Components). In this section, I give you a brief tour of these new features.

No Longer Required

First the good news: Some of the annoying features about working with Microsoft Transaction Server have been resolved with COM+. You don't, for instance, need to use CreateInstance to ensure that a component is created in the same transaction as the calling program. CreateObject is just fine. The SafeRef method is no longer required, either. Instead you can just use the Me keyword to return a reference to the object that the code is running in.

Not Yet Available

Now the bad news: In Windows 2000, object pooling is implemented but requires that components implement the Neutral Apartment Model for threading—which Visual Basic does not support. Should Visual Basic 7 support the Neutral Apartment Model, you will be able to configure a component so that it can be shared among several clients. In the meantime, you can't create pooled objects with Visual Basic.

LOAD BALANCING

Since load balancing has been removed from the initial release of Windows 2000, discussing it seems something like a tease. However, the long-term implications of load balancing are sufficiently important to introduce them here.

One of the more convenient features of the COM model is its location transparency. Location transparency allows you to load a component without having to know where the component's files are located. When a client loads an object, the client asks for the object by providing the object's progid, either in the CreateObject function or in the New command. Given a progid, Windows looks it up in the Windows registry to see where to find the component. If you moved a component to a completely different computer, you might have to change some registry entries, but no changes would be required to either the client or the component.

The one exception to this location independence was the version of the CreateObject function in Visual Basic 6. With this version of CreateObject, you could override the registry entries for an application and force a request for an object to be routed to a particular computer. The code to request the object MyComponent.MyClass on the computer MyServer, using the Visual Basic 6 version of CreateObject, would look like this:

```
Dim obj As MyComponent.MyClass
Set obj = CreateObject("MyComponent.MyClass", "MyServer")
```

COM+'s load balancing extends location transparency by providing a Router object that can let you invoke on an object on any one of several different computers. The Router object has a ServerName method that returns the name of the computer that the request for the object should be sent to.

The computer must be part of a cluster, which is a group of computers that can treated as a single machine.

The Router object accesses the computer designated as the router for a cluster. This router computer selects the next computer in the cluster to receive the request and returns the computer's name to the Router object. The Router object, in turn, returns the computer's name through its ServerName method. The CreateObject then routes the request for the object to be created to that computer.

Using the Router object with the CreateObject function to dynamically select a server looks like this:

```
Dim obj As MyComponent.MyClass
Set obj = CreateObject("MyComponent.MyClass", _
                       Router.ServerName)
```

In theory, load balancing should improve the scalability of your application. In practice, much depends on how requests are distributed around the computers in the cluster. So, a lot depends on the algorithm that the router computer uses to determine which computer in the cluster gets the next request. That decision, in turn, depends on what information is available to the router.

Microsoft has promised that load balancing will eventually include the ability to replace Microsoft's default algorithm for selecting computers with your own routine.

In addition, if you expect your objects to share information, you will need to make sure that they are all created on the same computer. If you are creating your objects through a series of calls, you have three ways of ensuring that all of your objects are created on the same computer:

1. Hardcode the server name into your code.
2. Accept the computer name in the registry.
3. Retrieve the computer name from the Router object and use that in your requests.

The following code demonstrates the third technique. The code retrieves a computer name from the Router object and then uses it to dynamically create two objects on the same computer:

```
Dim obj As MyComponent.MyClass
Dim obj2 As MyComponent.MyClass
Dim strServer As String

StrServer = Router.ServerName
Set obj = CreateObject("MyComponent.MyClass", strServer)
Set obj2 = CreateObject("MyComponent.MyClass", strServer)
```

Queued Components

One of the tools available to Windows 95/98/NT developers is the Microsoft Message Queue (MSMQ). The MSMQ allows a program to post or read a message on a queue—a kind of e-mail for components. Effectively, the MSMQ allows programs to communicate asynchronously: A program can post a message for a component and then continue processing without having to wait for the other component to execute, confident that the message will be delivered (see Figure 16–2).

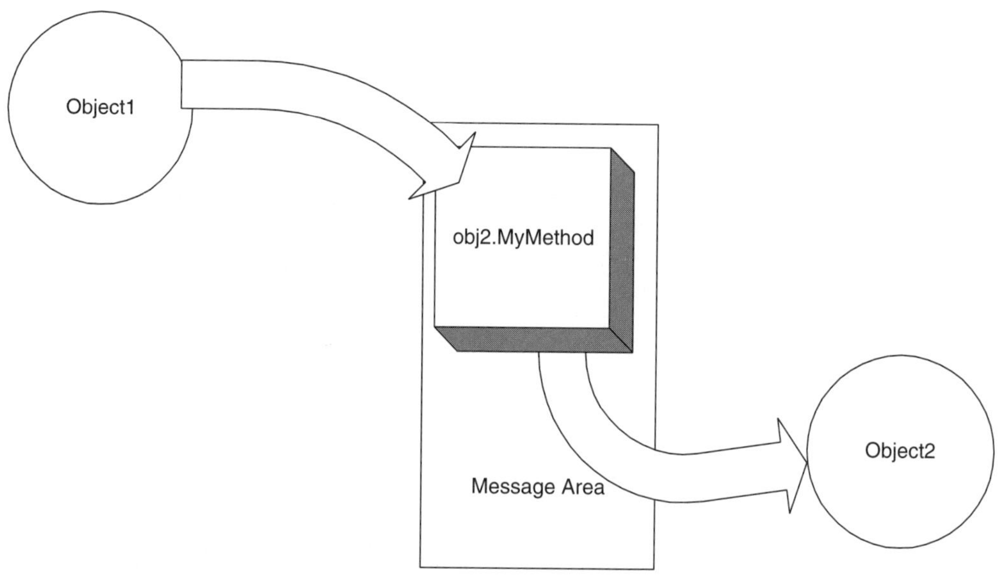

Figure 16–2 *The message queue architecture.*

Writing the code to post a message to MSMQ was straightforward, but creating a component to read messages was more complicated. To simplify the process of creating components that receive messages, COM+ has introduced Queued Components. Queued Components eliminate the need to write MSMQ dependent code in order to receive the message. Now, to create a component that will pick up messages, you need only configure it as a Queued Component using Component Services—no changes are required to the component's code.

CALLING A QUEUED COMPONENT

The queue options for a component appear on the Advanced tab of the Properties page for a component in Component Services. On this tab, you first check the option that indicates that the component can be reached through a queue. You then check the Listen option to have Windows 2000 create a queue for your component that will automatically deliver messages to your component.

To use Queued Components, MSMQ must be installed and users must be assigned MSMQ internal certificates that are used by MSMQ to authenticate messages.

There are some limitations around using Queued Components:

- The client program must still include MSMQ dependent code to create messages.
- The client can only pass data to the Queued Component. A Queued Component cannot return values, either through the parameters passed to it or through a method defined as a function. Properties may be set but not read.
- The client must use the Queued Component's default interface.

The request for the Queued Component's method is placed on the component's queue and waits there for the component to be activated and pick up its message. When the component does pick up the message (discussed in the next section), the component will execute its method or set its properties as if it had been called directly by the client.

COM+ will make three attempts to post the message after the client program writes it. If the message can't be posted, it isn't lost but is moved to a "dead letter" message queue. Using MSMQ administrative tools, you can browse that queue and delete or retransmit messages once you have determined what prevented the message from being posted.

For instance, a client that wanted to fire the method MyMethod on an object called MyComponent, passing two parameters, would use code like this:

```
Dim obj As Object
Set obj = GetObject("queue:/new:MyComponent.MyObject")
obj.MyMethod parameter1, parameter2
```

RECEIVING A MESSAGE

Once the message has been posted to the queue it will not be removed until the component that receives the message successfully processes it. If the component is normally running, it will pick up its messages as soon as it is free to do so.

If the component is loaded into memory, the message will be delivered almost immediately (i.e., the code for the requested method or property in the component will be run). If the component isn't running, then you'll need to provide some mechanism for creating the object so that it can process its messages. For instance, you can start a component by selecting it in the COM+ Applications folder in Component Services, right-mouse clicking on it, and selecting Start from the popup menu. This will cause the component to load and have all of its objects process any queued requests. You could also use a script running under the Windows Script Host (see the chapter on Script Components) or another Visual Basic program to create the receiving component. Your script or compiled program could be set to run from whatever scheduling package that you use.

Security for a Queued Component is handled through roles like any other Component Service or MTS object. However, you cannot assign a different identity to a Queued Component. With most COM+ objects, you can have it assume the security of some user in the server's security system for the period of time that it is executing. This lets the component's objects access resources that the user executing the program wouldn't be allowed to use. However, a Queued Component always reflects the security context of the user that created it.

Loosely Coupled Events

COM+ provides an additional way for objects to communicate with their clients by using COM+ Events. COM+ Events are said to be "loosely coupled" because the object firing the event and the client receiving the event don't have to be aware of each other or even running at the same time.

COM+ Events are implemented through Event objects. An Event object is any object that you establish a subscription for in the Component Services user interface. In your component, instead of using the RaiseEvent keyword to fire an event, you use the New keyword to create one of the Event objects that you've established. With the object created, you can then set the object's methods or properties and release it. The object, rather than being destroyed, is saved in the COM+ Event system. As soon as you release the object, any objects that subscribed to the event are notified and connected to the object that you created.

The same restrictions that applied to Queued Components also apply to Event objects.

Constructors

One of the deficiencies of Visual Basic object is the absence of constructors. Constructors are code called by the object as part of creating the object. The Initialize event fulfills some of the functions of a constructor, but the Initialize routine can't be passed any parameters. As a result, many of my objects have an ID property that must be set immediately after creating the object in order to tell the object what data it should use (i.e., by setting the ID property to a customer number in order to have the code work with the data for a particular customer). This ID property is, effectively, a kind of constructor called after the object is created. This raises the possibility that the object could be created with the New keyword but never have its ID property set—a situation guaranteed to generate errors.

COM+ provides the ability to define constructors for Visual Basic objects, but the parameter that's passed to the object is set in the Component Services user interface. As a result, the parameter is fixed for every invocation of the object. This severely limits the use of this feature, but does allow you to add your own "declarative programming" features to your object. Users of your component can control its behavior by setting the string to be passed to your object's constructor routine.

To add a constructor to your object, you must add the COM+ Services Type Library to your Visual Basic project's References list. You can then implement the IObjectConstruct interface in the Class modules that you want to accept constructor strings. The interface requires that you then implement its Construct method. This method is passed a single object (called pCtorObj) as a parameter when your object is created. The pCtorObj object has a ConstructString property that contains the string set in the Component Services User Interface.

A typical set of code to retrieve a constructor string would look like this:

```
Implement IObjectConstruct
Dim strConstruct As String

Private Sub IObjectConstruct_Construct( _
      ByVal pCtorObj As Object)
Dim obj As IObjectConstructString

     Set obj = pCtorObj
     strConstruct = obj.CounstructString
End Sub
```

If no constructor string is provided, no error is raised.

If your constructor string will contain more than one value, you should probably use the same format as ADO/ODBC connections strings. This format consists of the name of the value to be passed, an equals sign, the value being passed, and a semi-colon. This combination of name, =, value, ; can be repeated indefinitely:

```
value_name = value; value_name = value;….
```

For instance, to have your constructor accept two parameters, DSN and LogFileName, your user would enter this constructor string:

```
DSN=MyDSN;LogFileName=C:\MyFile.TXT
```

You can process the string using Visual Basic's Split function. Split accepts two parameters: a string to process and a delimiter. Split returns an array consisting of all of the strings between the delimiter. For instance, passed the string from my previous example and ";" as the delimiter, Split would return an array containing "DSN=MyDSN" in its first position and "LogFileName=C:\MyFIle.TXT" in its second position. To separate the value name from the value, you can use the Split function again with "=" as the delimiter.

Here's some code that could be used to process my sample constructor string containing the DSN and LogFileName values:

```
Dim ConstructStrings() As String
Dim ConstructItem() As String
Dim item As Variant

ConstructStrings = Split(strConstruct, ";")
For Each item In ConstructStrings
    ConstructItem = Split(item, "=")
    Select Case ConstructItem(0)
      Case "DSN"
        StrDSN = ConstructItem(1)
      Case "LogFileName"
        StrLog = ConstructItem(1)
    End Select
Next
```

The code first uses the Split function to create an array of all of the value_name/value pairs. With an array of all of the values loaded, the code runs through the array using Split to separate each pair into a new array. In the example just shown, the array ConstructItem will contain the name of the value in position 0 and the value of the parameter in position 1. Using this example, this means that, the first time through the For Each...Next loop, ConstructItem(0) would contain "DSN" and ConstructItem(1) would contain "MyDSN".

More Security Objects

COM+ provides you with more objects if you want to create custom security code to enhance or replace role-based security. In COM+ you have access to the SecurityCallContext object. Before using the SecurityCallContext object you must add the COM+ Services Type Library to your References list.

To get a reference to the SecurityCallContext object for the current call to your component, you must use the GetSecurityCallContext method. GetSercurityCallContext returns a reference to the current SercurityCallContext object (in the same way that GetContextObject returns a reference to the ObjectContext object). GetSecurityCallContext is used like this:

```
Dim sobj As SecurityCallContext
Set sobj = GetSecurityCallContext
```

The SecurityCallContext object effectively replaces the security-related properties that were part of ObjectContext object. From the SecurityCallContext object you can retrieve SecurityIdentity objects that represent the security of the client that called your object and the application that originally initiated the set of calls. SecurityIdentity objects give you access to the caller's Windows Security Identifier (SID), account name, and other related properties.

The SecurityCallContext is only valid for the current call to the object. You should always set the object to Nothing before your component finishes processing the current method call and reacquire the reference at the start of the next call.

Debugging COM+

COM+ makes debugging much easier in Visual Basic. You are able to debug several components in one session, with the debug control flowing from one component to another as each is called. The Initialize and Terminate event code, where debugging was awkward, are now treated like any other event. When a COM+ component fails, debugging for the component won't always be stopped and you will be able to reactivate the component to restart debugging by having it called from another client.

Deploying COM+ Applications

A new component of the Windows 2000 operating system is the Windows Installer. The Windows Installer is invoked by the operating system to control the process of installing new applications both during the initial install and in "install on demand" scenarios.

The Windows Installer also fundamentally changes the nature of the installation task. Instead of running a custom program that performs all the necessary updates, the Windows Installer uses what Microsoft calls a "data driven" approach. With this strategy, every registry entry is tied to some component. If that component is installed, the registry entries for it are made. If the component is removed, the registry entries for that component are also removed. The same approach is used for supporting files or any other resource required by the item being installed.

This new strategy allows for incremental installs and "install on demand." Previously, install packages were really little programs that had to be run from start to finish to accomplish their task. The Window Installer's data-driven approach allows individual components to be installed (or uninstalled) without rerunning the whole setup. Setup routines were like Wizards: You could run them but, if you were unhappy with the result, you couldn't rerun just part of the Wizard. The data-driven approach lets you pick a single component and install it along with the required registry keys, files, and components that it depends upon. In theory, if a component isn't functioning correctly because of missing support files, registry keys or other components, Windows can check the Windows Installer's repository for the damaged component and reinstall any missing parts.

Visual Studio Installer

The tool that creates Windows Installer setup packages is the Visual Studio Installer. It's available as a download from the Microsoft MSDN Website (*msdn.Microsoft.com*) or as part of the Windows 2000 Readiness kit. You can start using the Visual Studio Installer (see Figure 16–3) to deliver installation packages for Windows 95/98/NT and 2000 for all of the components types described in this book. While the user interface is certainly different, the end result from your point of view is the same: a setup disk (or, more likely, a CD-ROM).

Using Visual Studio Installer will require you to make sure that Windows Installer is present on your target computers. Windows Installer is installed as part of the Office 2000 package and with Windows 2000. For all other computers, you'll have to include Windows Installer as part of your installation. If you do include the Windows Installer in your setup, you cannot use 3.5-inch floppies as your installation medium.

The Visual Studio Installer offers you more options than the old Package and Deployment Wizard. These include:

- The ability to stipulate conditions under which your component will be installed (e.g., "requires Windows 2000")
- Creating new directories on the user's computer
- Installing several projects in one setup routine

On the other hand, Visual Studio does not automatically make the registry entries that DCOM needs, and requires you to use its Registry Editor to create your Registry entries by hand. For remote components, you're probably better off using Component Service's ability to create installation packages, though this still leaves you with the problem of installing any supporting files that your component requires.

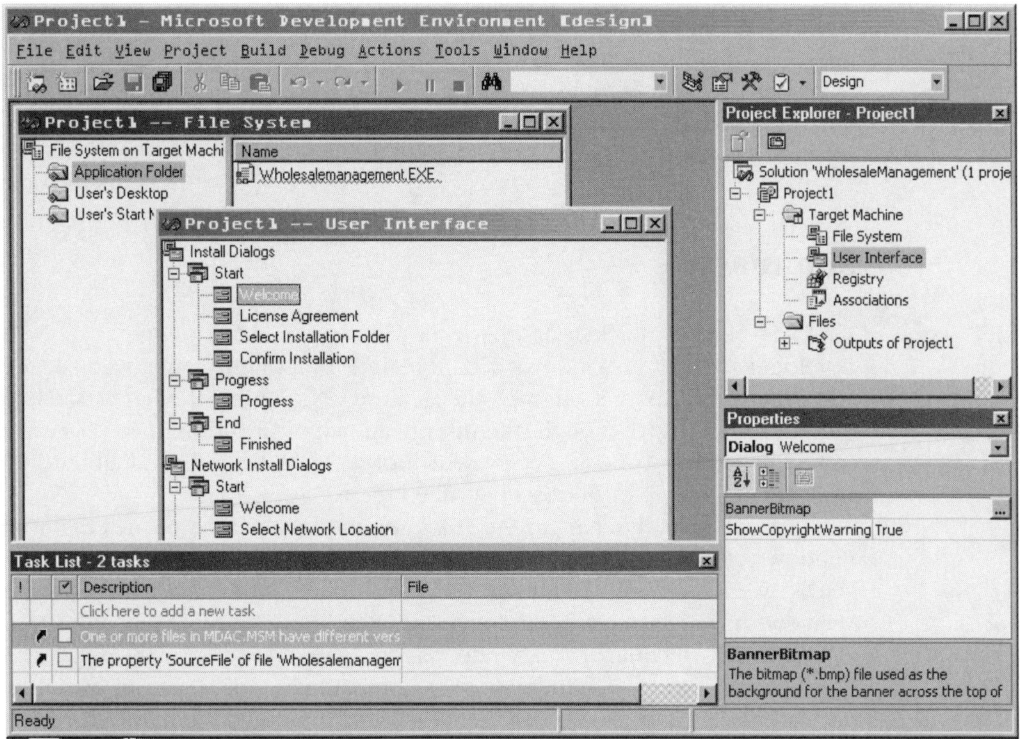

Figure 16–3 *The Visual Studio Installer.*

Unlike the Package and Deployment Wizard, Visual Studio Installer isn't an add-in. Instead, it's another development tool that works inside the Microsoft Development Environment (like Visual InterDev and Visual J++). Starting Visual Studio Installer starts the Microsoft Development Environment (MDE). When the MDE starts up you can choose to create a Visual Studio Installer project. From the initial Visual Studio Installer screen you pick a template as the basis for your new project. If you select the Visual Basic Installer template, you will be asked to select a Visual Basic project to create a Windows Installer package for Visual Basic projects. Once your Installer project is set up, you can define your installation using the project's properties or the ActiveX Designer-like tools that are included as part of the project.

Once you've finished modifying your Installer project, selecting Build from the Build menu will rebuild your application and generate the setup routine. You can debug your install by right-mouse clicking on the project name in the Microsoft Development Environment and selecting Launch Install.

Make sure that you check out the Readme file that comes with Windows Installer. This file lists known problems with the tool. Some problems you are unlikely to run into (you can't create a single installation package that will install more than 800 components), some are obvious (you can't create install packages with Visual Studio Installer unless you are a Visual Studio user), and some are more critical (Visual Studio Installer's Help files are not part of the MSDN help system for Visual Studio).

Summary

This has been a quick tour of the new features added to the component developer's toolkit in Windows 2000: queued components, enhanced security, and event subscriptions, among other features. Not much of what was already present has changed, though (the disappearance of CreateInstance is one welcome exception). You can decide which of these features are valuable to you and take advantage of them as you need them.

For this rapidly changing technology, the best source of material about Windows 2000 remains the Microsoft Developer Network CD-ROMs and the MSDN Website itself. To bring the information that you need together, Microsoft has released the Windows 2000 Readiness Kit which includes training materials, technical and white papers, the Windows 2000 application specifications, and the Windows 2000 Compatibility guide. It's an invaluable resource (the Visual Studio Installer comes with the Readiness Kit along with some other goodies, also). The kit can be ordered from your local Microsoft office for shipping and handling charges (more information, including contact information for Microsoft offices worldwide, is available on the MSDN Website at ***msdn.microsoft.com***)

And the best experience that you can get is to start creating components under Windows 2000.

PART FIVE

Appendices

In This Part

- **APPENDIX A**
  The Wholesale Management Database
- **APPENDIX B**
  Benchmark Code

The appendices cover two topics. Appendix A reviews the data design of the WholesaleManagement system that was used as the example in Part 2 of the book. This includes a brief discussion of the principles of database design that controlled the format of the tables in the system.

Appendix B discusses how the benchmarks that appeared in Part 2 were derived. The chapter begins with a general warning about the value of benchmarks. Samples of the code used to generate the data used in this book are included. The benchmarking code was generated by a Visual Basic add-in, which is also described in Appendix B (you can download the Add-in from my web site at www.phvis.com).

APPENDIX A

The Wholesale Management Database

The first seven chapters of this book develop an object model based on a fictitious company's data model as represented in the Wholesale-Management database. In this appendix, I describe the design decisions and some of the relational theory behind that data model in more detail than the quick references in the main chapters.

First, I should supply a quick description of the fictional business that required the WholesaleManagement database. The company is a wholesaler dealing in a variety of products. A wholesaler is a company that buys products from producers, warehouses them (for as little time as possible), and then sells them to retailers who, in turn, sell the products to consumers like you and me. The product's producers are referred to as vendors within the company and the retailers who buy the products are referred to as customers.

For a retailer, the benefit of using a wholesaler instead of buying directly from the producer is that the retailer can buy goods from a variety of producers at one place: the wholesaler. Not surprisingly then, a typical purchase from the wholesaler will consist of a number of goods (if the retailer was buying only one thing from the wholesaler, the retailer would probably deal directly with the product's producer).

In order to convince retailers that they should be buying their supplies from the company, a sales staff visits customers. These sales people help the retailer determine what products need to be reordered, try to convince the retailer to purchase additional products from the company, advise the retailer of any special pricing breaks or marketing support, work out delivery schedules, notify the customer of any problems with the customer's existing or projected orders, discuss pricing, and provide information on projected sales of the goods that the company carries.

To provide all of these services effectively, it's important that the sales representative be familiar with the retailer's business, the products that the retailer buys from the company, the plans that the retailer has, and the history that has developed between the retailer and the company. To support this, the company assigns customers to a single sales representative for any particular category of products. Each sales representative will be expected to be work with a particular group of customers and become familiar with the retailers' needs and wants for, at least, one category of products. For any particular category of products, a customer expects to deal with one sales representative from the company.

The company sells products in a wide variety of categories, so varied that a single sales representative can't be expected to be familiar with them all. To handle this, the company has divided its sales staff into groups based on the categories of products it sells. While this ensures that the representatives are knowledgeable about the products they sell, it also means that retailers that buy goods from several categories will get visited by several sales representatives. However, for any particular category, the customer is visited by only one sales representative.

When the retailer wants to buy goods from the company, the retailer will issue a sales order to the company, listing the products that they want to purchase and what price they expect to pay (based on the company's posted prices for its products). After the company delivers goods to the customer, the company will prepare an invoice to be sent to the retailer, asking for payment on goods sent to the retailer.

The Database

The WholesaleManagement database is a relational data model in third normal form. To use less jargon, that means that the data in the WholesaleManagement database is organized into a series of tables designed to reduce problems associated with updating and to make it easy to retrieve data. The result is a set of eight tables:

- The Customer table contains information about the company's customers. The information includes the customer's Id number, first and last name, and credit rating.
- The CustomerAddress table lists all the addresses associated with each customer, including the customer's billing address, delivery address, and so on.
- The OrderHeader table holds information for a particular order. This includes the Id of the customer who ordered the product, the date of the

order, the method of payment, and the address the order is to be delivered to. There are also several types of orders: standard, rush, and back orders (back orders are created when the products the customer ordered aren't in stock and the order has to be held until the product arrives).

- The OrderDetails table lists each product purchased on a sales order.
- The Invoices table contains information used in billing the customer for a purchase.
- The Products table lists the information about each product that the company sells. Product information includes the product Id, a description of the product, and its current price.
- The SalesRep table lists the various sales representatives who call on the company's customers. The rows in the SalesRep table contain the SalesRep Id, the representative's name, and what category of products the representative sells.
- The CustomerRep table contains a row for each customer served by a sales representative.

The need for some of the tables is obvious. The Customer, Invoices, SalesRep, and Product tables hold information about some of the principal entities in the company. However, it's worth looking at why the system also includes a CustomerAddress and CustomerRep table, and why information about an order is split between an OrderHeader and OrderDetails table.

Relational Tables

Each of the tables in the WholesaleManagement database contains information about an entity or information about a relationship between entities. For instance, the Customer table contains information about all of the Customers that the company does business with while the SalesRep table contains information about the company's sales staff. The CustomerRep table contains information about the relationship between customers and sales staff.

A table is organized into rows and columns. Each row in the table represents one instance of the entity or relationship described by the table. For instance, in the Customers table, each row in the table holds the information about one customer. In the SalesRep table, each row holds the information for one member of the sales staff. The CustomerRep table's rows hold the information about the relationship between one customer and one sales representative.

Each column in a table represents some information that the company wants to keep track of. For instance, the Customer table contains columns for First Name and Last Name. The CustomerRep table contains columns to hold the date of the last meeting between a sales representative and a customer.

Some tables represent both a relationship and an entity. The OrderDetail table's rows represent individual items purchased on a customer order. An order where the customer purchased three items from the company would have three rows in the OrderDetail table, one row for each item purchased as part of that order. The columns in the OrderDetail table hold information related to the OrderDetail: which sales order the detail belongs to, the name of the product that was ordered, and the quantity ordered by the customer. A typical OrderDetail row might say that this order detail is part of order 1572, that the product being ordered was Z98513, and that the customer ordered 5 units of the product.

While the OrderDetail is an entity in its own right, it also represents a relationship between orders and products. Each row in the OrderDetail table contains the information about a particular product purchased on a particular order. In this way, the OrderDetail table performs the same function as the CustomerRep table. In the same way that the CustomerRep table contains the information about the relationship between sales representatives and customers, the OrderDetail table contains information about the relationship between orders and products.

Some columns in the table are more important than others. Particularly important to the data design for each table is the table's primary key. Before a table can be considered to be "relational," it must have a primary key identified. The primary key for a table identifies one or more columns in the table that uniquely identify each row table. For instance, for the Customer table in the WholesaleManagement system, the Customer Id column uniquely identifies each row in the table: No two rows have the same value in the Id column. A primary key can consist of more than one column.

The term "relational" in "relational database management system" comes from the use of the primary key. In the branch of mathematics that is the basis for the relational database theory, a relation is a function that, given a number, returns a unique value. No two inputs to a relation will generate the same output. In the WholesaleManagement database, given a customer's Id, you will retrieve exactly one row from the Customer table and each Id will give you a different row.

The primary key for the OrderDetail table consists of two columns: the Order number that the detail belongs to and the Id of the product being bought. For any Order number, many rows in the OrderDetail table could be found because a typical Order consists of many products being bought. The same is true of the product Id: For any particular product Id, many OrderDetail rows could be retrieved because most products are purchased on a number of different orders (at least, the company hopes so). However, the combination of the Order number and product Id will retrieve exactly one row from the OrderDetail and will be the table's primary key.

The WholesaleManagement's database designers didn't have to produce the database design that I've described here, by the way. There are a number of different options that they could have taken. In the OrderDetail table, for instance, the primary key for the table could have been the Order number and the line number for each item on the Order instead of the Order number and product listed on that line. With the present design, it's impossible to purchase the same product twice on the same order. Attempting to do so would generate a duplicate primary key, which isn't allowed in a relational database.

Splitting Tables

As important as what appears in the tables is what doesn't appear in the tables. To begin with, no table has a column that contains multiple values. Each column in every table represents a single piece of information—no column holds a list or array or any other multiple value data type. Column data types are "scalar" data, data that can be represented with a single data value such as a name, quantity ordered, product weight, date of last meeting, and so on.

In addition, the tables contain no repeating columns. In the Customer table, for instance, you don't see BusinessAddress, HomeAddress, ContactAddress fields. Instead, this information is stored in a separate CustomerAddress table. This is an important part of the table design and ensures that the database's users can retrieve their data easily while keeping the costs of enhancing the database to a minimum.

Unfortunately, out in the real world it's not unusual to see tables that do have repeating columns. A typical example is a Customer table that includes a customer's sales over a period of time stored in a set of columns called JanSales, FebSales, MarchSales, and so on.

The problem with repeating data is that it makes it difficult, and occasionally impossible, to report on the data in the table. Using the table with repeated sales data as an example, trying to find the month with the largest sales is a trial. Someone would have to write a set of code that compared January's sales to February's and stored the name of the month that had the largest sales, then compared the sales for the winning month to the sales for March, storing the name of that winner, and then comparing the results to April, and so on for the rest of the twelve months.

In addition, table designs that use repeating columns are essentially inflexible. If the company decided to keep sales information for a two-year period, the table would have to be completely redesigned. Not only would another twelve columns have to be added to hold the additional data, the existing columns would have to be renamed to distinguish JanFirstYearSales from JanSecondYearSales.

Table designs with repeating columns are also prone to errors. If it's July and I look at a customer row with sales data in columns named JanSales, FebSales, through to DecSales, what am I to make of the sales data for August through to December? Since it's only July, data in the columns for the later months can't represent actual sales. Do those numbers represent the sales for the previous year still left in those columns? Or, are they forecasts for the expected sales for those months? (In that case the columns represent very different data from the January to June sales.) Should the company be running a program at the start of the year that sets all of those columns to zero until the data comes in? The scheduling of that initialization program would have to be carefully managed because the company wouldn't want to eliminate the year's sales data until all the sales reporting is complete.

The problems with maintaining a design with two years' worth of data are worse. Presumably, at year end the data from the year 1 columns must be copied to the year 2 columns before the year 1 columns are initialized to zero.

Repeating columns are also inefficient when it comes to storing data in the least amount of space. A new customer, for instance, will have no sales information. However, a table design with repeating columns requires that space be set aside to hold twelve months' worth of data anyway.

The relational database theory offers a solution to the problem of repeating columns. The alternative to repeating columns is to move the offending field to a table of its own. In this case, this would involve creating a CustomerSales table. This new table consists of three items: the repeating column from the original table, the primary key from the original table, and an identifier for the row. Rather than having twelve columns of sales data, the new table has one column to hold the data for one month for one customer.

The new table includes the primary key from the original table so that the information in the new table can be tied back to the original data. In the new design, it's still important the sales information for a customer be tied back to the rest of the customer's data. So, the new CustomerSales table will need to include the customer Id (the primary key from the Customer table) so that the customer that the sales information belongs to can be identified.

This process of refining the design of a table is called "normalizing" the design. The term is drawn from politics (as when two countries speak of "normalizing" their relationship). A table with no repeating columns is said to be in first normal form, for instance. Typically, business systems are taken to what's called third normal form, though higher normal forms exist (and so do different normalization processes than the one that I describe here).

Like any relational table, this new table must have a primary key. Since any customer will have multiple sales rows, the customer Id can't be used as the primary key—at least not by itself. Every sales row for a customer will have the same customer Id, so those fields do not uniquely define a customer row. A third column is added to the new table to become part of the primary key and distinguish among the various rows for the same customer. Typically, this identifier is related to whatever distinguished the repeating columns in the original table.

Since the various sales columns in the original design were distinguished by date (January sales vs. February sales vs. March sales, etc.), each row in the CustomerSales table should be distinguished by date. The column added to the CustomerSales table is a date field that gives the year and month that the sales information applies to. The final design for the CustomerSales table consists of three columns: the two primary key columns (Customer Id column and SalesDate) and the SalesAmount column.

This new design would solve all of the problems with the old table design with its repeating columns. To store more sales history data for a customer, rows for the additional dates can be added to the table. New customers can have rows added as they generate sales, and there's no need to delete last year's data to make room for this year's. A single SQL statement would find the month with the best sales—It's the first row returned by this query:

```
Select Date, Sum(Sales)
From CustomerSales
Group By Date
Order By Sum(Sales)
```

Returning to the WarehouseManagement database, the designers recognized that placing customer address fields (billing address, delivery address, and so on) in the Customers table would form a set of repeated columns. Instead, the database designers placed the address information in a CustomerAddress table. The primary key for the CustomerAddress table consists of the Customer Id column (so that addresses can be tied back to the customer that they belong to) and an identifier column that indicates what kind of address that is stored in the row: home address, billing address, and so on.

The OrderHeader table could also have contained a set of repeated columns, one set for each item ordered. Had the designers used that format, someone would have had to determine the maximum number of items that would ever be bought on a single order, and set aside that many columns. All the problems that I listed for the CustomerSales columns would have afflicted this design also. Instead, the designers placed the columns required for each product ordered in the OrderDetails table. The primary key for this table is the OrderNumber (the key from the OrderHeader table) and the product number.

In making these decisions, one of the questions that a database designer faces is recognizing repeating columns. For instance, do the FirstName, LastName columns in the Customer table constitute a repeating field? Most people would say no, but you need to understand the basis for that decision. Much of the time, the decision depends on understanding how the business views the data.

To begin with, a customer's first name and last name are really very different. For instance, you typically refer to strangers using their last name and to friends using their first name. As a result, you could say that the FirstName and LastName columns aren't repeating because they are different kinds of data.

Another way of recognizing whether a set of columns is repeating or not is to ask if there is a limit to the number of columns. For the CustomerSales data, as an example, company management could have asked for all sale information to be kept forever, generating an infinite number of sales columns (assuming that the company never goes out of business). For the OrderDetails table, there is also no limit on the number of items purchased on a single order (except for the size of the customer's wallet). And, since a customer can have multiple fax numbers, Websites, e-mail addresses, and second homes, there's no end to the number of addresses that a customer could have. For these reasons, the CustomerAddress and OrderDetails tables are part of the WholesaleManagement database design. there is, however, an expectation that a customer will have a limited number of names.

By the way, it's not impossible that the customer's name could be a repeating field and require a table of its own—it all depends on the nature of the business. A database system that was built kept track of a police department's customers, the people that the officers arrested. For that database, the customers could very easily (and frequently did) have a large number of names.

Relationships

Tables in a relational database have relationships with each other. The examples that I've discussed so far have already demonstrated one kind of relationship that two tables can have with each other. The Customer table, for instance, has a "one-to-many" relationship with the CustomerAddress. That is to say, each Customer row can have many CustomerAddress rows related to it.

Relationships between tables are established by repeating the primary key from one table in another table. The CustomerAddress table's primary key is made up, in part, of the primary key from the Customer table. While there is only one Customer row with any particular customer number, there can be many CustomerAddress records with the same Customer number.

From the other side of the relationship, however, a CustomerAddress can belong to only one customer. There's a practical business reason for this: When an order is shipped, it is going to one customer at one address and the database design reflects this. The CustomerAddress row holds the primary key for the Customer row that the address belongs to. Since a primary key identifies exactly one record in the Customer table, each CustomerAddress row refers back to exactly one Customer row.

The relationship between the OrderHeader and OrderDetails tables is also a one-to-many relationship (each OrderHeader can have many OrderDetails but each OrderDetail has only one OrderHeader row). The same is true of the relationship between the Product and OrderDetail tables, and the Customer and Invoices tables.

The tables in the WholesaleManagement database also include "many-to-many" relationships. Because of the way that the company is organized, one customer can be serviced by several sales representatives. The company has many divisions and the sales staff is organized by division. If a customer buys products from different divisions within the company, then that customer will be visited by sales representatives from each of those divisions. And, of course, each sales representative has many customers that they do business with. Since a customer can have many sales representatives and a sales representative can have many customers, the two tables are said to be in a "many-to-many" relationship.

Carrying the primary key over to another table can only create a one-to-many relationship, so a different technique is required to handle many-to-many relationships. This is the reason that the CustomerRep table exists—to hold the relationship between the Customers and SalesReps tables.

The primary key of the CustomerRep table consists of the SalesRep name (the primary key for the SalesRep table) and the Customer Id (the primary key for the Customers table). By placing the Customer Id in the CustomerRep table, the CustomerRep table has a one-to-many relationship with the Customer table: For each row in the Customer table, there can be many rows in the CustomerRep table. Similarly, by placing the SalesRep Id in the CustomerRep table, the CustomerRep table has a one-to-many relationship with the SalesRep table: For each row in the SalesRep table, there can be many rows in the CustomerRep table.

Putting those two relationships together, one-to-many from SalesRep to CustomerRep and one-to-many from Customer to SalesRep, gives a many-to-many relationship between the SalesRep and Customer tables. Each SalesRep row can have many rows in the CustomerRep table—one for each customer that the sales representative works with. Each Customer row can have many rows in the CustomerRep table—one for each sales representative that the customer works with.

The CustomerRep table may seem like an artificial construct to represent a very common relationship in the real world. However, it turns out that there is some information that can only be stored in the CustomerRep table. This is information about the relationship between the customer and the sales representative.

For instance, the company wants to store the date of the last visit by the sales representative to the customer. This information can't be stored in the Customer table because the customer is visited by many sales representatives. While the customer table could store the date of the last visit by any sales representative, without adding repeating columns it's not possible to record the date of the last visit for all the sales staff that work with the customer. The reverse is also true. In the SalesRep table, the company could store the last visit by the staff member to any customer. But, without adding repeating columns, it's not possible to record the date of the last visit for each customer that a sales representative visits in a single SalesRep row.

However, the CustomerRep table contains a single record for every Customer-SalesRep combination. Recording the last visit for a particular sales representative to a particular customer just means adding a "LastVisit" column to the CustomerRep table.

The OrderDetails table also acts as the representation of a many-to-many relationship. Each OrderDetail record contains the number for an Order, putting the OrderDetail on the many side of a one-to-many relationship with the OrderHeader table. The OrderDetail table also contains the Id for the product that was being purchased. As a result, the OrderDetail table is also on the many side of a one-to-many relationship with the product table. The OrderDetail table represents, then, the many-to-many relationship that exists between the OrderHeader table and the Product table: One order can be for many products and one product can appear on many orders. What's contained in the OrderDetail table is the information about the relationship between the order and the product: How many units of the product were purchased on this order.

Summary

In this appendix, I've provided some more detail on the case that I use for my examples in Chapters 1 through 7. I gave you an overview of the company's business and briefly described the tables that I refer to in the chapters.

I also described some of the design decisions that led to this table layout, along with the parts of the relational theory that were relevant to that discussion. The identification of a primary key for a table, for instance, converted the table from being a collection of rows into a relational table. Identifying and removing repeating columns began the process of making the table well-designed by normalizing it.

I then described how tables use primary keys to express the relationships that exist between the tables. You saw that the database design included several one-to-many relationships. These relationships were implemented by repeating the primary key for a table in the design of the related table. I also showed you how many-to-many relationships were expressed, using a table that included primary keys from the two tables involved in the relationship.

If you find the process of designing an effective database interesting there are a number of books out there that can help you understand the process. Prentice Hall publishes *Database Management and Design* by Gary W. Hansen and James V. Hansen. Another good book is *Database Design for Mere Mortals* by Michael J. Hernandex (Addison-Wesley). I edit the Smart Access newsletter and, while it is aimed at developers using Microsoft Access, the newsletter frequently includes articles on database design and effective use of SQL (you can check us out at *www.pinpub.com*).

Database design is a subject near and dear to my heart. It is also the basis for creating business systems that are reliable, maintain the integrity of their data, and give you the fastest possible performance. The time you spend in this area (and learning how to use SQL, the language of relational databases) will pay off in faster development, lower costs, and great performance.

APPENDIX B

Benchmark Code

You should always be suspicious of benchmarks. That may seem like an odd way to open a section that presents benchmark code, but it's a warning that you should always bear in mind. At the most basic level, the computer that the benchmarks were run on will have a dramatic impact on run times. Since you don't have access to that computer and won't be running your production code on it, the relevance of the benchmarks to you is immediately suspect. Nonetheless, benchmarks can provide you with useful information on the costs of making specific design decisions where performance is your primary criteria.

You should, for instance, be able to use the relative differences between different code sets in the benchmark (i.e. if one set of code takes longer to run than another set of code, it should do so on all computers). However, you can't count on either the absolute difference (one set of code takes five seconds longer) or the proportional difference (one set of code took twice as long) remaining constant from one computer to another.

When looking at benchmarks you should also realize that the assumptions of the programmer who created the benchmarking code can affect the results. Those assumptions are especially dangerous if they are unspoken. You may not be aware that the programmer is testing the code with all Visual Basic optimizations turned off, for instance, while you run with them all turned on.

One last warning: By definition, benchmark code is not production code. No production program every looked like benchmark code and so it's questionable how valid the results are when applied to "real" programs. The results of running my benchmark code that passes 100 parameters to a routine are suspect because:

1. The program contains code for measuring time to complete that a production program typically does not include
2. The program also contains calls to routines with 99 parameters, 98 parameters, and so on, which a production program wouldn't have.
3. The code is executed many more times in one run than it would be in a production environment.

To address these concerns, in this appendix I've included sample code from the programs that generated the benchmarks so that you can copy and generate the sections that are interesting to you. I haven't included all of the code (much of it is very repetitious) but I have tried to put enough in for you to see how I got my results. You can also check my code for errors if you feel the results are suspect. I'm sure that many readers will point out methodological flaws in the code, which will allow me to further refine these tests.

The Benchmark Add-In

The actual benchmark code is produced by a Visual Basic COM Add-In. I've also included some of the code for that Add-in that Add-in in this appendix. You can download the Add-in from my website at ***www.phvis.com*** and use it to regenerate the benchmark code. This will let you test my assumptions and see what results you get on your computer.

To use the Add-in you must first register it either by compiling it in Visual Basic or by downloading the Add-in's setup program from my website. Once the Add-in is registered, you will find it listed in Visual Basic's Add-ins Manager as VBOCHBenchmarks. After loading the Add-in from Visual Basic's Add-in Manager, the form shown in Figure B–1 will appear.

You must then create a Standard EXE Visual Basic project. With that project loaded, you should then display the Add-in. If the Add-in isn't visible you can display it by selecting the VBOCH Benchmarks item that will have been added to your Add-ins menu. You can then select the test that you want to run, enter an iterations and range number, and click on the Load Code command button. The Add-in will then delete any Forms from your project (that way the project will default to running a Sub Main routine on startup) add a standard module to your project, and fill that project with the benchmark code.

The Iterations and Range text boxes on the add-in control how much benchmark code is generated and how many times the test will be run. The Range entry controls how extensive the test is and how the code varies throughout the test. For instance, for the test that measures the effect of adding many parameters to a routine, the Range text box entry controls how many

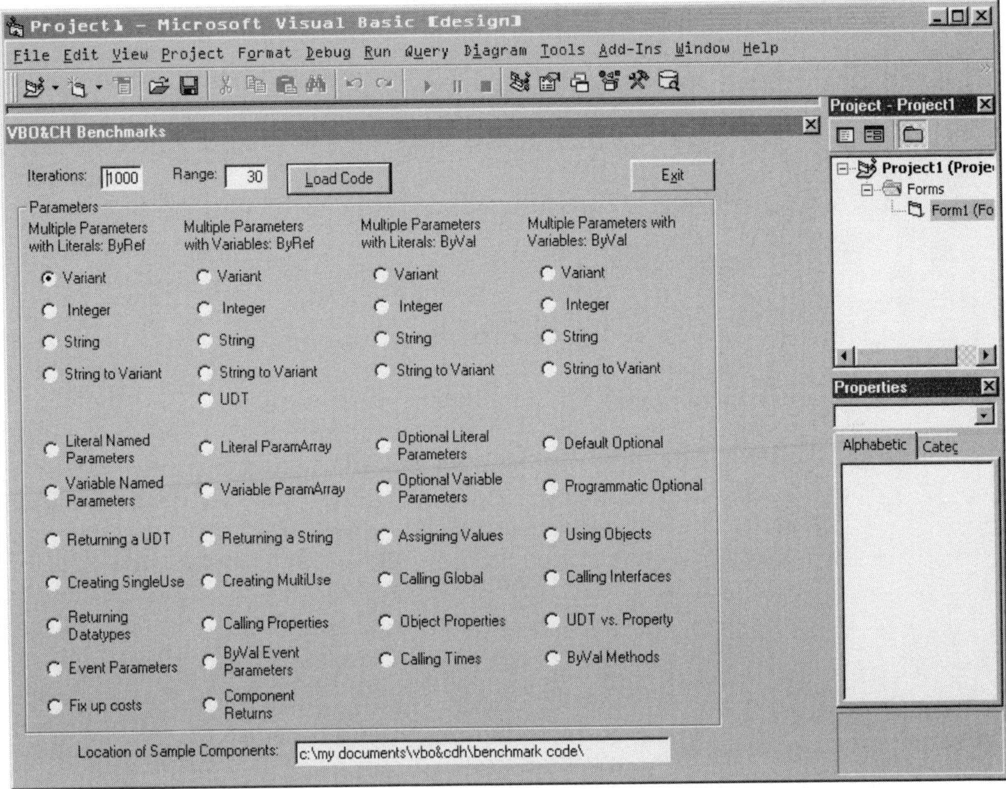

Figure B–1 *The Benchmark code Add-in.*

parameters are generated. Setting Range to 30 generates code to call routines with parameter counts varying from 1 to 30. For many tests, Range has no effect whatever and will be set by the Add-in when you generate the test code.

The Iterations entry controls how many times the code is run. Typically, for instance, I ran each test 1000 times to ensure that I got a measurable amount (e.g. over one millisecond of run time).

One effect that Range does have is to indirectly control the length of the lines in the sample code. Setting Range to 30 for the parameter test, as an example, will generate at least one line of code long enough to list 30 parameters. Since the Add-in makes no attempt to break up long lines, you may generate a line that exceeds Visual Basic's maximum for a single line if you set Range high enough.

Once you have generated the module by clicking on the Load Code button, you can run the code by either clicking on Visual Basic's Run button or pressing the F5 key. The test code will then execute all the tests for the specified number of iterations. As the code runs, the timings for each test are placed in an array call varArray. After the test finishes executing, the contents of varArray are printed to the Immediate Window, where you can view them. The code can be viewed, printed, or saved like any other Visual Basic program.

Every set of test code is unique but all tests include two routines: Main and RunTest. Main is present to be called automatically when you run the generated code in the Visual Basic IDE. The Main routine then calls the Run-Test routine (which controls execution of the test routines) and prints out the results of the second execution of RunTest from the varArray array. The Main routine is the same for every test and I've included it below in the sample code. The RunTest routine varies from test to test and I've included sections of each version, along with representative samples of the test code that goes with it, for each test. I have not included every version of the tests (for instance, the parameter tests included versions for integers, strings, and variants—I have included only the integer versions).

To work with the tests, I have also included some simple components. The code for these components can be downloaded from my website. Not included in this sample code is a form (frmWait) that displays a message asking the user to wait while the test code is generated. You can either create your own form, comment out the two references to the form in my code, or download the form from my website. The components will be automatically added to the test application's References list as part of generating the code. However, in order for this to work, you'll have to tell the Add-in where to find my sample components. You can specify the full path names to the compiled versions of the components in the text box at the bottom of the Add-in labeled "Location of Sample Components."

Sample Code

Main Routine

```
Option Explicit

Declare Function timeGetTime Lib "winmm.dll" () As Long
Dim varArray(100, 2) As Variant
Sub Main()
Dim ing As Integer

RunTest
RunTest
For ing = 0 To 60
    Debug.Print varArray(ing, 1) & ": " & varArray(ing, 2)
Next
End Sub
```

Multiple Parameters

```
Sub RunTest()
Dim ing As Integer
Dim lngStartTime As Long
Dim lngRunTime As Long


varArray(0, 1) = "Parameters"
varArray(0, 2) = "Milliseconds"
lngStartTime = timeGetTime
For ing = 1 To 1000
    Test1 1
Next
lngRunTime = timeGetTime - lngStartTime
varArray(1, 1) = 1
varArray(1, 2) = lngRunTime


lngStartTime = timeGetTime
For ing = 1 To 1000
    Test2 1, 2
Next
lngRunTime = timeGetTime - lngStartTime
varArray(2, 1) = 2
varArray(2, 2) = lngRunTime


lngStartTime = timeGetTime
For ing = 1 To 1000
    Test3 1, 2, 3
Next
lngRunTime = timeGetTime - lngStartTime
varArray(3, 1) = 3
varArray(3, 2) = lngRunTime

End Sub
Public Sub Test1(p1)
End Sub
Public Sub Test2(p1, p2)
End Sub
Public Sub Test3(p1, p2, p3)
End Sub
```

Optional Parameters

```
Sub RunTest()
Dim ing As Integer
Dim lngStartTime As Long
Dim lngRunTime As Long


varArray(0, 1) = "Optional Parameters"
varArray(0, 2) = "Milliseconds"
lngStartTime = timeGetTime
For ing = 1 To 1000
    Test1 "1"
Next
lngRunTime = timeGetTime - lngStartTime
varArray(1, 1) = 1
varArray(1, 2) = lngRunTime

lngStartTime = timeGetTime
For ing = 1 To 1000
    Test2 "1", "2"
Next
lngRunTime = timeGetTime - lngStartTime
varArray(2, 1) = 2
varArray(2, 2) = lngRunTime

lngStartTime = timeGetTime
For ing = 1 To 1000
    Test3 "1", "2", "3"
Next
lngRunTime = timeGetTime - lngStartTime
varArray(3, 1) = 3
varArray(3, 2) = lngRunTime
End Sub
Public Sub Test1(Optional p1 As String)
End Sub
Public Sub Test2(Optional p1 As String, Optional p2 As String)
End Sub
Public Sub Test3(Optional p1 As String, Optional p2 As
String, Optional p3 As String)
End Sub
```

Default Parameters

```
Sub RunTest()
Dim ing As Integer
Dim lngStartTime As Long
Dim lngRunTime As Long


varArray(0, 1) = "Default Parameters"
varArray(0, 2) = "Milliseconds"
lngStartTime = timeGetTime
For ing = 1 To 1000
    Test1
Next
lngRunTime = timeGetTime - lngStartTime
varArray(1, 1) = 1
varArray(1, 2) = lngRunTime

lngStartTime = timeGetTime
For ing = 1 To 1000
    Test2
Next
lngRunTime = timeGetTime - lngStartTime
varArray(2, 1) = 2
varArray(2, 2) = lngRunTime

lngStartTime = timeGetTime
For ing = 1 To 1000
    Test3
Next
lngRunTime = timeGetTime - lngStartTime
varArray(3, 1) = 3
varArray(3, 2) = lngRunTime
End Sub
Public Sub Test1(Optional p1 As String = "X")
End Sub
Public Sub Test2(Optional p1 As String = "X", _
Optional p2 As String = "X")
End Sub
Public Sub Test3(Optional p1 As String = "X", _
Optional p2 As String = "X", _
Optional p3 As String = "X")
End Sub
```

ByVal Parameters

```
Sub RunTest()
Dim ing As Integer
Dim lngStartTime As Long
Dim lngRunTime As Long


varArray(0, 1) = "ByVal Parameters"
varArray(0, 2) = "Milliseconds"
Dim v1 As Integer
Dim v2 As Integer
Dim v3 As Integer
lngStartTime = timeGetTime
For ing = 1 To 1000
    Test1 v1
Next
lngRunTime = timeGetTime - lngStartTime
varArray(1, 1) = 1
varArray(1, 2) = lngRunTime

lngStartTime = timeGetTime
For ing = 1 To 1000
    Test2 v1, v2
Next
lngRunTime = timeGetTime - lngStartTime
varArray(2, 1) = 2
varArray(2, 2) = lngRunTime

lngStartTime = timeGetTime
For ing = 1 To 1000
    Test3 v1, v2, v3
Next
lngRunTime = timeGetTime - lngStartTime
varArray(3, 1) = 3
varArray(3, 2) = lngRunTime
End Sub
Public Sub Test1x(ByVal p1 As Integer)
End Sub
Public Sub Test2(ByVal p1 As Integer, ByVal p2 As Integer)
End Sub
Public Sub Test3(ByVal p1 As Integer, ByVal p2 As Integer, _
ByVal p3 As Integer)
End Sub
```

User Defined Types as Parameters

```
Type T1
E1 As String
End Type

Type T2
E1 As String
E2 As String
End Type

Type T3
E1 As String
E2 As String
E3 As String
End Type
Sub RunTest()
Dim ing As Integer
Dim lngStartTime As Long
Dim lngRunTime As Long


varArray(0, 1) = "UDT Parameters"
varArray(0, 2) = "Milliseconds"
Dim v1 As T1
v1.E1 = "X"
Dim v2 As T2
v1.E1 = "X"
v2.E2 = "X"
Dim v3 As T3
v1.E1 = "X"
v2.E2 = "X"
v3.E3 = "X"
lngStartTime = timeGetTime
For ing = 1 To 1000
    Test1 v1
Next
lngRunTime = timeGetTime - lngStartTime
varArray(1, 1) = 1
varArray(1, 2) = lngRunTime

lngStartTime = timeGetTime
For ing = 1 To 1000
    Test2 v2
Next
lngRunTime = timeGetTime - lngStartTime
varArray(2, 1) = 2
varArray(2, 2) = lngRunTime

lngStartTime = timeGetTime
```

```
For ing = 1 To 1000
    Test3 v3
Next
lngRunTime = timeGetTime - lngStartTime
varArray(3, 1) = 3
varArray(3, 2) = lngRunTime
End Sub
Public Sub Test1(p1 As T1)
End Sub
Public Sub Test2(p2 As T2)
End Sub
Public Sub Test3(p3 As T3)
End Sub
```

User Defined Types as Return Values

In this test, you will notice that the various subroutines that are called from RunTest. Each subroutine has sets the value of one more element than the previous routine. While this ensures that the test doesn't test just the cost of returning a multiple element UDT, it seems to me that the results are more useful. My attitude was that, if you are expecting a multiple element UDT from the function, that you are expecting that function to set all of those elements (or you would have used a UDT with fewer elements) and so setting those elements is a real cost of using more elements.

```
Type T1
E1 As String
End Type

Type T2
E1 As String
E2 As String
End Type

Type T3
E1 As String
E2 As String
E3 As String
End Type
Sub RunTest()
Dim ing As Integer
Dim lngStartTime As Long
Dim lngRunTime As Long


varArray(0, 1) = "UDT Return Value"
varArray(0, 2) = "Milliseconds"
Dim v1 As T1
Dim v2 As T2
Dim v3 As T3
```

```
lngStartTime = timeGetTime
For ing = 1 To 1000
    v1 = Test1()
Next
lngRunTime = timeGetTime - lngStartTime
varArray(1, 1) = 1
varArray(1, 2) = lngRunTime

lngStartTime = timeGetTime
For ing = 1 To 1000
    v2 = Test2()
Next
lngRunTime = timeGetTime - lngStartTime
varArray(2, 1) = 2
varArray(2, 2) = lngRunTime

lngStartTime = timeGetTime
For ing = 1 To 1000
    v3 = Test3()
Next
lngRunTime = timeGetTime - lngStartTime
varArray(3, 1) = 3
varArray(3, 2) = lngRunTime
End Sub

Public Function Test1() As T1
Dim v1 As T1
v1.E1 = "X"
Test1 = v1
End Function
Public Function Test2() As T2
Dim v2 As T2
v2.E1 = "X"
v2.E2 = "X"
Test2 = v2
End Function
Public Function Test3() As T3
Dim v3 As T3
v3.E1 = "X"
v3.E2 = "X"
v3.E3 = "X"
Test3 = v3
End Function
```

Using Enums, Constants, and Variables

```
Sub RunTest()
varStr = "X"
varInt = 1
TestEnum
TestLitStr
TestLitInt
TestVarStr
TestVarInt
TestConStr
TestConInt

End Sub
Sub TestEnum()
Dim v As enm
v = enmValue
End Sub
Sub TestLitStr()
Dim v As String
v = "X"
End Sub
Sub TestLitInt()
Dim v As Integer
v = 1
End Sub
Sub TestVarStr()
Dim v As String
v = varStr
End Sub
Sub TestVarInt()
Dim v As Integer
v = varInt
End Sub
Sub TestConStr()
Dim v As String
v = conStr
End Sub
Sub TestConInt()
Dim v As Integer
v = conInt
End Sub
```

Assigning Variables, Constants, and Enums

```
Sub RunTest()
Dim ing As Integer
Dim lngStartTime As Long
Dim lngRunTime As Long


varArray(0, 1) = "Assigning Values"
varArray(0, 2) = "Milliseconds"
lngStartTime = timeGetTime
For ing = 1 To 1000
Test1
Next
lngRunTime = timeGetTime - lngStartTime
varArray(1, 1) = "Enum"
varArray(1, 2) = lngRunTime

lngStartTime = timeGetTime
For ing = 1 To 1000
Test2
Next
lngRunTime = timeGetTime - lngStartTime
varArray(2, 1) = "Literal String"
varArray(2, 2) = lngRunTime

lngStartTime = timeGetTime
For ing = 1 To 1000
Test3
Next
lngRunTime = timeGetTime - lngStartTime
varArray(3, 1) = "Literal Integer"
varArray(3, 2) = lngRunTime

lngStartTime = timeGetTime
For ing = 1 To 1000
Test4
Next
lngRunTime = timeGetTime - lngStartTime
varArray(4, 1) = "Variable String"
varArray(4, 2) = lngRunTime

lngStartTime = timeGetTime
For ing = 1 To 1000
Test5
Next
lngRunTime = timeGetTime - lngStartTime
varArray(5, 1) = "Variable Integer"
varArray(5, 2) = lngRunTime
```

```
lngStartTime = timeGetTime
For ing = 1 To 1000
Test6
Next
lngRunTime = timeGetTime - lngStartTime
varArray(6, 1) = "Constant String"
varArray(6, 2) = lngRunTime

lngStartTime = timeGetTime
For ing = 1 To 1000
Test7
Next
lngRunTime = timeGetTime - lngStartTime
varArray(7, 1) = "Constant Integer"
varArray(7, 2) = lngRunTime

End Sub
Sub Test1()
Dim v As enm
v = enmValue
End Sub
Sub Test2()
Dim v As String
v = "X"
End Sub
Sub Test3()
Dim v As Integer
v = 1
End Sub
Sub Test4()
Dim v As String
v = varStr
End Sub
Sub Test5()
Dim v As Integer
v = varInt
End Sub
Sub Test6()
Dim v As String
v = conStr
End Sub
Sub Test7()
Dim v As Integer
v = conInt
End Sub
```

Using Objects as Parameters

```
Sub RunTest()
Dim ing As Integer
Dim lngStartTime As Long
Dim lngRunTime As Long


varArray(0, 1) = "Objects as Parameters"
varArray(0, 2) = "Milliseconds"
Dim objExe As VBOCHEXE.TestObject
Dim objDLL As VBOCHDLL.TestObject
Set objExe = New VBOCHEXE.TestObject
Set objDLL = New VBOCHDLL.TestObject
lngStartTime = timeGetTime
For ing = 1 To 1000
Test1 objDLL
Next
lngRunTime = timeGetTime - lngStartTime
varArray(1, 1) = "ByRef DLL"
varArray(1, 2) = lngRunTime

lngStartTime = timeGetTime
For ing = 1 To 1000
Test2 objExe
Next
lngRunTime = timeGetTime - lngStartTime
varArray(2, 1) = "ByRef EXE"
varArray(2, 2) = lngRunTime

lngStartTime = timeGetTime
For ing = 1 To 1000
Test3 objDLL
Next
lngRunTime = timeGetTime - lngStartTime
varArray(3, 1) = "ByVal DLL"
varArray(3, 2) = lngRunTime

lngStartTime = timeGetTime
For ing = 1 To 1000
Test4 objExe
Next
lngRunTime = timeGetTime - lngStartTime
varArray(4, 1) = "ByVal EXE"
varArray(4, 2) = lngRunTime

End Sub
Sub Test1(ByRef InValue As VBOCHDLL.TestObject)
End Sub
Sub Test2(ByRef InValue As VBOCHEXE.TestObject)
End Sub
Sub Test3(ByVal InValue As VBOCHDLL.TestObject)
End Sub
Sub Test4(ByVal InValue As VBOCHEXE.TestObject)
End Sub
```

Returning Different DataTypes From Functions

```
Sub RunTest()
Dim ing As Integer
Dim lngStartTime As Long
Dim lngRunTime As Long


varArray(0, 1) = "Returning Datatypes"
varArray(0, 2) = "Milliseconds"
Dim stz As String
Dim inr As Integer
Dim byt As Byte
Dim dat As Date
Dim bol As Boolean
Dim cur As Currency
Dim dbl As Double
Dim sng As Single
Dim vrt As Variant
Dim lng As Long

lngStartTime = timeGetTime
For ing = 1 To 10000
stz = Test1
Next
lngRunTime = timeGetTime - lngStartTime
varArray(1, 1) = "Returning String"
varArray(1, 2) = lngRunTime

lngStartTime = timeGetTime
For ing = 1 To 10000
inr = Test2
Next
lngRunTime = timeGetTime - lngStartTime
varArray(2, 1) = "Returning Integer"
varArray(2, 2) = lngRunTime

lngStartTime = timeGetTime
For ing = 1 To 10000
byt = Test3
Next
lngRunTime = timeGetTime - lngStartTime
varArray(3, 1) = "Returning Byte"
varArray(3, 2) = lngRunTime

lngStartTime = timeGetTime
For ing = 1 To 10000
dat = Test4
Next
lngRunTime = timeGetTime - lngStartTime
varArray(4, 1) = "Returning Date"
varArray(4, 2) = lngRunTime
```

```
lngStartTime = timeGetTime
For ing = 1 To 10000
bol = Test5
Next
lngRunTime = timeGetTime - lngStartTime
varArray(5, 1) = "Returning Boolean"
varArray(5, 2) = lngRunTime

lngStartTime = timeGetTime
For ing = 1 To 10000
cur = Test6
Next
lngRunTime = timeGetTime - lngStartTime
varArray(6, 1) = "Returning Currency"
varArray(6, 2) = lngRunTime

lngStartTime = timeGetTime
For ing = 1 To 10000
dbl = Test7
Next
lngRunTime = timeGetTime - lngStartTime
varArray(7, 1) = "Returning Double"
varArray(7, 2) = lngRunTime

lngStartTime = timeGetTime
For ing = 1 To 10000
sng = Test8
Next
lngRunTime = timeGetTime - lngStartTime
varArray(8, 1) = "Returning Single"
varArray(8, 2) = lngRunTime

lngStartTime = timeGetTime
For ing = 1 To 10000
vrt = Test9
Next
lngRunTime = timeGetTime - lngStartTime
varArray(9, 1) = "Returning Variant"
varArray(9, 2) = lngRunTime

lngStartTime = timeGetTime
For ing = 1 To 10000
lng = Test10
Next
lngRunTime = timeGetTime - lngStartTime
varArray(10, 1) = "Returning Long"
varArray(10, 2) = lngRunTime

End Sub
Function Test1() As String
End Function
Function Test2() As Integer
```

```
End Function
Function Test3() As Byte
End Function
Function Test4() As Long
End Function
Function Test5() As Boolean
End Function
Function Test6() As Currency
End Function
Function Test7() As Double
End Function
Function Test8() As Single
End Function
Function Test9() As Variant
End Function
Function Test10() As Long
End Function
```

Comparing Property Implementations

```
Sub RunTest()
Dim ing As Integer
Dim lngStartTime As Long
Dim lngRunTime As Long


Dim strTest As String
varArray(0, 1) = "Calling Properties"
varArray(0, 2) = "Milliseconds"

Dim obj As VBOCHEXE.TestObject
Set obj = New VBOCHEXE.TestObject

lngStartTime = timeGetTime
For ing = 1 To 1000
    strTest = obj.MyMethodFunction()
Next
lngRunTime = timeGetTime - lngStartTime
varArray(1, 1) = "Reading: Property Procedure"
varArray(1, 2) = lngRunTime

lngStartTime = timeGetTime
For ing = 1 To 1000
    obj.StrProcProp = strTest
Next
lngRunTime = timeGetTime - lngStartTime
varArray(2, 1) = "Writing: Property Procedure"
varArray(2, 2) = lngRunTime

lngStartTime = timeGetTime
For ing = 1 To 1000
    strTest = obj.StrProcProp
```

```
Next
lngRunTime = timeGetTime - lngStartTime
varArray(3, 1) = "Reading: Public Variable"
varArray(3, 2) = lngRunTime

lngStartTime = timeGetTime
For ing = 1 To 1000
    obj.StrVarProp = strTest
Next
lngRunTime = timeGetTime - lngStartTime
varArray(4, 1) = "Writing: Public Variable"
varArray(4, 2) = lngRunTime

lngStartTime = timeGetTime
For ing = 1 To 1000
    strTest = obj.MyMethodFunction()
Next
lngRunTime = timeGetTime - lngStartTime
varArray(5, 1) = "Reading: Function"
varArray(5, 2) = lngRunTime

lngStartTime = timeGetTime
For ing = 1 To 1000
    obj.MyMethodSub (strTest)
Next
lngRunTime = timeGetTime - lngStartTime
varArray(6, 1) = "Writing: Subroutine"
varArray(6, 2) = lngRunTime

End Sub
```

Setting Object Properties Using Set and Let

```
Sub RunTest()
Dim ing As Integer
Dim lngStartTime As Long
Dim lngRunTime As Long


varArray(0, 1) = "Set and Let Procedures"
varArray(0, 2) = "Milliseconds"

Dim obj As VBOCHEXE.TestObject
Dim objPass As VBOCHEXE.TestObject

Set obj = New VBOCHEXE.TestObject
Set objPass = New VBOCHEXE.TestObject
lngStartTime = timeGetTime
For ing = 1 To 1000
    obj.objProcPropLet = objPass
Next
lngRunTime = timeGetTime - lngStartTime
```

```
varArray(1, 1) = "Using Let"
varArray(1, 2) = lngRunTime

lngStartTime = timeGetTime
For ing = 1 To 1000
    Set obj.objProcProp = objPass
Next
lngRunTime = timeGetTime - lngStartTime
varArray(2, 1) = "Using Set"
varArray(2, 2) = lngRunTime

End Sub
```

Returning Multiple Parameters from an Event

This test involved an internal object that fired events using multiple parameters. Here's the code for the object:

```
Dim ing As Integer
Dim lngStartTime As Long
Dim lngRunTime As Long
Dim WithEvents objEvent As VBOCHDLL.TestEvent

Public Sub RunTest()
varArray(0, 1) = "Event Parameters"
varArray(0, 2) = "Milliseconds"

Set objEvent = New VBOCHDLL.TestEvent

lngStartTime = timeGetTime
For ing = 1 To 1000
    objEvent.EventMethod 1
Next
lngRunTime = timeGetTime - lngStartTime
varArray(1, 1) = "1"
varArray(1, 2) = lngRunTime

lngStartTime = timeGetTime
For ing = 1 To 1000
    objEvent.EventMethod 2
Next
lngRunTime = timeGetTime - lngStartTime
varArray(2, 1) = "2"
varArray(2, 2) = lngRunTime

lngStartTime = timeGetTime
For ing = 1 To 1000
    objEvent.EventMethod 3
Next
lngRunTime = timeGetTime - lngStartTime
```

```
varArray(3, 1) = "3"
varArray(3, 2) = lngRunTime
End Sub
Private Sub E1(p1 As String)
'
End Sub
Private Sub E2(p1 As String, p2 As String)
'
End Sub
Private Sub E3(p1 As String, p2 As String, p3 As String)
'
End Sub
```

Here's the code that called the object's RunTest method to fire the events:

```
Sub RunTest()
Dim ing As Integer
Dim lngStartTime As Long
Dim lngRunTime As Long


Dim obj As VBOCHClass1

Set obj = New VBOCHClass1
obj.RunTest
End Sub
```

Using ByVal Parameters on an Event

Again, this involved a test object and a routine to call the test object's RunTest method. The code to call the RunTest method is identical to the previous test, so I've omitted it. Here's the object's code:

```
Dim ing As Integer
Dim lngStartTime As Long
Dim lngRunTime As Long
Dim WithEvents objEvent As VBOCHDLL.TestEventByVal

Public Sub RunTest()
varArray(0, 1) = "Event Parameters"
varArray(0, 2) = "Milliseconds"

Set objEvent = New VBOCHDLL.TestEventByVal

lngStartTime = timeGetTime
For ing = 1 To 1000
     objEvent.EventMethod 1
Next
lngRunTime = timeGetTime - lngStartTime
varArray(1, 1) = "1"
varArray(1, 2) = lngRunTime

lngStartTime = timeGetTime
For ing = 1 To 1000
     objEvent.EventMethod 2
Next
lngRunTime = timeGetTime - lngStartTime
varArray(2, 1) = "2"
varArray(2, 2) = lngRunTime

lngStartTime = timeGetTime
For ing = 1 To 1000
     objEvent.EventMethod 3
Next
lngRunTime = timeGetTime - lngStartTime
varArray(3, 1) = "3"
varArray(3, 2) = lngRunTime
End Sub
Private Sub E1(p1 As String)
'
End Sub
Private Sub E2(p1 As String, p2 As String)
'
End Sub
Private Sub E3(p1 As String, p2 As String, p3 As String)
'
End Sub
```

Comparion of SingleUse and MultiUse Load

This test compared the load on the computer made by MuliUse and SingleUse objects. The test determined how many objects could be created before the system crashed I've included the code for creating the SingleUse object here.

```
Sub RunTest()
Dim ing As Integer
Dim lngStartTime As Long
Dim lngRunTime As Long


varArray(0, 1) = "Creating Objects"
varArray(0, 2) = "Milliseconds"

Dim objMulti(3) As VBOCHSize.TestMulti
Dim objSingle(3) As VBOCHSize.TestSingle

lngStartTime = timeGetTime
For ing = 1 To 3
     Set objSingle(ing) = New VBOCHSize.TestSingle
Next
lngRunTime = timeGetTime - lngStartTime
varArray(1, 1) = "Creating SingleUse"
varArray(1, 2) = lngRunTime

End Sub
```

Calling Methods on Global and MultiUse Objects

```
Sub RunTest()
Dim ing As Integer
Dim lngStartTime As Long
Dim lngRunTime As Long


varArray(0, 1) = "Calling Interfaces"
varArray(0, 2) = "Milliseconds"

Dim objM As VBOCHEXEI.ITestObject
Dim objG As VBOCHEXEI.GTestObject

Set objM = New VBOCHEXEI.ITestObject
Set objG = New VBOCHEXEI.GTestObject

lngStartTime = timeGetTime
For ing = 1 To 1000
    objG.MyGlobalMethod
Next
lngRunTime = timeGetTime - lngStartTime
varArray(1, 1) = "Calling a method on Global Class"
varArray(1, 2) = lngRunTime

lngStartTime = timeGetTime
For ing = 1 To 1000
    objM.MyMethod
Next
lngRunTime = timeGetTime - lngStartTime
varArray(2, 1) = "Calling a method on a MuliUse Class"
varArray(2, 2) = lngRunTime

End Sub
```

Implemented vs. Native Methods

```
Sub RunTest()
Dim ing As Integer
Dim lngStartTime As Long
Dim lngRunTime As Long


varArray(0, 1) = "Calling Interfaces"
varArray(0, 2) = "Milliseconds"

Dim objIO As VBOCHEXEI.ITestObject
Dim objII As VBOCHEXEI.ITestObject
Dim objO As VBOCHEXEI.TestObject

Set objIO = New VBOCHEXEI.ITestObject
Set objII = New VBOCHEXEI.TestObject
Set objO = New VBOCHEXEI.TestObject

lngStartTime = timeGetTime
For ing = 1 To 1000
    objIO.MyMethod
Next
lngRunTime = timeGetTime - lngStartTime
varArray(1, 1) = "Calling a method on an interface class"
varArray(1, 2) = lngRunTime

lngStartTime = timeGetTime
For ing = 1 To 1000
    objII.MyMethod
Next
lngRunTime = timeGetTime - lngStartTime
varArray(2, 1) = "Calling an implemented method"
varArray(2, 2) = lngRunTime

lngStartTime = timeGetTime
For ing = 1 To 1000
    objO.MyMethod
Next
lngRunTime = timeGetTime - lngStartTime
varArray(3, 1) = _
"Calling a native method on an implemented class"
varArray(3, 2) = lngRunTime

End Sub
```

Methods Implemented as Functions and Subroutines

```
Sub RunTest()
Dim ing As Integer
Dim lngStartTime As Long
Dim lngRunTime As Long


varArray(0, 1) = "Calling Times"
varArray(0, 2) = "Milliseconds"

Dim objEXE As VBOCHEXE.TestObject
Dim objDLL As VBOCHDLL.TestObject

Set objEXE = New VBOCHEXE.TestObject
Set objDLL = New VBOCHDLL.TestObject
lngStartTime = timeGetTime
For ing = 1 To 1000
     MyRoutine "x"
Next
lngRunTime = timeGetTime - lngStartTime
varArray(1, 1) = "Internal: Subroutine Call"
varArray(1, 2) = lngRunTime

lngStartTime = timeGetTime
For ing = 1 To 1000
     objDLL.MyMethodSub "x"
Next
lngRunTime = timeGetTime - lngStartTime
varArray(2, 1) = "DLL: Method Call"
varArray(2, 2) = lngRunTime

lngStartTime = timeGetTime
For ing = 1 To 1000
     objEXE.MyMethodSub "x"
Next
lngRunTime = timeGetTime - lngStartTime
varArray(3, 1) = "EXE: Method Call"
varArray(3, 2) = lngRunTime

lngStartTime = timeGetTime
For ing = 1 To 1000
     varStr = MyFunction("x")
Next
lngRunTime = timeGetTime - lngStartTime
varArray(4, 1) = "Interal: Function Call"
varArray(4, 2) = lngRunTime

lngStartTime = timeGetTime
For ing = 1 To 1000
```

```
    varStr = objDLL.MyMethod("x")
Next
lngRunTime = timeGetTime - lngStartTime
varArray(5, 1) = "DLL: Method Call, Function"
varArray(5, 2) = lngRunTime

lngStartTime = timeGetTime
For ing = 1 To 1000
     varStr = objEXE.MyMethodFunction
Next
lngRunTime = timeGetTime - lngStartTime
varArray(6, 1) = "EXE: Method Call, Function"
varArray(6, 2) = lngRunTime

End Sub
Function MyFunction(p1 As String) As String
'
End Function
Sub MyRoutine(p1 As String)
'
End Sub
```

Parameters with Out-Of-Process and In-Process Components

```
Sub RunTest()
Dim ing As Integer
Dim lngStartTime As Long
Dim lngRunTime As Long


varArray(0, 1) = "ByVal/ByRef Call"
varArray(0, 2) = "Milliseconds"

Dim obj As VBOCHEXEI.TestObject
Dim objEXE As VBOCHEXE.TestObjectByVal
Dim objDLL As VBOCHDLL.TestObjectByVal

Set obj = New VBOCHEXEI.TestObject
Set objEXE = New VBOCHEXE.TestObjectByVal
Set objDLL = New VBOCHDLL.TestObjectByVal
lngStartTime = timeGetTime
For ing = 1 To 1000
     objDLL.MyMethodSubByRef varStr
Next
lngRunTime = timeGetTime - lngStartTime
varArray(1, 1) = "DLL: ByRef Method Call, String"
varArray(1, 2) = lngRunTime

lngStartTime = timeGetTime
For ing = 1 To 1000
     objEXE.MyMethodSubByRef varStr
Next
lngRunTime = timeGetTime - lngStartTime
varArray(2, 1) = "EXE: ByRef Method Call, String"
varArray(2, 2) = lngRunTime

lngStartTime = timeGetTime
For ing = 1 To 1000
    varStr = objDLL.MyMethodByRef(varStr)
Next
lngRunTime = timeGetTime - lngStartTime
varArray(3, 1) = "DLL: ByRef Method Call, Function, String"
varArray(3, 2) = lngRunTime

lngStartTime = timeGetTime
For ing = 1 To 1000
    varStr = objEXE.MyMethodByRef(varStr)
Next
lngRunTime = timeGetTime - lngStartTime
varArray(4, 1) = "EXE: ByRef Method Call, Function, String"
varArray(4, 2) = lngRunTime

lngStartTime = timeGetTime
For ing = 1 To 1000
     objDLL.MyMethodSubObjByRef obj
```

```
Next
lngRunTime = timeGetTime - lngStartTime
varArray(5, 1) = "DLL: ByRef Method Call, Object"
varArray(5, 2) = lngRunTime

lngStartTime = timeGetTime
For ing = 1 To 1000
     objEXE.MyMethodSubObjByRef obj
Next
lngRunTime = timeGetTime - lngStartTime
varArray(6, 1) = "EXE: ByRef Method Call, Object"
varArray(6, 2) = lngRunTime

lngStartTime = timeGetTime
For ing = 1 To 1000
    varStr = objDLL.MyMethodObjByRef(obj)
Next
lngRunTime = timeGetTime - lngStartTime
varArray(7, 1) = "DLL: ByRef Method Call, Function, Object"
varArray(7, 2) = lngRunTime

lngStartTime = timeGetTime
For ing = 1 To 1000
     varStr = objEXE.MyMethodObjByRef(obj)
Next
lngRunTime = timeGetTime - lngStartTime
varArray(8, 1) = "EXE: ByRef Method Call, Function, Object"
varArray(8, 2) = lngRunTime

lngStartTime = timeGetTime
For ing = 1 To 1000
     objDLL.MyMethodSubIntByRef ing
Next
lngRunTime = timeGetTime - lngStartTime
varArray(9, 1) = "DLL: ByRef Method Call, Integer"
varArray(9, 2) = lngRunTime

lngStartTime = timeGetTime
For ing = 1 To 1000
     objEXE.MyMethodSubIntByRef ing
Next
lngRunTime = timeGetTime - lngStartTime
varArray(10, 1) = "EXE: ByRef Method Call, Integer"
varArray(10, 2) = lngRunTime

lngStartTime = timeGetTime
For ing = 1 To 1000
    varStr = objDLL.MyMethodIntByRef(ing)
Next
lngRunTime = timeGetTime - lngStartTime
varArray(11, 1) = _
"DLL: ByRef Method Call, Function, Integer"
varArray(11, 2) = lngRunTime
```

```
lngStartTime = timeGetTime
For ing = 1 To 1000
     varStr = objEXE.MyMethodIntByRef(ing)
Next
lngRunTime = timeGetTime - lngStartTime
varArray(12, 1) = _
"EXE: ByRef Method Call, Function, Integer"
varArray(12, 2) = lngRunTime


lngStartTime = timeGetTime
For ing = 1 To 1000
     objDLL.MyMethodSub varStr
Next
lngRunTime = timeGetTime - lngStartTime
varArray(13, 1) = "DLL: ByVal Method Call, String"
varArray(13, 2) = lngRunTime

lngStartTime = timeGetTime
For ing = 1 To 1000
     objEXE.MyMethodSub varStr
Next
lngRunTime = timeGetTime - lngStartTime
varArray(14, 1) = "EXE: ByVal Method Call, String"
varArray(14, 2) = lngRunTime

lngStartTime = timeGetTime
For ing = 1 To 1000
    varStr = objDLL.MyMethod(varStr)
Next
lngRunTime = timeGetTime - lngStartTime
varArray(15, 1) = "DLL: ByVal Method Call, Function, String"
varArray(15, 2) = lngRunTime

lngStartTime = timeGetTime
For ing = 1 To 1000
     varStr = objEXE.MyMethod(varStr)
Next
lngRunTime = timeGetTime - lngStartTime
varArray(16, 1) = "EXE: ByVal Method Call, Function, String"
varArray(16, 2) = lngRunTime

lngStartTime = timeGetTime
For ing = 1 To 1000
     objDLL.MyMethodSubObj obj
Next
lngRunTime = timeGetTime - lngStartTime
varArray(17, 1) = "DLL: ByVal Method Call, Object"
varArray(17, 2) = lngRunTime

lngStartTime = timeGetTime
For ing = 1 To 1000
     objEXE.MyMethodSubObj obj
Next
```

```
lngRunTime = timeGetTime - lngStartTime
varArray(18, 1) = "EXE: ByVal Method Call, Object"
varArray(18, 2) = lngRunTime

lngStartTime = timeGetTime
For ing = 1 To 1000
    varStr = objDLL.MyMethodObj(obj)
Next
lngRunTime = timeGetTime - lngStartTime
varArray(19, 1) = "DLL: ByVal Method Call, Function, Object"
varArray(19, 2) = lngRunTime

lngStartTime = timeGetTime
For ing = 1 To 1000
     varStr = objEXE.MyMethodObj(obj)
Next
lngRunTime = timeGetTime - lngStartTime
varArray(20, 1) = "EXE: ByVal Method Call, Function, Object"
varArray(20, 2) = lngRunTime

lngStartTime = timeGetTime
For ing = 1 To 1000
     objDLL.MyMethodSubInt ing
Next
lngRunTime = timeGetTime - lngStartTime
varArray(21, 1) = "DLL: ByVal Method Call, Integer"
varArray(21, 2) = lngRunTime

lngStartTime = timeGetTime
For ing = 1 To 1000
     objEXE.MyMethodSubInt ing
Next
lngRunTime = timeGetTime - lngStartTime
varArray(22, 1) = "EXE: ByVal Method Call, Integer"
varArray(22, 2) = lngRunTime

lngStartTime = timeGetTime
For ing = 1 To 1000
    varStr = objDLL.MyMethodInt(ing)
Next
lngRunTime = timeGetTime - lngStartTime
varArray(23, 1) = "DLL: ByVal Method Call, Function, Integer"
varArray(23, 2) = lngRunTime

lngStartTime = timeGetTime
For ing = 1 To 1000
     varStr = objEXE.MyMethodInt(ing)
Next
lngRunTime = timeGetTime - lngStartTime
varArray(24, 1) = "EXE: ByVal Method Call, Function, Integer"
varArray(24, 2) = lngRunTime

End Sub
```

Returning Values from Out-of-Process and In-Process Components

```
Sub RunTest()
Dim ing As Integer
Dim lngStartTime As Long
Dim lngRunTime As Long


varArray(0, 1) = "Return Data"
varArray(0, 2) = "Milliseconds"

Dim stz As String
Dim ing2 As Integer

Dim objDLL As VBOCHDLL.TestObjectFunction
Dim objEXE As VBOCHEXE.TestObjectFunction
Dim obj As VBOCHEXEI.TestObject
Set objEXE = New VBOCHEXE.TestObjectFunction
Set objDLL = New VBOCHDLL.TestObjectFunction
Set obj = New VBOCHEXEI.TestObject

objEXE.ing = 0
objEXE.stz = "x"
Set objEXE.obj = obj

objDLL.ing = 0
objDLL.stz = "x"
Set objDLL.obj = obj

lngStartTime = timeGetTime
For ing = 1 To 1000
stz = objEXE.MyMethodStr
Next
lngRunTime = timeGetTime - lngStartTime
varArray(1, 1) = "EXE: String"
varArray(1, 2) = lngRunTime

lngStartTime = timeGetTime
For ing = 1 To 1000
ing2 = objEXE.MyMethodInt
Next
lngRunTime = timeGetTime - lngStartTime
varArray(2, 1) = "EXE: Integer"
varArray(2, 2) = lngRunTime

lngStartTime = timeGetTime
For ing = 1 To 1000
Set obj = objEXE.MyMethodObj
```

```
Next
lngRunTime = timeGetTime - lngStartTime
varArray(3, 1) = "EXE: Object"
varArray(3, 2) = lngRunTime

lngStartTime = timeGetTime
For ing = 1 To 1000
stz = objDLL.MyMethodStr
Next
lngRunTime = timeGetTime - lngStartTime
varArray(4, 1) = "DLL: String"
varArray(4, 2) = lngRunTime

lngStartTime = timeGetTime
For ing2 = 1 To 1000
ing = objDLL.MyMethodInt
Next
lngRunTime = timeGetTime - lngStartTime
varArray(5, 1) = "DLL: Integer"
varArray(5, 2) = lngRunTime

lngStartTime = timeGetTime
For ing = 1 To 1000
Set obj = objDLL.MyMethodObj
Next
lngRunTime = timeGetTime - lngStartTime
varArray(6, 1) = "DLL: Object"
varArray(6, 2) = lngRunTime

End Sub
```

ABOUT THE AUTHOR

Peter Vogel (MBA, MCSD) is a principal in PH&V Information Services, specializing in system design and development for VBA-based systems. PH&V is involved in creating intranet and component based applications. Peter has designed, built, and installed systems for Bayer AG, Exxon, Christie Digital, and the Canadian Imperial Bank of Commerce. In addition to his consulting activities, Peter also edits two newsletter from Pinnacle Publishing (*www.pinpub.com*). Smart Access is the authority for in-depth technical information for Microsoft Access developers and XML Developer for programmers using XML to build N-tier and Web-based applications. Peter teaches Visual Basic, XML, and database design for Learning Tree International and wrote their Web application development course. His articles have appeared in every major magazine devoted to VB based development, several business magazines, and in the Microsoft Developer Network libraries. Peter also sits on the editorial advisory board for the "Information System Consultant" newsletter.

INDEX

A

B

K

L

M

Q

R

V

W

X

Prentice Hall: Professional Technical Reference
Back
Forward
Home
Reload
Images
Open
Print
Find
Stop
http://www.phptr.com/
What's New?
What's Cool?
Destinations
Net Search
People
Software

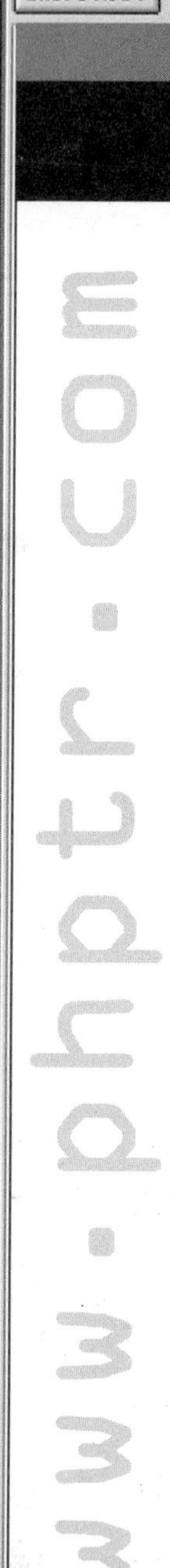
www.phptr.com